Houston Dining on the Cheap

A Guide to the 300 Best Inexpensive Restaurants in Houston

3rd Edition

Revised, Expanded and otherwise Updated for 2007 and beyond

Riccetti, Mike.
Houston dining on the cheap : the guide to the best inexpensive restaurants in Houston / Mike Riccetti. -- 3rd ed.
p. cm.
LCCN: 2001118839
ISBN: 978-0-9714040-4-5 / 0-9714040-4-6

1. Restaurants—Texas—Houston—Guidebooks. 2. Houston (Tex.)—Guidebooks. I. Title.

TX907.3.T42H687 2001 647.95764'1411
QBI01-201212

Cover Design - Sheila Kwiatek
Cover Photograph - Russ Andorka

Published by Tempus Fugit Press
P.O. Box 540306
Houston, Texas 77254

www.HoustonDiningontheCheap.com
Info@HoustonDiningontheCheap.com

Printed in the United States of America.

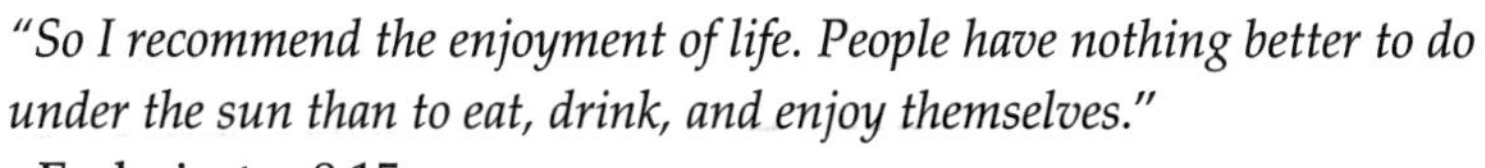

"So I recommend the enjoyment of life. People have nothing better to do under the sun than to eat, drink, and enjoy themselves."
- Ecclesiastes 8:15

"You cannot think well, you cannot love well, if you do not eat well."
- Virginia Woolf, ***A Room of One's Own***

"There is nothing in the world that we do as much as we do eating."
- Will Rogers

Praise for Past Editions of Houston Dining on the Cheap

"Each restaurant is reviewed in gut-wrenching detail and Riccetti pulls no punches. It's a fun book to read because **Riccetti eats - and writes - like a regular guy**."
- **Ken Hoffman**, *Houston Chronicle*, January 10, 2002

"*Houston Dining on the Cheap* is **remarkably comprehensive**.... Nicely done."
- *My Table Magazine*

"...**a worthwhile guide** to...inexpensive eateries of every variety."
- *Paper City*

"...[an] **excellent** book."
- **Tony Vallone**

"For the budget conscious, Mike Riccetti's book, *Houston Dining on the Cheap - A Guide to the Best Inexpensive Restaurants in Houston* **is an excellent source**."
- **Greater Houston Partnership**, *Here is Houston*

"Local gourmand and tightwad Mike Riccetti...[provides with his new edition] a **great road map and a fun read**...."
- **Ken Hoffman**, *Houston Chronicle*, April 13, 2004

Praise for The Guide to Ridiculously Easy Entertaining - Tips from Marfreless **by Mike Riccetti & Michael Wells**

"In a tone that is informative and reassuring, **the book allays fears about giving a party, explains everything you need to know to throw a great bash**...."
- *New York Daily News*

"**A must-have guide** to creating a classy and memorable social gathering with great drink and food...."
- *Midwest Book Review*

"The tone is light-hearted and fun.... Don't be fooled by the humor; **the information is comprehensive**."
- *Austin American-Statesman*

"...lots of flavor and great ideas....**an excellent reference guide**."
- *Contra Costa Times*

"...**bulging with advice on party-giving**...there's plenty of sensible, less obvious information here that hosts will find handy."
- *Houston Chronicle*

Recommended as a Christmas gift for 2005; "...**there's a lot of good info here**."
- *Wichita Eagle*

"Tips can help you **maintain your sanity** while keeping your holiday visitors happy."
- *Tucson Citizen*

"It has the goods to **make even the novice party planner look like a pro**."
- *The Montana Standard*

"**Tips on how to throw a last-minute bash** and save your sanity, too".
- *Miami Herald*

"I've always had an analogy that running a restaurant is like having a party. When I throw a party at my home, **this is my play book for a successful event**."
- **Johnny Carrabba**

"*The Guide to Ridiculously Easy Entertaining* **has it all**.... **full of sly humor**.... it even tells you how to pronounce cheese and wine names such as mohn-truh-SHAY."
- **Teresa Byrne-Dodge**, Editor & Publisher, *My Table Magazine*

"**This is the ultimate entertaining book**."
- **Brock Wagner**, founder and owner of Saint Arnold Brewing Company

---

"**very informative**...very funny"
- **Giuseppe Pezzotti**, Cornell University Hotel School

Table of Contents

Main Sections

Asides & Ramblings

Preface

Some Observations of Dining Cheaply in Houston

It's been reported that Americans on average dine out about three-and-a-half times per week, while Houstonians are at roughly five times per week. This is more than the residents of any other metropolitan area. Given the number of very good and affordable restaurants featuring nearly every cuisine imaginable, it's no wonder. Though Houston cannot match New York and San Francisco in terms of the number of exemplary fine-dining restaurants, and lags behind Chicago, celebrity chef mecca Las Vegas and resurgent New Orleans in expense account destinations, these cities doubtfully approach Houston in terms of quality inexpensive restaurants. Though I might be biased towards my hometown, this was my experience during the past decade or so when I worked and traveled to those cities on a somewhat regular basis. And, it's not just me, as several years ago *USA Today* wrote, "Houston just might be the people's dining capital [of the country]". Since Houston is inexpensive, as far as big cities go, and increasingly diverse, it is a great place for those who want to dine on the cheap.

Some of the hallmarks of Houston's restaurant scene are robust flavors, high quality, a lack of pretense, amazing diversity and great value. Though many large cities can claim multiple cuisines done well, it's hard to think of any city that does as many cuisines so well, especially for such reasonable prices. And, no other city might incorporate influences from Mexico, the Gulf, South Louisiana, rural Texas, Central America and, at the more expensive restaurants, second-generation Sicilian-Americans, sometimes on the same menu, as does Houston. Though great for Tex-Mex and Texas barbecue, those are just the tip of the iceberg. As most familiar with the dining scene will know, the most individualistic, eclectic and interesting restaurants are those that are individual operations.

Not surprisingly, with about a third of the population of Mexican descent, the almost surfeit of Mexican restaurants, and the relatively high ratio of quality-to-price in these types of eateries, Mexican restaurants make a relatively large percentage of restaurants that were deemed to be among the best inexpensive restaurants. Mexican and Vietnamese, and often Chinese cuisines use generally inexpensive ingredients and cooking techniques. Most of these are humble establishments that serve flavorful food for a song to recent immigrants, and service and décor are seemingly often an afterthought. Thai restaurants, though generally pricier than Mexican and Vietnamese ones, include a large percentage that offer high quality cooking coupled with reasonable prices. Conversely, though I enjoy Japanese and Korean restaurants, most of the ones worth recommending are too expensive for the purposes of this guidebook. Some cuisines represented locally such as those from western Africa, for example, that mostly serve their immigrant communities have not provided the overall quality dining experience to warrant inclusion though these can be interesting and enjoyable places to visit. For this guidebook, I've tried not to be partial toward any particular areas of town, but the simple fact is that most of the best inexpensive (and expensive) restaurants are located inside the Loop, west of downtown, or in the Galleria area. New Chinatown around Bellaire Boulevard on the west side is a very notable exception for inexpensive restaurants. There are also many interesting and worthwhile places near the Westheimer and Beltway intersection and a few miles west. Though I wish I could have found more to recommend in the outlying areas, there are not as many of the best restaurants out there, as is the case with most cities.

New for the Third Edition

Since the second edition was published in late 2003, many restaurants have opened, a good number have closed, some have improved, and others have declined or otherwise become less interesting. **The changes for this new edition include**:

- The **restaurant profile template has been changed** for easier use.
- **Profiles have been updated** to reflect the most recent information.
- **New restaurants have been added**. This includes ones that have opened since 2004, some restaurants that have impressed after re-evaluation, and even some that had escaped previous notice. There are **72** new restaurants profiled in this edition.
- **Some restaurants previously profiled are not included in this edition**:
    - **Some have closed** like A Taste of Portugal, Canton Seafood, Lockwood Malt Shop and Green's Barbecue.
    - **Some have become too expensive** for inclusion. These restaurants are such long-time favorites Café Montrose, Mardi Gras Grill (formerly Floyd's), Bayou City Seafood N' Pasta, divino, and some others that I would not hesitate to recommend. These are just not inexpensive.
    - **Some have become less proficient or too inconsistent** compared to other local inexpensive restaurants.
- A greater effort was made to **visit restaurants in outlying areas**. Galveston and points nearly that south, Tomball to the northwest and

Richmond and Rosenberg were too far out, but nearly everywhere else in the Houston area was fair game for investigation. During the research I've navigated most of the sprawl.

- Instead of trying to list every very good inexpensive restaurant, as was done in the previous editions, **this edition has the best 300 inexpensive restaurants in the Houston area**. There are many other worthwhile inexpensive eateries in Houston, but the ones profiled here are the best.
- All of the **asides are new** or updated.
- "Chinatown Southwest" has acceded to "**New Chinatown**", which has come into use, at least in some sectors, to describe this area.

About this Guidebook

This guide is written from the viewpoint of a dedicated diner, and a generally cheap, if mostly discriminating, wide-ranging and fairly experienced one at that. The restaurant profiles are written for the average at-least-somewhat-adventurous local restaurant-goer. These profiles are meant to describe each restaurant in a useful and critical fashion. Explanations of cuisines and dishes are provided when I believe it will be helpful for the majority of readers. To find the restaurants and create the profiles I have done **a lot of comparative research**: I have eaten at a great many restaurants in the Houston area, over **1,300** different restaurants and around **3,400** meals and counting, since the dedicated research began for the very first edition several years ago. (And, I was much chagrined to recently learn that many studies have shown that low-calorie lifestyle leads to longevity). In a testament to the quality of inexpensive restaurants in Houston, I have only had a fairly small number of bad meals, excepting late night fast-food stops, of course.

The hope for this guide was to be as comprehensive as possible in trying to name the best 300 inexpensive restaurants throughout the Houston area. I've tried very hard to be thorough, but I don't have the hubris to believe that I have not missed anything. But, this third edition is more inclusive and better than the previous two. In trying to find restaurants worthy of a visit, I have acted on the articles from generally reliable local, regional and sometimes national publications and web sites, and the tips of food savvy friends and family. Some of the resources I found most useful for my investigative purposes were the Dining Guide in the *Houston Chronicle*, especially Alison Cook's columns, Robb Walsh's articles in the *Houston Press*, *My Table - Houston's Dining Magazine*, and for basic contact information and maps, the B4-U-EAT.com web site. **I visited the restaurants anonymously**, and **I paid for the meals myself**; or, if I was lucky, by one of my dining partners. I have eaten at each restaurant profiled in this guide at least twice, in many cases, numerous times. For those restaurants with several locations, I tried to visit each one if it seemed necessary to do so. Though I've made it a point to be as objective as possible, this guide is inherently subjective, and opinionated. You will also notice that there are no advertisements in this book.

A **note about the menu items at local Middle Eastern and Greek restaurants**, which are numerous in this guide: Since the names are originally in Arabic, Greek, Turkish, Hebrew or Farsi, the English terms for the dishes shared by the Middle Eastern, Greek and Persian cuisines appear in different ways in their English translations on the various menus. To avoid confusion in the profiles among the myriad of places that offer these dishes, I thought that it was best to standardize the names. I chose the one that I thought was the easiest to pronounce and remember in English. Since these are consistent among all places in this guidebook, the spellings will often be slightly different than what is shown on a restaurant's menu.

Criteria for Inclusion

The restaurants in this guide were selected on the basis of overall quality and cost. There was more than a plethora of candidates for inclusion. Of the thousands of restaurants, I strove to select **the best 300 inexpensive restaurants in the Houston area** regardless of cuisine, but with the hope that the list would be very diverse. It was difficult to get down to 300. There are many other very good inexpensive restaurants; some are just more ethnic and less refined, for example.

Being a guide for inexpensive dining, cost was obviously a significant criterion. To be eligible for inclusion, it had to have an average meal price or rather, an **average entrée price at dinner of $13 or less.** Dinner, of course, is never cheaper than lunch. You might ask, why $13 at dinner? Using some very unscientific sampling methods, I came to the conclusion this average was an appropriate cut-off, separating generally "inexpensive" from "moderately priced" or "not cheap". Eligibility was determined by calculating the costs from each restaurant's menu (tedious, but useful) and knowing the restaurants to a certain degree. The first question that I asked myself in reviewing each restaurant for possible inclusion was, "would I want to return?" **Food quality** was the primary factor. For these generally inexpensive restaurants, **value** had to be very good (i.e. portions sufficiently sized). This $13 is for a meal, excepting drink(s), tax and tip, which might be an entrée and sides, a hamburger and fries, or a sandwich and side. Restaurants at the upper end of the price scale probably would not have made this list if they were only of comparable quality to places that were more inexpensive. Some other factors played a part, in order of importance, such as **consistency**, **service time**, **accessibility**, **service quality**, **menu variety** and **uniqueness of the dishes**; and, any other features that made it compelling to return and recommend that others visit. For example, if the staff was noticeably friendly and accommodating, or the setting was inviting or especially comfortable these could help entice future visits. Décor and atmosphere were of less importance. But, the greater the cost, the higher were the expectations for quality, service, décor and ambience or convenience. To be noted, mobile food trucks, which are mostly taco trucks in this area, were not eligible. These are entirely too mobile.

How to Use this Guidebook

If it is profiled in this guide, it is recommended. You can visit any one of the 300 restaurants that are profiled with a reasonable sense of confidence that you will receive a quality meal that is a good value. The fifteen restaurants with a star are highly recommended. Each entry provides the basic pertinent data for the restaurant such as address, phone number, and hours of operation, plus a descriptive profile. The **restaurants profiled are listed in alphabetical order**. Though this guidebook celebrates many restaurants that begin with *El, Il,* and *La,* it is written in English, not Spanish, Italian, or French, and it lists these restaurants by the order of the first letter. For example, *La Tapatia* is listed among the other restaurants beginning with an *L* not *T*. Also, restaurants named after a person are listed by the first letter of the name. *Maria Selma's* is shown with other restaurants whose name begins with an *M* rather than the *S*. Maybe not entirely in accordance with Strunk & White, this is how my spreadsheet software arranges names. An abbreviated example of the header for a profile is shown below. Most of it should be self-explanatory, but some illumination might be useful for the few lines that are shown below.

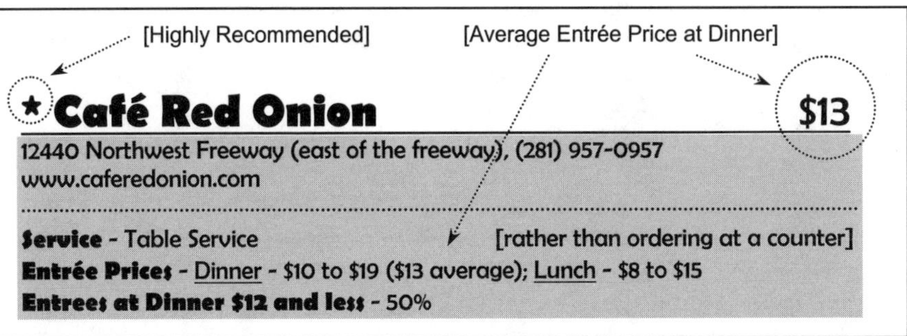

To make this guidebook more user-friendly, **indices of the recommended restaurants organized by both cuisine and location are near the end** (pages

457-468). There are also **lists of miscellaneous information** (pages 469-471) that might be helpful related to the recommended restaurants.

The information is accurate to the best of my knowledge at the time of printing, but the restaurant scene is Houston is dynamic. There is a chance that **prices will have increased** or that the restaurants profiled have closed, moved or changed in some other appreciable way. It pays to **call ahead**. There are 300 restaurants that are recommended and profiled, so this book should be useful for a while to come.

Acknowledgments

I would like to thank the following people for their help in suggesting restaurants, providing insight either knowingly, or otherwise, or supplying any other assistance along the way: Jack Thetford, Michael Wells, Gene and Cara Riccetti, Richard and Shirl Riccetti, Hank and Jennifer Fuselier, Dan and Sheila Berggren, Paul and Kristen Heyburn, Sameer Mehta, Greg and Carrie Hart, Brian Parizot, Keith and Sharon Leonard, Kathy Haveman, Mark Herrin, David Hinsley, Dave Feliciano, John Beach, Jeff Fetzer, Jay and Shannon Caldwell, Ed Taussig, Wayne and Elaine Herff, Miya Shay, Jane Kremer, Joe Strummer, Chantal Duke, Ashley Womack, John Moss, Enrico Bracalente, Lori Sebastian and Teresa Byrne-Dodge.

About the Author

Mike Riccetti has authored, now, three editions of ***Houston Dining on the Cheap***. He grew up in Houston, and is a product of public schools in Spring Branch and Strake Jesuit College Preparatory. He has degrees from The University of Texas at Austin and Cornell University. He is a regular contributor to *My Table* and an irregular contributor to other local and national publications, often concerning Houston-area restaurants. He is also the co-author of ***The Guide to Ridiculously Easy Entertaining - Tips from Marfreless*** published in 2005. He currently lives, works, and dines cheaply and sometimes not-so-cheaply in Houston.

Restaurant Profiles

The restaurants profiled in the succeeding few hundred pages are all recommended, if not necessarily unconditionally.

Abe's Cajun Market $9

1080 Clear Lake City Boulevard (just east of Galveston Rd.) 77062, (281) 480-2237
www.abescajunmarket.com

Cuisine - Cajun
Hours - Mon-Thu 8AM to 9PM; Fri 8AM to 10PM; Sat 9AM to 10PM; Sun 11AM to 9PM
Credit Cards - Amex, Diners, Discover, MC, Visa
Service - Table Service
Alcohol - Beer & Wine

Entrée Prices - $6 to $15 ($9 average)
Entrées $12 and less - 90%

Atmosphere & Décor - Casual
Appeal - Quality South Louisiana food in Clear Lake
Useful to Note - It's a good stop for prepared dishes to take home.
Menu Suggestions - Chicken and Sausage Jambalaya; Shrimp Creole (shrimp stewed in a tomato sauce); Shrimp Muffaletta; Shrimp Étouffée; Chicken and Sausage Gumbo

As the name indicates Abe's Cajun Market not only serves meals, but also sells Cajun-oriented products, attractively prepared and packaged foods for heating and eating at home such as stuffed chickens and turkeys, dips, sausages, and much more. But, most folks visit for the foods to be eaten at the inviting low-key restaurant, and Abe's does a bristling lunchtime business. The best things to order, and probably the best values, too, as these are well under ten dollars, are the plate specials that change each day. These can be very good versions of jambalaya, shrimp Creole and the like. Each are served with steamed white rice, good cornbread and a usually listless side vegetable. The expected South Louisiana favorites are served here plus a half-dozen entrée-style salads, almost twenty sandwiches and fried seafood platters. The étouffées and gumbos begin with a properly dark and flavorful roux. Unfortunately, the po boys are somewhat marred by bread that's not as crusty, nor as flavorful as it should be. But, the sausage po boy features sausage that is made in-house. That garlicky sausage enhances the red beans and rice, and can also be ordered separately and deep-fried. Abe's has a few different takes on some familiar items. One is a muffaletta with fried shrimp, which is much better than the shrimp po boy, another is a po boy with grilled pork, grilled onion, jalapeños, Monterey Jack cheese and spicy mustard, and baked potatoes that can be filled with steak, grilled chicken, fried shrimp or shrimp étouffée. The fried seafood platters featuring shrimp, oyster, crawfish and catfish served with fries, cornbread and cole slaw are also reliably well-done.

Addisaba $7

7668 De Moss (east of Fondren, west of Sharpstown Mall) 77036, (713) 995-0333

Cuisine - Ethiopian
Hours - Mon-Thu, Sun 11AM to 10PM; Fri-Sat 11AM to 2AM
Credit Cards - MC, Visa
Service - Table Service
Alcohol - Beer & Wine

Entrée Prices - $4 to $9 ($7 average)
Entrées $12 and less - 100%

Atmosphere & Décor - Barely functional
Appeal - Very inexpensive, flavorful food
Menu Suggestions - Alicha Fitfit (pieces of lamb and injera with braised onions in a mild curry sauce); Tibs (cubed beef sautéed with onions, tomato and green pepper): Kifto (ground beef with spiced butter); Quanta Firfir (dried cubes of beef simmered in berbere sauce with injera, onions and spiced butter)

In this bland and somewhat derelict strip center near the forlorn Sharpstown Mall, Addisaba turns out some interesting, good value food. Addisaba is a spelling of the capital of Ethiopia, and the fare here is from that usually misunderstood cuisine. The food is exotically spicy, uniquely flavored, and, yes, even filling. That is it is inexpensive and served, in small bowls with accompanying plates filled with *injera*, the spongy flat bread that is used as a utensil, and ripe for sharing makes this a potentially enjoyable place with an adventurous group. The setting and atmosphere are not likely to help, though. With the exception of a few noticeable remnants of its previous occupant, a Chinese restaurant, the décor is East Berlin, 1955; maybe an Ethiopian restaurant in East Berlin in 1955. It's fairly bleak. But, it is also dimly lit. There is a stage and it seems that an East African band plays from time-to-time, which probably helps if they are not too loud as the big television placed in the middle of the main dining room can often be, during other times. Not that it is drowning out too many conversations, other than that from the affable staff, as the spacious dining area seems usually entirely uncluttered with diners.

The fare is meat- and beef-heavy, which might entice some more Texans to visit. The printed descriptions for each dish do a good job providing explanation, but it's good to note that there are only entrées in Ethiopian cuisine, no appetizers nor desserts, so be prepared to eat your main dish until satiation. The hot and spicy *berbere* sauce is featured in many of the dishes. It's made with the seeds of cumin, cardamom, coriander, and fenugreek that are combined with garlic, ground cloves, turmeric, grated gingerroot, black pepper, salt, cinnamon, and dried red chiles. The *awaze* sauce is a combination of Ethiopian honey wine, garlic, onions and berbere sauce. The limited menu with just under twenty entrées has a single dish with chicken, seven featuring beef, a couple lamb, and a half-dozen vegetarian ones. Beef is cubed for many of the dishes and cooked, sautéed or stewed, with spices and other items. There is an excellent version of *Tibs*, beef sautéed with spices then cooked slowly with onions, tomatoes and green pepper for a wonderfully savory dish with at least a couple layers of flavor. Please remember that tartar means raw, which is how the ground beef *kifto* is traditionally prepared. The restaurant is quick to comply in friendly fashion if you'd like the *kifto* cooked. It tastes very good that way, too. It's tough to go wrong with any of the beef dishes. The *Alicha Fitfit*, tender and tasty pieces of lamb cooked with onions and served in a tasty curry sauce is one of the highlights here. Many of the plates are served with a small shredded green lettuce salad that is surprisingly good. Service is gracious, if sometimes a little too low key. There is a bar with spirits and beer including a few decent ones from Ethiopia.

Adrian's Burger Bar $9

5311 Sonora (west of Lockwood, south of I-10) 77020, (713) 674-1488

Cuisine - Hamburgers; Soul Food
Hours - Mon-Fri 11AM to 6PM; Sat 10AM to 5PM
Credit Cards - NONE
Service - Counter Service
Alcohol - NONE

Entrée Prices - $6 to $11 ($9 average)
Entrées $12 and less - 100%

Atmosphere & Décor - Barely functional
Appeal - One of the best burgers in town; some very good soul food dishes, too
Useful to Note - The hamburgers take at least twenty-five minutes.
Menu Suggestions - Hamburger; Cheeseburger; Double Meat Cheeseburger; oxtails; macaroni and cheese

The adage that things are bigger in Texas has been ringing true at Adrian's Burger Bar since the mid-1980s. The tasty regular burger here seems to be at least one full pound when cooked. These monstrosities are more than freakishly large; these are very good. Moist and flavorful, the enormous patties are cooked all of the way through, quite possibly the result of some time in the oven. Made to order, the burgers can easily take twenty minutes or more, even when the restaurant is empty. The kitchen has a heavy hand with the bright yellow mustard, even for such a large amount of meat, so it is a good idea to ask for them to go light on this condiment when ordering. Also be sure to ask for extra portions of your preferred condiment. Otherwise, you find your hands covered in mustard when trying to eat these burgers, as the basic buns are never quite up to the task. These burgers are a mess, no matter how you try to eat them. But, it is certainly worth it. If a regular burger is not enough, you can try versions with cheese, bacon, mushrooms or the Adrian's Deluxe Burger that comes with bacon, mushrooms, grilled onions and a lot of cheese. All are well crafted. Amazingly, there is even a double meat burger. More amazingly, is that the staff reports they receive a few orders each week for these. If you need a side with one of these massive burgers, skip the very greasy and limp fries, and go for the well-made and hearty macaroni and cheese, or the baked beans.

In addition to the burgers, there is also a steam table with offerings that change daily. Food from the steam table costs nine dollars and it includes an entrée, three sides and cornbread. A meal from the steam table is even more caloric than a burger and fries. Adrian's is certainly not a place for those with delicate appetites. The meat entrées such as the oxtails and smothered steak are very good here, and worthy of a trip, also. The sides including the expected greens, though, are often disappointments with the notable exception of the aforementioned macaroni and cheese. In addition to the burgers and soul food dishes, there are enchiladas, lasagna and spaghetti. All are large portions that come with a salad. And, if you somehow have room, the rich desserts are quite good. There is peach cobbler, pound cake, tea cake, and banana puddin'. Located in the Fifth Ward, and not very far south of I-10, Adrian's is easily accessible from downtown. It might be good to call ahead for a to-go order when getting a burger, as it does take time to cook that large a portion of meat, plus the dining area is something less than spartan. Set in a small part of a small building (a barber shop is next door), and populated with uncomfortable chairs and tiny tables, it is not really designed for lingering.

Aladdin $8

912 Westheimer (at Montrose) 77006, (713) 942-2321
www.aladdinhouston.com

Cuisine - Middle Eastern
Hours - Mon-Wed, Sun 11AM to 10:30PM; Fri-Sat 11AM to 3AM
Credit Cards - Amex, Discover, MC, Visa
Service - Counter Service
Alcohol - NONE; BYOB

Entrée Prices - $5 to $11 ($8 average)
Entrées $12 and less - 100%

Atmosphere & Décor - Pleasant, attractive; patio, which can be noisy at night
Appeal - Tasty and healthy Middle Eastern food in Montrose
Useful to Note - It's run by the same family that runs Fadi's.
Menu Suggestions - Greek salad; cabbage salad; hummus; beef shawarma; chicken shawarma

At the bustling corner of Montrose and Westheimer, Aladdin is a solid, inviting and attractively casual oasis of usually well prepared Lebanese food amidst the traffic and the often too interesting street parade. As with other local Middle Eastern restaurants, it's easy to eat healthy here. It's actually easier than most, as Aladdin sports a beautiful and bountiful spread of vegetables, salads and dips, typically fifteen to twenty items each day, which is not unlike those offered at the long-standing Fadi's restaurants. This is no coincidence, as the owners are related. Nicely, you can peruse the buffet offerings before you select. Aladdin is also user-friendly with its ability to create meals in a variety of different combinations with items from the vegetable-laden buffet and the grill, which includes the meats, plus the seafood of the day. There are kabobs, *shawarmas* and *falafels*, each available as pita-wrapped sandwiches. These are noticeably quite popular, and are served with a generous amount of pickles, tomatoes, onions, lettuce and *tahini*. Aladdin has a gas-fired brick oven in a corner of the restaurant that is put to good use. In addition to the basic pita bread, they offer ones studded with oregano, feta cheese, ground meat, and spinach and feta. The oven helps to provide finger-friendly starters such as *empanada*-like baked pies, *kibbe* balls, *falafel* and stuffed grape leaves. Aladdin is not as proficient as its progenitors. For example, the lamb kabobs might have a piece of gristle or two; though just out of the oven, the pita bread has not been as flavorful as at other places; and some of the items on the buffet might dry out before the end of the lunch hours. But, given the pedigree of the owners and the evident graciousness and hard work of the managers, there is plenty reason to believe that this restaurant will continue to improve.

Altamirano $7

8338 Southwest Freeway (at Gessner, northeast corner) 77074, (713) 484-5683

Cuisine - Mexican (taqueria)

Hours - Mon-Wed 6AM to 3:30PM; Fri-Sat 8AM to 3:30AM; Sun 6AM to 3:30AM
Credit Cards - Amex, MC, Visa
Service - Table Service
Alcohol - Beer

Entrée Prices - Dinner & Lunch - $4 to $12 ($7 average); Breakfast - $4 to $6
Entrées at Dinner $12 and less - 100%

Atmosphere & Décor - Pleasant for a taqueria
Appeal - Often very good Mexican food for cheap
Menu Suggestions - Tostadas de Ceviche de Cameron (cured shrimp on fried corn tortillas); Carne Adobada (a marinated pork slice); Quesadilla Latina al pastor (large flour tortillas filled with roast pork)

Altamirano Restaurante y Taqueria is one of those unassuming and easily overlooked small restaurants, quite often *taquerias,* which serves usually very good food for very low prices. Altamirano is a very proficient *taqueria* that cooks up some very tasty Mexican food in the style of central Mexico. Not to short-change this place, as the menu states that it is also a *restaurante* in addition to a *taqueria.* But, since *taqueria* is on the marquee above the entrance, *Taqueria* will have to do. Not that there is a difference at all for the Houston market. You will not visit Altamirano for its atmosphere or décor. It is a comfortable, if relatively unattractive place. You are here for the value-laden and tasty food, as are the recent immigrants from the interior of Mexico and Central America who make up the vast majority of the clientele.

The focused menu has many of the common items found at most *taquerias* with the addition of over a dozen seafood dishes. There is the *taqueria*-requisite cocktail, though just featuring shrimp. Their *ceviche* on a tostada, two to an order, is better than most. The cooling and zesty shrimp *ceviche* provides a wonderful textural and taste contrast to the deep-fried, crisp corn tortilla. The other seafood items include a variety of fried or sautéed dishes, and soups, mostly with tilapia and shrimp. What should satisfy anyone's taste in Mexican food, there are tacos and *tortas* in a number of ways, enchiladas, *Guisado de Puerco* (stewed pork with a choice of sauce), and less-than-stellar grilled steaks and fajitas, plus some hearty egg-based breakfast plates that are served with refried beans and rice. One of the specialties is quail (*guilotas*) served in red or green salsa or in a dark brown *mole.* The quail is also available in an enchilada. As with other *taquerias,* the tacos and *tortas* are especially good values and come with a variety of fillings. The large *tortas* feature fresh buns made with *bolillo* bread, and are accompanied with refried beans, shredded lettuce and chunks of fresh tomatoes. The array of fillings for the *tortas* and *gorditas* include shrimp, fajita, chicken, *lengua* (beef tongue) and pastor. With the tacos you can also order *barbacoa* and *chicharron* (pork skin). With the exception of the fajita, grilled chicken and shrimp tacos that are served with shredded lettuce and tomatoes, the rest are served Mexican-style with cilantro and diced raw onions.

The large, thick corn tortillas are made on the premises, and are noticeably tasty and a benefit to any dish here. The complementary salsa is a thin, tomato-based salsa that is presented at the table warm and features a slightly smoky taste with a very good flavor overall. In case there are any doubts that Tex-Mex is secondary here, the accompanying chips are too often not as fresh as they should be. To note, though the menu is in English, it helps to speak at least a minimal amount of Spanish, as the waitstaff might not speak English.

Amazon Grill $11

5114 Kirby (between Westpark and Bissonnet) 77005, (713) 522-5888
9600 Westheimer (just north of Gessner) 77063, (713) 933-0980
www.cordua.com

Cuisine - Pan Latin
Hours - Mon-Thu, Sun 11AM to 10PM; Fri-Sat 11AM to 11PM
Credit Cards - Amex, Diners, MC, Visa
Service - Counter Service
Alcohol - Full Bar

Entrée Prices - Dinner & Lunch - $8 to $16 ($11 average); Brunch - $6 to $9
Entrées at Dinner $12 and less - 90%

Atmosphere & Décor - Very nice, yet informal; patios
Appeal - Unique, quality food that you won't make at home; great tres leches
Useful to Note - The Kirby location is popular with families with young kids.
Menu Suggestions - Chinita (Asian-style slaw with lettuce greens, chicken and a sweet chile sauce); Tamarindo (grilled salmon with a tamarind-lime sauce); Peru (potato-crusted chicken breast); Puntas (spicy grilled pieces of beef); Puffy Tacos; Tres Leches (moist white cake made with three types of milk); Tabletop S'mores

Amazon Grill, from Michael Cordua, who brought us the well-loved Churrascos and Americas restaurants, is another example of a success from a top local restaurateur at a more casual level. Serving a great variety of interesting dishes, this is far from your typical counter-service restaurant, both in design and ambition. Starting life, fittingly, in what was a Café Express, before moving on, Amazon Grill usually hits all of the right notes, but in its move to more dramatic digs near West University and a second location in Westchase, it has not been as consistent, though the concepts and restaurant seem to continue to evolve. The dishes, though, are enticing pan-Latin fare that hardly anyone would attempt at home. The dishes are mostly well prepared, well presented and served in generously sized portions. For such pleasingly unique and usually good food and décor, Amazon Grill is a nice bargain. At the very least it allows diners to avoid having to dress up to have their luscious *tres leches*. But, the salad greens are always fresh and bountiful, the several dressings made in-house are zesty and unique, and the plantain chips are free.

The most artful of the forty-plus dishes are those with tropical Latin American notes such as grilled beef tips served with jalapeños and a spicy bean sauce, plantain- and potato-encrusted chicken and grilled breasts with interesting and often zesty fruit and sauce combinations. There is also clean-tasting tilapia served with a spicy Central American-style relish, pecan-encrusted and grilled salmon glazed with a tamarind sauce, which has been served here for years. Much of the menu has evolved since inception to include more recognizably Mexican and Tex-Mex dishes such as enchiladas, fajitas, tacos al carbon, fish tacos and that San Antonio specialty done Cordua-style, puffy tacos. These are adorned with shredded cheese and *crema fresca,* and delicious with either ground beef or roasted chicken. For any entrée, you will also get a noticeably fresh house salad with a choice of about a dozen freshly made, high quality dressings, the well-known fried plantain chips with *chimi-churri* sauce and several other sauces. For dessert, in addition to the Cordua-signature *tres leches,* there are several types of ice cream and sherbet, and the very popular campfire favorite, s'mores. There is a good value and mostly Mexican item brunch served on both Saturday and Sundays until 2PM. The high quality is not limited to the food. The plating of the dishes, not to mention the plates themselves, are befitting a far more expensive restaurant. These restaurants are quite attractive, a handsome, well-designed establishment that just happens to have counter service rather than service at the tables and booths. When the weather is nice, the patios are usually packed. To note, there is live music on Thursdays at the Gessner location.

Andros Deli $7

3828 Fondren (just north of Westpark) 77063, (713) 977-1440

Cuisine - Sandwiches; Greek
Hours - Daily 7AM to 10PM
Credit Cards - MC, Visa
Service - Counter Service
Alcohol - NONE

Entrée Prices - $5 to $8 ($7 average)
Entrées $12 and less - 100%

Atmosphere & Décor - Functional

Appeal - Inexpensive and tasty sandwiches and Middle Eastern specialties
Menu Suggestions - Greek Gyro sandwich; Fat Boy po boy

Like its scruffy commercial neighborhood, the Andros' exterior is not terribly attractive. That shouldn't deter a visit, as Andros is a proficient and good value purveyor of sandwiches, as it has been since 1977. A sign in 2006 announced that the original owner is back. The customers are still here, though the grocery section is long gone and the menu is pared down. A big attraction is the variety of the local version of the cold po boy sandwiches, convenient both for dine in and take out. It starts with the house special Fat Boy, made with ham, salami, provolone, mayonnaise, sweet relish, and a crusty-enough roll. The Skinny Boy is the same as the Fat Boy, but, not surprisingly, made with less ham and salami. Other possibilities include turkey, ham, *mortadella*, chicken salad, salami, roast beef and a Reuben. The other hot sandwiches are an eclectic array, but all are seemingly well prepared, and inexpensive. There is a gyro sandwich that is probably one of the best gyros in town, a Cuban shrimp sandwich, a grilled chicken breast sandwich, a half-pound cheeseburger, and a *souvlaki* sandwich (marinated and grilled beef cubes). For salads there are the chicken and tuna salad, and, befitting the owner's homeland, of course, the requisite zesty Greek salad. For heartier appetites Andros offers a number of other choices, many involving the grill and olive oil. Andros also makes different soups daily, which seem to work better during the cooler months.

Antone's Import Co. $5

2424 Dunstan (west of Morningside) 77005, (713) 521-2883
8057 Kirby (north of the Astrodome) 77054, (713) 667-3400
3823 Bellaire (between Buffalo Speedway and Weslayan) 77025, (713) 218-8383

Cuisine - Sandwiches
Hours - Dunstan - Mon-Fri 8AM to 8PM; Sat-Sun 9AM to 6PM; Kirby - Daily 8:30AM to 7PM; Bellaire - Daily 8:30AM to 7PM
Credit Cards - Amex, Diners, Discover, MC, Visa
Service - Counter Service
Alcohol - Beer & Wine

Entrée Prices - $4 to $7 ($5 average)
Entrées $12 and less - 100%

Atmosphere & Décor - Spartan, but pleasant
Appeal - Slowly disappearing long-time local favorite for cheap cold sandwiches
Useful to Note - The similarly named Antone's Po Boys & Deli isn't as good.
Menu Suggestions - Piggy Po Boy; Super Original Po Boy; Tuna Po Boy

---

Since its inception as a single grocery store on the edge of the Fourth Ward, Antone's Import Co. has long been the standard in Houston for cheap and tasty prepared sandwiches. A Lebanese family bought the first Antone's many years ago (the site of the current Gravitas) and successfully expanded the concept into a good number of branches throughout the city. In the 1990s during the settlement of the estate of the founder's widow, Antone's became two separate companies, Antone's Import Co. and Antone's Po'Boys & Deli, the slicker and larger operation. Though each chain has similar menus and recipes, Antone's Import Co., now down to just three stores, more closely the original concept of a food import company and deli, is clearly the one to visit.

The offerings consist of the locally famous po boys, salads, cold pasta salads and Middle Eastern items such as *tabouli* and *hummus*. The po boys are cold sandwiches featuring a long, fresh hero-style bun. These fresh buns are distinctively a tad dry and slightly crunchy, and help to distinguish Antone's sandwiches from lesser competitors. These crusty small loafs, which are similar at all Lebanese-run po boy purveyors, might be a legacy of the French influence in Lebanon in the last century. The po boys come in a number of variations: Original, roast beef, tuna, etc. All come with pickle slices, and many with Antone's popular and unique Hot Chow Chow, a fairly spicy mixture of pickled cabbage, onions, sweet green peppers and paprika. The sandwiches are inexpensive and easy to grab for a quick and satisfying meal. The Original, filled with salami and ham with provolone, pickles, relish and mayonnaise is the biggest seller. Another winner is the Super Po Boy, which is just like the Original, with a little more between the buns. Their version of the tuna sandwich is satisfying, with the crispness of the pickles providing a good contrast to the soft canned tuna. The Piggy is apparently either loved or, well, not loved. It's not really a good idea to look at the heart of the sandwich, at least for the squeamish. Its filling is a surprising pinkish mixture of ham, hard salami, dried oregano and mayonnaise. The sandwich is finished with jalapeño jack cheese and slices of pickles, and is a favorite among many long-time customers. There is also the Nature Boy, which is filled with *tabouli* and feta cheese. One potential drawback with the sandwiches here is that some could be sitting in the refrigerator a little too long. After which, they tend to become a bit soft and rather bland. But, that doesn't happen too often during lunch, as turnover is usually pretty high and it is easy to pick a fresher one out of the cooler or ask them to make you one. In addition to the well prepared food, the staff always seems friendlier than just about any other similarly priced place.

When visiting an Antone's the drill is straightforward: work your way to the refrigerated case, select from one of the half-dozen or so types of pre-made sandwiches; pick up chips or freshly made *hummus* or potato salad; get a drink from the refrigerator, and maybe *baklava* or another Middle Eastern dessert; and then wait in line to pay at the cashier. As an import company, Antone's stores have a decent selection of imported cheeses, cold cuts, pastas, olive oils and wine. Most of the items are Mediterranean: Italian and Middle Eastern. The sandwich wrapper has announced for years, even it's no longer true, "South's greatest selection of Italian, Greek, Armenian and Middle East food". In addition to a reliable po boy, Antone's are good places to pick up some lunchmeat, cheese, olive oil, dry pasta, or even some spices or dried herbs.

Antonio's Flying Pizza $13

2920 Hillcroft (between Richmond and Westheimer) 77057, (713) 783-6080
www.antonios.com

Cuisine - Pizza; Italian-American
Hours - Tue-Thu 11AM to 10PM; Fri 11AM to 11PM; Sat 12 to 11PM
Credit Cards - Amex, MC, Visa
Service - Counter Service
Alcohol - Beer & Wine

Entrée Prices - Dinner - $6 to $26 ($13 average); Lunch - $5 to $11
Entrées at Dinner $12 and less - 50%

Atmosphere & Décor - Nice for a pizza parlor
Appeal - Long-time favorite for good pizza and Southern Italian-American food
Menu Suggestions - Sausage Sandwich; Veal Parmigiana Sandwich; Eggplant Parmigiana Sandwich; Sicilian-style pizza; thin crust pizza; Cannelloni; Baked Ziti

Antonio's Flying Pizza has been tossing and serving some of the better pizza in the area for quite a while. The restaurant first opened in 1971, and it does not seem like much has changed there since then. Décor and menu are definitely retro. That's not at all a bad thing for a place that is well known for delicious pizza, unpretentious, and familiar Southern Italian-American food. Tables are covered with vinyl red-and-white checkered tablecloths and there is a wood-paneled bar in the back. On the walls are attractive black-and-white photos of hardscrabble villages in Sicily or elsewhere in the *mezzogiorno* that are romantic places to be *from*, at least before immigrating to cook for Americans.

Fitting for a place with "pizza" in the name, the pizzas alone make a trip here worthwhile. Both the thin crust and the thicker crust, slightly doughy Sicilian-style pizzas, are worth ordering. It begins with the crusts, which for both are light and tasty, with a welcome hint of butter. Maybe the crusts are so good because these are hand-tossed. At the very least, it can make for a fun show, and the pizza-makers often entertain kids with their dough-tossing antics. Even during lunch, flying pizza dough is much in evidence. Antonio's offers all of the popular toppings, and they are used in a judicious fashion, as is the mozzarella and slightly sweet tomato sauce; no skimping, nor excess to unbalance. The result might be what is described as New York-style, but a little heftier. The pizzas' *cugino*, the calzone, is also served here. On the full dinner menu, there are also pastas, listed under the headings of "Pasta", "Baked Dishes" and "Classics" that can be pretty appetizing. The "Pasta" section provides the opportunity to mix and match. It lists about ten popular sauces such as fresh tomato, marinara, pesto, meat sauce, a red or white seafood sauce with a choice of over a half-dozen pastas: spaghetti, ziti, linguini, fettuccine, rigatoni, cappellini and even the stuffed tortellini. Going beyond the pastas can be fairly pricey, especially with the veal and seafood items. Lobster tails are never cheap. Conversely, price-wise, lunch is a good time to visit, in part, because their well prepared thin crust individual-sized pizzas begin at around $6. With a topping, it is usually enough for most people at lunch. There are also other lunch specials under ten bucks, and even cheaper sandwiches. The pastas are all red and white and include ravioli, manicotti, fettuccine Alfredo, spaghetti and meat sauce and the like. The reliable cannelloni here is baked in a small casserole dish with plenty of gooey, melted mozzarella. The Italian-American hot sandwiches, with good bread, tomato sauce and gooey melted white cheese, are a very tasty and satisfying bargain. These are large-sized hoagie buns filled with Italian sausage, meatballs, or eggplant and topped with marinara sauce and melted provolone. The one with sausage is especially tasty. The service is usually attentive, if sometimes not overly friendly.

Armadillo Palace $10

5015 Kirby (between Westpark and Bissonnet) 77098, (713) 526-9700
www.thearmadillopalace.com

Cuisine - Texan
Hours - Mon-Wed 11AM to 12AM; Thu 11AM to 1AM; Fri 11AM to 2AM; Sat 12PM to 2AM; Sun 12PM to 12AM
Credit Cards - Amex, Diners, Discover, MC, Visa
Service - Table Service
Alcohol - Full Bar

Entrée Prices - $6 to $20 ($10 average)
Entrées $12 and less - 70%

Atmosphere & Décor - Casual; more of a bar at night
Appeal - Good food and an often lively Texas-themed bar
Useful to Note - Live Texas music most nights of the week; 18 and over after 8PM

Menu Suggestions - Campechana Extra (cured shrimp and crab with avocado, chiles and onions); Michael Berry Burger (grilled half-pound burger); Country Fried Steak; Venison Chili

---

Across a side street from his first and still amazingly popular barbecue restaurant and announced by a giant metal-skinned armadillo, Jim Goode has created yet another unique and successful dining concept that is especially well-suited to the Houston area. Armadillo Palace combines good food with an attractive and stylized Texas-themed bar that often features regional Texas music acts. Much of the time, it's actually more of bar, but the food is still worthy of a visit. As a bar, the small menu offers a focused number of appealing appetizers. This being a Goode operation, you can expect that these will be much better than their descriptions connote. The entirety is Tex-Mex in nature: nachos, chips and guacamole, *queso fundido, empanadas* and *flautas*. Goode Co. Seafood's signature *campechana* is also served here and tastes as it does there. The wonderful mixture of shrimp, crab, avocado, onion, chile and salsa is a nearly perfect complement for the crisp chips that are served with it, not to mention a cold lager beer. Unlike most bars, the nachos are actually pretty good here, even if the plentiful and far-better-than-usual toppings overwhelm the chips. One quibble is that you have to pay four bucks for chips and salsa; one of the few places in town that charges for this. But, it's a drinking establishment during a significant portion of its time open. The entrées are regionally Texan with those expected robust and on-target Goode Co. touches. Of the roughly ten entrées, there is a very good, juicy grilled half-pound burger served with choice of a variety of toppings, including smoked bacon and avocado slices, and an fresh, airy homemade bun, an attractive and tasty chicken fried steak made with a strip steak, a smoked chicken breast sandwich, a chicken salad sandwich made with toasted pecans and apple slices, venison chili in the properly Texas fashion with cubed meat and an absence of beans, and, for those big spenders, a tender 12-ounce USDA choice ribeye steak. Possibly the most interesting item is the Peace Maker, toasted French bread slices slathered with horseradish and topped with strip steak that has been smoked. For dessert, there is the excellent Goode Co. pecan pie. Though it can get crowded in the evening both for the music and as a singles scene, the service is usually very attentive. Other attractions here are the many feet of bar space, several taps including the hometown Saint Arnold, and many easy-to-view flat-screen televisions. To note, Armadillo Palace is quite kid-friendly until 8PM when those under 18 are not allowed.

Avalon Diner $8

2417 Westheimer (east of Kirby) 77098, (713) 527-8900
12810 Southwest Freeway (in the Fountains Center) 77477, (281) 240-0213
www.avalondiner.com

Cuisine - Diner
Hours - Westheimer - Mon-Fri 6:30AM to 5PM; Sat-Sun 7AM to 4PM; Stafford - Mon-Thu, Sun 7AM to 9PM; Fri-Sat 7AM to 10PM
Credit Cards - Amex, MC, Visa
Service - Table Service
Alcohol - NONE

Entrée Prices - $5 to $15 ($8 average)
Entrées $12 and less - 90%

Atmosphere & Décor - Nice, diner-esque
Appeal - Filling the diner bill for nearby residents
Useful to Note - Each location has a slightly different, but similar, menu.
Menu Suggestions - breakfast; French toast; Jalapeño Cheeseburger; milkshakes

---

Avalon Diner has aptly and consistently satisfied the need for American comfort food in one location or another in the River Oaks area since 1938. The currrent one fittingly sits adjacent to, and adjoining an Avalon Drugs and earns nostalgic style points in never-look-back Houston. Though the setting ensures that the Avalon Diners cannot be mistaken for anything other than a diner, the restaurants themselves are fairly attractive with photos of yesteryear, a clean décor, and nicely upholstered booths. These are probably the cleanest and nicest diners in town. In part, because of this, and the kid-friendly American menu, these restaurants are popular with families with younger children on the weekends. The fare is typical diner fare for this part of the country. It won't excite some folks, but many others will find it comfortable and familiar. As with most diners, one of the most compelling about the Avalon Diner is that breakfast is served all the time.

The breakfasts are the well-worn, expected favorites that Avalon does well: eggs, pancakes, omelets, waffles, French toast, and all of the requisite sides. For regional flavor, there is also the Mexican and Tex-Mex breakfast items like *Huevos Rancheros* and *Migas*. The French toast is one of the highlights of the these offerings, and is one of the better versions in town. The numerous egg dishes are properly cooked, and any one can be made with egg whites or an egg substitute for an additional charge. The hash browns really are hash browns, made with shredded potatoes, but are too often undercooked. For the meat, choose the sausage, as the bacon is prepared en masse in batches and might arrive very dry and less-than-tasty. The numerous non-breakfast offerings include a range of hamburgers, hot dogs, hot and cold sandwiches, salads, vegetable soup of the day, frito pie and dinner plates. Some of the sandwiches are old-time regional diner items such as the patty melt, pimento cheese and egg salad. The hamburgers are diner-quality and pretty decent, made with griddle-fried hamburger patties. Jalapeños can readily add more zest and flavor. The full dinners include an eight-ounce steak, the ubiquitous chicken fried steak, an open-faced roast beef sandwich, meatloaf, grilled frankfurters with baked beans and a couple of chicken dishes. The more elaborate and fine value daily specials that change daily include baked chicken and dressing, fried chicken, roast turkey and dressing, roast beef and dressing, chicken and dumplings, tuna croquettes, and a stuffed bell pepper. The accompaniments for these can include: fried okra, red beans and rice, jalapeño cheese grits, baked sweet potato and black-eyed peas. Cajun Chef hot sauce and a couple flavors of Tabasco will be a necessary addition for many, as the flavors are rarely bold (the service at times might be more so), much less exotic. But, the patrons, most of them long-time, are happy with what they're getting here. In any case, it's good to remember that Avalon Diner still serves the old-fashioned fountain drinks such as milk shakes, cherry Coke, ice cream sodas and ice cream floats.

Baba Yega $10

2607 Grant (block east of Montrose, north of Westheimer) 77006, (713) 522-0042
www.babayega.com

Cuisine - American
Hours - Mon-Thu, Sun 11AM to 10PM; Fri-Sat 11AM to 11PM
Credit Cards - Amex, Diners, Discover, MC, Visa
Service - Table Service
Alcohol - Full Bar

Entrée Prices - $8 to $16 ($10 average)
Entrées $12 and less - 80%

Atmosphere & Décor - Comfortable; patio
Appeal - A friendly neighborhood restaurant in the heart of Montrose
Useful to Note - Good value steak night on Monday and pastas on Tuesday
Menu Suggestions - salads; Baba Yega Caesar (served with strips of marinated, grilled chicken breast); Bacon Burger; California Sandwich (avocado, tomato, sprouts and provolone cheese); The Fantasy Sandwich (avocado, tomato, mayonnaise, provolone cheese and ham)

Baba Yega can be best described as an informal, somewhat cozy neighborhood restaurant in the heart of Montrose. Located in an old house with several dining rooms, a small bar area and two large outdoor patios, Baba Yega has a very comfortable feel. And, the menu with many enticing, familiar items, and the generally attentive and friendly service reinforces this. Since 1975 Baba Yega has been popular with not just neighborhood denizens, but all downtown office workers, and others in search of an honest meal in a welcoming and cozy setting.

The fare here is casual American cooking with a healthy bent. The menu has grown over the years to include a fair number of salads, a number of vegetarian dishes, a handful of hamburgers and meat-laden sandwiches, several grilled entrées, and desserts with varying amounts of fat grams. Many of the starters are local favorites, which results in an eclectic array of choices: artichoke and spinach dip, chips and *queso,* Tomatoes Caprese (mozzarella cheese with fresh tomatoes and basil), brie and feta cheese, *ceviche,* grilled portobello mushrooms, pizza, and cold smoked salmon The enticing, but healthy, salads include a fruit plate, twists on the garden salad, a spinach salad, the Chef's Salad with ham, turkey and cheddar cheese. Two of the more popular are the zesty Greek Salad with red onions and tomato, and their version of the Caesar salad with strips of marinated and grilled chicken. For a place with such an emphasis on low-calorie and low-fat dining, it serves an excellent burger. These began with a hand-crafted half-pound patty cooked to order with American cheese and mayonnaise with lettuce and tomato and a choice of bacon, mushrooms or avocado, on a large, toasted bun. Baba Yega is very generous with the bacon, as an order with it comes to around a half-dozen large, crisp slices. The sandwiches include a cheese-steak, a chicken breast, smoked turkey and brie, a muffaletta and a turkey burger. One of the long-time favorites and best choices is The Fantasy, consisting of ham with avocado, provolone cheese, tomato and mayonnaise. All of the burgers and sandwiches come with a choice of potato salad or fries. The crispy fries are usually the better option.

The entrées listed under "Vegetarian's Delight" are mostly sandwiches, and some of the most popular dishes. The vegetarian sandwiches include one with a grilled portobello mushroom, a vegetarian club with "turkey style gluten & fakin' bacon", the Boca Burger with a vegan patty and choice of avocado or sautéed mushrooms, the Black Bean Burger, and the California, that has been on the menu since inception, made with avocado, provolone cheese, tomato and sprouts. There is also a pasta served with vegetables and another dish with grilled vegetables and rice. The "Grilled Entrées" include salmon, rainbow trout, grilled yellow fin tuna over pasta in a cream sauce with vegetables, a chicken breast, and grilled chicken pasta in a tomato sauce. To be inclusive of those who want to eat heavy, in addition to the top-notch burgers, there is also a twelve-ounce ribeye that is marinated then grilled. In case you were wondering about the name, according to the menu, Baba Yega is a witch in some part of Slavic mythology. This was the subject of the AOR-era Emerson, Lake and Palmer song entitled, "The Huts of Baba Yega", which apparently inspired the restaurant's founders.

Baker's Ribs $8

2223 S. Voss (between Westheimer and San Felipe) 77057, (713) 977-8725
www.bakersribs.com

Cuisine - Barbecue
Hours - Mon-Sat 10AM to 8PM; Sun 10AM to 3PM
Credit Cards - Amex, Discover, MC, Visa
Service - Counter Service
Alcohol - NONE

Entrée Prices - $5 to $11 ($8 average)
Entrées $12 and less - 100%

Atmosphere & Décor - Scruffy; patio
Appeal - Interesting and generally well-done barbecue helped by a great sauce
Menu Suggestions - pork ribs; pork sandwich; chopped beef sandwich; sausage; dirty rice; marinated tomatoes

Baker's Ribs, part of a small Dallas-based chain that re-opened locally after shuttering a few years ago, is not a barbecue temple, but a somewhat unique, generally proficient part of the local smoked meats landscape. There is hickory-smoked pork, beef, turkey, sausage, chicken and ribs here. Ribs are in the name for a reason, and these are suitably meaty, moist and flavorful. Unusual for local barbecue restaurants, Baker's also serves non-rib pork. This, and each of the meats, is pretty good, if not as succulent or as smoky, as is found at the top places. The meats are almost necessarily complemented with a number of squirts from the plastic squeeze bottle containing their warmed vinegar-y barbecue sauce. That addition makes for a nearly always enjoyable combination. The sandwiches, with the sauce, of course, might be a better way to enjoy the meats, as these nicely feature an airy, tasty, toasted bun. The sides set in the steam table as you order can include an interesting array, such as black beans, zesty stewed tomatoes, cole slaw, pasta salad, marinated cucumbers and a sugar-laden peach cobbler. The cool, juicy tomatoes can be especially tasty, and a nice contrast to the warm barbecue. Though conveniently located near some nice neighborhoods, Baker's is sufficiently scruffy: there is lots of rough-hewn woods, concrete floors, low lighting, lame decorations, televisions tuned to an uninteresting program, and tables are that are often un-bussed for a while, which is probably more easily overlooked at a barbecue joint. Conversely, Baker's is convenient for take-away as it has easy-to-order family meals for various sized groups.

Bamboo House $11

540 Waugh (between Allen Parkway and W. Dallas) 77019, (713) 522-3442

Cuisine - Pan Asian
Hours - Mon-Thu, Sun 11AM to 9PM; Fri-Sat 11AM to 10PM
Credit Cards - Amex, Diners, Discover, MC, Visa
Service - Table Service
Alcohol - Beer & Wine

Entrée Prices - Dinner - $7 to $18 ($11 average); Lunch - $8 to $9
Entrées at Dinner $12 and less - 60%

Atmosphere & Décor - Pleasant
Appeal - Well-executed, accessible Asian food in a nice setting
Useful to Note - Lunch specials are offered during the weekends, too.
Menu Suggestions - Crispy Crab Dumplings with Cream Cheese; Crispy Salmon Roll; Orange Beef (quickly fried pieces of beef in an orange-tinged sauce); Wok Seared Beef and Leeks; Hot Fish (crispy slices of fish in a spicy tomato sauce); Walnut Shrimp (crispy shrimp in a spicy sauce with caramelized onions); Thai Curry Chicken (with a spicy red curry in coconut milk)

The charms of Bamboo House belie its exterior in a nearly faceless double-decker strip center across from the towering AIG complex on Waugh. This is one of the better Inner Loop Asian restaurants. And, a good amount of Asia is represented, mostly seamlessly and in complementary and attractively presented fashion. There are popular Chinese, Thai, and Japanese dishes and influences on their focused and very approachable menu, in addition to Vietnamese. Bamboo House will certainly have a dish, or several, that will appeal to the most casual fan of Asian cuisines. Décor is attractive, inviting and soothing. Sturdy dark tables and chairs share the small dining room with banquettes and walls in pleasant earth tones. Service is friendly and generally attentive, a far cry from Chinatown.

There are a number of tempting ways to start here, more so than at other restaurants, it seems: *edamame*, pork dumplings, spring rolls with shredded vegetables or with shrimp, chicken, rice noodles, the deep-fried Imperial rolls, shrimp tempura, fried dumplings filled with crab and cream cheese, deep-fried rolls with salmon and spinach, and the Philly Roll with the great match of smoked salmon and cream cheese. Before starting, it's good to know that the Vietnamese dishes are probably the least interesting, which is fairly surprising since the owners are Vietnamese. For example, the Imperial Rolls, which elsewhere are thick rolls of crunchy dough bursting with flavor are small and thin here with somewhat a different, though enjoyable taste, maybe due to the taro. For the entrées, the vermicelli dish has very tasty chicken or beef, but does not sport the delicacy that's found in versions of the dish at the innumerable Vietnamese restaurants around. Conversely, the Chinese-inspired dishes might be the best.

The entrées feature chicken, beef, seafood, vegetables, noodles and rice. There are Chinese egg and rice noodles, Japanese *soba* and *udon* (wheat and buckwheat, respectively), and the thin rice Vietnamese vermicelli. A number of the entrées are usually lighter and more pleasing versions of the familiar Chinese-American staples such as General [Tso's] Chicken (breaded chicken with dried chiles in a spicy soy and garlic sauce), Sweet and Sour Chicken, Spicy Chicken with Peanuts, fried rice, *lo mein* (stir-fried egg noodles), and Orange Beef. This features thin slices of very flavorful orange-tinged beef that is tender, moist, and certainly much higher quality than similar versions elsewhere, which avoids most of the gloppiness that usually affects this dish. The Wok Seared Beef and Leeks dish uses similarly well prepared slices of beef in a lighter presentation with red peppers, leeks and a slightly sweet sauce. For the steak-and-potatoes person in the group, there is a tender, marinated 8-ounce ribeye served with teriyaki sauce. The handful of fish dishes are quite good; available pan-fried, baked or in a clay pot. The fried rice dishes are very good, including the one that features pieces of ham, shrimp and pineapples. The stir-fried *soba* noodles with greens and chicken are attractively presented, as are the half-dozen or so other pan-Asian noodle dishes. Lunch is a wise time to visit, as there are about twenty lunch specials, including most of the entrées, and each are priced under ten bucks.

Barbecue Inn $10

116 W. Crosstimbers (west of N. Main) 77018, (713) 695-8112

Cuisine - Texan; Barbecue
Hours - Tue-Sat 10:30AM to 10PM
Credit Cards - Amex, Diners, Discover, MC, Visa
Service - Table Service
Alcohol - Beer

Entrée Prices - $6 to $19 (average is $10)
Entrées $12 and less - 80%

Atmosphere & Décor - Pleasant, retro
Appeal - Well-done Houston favorites from the 1940s and 50s
Useful to Note - Don't let the parking lot security guard deter you.
Menu Suggestions - Chicken Fried Steak; Fried Shrimp Basket; pork ribs; coconut cream pie

Featuring Southern, Texas and Gulf Coast cooking, Barbecue Inn is the type of restaurant that probably appealed to most Houstonians after the Second

World War and well into the Eisenhower Administration. And, actually, up to the present, too. It's usually crowded most nights of the week, often like it has been since it opened since 1946. Once fate had a witness, the years seemed like friends. Well prepared, familiar and tasty food, a pleasant atmosphere and very efficient and friendly service are some of the keys to its continued popularity. The restaurant occupies a very tidy space in a neighborhood that has seen better days. The interior is nice and tidy, too. The dining room is pleasantly decorated and comfortable. Booths provide most of the seating. There is also a counter with stools for the single diner, and a section for takeout orders. As with the décor and atmosphere, the food is decidedly untrendy, homey, and comfortable. A menu from 1965 on display in the hallway leading into the restaurant is evidently just a shortened version of today's menu, excepting the very scanty prices, of course. The fryer gets a workout here. The highlights of the menu are barbecue, fried chicken, chicken fried steak and fried shrimp. These items are not the trendiest, but are immensely satisfying to many, especially the fried shrimp, which are large and succulent, and some of the best in the area. The same can be said for the chicken fried steak, which is another reason to visit. It's possible to eat heartily and fairly cheaply here, if not in heart-healthy fashion. The inexpensive items include beef, pork and fried catfish sandwiches, and hamburgers. The priciest items are the steaks, an eight-ounce filet mignon and a twelve-ounce rib-eye, which are not cheap, but are still a fine value. The salads are of the basic iceberg variety, but they are large by dinner salad standards, and they feature fresh lettuce and tomatoes, something often lacking at many similar establishments. A drawback might be that it can be difficult to eat light here. Even the Chef's Salad features barbecued beef or ham. The Barbecue Inn is discernibly popular with most age groups. A typical evening will find both young families and older couples. What they have in common is that they seem to be preparing for winter hibernation, even during the depths of summer. This is the type of food that will do that to you.

Barnaby's Café $9

602 Fairview (between Taft and Montrose) 77006, (713) 522-0106
1701 S. Shepherd (south West Gray) 77019, (713) 520-5131
414 West Gray (between Taft and Montrose) 77006, (713) 522-8898
www.barnabyscafe.com

Cuisine - American
Hours - Mon 11AM to 10PM; Tue-Thu 7AM to 10PM; Fri 8AM to 11PM; Sun 8AM to 10PM
Credit Cards - Amex, Diners, Discover, MC, Visa
Service - Table Service
Alcohol - Beer & Wine

Entrée Prices - Dinner & Lunch - $7 to $18 ($9 average); Breakfast - $4 to $7
Entrées at Dinner $12 and less - 90%

Atmosphere & Décor - Nice
Appeal - Good comfort food for Montrose and the Shepherd corridor
Useful to Note - It can be fine choice for a casual Sunday brunch.
Menu Suggestions - Chinese Chicken Salad; Chicken Mediterranean Salad; Turkey Breast with Cranberry Mayonnaise Sandwich; Doctor Gale's Meatloaf; Newport Chicken; hamburgers; breakfast; apple pie; chocolate cake; brownie á la mode

---

In its more recent additions on Shepherd and West Gray, and in its homier original one(s) in the heart of Montrose, Barnaby's serves well prepared, comfortable American food. Though the menu items might be described as diner-esque, the delivery, presentation and range of the dishes, plus the feel of the restaurants, won't be confused with anyone's idea of a greasy diner. The food is generally better, and the restaurants are nicer and cleaner, and the service is unfailingly more friendly and cheerful than any diner.

Barnaby's creates very satisfying (and often very large) versions of familiar dishes. And, some twists to liven up those familiar plates. The menu is neatly divided among salads, cold sandwiches, hamburgers, dinner plates and desserts. There are no appetizers. But, given the healthy-sized portions, these are not really necessary. There are no soups, either, which might be another matter. The salads include a Caesar, both with and without grilled chicken, a chef's salad, the Chinese Chicken Salad, Chicken Mediterranean Salad and the California Salad. The handful of cold sandwiches is not what you will find at most diners. There is Turkey Breast with Cranberry Mayonnaise, Honey Baked Ham with Honey Mustard, Albacore Tuna with Pecans, Pesto Chicken Salad and Artichoke Hearts, plus a comparatively boring club sandwich. The hamburgers, made with hormone-free ground chuck, are cooked to a tastier and juicy medium, and the toppings include an interesting array: guacamole, green chile and hickory barbecue sauce. For those trying to contain their waistlines, there are also the non-traditional turkey burger, a grilled chicken sandwich, a buffalo burger and a vegetarian burger. All come with fries. The various dinner plates are recognizable mainstream regional fare. Among the nearly twenty choices include ribs, meatloaf, steak, a variety of chicken breast preparations, salmon, pork chops, a stir-fry, a couple of different lasagna dishes, other pastas, *tostadas* and a burrito. There are not too many places around where you can always get a well prepared twelve-ounce steak with fries and a salad for twelve bucks. If you have room for dessert, the selections are the pie *du jour*, available with a scoop of Amy's ice cream, carrot cake, cheesecake, Italian cream cake, a chocolate dish and the old soda fountain classic Black Cow, a vanilla ice cream soda.

The original Fairview location and the twenty-seat or so Baby Barnaby's next door in the heart of Montrose have the comfortable well-worn feel to them. The Shepherd and West Gray Barnaby's are sleeker, but similarly comfortable. Breakfast is served on the weekends, though quite good, does not seem as satisfying as the lunch and dinner offerings. A couple of the pluses are the bacon is thick, crisp and excellent, and coffee is charmingly served in small individual pots. During other times, beers and wine are available, and at all times, fresh lemonade.

Barry's Pizza $9

6003 Richmond (at Fountain View) 77057, (713) 266-8692
11303 Fountain Lake Drive (Fountains Shopping Center) 77477, (281) 494-0666
www.barryspizza.com

Cuisine - Pizza
Hours - Mon-Fri 11AM to 11PM; Sat 12 to 11PM; Sun 12 to 10PM
Credit Cards - Amex, Discover, MC, Visa
Service - Table Service
Alcohol - Beer & Wine

Entrée Prices - Dinner - $6 to $13 ($9 average); Lunch - $6 to $8
Entrées at Dinner $12 and less - 90%

Atmosphere & Décor - Pizza parlor
Appeal - Good pizza joints
Useful to Note - There are plenty of televisions to catch the game.
Menu Suggestions - deep dish pizzas

With two unpretentious locations, Barry's serves some of the better pizzas in town. The settings fit the bill, as it is tough to mistake these for anything other than pizza parlors; not a bad thing at all. These are fairly large, open, and, of course, very informal. The tables are covered with red and white checkered tablecloths. Televisions, usually turned to a sporting event featuring a local team, are conveniently perched throughout the restaurants. Good pizza, beer and the game on the tube make for a great mix. Barry's offers thin crust and rectangular Sicilian-style deep-dish pizzas. Both can be very good, especially the deep-dish versions, which are the best pizzas of this type in town. The quality of the pizza begins with the crust. For the deep-dish version, it is especially buttery tasting and crispy. Even the whole-wheat crusts are pretty scrumptious. The toppings are of high quality and judiciously used. The menu states that the pizzas are cooked on stone deck ovens, just like they do in Naples, the birthplace of pizzas. Though

Barry's might not be using the traditional wood-burning ones, as they do there, you can't tell otherwise. The smallest of the deep dish pizza size, eight-by-ten, will usually satisfy two hungry adults. The specialty pizzas include Barry's Special (pepperoni, Italian sausage, mushrooms, ham, bell pepper and onion), Barry's Beef Fajita (grilled beef fajitas with *pico de gallo* and avocado) and the Hawaiian (with ham and pineapple). If these or the other specialty pizzas do not fit your fancy, Barry's has the full range of toppings to help create your own. In addition to the obvious toppings, there are artichoke hearts, jalapeños, anchovies and feta cheese. The pizzas are the real reason to visit Barry's, but they also serve the popular Southern Italian-American dishes for those who want something different. They have salads, Italian-American subs and the popular and familiar pasta dishes. If you need some starters before the pizza or the pastas, there are Buffalo wings, breaded and fried mozzarella sticks, fried mushrooms and a regional twist on the St. Louis specialty of toasted ravioli, Spicy Fried Ravioli. These are ravioli made with ricotta, mozzarella and jalapeños, deep-fried and served with the house-made marinara sauce. Only a cardiologist could find fault with that combination.

Bellaire Broiler Burger $6

5216 Bellaire (near the Bissonnet and Bellaire intersection) 77401, (713) 668-8171

Cuisine - Hamburgers
Hours - Mon-Sat 11AM to 8PM
Credit Cards - MC, Visa
Service - Counter Service
Alcohol - Beer & Wine

Entrée Prices - \$5 to \$7 (\$6 average)
Entrées \$12 and less - 100%

Atmosphere & Décor - Spartan and unintentionally retro
Appeal - Excellent, inexpensive burgers; some of the best burgers in town
Some Menu Highlights - hamburgers; Combination Special (hamburger patty with two grilled hot dogs and chili, grated cheddar cheese and chopped onions in a bun)

Some delicate types might describe Bellaire Broiler Burger as a greasy dump. Though that terminology might have a lot of merit, it's a very good greasy dump. The restaurant consists of a grill in an open kitchen, which is visible behind the counter where you place your order, Formica booths, a small moveable bar area displaying a couple of beer taps, a television set in a corner, wood paneling, a moderately sized dining room, and a low ceiling. It feels like something out of the early 1950s. Apparently, the place has not been substantially remodeled since that time. It does not detract at all from the enjoyment of the meal. In fact, this might even enhance it. The reason to visit, the relatively thin burgers are grilled and excellent. These are your basic all-American-style burgers. Messy, juicy enough and nothing fancy, these are nonetheless always very satisfying. That the hamburgers are grilled is evident, as flames more-than-occasionally jump from the grates. These attractively charred patties seem to meld perfectly with the toasted buns, ripe and juicy tomato slices and crisp lettuce to become some of the very best burgers in town. These basic burgers are available with just a handful of additions such as cheddar cheese, bacon, chili, mushrooms and barbecue sauce. For the hungry patron, a nice value is the Half Pounder. For just more than five bucks you get a hamburger with a delicious half-pound patty adorned with mustard, mayonnaise, onions, pickles, lettuce and tomatoes. A treat, though certainly not for the cholesterol level, is the Combination Special. It consists of a charcoal broiled hamburger patty with two grilled hot dogs and chili, grated cheddar cheese and chopped onions in a bun. The grilling of the hot dogs, as with the hamburgers, does make a difference, and a very savory, and potentially, very sloppy, sandwich. The majority of the items offered are hamburgers, and these are the chief draw. Bellaire Broiler Burger does serve other unpretentious items: a marinated and grilled chicken breast sandwich, a BLT, a fried fish sandwich, chili, deep-fried chicken strips, grilled ground chuck with barbecue sauce, and a loaded chef's salad. The onion rings are probably a better bet than the fries that are crisp enough but lacking any salt or seasoning. For beverages, there is inexpensive, industrial-style beer and wine, soft drinks, and also milk shakes. Bellaire Broiler Burger can be a very gratifying place to visit when you have the taste for hamburgers, or just a sense of nostalgia.

Berryhill Baja Grill $9

2639 Revere (just south of Westheimer) 77098, (713) 526-8080
1717 Post Oak Boulevard (at San Felipe) 77056, (713) 871-8226
3407 Montrose (at Hawthorne, south of Westheimer) 77006, (713) 523-8226
13703 Southwest Freeway (at Sugar Creek) Sugar Land, 77479, (281) 313-8226
5110 Buffalo Speedway (at Westpark) 77005, (713) 667-8226
11660 Westheimer (between Hayes and Kirkwood) 77077, (281) 759-2242
5482 FM 1960 W (at Champions Forest) 77069, (281) 444-2323
702 E. 11th (between Studewood and Heights) 77008, (713) 225-2252
716 Kingwood (east of 59 and 494) Kingwood, 77339, (281) 359-8226
9595 Six Pines (at Research Forest) The Woodlands, 77380, (281) 298-8226
www.berryhillbajagrill.com

Cuisine - Mexican (Baja-influenced)

Hours - Revere - Mon-Fri 10AM to 10PM; Sat 9AM to 10PM; Sun 9AM to 9PM; Post Oak - Mon-Sat 9AM to 10PM; Sun 9AM to 9PM; Montrose - Mon-Thu, Sun 10AM to 10PM, (Bar open until 11PM); Fri-Sat 10AM to 11PM (Bar open until 12AM); Sugar Land - Mon-Thu 9AM to 10PM; Fri 9AM to 11PM; Sat 8AM to 11PM; Sun 8AM to 9PM; Buffalo Speedway - Mon-Thu 9AM to 10PM; Fri-Sat 9AM to

11PM; Sun 9AM to 9PM; Westheimer - Mon-Sat 9AM to 10PM; Sun 9AM to 9PM; Heights - Mon-Thu 11AM to 10PM; Fri-Sat 8AM to 11PM; Sun 8AM to 10PM; Champions, Kingwood & Woodlands - Mon-Thu, Sun 10AM to 10PM; Fri-Sat 10AM to 11PM
Credit Cards - Amex, Discover, MC, Visa
Service - Counter Service
Alcohol - Full Bar

Entrée Prices - Dinner & Lunch - $5 to $13 ($9 average); Breakfast - $4 to $7
Entrées at Dinner $12 and less - 90%

Atmosphere & Décor - Nice, especially for fast-casual restaurants
Appeal - Exceptional fish tacos and good Tex-Mex breakfasts
Menu Suggestions - Original Fish Taco (fried fish with red cabbage); Crispy Shrimp Taco; Original Shrimp Taco (shrimp sautéed in white wine); Chicken Quesadilla; Chipotle Shrimp Quesadilla; Spinach Enchiladas; Corn Enchiladas; Chicken Enchiladas; soups; breakfast tacos

---

The name change from Berryhill Hot Tamales to Berryhill Baja Grill several years ago reflects the fact that it was the fish tacos that brought Berryhill its popularity. In fact, Berryhill helped to introduce and popularize the southern Californian favorite in Houston during the 1990s. The fish tacos are excellent, and the best things to order at Berryhill. These consist of fish or shrimp, either breaded and deep-fried or grilled, served with shredded red cabbage and a spicy mayonnaise- or mustard-based dressing wrapped within two corn tortillas. Both the original fried and grilled fish versions are excellent. Surprisingly, these are made with farm-raised catfish, which is usually not anyone's first choice for a fish taco (especially so on the Left Coast). But, the tacos are so clean-tasting and delicious it is tough to imagine that they could be much better with any kind of substitution. The tacos with shrimp, especially the fried ones, are also quite commendable. An order of two tacos, plus the complimentary chips and salsa, make for a sufficient meal for most people. Given the very high quality of the Mexican food in town, and especially when compared with West Coast fare, it is not surprising that the fish tacos at Berryhill are at least as good, or better than you would typically find throughout much of southern California, at least what I've found north of Ensenada. The fish tacos are that tasty. The nearly artful and bounteous breakfast tacos on fresh flour tortillas are nearly as good of a reason to visit.

For all of the dishes, the ingredients, preparation and even the presentation are very good. In addition to the seafood and breakfast tacos, there are soups and salads including an interesting corn and poblano pepper chili chowder, *quesadillas,* enchiladas, burritos, deliciously deep-fried chimichangas and desserts. The Tex-Mex-style *quesadillas* featuring large flour tortillas filled with several choices can be very good, and have more flair than typical *quesadillas*. The chicken version features shredded chicken and red onions, Anaheim chiles and Monterey Jack and cream cheese. The *Chipotle* Shrimp *quesadilla* is made with poblano peppers, leeks, grilled onions and Monterey Jack cheese in addition to the shrimp sautéed with *chipotle* peppers. The combination dishes, with tamales, tacos and enchiladas are for those who do not want to make too many decisions. The former signature items, the tamales, are less flavorful with the absence of the lard, but these still have plenty of fans. These comparatively healthful, if far from the best local commercial versions, are properly served in cornhusks and a choice of several stuffings. There are more than enough dishes to satisfy the vegetarians and health conscious, even during breakfast. For those not interested in healthful dining and a nice complement to their ice cold Mexican beers and tasty margaritas, there are a couple of enticing appetizers in addition to the expected queso and nachos: small hard-shell tacos filled with chicken and guacamole, and roasted bacon-wrapped jumbo shrimp.

The settings for the Berryhill restaurants are probably nicer than what can be expected from the menu prices. The original Revere location, with namesake Walter Berryhill's tamale cart situated in front, is a small sliver of a restaurant with counter space and a handful of tables, both inside and around the small patio area outside. The Post Oak Berryhill's is larger, and more user-friendly with better service. But given that it is in the heart of the Galleria area, it is always crowded during the lunchtime hours. The Montrose location has become part of the landscape, and is another option for a festive Sunday brunch. The 11th Street location has been a very welcome addition to the Heights, which certainly still does not have an overabundance of alluring dining spots. There are other Houston area locations and ones in Austin and Dallas, plus plans for greater expansion locally and throughout the state. Hopefully, the quality that has made Berryhill's successful will not suffer as the number of restaurants and franchises increase.

Bibas Greek Pizza $10

5526 Memorial (east of Wescott) 77007, (713) 861-2266

Cuisine - Pizza; Greek
Hours - Daily 11AM to 10PM
Credit Cards - Amex, Diners, Discover, MC, Visa
Service - Table Service; Delivery
Alcohol - Beer & Wine

Entrée Prices - $6 to $14 ($10 average)
Entrées $12 and less - 80%

Atmosphere & Décor - Nice enough for a pizza joint; patio
Appeal - Very good pizza near Memorial Park
Useful to Note - Take-away is a good option for a pizza.
Menu Suggestions - pizza

Situated in an unusual A-frame structure almost encroaching on Memorial Drive, not too far from the park, Bibas Greek Pizza, or whatever the signage currently shows, serves up just that, pizza with a Greek intonation, and a fairly large number of standard Greek dishes. With more than a dozen tables on the patio in front of the restaurant, this is a pleasant enough place to enjoy a pizza and a beer on a nice day. There is not much seating inside, anyway. The menu brags about serving the best Greek pizza in town; not that there are any other places that immediately come to mind advertising Greek pizza. The pizza here is some of the best pizza in town, Greek or otherwise. The restaurant is justifiably proud of their crusts, the requisite base for any worthy pizza, which are noticeably buttery and properly crispy. Though called thin crust pizzas, these are healthy and suitably sturdy thin crust pizzas. The pizzas are usually expertly cooked, neither underdone in the middle nor overdone at the edges, as sometimes disappointingly happens at other purveyors of American-style pizzas. The best ones here seem to have a Greek flavor, for some reason. A version with pepperoni and feta cheese shows what Bibas Greek Pizzas does very well. It comes with plenty of slightly melted feta cheese, which greatly complements the tomato sauce, and a fair amount of thinly sliced pepperoni. Though loaded with toppings, the pizza is balanced and very tasty. Also very good are the specialty pizzas such as the classically named Acropolis (pepperoni, sausage, beef, bell peppers, onions, olives and mushrooms) and Aphrodite (tomatoes, grilled chicken and feta). A large pizza should be at least enough to satiate two hungry adults. If excellent pizza is not in order, Bibas also serves a large menu of traditional Greek dishes. These include various appetizers, salads and entrées. Among the choices are *spanikopita* (phyllo pastry filled with feta and fresh spinach), *tiropita* (phyllo pastry filled with marinated chicken with grilled onions), cucumbers with *tzaziki* (a yogurt-based dip), *kalzones* with several different fillings, gyros, *souvakli* (grilled, marinated beef cubes), *dolmades* (stuffed grape leaves), Greek salad, *moussaka* (eggplant casserole with ground beef and béchamel sauce), zesty boiled and marinated octopus, plus some pastas and Greek fajitas that are seasoned chopped lamb and beef served with onions, green peppers, tomatoes and feta cheese.

Bibas Greek Restaurant $9

607 West Gray (between Taft and Montrose) 77019, (713) 523-8432

Cuisine - Greek; Diner
Credit Cards - Amex, Diners, Discover, MC, Visa
Hours - Open 24 Hours
Service - Table Service
Alcohol - Beer & Wine

Entrée Prices - Dinner & Lunch - $5 to $25 ($9 average); Breakfast - $5 to $9
Entrées at Dinner $12 and less - 80%

Atmosphere & Décor - Comfortable, but friendly; patio
Appeal - Well prepared Greek food, and breakfast at all hours, too
Useful to Note - Don't ask John about that Anatolian favorite, hummus
Menu Suggestions - Greek Salad; Greek Salad with gyro meat; octopus; Shish Kabob; Gyro Sandwich; Gyro Platter; Lamb Shank

---

About a mile west of downtown, situated in an old house on West Gray between Taft and Montrose marked by an ambiguous sign reading "One's a Meal / (BIBAS) / OPEN 24 Hrs.", Bibas Greek Restaurant serves generally well prepared Greek food at all hours. In sprawling, auto-centric Houston, it's a neighborhood restaurant with a personality. A big part of the attraction at Bibas is a couple of long-time Greek waiters who have been with the restaurant many years, even before the Bibas named graced the signage. Unlike the waitstaff in most restaurants, they are professional waiters who are personable, very helpful and efficient, and aid in giving this place a lot of character. Along with the friendly owner, they help to make dining at Bibas a pleasant experience. In a city of surprisingly limited restaurant hours, Bibas is one of the too-few stops in the area for late night grub, either for breakfast, or certainly, Greek.

Although it offers other dishes, the main menu at Bibas is Greek, and this is where the kitchen shines. Offerings include the familiar Greek appetizers, sandwiches and entrées. The starters include *dolmades* (stuffed grapes leaves), *tzatziki* (the yogurt-based dip), *taramosalata* (a creamy carp roe mixture), *melintzanosalata* (whipped eggplant and herbs), and the stuffed phyllo pastries: *spanakopita* (spinach), *tiropita* (feta), *kotopita* (grilled chicken and onions), and *kreatopita* (ground beef). Sautéed octopus, a Greek staple, is also available upon request. The sandwiches include a competent gyro, and beef and chicken *souvlaki,* featuring meat that has been marinated then grilled, and a grilled cheese sandwich served in pita bread. Both the gyro and *souvlaki* are available as plates served with a Greek salad. Beyond the more casual items, the best, and most expensive items, are the Greek entrées such as the kabobs with shrimp, chicken and beef. There is also the heavy *moussaka* (layers of eggplant, potato and meat sauce), *Keftedakia* (meatballs in tomato sauce), plus larger portions of several of the appetizers. The calzones (or kalzones on the menu) seem to be made with a large pita-style bread folded over toppings. Certainly different than the Italian-American version, these can be satisfying, especially the gyro-filled version. There are also several, mostly Greek-flavored pizzas, which might not be as good as the excellent pizzas Bibas Greek Pizza a few miles to the west, but you can order small individual-sized pizzas, an attraction for solo diners in need of a pizza fix. To wash the food down, Bibas has several cold bottled beers, and a number of Greek wines of debatable quality.

Also on the menu are items from the long-gone One's a Meal restaurants, a once-popular Greek-operated diner with several area locations. This section of the menu consists of the basic American breakfast and dinner options. Though not as reliable as the Greek dishes, these are nonetheless sufficiently prepared, and best of all, served at all hours. There are a number of three-egg omelets, a fine value that are served with basic diner coffee, a choice of toast or biscuits, and a choice among hash browns (just bland sautéed potatoes here), grits and fries. Chili can be slathered atop any omelet for an additional charge. Bibas also serves most of the other expected breakfast highlights you would expect from a diner: French toast, pancakes, waffles and the like in combination meals. Bibas also serves a decent one-third pound burger and cheeseburger. Sides of fries or onion rings can make a fine accompaniment. To note, though it shares a name with Bibas Greek Pizza, it has different owners and generally different proficiencies.

Bijan Persian Grill $9

5922 Hillcroft (between Southwest Freeway and Harwin) 77036, (832) 242-5959

Cuisine - Persian
Hours - Daily 10AM to 12AM
Credit Cards - Amex, Discover, MC, Visa
Service - Counter Service
Alcohol - NONE

Entrée Prices - $6 to $12 ($9 average)
Entrées $12 and less - 100%

Atmosphere & Décor - Comfortable
Appeal - An informal and comfortable stop for well prepared kabobs
Useful to Note - Only quality halal meat is served, which should be expected
Menu Suggestions - hummus; Koobideh (ground beef kabob); Chicken Barg (chicken kabob); Lamb Shish Kabob

Busy since opening in 2003, Bijan Persian Grill is a nicely appointed, comfortable and airy eatery that has aptly filled a niche for a place with good, zesty grilled meats. It's more upscale than its predecessors at this price range. This is the type of casual, approachable restaurant, especially given its proximity to the Southwest Freeway, which should appeal to many more than just those who grew up with this type of food. If you are unfamiliar with Persian cuisine, the focused menu shown above the counter has a number of items listed with brief descriptions for each under the appropriate headings: cold appetizer, hot appetizer, kabobs, stews, desserts. There are also photos for the entrées, and the accommodating staff will be quick to help, if needed. There are plentiful sides of over a half-dozen cold appetizers like a well-made *hummus, tabouli,* pickled vegetables, a salad, and several yogurt-based dips, well suited for this climate. There is yogurt with cucumber (*Must-o-Mooser*), yogurt with shallots (*Must-u-Khiyar*), and the popular spinach and yogurt (*Borani Essfenaj*). Each serves as a fine complement to the fresh flat bread. The grilled items are the main attraction, which is not surprising with the name Bijan Persian Grill. There are versions with ground beef (*Koobideh),* beef, lamb, lamb shank, chicken fillet (*Barg*), ground chicken (chicken *Koobideh*), Cornish hen (*Juoujeh*), salmon, and combinations. The meats are prepared on an indoor grill behind the counter, and are served properly moist and flavorful. The juices and tartness of the accompanying lemon wedge and grilled tomato-half help to enhance the typically clean, meaty flavors of these dishes. The beef kabobs are probably better than the ones with chicken. The other entrées are a handful of beef stews with lentils or eggplant. These can also be made as vegetarian dishes. To finish, there are several sweet pastries and Persian ice cream.

Black Walnut Café $9

5510 Morningside (near University) 77005, (713) 526-5551
2520 Research Forest (west of Grograns Mill) The Woodlands, 77381, (281) 362-1678
www.bwcafe.com

Cuisine - American
Hours - Mon-Sat 8AM to 10PM; Sun 8AM to 9PM
Credit Cards - Amex, Discover, MC, Visa
Service - Counter Service
Alcohol - Beer & Wine

Entrée Prices - Dinner & Lunch - $5 to $17 ($9 average); Breakfast - $5 to $10
Entrées at Dinner $12 and less - 90%

Atmosphere & Décor - Pleasant
Appeal - Well-made comfort food
Useful to Note - Breakfast is served all the time.
Menu Suggestions - omelets; salads; gelato

The important thing to note about Black Walnut Café is that it provides flavorful food to suit most tastes for a reasonable price with some very welcome amenities, including a noticeably friendly staff. The offerings include egg-centric breakfasts served all day (freshly squeezed orange juice, too), and salads, hot sandwiches, burgers, soups, pastas, flatbreads, and a few heartier entrées, most with the expected regional zest during the afternoon and evening hours. Large, thick glassware is used for drinks and the flatware and utensils are a cut above most restaurants in this price range. And, the sturdy table and chairs are quite comfortable, which is a big plus. The well-attended dining rooms attest to the fact it is doing things right for most diners.

But, it certainly can stand some tweaking. In several ways the restaurant can be too cute for its own good, in slightly irritating fashion. The décor, which might be mistaken for cozy-sophisticated in a setting many miles from a city center, is neo-fern bar. With the opening of the second location, it already felt like these were chain restaurants. Featuring dark wood, black walnut, maybe, it is not at all unattractive. It's just not that easy cool, exhibited at places like (the much pricier) Gravitas or Café Express that it seems the owners were striving for. This misstep extends to the menu's presentation, which is cluttered and overly cutesy to the point of near-confusion. Many names and titles are presented in both cases (e.g. "corn PoBlaNo chOwDer"). Prices are listed without dollar signs and the decimals are extended to four places (8.9562, for example). There are the many seemingly incongruous food terms such as the northern Italian-originated pesto and gorgonzola pastas prominent in dishes listed as Greek, and the "Insaladas", misspelled in both Italian and Spanish, but, thankfully, are identifiably salads. Plus, there are a good number of items and phrases that are not found in any food dictionary and certainly result in some customer bewilderment ("marie cheese", "pesto pavia", "gb", "tpg cut", etc.). The set-up, with only a small counter area to take orders not noticeably identified and a large menu just inside the door that helps to back up traffic to outside the restaurant during peak dining hours, makes it obvious that no industrial engineer was involved in the design.

These demerits are generally minor irritants compared to the quality of the food and the amiability of the staff. In addition to the breakfast fare, the wide-ranging menu has appealing items like a Southwestern Lasagna with chicken, black beans and jalapeños, corn poblano chowder, a blackened salmon Caesar salad, pot roast, and pasta with crawfish tails, sausage and plenty of cayenne pepper. There is beer and a strangely selected list of wines. There are also fresh fruit drinks, smoothies, espresso and espresso-based drinks, and even *gelato*, the Italian take on ice cream, which is made at the Woodlands location.

Blue Nile $10

9400 Richmond (between Fondren and Gessner) 77063, (713) 782-6882
www.bluenilerestaurant.com

Cuisine - Ethiopian
Hours - Daily 11AM to 11PM
Credit Cards - Amex, MC, Visa
Service - Table Service
Alcohol - Full Bar

Entrée Prices - $5 to $15 ($10 average)
Entrées $12 and less - 90%

Atmosphere & Décor - Spartan
Appeal - Very good food from a cuisine unfamiliar to most
Useful to Note - It's best to eat with your hands here.
Menu Suggestions - Yessiga Wot (a beef stew); Banatu (a stew with minced beef and bread); Doro Wot (a chicken stew); Kifto (a lamb stew)

Though Ethiopian restaurants have been around in this country for a number of years, they are still not perceived as a tempting option for most people. It is unfortunate, for one, because Ethiopian cuisine reflects a unique heritage and cuisine that extends back to biblical times. The trepidation of trying this cuisine might increase upon entering the usually empty dining room at the Blue Nile, which is located in an older strip center on Richmond. It might give someone pause to wonder whether they made the right choice. But ignoring the sparse décor and lack of fellow patrons, you will enjoy some interesting, very tasty, and, yes, filling food. Suitable for local tastes, most of the dishes are meat-based and spicy. Décor is at a minimum at Blue Nile. And, unlike some nicer Ethiopian restaurants in other cities, (the more comfortable) standard tables and chairs are used rather than the traditional low tables with backless stools or hassocks.

The manner of presentation and eating are different than at most restaurants. All of the entrées are served with *injera*; the common Ethiopian bread that doubles as the eating utensil for the food. *Injera* is a flat bread that has a spongy consistency, made with the staple grain of northeast Africa, teff (the smallest grain in the world that is high in calcium, protein and iron content, in case you were wondering). Most dishes are served in small bowls that accompany a large plate covered with a big piece of *injera* and dotted with what looks like a yellow mess and a green mess. These are flavorful, if somewhat indescribable, accompaniments to, rather than condiments for, the dishes. The drill is to tear off a piece of *injera* from the basket, scoop some of the entrée onto the outstretched *injera*, then add the yellow or green side and eat. This should be easy to handle for most

Houstonians used to filling tortillas. The presentation leads easily to sharing of dishes, and a wise strategy for a group might be to order several dishes so as to taste the many different flavors. There are no appetizers or desserts in Ethiopia, just main dishes.

One of the best and most accessible dishes on the short menu is the *Yessiga Wot*, which is beef stewed with the flavorful and slow-burning *berbere* sauce. It is delicious and fairly spicy, with some unusual flavors due to the components of cardamom, cumin, and chile peppers. It looks similar to a long-simmered goulash. Like goulash, it is hearty and filling, though the spicing is quite different. The other *wot* on the menu is also a stew-like dish flavored with the *berbere* sauce, and it's also very appetizing. The *Doro Wot* is a similar dish made with chicken; a chicken leg and a hard-boiled egg are substituted for the beef. The *Banatu* is another very good dish consisting of minced beef in the *berbere* sauce mixed together with pieces of *injera*. If you doubt that Ethiopian food cannot be filling, you need to try this dish. Maybe not as flavorful as these, but certainly tasty, is the *Tibs*, marinated beef cubes served with sautéed onions, slices of jalapeño and fresh rosemary. The beef in this dish can be a little tough, but it is flavorful. Given the common knowledge of the country, it is not surprisingly that there are several vegetarian dishes. These seem much more flavorful than most vegetarian fare. There is *Timatim Fitfit* that is made with fresh tomatoes, jalapeños, bell peppers, and olive oil mixed in with pieces of *injera* and the unique Ethiopian herbs and spices. Another interesting dish is the *Yemisser Wot*, a meatless version of the Ethiopian stews with lentils replacing the beef or chicken, and served with the *berbere* sauce, green peppers, garlic and ginger. Unfortunately for the Ethiopian food aficionados, though probably not for most Houstonians, the *Doulet* is only served on the weekends. Considered a delicacy, it consists of minced lamb liver, lamb tripe and beef sautéed with butter, hot pepper and herbs and spices. Also on weekends, at night, Blue Nile might have bands and music. And, presumably more patrons than during the lunch hours. If you have time, you might want to indulge in the Ethiopian Coffee. That beverage that helps make the modern world work, originated in Ethiopia, after all.

Bombay Sweets $6

5827 Hillcroft (between Southwest Freeway and Harwin) 77036, (713) 780-4453

Cuisine - Indian; Vegetarian
Hours - Daily 11AM to 9:30PM
Credit Cards - Amex, Discover, MC, Visa
Service - Buffet
Alcohol - NONE

Entrée Prices - Buffet is $6 throughout the day
Entrées $12 and less - 100% (there is only the buffet)

Atmosphere & Décor - Functional
Appeal - Excellent, all-you-can-eat South Indian vegetarian food for cheap
Useful to Note - They also serves great Indian sweets in bulk.
Buffet Suggestions - vegetable samosa; chana masala (curried chickpeas with ginger and garlic); vegetable korma (a curry with crisp vegetables); saag paneer (spinach with fresh cheese); maleen paneer (cubes of fresh cheese in an orange curry sauce); kheer (rice pudding)

The full name is Bombay Sweets & Pure Vegetarian Restaurant, a very descriptive moniker for an establishment that is both a South Indian vegetarian restaurant and a retail purveyor of Indian dessert items. The prime attraction is that the meals are a great value via the self-serve buffet for a comparative song. It is all vegetarian, but with a noticeably generous use of *ghee* (clarified butter used in Indian cooking) and *paneer* (cheese), the food will have enough fat content to satisfy most carnivores. You will feel satiated after a visit here, often stuffed. One of the several similar storefront restaurants on Hillcroft near the Southwest Freeway, Bombay Sweets is the best of the lot.

All orders of the buffet come with freshly baked *naan* and the thin, crispy *papadum*. The *papadum* works well as the chip to the spicy or sweet chutneys dip. The *naan* is useful for the remainders of the sauces from the buffet items. The items on the short buffet vary daily. This is not as extensive as most buffets (which are standard at nearly all Indian restaurants at lunch), but almost everything is well prepared and fairly appealing. Some of the better dishes that appear in the steam trays are the very dark *saag paneer* (spinach with cheese), *chana masala* (chickpeas in a curry sauce), vegetable *korma* (crisp vegetables cooked in a zesty sauce with yogurt and nuts), *maleen paneer* (fresh cheese in an orange-colored curry), and the several lentil (*dal*) dishes. With a name like Bombay Sweets, you can expect that the complimentary dessert on the buffet line will be good. The *kheer*, though slightly runny, is very flavorful. The several *dosas*, large Indian-style crêpes, are extra. These are tasty, too. So are the vegetable *samosas* (fried potato-filled pastries). Bombay Sweets is also a popular stop for Indian sweets. These are usually sold in bulk, at least in family-sized portions, but an individual dessert can be wrangled from the display if something sweet is needed after the buffet.

Brasil — $8

2606 Dunlavy (at Westheimer) 77006, (713) 528-1993

Cuisine - American
Hours - Daily 7AM to 2AM
Credit Cards - Amex, MC, Visa
Service - Counter Service
Alcohol - Beer & Wine

Entrée Prices - Dinner & Lunch - $6 to $10 ($8 average); Breakfast - $4 to $7
Entrées at Dinner $12 and less - 100%

Atmosphere & Décor - Comfortable; patio
Appeal - A funky coffeehouse-type café with better-than-expected food
Useful to Note - Street parking only; it's usually easy to find a place nearby.
Menu Suggestions - Brasil Caesar Salad (with basil, manchego cheese and chicken); Spicy Chicken Salad Sandwich; Fresh Mozzarella Sandwich; Sausage and Goat Cheese Pizza; Four Cheese Pizza; Classic Pepperoni Pizza

---

Brasil is a cool, coffeehouse-type café with well-made, enticing casual food, some decent wines and very nice beers. It is an airy place that is popular with students and those who rarely seem pressed for time, if not looking crude and feckless. Local artwork decorates the walls on a rotating basis in a variety of styles that helps to give the restaurant some constant freshness. There are a couple dining rooms in an L-shape around a small patio that faces Westheimer, and usually enough room to accommodate those reading poetry in near solitary or those studying within groups. Musicians such as legendary jazz vibraphonist Harry Sheppard play or DJ's spin tunes in the larger of the dining areas, usually on Monday nights.

Lest there be any confusion, the food at Brasil, the Portuguese spelling of Brazil, is not Brazilian. The choices at this very informal restaurant run the range from mostly Mediterranean-influenced, and with somewhat of a health food bent, appetizers, soups, salads, sandwiches and pizzas during the fully waking hours. Brasil is distinctive in that it bakes its own bread. For starters, or to munch on with wine or beer, are combinations with *hummus, tabouli* and *baba ganoush* and bagel chips, freshly baked bread, garlic bread, a warm brie wedge served with a dried fruit compote, marinated goat cheese, and an olive and cheese plate. Brasil has over a half-dozen interesting salads, such as a couple versions of the Caesar, a Greek, a Chef's salad also with garbanzo beans, daikon radish sprouts and toasted pumpkin seeds. Several can be made more filling with the addition of chicken or tuna. The sandwich options are mostly vegetarian, and served on a choice of either sturdy *ciabatta* or a decent *focaccia* bread. The surprisingly tasty Spicy Chicken Salad sandwich with jicama, poblano pepper, cilantro, and pumpkin seeds is one of their best. It's certainly not your standard version. The Fresh Mozzarella sandwich is another one to consider with fresh mozzarella, pesto, artichoke hearts, tomato and fresh spinach. It can be upgraded with prosciutto for a couple bucks more. Other sandwiches include the Classic Turkey, Fresh Dill Egg Salada, Marinated Tuna (without mayonnaise), Heart of Palm, Baked Eggplant, a BLT with blue cheese and avocado, and a pita stuffed with a choice of *hummus, tabouli* or *baba ganoush.* If you are hungry, you probably need an appetizer or a cup of soup along with a sandwich. The eight-inch personal-sized pizzas with a usually thick, crispy crust and a soft interior are more filling, and pretty good, too. These come in nearly a dozen versions such as Classic Pepperoni, Four Cheese that includes feta and manchego, and Margherita. Plus there are some more unusual combinations: Spinach and Feta; Alsace, with pesto, red onions, roasted garlic and prosciutto; Verde, with mozzarella and fontina cheeses with a salad mixture of basil, parsley and chives; and one featuring *hummus.*

Brasil serves a good cup of coffee and a limited, but appealing selection of breakfast dishes seven days a week. Going beyond its coffeehouse setting, Brasil offers a decent array of beers and wines. The well chosen, fair-sized selection of beers, available in bottles include the distinctive Bavarian wheat beers Schneider Weisse and Julius Echter, the excellent and distinctive Belgian Duvel, a couple of the Chimay Trappist ales, and four of the well crafted Samuel Smith beers from the historic brewing center of Burton-on-the-Trent in northern England.

Breakfast Klub $8

3711 Travis (at Alabama) 77002, (713) 528-8561
www.thebreakfastklub.com

Cuisine - American (regional)
Hours - Mon-Fri 7AM to 2PM; Sat 8AM to 1PM
Credit Cards - Amex, Discover, MC, Visa
Service - Counter Service
Alcohol - NONE

Entrée Prices - $5 to $12 ($8 average)
Entrées $12 and less - 100%

Atmosphere & Décor - Pleasant, low-key and even somewhat hip
Appeal - Cool, friendly eatery that serves excellent breakfast fare
Useful to Note - Expect very long lines on Saturday.
Menu Suggestions - Breakfast Kroissant (eggs, cheese, tomato with bacon on a freshly baked croissant); Biskits & Gravy (two buttermilk biscuits with sausage-inflected gravy); French toast; roasted potatoes; Wings & Waffles (six fried chicken wings and a Belgian waffle); Katfish & Grits (a fried catfish fillet and side of grits with an egg or roasted potatoes)

On the weekends lines form well outside the entrance; some evidence that this has become a local fixture since its opening in 2001. The Breakfast Klub serves excellent and interesting, fun and unpretentious food in an informal setting with a certain amount of cool. Though stylish, the owners and staff are noticeably very friendly, and the restaurant always seems to have a warm vibe to it. Dark wood tables, chairs and some even more comfortable seats are set amidst the industrial chic type of décor, and African-inspired art adorns some of the walls, above the concrete floors. Located in Midtown near the spur to downtown for the Southwest Freeway, the Breakfast Klub is quickly accessible to those on the southwest side of town during the weekend, not just those downtown and in town.

Though not soul food in the traditional sense, the offerings have a noticeable African-American feel, and are divided neatly among breakfast plates, omelets, breakfast sandwiches, salads, and lunch sandwiches. Befitting their old menu blurb about being "a coffee shop that happens to serve great food", the now requisite Italian espresso-based coffees are served along with the other necessary, non-alcoholic beverages including cranberry and cranberry-apple juice. Only open until the early afternoon, breakfast is served all of the time and comprises most of the menu. Almost all of the breakfast choices are very good. Featuring noticeably freshly baked goods nicely complemented with tasty fat, the French toast and biscuits and gravy are among the best in town, as is the Breakfast Kroissant. This is a scrambled egg-filled sandwich featuring a buttery croissant and a choice of meats served with a properly ripe, juicy and flavorful roma tomato slice. The latter is a nice feature of all their sandwiches. In fact, each of the ingredients is noticeably fresh and top-notch here. There are several other breakfast sandwiches, pancakes and waffles, omelets made with three eggs, and some other, more eclectic options. There is even Green Eggs & Ham. The eggs get their color from the hearty addition of chives, spinach and bell peppers, in case you are curious. The Katfish & Grits feature an expertly breaded and fried clean-tasting and moist catfish fillet served with some well-made grits. The Wings & Waffle is a take on the jazzy combination of fried chicken and waffles. More so the Belgian waffle, but the tasty fried chicken wings, too, benefit from a dash of maple syrup. The breakfast sides are much more than an afterthought here. The cubed roasted potatoes are good, possibly the best breakfast potatoes outside of very good hash browns. And good for any place specializing in breakfast, the bacon is thick and crispy. The lunch-style items are also worthy of a visit. There are a handful of artful sandwiches and salads from which to choose: a club, a chicken club, grilled chicken, tuna salad, chicken salad, and the increasingly familiar BLT with avocado. The salads are a Chef Salad, Caesar with grilled chicken and Grilled Chicken Salad with grilled chicken breast, bacon, chopped hard-boiled eggs, cheese and tomatoes among salad greens. The salads and sandwiches can also be fitted half-size with the soup of the day. Whenever you come, the Breakfast Klub will offer likely offer a warm and enjoyable dining experience that should be worth the wait. To note, there are daily specials: red beans and rice on Mondays; pasta with sliced chicken in a cream sauce on Tuesday; crawfish étouffée on Wednesday, chicken fried chicken on Thursday, and fettuccine with crawfish and grilled shrimp on Friday. Check their web site for any changes.

Brown Bag Deli $6

2036 Westheimer (just east of Shepherd) 77098, (713) 807-9191
2540 Amherst (east of Kirby, between Rice & University) 77005, (713) 520-6100
13169 Northwest Freeway (between Pinemont & Hollister) 77040, (713) 690-8600
www.thebrownbagdeli.net

Cuisine - Sandwiches
Hours - Mon-Sat 11AM to 6PM
Credit Cards - Amex, Diners, MC, Visa
Service - Counter Service
Alcohol - NONE

Entrée Price - $6
Entrées $12 and less - 100%

Atmosphere & Décor - Pleasant
Appeal - Quick and tasty cold sandwiches for cheap in a friendly setting
Useful to Note - You can order via the clipboard.
Menu Suggestions - chicken salad sandwich; roast beef sandwich

Since 2003 Brown Bag Deli has offered Houston a welcome, casual concept for well prepared cold sandwiches and another winner from the folks who own the nearby Barnaby's restaurants. The sandwiches are all design-it-yourself. You tell the counter person what ingredients to include among the choices for bread, meats, cheeses, and condiments from the fairly numerous choices listed on the brown bags cutely affixed to a clipboard near the counter. The breads are white, wheat and jalapeño cheddar, each of which are slightly sweet and always fresh, and a good starting point. The "meats", or rather sandwich fillings, are slightly eclectic and there should be one for nearly every palate: roasted turkey, roast beef, chicken salad, egg salad, maple-glazed honey baked ham, albacore tuna with pecans, pimento cheese, and beef salami. These fillings are all top quality, as are all of the sandwich ingredients. The moist, noticeably medium-rare roast beef and the chicken salad are especially good. The cheese slices include cheddar, jalapeño jack, Monterey Jack, and horseradish white cheddar. The condiments and other accompaniments are mayonnaise, horseradish sauce, honey mustard, brown deli mustard, lettuce, tomato, raw red onion slices and pickle slices. For an extra charge, you can add additional cheese and double meat, though the regular-sized sandwiches will be enough for most people. The sides include potato salad made with skin-on red potatoes, cole slaw, fresh fruit, or one of the tasty Louisiana-crafted Zapps chips. The house-made sides are fairly substantial, and conveniently served in a heavy plastic container, well-suited for takeaway. You can finish the meal with a chocolate cake, coconut cream cake, lemon cream cake, or an Apple Spice Cake. Fountain drinks, iced tea, and Starbucks coffee are there to help wash it down. Service is quick and the staff is noticeably friendly and efficient. Brown Bag Deli is a far cry from most inexpensive, often dreary sandwich shops. Not incidentally, the resulting cold sandwiches are generally much better, too. The small restaurants are functional, but more than pleasant enough for dining in.

Buffalo Grille $8

3116 Bissonnet (east of Buffalo Speedway) 77005, (713) 661-3663
1301 Voss (at Woodway) 77057, (713) 784-3663
www.thebuffalogrille.com

Cuisine - American (regional)
Hours - Mon 7AM to 2PM; Tue-Fri 7AM to 9PM; Sat 8AM to 9PM; Sun 8AM to 2PM
Credit Cards - Amex, Diners, Discover, MC, Visa
Service - Counter Service
Alcohol - Beer & Wine

Entrée Prices - Dinner & Lunch - $5 to $16 ($8 average); Breakfast - $3 to $9
Entrées at Dinner $12 and less - 90%

Atmosphere & Décor - Pleasant, but casual
Appeal - Reliable American breakfasts in a nicer-than-typical-diner-type place
Useful to Note - Only the breakfast menu on Sundays at the Bissonnet location.
Menu Suggestions - French toast, pancakes, breakfast #3B (eggs scrambled with bacon and cheddar); bacon, Cinnamon Coffee; Peppered Pork Chops; King Ranch Spinach Enchiladas; Chicken Araniva (chicken breast over rice with green chile sauce and cheese)

Open since 1984, and seemingly crowded during the weekend morning hours since then, The Buffalo Grille, as it's formally known, is not a grill, or a diner *per se*. It's a quaint and informal restaurant that serves regional diner fare for breakfast, lunch and dinner. The quality at the Buffalo Grille is generally higher than what you will find at a typical diner. The tariff is a tad higher than a typical diner, too. And, the crowd is also a lot more well-heeled and well-scrubbed than the typical diner patron, and one that does not seem to mind to pay for a little extra, such as for the extraneous "e" at the end of "Grille". The original Buffalo Grille, located on Bissonnet near Buffalo Speedway (hence the restaurant name), is across the street from West University Place. This location, especially, is packed for breakfast each weekend morning.. A line usually stretches well outside the restaurant waiting to order food at the counter. Their breakfast business is pretty brisk during the week, too. The lengthy weekend line usually moves quickly because the friendly counter staff and kitchen are quite efficient at dealing with crowds.

Breakfast, served all the time, features the basic Houston-area morning meal options: pancakes, French toast, bacon, potatoes, a variety of omelets, and some Mexican egg dishes. Some things work better than others. The French toast, large whole slices of thick bread that is surprisingly light, is among the best in town. The pancakes and the create-it-yourself omelets with three very large eggs are generally good, too. The hash browns, though not the home fries that are often served under the guise of hash browns, should usually be avoided. Too often these are strangely gray in color, and rather listless and unappealing. The thick pecan-smoked peppered bacon, however, is excellent, if not cheap. The pecan-smoked sausage is not quite as good. For the health-conscious there is also chicken apple sausage. The Mexican breakfast dishes are decent-sized, but rather bland compared to local Mexican restaurants. But, Buffalo Grille provides some nice touches that you would certainly not find at a diner. The syrup is heated. You have the option between regular coffee and that flavored with a little bit of cinnamon; both coffees are quite palatable. Though quaint, the old tables and chairs at the original location, an assortment of finds at garage sales and antique shops, can be a bit uncomfortable. The lunch and dinner menu is not as enticing as the breakfast one, and the restaurant is less crowded during these hours, but the casual regional, American fare is generally well prepared and a fine value. They serve tasty one-third pound burgers, a few salads, sandwiches like grilled cheese and chicken salad, baked potatoes and entrées such as chicken fried steak, burritos, moist and piquant pork chops, grilled chicken breast, fajitas, red beans and rice, and catfish fillets.

Burns Bar BQ — $8

8397 De Priest (between Victory and DeWalt) 77088, (281) 445-7574

Cuisine - Barbecue
Hours - Tue-Sat 10:30AM - 7PM (later on Saturday nights)
Credit Cards - Discover, MC, Visa
Service - Counter Service
Alcohol - NONE

Entrée Prices - $5 to $14 ($8 average)

Entrées $12 and less - 90%

Atmosphere & Décor - Old School barbecue stand; just outside dining
Appeal - Excellent Texas barbecue off the beaten track
Useful to Note - There's not a lot of parking here.
Menu Suggestions - Chopped Beef Sandwich; Sliced Beef Sandwich; Plate with beef brisket; ribs; baked beans

---

Situated in the still almost rural Acres Homes neighborhood not too far from I-45 and Little York, Burns Bar BQ serves some of the best barbecue in the area from a converted wood-frame house. A proper restaurant since around 1990, it has long been popular within the community, but it's mostly unknown outside of the nearby vicinity. But, Burns did manage to get the attention of the Food Network, which featured it on a show in 2003. Set amidst tall pine trees, small houses and tiny churches, Burns might not seem like much. Aside from the unseen cinder block pit and its companion metal pit, there's not much to Burns. The billowing smoke gives indication that you're at a serious barbecue joint. Once you've found it, you place your order in the air conditioned interior, and then wait for it there on one of the plastic chairs amidst somewhat faded, photos (Johnnie Cochran, Whoopi Goldberg, and former Rocket Bobby Joe Ried among others), plaques and accolades such as a couple Majic 102 Best of the Hood awards for "the best barbecue stand". After receiving the order you eat it on one of the covered picnic benches outside or take it back home or to work. Takeout is popular.

One of the best ways to enjoy the brisket is on a sandwich. The hefty chopped beef brisket sandwich is served with a bountiful amount of coarsely minced meat, with both black charred pieces and some others juicy with noticeable pink smoke rings. This is topped with plenty of house-made sauce between two hamburger buns for a messy, delicious sandwich. The similar sliced beef sandwich is also very good. Actually, the brisket here is excellent in any manner. It's the best of the meat choices, though everything is done in fine fashion. Along with the other barbecued meats, the brisket is also available as a plate. These plates come as 1-meat, 2-meat, 3-meat, and rib short ends, each with the barbecue baked beans and potato salad sides, and a few slices of super-processed white bread. The 3-meat plate comes with a hefty serving each of the beef brisket, beef links, and pork ribs. The ribs are moist and tasty, if not quite the quality of Williams Smokehouse, at the southern end of Acres Homes. The ribs are popular, and Burns even sells those rib short ends for a little more. The crumbly beef links are tastier than most. As good as the meats are, it gets even better when swimming in Burns' sauce. The smoky barbecue beans, cooked with onions and pieces of sausage, make for an excellent complement to a barbecue plate or sandwich. The yellow, mayonnaise-heavy potato salad is good, too. As popular as takeout is here, barbecue is also sold by the pound, sides are sold by the quart, and the restaurant even lists special dinners for 25, 50, 100, and 150. It would be enviable to treat your workplace or extended family to Texas food like this.

Burt's Meat Market & Cajun Foods $7

5910 Lyons (between Lockwood and Kress) 77020, (713) 674-0064

Cuisine - Cajun; Soul Food
Hours - Mon-Fri 9AM to 7:30PM, Sat 9AM to 8:30PM; Sun 9AM to 6PM
Credit Cards - Discover, MC, Visa
Alcohol - NONE
Service - Counter Service

Entrée Prices - $4 to $8 ($7 average)
Entrées $12 and less - 100%

Atmosphere & Décor - A meat market in a working class neighborhood
Appeal - Some of the best soul food in town, and possibly better Cajun items
Useful to Note - This is strictly a take-away operation, there is no seating.
Menu Suggestions - boudin in a cup; boudin; beef tips over rice with gravy; fried chicken; gumbo; peach cobbler

Burt's Meat Market & Cajun Foods serves food good enough for people to drive a ways not only to get it, but to eat it, too, as Burt's is strictly a take-out operation. Burt's is a butcher shop specializing in Cajun items with a soul food steam table with a similar South Louisianan bent. There are no tables and no loitering. But, the food is good enough and the prices low enough, for lines to form during lunch hours to purchase the food to take to eat at home or to the office or work site. It possesses the prettiest and most enticing steam table in the area. Located near the boundary between the African-American Fifth Ward and the Hispanic Denver Harbor neighborhoods, Burt's serves both communities, plus displaced Cajuns and Cajun and soul food aficionados. Hearty, satisfying and a great value are the best adjectives to describe a meal here. For less than seven bucks you can get a meat, two sides from a changing array of local soul food favorites accompanied with a couple cornbread muffins or less interesting white bread. There can be chicken and dumplings, lean but tender beef tips with a light brown gravy over rice, stuffed pork chops, gumbo, barbecued chicken, barbecued pork ribs, andouille sausage and a Flintstone-esque Cajun smoked turkey leg, complemented with zesty greens, cabbage, moist corn seemingly just cut from the cob, candied yams, steamed cabbage, mashed potatoes, and macaroni and cheese. There are also several sandwiches, boudin and the unique and much easier to eat on the run, boudin in a cup, which is always flavorful. A cup is a fair amount more than a snack for just three dollars or so. Boudin is made here in several styles, Cajun that can be mild or hot, which might be too spicy for most purists, and beef and seafood. To note, Burt's is a good stop for your Cajun cooking needs, as they make tasso, boudin in several styles, and andouille sausage. Chitterlings, too.

Busy Boy Sandwiches $8

5722 Hillcroft (between Westpark and Harwin) 77036, (713) 783-1188

Cuisine - Sandwiches (with a Middle Eastern bent)
Hours - Mon-Sat 11AM to 5PM
Credit Cards - Amex, Discover, MC, Visa
Service - Counter Service
Alcohol - NONE

Entrée Prices - $6 to $9 ($8 average)
Entrées $12 and less - 100%

Atmosphere & Décor - Comfortable, but not meant for lingering
Appeal - Satisfying sandwiches from a well-run enterprise
Menu Suggestions - Mamma's Meatball Sandwich; Shawarmawich (chicken shawarma on a French roll)

Busy Boy Sandwiches is a slicker operation than most on the stretch of Hillcroft that extends from Southwest Freeway north to Westheimer and is filled with spartan Indian, Persian and Middle Eastern shops and restaurants. The less adventurous diners will certainly find this most approachable of the lot. Busy Boy is a nicely put together fast-casual restaurant with an efficient staff and kitchen, and an attractively printed and well thought out small menu that makes it possibly well-poised for expansion. There is undoubtedly something from the list of Middle American- and Middle Eastern-leaning offerings that will appeal to anyone from the office. It's easy to believe that you can eat in a more healthy fashion here than at most other sandwich shops with its roughly twenty sandwiches in several forms, salads and soups. The sandwiches are divided among subs that use 7-inch buns, *panini*-style that are served on toasted Italian-esque flat bread, and *shawarmas*. There are cold and hot sandwiches with turkey breast, ham and salami, tuna salad, chicken salad, a Rueben and a battered-and-fried chicken breast. The meats are all quality *halal*. The basic meatball sandwich is enjoyable, if somewhat dainty. The *shawarmas,* slowly roasted slices of chicken, turkey or beef, are served in a traditional pita, as a plate, and also on top of a salad and, in unusual fashion, in a French bread roll. These are good, though not in the same league as ones from restaurants further up Hillcroft. The small condiment area includes a tasty, but not very hot, hot sauce that works as a welcome complement to most of the sandwiches, and a light mango salsa with a hint of mangos. The former has an Indian flavor, which is quite interesting given the Middle Eastern pedigree that is advertised. The portions are not terribly large. The fries are a little bland, but freshly fried; the *hummus* might be a better side. The staff is friendly, and the restaurant is very clean and well-kept.

Cabo $11

419 Travis (at Texas) 77002, (713) 225-2060
www.cabomixmex.com

Cuisine - Mexican (Baja-influenced)
Hours - Mon-Wed 11AM to 12AM; Thu - Sat 11AM to 2AM; Sun 11AM to 10PM
Credit Cards - Amex, MC, Visa
Service - Counter Service
Alcohol - Full Bar

Entrée Prices - $6 to $21 ($11 average)
Entrées $12 and less - 70%

Atmosphere & Décor - Attractive and somewhat stylish, fun; patio
Appeal - Surprisingly good and interesting Mexican food in a lively setting
Useful to Note - It's primarily a bar at night.
Menu Suggestions - Grilled Chicken Sandwich; Habanero Shrimp Taco; Grilled Shrimp Taco; Grilled Fish Taco; Shrimp Quesadillas; margarita

Though primarily a bar, the food at Cabo is worthy of a special trip. It's especially well prepared and imaginative for a generally inexpensive, lively and stylishly decorated place that is as much a bar as a restaurant. It can get crowded, and can be fairly rowdy on weekend nights with a relatively younger crowd that has seemingly driven in from the suburbs. A crowd that starts at Cabo is usually along its way to hit the town to drink its wages. Though housed in a fairly large, two-story building, it's best to get there early if you want to have space to enjoy the food. But, it's not too raucous for lunch during the week, or often prior to a baseball game.

As the number of Cabo locations has contracted in recent years, the menu has greatly expanded. The offerings are primarily Mexican or Tex-Mex, but, showing the influence of former consultant Arturo Boada, more recently of Beso and Arturo's, these are strongly influenced from the Caribbean South America. The menu has accurately proffered that the kitchen offers, "traditional Tex-Mex recipes, those found in the coastal fishing villages and selected favorites from Central and South America". The menu is divided among appetizers, soups, salads, grilled sandwiches, tacos, burritos, fajitas, enchiladas and the larger plates. The appetizers provide things on which to munch while drinking, and some dishes that can make for a meal. Zesty *ceviche* with red snapper, shrimp and scallops is a reliable choice. The soups are the popular tortilla soup and the Roasted Corn and Hot Pepper Soup. The artful fish tacos are especially good. These, and all of the seafood tacos, consist of shredded cabbage, mayonnaise, and the choice of fillings supported between two corn tortillas. Among the best of the tacos are the Habanero Shrimp Tacos. These can be quite spicy, as you should expect with anything prefaced with "habanero". The *quesadillas* with shrimp are excellent. The regular shrimp tacos are very good, also. These tacos are somewhat expensive at around $4 and $5 (or $7 for the lobster versions). A couple tacos are usually needed to satiate an average hunger. In contrast, only one of the large burritos can satisfy most people. These are available with the same fillings as the tacos, except the grilled fish. The sandwiches, especially the Grilled Chicken Sandwich, are great. This is probably one of the best hot sandwiches in town. It features moist char-grilled strips of chicken with shreds of crisp lettuce and slices of tomato on toasted, fresh, distinctive Mexican *bolillo*-style bun. This uniquely flavored and tasty bread helps to makes these much better than the typical sandwich. The plates, or "Favorites", are the most ambitious of offerings with grilled yellowfin tuna, plantain-crusted mahi mahi, a unique version of barbecue shrimp, and a coastal Mexican-inspired take on surf-and-turf among the choices. Each can be complemented in spicier fashion by toppings in the tradition of Floyd's restaurants. Bottles of house-made habanero hot sauce line much of the dining areas. This very spicy and flavorful sauce enhances just about everything on the menu. It is hot, though. Make that very hot.

Cabo has a full bar with an emphasis on margaritas, sangria, Cuba Libres, Screwdrivers and Salty Dogs. The margaritas are notoriously potent. There is a wide variety of bottled Mexican beers. For those not interested in imbibing, there are fresh fruit juices: freshly squeezed orange and grapefruit juices; *limonade*; and fruit smoothies. The rabid bar scene can be off-putting to many, and it can be distracting for dining on weekend nights, but it does not obscure the high quality of the food.

Cadillac Bar $12

1802 Shepherd (just south of I-10) 77007, (713) 862-2020
www.cadillacbar.com

Cuisine - Tex-Mex
Hours - Mon-Thu, 11AM - 10:30PM; Fri-Sat 11AM - 12AM; Sun 12 - 10:30PM
Credit Cards - Amex, MC, Visa
Service - Table Service
Alcohol - Full Bar

Entrée Prices - $8 to $22 ($12 average)
Entrées $12 and less - 60%

Atmosphere & Décor - Lively, loud
Appeal - Surprisingly very good Mexican food in very festive surroundings
Useful to Note - Bachelorette parties visit the bar area most weekend nights.
Menu Suggestions - Fajita Nachos; Cabrito al Horno (baked goat); Cabrito al Pastor; Quail; Quesadillas; Pollo Rufino (marinated chicken breast in a sauce of white wine, garlic and mushrooms); Enchiladas Suizas; Enchilada Combo; Spinach Enchiladas; Frog Legs; Cadillac Chile Relleno

For a long time, the Cadillac Bar had enjoyed the reputation for being a very fun, noisy restaurant, but one that served less-than-stellar Tex-Mex. The prominence of the "Bar" in the name was very fitting. Hopefully this reputation in regards to the food has changed, because the kitchen has been turning out high quality food, including some dishes that might be without peer in town. One of those dishes features the northern and central Mexico favorite, *cabrito*, goat. This is somewhat ironic considering that Cadillac has long had a reputation for being brashly Tex-Mex. Though *cabrito* is always going to be somewhat greasy and somewhat uniquely flavored, *cabrito* served in a great many Mexican restaurants in the area are too often so. By contrast, it is consistently exceptional at Cadillac. Since they are committed to serve only top quality milk-fed *cabrito,* it is sometimes unavailable. Another indication that this restaurant takes these dishes seriously is that it has a neon sign with "CABRITO" in bold letters in front of the glassed-in preparation area when it's available. The better of the two *cabrito* dishes offered, the *Cabrito al Pastor*, the mesquite-roasted version, is excellent. The other one, the baked *Cabrito al Horno,* is also more than satisfactory. This is something that will probably even appeal to most previously goat-adverse *gringos*. Both versions are usually very moist and flavorful, especially the crisp skin. A few other somewhat unexpected items here are frog legs, quail and crawfish, which make it into enchiladas. The quail is excellent either mesquite-grilled or deep-fried. The crawfish enchiladas are best avoided. But, most items on the primarily Tex-Mex menu are worth ordering. There are also fajitas, *chile con queso*, tacos and crispy tacos. The large Tex-Mex-style *quesadillas* and the spinach enchiladas are also very good entrées. Yet another winner is the Cadillac *Chile Relleno,* a poblano pepper that has been stuffed with seasoned ground beef, then deep-fried and covered with plenty of melted Monterey Jack cheese and salsa. Maybe even a little more refined is the excellent *Pollo Rufino,* chicken breast that has been marinated in white wine and garlic mushroom sauce and then grilled. The sides, the rice and beans, and the chips and salsa, are always good.

Though the food is good, the place has lost none of its party atmosphere. That should be expected from a place whose matchbox covers proclaim,

"¡Damas desnudas toman gratis!" You can still write on the walls, and there is no shortage of graffiti. Don't come here expecting to converse quietly. Cadillac is evidently a required stop for every bachelorette party in town. It is always very crowded during weekend nights. The bar is very proficient, up to meeting the demands of the thirsty crowds. Though they could probably get away with less, the margaritas, especially the top-shelf versions, are excellent. In a place like this, it helps to have competent bartenders who do a great job helping keep the thirsty throngs plied with tasty libations. But, unlike in the past, those libations are not the sole reason to visit. You can really enjoy Cadillac with nary a single drop; or, maybe not.

Café Artiste $8

1601 W. Main (at Mandell, north of Richmond) 77006, (713) 528-3704

Cuisine - American (with strong South Louisiana accents)
Hours - Mon-Thu, Sun 8AM to 11PM; Fri-Sat 8AM to 1AM
Credit Cards - MC, Visa
Service - Counter Service
Alcohol - Beer & Wine

Entrée Prices - Dinner & Lunch - $4 to $10 ($8 average); Breakfast - $4 to $10
Entrées $12 and less - 100%

Atmosphere & Décor - Functional, but comfortable
Appeal - Very good breakfasts with interesting coffees; and after, too; patio
Menu Suggestions - Eggs New Orleans (poached eggs on a crab cake with spinach, tomato, Canadian bacon and a spicy Hollandaise sauce); Eggs Benedict; Croissant Sous Du Lait (a warmed croissant with a blend of eggs and yogurt); Cajun Scrambled Eggs (eggs scrambled with green onion, tomato, jalapeño and sausage); Artiste Steak Po-Boy; coffee

The name reflects its proximity to the museums of the Menil Collection that are a few blocks away. And, Café Artiste is a nice place to get some food or a drink, or coffee after getting your fill of the works of Magritte, Rothko, or even Cy Twombly. It's an informal and comfortable restaurant exhibiting the locally popular Louisiana flavors adjoining the west Montrose neighborhood with a number of large booths and several tables in the average-sized dining area.

Café Artiste takes pride in its breakfasts, and the menu states that their "award-winning breakfasts use only the freshest ingredients and feature food prepared in the style of Southern Louisiana". This is quite evident, as their breakfasts are indeed very good. Some of the breakfast offerings are somewhat unique, at least their names: *Crossaint Sous Du Lait, Pain DeVille*

Stack, and *Thibodeaux* Stack. The Eggs Arnold is their version of Eggs Benedict (get it?), poached eggs on grilled English muffins with spinach, tomato or Canadian bacon with a spicy Hollandaise sauce. Even tastier is the Eggs New Orleans with poached eggs atop fried crabcakes with spinach, tomato slices, Canadian bacon and the piquant Hollandaise sauce. The somewhat unique *Croissant Sous Du Lait* is a blend of eggs and light yogurt that is baked and served on a croissant, and is also available with spinach and ham. The *Pain DeVille* Stack consists of buttermilk pancakes that are blended with cornmeal. The *Tibodeaux* Stack is the basic buttermilk pancakes. Both pancake dishes can be topped with bananas or blueberries for an extra dollar. As a nod to the popularity of Mexican breakfasts, Café Artiste serves *migas* (scrambled eggs with corn tortilla strips and onions, tomatoes and jalapeños) and eggs with salsa. There is also a wide range of omelets. Even commendable is the simple dish with two eggs over easy with sausage patties and sliced and sautéed potatoes. The basic biscuits and gravy are not on the menu, but can appear as part of one of the morning specials. The zesty sausage-infused gravy and the fresh large biscuit make this an excellent indulgence. Necessary for a café, Café Artiste offers a variety in freshly brewed coffee beverages. All of the coffee (and tea, too) is brewed by the cup, glass or pot, individually, only when ordered. They have Danesi-supplied espresso and a large number of espresso-based drinks. There are also drip coffees available for around a buck-and-a-half. There are about a dozen flavored coffees plus regular coffee from several different regions. Surprisingly, this even includes the pricey Hawaiian Kona and the very flavorful and very expensive Jamaican Blue Mountain, which is why Café Artiste needs to charge for coffee refills.

Breakfasts are the biggest attraction, but you can still get a satisfying meal for lunch and dinner, though the kitchen is less consistent for these. They offer salads, sandwiches, hamburgers, individually sized pizzas and an eclectic small number of dinner plates. Among the sandwiches, one of the best ones is the Artiste Steak Po-Boy, made with good quality, sliced steak, sweet peppers, onions, and melted Swiss cheese. Others include a club, a cold po boy with cold cuts, a grilled shrimp po boy, grilled cheese, a hamburger, and a couple of vegetarian options. Most are served with tasty, skin-on potatoes. The dinner plates include a wide range of culinary influences that are right at home in Houston: vegetarian cheese enchiladas; vegetable lasagna; *quesadillas*; a plate featuring *hummus, cous-cous* and char-grilled vegetables; black beans and rice; and chicken and rice. Café Artiste is well-suited for a quick meal at most times, or a leisurely time lingering over coffee and reading material or chatting. As such it is often filled with students and artsy types; some of which might know or care that Federico Lorca is dead and gone.

Café Caspian $13

12126 Westheimer (between Kirkwood and Dairy Ashford) 77077, (281) 493-4000
www.cafecaspian.com

Cuisine - Persian
Hours - Tue-Thurs, Sun 11AM to 10PM; Fri-Sat 11AM to 11PM
Credit Cards - Amex, MC, Visa
Service - Table Service
Alcohol - Beer & Wine

Entrée Prices - Dinner - $10 to $18 ($13 average); Lunch - $7 to $14
Entrées at Dinner $12 and less - 30%

Atmosphere & Décor - Very Pleasant
Appeal - Tasty Persian food in an attractive setting
Useful to Note - They are closed on Mondays.
Menu Suggestions - Koobideh with beef (skewered rolls of spiced ground beef); Ghormeh Sabzi (stew with beef, kidney beans, dried limes and sautéed herbs)

Café Caspian serves the hearty cuisine of Iran, the formerly named Persia. The usually robust and meat-based Persian food will have a pleasing familiarity, especially if you occasionally frequent the area Greek and Middle Eastern restaurants. Café Caspian is a fine choice to help explore this cuisine. It occupies a surprisingly attractive space in an otherwise undistinguished strip center in west Houston. The handsome interior is highlighted by the ceilings, which are attractively painted light blue and white to mimic clouds in the sky. This is a pleasant restaurant with consistently well-made food and proficient service. And, it provides a nice dining value.

Many of the entrées feature beef or chicken that is stewed or grilled, and served with the long-grain basmati rice. The small menu provides fairly useful descriptions of each item, even if the names might seem unusual. To start the meal, and usually generously when done with those, each table receives a large, fresh piece of *taftoon* bread (somewhat similar to the more common Indian *naan*), and a plate with chunks of feta-like cheese, small turnips and fragrant, fresh herbs like basil and parsley. The bread makes for a nice appetizer when wrapped around some of the herbs and pieces of the feta cheese. As the former Persia can also be very hot during the summer, the formal appetizers at Café Caspian are soothing for the Houston climate. These include *hummus, tabouli* and other dips like the *Mast-o Khiyar*, yogurt with chopped cucumbers and mint. The similar *Mast-o Mooseer* is yogurt with chopped shallots. There is also the Shirazi Salad that is made of diced cucumbers, tomatoes, onions, cilantro, vinegar and olive oil. The stews and kabobs, though served in large portions, are not terribly heavy. The stews include *Gheymeh* that consists of sautéed beef, split peas in a tomato-based brown sauce and topped with shoe-string potatoes; the *Fesenjan* is baked chicken served with a sauce that is a purée of walnuts and pomegranates; and the third, *Ghormeh Sabzi,* is a tasty and zesty stew with chunks of beef with kidney beans, dried limes and sautéed herbs. Vegetarian versions are available. White basmati rice is served with each of the stews, but interesting rice plates incorporating a range of contrasting flavors and textures can be had for an additional few dollars. These include the rice with sweet and sour cherries, saffron, almonds and pistachios; another with sour barberries and saffron; and one with lentils, sautéed raisins, dates and onions. Though these can be very good, the more familiar-sounding kabobs might be more appealing to most. There are several varieties each served with plentiful basmati rice and grilled tomato halves. When eating these it's good to incorporate the juice and acidity of the tomatoes with the meat and rice. The *Koobideh* is two large rolls of moist, spiced ground beef that is skewered and grilled. The beef version is better, but it's also available with chicken. The beef version of *Barg* is marinated filet that is sliced, skewered then broiled. There are also kabobs with salmon and shrimp. In addition to the stews and kabobs, Café Caspian serves Cornish hen that has been marinated in saffron, olive oil and lemon juice then grilled, and a meaty lamb shank.

Café Chino $12

6140 Village Parkway (north of University, east of Kirby) 77005, (713) 524-4433
www.cafechinohouston.com

Cuisine - Chinese
Hours - Mon-Fri 11AM to 10PM; Sat-Sun 12 to 10PM
Credit Cards - Amex, Discover, MC, Visa
Service - Table Service; Delivery
Alcohol - Full Bar

Entrée Prices - Dinner - $7 to $19 ($12 average); Lunch - $6 to $10
Entrées at Dinner $12 and less - 50%

Atmosphere & Décor - Very Nice
Appeal - Chinese in pleasant surroundings
Menu Suggestions - Hunan Noodle; Lamb in Curry Basil Sauce; Moo Shu Pork with plum sauce; General Chicken (battered and deep-fried chicken in a hot and sweet sauce); Chino Beef (crispy beef with a sweet orange sauce); Wok-Seared Eggplant Garlic

The décor and atmosphere at Café Chino are nicer than all but the most upscale area Chinese restaurants. Correspondingly, service at Café Chino is prompt and attentive. The menu provides many appealing options, and the kitchen is efficient. With lights usually dimmed in the evening, Café Chino is a somewhat intimate, yet warm and inviting restaurant that has long fit in very nicely in the Rice Village. It provides a good neighborhood outlet for comfortable Chinese food for the nearby residents of the West University and Southampton. Café Chino, subtitled Hunan Cuisine, serves the type of Chinese food that is recognizable and well-liked by most Americans. There are Fried Wontons, Hot and Sour soup, Sesame Chicken, Beef with Broccoli, Moo Shu Pork, Shrimp Fried Rice, and the ubiquitous General Tso's Chicken. The last is probably the most recognized "Hunan" dish, though it began life in a kitchen in Manhattan in the 1970s. Tellingly, there are no Chinese characters on the menu, and chopsticks are available only upon request. But, the execution is generally better at Café Chino than at most similar restaurants. The touch is somewhat lighter. The ingredients are of noticeably high quality; the vegetables are reliably fresh and cooked quickly so that they retain their texture and flavor. And, the portions are generous. The menu is divided among hot and cold appetizers, soups, specialties, poultry, meat, noodles and rice, seafood and vegetable dishes. There are many familiar and interesting items. In addition to chicken, beef and pork, Café Chino also prepares dishes with lamb and duck. There is both a half and a whole Crisp Duck available, and even a dish called Grilled Cinnamon Apple Baby Ribs. For seafood, shrimp predominates, but there are some entrées with scallops, and some of the specialties include salmon, lobster, soft shell crab, and a Crispy Whole Fish. None of the food is very hot, even the ones designated as such, fitting the inclination of the most of the regular patrons. There are several curry dishes featuring lamb, chicken, shrimp and vegetables. The curry is quite mild, and light. With almost sixty entrées from which to choose, Café Chino will probably have several dishes to appeal to most patrons. And, most everyone will certainly enjoy the additional aspects that make Café Chino a good restaurant.

Café Express $9

5601 Main (at Bissonnet, in the Museum of Fine Arts) 77005, (713) 639-7370
1422 West Gray (east of Waugh) 77019, (713) 522-3100
1101 Uptown Park Boulevard (in Uptown Park) 77056, (713) 963-9222
4700 Beechnut (in Meyerland Plaza) 77096, (713) 349-9222
3200 Kirby (between Richmond and W. Alabama) 77098, (713) 522-3994
780 W. Sam Houston Parkway N. (north of Memorial) 77024, (713) 586-0800
6750 Woodway (just east of Voss) 77057, (713) 935-9222
650 Main (between Texas and Walker) 77002, (713) 237-9222
19443 I-45 S. (at Bay Area Boulevard) 77598, (281) 554-6999
5311 FM 1960 W. (east of Champions Forest) 77069, (832) 484-9222
9595 Six Pines (at Research Forest) The Woodlands, 77380, (281) 298-2556
15930 City Walk (in Sugar Land Town Square) Sugar Land, 77479, (281) 980-9222
www.cafe-express.com

Cuisine - American
Hours - MFAH - Tue-Wed, Fri, Sun 11AM to 4PM; Thu-Fri 11AM to 9PM; West Gray - Mon-Thu, Sun 11AM to 11PM; Fri-Sat 11AM to 12AM; Uptown Park - Daily 11AM to 11PM; Beechnut - Daily 11AM to 10PM; Kirby - Daily 11AM to 11PM; Sam Houston Parkway - Daily 11AM to 11PM; Woodway - Daily 11AM to 11PM; Main - Mon-Sat 11AM to 10PM; Sun 11AM to 8PM; Webster - Daily 11AM to 11PM; FM 1960W - Daily 11AM to 11PM; The Woodlands - Daily 11AM to 11PM; Sugar Land - Daily 11AM to 11PM
Credit Cards - Amex, Diners, Discover, MC, Visa
Service - Counter Service
Alcohol - Beer & Wine

Entrée Prices - $6 to $14 ($9 average)
Entrées $12 and less - 90%

Atmosphere & Décor - Nice, casual
Appeal - Good, healthy food in nicely informal, quick and convenient locations
Menu Suggestions - Roast Beef with Swiss Cheese Sandwich; burgers; baked potato soup; chili; vegetable tart; chicken salad; Triple Deli Salad (chicken salad, tuna salad, pasta with pesto on lettuce greens)

Café Express began what has become a welcome trend of high-end restaurateurs (Café Annie in this case) opening informal, inexpensive counter-service restaurants that serve high quality, interesting, and freshly prepared food. These still do it better than most. The concept is excellent and portable; there are currently a number of Café Expresses in Houston, plus a handful of locations in the Dallas-Fort Worth area.

The casual yet evidently substantial style of the ever-evolving offerings seems to aptly match the décor. There are plenty of salads, sandwiches, burgers, soups, healthy sides, pastas and chicken dishes to match most cravings. The food is artfully prepared to order with very good, and very fresh ingredients, a big part of Café Express' long-standing popularity. There are about ten different, imaginative entrée-size salads, each with a multitude of components. There is the popular, requisite Caesar available with grilled chicken or shrimp; a version of the Greek salad; the Shrimp and Avocado Salad with avocados, bacon, jicama, tomatoes, spicy salsa and Parmesan cheese. Sandwiches are generally quite good. These are basic sandwiches tweeked to be more interesting. The Roast Beef sandwich with Swiss cheese, lettuce, tomatoes and roasted tomato pesto on garlic bread, is one of their best. The Club Sandwich is a proper triple decker, made with roasted turkey, Monterey Jack cheese, bacon, tomato and mayonnaise and a creamy Parmesan dressing. There are also Café Express' versions of the BLT, grilled chicken sandwich, roasted turkey sandwich. The sandwiches come with either chips or pretty decent fries. The burgers are generally good, and can also be ordered with turkey or vegetable patties. The soups served daily, the Chicken Soup and the Vegetarian Black Bean, can work as complements to a salad or sandwich. The sides are much more than chips and fries. Café Express serves broccoli, spinach, roasted mushrooms, French-style green beans, roasted artichoke hearts with spinach and tomatoes. Most are tastily cooked in garlic and butter. Other sides include house-made guacamole, *hummus*, fruit salad, and a tasty vegetable tart that might be an off-the-menu item. The American-style pasta dishes featuring linguini or penne are decent, and seemingly popular. There should be one that satisfies your current taste. Linguine is served with a choice of sauces: pesto; four cheeses; roasted tomato cream; a Bolognese-inspired *ragù* interestingly made with turkey; marinara; and marinara with mushroom. Another, the Pasta Capri, is linguine with shrimp, spinach in a roasted tomato cream sauce. The heartiest dishes feature grilled chicken made with a boneless chicken breast, and the roasted half of chicken. For around $10, these make hearty meals when combined with side salads, mashed potatoes, vegetables or pastas. To put the finishing touch on any order, Café Express thoughtfully provides a plentiful number of sauces, olive oil, mustards, vinegars, pickles, pepperoncini, capers, cornichons, sun-dried tomatoes and the like to help enliven any dish. This is far from the typical "fixin's" station that you will find at many other counter-service establishments. Café Express aptly describes it as an "Oasis table". Café Express has several beers and wine by the glass.

Café Lili $11

5757 Westheimer (west of Chimney Rock) 77057, (713) 952-6969
www.cafelili.com

Cuisine - Middle Eastern
Hours - Mon-Thu 11AM to 9PM; Fri-Sat 11AM to 10PM
Credit Cards - Amex, Discover, MC, Visa
Service - Counter Service
Alcohol - Beer & Wine; BYOB

Entrée Prices - $8 to $24 ($11 average)
Entrées $12 and less - 80%

Atmosphere & Décor - Pleasant
Appeal - Good Lebanese food in a friendly and informal environment
Menu Suggestions - baba ganoush; fatoosh (lettuce, tomatoes, parsley and pita chips); Kafta Kabob Sandwich; Chicken Kabob Sandwich; Falafel Sandwich

Friendly and efficient counter service and fresh, well prepared Middle Eastern food are hallmarks of Café Lili. The decent-sized place is clean and often crowded during lunchtime. It seems that the local Lebanese community makes up a good portion of the business at other times. Café

Lili is a nice choice in the Galleria area when the mood strikes for increasingly familiar Levantine food. That anachronistic term might not draw the interest of friends and co-workers, but the thought of Café Lili's *tabouli, baba ganoush* and grilled dishes should.

The items served at Café Lili are similar to many of the other local Middle Eastern restaurants: salads, dips, pita sandwiches and kabobs make up much of the menu. There are a large number of small dishes, so there is an array of choices that can work as an appetizer or a side dish to a sandwich. In addition to the popular *hummus, baba ganoush, tabouli* and stuffed grape leaves, Café Lili serves *fatoosh* salad (lettuce, tomatoes, parsley and fried pita chips); *moussaka* (a hearty dish of eggplant and béchamel sauce); fried *kibbe; laban* (a house-made yogurt dip); meat pies; spinach pies; and various salads of yogurt and cucumber, lettuce, feta cheese, lima beans and green beans. Café Lili does a fine job with salads of all varieties here. Both the *baba ganoush* and the *hummus* are less creamy than most other versions in the area. But, both are commendable, especially with some additional olive oil poured on top. The hot sandwiches, wrapped in pita bread, are a *falafel,* beef *shawarma* (no chicken *shawarma* here) adorned with tomatoes, and kabobs of flame-broiled beef, chicken and a *kafta kabob* (ground beef). Café Lili's version of the *falafel* sandwich comes loaded with shredded lettuce, tomatoes, marinated peppers, cucumbers and *tahini* dressing. All are good, though one drawback is that the pita bread is packaged, and not fresh-from-the oven or as flavorful as at some other local restaurants. More substantial, and larger dishes include the kabob plates featuring beef, chicken, *kafta* or a combination of kabobs served with rice and a choice of *hummus* or green salad. These are pricier, but are still a good value given the amount of food that is served. There is also a Chicken Kabob Salad with romaine lettuce, feta cheese, green onions and tomatoes with grilled chicken breast, and Chicken and Rice, boiled, shredded chicken served over rice and topped with cinnamon and pine nuts. Desserts include *baklava,* plus rice pudding, caramel custard and date and coconut cookies. Though the décor is somewhat spartan, for an unpretentious restaurant located in a strip center, Café Lili has some charm. Photographs of the members of the owners' family along with those of the formerly beautiful city of Beirut adorn the walls. Televisions are located above the dining area, but are not obtrusive, as they are often tuned, with low volume, to one of the financial news stations for the crowd of mostly office workers.

Café Malay — $11

10234 Westheimer (at Seagler, just inside the Beltway) 77042, (713) 785-7915
www.cafe-malay.com

Cuisine - Malaysian
Hours - Mon-Thu, Sun 11AM to 10PM; Fri-Sat 11AM to 11PM
Credit Cards - MC, Visa
Service - Table Service; Delivery
Alcohol - NONE; BYOB

Entrée Prices - Dinner - $6 to $18 ($11 average); Lunch - $5 to $7
Entrées at Dinner $12 and less - 60%

Atmosphere & Décor - Pleasant
Appeal - Tasty and fairly authentic Malaysian food
Useful to Note - Order the Roti Canai to start the meal.
Menu Suggestions - Satay Chicken; Roti Canai (pan-fried bread with a curry dipping sauce) Beef Rendang; Nasi Lemak (flavored rice with anchovies, chicken and a hard-boiled egg); Chow Kueh Teow (rice noodles with shrimp, squid, bean sprouts and egg); Hainan Chicken (half-chicken steamed with sesame oil); Hainan Chicken Rice (steamed chicken and rice with chiles, ginger and soy sauce)

Café Malay is a well-run small restaurant, and a welcome addition to the constellation of interesting ethnic restaurants within a short few miles from the intersection of Westheimer and the Beltway. The setting, featuring subdued greens and browns in the main dining room and red in the back room, is comfortable and fairly attractive. Though Malaysian food is somewhat unique on the local restaurant scene, visitors to local Thai, and to a lesser extent, Chinese restaurants will notice familiar dishes. The Indian influences to the cuisine are more apparent with the flavors than the actual dishes. Sweet, spicy and sometimes salty and sour flavors interplay in many of the preparations. Curry flavored dishes, usually thickened with coconut milk, are common. Chiles, turmeric and tamarind are used in many items. Long-simmering, frying and steaming are all employed. Steamed rice is a common part of each table. Rice and egg noodles are featured in a number of items. Meats, seafood and vegetables can be centerpieces of the meal here. Fish heads feature prominently in about a half-dozen dishes. These seem more accessible when deep-fried. The menu with over 100 items is well-laid out and divided among soup, appetizers, casserole, chicken, beef, pork, crab, squid, shrimp, fish, fried rice, noodles, vegetables, and sizzling plates. The most enjoyable for many will be Beef Rendang, the long-simmered spicy beef that is also very popular in neighboring Indonesia. Another deserved favorite is the Hainan Chicken, chicken that has been stewed in a soy sauce-laden broth. It is very good, though requires a little work to separate the moist, delicious meat from the bones and cartilage. According to the menu, the dozen or so fish dishes allow for a choice among the familiar tilapia, flounder, striped bass, red snapper, and something called white promets. These are available deep-fried or steamed with several different sauces. Whatever you order for your main dish, it's wise to start with an order of the *roti canai*, the puffy, freshly baked flat bread that is pan-fried on one side and nearly irresistible when dipped in the light, thin curry sauce or the homey peanut sauce, the latter which has to be requested. It's obvious some planning and care went into the creation of this restaurant. The service, though, can sometimes be more earnest than polished. For those new to the cuisine, lunchtime is a good time to visit, as there are a dozen Malaysian and nearly thirty more popular Chinese lunch specials, all quite inexpensive. The latter are also served with fried rice, an egg roll, and a soup.

Café Mezza & Grille $10

6100 Westheimer (between Fountain View and Voss) 77057, (713) 334-2000
www.cafemezza.net

Cuisine - American (with strong Eastern Middle Eastern aspects)
Hours - Mon-Thu, Sun 10:30AM to 12AM; Fri-Sat 10:30AM to 4AM
Credit Cards - Amex, Discover, MC, Visa
Service - Table Service
Alcohol - Beer & Wine; BYOB

Entrée Prices - $6 to $20 ($10 average)
Entrées $12 and less - 80%

Atmosphere & Décor - Functional, but pleasant
Appeal - Wide-range of enticing options
Useful to Note - The cakes are baked daily.
Menu Suggestions - Tomato and Basil Soup; Mezza Red Pepper Dip (red pepper, pomegranate molasses and olive oil); Mezza Salad (greens, toasted almonds, pineapple); Beef Tenderloin Salad (greens, sun-dried tomatoes, chickpeas, feta and tenderloin); Kufta Kabob Platter (marinated ground sirloin kabab); Mixed Grille (shish kabob, grilled diced chicken breast and grilled shrimp)

The oddly named, well-designed, well-staffed and laid back Café Mezza & Grille offers what is accurately subtitled, "American cuisine with Mediterranean flare". Café Mezza's unique, if mostly familiar, menu is eclectically filled with an array of casual items with an Eastern Mediterranean bent. There is literally something for nearly everyone here. With a Houston-highlights approach, there is Caesar salad, tomato and basil soup, chicken tortilla soup, Buffalo wings, pastas including the fettuccine Alfredo, a Reuben sandwich, shrimp *Campechana,* hamburgers, fish tacos, spinach dip, fried calamari, grilled chicken breast, and more, plus a kids menu and a number of potentially distracting televisions placed around the tiled and often-loud dining room, all of which makes it especially family-friendly. That, and its BYOB policy, which can help pacify Mom and Dad.

A visit here begins with a savory, tough-to-resist dip of olive oil, sesame seeds and powdered oregano that is served with crisp pita chips. There are a number of other tempting starters to allow you additional time to select an entrée from the lengthy menu. There is *hummus, baba ganoush, bruschetta, tabouli* and the unique Mezza Red Pepper Dip made with red pepper, olive oil and pomegranate molasses. The restaurant's very wide-ranging approach might ensure some rough spots, but the salads and grilled items are reliably well done, especially those with a Turkish pedigree, such as the *kafta* with marinated ground sirloin mixed with parsley and minced onions, *tawook* with marinated diced chicken breast, and the kabob with filet mignon. Café Mezza also has a couple of more ambitious and pricier entrées each day. At the lower end of the price range, the burgers and unusual *shawarma* and *falafel* wraps are decent, if hefty, but nothing special. Though the portions are large, it's easy to eat healthy here, or to feel that you are eating in a healthy fashion. There are roughly a dozen vegetarian entrées, plus entrée-size salads. Many of the dishes are cooked in olive oil or grilled, and most seem clean-tasting. The popular sandwiches are served with a choice among chopped fresh fruit topped with a light poppy seed dressing, crisp potato wedges, sweet potato fries, potato, or a cup of soup or the house salad for a small, additional charge. That house salad is an interesting mix of greens, toasted almonds, shredded carrots and pieces of grilled pineapple in a buttermilk-garlic-Parmesan dressing. To finish a meal, there are cakes, chocolate and otherwise, and other items that are created daily.

Café Piquet $12

5757 Bissonnet (between Chimney Rock and Hillcroft) 77081, (713) 664-1031

Cuisine - Cuban
Hours - Tue-Thu 11AM to 9PM; Fri-Sat 11AM to 10PM; Sun 11AM to 7PM
Credit Cards - MC, Visa
Service - Table Service
Alcohol - Beer & Wine

Entrée Prices - $7 to $22 ($12 average)
Entrées $12 and less - 70%

Atmosphere & Décor - Pleasant
Appeal - Serving possibly the best Cuban food in town in a nice setting
Menu Suggestions - Empanada; Grilled Chicken Breast; Roasted Pork; Picadillo (ground beef in a tomato sauce); Ropa Vieja (shredded, stewed beef); black beans; café cubano (Cuban-style espresso); sangria; batidos (thick fruit shakes)

Café Piquet serves up what might be the best Cuban food in town. Popular with Cuban food aficionados and food lovers in general since it opened in 1996, it's now in its third, largest and nicest location in the neighborhood;

finally in a very pleasant and comfortable place. Service is efficient, and the oft-present owners are very friendly. Attentive waiters speak decent enough English, and more readily, Spanish in the clipped, rapid-fire Cuban dialect. The menu is user-friendly, as all of the dishes have descriptive names in English, which often seem less appetizing than their more melodic, original Spanish names.

The menu has grown to be fairly extensive and includes most of the popular Cuban favorites, most hearty, further made so with the nearly requisite side of black beans, and often with tropical flavors. For lunch and lighter meals, Café Piquet serves several varieties of the Cuban sandwich. One of these sandwiches, plus a side, or one of the tropical fruit shakes will make for a satisfying and filling meal. A good way to begin a bigger meal is with an *empanada* enlivened with a few splashes from the bottled hot sauce. Here these are filled with *picadillo,* long-simmered, seasoned ground beef, and a noticeable number of peas, then deep-fried. Other appetizers of the nearly ten served include yucca in garlic sauce, fried yucca and deep-fried plantain chips. The latter two are served with a *mojo* sauce for dipping made with minced garlic, lime and olive oil. All of the entrées are served with a form of rich, smooth-tasting black beans, rice, and either plantains or relatively bland steamed yucca, and are usually quite filling. The chicken entrées are seemingly popular. These include a butterflied and grilled chicken breast, the breaded chicken breast, and something described as "Lite" Chicken. There are pork chops, two in an order, roasted pork, and *masitas,* which are fried pork chunks. The roasted pork is reportedly cooked for ten hours, and results in a tender and tasty dish. The *masitas* avoid the dryness that can plague this dish, and are flavorful. Café Piquet has grilled steak items, a filet mignon and a rib-eye, some sautéed ones, a sirloin and an eye of the round, a breaded steak, and a couple other beef dishes, *picadillo* and *Ropa Vieja,* shredded beef. The steaks are decent, though not steakhouse quality. The *picadillo* plate can be enjoyable, but might work better as the filling for the *empanadas.* The seafood offerings are Cuban Shrimp Creole, Lobster Cuban Creole, breaded and fried shrimp, breaded and fried red snapper fillet, an entire red snapper either steamed or fried, and fried fillets of seldom seen Gulf fish, kingfish and grouper. If the large amount of food is not enough, the desserts feature bread pudding, rice pudding, flan, guava shells, guava marmalade, and the ubiquitous *tres leches.* A fitting end to any meal is with Café Piquet's excellent espresso-like Cuban coffee, *café cubano.*

Café Pita+ $7

10890 Westheimer (between the Beltway and Wilcrest) 77042, (713) 953-7237

Cuisine - Bosnian

Hours - Mon-Thu 11AM to 10PM; Fri 11AM to 11PM; Sat-Sun 12 to 10PM
Credit Cards - Amex, Discover, MC, Visa
Service - Table Service
Alcohol - NONE

Entrée Prices - $4 to $9 ($7 average)
Entrées $12 and less - 100%

Atmosphere & Décor - Generally quaint
Appeal - Hearty, flavorful and sometimes healthy food for a great price
Menu Suggestions - Hummus; Eggplant Dip (baba ganoush); red pepper and sun-dried tomato dip; Cevap (sausage-like ground beef rolls served with plenty of fresh bread); pizzas

---

The moniker for the small Westchase-area Café Pita+ is a tad misleading. It is a café in that the Italian-style coffees are lingered over here, and several of its dishes are commonly accompanied by pitas, but there are no pitas here. This is a Bosnian restaurant featuring hearty and flavorful cooking that is a great value. The mention of Bosnian fare is unlikely to draw a crowd outside of that emigrant community, so some background is helpful, even if the cooking will be readily enjoyable for most Houstonians. Bosnia (or Bosnia and Herzegovina) is mostly known here for the war and atrocities in the 1990s, and maybe its capital, Sarajevo, either for hosting Winter Olympics or the event that triggered World War I. The country is populated by Slavs (following three different religious traditions) and several of the hearty dishes here are common to most Slavic cuisines. It was governed by the Sublime Porte in Istanbul for several centuries and a portion of the offerings are Middle Eastern. Lying close to the Adriatic and across from the culinary juggernaut of Italy, a significant portion of the dishes is Italian or Mediterranean. These three distinct influences are joined on the small menu with a couple of nearly all-American creations such as a Chicken Caesar and a Cobb Salad. It might seem a bit discordant to first-time visitors. But, with recognizable, consistent and appealing flavors, and good ingredients, it all comes together rather naturally on your table. This is tasty home cooking from the Balkans paired with presentation that is surprisingly quite nice.

The small restaurant consists of an open kitchen and maybe a dozen small tables with a flat screen television in back. It is popular with local Bosnians most of the time, and nearby office workers during lunchtime. The restaurant itself might not be the most inviting around, but the affable, usually present owner makes a good effort to be accommodating and informative. Though the entrée portions are generous, the Middle Eastern dips are an excellent way to begin a meal. The *hummus* can be especially good. It is served with *lepinja* bread that is very aptly described as a cross between pita bread and *ciabatta* bread. It's fluffy and airy and a good complement to the dips and the sandwiches. The most popular item is the *cevap*, which is seasoned ground beef rolls served with plenty of the fresh *lepinja* bread. It looks like a huge sandwich, but it's expected that you tear off a piece of the bread and eat it with one of the sausage-like rolls and some of the accompanying butter. *Burek* is a lengthy coiled stretch of puff pastry filled with ground beef or cheese; somewhat similar to a giant elongated *spanikopita*, and a lot of food for the price. The hand-crafted 10-inch individually sized thin-crust pizzas are quite tasty, and can be ordered with a few unique toppings. For entrées there are shish kabobs with beef and chicken breast, stuffed peppers and stuffed cabbage, both filled with ground beef, and from the deep blue sea (or out of the blue for some), grilled sardines. If you have room for a sweet finish, there is *baklava*, rice pudding, and crêpes with a chocolate and hazelnut mix, topped with a berry sauce.

* Café Red Onion $13

12440 Northwest Freeway (between W. 43rd and Bingle) 77092, (281) 957-0957
3910 Kirby (between Richmond and Southwest Freeway) 77098, (713) 807-1122
1111 Eldridge Parkway (south of Memorial) 77077, (281) 293-9500
www.caferedonion.com

Cuisine - Pan Latin (Innovative Central American and Mexican)
Hours - Mon-Thu, Sun 11AM to 10PM; Fri-Sat 11AM to 11PM
Credit Cards - Amex, MC, Visa
Service - Table Service
Alcohol - Full Bar

Entrée Prices - Dinner - $10 to $19 ($13 average); Lunch - $8 to $15
Entrees at Dinner $12 and less - 50%

Atmosphere & Décor - Nice, inviting
Appeal - Zesty, high quality Central American-inspired fare
Useful to Note - If you like these, check out Café Red Onion Seafood & Mas.
Menu Suggestions - Shrimp Ceviche; Cream of Roasted Poblano Pepper Soup; Cream of Roasted Red Pepper Soup; quesadillas; Seafood Enchiladas; Beef Enchiladas; Jalapeño Steak; Jalapeño Chicken; Chicken Tikal; Roatan Crab Cakes; Pupusa Revueltas (pan-fried stuffed corn pockets); Southwest Snapper (pan-fried snapper with a cheese sauce and cabbage relish); Medallion de Beef Colombia; Tres Leches Centro America

The three Café Red Onion locations are interesting, attractive, reasonably priced, well-run and great value restaurants. Reflecting the gracious owner, these are friendly, comfortable and noticeably hard-working places. The cooking, the main reason to visit, can loosely be characterized as creative and somewhat sophisticated Mexican with a strong Central American influence. The result is innovative, fairly unique, pan-Latin, extremely well-executed and very well-presented. The artfulness and attractiveness of the dishes are probably the most pleasantly surprising aspects of dining at Café Red Onion. Mexican food, especially with strong Tex-Mex leanings, no matter how tasty it is, is rarely attractive at other restaurants. It is here, as are all of the plates. In addition to those numerous Mexican items, other dishes include Salvadoran *pupusas*, an Argentine-style steak served with *chimi-churri* sauce, and many engaging dishes of the owner's creation. What all of the entrées have in common are robust flavors arranged in complementary patterns with a presentation quality that belies the owner's long Escoffier-esque hotel background.

The meal begins, in Tex-Mex fashion, with chips and salsa. The chips are thick corn chips that are served with a flavorful tomato-based salsa and another one, a slightly sweet pineapple- and tomatillo-based yellow salsa, reflecting tropical Central America. The list of dishes is suited very well for the city that likes bold and often spicy flavors. Though the entrées are satisfyingly large, some of the appetizers and soups can be a tempting way to start the meal. The cream of roasted poblano pepper and cream of roasted red pepper are especially flavorful and not heavy at all. The *empanadas* are good, and here are fried pastry squares filled with one each of ground beef, chicken or tropical guava presented very nicely on a large plate, each *empanada* sitting near its own zesty sauce. The shrimp *ceviche* is another good choice. Fried yucca, fried plantains, and gourmet small tacos are some of the other starters. The Mexican entrées described on the menu as "South of the Border Plates" include various preparations of *quesadillas*, tacos, *flautas* and enchiladas. These are all far more than palatable. The *quesadillas* are prepared in the Tex-Mex fashion with flour tortillas sandwiching a variety of fillings, but with quite a bit more panache than usual. In addition to admirable versions with chicken and cheese, and chicken and spinach, Café Red Onion also has one with pesto, grilled chicken breast and cheese, and another with portobello mushrooms, *chipotle* salsa, grilled chicken breast and cheese. The enchiladas come in beef, chicken, spinach and seafood versions, the last of which is excellent.

The rest of the menu is divided among House Specialties, grilled beef and pork, and grilled chicken. Many of the dishes deserve mention, and nearly all are satisfying, at the very least. One of the most interesting of the specialties is the Medallion de Beef Colombia, a four-ounce filet mignon medallion that has been coated with freshly ground coffee, seared quickly, and served with a mango-based sauce and grilled zucchini, squash, sautéed plantains and covered with shredded and fried onions. The steak itself is not very large, but the entire dish includes a fair amount of food. The excellent sauce complements everything on the plate and helps to tie the disparate flavors together. The other steak listed as a specialty is the increasingly popular *chimi-churri*-basted steak. It is a marinated and grilled seven-ounce strip steak served with the *chimi-churri* sauce with sides of black beans and fried plantains. The very good and filling *Pupusa Revueltas* is quite a bit more attractive than the *pupusas* served at local Salvadoran restaurants. These *pupusas* are the pan-fried, stuffed corn masa pockets filled with shredded pork tenderloin and Monterey Jack cheese (*revueltas* meaning the mixing of the two fillings), served over refried beans, topped with an upscale version of the traditional Salvadoran cabbage relish, and sides of fried plantains and rice. The Jalapeño Chicken, a grilled boneless chicken breast topped with a *jalapeño* and Monterey Jack Cheese sauce, is usually delicious. Somewhat surprisingly, it's even better than a similar preparation with steak. These are just some of the highlights. For dessert, there is a very good rum-laden version of Houston's favorite dessert, *tres leches*.

25 a little too expensive for this guidebook

Houston has excellent restaurants at nearly every price range, but the hallmark is value. These twenty-five restaurants listed below fall just beyond the price guidelines for this book, but provide a very good dining experience and are a fine value. Approximate average prices per meal, excluding drinks, tax and tip, are shown parenthetically.

- **Ashiana** - Indian - 12610 Briar Forest **($18)**
- **Bayou City Seafood n' Pasta** - Seafood, Cajun - 4730 Richmond **($16)**
- **Café Montrose** - Belgian - 1609 Westheimer **($17)**
- **Clementine's** - American - 6448 FM 1960 W **($15)**
- **Cyclone Anaya's** - Tex-Mex - 1710 Durham & other locations **($14)**
- **divino** - Italian - 1803 W. Alabama **($17)**
- **El Meson** - Spanish, Cuban, Tex-Mex - 2425 University **($17)**
- **Floyd's Cajun Seafood** - Cajun, Seafood - 20760 I-45 S. **($15)**
- **Frenchie's** - Italian - 1041 NASA Road 1 **($18)**
- **Fung's Kitchen's** - Chinese - 7320 Southwest Freeway **($15)**
- **Goode Co. Seafood** - Seafood - 2621 Westpark & 10211 I-10 W. **($18)**
- **Isla Coqui** - Puerto Rican - 1801 Durham **($16)**
- **Joyce's** - Seafood - 6415 San Felipe & 3736 Westheimer **($16)**
- **Khyber** - Indian - 2510 Richmond **($17)**
- **Korea Garden** - Korean - 9501 Long Point **($14)**
- **Kubo's** - Japanese - 2414 University **($18)**
- **Laurenzo's 1308 Cantina** - Tex-Mex - 1308 Montrose **($15)**
- **Mardi Gras Grill** - Cajun, Seafood - 1511 S. Shepherd **($15)**
- **Perbacco** - Italian - 700 Milam **($15)**
- **Pico's** - Mexican - 5941 Bellaire **($15)**
- **Rudi Lechner's** - German - 2503 S. Gessner **($14)**

- **Santos - The Taste of Mexico** - Tex-Mex - 10001 Westheimer (**$17**)
- **Tila's** - Tex-Mex / Mexican - 1111 S. Shepherd (**$16**)
- **Vietopia** - Vietnamese - 5176 Buffalo Speedway (**$15**)
- **Yatra** - Indian - 706 Main (**$15**)

Cahill's on Durham $7

903 Durham (just south of Washington) 77007, (713) 864-9400

Cuisine - Hamburgers
Hours - Mon-Thu 11AM to 11PM; Fri-Sat 11AM to 1AM
Credit Cards - Amex, Diners, Discover, MC, Visa
Service - Table Service
Alcohol - Full Bar

Entrée Prices - $6 to $12 ($7 average)
Entrées $12 and less - 100%

Atmosphere & Décor - Spartan; it's a neighborhood bar
Appeal - Some of the very best hamburgers in Houston
Useful to Note - Cahill's is a bar, first and foremost.
Menu Suggestions - Ranch Burger; Mushroom Burger; Jalapeño Burger; fries

Cahill's on Durham is primarily a neighborhood bar located in a large old house on Durham, just south of Washington. Its interior with beer signs and ordinary appearance (excepting the attractive pressed tin ceiling), gives no sign that the kitchen is so proficient. While Cahill's could probably get by with lesser food that passes at many bars, they serve some of the best hamburgers in the Houston area. The quality of the burgers in their several guises is tough to match. It begins with the good-sized patties that are hand-crafted with quality ground chuck beef with the proper amount of fat. These are grilled over an open flame resulting in a beautifully and suitably charred exterior and a juicily interior. The buns are large, properly sized and toasted, and the toppings are top-notch and plentiful. The basic burger, the Hammerburger, comes with the expected and perfectly suitable mayonnaise, mustard, lettuce, tomatoes, pickles and onions. For a slight additional charge you can get cheese with the choice among, American, cheddar, Swiss, provolone and Pepper Jack. The Mushroom Burger, served with plenty of mushrooms, caramelized onions and Swiss cheese is especially good. The Ranch Burger is topped with cheddar cheese, thick, smoked bacon and ranch dressing. There is also the Jalapeño Burger that has pepper jack cheese, onions, tomatoes, and sliced fresh jalapeños that have been sautéed in garlic. Though loaded with jalapeños, this is spicy and very flavorful without being overly hot. In addition to the hamburgers, Cahill's serves a couple of entrée-sized salads and about a dozen hot and cold sandwiches including an overstuffed cheesesteak, Hot Roast Beef with grilled onions and Swiss cheese, and a club sandwich. The sandwiches, along with the hamburgers, come with a choice among very good onion rings, potato chips and probably best of all, fries, which are suitably crisp and long. These are a very fine accompaniment to a burger, especially when eaten at Cahill's rather than take-away. Not just the fries, but the onion rings and potato chips are made from scratch; quite unusual these days, except for neighbored pubs on Shepherd, it seems.

The owner of Cahill's is originally from Chicago, which might be easy to discern from the nearly overwhelming mass of Chicago sports memorabilia on the wall. It's interesting that three bars run by three Chicagoland natives (Cahill's, Market Square Bar & Grill, and Kenneally's), none of whose names ends in vowel, turn out such good food. Being primarily a bar, there is a full range of liquor and a number of pretty decent beers on tap. On Wednesdays, Cahill's provides one of the better values in town by offering a well prepared ten-ounce Black Angus New York strip steak that is cooked to order, plus a salad and mashed potatoes, which is not only better than nearly every other steak nights at local bars, at around twelve bucks, it's probably cheaper, too. To note, in part since so many items are made from scratch, the small kitchen can sometimes get backed up when the bar is crowded.

Cali $5

3030 Travis (between Tuam and Elgin) 77006, (713) 526-0112

Cuisine - Vietnamese
Hours - Mon-Sat 11AM to 8PM
Credit Cards - MC, Visa
Service - Counter Service
Alcohol - NONE

Entrée Prices - Dinner - $2 to $9 ($5 average); Lunch - $2 to $7
Entrées at Dinner $12 and less - 100%

Atmosphere & Décor - Very Spartan
Appeal - Cheap Vietnamese sandwiches in Midtown
Menu Suggestions - Banh Mi Thit Nuong (grilled BBQ pork sandwich); Cali Special Sandwich; Bo Luc Lac Diet (spicy garlic sliced beef); fried banana

Cali is a small, sparse, but generally clean and often bustling Vietnamese restaurant located on Travis in Midtown among many other Vietnamese businesses. The popularity of Cali, especially for the non-Asian patrons, is due to their reliability of their *banh mi*, the Vietnamese sandwiches that are served on a fresh, crusty small French baguette with shredded, marinated carrots, large slices of fresh jalapeños, fresh cucumber and a choice of different fillings. There are a dozen different fillings for these, more than most restaurants that serve these sandwiches. These include those filled with the very popular char-grilled pork (*thit nuong*), pâté, steamed pork (*thit xa xiu*), shredded grilled chicken (*ga*), pork meatball, a vegetarian, and even one with sardines and tomato sauce. The char-grilled pork sandwich, like most of the other Vietnamese sandwich shops, is the best. Not quite as delectable, but still good, is the steamed pork.

In addition to the sandwiches, Cali offers many different items, nearly 100, many more than most of the other restaurants specializing in Vietnamese sandwiches. These other dishes are favored by most of the Vietnamese customers, and range from spring rolls, the wonderful Vietnamese deep-fried Imperial rolls, the vermicelli noodle bowls (*bun*), egg noodle and wonton soup dishes, the beef noodle soup (*pho*), the rice *congee* soup (*chao*), a large number of rice plates with a variety of toppings (*com dia*), vegetarian dishes (*mon chay*), and the large family plates (*com gia dinh*). These are all very reasonably priced, and many easy to order for the non-Vietnamese speaker courtesy of large color photos with numbers that adorn one of the counter areas. The two dozen or so specials on the white board near the counter might be more difficult to discern for some, though. There are also a number of Chinese-inspired dishes offered, which will likely be of greater familiarity for downtown office workers at lunchtime. Whatever is ordered for the main dish, a fitting end to the meal, ignoring the calorie count, is a battered and deep-fried banana for dessert. Cali also offers an array of freshly squeezed fruit drinks, including smoothies, and other Southeast Asian and Vietnamese drinks including excellent dark roasted French coffee that is available over ice, too.

Candelari's Pizzeria $9

4505 Bissonnet (at Newcastle) 77401, (713) 662-2825
6002 Washington (east of Wescott) 77007, (832) 200-1474
6825 S. Fry Road (north of FM 1093) Katy, 77494, (281) 395-6746
www.candelaris.com

Cuisine - Pizza
Hours - Bissonnet - Mon-Thu 5 to 10PM; Fri-Sat 11Am to 10PM; Sun 11AM to 9PM; Washington - Mon-Thu, Sun 11AM to 10PM; Fri-Sat 11AM to 11PM; Fry - Mon-Thu, Sun 11AM to 9:30PM; Fri-Sat 11AM to 10:30PM
Credit Cards - MC, Visa
Service - Counter Service
Alcohol - Bissonnet & Fry - Beer & Wine; Washington - Full Bar

Entrée Prices - Dinner - $7 to $11 ($9 average); Lunch Buffet - $9

Entrées at Dinner $12 and less - 100%

Atmosphere & Décor - Pleasant (dine-in at the Bissonnet location is limited)
Appeal - Excellent pizzas
Useful to Note - Dine-in buffet is served for lunch, Monday through Saturday.
Menu Suggestions - Surfer Pizza (pineapple, Canadian bacon, artichoke hearts, feta and pesto); King Mike's Pizza (Italian sausage, sun-dried tomato chicken sausage, pesto, roasted garlic, bacon, portobello mushrooms and feta); Spinaci Pizza (spinach, fresh tomatoes, basil, feta and Parmesan); T-Rex (Italian sausage, andouille sausage, pepperoni, ground beef, bacon and Canadian bacon); Pollo Arrosto (roasted chicken, roasted garlic, roasted red peppers, sun-dried tomatoes and feta)

Candelari's is one of the best pizzerias in the area. The genesis for some of the quality is that Candelari's is also a sausage maker, the self-proclaimed, "King of Sausages" for the Houston area. These top quality sausages, more than just the fennel-specked Italian sausages, are made in-house, and find their way into several of the pizzas. But, a very tasty pizza from Candelari's doesn't have to contain their sausages, and almost every version is quite good, even a different version such as the Surfer Pizza with pineapple, Canadian bacon, artichoke hearts, pesto and feta cheese. The foundation for any tasty pizza is the crust, and Candelari's crusts are sufficiently crisp and sturdy, buttery and very good. On top of that solid foundation Candelari's uses top-notch ingredients. And, importantly, unlike some other area pizzerias, the ingredients are used in a fairly judicious fashion. The pizzas have a balance of tastes and texture in proportion; there is not an overwhelming amount of one topping or cheese that dominates. Since Candelari's pizzas are not overloaded with cheese, these will taste great the next morning for breakfast, and not too soggy with the moisture from excess cheese, if you somehow manage not to scarf it all once it arrives. Pizzas on their New York Style thin crust are generally a better option than the Deep Dish. Those crusts are just a bit overly doughy, and for that reason seem to become flaccid somewhat more quickly than the New York Style, but are still quite tasty, though. Good to note, especially when in the throes of hunger, the Deep Dish pizzas take about forty-five minutes to prepare versus the twenty-five minutes for the New York Style pizzas. For the health-conscious, Candelari's does an excellent job with their wheat crusts, which might be the best in the area.

Though the pizzas are easily is the biggest draw, there are also appetizers, salads, hot and cold sandwiches, and several pasta dishes that make Candelari's more convenient for lunch, and other times when pizza doesn't seem to be in the cards. The large green salads can be made heartier with roasted chicken breast for an additional couple of dollars. The sandwiches include the Italian-American standard, sausage with peppers, onions and melted mozzarella cheese, a meatball sandwich, a club featuring smoked turkey and bacon, and the regionally popular muffaletta, which is served warm. Some of the ten or so pastas are the basic thin pasta in marinara sauce with meatballs, and even better, the signature Italian sausage instead of the meatballs, lasagna with sausage and spinach, and Penne Perfetto, penne with Italian sausage in a tomato cream sauce. There are also a handful of desserts, appetizers and side salads to complete any meal. To note, Candelari's offers a very good value all-you-can-eat pizza buffet with actually good pizza, with a side salad and drink for around nine bucks Monday through Saturday.

Caribbean Cuisine $7

7433 Bissonnet (between Fondren and S. Gessner) 77074, (713) 774-7428

Cuisine - Caribbean
Hours - Mon-Thu 10AM to 8PM; Fri-Sat 10AM to 10PM
Credit Cards - Amex, Diners, MC, Visa
Service - Counter Service
Alcohol - Beer

Entrée Prices - $4 to $10 ($7 average)
Entrées $12 and less - 100%

Atmosphere & Décor - Spartan
Appeal - Reliable Jamaican fare with inexpensive sweets
Useful to Note - Hakeem Olajuwon has recommended it in the past.
Menu Suggestions - Jerk Chicken; Oxtails; cookies; bread pudding

Located in a run-down strip center in Sharpstown, Caribbean Cuisine might not seem too promising at first sight. But, it has been a reliable provider of Jamaican standards for quite a while now; "De Real Ting" as advertised. It's a friendly, small and tidy counter-service restaurant that does steady business for lunch. Takeout is popular, though the dozen or so tables provides a pleasant enough setting. A small retail section occupies a corner of the restaurant. The relatively small menu has most of the island favorites. There are patties, the deep-fried turnovers filled with beef, chicken or vegetables, *roti* (very flat, Indian-style pan bread) with several different fillings, jerk chicken, fried plantains, curries, stews and seafood. The spicy and flavorful jerk chicken (marinated with very hot peppers then grilled) comes in several guises. There are jerk chicken wings, a jerk chicken sandwich, jerk chickens (a quarter, half and whole), and a jerk chicken plate. The sandwich on a piece of folded coco bread (the slightly sweet bread made with coconut milk) is an enjoyable, if not a very large sandwich. And, overall, the portions at Caribbean Cuisine are not very large, at least not by

Houston restaurant standards. There are plates denoted "Yard Specialties" that are served with rice and red peas, and a couple pieces of fried plantains. In addition to the jerk chicken and jerk wing, these choices include curry goat, curry chicken, curry shrimp, brown stew chicken, oxtails, jerk pork, red snapper fillet, and an entire red snapper. If you cannot decide on one, the "Round de Yard" is a choice of three of the entrées, excluding the seafood. There are usually a couple daily specials in addition to the menu items. The bottled Caribbean red chili sauce will definitely help if you need things spicier than is served. Though the portions might not be large, desserts and beer are especially inexpensive at Caribbean Cuisine. If you are still not quite satiated after the meal, one of the sweets can help. Portions of the luscious bread pudding, banana bread, and most cakes are just around a buck. Three freshly baked cookies are similarly cheap. The chocolate chip, sugar and oatmeal cookies all provide a fitting reward at the end of the meal. It's also not much of financial commitment to finish sweetly with a slice of cheesecake, rum and raisin or the unusual grape nut ice cream. There is Red Stripe, Heineken, Bud Light, a couple of shandies, and Guinness Extra Stout for a pittance. Non-alcoholic beverages include ginger beer and other Caribbean favorites.

Carter & Cooley Co. $8

375 W. 19th (west of Heights) 77008, (713) 864-3354

Cuisine - Sandwiches
Hours - Mon-Fri 9AM to 3:30PM; Sat 9AM to 5PM
Credit Cards - Amex, Discover, MC, Visa
Service - Counter Service
Alcohol - NONE

Entrée Prices - $6 to $10 ($8 average)
Entrées $12 and less - 100%

Atmosphere & Décor - Comfortable
Appeal - Well-made sandwiches in a cool space
Useful to Note - There's just street parking, but there is plenty within a block.
Menu Suggestions - Muffaletta; BLT sandwich; Ham and Brie sandwich

Located in a charming structure built in 1921, ancient by Houston standards, Carter & Cooley is in the main business district in the Heights. Carter & Cooley has been in operation since 1989. It looks like what an old-stye sandwich shop, or malt shop, should look like. Fairly spacious for such an operation, there is room for plenty of tables, the requisite deli counter and an attractive, soaring pressed tin ceiling that seems to be nearly twenty feet from the floor. This is certainly not an antiseptic chain sandwich shop. It's tough to think of a nicer and more distinctive place in which to eat a sandwich in town. The interior of Carter & Cooley is a testament to the history of the Heights neighborhood in its early development. And, not just with the architecture. Numerous, interesting photographs of the early days of the Heights from the late nineteenth and early twentieth centuries when it was a separate muncipality apart from Houston are shown on the walls. But, this relative charm would be for naught if the food was not worth a visit. It is. Carter & Cooley can be described as an American deli, rather than a Jewish or Italian one. There are several well crafted Jewish-American sandwiches, and the New Orleans-Italian muffaletta, but the emphasis is on the middle American favorites. There are over twenty-five sandwiches on the menu that includes hot pastrami, Reuben, egg salad, tuna salad, BLT, liverwurst, smoked turkey breast, and a couple vegetarian sandwiches. The sandwiches are good because Carter & Cooley uses quality ingredients. The foundation, the breads are baked daily. The lunch meats are top-notch. The accompanying lettuce and tomato slices always seem suitably fresh and green and red, respectively. The bacon that is used for the BLT is not the thin, crumbly bacon hidden among the lettuce and toast, but rather thick hickory-smoked bacon. Unlike many other so-called BLT sandwiches at lesser places, the bacon is prominent. A generous number of slices find their way onto each of these. All of the sandwiches come with a decent potato salad, and a pickle slice. Carter & Cooley also has house-made chili and a daily soup. There are also several sides and salads such as macaroni, fruit salad, pasta salad and an artichoke and pasta salad. If you need a sweet finish, there are individual pies baked in-house and several cakes and brownies.

Casa de Leon $6

9217 Long Point (at Campbell) 77055, (713) 461-1955

Cuisine - Mexican (taqueria)
Hours - Mon-Fri 6AM to 2AM; Sat-Sun 6AM to 3AM
Credit Cards - Amex, MC, Visa
Service - Table Service
Alcohol - Beer

Entrée Prices - Dinner & Lunch - $3 to $10 ($6 average); Breakfast - $3 to $5
Entrées at Dinner $12 and less - 100%

Atmosphere & Décor - Spartan
Appeal - Often very good Mexican food at very low prices
Useful to Note - Nearby clubs empty into the restaurant on weekends.
Menu Suggestions - Enchiladas Supremas; Enchiladas Verdes; Chuletas de Puerco (pork chops); Carne Guisada (stewed beef)

The proficient and inexpensive Casa de Leon is a family run operation, which is noticeable in that the staff seems more intent than most in serving the customers, quickly and in a friendly manner. As is a near requirement for a capable *taqueria,* the flour tortillas are handmade daily, and nicely complement many dishes. The complimentary salsas on the tables are more than satisfactory. The only letdown is that the chips are too often stale. If so, the waitstaff will be happy to bring you some fresh ones. The relatively small menu sports some winners at virtually all stops. In addition to being very palatable, the dishes are typically larger-than-expected. With almost all of the plates most around $6, you certainly get more than your money's worth in terms of quality and quantity. The one enchilada dish on the menu, the *Enchiladas Supremas,* and the ones that make it as daily specials, are consistently excellent. These are probably as good as any other enchiladas, certainly any for under $10. The *Enchiladas Supremas* consist of four enchiladas, one each of grilled beef, chicken, bean and *queso fresco,* the white Mexican cheese that does not melt. The one with grilled beef is especially good. The *Enchiladas Verdes* consist of three large enchiladas, corn tortillas filled with moist chicken cooked in the Mexican-style with a red sauce, and then topped with a sweet green salsa and covered with chopped fresh onions. The *Chuletas de Puerco* consists of two fairly large, moist pork chops. The *Carne Guisada* is a big dish of expertly stewed beef served with a flavorful, rich gravy. In addition to these, there are other interesting dishes: a fajita plate with beef, chicken or shrimp; *Alambres,* a shish kabob dish with beef and shrimp; *flautas;* a grilled T-bone steak served Mexican-style with grilled onions and green peppers; breaded and fried catfish, fried perch (*mojarra*); breaded and fried shrimp; a *milanesa* (a thin breaded steak); and *Cabrito Adobabo,* marinated and stewed goat. Most of the plates come with rice and thick refried beans.

You can also get tacos, *tortas,* burritos, *tostadas,* and *quesadillas* with a choice of meat. The array of meat choices should satisfy almost all tastes: fajitas, *pastor* (pork), *lengua* (beef tongue), *barbacoa* (here, stewed beef cheek), chicken, *pierna* (pork leg), *sesos* (cow brains), *chicharron* (pork skin), *carne guisada* and *birria* (baby goat). The *tortas* are a great value at around $2.50. Also a value, there are several combination plates for around five bucks with enchiladas, burritos, and tacos. Unlike many Mexican eateries that serve it only on weekends, the *menudo* is served daily along with a hearty beef soup, a soup featuring shrimp, and another, *Birria en Caldo,* Jalisco-style goat soup. Breakfast is also served daily, primarily from 6AM to 11AM. After 11AM, the price of the basic scrambled egg combinations goes up to three dollars. Though generally a family place, similar to many *taquerias,* it can get fairly raucous late on weekend nights, as it is located near many Hispanic night clubs.

Casa Grande $9

3401 N. Main (just east of I-45 N.) 77009, (713) 227-8801

Cuisine - Mexican
Hours - Mon-Fri 7AM to 12AM; Sat-Sun 7AM to 2AM
Credit Cards - Amex, Discover, MC, Visa
Service - Table Service
Alcohol - Full Bar

Entrée Prices - Dinner - $5 to $17 ($9 avg.); Lunch - $5 to $8; Breakfast - $2 to $6
Entrées at Dinner $12 and less - 90%

Atmosphere & Décor - Appropriately Tex-Mex; often loud
Appeal - Solid Mexican food in festive surroundings
Useful to Note - There is also an adjoining club open on the weekends.
Menu Suggestions - Cabrito a la Parilla (grilled goat); Bisteck Ranchero; Enchiladas Suizas; Enchiladas Casa Grande (enchiladas covered in a creamy mushroom sauce); Huevos a la Mexicana; Huevos con Machacado (eggs scrambled with dried beef); Migas

Perched just above I-45 North at Main Street, with older billboards advertising the restaurant, the vast majority of commuters driving to and from downtown are probably not enticed to visit Casa Grande, even though it is a short distance to the downtown office towers. Virtually all of the patrons are presumably from the surrounding, predominantly Hispanic neighborhood. Those just driving past Casa Grande are missing some very well prepared and value-priced Mexican food in an often fun, appropriately somewhat scruffy and festive atmosphere.

The relatively small menu is heavy on seafood and steaks. With the exception of the appetizer nachos, *chile con queso* and the Tex-Mex *quesadillas,* the dishes are Mexican rather than Tex-Mex. The seafood offerings include grilled and fried shrimp, catfish and red snapper, *caldos* (brothy, straightforward soups), and *cocktels,* (marinated, raw seafood) with shrimp, oysters and octopus. Other daily soups include beef, chicken, spicy chicken (*Caldo Tlalpeño*), *posole* (pork and hominy), and *menudo* (beef tripe). There are also plates that are reasonably priced and served with refried beans and rice that feature *flautas,* a burrito, *Bistek Ranchero* (beef fajitas in a spicy sauce), *tampiqueña* (a small, grilled steak) served with an enchilada and a tamale, and *Barbacoa de Pozo* (a dish of steamed beef). From the grill are t-bones, sirloin, club steak, the breaded beef *milanesa,* and pork chops. All of these are complemented with grilled onions, guacamole, *pico de gallo,* charro beans and fries. If you are a fan of *cabrito* you should try Casa Grande's very commendable version. This will probably even satisfy most patrons from Monterrey, Mexico where *cabrito* is a very popular dish. Enchiladas come in only three styles filled with either chicken or beef. The *Enchiladas Casa Grande* features a unique, flavorful, rich mushroom sauce. There are a handful of lunch specials avialable during the work week for around six bucks; plates with tacos, taco salad, enchiladas, burritos, fajitas, and pork chops. And, they serve the standard Mexican scrambled egg breakfasts every morning including *migas, huevos rancheros, huevos a la mexicana,* and *huevos con machacado* (with dried beef), which are always on the mark. The kitchen handles just about everything quite aptly, including the basics, of course: the flour tortillas are freshly made in-house; and the salsas are flavorful. Everything is cooked to order, and you'll probably wait just a little longer than at most places, which is not necessarily a bad thing. In addition to the food, there is live music nearly every night. Though entertaining, the restaurant can get very loud with its low ceilings and tiled floors. A quiet conversation is usually out of the question. For some reason, even without the live music, the stereo is usually blaring. However, the food is noticeably good and enjoyable, regardless of the distraction.

Central China $8

9390 Bellaire (between Ranchester and Corporate) 77036, (713) 541-9612

Cuisine - Chinese
Hours - Daily 7:30AM to 9:30PM
Credit Cards - MC, Visa
Service - Counter Service
Alcohol - Beer & Wine

Entrée Prices - Dinner - $4 to $17 ($8 average); Lunch - $3 to $5
Entrées at Dinner $12 and less - 90%

Atmosphere & Décor - Pleasant
Appeal - Consistently good, inexpensive Chinese food in New Chinatown
Useful to Note - Lunch is an amazing value; very little English is spoken.
Menu Suggestions - Curry Beef; Curry Chicken; Pepper Chicken; Pepper Beef; Fried Shrimp with Walnut; Sesame Chicken; pan-fried pork dumplings; steamed pork dumplings

Central China may serve specialties from central China. With the inclusion of mutton among its offerings and the propensity of noodle dishes, it seems so, but it's tough to state with certainty, as a good portion of the menu is only in Chinese. It's nearly pointless to ask the waitstaff since they all seem to lack conversational ability in English. No matter, as the food that is easy to select from the menu is very well prepared whatever its origins might be. And, much of it is very inexpensive. Visiting Central China during lunchtime you will even find some non-Chinese patrons occupying some of the two dozen tables. It's a low-key, pleasant place for a meal with an earnest, if nearly non-English speaking staff in the heart of New Chinatown.

The list of around two dozen lunch specials contains many of the familiar Cantonese-inspired dishes, plus a handful of other ones. Amazingly, most are around $4, and come with a crispy, noticeably just-made egg roll, rice and soup. Lunch is a really great value here. There are the American Chinese restaurant staples such as Sweet and Sour Chicken, Moo Goo Gai Pan, Lemon Chicken, General Tso's Chicken, Pork with Garlic Sauce, and Kung Pao Chicken. The better choices from the lunch menu are Curry Beef, Scallion Beef, Sesame Chicken, Pepper Chicken and the Pepper Beef. The Pepper Beef consists of moist, thin pieces of tender and flavorful beef. Its quality is far superior to similarly priced beef dishes along Bellaire Boulevard. It is served with quickly stir-fried and crisp pieces of bell pepper and green peppers. The curry dishes, with beef, chicken or shrimp, feature a light subtle curry. The Hunan Chicken is prepared with pieces of dried chile peppers. The shrimp in the Fried Shrimp with Walnuts are medium-sized, breaded, and perfectly fried, and wonderfully complemented both with the crunchy, pan-fried walnuts and a slightly sweet and viscous sauce that is judiciously applied. The sides to the lunch specials are a cut above average: the rice is moist; the egg rolls are properly crusty and savory; and the hot and sour soup is very flavorful. Even in English, there are many enticing items on the non-lunch special menu. Among the more recognizable side items are the dumplings, steamed buns, and a fried cake with Chinese chives, which are listed under the title "Breakfast". Encased in a sturdy and tasty sheath, the dumplings are plump and very enjoyable. One order of eight dumplings makes for a filling lunch. The rest of the menu that can be discerned by those who don't read Chinese consists of the sections with titles of Appetizers; Soup; Seafood; Pork, Beef & Mutton; Chicken; Vegetables & Bean Curd; Noodles; and Hot Pot. Under these headings are Chicken Lo Mein, Eggplant with Garlic Sauce, Spicy Pork Lo Mein, Beef with Orange Peel, Salt Tossed Crispy Pork Chop, Crispy Squid with Spicy Salt, and Beef with Green Peppers; surely some are good choices given the kitchen's proficiency with the translated-into-English items. The Hot Pots and chef's specials are limited to those who can read some Chinese, or the very adventurous.

Chacho's $6

6006 Westheimer (west of Fountain View) 77057, (713) 975-9699
www.chachos.com

Cuisine - Tex-Mex
Hours - Open 24 hours

Credit Cards - Amex, Diners, MC, Visa
Service - Counter Service, Drive Thru
Alcohol - Full Bar

Entrée Prices - Dinner & Lunch - $3 to $10 ($6 average); Breakfast - $3 to $5
Entrées at Dinner $12 and less - 100%

Atmosphere & Décor - Spartan
Appeal - Solid, freshly made Tex-Mex fast food; strong margaritas
Useful to Note - It can get boisterous late night.
Menu Suggestions - Beef Fajita Nachos; Shredded Beef Quesadillas; enchiladas

---

Chacho's is a big improvement upon the fast-food Tex-Mex concept pioneered by Taco Cabana. Chacho's serves unpretentious Tex-Mex and Mexican favorites that are freshly prepared with fresh ingredients for low prices, in a large and convenient location for long hours. All hours, in fact. Unlike Taco Cabana, the food is reliably quite good, the ingredients are very fresh, and the portions are large.

Something from Chacho's extremely large menu should satisfy almost any Tex-Mex and even Mexican food craving. Emblematic of the focus on quality, a number of salsas, made in-house, are available at the condiments station. Very nicely, both flour and corn tortillas are also made in the restaurant. There is even a full bar that dispenses surprisingly well crafted and potent margaritas. The menu has a number of nachos (truly "made with an enormous amount of aged cheese"), salads, soups, *chalupas,* tacos, burritos, *quesadillas,* Tex-Mex plates, and seafood items. The toppings and fillings include *carne guisada* (stewed beef), shredded beef, grilled chicken, shredded chicken and shrimp. It is a far cry from the miscellanea found in similar dishes at other fast food places. Full orders of *quesadillas* and burritos are both huge. Perfect takeout for a group are the orders by the pound, or half-pound, of beef fajitas, chicken fajitas, shredded beef, *carne guisada* (stewed beef) and *barbacoa* (Mexican-style barbecue from somewhere on the cow's head). Along with the expected Tex-Mex items, there are also more traditional Mexican dishes like *gorditas* (fried stuffed corn *masa* pockets), *sopes* (fried corn *masa* rounds topped with beans and meat) and the Mexican sandwiches, *tortas. Menudo* (beef tripe and hominy soup) is even served all the time. A godsend to many, the entire breakfast array is also served all the time. There are plenty of different choices of breakfast tacos including *machacado* (dried beef) and egg. Breakfast plates include *huevos rancheros, migas,* plates with *barbacoa,* and eggs scrambled with *machacado,* American-style bacon or sausage and eggs and the Macho Chacho Plate, very accurately described as an improvement over Denny's Grand Slam

Breakfast. The breakfast items are dirt cheap Monday through Friday between 5AM and 10AM, and just plain cheap at other times.

In addition to the ample-sized portions, the food is generally heavy. It's true that Tex-Mex by definition is heavy food, but it is more so at Chacho's. This is probably due to the fact that most everything seems to be laden with mounds of melted shredded cheddar cheese, which is not necessarily a bad thing. A big part of its appeal is that Chacho's strives for customer convenience. The turnaround time from ordering to feasting is quick. It is open twenty-four hours every day. To accommodate the masses, there is not just one drive-thru lane, but two, and there is even an ATM inside the restaurant. There are also sections on the menu for vegetarians, and now low carb diets; a few years ago it was for those following low-fat diets, and one of the faddish protein-laden diets like Atkins or Protein Power. Though convenience is the goal, it might be less so late at night when lines can get quite long.

Champ Burger $6

304 Sampson (between Harrisburg and Canal) 77003, (713) 227-7737
www.champburger.net

Cuisine - Hamburgers
Hours - Mon-Fri 7AM to 4:30PM
Credit Cards - NONE
Service - Counter Service
Alcohol - NONE

Entrée Prices - Lunch - $4 to $8 ($6 average); Breakfast - $3 to $5
Entrées at Lunch $12 and less - 100%

Atmosphere & Décor - Not Much
Appeal - Friendly, long-standing working class hamburger joint
Useful to Note - The only seating available is outside.
Menu Suggestions - Champ Burger; Champ Burger with bacon; onion rings

Champ Burger is a tidy oasis in the East End that has been serving more-than-satisfying hamburgers and other easy-to-eat foods since 1963. Under a large awning, there are usually a number of patrons waiting to place or pickup an order, which are dispensed in brown bags. Champ's has a friendly egalitarian atmosphere. Takeaway is popular with the mostly working class clientele who might not have much time for lunch. This is aided by the fact that the only seating at Champ Burger is around the side from the counters, outside on concrete tables under large umbrellas. Even during the hot and humid summer months, there will be folks eating here. Though there is not much in the way of offerings at Champ Burger, it is still very busy during each lunchtime weekdays. With a name like Champ Burger, you can expect that the burgers are popular, and these are the biggest draw. The menu advertises that they use one-third prime ground chuck for their hamburgers. These are properly cooked with a crust around the juicy patties, and are available with cheese, bacon, and chili. Of course, unadorned is quite good, too. Also popular at Champ Burger is the Texas Size Steak Sandwich, which is basically a hamburger with a patty that is breaded and served like a chicken fried steak. There are hamburgers, several hot sandwiches, hot dogs, baskets with fried chicken, breaded and deep-fried steak fingers and fish, and a couple salads for the afternoon, and breakfast tacos and breakfast sandwiches for the morning. For sides, the pre-cut fries are served hot and crispy, but nothing special. Much better for an additional fifty cents are the thick, deep golden-hued, and very tasty onion rings. To finish or complement a meal there are also shakes and a hot apple turnover.

Chez Beignets $3

5243 Buffalo Speedway (just north of Bissonnet) 77005, (713) 592-9777

Cuisine - Café
Hours - Mon-Thu 6:30AM to 10AM, 5 to 11:30PM Fri 6:30AM to 10AM, 4PM to 2AM; Sat 6:30AM to 2AM; Sun 6:30AM to 12PM
Credit Cards - NONE
Service - Counter Service
Alcohol - NONE

Entrée Prices - Beignets are three for $3, and a dozen for $11
Entrées $12 and less - 100%

Atmosphere & Décor - Comfortable; patio
Appeal - Scrumptious beignets in a pleasant café setting
Useful to Note - Beignets are often cooked to order; it could be a few minutes.
Menu Suggestions - beignets

As one more local food item that was popularized in nearby New Orleans, most notably from the famous Café du Monde well known by all tourists, beignets, the French take on donuts, are a nice alternative to the morning pastry fare. And, Chez Beignets is evidently always ready to dispense tasty, hot beignets whenever you might have the craving for them: early in the morning during the week before work; late at night during the weekend; late at night during the week, etc. Run by an affable German couple, Chez Beignets has very long hours. It's open until midnight or nearly so from Sunday through Thursdays and 2AM on the weekends. The beignets are excellent; slightly heavier than other local versions, and a little more flavorful. Usually fresh from the deep fryer, the soft doughy exteriors are ladled with an impressive amount of powdered sugar. Though delicious, these are probably not recommended on a daily basis. Two beignets are usually enough for most, though three for only three bucks is tough to resist, though the sugar rush or feeling of tightening arteries might be palpable. If some more sugar is needed you can get the beignets stuffed with chocolate mousse, vanilla-hazelnut or a raspberry filling for an additional charge. Chez Beignets occupies a very pleasant, small space in the shopping center at the outskirts of West University at Buffalo Speedway and Bissonnet. It's a pleasant place to sit and enjoy the beignets with the morning paper and a drink, be it an espresso or espresso-based drink, chicory coffee, hot chocolate, iced coffee, the more familiar drip coffee, tea or *granita* (a flavored, mostly frozen drink). The friendliness of the owners extends to the fact that most of the refills are free to allow you to finish that paper. Chez Beignets also serves the bubble tea drinks that were initially popular in Taiwan and Hong Kong, and have spread in the past decade to the Chinese and Vietnamese restaurants on Bellaire and Midtown, and beyond.

China Garden $11

1602 Leeland (at Crawford) 77003, (713) 652-0745

Cuisine - Chinese
Hours - Mon-Fri 11AM to 9:30PM; Sat-Sun 12 to 9:30PM
Credit Cards - Amex, Discover, MC, Visa
Service - Table Service
Alcohol - Beer & Wine

Entrée Prices - Dinner - $6 to 19 ($11 average); Lunch - $6 to $10
Entrées at Dinner $12 and less - 80%

Atmosphere & Décor - Functional
Appeal - Familiar and proficiently prepared Chinese-American food
Useful to Note - Access might be tough before a big event at the Toyota Center.
Menu Suggestions - Hunan Beef (lightly battered, deep-fried cubes of beef in an orange-flavored sauce); Mongolian Beef (marinated beef stir-fried with onion and carrots); Lemon Chicken (lightly battered grilled pieces of chicken and topped with a lemon-based sauce); egg rolls; crawfish fried rice

Located across the street from the parking garage for the downtown basketball arena, China Garden has seen many changes in the area since its start in the mid-1960s, without markedly changing much itself, aside from a long ago move. It's good-sized and comfortable dining room that could be a fine museum piece representing a typical 20th century Chinese restaurant in the US. Though situated not too far from the original Chinatown, China Garden is geared mostly toward a non-Chinese clientele. Knives and forks are set on the table, not chop sticks. China Garden serves the familiar

Cantonese-inspired Chinese food that will be familiar with most Americans. Long-standing China Garden just prepares these popular dishes with a lighter and defter touch than the vast majority of restaurants that serve a similar menu. It seems that a great many of the patrons have long-since become regulars, and have been visiting for years.

There should be something for anyone who likes this fairly standard type of Chinese fare. The extensive dinner menu consists of nearly 120 items plus appetizers and soups. The lunch menu lists almost thirty dishes. There are dishes featuring chicken, pork, beef, shrimp, fish, and vegetables, plus clay pots and *chow mein*s with house-made noodles (that are fried and served with other stir-fried items). Among the better and most popular dishes are meat-based and include Hunan Beef, Mongolian Beef, and Lemon Chicken. The Hunan Beef really is lightly battered as described on the menu. Featuring tender and moist pieces of beef in a fairly light orange-flavored sauce, this is a dish that will appeal to most casual fans of Chinese foods. The Mongolian Beef consists of marinated beef stir-fried with onion and carrots. The Lemon Chicken is lightly battered grilled pieces of chicken and topped with a gooey, brown lemon-based sauce. Along with the beef, the chicken is of high quality. There is also Green Pepper Steak, Kung Pao Chicken, Spicy Chicken (fried strips of chicken topped with a sweet garlic-based sauce), Sweet & Sour Pork, Fried Hot Pork (fried cubes of pork in a spicy brown, onion sauce), Shrimp Fried Rice, Curry Beef, Curry Chicken, Seafood Lo Mein, Tangy Orange Peel Chicken, Crab Meat Fried Rice, Fried Shrimp in Tomato Sauce, Young Chow Fried Rice, Spiced Crispy Duck, and many others. Most of the entrées are served with the expected plentiful fried rice and a plump egg roll.

Chinese Café $8

9252 Bellaire (between Ranchester and Corporate) 77036, (713) 771-4330
5092 Richmond (just outside Loop 610) 77056, (713) 621-8877
3338 Highway 6 S. (at Williams Trace) Sugar Land, 77478, (281) 980-6663

Cuisine - Chinese
Hours - Mon-Fri 11AM to 9:30PM; Sat-Sun 12 to 9:30PM
Credit Cards - Amex, MC, Visa
Service - Counter Service
Alcohol - Beer & Wine

Entrée Prices - Dinner - $6 to $10 ($8 average); Lunch - $4 to $6
Entrées at Dinner $12 and less - 100%

Atmosphere & Décor - Functional
Appeal - Freshly prepared Chinese food for very cheap
Useful to Note - Bellaire location is next to Olympic Chinese Bakery for dessert.

Menu Suggestions - Lunch Specials (two meats, a vegetable and soup that changes daily); Shrimp Fried Rice; Double Spicy Chicken; Pork with Bamboo Shoot; Kung Pao Chicken; Shrimp with Pelt Bean

If you plan to eat lunch at the Chinese Café location on Bellaire in New Chinatown, you should try to arrive before noon, because from then until one it is usually quite crowded both with Chinese and non-Chinese patrons. And, with good reason. For a pittance, around $5, you can get a lunch special consisting of two kinds of meats, a vegetable, and a soup plus rice. This is fresh, well prepared and apparently authentic Chinese food (if served in a multi-part plate). The lunch special changes daily, but it is always worthwhile. It might be barbecued chicken or beef stir-fried with onions, bok choy or cabbage, etc. The lunch specials are certainly not the only things that are worth ordering at the Chinese Café, however. For each of the dishes, the vegetables are fresh and properly crisp, the meats and seafood are of decent quality, and just about everything is prepared with a deft touch.

If you eschew the lunch special, or you are dining during the evening, you will need to select your choice from the menu board, or better yet pick up a menu before arriving at the counter to order. The well-organized menu is divided among the headings: Chicken, Pork, Beef, Bean Curd, Seafood, Fish, Vegetable, Diet Dishes, Fried Rice, Fried Noodle, Soup and Various Dishes. There are between roughly five and fifteen entrées listed under each heading in Chinese and with a fairly descriptive English name. Many of the dishes are of the popular Chinese-American variety. Those are usually lighter and have a fresher taste than most of their counterparts elsewhere. Even the egg rolls are surprisingly good for a Chinese restaurant, if not quite the level of the better Vietnamese restaurants. Many of the other dishes seem to be influenced by most of the main regions in China or at least reference those in some way. Some of the better, or more interesting, dishes from the fairly large number of choices are: Double Spicy Chicken, Hot Pepper Chicken, Pork with Bamboo Shoot, Beijing Style Sweet and Sour Loin, Beef Shredded with Hot Pepper, Shrimp with Pelt Bean, Celery with Fresh Squid, Stir-Fried Egg with Tomato, Pork and Egg Fried Rice, Shrimp Fried Rice, and Chicken Fried Noodle. In addition to the daily lunch special mentioned above, there is also a lunch menu that is available from 11AM to 3PM from Monday to Friday. Consisting of around two dozen dishes from the main menu, these are a couple of dollars cheaper.

The straightforward, counter-service Chinese Café restaurants are nothing fancy. The settings are functional and utilitarian, but are clean and brightly lit. The turnaround time from the kitchen is very fast. Not surprisingly, the New Chinatown location features the most consistent kitchen and generally the best food of the three branches. This is one Chinese restaurant in New Chinatown that has long been popular with non-Chinese patrons. Maybe this is because much of the food is somewhat Americanized, but a little less so than many of the other Chinese lunch specials that are offered in the neighborhood. Probably the biggest reason is that the food is just good, and inexpensive.

Christian's Tailgate Bar & Grill $9

7340 Washington (just north of I-10) 77007, (713) 864-9744
2000 Bagby (at Pierce) 77002, (713) 527-0261

Cuisine - Hamburgers
Hours - Washington - Mon-Sat 9AM to 9PM; Bagby - Daily 11AM to 2AM
Credit Cards - Amex, Diners, Discover, MC, Visa
Service - Table Service
Alcohol - Beer & Wine

Entrée Prices - $6 to $12 ($9 average)
Entrées $12 and less - 100%

Atmosphere & Décor - Sports bar
Appeal - Good, straight-forward burgers
Menu Suggestions - hamburgers; Grilled Chicken Sandwich

The two locations of Christian's are far from the well-scrubbed antiseptic sports bars that are too easy to find across the country. Christian's has personality. The gruff clerk at the original Washington location is a welcome part of the atmosphere for many, and a necessary annoyance for others. Though very popular, the Bagby location is much different than many of its sleek and hip neighbors that have come to populate the Midtown nightlife. It retains the working class feel of the original. "Tailgate", after all, is a NASCAR reference, though the other sports get more television time. When one of the local teams is not playing, each of those numerous televisions is turned to one of the ESPN channels during the day with the air usually filled with commercial 1970s rock. You can always catch the score here. The kitchen, or more specifically the burgers, is also a big draw, possibly a bigger draw for most than the game and some beer. The much-lauded burgers properly feature a thoroughly cooked to brown, but still juicy and flavorful patty, large pieces of green and white iceberg lettuce, thick slices of a reddish tomato on a white bun slathered with plenty of bright yellow mustard. The rest of the deep-fried fare is pretty much as you would expect, and matches well with the easy-pouring beers from the tap. Fries and onion rings are perfunctory.

Chuy's $10

2706 Westheimer (just west of Kirby) 77098, (713) 524-1700
18035 I-45 N. (north of FM 1960) Spring, 77090, (936) 321-4440
www.chuys.com

Cuisine - Tex-Mex
Hours - Mon-Thu, Sun 11AM to 11PM; Fri-Sat 11AM to 12AM
Credit Cards - Amex, Diners, Discover, MC, Visa
Service - Table Service
Alcohol - Full Bar

Entrée Prices - $7 to $13 ($10 average)
Entrées $12 and less - 90%

Atmosphere & Décor - Nice, lively
Appeal - Very good Tex-Mex in a lively atmosphere
Useful to Note - There's some street parking on Virginia across busy Westheimer.
Menu Suggestions - Deluxe Chicken Enchiladas; 9-1-1 Hot Plate (blue corn tortilla enchiladas with grilled chicken, cheese and a very spicy salsa); Chuychanga; Chile Rellenos with Shrimp & Cheese; Green Chili Burrito; Deluxe Tomatillo sauce

Though it doesn't feel like a chain, Chuy's began in Austin in the early 1980s, and it's been a very popular part of the Houston dining landscape for quite a while. In a time where it has become fashionable to proclaim authentic or regional quality of the Mexican dishes, the food is unabashedly and stylishly kitchy Tex-Mex. And, it is consistently satisfying. The ingredients are always fresh and top-notch, the cooking is well-executed, the flavors are expectedly and properly robust and the dishes are always pleasing, and large. In addition to the well-known quality of the food, Chuy's is very popular for being a fun and lively place in which enjoy yourself whether or not you are planning to eat. The restaurants are well crafted, intentionally tacky shrines to Elvis Presley. It helps make for a fun, and not so serious, often boisterous atmosphere. Because of this, the Westheimer location is just about always packed during happy hour and into the night late during the week and on weekends.

Chuy's provides one of the best dining values around. Most entrées, which are almost always enough food for a hungry adult, average around $10. The offerings are all of the Tex-Mex favorites. The appetizing fat-laden starters include *chile con queso*, nachos, and *quesadillas*, and there are tacos, enchiladas, *chile rellenos*, and combination plates, Tex-Mex salads and fajitas, of course. The burritos advertised "Big as Your Face", are nearly that and filled with a choice of just bean and cheese, ground beef or grilled chicken, and topped with a variety of sauces. The deep-fried version, the Chuychanga gives even more fat grams, and probably taste, for the money.

But, the enchiladas are possibly the best of the entrées at Chuy's. The Deluxe Chicken, made with grilled chicken and the Deluxe Tomatillo sauce, might be the best of the enchilada dishes. The creamy slightly piquant Deluxe Tomatillo sauce is made with tomatillos and sour cream, and can be addictive, and it works well as a sauce for the chips. The 9-1-1 Hot Plate consists of enchiladas made with blue corn tortillas, filled with grilled chicken and topped with melted cheese and a very spicy green salsa. The Southwestern Enchiladas are stuffed with grilled chicken, green chile sauce and topped with a fried egg. In addition to the enchiladas the *chile rellenos* can be excellent. These consist of a large, breaded deep-fried poblano pepper cooked the familiar Tex-Mex fashion. The best of the fillings is the Shrimp and Cheese, topped, again, with Deluxe Tomatillo Sauce.

Befitting its spot on Westheimer, just west of Kirby, the River Oaks location still seems hip and cool after being open since the early 1990s, an eternity by Houston restaurant standards. A fun diversion is the annual Hatch Green Chile Festival each September where Chuy's celebrates the source of their green chiles (Hatch, New Mexico) with a variety of dishes made with those flavorful chiles. It's an especially worthwhile time to visit, as is the much more crowded celebration of the King's birthday.

Collina's $8

2400 Times (at Morningside) 77005, (713) 526-4499
3835 Richmond (east of Weslayan) 77027, (713) 621-8844
12311 Kingsride (west of Gessner) 77024, (713) 365-9497
4990 Beechnut (west of Loop 610) 77096, (713) 349-0404
502 W. 19th (between Heights and N. Shepherd) 77008, (713) 869-0492
12002 Richmond (at Kirkwood) 77082, (281) 679-5800
www.collinas.com

Cuisine - Pizza
Hours - Mon-Sat 11AM to 10PM
Credit Cards - Amex, Diners, MC, Visa
Service - Table Service; Take-away is popular
Alcohol - Richmond & W. 19th - BYOB; Other Locations - Beer & Wine, BYOB

Entrée Prices - $5 to $15 ($8 average)
Entrées $12 and less - 90%

Atmosphere & Décor - Comfortable; patio (Times)
Appeal - Good pizzas and a BYOB option at several locations
Useful to Note - The original Richmond location might be the best; strictly BYOB.
Menu Suggestions - pizzas; focaccia; Chicken Tetrazini

The best reason to visit one of Collina's informal, popular and sometimes boisterous locations is their pizza. Well, the pizza and their well-known BYOB policy. As wine and food, especially Italian food, are nearly inseparable, Collina's BYOB policy is very commendable. It's nice to be able to have that extra glass of *vino* to help wash down the food, and to make the meal more enjoyable, without having to pay the typical egregious restaurant markup for wine. With the exception of the original spot on Richmond and the one in the dry part of the Heights, the other locations also sell wine and beer if you have not stopped for provisions beforehand.

The Collina's restaurants are some of the best pizza places in the area. A scan of the dining room on most evenings will show it full, or nearly so, of patrons enjoying pizzas. The base, and basis, for their pizzas is a very good crust. These are generally thin crusts, not quite as thin as a typical New York-style, but slightly doughy and very tasty. A whole-wheat version is also offered, which is decent, though quite not as flavorful. Most pizzas are fitted with mozzarella, provolone, and grated Romano cheeses. The rest of the toppings are fresh and of high quality. There are over a half-dozen interesting specialty pizzas. If one of those does not fit the bill, then Collina's offers a wide range of additions from which to choose, so almost anything can be created (within the realm of proper American pizza decorum). The large pizza is larger than at other pizzerias, a full twenty inches in diameter, and is almost enough for four adults. In addition to pizza, they do serve the range of typical Southern Italian-American dishes that you would expect at a place that bills itself as an Italian restaurant in Houston. But, these are generally disappointing. Gooey and bland marinara-esque sauce touches most of them. The pastas are cooked to an overly soft texture, and the stuffed ones can seem too doughy. The decidedly retro Chicken Tetrazini is one of the few non-pizza items worth ordering. The décor at Collina's is nothing fancy, but appropriate for a pizza joint. The somewhat expected red-checkered tablecloths cover each table, and large cans of tomatoes and other Italian food items are placed prominently on the shelves near the dining areas. These are informal places, and the settings are functional, yet fitting. Service is usually efficient, better than most pizza places, and almost always friendly.

Colombian Cuisine $13

13920 Westheimer (between Eldridge and Highway 6) 77077, (281) 584-0437

Cuisine - Colombian
Hours - Mon-Sat 11AM to 9PM; Sun 12 to 8PM
Credit Cards - MC, Visa
Service - Table Service

Alcohol - Beer & Wine

Entrée Prices - $8 to $15 ($13 average)
Entrées $12 and less - 50%

Atmosphere & Décor - Pleasant, quaint
Appeal - Tasty Colombian food on far Westheimer
Menu Suggestions - Lomo Empanizado (deep-fried breaded pork loin); Bistec Empanizado (deep-fried breaded skirt steak); Steak Chimichurri (grilled strip steak with sautéed mushrooms and chimi-churri sauce); Sobrebarriga Criolla (grilled steak served with a creamy tomato sauce)

In one of the many unassuming and bland strip centers on the western expanse of Westheimer, Colombian Cuisine somehow stands out for its tasty and well prepared food served in a quaint white table-clothed restaurant. As the name suggests Colombian Cuisine mostly features the food of Colombia, which at times receives some more spicing courtesy of the locally popular poblanos, *chipotles* and even hotter *chiles*. Though the dish names here might be unfamiliar for many, the preparations and flavors will be recognizable and engaging with steaks, cream sauces, sautéed and caramalized onions, grilled Gulf seafood, and some mild tropical flavors; at the very least for the several straightforward pasta dishes. The large menu is neatly divided among appetizers, *ceviches*, soups, Colombian specialties (that are mostly meat-laden), steaks, salads, Chef's specialties of seafood and chicken breasts, rice dishes, pork loins, shrimp, chicken breast dishes, pastas, fish fillets and entire fish preparations. For starters there are *arepas* (thick corn patties), *empanadas*, and fried plantains and bananas. The soups feature Colombian specialties such as *Sancocho de Gallina* (a spicy soup of hen, or maybe just chicken) plus other soups featuring oxtail, seafood with coconut milk, and *Mondongo*, a soup filled with honeycombed beef tripe. Beef liver and *Lengua en Salsa Criolla* (beef tongue served with a creamy tomato sauce) are a couple of other dishes that might appeal strictly to the Colombian clientele. The steaks, and most of the other meat dishes, are even better with the addition of some of the piquant parsely and vinegar sauce that's on the table. Colombian Cuisine has nearly ten shrimp dishes, mostly sautéed, and over a dozen with fish fillets which are primarily grilled, but also blackened and breaded and pan-fried (*empanizado*). Each of the numerous entrées is served with white rice, vegetables, fried plantains, and a small green salad, which make for a usually very filling meal. The handful of pasta dishes feature fettuccine, with several toppings, half with that American favorite, fat-laden Alfredo sauce.

Connie's Seafood House $8

2525 Airline (between Cavalcade and Loop 610 N.) 77009, (713) 868-2144
7502 Long Point (between Antoine and Wirt) 77055, (713) 688-3318
340 S. 69th Street (at Canal) 77011, (713) 921-4622
8520 Gulf Freeway (between Bellfort and Winkler) 77017, (713) 641-5003
1617 Spencer Highway (at Shaver) Pasadena, 77504, (713) 910-0100

Cuisine - Seafood (with a Mexican influence)
Hours - Mon-Thu 10AM to 9:30PM; Fri-Sat 10AM to 11PM; Sun 10AM to 10PM
Credit Cards - NONE
Service - Counter Service
Alcohol - Beer

Entrée Prices - Dinner - $3 to $13 ($8 average); Lunch - $4
Entrées at Dinner $12 and less - 80%

Atmosphere & Décor - Functional
Appeal - Fresh seafood for not a lot of money
Useful to Note - Shares same owners as the Mambo restaurants and Mak Chin's.
Menu Suggestions - fried shrimp; fried redfish; fried red snapper; fried scallop; Special Fried Rice

Connie's Seafood House with several locations with slightly different marquees for each such as Connie's Seafood Market & Restaurat, Connie's Seafood & Oyster Bar, and Connie's Seafood Restaurant & Oyster Bar is a place to come for fresh, mostly fried, seafood. It might be the best of the local, "you buy, we fry" establishments and a reliably good value. Though primarily geared toward a Hispanic customer base, Connie's is a good place to visit for anyone who likes tasty fried fresh Gulf seafood in an informal setting.

Actually not everything is fried. You do have a choice among cooking styles. Steamed fish, grilled shrimp, shrimp sautéed in butter, or not too often seen cooked with ketchup are all available. Frying is just the best choice for many of the items. The menu offers a number of selections such as raw oysters, *ceviche*, Mexican-style seafood cocktails, seafood soup, seafood gumbo, platters with fish, shrimp and shellfish that are served with fries and a somewhat green salad, combination platters, and a variety of cooked items for sale by the pound. These include shrimp, scallops, frog legs, mussels, squid, crawfish tails and small octopi that are fried, sautéed in garlic and butter (*al mojo*) or served with a tomato-based *ranchero* sauce. Some of the better platters are the large order of fried red snapper, and the fried scallops. Fried rice makes it onto the menu, and is a popular and tasty side, much better than the fries. It is no surprise, then, that the menus are printed by Chinatown Printing & Graphics. Some of the best deals are under the menu section, "Special". These include two fairly sized pieces of fish, six butterflied medium-sized shrimp with a side of seafood fried rice. All breaded and fried, of course. The fish might even be the flavorful redfish, surprisingly enough. Other specials include fifteen shrimp and fries, and an entire fried tilapia served with fried rice.

These restaurants are clean, and fairly inviting, if functional. Most are here to eat rather than dine. You order at the counter, and wait for your dish to be cooked, which is then brought to your table. A handful of hot sauces are on the tables, and, nicely, all the tartar sauce you need is available by dispenser (it's on ice). The location on Airline near the farmers market is also a seafood market with fresh whole fish and other seafood on display. Depending on the season and the catch, the bounty behind the glass case might be drum, trout, redfish, red snapper, flounder, sheepshead, gar, catfish, scallops, mussels, octopus, oysters, and several sizes of shrimp.

Dacapo's Café $8

1141 E. 11th (at Studewood) 77008, (713) 869-9141

Cuisine - Café / Bakery
Hours - Tue-Fri 11AM to 6PM; Sat 10AM to 5PM
Credit Cards - Amex, Discover, MC, Visa
Service - Counter Service
Alcohol - NONE

Entrée Prices - $5 to $12 ($8 average)
Entrées $12 and less - 100%

Atmosphere & Décor - Comfortable, though small
Appeal - Excellent freshly baked pastries
Menu Suggestions - Cinnamon Rolls; croissants; cakes; Roast Beef Sandwich; Corned Beef Sandwich; Chicken Salad Sandwich

The phrase on Dacapo's Café's menu is "a pastry café", a very apt description. The setting looks like a café, and the emphasis is on light fare and baked items. The restaurant has a proper setting: it's located in an older commercial building in the heart of the Heights, and the dining area consists of only about a dozen small tables and booths set across and around the display counters. For lunch there are sandwiches, salads, quiches, and combinations thereof each made to order. The sandwiches are spruced-up variations of traditional ones. A key and welcome differentiator is that the sandwiches are served on Dacapo's noticeably fresh and tasty house-made bread. There is a BLT, a hot roast beef, hot corned beef, chicken salad, a tuna salad, a club, ham and cheese, and then an ALT (avocado, lettuce, tomato, provolone cheese and mayonnaise) and Dacapo's Santa Fe (marinated turkey breast, lettuce and tomato and mango chutney). The spiced-up roast beef sandwich is made with beef that has been marinated, roasted and shredded and served with a small amount of melted provolone cheese, sliced red onions, mustard and horseradish-mayonnaise. The result is a pleasing and spicier version of a familiar sandwich. Another winner is the Vegetarian Special that consists of alfalfa sprouts, mushrooms, cucumbers, zucchini, provolone cheese and sun-dried tomato vinaigrette sauce on peppered herbed bread. These are all a significant cut above the norm, though there might be an occasional misstep like a barely red tomato slice during the winter months. Each of the sandwiches comes with a choice of chips, cold pasta salad or a mild potato salad. The salads include their house salad of romaine lettuce, tomato with avocado and slices of marinated chicken with a vinaigrette dressing. There is also a Caesar salad and a variation made with fresh fruit, chicken and toasted pecans. They do a steady business with their cakes and pastries. Some are Chocolate Mousse Cake that features a couple inches of chocolate mousse, a Carrot Cake, a three-layer Chocolate Fudge Cake, a Banana Split Cake topped with chocolate, caramel and fresh strawberries, Cheesecake, and an Italian Crème Cake. Dacapo's also serves a nice cup of coffee, either the drip House Blend or one of the espresso-based coffees.

Daily Grind $11

4115 Washington (between Heights and Shepherd) 77007, (713) 861-4558

Cuisine - American
Hours - Mon-Thu 6AM to 10PM; Fri 6AM to 11PM; Sat-Sun 8AM to 10PM
Credit Cards - Amex, MC, Visa
Service - Table Service
Alcohol - Beer & Wine

Entrée Prices - $7 to $13 ($11 average)
Entrées $12 and less - 80%

Atmosphere & Décor - Casual; patio
Appeal - Very good omelets and an inviting coffeehouse on Washington
Useful to Note - Orders can take a while to fill during weekend breakfast times.
Menu Suggestions - omelets; jalapeño-cheese grits; muffaletta

Crowded on the weekends and doing a brisk weekday lunch business, Daily Grind has been a welcome addition to gentrifying Washington Avenue. The food is one attraction, as is the coffeehouse set up, especially during the day. The building is airy and comfortable enough to encourage lingering. And, it has a good amount of outside seating for those nicer days. Occupying an older house, and filled with mismatched furniture from banquet halls past, it has the proper laid-back feel, except, maybe, when the hungry throngs overwhelm the place during lunchtime and for breakfasts on the weekends. The menu at this counter service restaurant includes salads, hot sandwiches, and design-it-yourself pastas and omelets, plus some morning Tex-Mex flair. The pasta dishes can be either penne or linguine and personalized with a choice of one of several Italian-American sauces, over a dozen vegetables, cheese or mushrooms additions and Italian sausage, grilled chicken or shrimp. The omelets can be customized into a possibly even greater array of finished dishes. Daily Grind is on the mark for the breakfasts, less so with the other items. The tasty, sufficiently fluffy and moist four-egg omelets are some of the best around, and easily the best items on the menu. Smaller-appetite-friendly, these are also available in half-orders. It's wise to note that you will likely need to be patient during the weekend breakfast crunch times as the small kitchen can quickly get backed up. The food is almost always worth that wait. Drip coffees, available in several styles and flavors, will likely be brewed too weakly for those who like robust coffee.

D'Amico's Italian Market Café $13

5510 Morningside (north of University, in Village Arcade II) 77005, (713) 526-3400
www.damico-cafe.com

Cuisine - Italian-American
Hours - Mon-Thu 11AM to 10PM; Fri-Sat 11AM to 11PM; Sun 5 to 10PM
Credit Cards - Amex, Diners, Discover, MC, Visa
Service - Table Service
Alcohol - Beer & Wine

Entrée Prices - Dinner - \$8 to \$22 (\$13 average); Lunch - \$6 to \$11
Entrées at Dinner \$12 and less - 50%

Atmosphere & Décor - Think red-checkered tablecloths and lively, but quaint
Appeal - Satisfying, familiar Southern Italian food in a casual setting
Useful to Note - You might have to pay for parking in the garage.
Menu Suggestions - Marilyn Salad (Caesar salad topped with fried calamari); Honey Mustard Chicken Salad (romaine, grilled chicken, tomatoes and cucumbers with a honey-mustard dressing); Chicken Parmesan; Focaccia Panino; Wild Mushroom & Walnut Tortellini; Tortellini Genovese (stuffed pasta with pesto); Fettuccine Alfredo with crab; Mezzaluna (pasta filled with smoked chicken and cheese in an Alfredo sauce with sundried tomatoes); Crawfish Ravioli

Located in the Village Arcade facing the bustling Morningside, D'Amico's is a charming comibination of a small Italian grocery store and deli, and an informal Southern Italian-American restaurant. The deli with cold cuts and cheeses in refrigerated display cases is immediately to the right of the entrance, and the shelves loaded with grocery items are to the left. Tables are located in a back section of the space and behind the stacks of grocery items. There is also a pleasant umbrella-bedecked patio with a few tables on the sidewalk in front of the restaurant. It is popular when the weather is bearable, and a nice place to view the often busy evening street scene.

The cooking at D'Amico's is recognizable Southern Italian-American with a dash of southeast Texas Gulf Coast influences. The fairly long menu has a few antipasto dishes, salads, pizzas, sandwiches, pastas and veal, pork, chicken and seafood dishes. The salads, available for lunch and dinner, include Fresh Mozzarella, Tomato and Basil, a marinated seafood salad, Honey Mustard Chicken Salad, and the ubiquitous Caesar Salad with a couple different toppings. The pizzas are decent, and crafted in the traditonal fashion: cooked in a wood-burning oven, featuring a thin crust, and about ten inches in diameter. There are several versions, and you can create your own from the list of Italian toppings. There are also several pastas available for lunch, and many more for dinner. The list of sandwiches includes a fried shrimp po boy, Muffaletta, a meatball, sausage and peppers, a cold sub with the artery-clogging trio of *capocollo, mortadella* and *sopressata* with provolone, and several Italian-style *panini*. One of the best of these is the *Focaccia Panini*, featuring *capocollo*, smoked mozzarella, basil, ripe roma tomato slices, lettuce and a vinaigrette on a spongy *focaccia* bread. In addition to the menu items, the daily lunch steam table selections can make for a satisfying and inexpensive lunch. Advertised as the "best lunch value in the Rice Village", these include a choice of three items among ten that change daily and weekly. The steam table may include lasagna, pasta carbonara, chicken piccata, manicotti, rigatoni, Italian sausage, and Red Snapper Picatta. And, it can also feature fried chicken, beef brisket, fried okra, mashed potatoes, bean salad, New England clam chowder, potato salad and meatloaf. Check the web site for weekly specials.

The dinner menu is larger and generally heartier. In addition to the salads and pizzas served for lunch there are nearly twenty pastas and about a dozen meat or seafood dishes. The pastas include dishes with dried and freshly made pastas, and thin and stuffed pastas. Along with the familiar spaghetti and meatballs and lasagna, there is D'Amico's version of the San Franciscan *cioppino* (seafood and tomato sauce over housemade red pepper pasta), plus the regionally oriented ravioli stuffed with crawfish and poblano peppers. One of the best pasta dishes is the Wild Mushroom and Walnut Tortellini, which is freshly made tortellini pasta stuffed with wild mushrooms, walnuts and cheese in a sauce of white wine and lemon butter. The "House Favorites", include popular Italian-American presentations of veal, including osso buco, and chicken along with several other nontraditonal dishes. Though not inexpensive, these are also served with a house salad. D'Amico's does a brisk takeout business, both for the prepared food and grocery items. These are primarily Italian: dried pastas, olive oils, balsamic vinegar, *biscotti*, Italian cookies, wine and the like. The deli provides mostly Italian and Italian-style lunch meats and cheese. The grocery and deli are more than just attractive show pieces. For example, they sell *prosciutto di Parma* for usually a few dollars cheaper than most area stores. It is a convenient stop for delicious Italian lunch meats and cheeses, so to help craft the perfect sandwich at home.

Daniel Wong's Kitchen $11

4566 Bissonnet (west of Newcastle) 77401, (713) 663-6665
www.danielwongskitchen.com

Cuisine - Chinese
Hours - Mon-Fri 11AM to 9:30PM; Sat-Sun 12 to 9:30PM
Credit Cards - Amex, Discover, MC, Visa
Service - Table Service
Alcohol - Beer & Wine

Entrée Prices - Dinner - $8 to $17 ($11 average); Lunch - $6 to $9
Entrées at Dinner $12 and less - 99%

Atmosphere & Décor - Nice, comfortable and low-key
Appeal - Innovative and lighter-than-usual Chinese and Chinese-inspired fare
Menu Suggestions - Puffs (crab inside a crispy shell); Sparkling Chicken (chicken covered in honey and cooked in aluminum foil); Velvet Corn Soup (corn chowder); Rio Grande Valley Beef (pieces of beef with orange and wine); South of the Border Turkey (with basil, cilantro and rosemary in a wine sauce); Fresh Pineapple Sweet & Sour Duck; Hunan Fried Rice; "Road Kill" Chicken (sliced chicken cooked with garlic and finished with fermented beans, onions and gin); "Road Kill" Pork

Proprietor Daniel Wong, originally from southern China, has been cooking Chinese food in Houston since 1960. By all accounts, his cooking seems to have been evolving during his entire lengthy tenure. The food at comfortable Daniel Wong's is Chinese food somewhat tailored to the local clientele, and reflective of this area's regional influences. But, it is more innovative, and apparently, lighter than the fare offered by most Chinese restaurants that cater to a non-Chinese crowd. The menu does proclaim, "Healthy food for you". The ingredients always seem very fresh, and are prepared without an excess of oil or sugar. The list of dishes is different than most area Chinese restaurants. The entrées feature not only chicken, but also turkey. There is pork, of course, but plenty of beef and lamb dishes. For seafood, there is shrimp, crab, scallops, red snapper and salmon. Some dishes can be deemed Chinese-inspired rather than Chinese. Some have no

Chinese antecedants at all, like the seafood gumbo, a local staple. In many ways, Daniel Wong's is a restaurant that has its roots in Chinese cooking and uses that to provide satisfyng and healthy food to their customers. Indicative of the direction of the kitchen, and maybe more so, the clientele, there is only silverware on the tables, no chopsticks.

There are many interesting preparations that will appeal to most any patron. The menu is clearly laid out with sections for appetizers, poultry, beef and pork, seafood, "healthy food", and rice and noodles. Each dish, and section, is explained with a long sentence or two. The beef and pork section states, "Trimmed of excess fat. Selected for its tenderness and taste. Cooked in unique ways you will enjoy". These are true statements. One thing that might not seem as veracious to those used to eating spicy food is that the dishes indicated as being "hot and spicy" are really not at all. This might be due in deference to the residents of Bellaire and nearby West University, or more likely, the fact that the namesake's regional Cantonese cuisine is not very spicy. Similarly, for the dishes described as being cooked with garlic, the kitchen also has a fairly light hand with it, unlike many places in the Chinatowns. One dish, or dishes, as it comes with a pork and chicken versions that does have a garlic bite are the "Road Kill" Pork and Chicken. It is thinly sliced meat, quickly cooked with fresh garlic and spices. Another interesting, very good and very popular appetizer is the Sparkling Chicken. It is a half-dozen shreds of chicken slathered in honey, lightly seasoned, garnished with green onion shreds and quickly cooked inside aluminun foil for a unique and delectable effect. Another worthy entrée is the Rio Grande Valley Beef consisting of crispy chunks of tender beef served with pieces of oranges and orange peels in a slightly spicy brown sauce. This dish, and all of the entrées at Daniel Wong's, are very large. Dinner can often result in leftovers for lunch the next day. In addition to the chicken, turkey, pork, and beef dishes, there are about a dozen seafood items, vegetarian dishes, and a handful of fried rice dishes. The Hunan Fried Rice, available with small chunks of pork, beef and chicken, is somewhat spicy and very flavorful.

Lunch specials are a good deal, and nicely, these are also offered on Saturday and Sunday. Many of the twenty-odd lunch specials are the same dishes as those offered for dinner, but for a few dollars less. These plentiful dishes come with rice and a crispy spring roll, plus the entrée. For the price, these are an especially nice deal. To add a soup will set you back an additional two dollars. You can get seafood gumbo and a somewhat bland corn chowder in addition to hot-and-sour or wonton soup. The setting in a small, stand-alone building is nice. It is a charming, small restaurant decorated with abstract paintings whose interior could pass for any nice restaurant, regardless of cuisine. Service is proficient, and gracious.

Darband Shishkabob $7

5670 Hillcroft (between Harwin and Westpark) 77036, (713) 975-5670

Cuisine - Persian
Hours - Mon-Thu 11AM to 10PM; Fri-Sun 11AM to 11PM
Credit Cards - Amex, Discover, MC, Visa
Service - Counter Service
Alcohol - NONE

Entrée Prices - $5 to $10 ($7 average)
Entrées $12 and less - 100%

Atmosphere & Décor - Functional
Appeal - Tasty Persian-style kabobs for cheap
Menu Suggestions - Chengeh Kabob (two skewers of grilled lamb); Darband Special (a skewer of grilled lamb and a skewer of grilled beef cubes)

Since 1986 Darband Shishkabob has specialized in Persian-style kabobs. Most days and especially Sunday afternoons will find the small restaurant crowded with members of the local Iranian community; tables are filled with diners eating, discussing and drinking tea. Darband is set in an often lively strip center location among a number of other ethnic eateries and shops. It features a slightly vaulted ceiling and small fountain in the center of the dining room that gives the restaurant some more pizzazz than many counter-service places. Darband is all about grilled meat. Beef, lamb and chicken, both in pieces and ground, make it onto skewers, which comprise almost all of the ten or so entrées. If you are not familiar with the names of these dishes, there are photos above the counter. Unfortunately, the items are tough to discern, at least to distinguish between the beef and lamb ones. The cashier is quick to answer questions, though, and the various skewers ready for the grill are arrayed in a refrigerated case for you to peruse. Each of the skewered dishes is served with a large amount of long-grain rice sprinkled with relatively mild ground sumac, fresh flat bread, and lime quarters, sprigs of cilantro, parsley, slices of radish, a quarter of white onion and usually roasted tomato halves. The juice and acidity of the tomatoes and limes help enliven both the meats and rice. The meat, rice and bread make for a filling meal. The dishes aren't spicy, and the flavors will be quite recognizable for most area diners. The food will rarely wow here, but it rarely fails to satisfy, especially given the value (part of this is evidenced in the Styrofoam plates). Each of the skewers is properly cooked, and the meats remain moist. The clean-tasting lamb skewers are probably the best of the lot.

Middle Eastern, Persian...it's all Greek to me

Customers at the numerous Middle Eastern, Turkish and Persian restaurants both here and around the country will find quite similar fare at these regardless of country of origin, be it Lebanon, Syria, Jordan, Egypt, and even Israel. This probably comes as a surprise to most patrons. The reason for this is explained in 2005 article in *Gourmet*: "Unlike…Europe, which boasts stunning culinary diversity in a relatively compact area, the Middle East demonstrates broad gastronomic parallels from North Africa all the way to Central Asia. There is more dissimilarity between Italy and France, which are adjacent, [and just along the Italian peninsula] than there is between Egypt and Iran, which are separated by nearly 1,000 miles. Owing to a harsh desert climate interrupted by pockets of fertility, as well as more than a millennium of shared religious and cultural traditions, most Middle Eastern countries consume the same staples: freshly baked flatbread; rice and beans; a limited number of fruits, vegetables and dried nuts; rare treats of beef and lamb; and an infinite variety of sweet, sticky cakes and porridge." Greek food is very similar, and many dishes are nearly identical, as there were numerous Greek communities on the Anatolian peninsula for several millennia until last century.

Dimassi's Mediteranean Buffet $11

8236 Kirby (between OST and McNee) 77054, (713) 526-5111
5064 Richmond (just west of Loop 610) 77056, (713) 439-7481
4654 S. Highway 6 (at Dulles / Austin Parkway) Sugar Land, 77479, (281) 277-2184
1640 Lake Woodlands (east of Six Pines) The Woodlands, 77380, (281) 363-0200
11335 I-10 W. (between Wilcrest and Kirkwood) 77024, (713) 465-8222
907 Franklin (at Travis) 77002, (713) 224-0588
www.dimassisbuffet.com

Cuisine - Middle Eastern
Hours - Daily 11AM to 10PM
Credit Cards - Amex, Discover, MC, Visa
Service - Buffet Service
Alcohol - Beer & Wine

Entrée Prices - Dinner - $11 (all-you-can eat); Lunch - $10 (all-you-can eat)
Entrées at Dinner $12 and less - 100%

Atmosphere & Décor - Functional
Appeal - Array of appetizing Middle Eastern food, buffet-style; all-you-can-eat
Menu Suggestions - Greek Salad; hummus; tabouli; lamb; baklava

Dimassi's is the local progenitor of the Middle Eastern cafeteria-style restaurants. These are now strictly self-service, all-you-can-eat operations. Clean, bright and pleasant places, Dimassi's are a generally step up from the usually sterile or dull environment of the typical cafeteria (though the faded and slightly scruffy Galleria area location is an exception to this). The food here is not nearly as good as at some of the better Middle Eastern restaurants in town, but you eat as much as you'd like, the fare is healthy, and the price is fair. As long demonstrated by Dimassi's, Middle Eastern fare is well suited to cafeteria service since many dishes are best created in batches such as the items you'll find at the start of the buffet line like *tabouli* (cracked wheat, tomato, cucumber, mint, lemon and olive oil), the dips like *hummus* and *baba ganoush*. And, these popular items are reliably good here. Other appetizers, on what Dimassi's describes as, "the biggest buffet in North America", can include deep-fried *kibbe* balls, grape leaves stuffed with beef and rice, similarly stuffed cabbage rolls, vegetarian grape leaves, *falafel*, *spanikopita* (spinach-filled phyllo pies). In addition to the dips and the accompanying fresh-enough pita bread, the vegetables and crisp salads are the draw for many. There might be a half-dozen vegetables each day, such as pan-fried eggplant, Parmesan Spinach, Italian-style green beans, squash with mushrooms, baby okra, cauliflower, Cilantro Lentils, Coriander Potatoes, and *Tahini* Eggplant. The salads are *fatoosh* (lettuce, cucumber, tomatoes, parsley, mint and pita) *tabouli*, pasta salads, cabbage salad and a familiar Greek salad and a less so Lebanese salad. Most of the meats are decent, and you might find a leg of lamb, different preparations of chicken, plus kabobs of chicken, beef and ground beef. Unfortunately, the lamb shank is variable; it can often be stewed too long and lacking in flavor. If you have room, Dimassi's also has an array of Middle Eastern sweets such as *baklava*, date cookies and lady fingers, and you've already paid for it.

* Dolce Vita $13

500 Westheimer (between Taft and Montrose) 77006, (713) 520-8222
www.dolcevitahouston.com

Cuisine - Italian; Pizza
Hours - Tue-Thu, Sun 5 to 10PM; Fri-Sat 5-11PM
Credit Cards - Amex, Discover, MC, Visa
Service - Table Service
Alcohol - Full Bar

Entrée Prices - $10 to $20 ($13 average)
Entrées $12 and less - 30%

Atmosphere & Décor - Nice, but comfortable
Appeal - The best Italian-style pizza in town; authentic flavors of Italy

Useful to Note - Reservations for 6+; no take-away; almost valet parking only.
Menu Suggestions - Pizza Vongole (with small clams, cherry tomatoes and mozzarella); Pizza Calabrese (with spicy salami, tomatoes and mozzarella); Pizza Robiola (with robiola cheese, pancetta and leeks); Pizza Margherita; Pizza Salsiccia e Friarielli (with sausage, broccoli rabe and pecorino cheese); salad with escarole and pecorino; salad with parsley and pancetta; mozzarella in carozza (Italian-style grilled cheese); speck (cured and smoked sliced ham); mushrooms with mint and ricotta; cheese plate (ricotta, taleggio, gorgonzola, pecorino and Parmesan served with honey)

Proprietor Marco Wiles, who runs the best Italian restaurant in the state, Da Marco, just down the street, has created an upscale pizzeria that serves excellent and authentically flavored Italian-esque pizzas. In fact, the pizzas here are better than I've had in my several trips to Italy. These are truly Italian, as are all of the offerings, but too creative and wide-ranging to be authentically Neapolitan. The pizza-makers in Naples, the birthplace of pizza, stick to a few simple favorites. Dolce Vita gets inspiration from there and also well beyond Campania to much of the Italian peninsula.

These individual-sized pizzas are cooked in a very hot wood-burning oven, in the true Italian fashion; and, the crusts are light, flavorful, crisp at the edges and softer in the middle. The very high quality toppings are properly parsimoniously placed around the top. The toppings are easily the best among local pizza joints. The interesting pizzas are different than what you'll find at other local pizzerias and Italian restaurants, not just with the Italian-style crust. The nearly dozen choices have a selection of wonderfully complementary toppings and include *Robiola* with robiola cheese, leeks and pancetta; *Vongole,* small clams, cherry tomatoes and mozzarella; and the *Taleggio* with the pungent, soft *taleggio* cheese, arugula, slices of pear and some truffle oil. You can also create your own, and each of the pizzas can be topped with a fried egg for an additional buck. For those looking for something familiar, there is the now-familiar Pizza Margherita with just tomato, large leaves of basil and mozzarella (actually the traditional, higher quality *mozzarella di bufula),* and the Pizza Calabrese is essentially the Italian version of the American pepperoni pizza.

Dolce Vita is really a *ristorante* that features pizzas, as it's grander than a pizzeria. There is no *birra alla spina* (draft beer) that is seemingly required by law in Italy for pizzerias, but rather artful cocktails and an interesting wine list, and the pizzas are just one of the caloric attractions. Salads, appetizer plates, pastas and the daily specials, a meat and fish, are also a cut above. The appetizer plates are a great way to start, and the dishes are listed among vegetables, cured fish, cured meats, fried items and cheeses. These are far removed from the fried mozzarella sticks. Some of the items include roasted parsnips with wine must, shaved Brussels sprouts with pecorino cheese, preserved fried whitefish, *baccala,* the sweet *prosciutto di San Daniele,* domestic artisanal speck (think smoked prosciutto), fried croquettes of pumpkin and goat cheese, fried anchovies, the deep-fried rice and cheese *supplì,* and several tasty Italian cheeses that can be complemented with honey, if you'd like. In addition to selecting these individually, Dolce Vita encourages you to order an entire theme such as cheese, vegetables and fish. The straightforward salads are noticeably far more than the sum of their simple components. The pastas are a pan-Italian collection of simple, amazingly flavorful dishes. There is Puglia-inspired hand-made shell-like *orecchiette* with escarole and sweet sausage; the Roman favorite of spaghetti with grated cheese and black pepper; *bucatini* (thick spaghetti with holes) with octopus, chiles and tomatoes, and the hearty gnocchi with *ragù,* and *paccheri* (wide hollow pasta tube) with tomato, basil and Parmesan. The meat specials might be braised pork served with polenta, beef *braciola,* braised lamb, and that Southern Italian feast day favorite, grilled sausage with peppers. The fish might be a fillet of the extremely tasty Chilean sea bass. These specials might not be as consistent as the pizzas, but can still be well worth ordering.

The wine list is chauvinistically and gloriously solely Italian in a great array of styles and regions, most of which will complement the pizza or other Italian fare. The wines are not just the expected Chiantis, Pinot Grigios and Barolos, but include food-friendly wines from nearly every region in Italy. There are some interesting and inexpensive wines including Nero D'Avola from Sicily, Barbera from Piedmont, Lugana from the Veneto and Verdicchio from the Marches, plus a half-dozen dessert wines. Set in an old house, Dolce Vita is a comfortable place. But, the service is somewhat fitting of the not-high-dollar price. It can be a bit ragged at times, but it's usually earnest and quite sufficient.

Don Café Sandwich $5

9300 Bellaire (between Ranchester and Corporate) 77036, (713) 777-9500

Cuisine - Vietnamese; Sandwiches
Hours - Daily 8AM to 9PM
Credit Cards - Discover, MC, Visa
Service - Table Service
Alcohol - NONE

Entrée Prices - $2 to $7 ($5 average)
Entrées $12 and less - 100%

Atmosphere & Décor - Pleasant
Appeal - Cheap and well-made sandwiches in a tidy comfortable setting

Menu Suggestions - banh mi (Vietnamese sandwiches); Banh Mi Curry Ga (chicken served in a green curry broth and a small baguette)

The fact that often-bustling Don Café could open up within thirty yards of two long-standing Vietnamese sandwich shops and become a success is some indication of its quality. Their sandwiches are just about as good as its immediate neighbors, and with about twenty tables and high ceilings, Don Café is a larger and more comfortable place to dine. Though take-away is very popular, you can actually linger here, as many of the polyglot patrons do. Don Café serves all of the requisite Vietnamese sandwiches plus the somewhat unique versions with char-grilled beef *(banh mi thit bo nuong)* and char-grilled chicken (*banh mi thit ga nuong*). There is the delectable char-grilled pork, shredded pork, steamed pork, pork meatballs, chicken (which is served shredded), ham and pâté and the Special with the brightly colored Vietnamese-style ham. Similar to most area Vietnamese sandwiches, these feature a crusty fresh baguette, a big slice of fresh jalapeño and plenty of marinated, shredded carrots. Almost needless to state, this Vietnamese sandwich shop is a great value, especially so since it is one of the few that still offers a free sandwich for every five purchased. This fact is announced in English, Vietnamese and Spanish, perfect for that work crew. In addition to the sandwiches, there are about two dozen items on the menu and a few brightly colored packaged items near the counter. One excellent non-sandwich dish, though listed as a sandwich, is the stewed chicken legs in a very flavorful, though not spicy, green curry broth peppered with chopped scallions and cilantro leaves (*banh mi curry ga*) and served with a small baguette. The bread serves as a sop for the tasty soup, and can be used to craft a simple sandwich. Additionally, Don Café has the hearty soups such as *pho* with several variations that seem to adorn many tables, the popular rice plates (*com dia*) and vermicelli dishes (*bun*) and spring, summer and the deep-fried Imperial rolls to start. The small menu also has room for the central Vietnamese spicy beef and noodle soup, *bun bo hue*, a vermicelli dish with crab meat and snails (*bun rieu oc*), and freshly squeezed sugar cane juice.

Don Carlos $11

416 76th (north of Harrisburg) 77012, (713) 923-1906
8385 Broadway (south of Bellfort) 77061, (713) 641-2084
6501 Southwest Freeway (east of Hillcroft on the south side) 77074, (713) 776-2891

Cuisine - Tex-Mex
Hours - Mon-Thu 8AM to 11PM; Fri 8AM to 3:30AM; Sat 7AM to 3:30AM; Sun 7AM to 12AM
Credit Cards - Amex, MC, Visa
Service - Table Service

Alcohol - Full Bar

Entrée Prices - Dinner - $7 to $14 ($11 avg.); Lunch - $5 to $9; Breakfast - $3 to $11
Entrées at Dinner $12 and less - 80%

Atmosphere & Décor - Comfortable, often lively
Appeal - Satisfying Mexican food in large and lively restaurants
Menu Suggestions - Fajitas; Tacos al Carbon; Enchiladas Banderas (enchiladas, one topped with white cheese, one with white cheese and tomatillo sauce, and one with yellow cheese and chili sauce); Cheese Enchiladas; Tacos al Trompo (tacos with pork meat from the snout)

Sporting more flair and better food than most small local Tex-Mex chains, Don Carlos is a reliable and often fun place to dine. Festooned in aqua and pink as are seemingly most of the Mexican restaurants on Houston's east side and in northern Mexico, the first Don Carlos restaurant in the heart of the Hispanic Second Ward can be worth a drive for a meal. This and the other two locations are large and rambling places meant to serve groups and families. The crowds can be big and lively on weekend nights, especially at the original location. Though the atmosphere is certainly a draw, the crowds would not return if the food was not good.

The large dinner menu is divided among appetizers, soups and salads, combination plates, *Orginales Tacos al Carbon,* burritos and enchiladas, fajitas, *Parrilladas Combinadas* (grilled combination plates), *De la Parrilla* (other grilled items), seafood, and specials. The portions are hearty, and value is evident here. Fajitas and the other grilled beef items are big draws at Don Carlos. Before grilling, the flank steak for the fajitas and *tacos al carbon* is marinated for a couple days in a mixture that consists mostly of lemon juice, soy sauce, garlic, and pineapple juice. The fajitas include the basic version, simply called *Carne Asada,* plus ones with slices of poblano peppers, onions and mushrooms, and another with bell pepper, onion and melted cheese. The specials include the eponymous *Don Carlos Especial* with barbecue pork slices cut from the snout (called *trompo*), and Steak *a la Mexicana,* slices of fajita meat marinated in a hot sauce and then sautéed. Along with the fajitas and steak specials are a number of *parilla,* or mixed grill, items. At Don Carlos these are mostly combination plates featuring a variety of grilled items like several different steak preparations, chicken, shrimp, beef short ribs, and tripe. There are *parilla* combinations for one, two and four people. This can be a great way to feed a small group. There are many enchilada dishes, usually with a choice of fillings between chicken or ground beef. Some of the notable ones are the *Enchiladas Mexicanas* (four enchiladas filled with white cheese and served with fried potatoes), *Entomatadas de Pollo* (here, three shredded chicken enchiladas in a spicy tomato sauce), and *Enchiladas de Fajita* (with a choice of beef or chicken, and a chili or tomatillo sauce). Another worthy choice is the *Enchiladas Banderas*. These are three enchiladas made with a choice among ground beef, chicken and cheese that are assembled to resemble the Mexican flag (one topped with white cheese, one with tomatillo sauce and the white cheese, and one with yellow cheese and chili sauce). Though meat dishes predominate, there are spinach enchiladas plus several shrimp dishes including the appealing *Camarones Gratinados* (grilled jumbo shrimp wrapped in bacon and with melted cheese that is called brochette on other local menus).

Lunchtime is a good time to visit Don Carlos, as there are around twenty-five substantial and fairly inexpensive specials. Among the choices are some of the most popular Tex-Mex dishes, such as fajitas, tacos, burritos, taco salad, and *chimichangas*, but there is also *Caldo de Res* (a hearty beef soup) and *Carne Adobado* (a marinated steak). In addition to lunch and dinner, breakfast is also served daily, beginning at 8AM. Don Carlos provides a large number of choices including many hearty Mexican scrambled egg breakfast combinations plus omelets and pancakes. Almost all of the nearly twenty Mexican breakfast dishes (called *Almuerzos* here) prominently feature meat, and nearly all of them are served with *papas con chorizo*, roasted potatoes with the Mexican sausage. Among these dishes are *Almuerzo Monterrey* (fajita meat, *huevos rancheros, papas con chorizo* and refried beans), *Chuleta y Huevos* (a pork chop, *huevos rancheros, papas con chorizo* and refried beans), and *Machacado Norteño* (marinated dried beef, two eggs, *papas con chorizo* and refried beans). Some of the specialties, *Menudo* (beef tripe soup) and *Barbacoa de Cabeza* (barbecued cow head), are served only on the weekend. As might be expected, the location on 76th Street has the most character. Another location is situated close to Hobby Airport. The spiffiest location is on the Southwest Freeway at Hillcroft not too far from the Galleria area.

Doña Tere Tamales $4

8331 Beechnut (just west of Southwest Freeway) 77036, (713) 270-8501
13238 Bellaire (between Dairy Ashford and Eldridge) 77083, (832) 328-0761

Cuisine - Mexican (taqueria - Mexico City-style tamales)
Hours - Mon-Fri 6AM to 10PM; Sat-Sun
Credit Cards - MC, Visa
Service - Counter Service
Alcohol - NONE

Entrée Prices - $2 to $6 ($4 average)
Entrées $12 and less - 100%

Atmosphere & Décor - Not really

Appeal - Giant, tasty tamales for very cheap
Useful to Note - You will also need to order the salsa along with the tamales.
Menu Suggestions - dulce con pana tamales; chicken-mole tamales; oaxacaño tamales (giant square tamales filled with shredded pork)

Doña Tere's bare-bones operations are essentially enclosed tamale stands serving the Mexico City-style tamales to recent immigrants and migrants. When visiting, you'll likely join the short queue and place an order from the limited menu hung behind the counter. There are no descriptions to help, and there is a good chance that the cashier will not speak any English. No matter, you can't go wrong here. What's probably the most important thing for first time customers to understand is that you'll only need to order two or maybe three tamales per person. For those who are used to eating tamales in Houston, the size of the ones here might come as a shock. These are huge, at least double the size of most tamales served in area restaurants and shops. Lifting a hefty tamale, and peeling away the large corn husks you'll find very thick rolls of *masa* dough enclosing a small variety of very tasty fillings. Pork, white cheese and fresh jalapeños, and shredded chicken with dark brown *mole* are several of the tasty choices. Most are complemented by the light, slightly sweet and spicy green salsa, which, in unusual fashion, will have to be ordered separately. The most unique tamale of the few that are offered is probably the purple-hued *dulce con pana* version. These are not very *dulce* (sweet) though, but are a very tasty, mostly savory concoction with some sweetness provided by the raisins and a touch of cinnamon. The even larger, square-shaped *oaxacaño* tamale comes in a dark green banana leaf. One of these might be enough for many appetites.

Doozo Noodle & Dumplings $6

1200 McKinney (at San Jacinto; Houston Center, 3rd Floor) 77002, (713) 759-0103

Cuisine - Chinese (dumplings and noodles)
Hours - Mon-Fri 11AM to 3PM
Credit Cards - NONE
Service - Counter Service
Alcohol - NONE

Entrée Prices - $4 to $7 ($6 average)
Entrées $12 and less - 100%

Atmosphere & Décor - Mall food court
Appeal - Good dumplings in the Houston Center downtown
Useful to Note - The line moves quickly, have no fear.
Menu Suggestions - Steamed Pork Dumplings; Steamed Vegetable Dumplings; Steamed Chicken Dumplings

---

Doozo Noodle & Dumplings is mostly just that, a small eatery dispensing Chinese noodle and dumpling dishes. Actually, for most patrons, it's only half that phrase, the dumplings. Doozo's rendition of the steamed Chinese dumplings draws huge lines during the long lunchtime hours at the Houston Center downtown. Doozo efficiently serves the crush of patrons with dumplings that have been made shortly beforehand in various combinations. Since there are just steamed pork, vegetable and chicken, and then combinations thereof (half pork, half vegetable, etc.), the number of permutations is easily manageable. The very prompt service, in addition to the tasty and quick-to-consume dumplings, is part of the attraction to office workers with tight schedules.

The pork dumpling is filled with shredded pork and some type of greens. The vegetable dumplings have greens, clear, thin rice noodles and what seems to be bean curd. The chicken is just shredded chicken, and comparatively somewhat bland. The pork is probably the most flavorful of the three, though each is tasty. These dumplings are great when downtown and pressed for time, but are not quite as good as those at the Dumpling King on Westheimer or San Dong Noodle House in New Chinatown, which are cooked to order. Since Doozo's has to pre-cook the dumplings to satisfy the dramatic lunchtime spike in business, the dumpling cover often becomes slightly gummy. But, no matter, this fact will not deter you from coming again, when downtown. You have a choice of spicy or mild dipping sauce to accompany the dumplings. In the Cantonese-style, the spicy is not very spicy at all, but it's more flavorful than the mild sauce. Both are primarily soy sauce and make for nice complements to the dumplings, as the sauce is quickly absorbed through those fairly thin wrappings. If the popular dumplings are not for you, there are also four types of pre-packaged sushi (doesn't it seem most every Asian restaurant serves sushi these days), and several noodle dishes. Everything is inexpensive here, and served very quickly.

Dot Coffee Shop $11

7006 Gulf Freeway (just north of Loop 610 S.) 77017, (713) 644-7669

Cuisine - Diner
Hours - Open 24 hours daily
Credit Cards - Amex, Diners, MC, Visa
Service - Table Service
Alcohol - NONE

Entrée Prices - Dinner & Lunch - $5 to $21 ($11 average); Breakfast - $5 to $16
Entrées at Dinner $12 and less - 70%

Atmosphere & Décor - Nice, for a diner
Appeal - Diner food in a comfortable setting
Menu Suggestions - French toast; Houston Omelet (with bacon, ham and pork sausage); eggs; hash browns; Jumbo Chicken Fried Steak

---

The Dot Coffee Shops were the restaurants that got the Pappas corporate juggernaut rolling in the 1960s. There were once several locations, but these eventually closed as the Pappas' restaurants and concepts expanded and grew more upscale. The only location left is the one just off the Gulf Freeway, near the Gulfgate Mall. It's the product of very successful restaurateurs who have the knack for giving the customers just what they want and maybe a bit more. Dot is a good version of the traditional American diner. For one, it is a lot nicer than most diners (and probably too nice to spot anyone with a resemblance to Vic Tayback, for example). It's an attractive place with noticeably good quality furniture. These tables are quickly bussed, and the place is much cleaner than most diners. Large framed color photographs of Houston from the mid-twentieth century decorate the walls at modest intervals. As with most of the Pappas establishments, the restaurant is quite large, even big for a diner. It seems spacious, though usually crowded with patrons. The service is usually a little better than other local diners.

The utility of the relatively attractive diner would come to naught if the food wasn't satisfying, and not worth the price. The kitchen does not quite have the deftness of the much humbler Frank's Grill, but it does well enough. The basic American diner offerings echo their neon sign proclaiming, "Steaks, Shakes & Pancakes", are well executed here, plus some interesting twists. There are Strawberry Pancakes, Pecan Nut Pancakes, French toast & Bananas, and the Croissant Breakfast. The eggs are very large and even the simple eggs over-easy have a surprisingly amount of flavor. The egg dishes are the best breakfast items. The French toast is nearly as good; some of the best around, in fact. The small-sized regular pancakes are nothing special, though. And, the bacon, at times can seem like it has spent too much time under a heat lamp, could be better. And, for some reason, vegetable oil spread is used instead of butter. Otherwise, Dot seems not to have left a detail unnoticed. The hash browns are the real hash browns, shredded and properly browned on the griddle, not the home fries that many places masquerade as hash browns. The lettuce used for the salads might be iceberg lettuce, but it is fresh and greener than similar versions of this basic garden salad. Sliced, ripe, red roma tomatoes accompany the crisp green lettuce on the salads. Coffee is served in small pots that are deposited on each table. As with the breakfasts, the lunch and dinner menu includes of all the local diner favorites. There are hamburgers, hot sandwiches, fried chicken, catfish, and, of course, chicken fried steak. Then there is a 12-ounce ribeye steak, a 12-ounce strip steak, and various fried Gulf seafood including the Deluxe Fried Seafood Platter with shrimp, catfish and crawfish. The dishes are not terribly inexpensive, but the value is there, as these are invariably well prepared and plentiful. For the best non-breakfast values, there are a half-dozen specials each day featuring entrées such as Baked Chicken & Rice, Fried Catfish Fillet, Liver and Onions, Beef Pot Roast, Meatloaf, and Country Fried Chicken Breast. An entrée and three vegetables are cheaper from 11AM to 3PM than it is afterwards. In addition to the breakfast and nighttime fare, there are also pies and cakes made in-house.

Dot does a brisk business and is packed on weekend mornings, and fairly busy at most other times. There can be a surprisingly big crowd at a random time like nine on a Wednesday evening. It is easy to get to from downtown and the neighborhoods south of town. The busy area on the feeder of the Gulf Freeway is a small nexus for worthwhile cheap eats; Dot is next door to a Pappas Bar-B-Q, and just around the corner from a Taqueria Mexico.

Droubi's Bakery and Deli $6

7333 Hillcroft (south of Bellaire) 77081, (713) 988-5897
2721 Hillcroft (just south of Westheimer) 77057, (713) 782-6160

Cuisine - Middle Eastern
Hours - 7333 Hillcroft - Mon-Sat 8AM to 8PM; Sun 8AM to 7PM; 2721 Hillcroft - Mon-Sat 8AM to 8PM; Sun 10AM to 7PM
Credit Cards - Amex, Discover, MC, Visa
Service - Counter Service
Alcohol - Beer

Entrée Prices - $4 to $8 ($6 average)
Entrées $12 and less - 100%

Atmosphere & Décor - Spartan
Appeal - Decent Middle Eastern food for cheap
Useful to Note - The downtown Droubi's are not nearly as reliable.
Menu Suggestions - Chicken Shawarma; Beef Shawarma; Falafel Sandwich; Lamb Shanks

At the bustling main location on south Hillcroft, south of Bellaire, Droubi's Imports and Deli provides a grocery, a fairly large deli, cheese counter and hot food from the steam table for a mixed clientele, Arabs along with non-Arabs from the general neighborhood. It's a good place to stop for a quick inexpensive meal whether or not you need to also shop for cheese, quality *halal* meats and other Middle Eastern specialties. Prices are low and the number of choices is more than sufficient for lunch. The offerings are the locally popular cold po boys in the Antone's tradition, plus pita sandwiches and Middle Eastern plates from the steam table. A couple selling points for Droubi's is that the cooked meats are all *halal* ensuring a certain level of quality, and Droubi's bakes all of its own bread. In fact, many other restaurants purchase their pita bread. The pretty good *shawarmas* are made with roasted meat that is sliced from the nice-looking spinners across the counter, and then grilled for finishing and assembled in front of your eyes. The *shawarmas* are available in either beef or chicken, and are served with slightly roasted tomatoes, onions and pickles inside the pita bread. Droubi's also serves most of the familiar Middle Eastern items such as *falafel, hummus, baba ganoush, tabouli,* stuffed grape leaves and the like, and does a solid job with these. Heartier Middle Eastern fare is also available from the steam table including a lamb shank, Cornish hen, a fish dish, and even a Persian-style *koobideh* made with seasoned ground beef. Attractive house-made pastries from the tough-to-miss pastry counter such as *baklava* are a tempting finish to a satisfying meal. The crumbly *baklava* is delicious. The settings are very informal and functional. Tables are placed near the food counter, surrounded by the stations for meats, cheeses and pastries. The décor is the surrounding grocery and market. The newest Droubi's, that took a very long time to open, is a fairly good-sized operation on Hillcroft just south of Westheimer.

Dumpling King $7

6515 Westheimer (just east of Hillcroft / Voss) 77057, (713) 266-1468

Cuisine - Chinese
Hours - Mon-Thu, Sun 11:30AM to 10PM; Fri-Sat 11:30AM to 11PM
Credit Cards - Amex, MC, Visa
Service - Table Service
Alcohol - Beer & Wine

Entrée Prices - Dinner - $5 to $10 ($7 average); Lunch - $4 to $7
Entrées at Dinner $12 and less - 100%

Atmosphere & Décor - Spartan
Appeal - Some of the best Chinese dumplings in town
Menu Suggestions - Shrimp and Pork Dumplings; Chicken and Cheese Dumplings; Fried Beef Dumplings; Fried Pork Dumplings; most dumpling dishes

Dumpling King is a fitting name for this restaurant. It serves some of the best Chinese dumplings in town. These are the dough pockets that are filled with several different minced meats or vegetables, then steamed or pan-fried. There are over fifteen different combinations: chicken, pork, beef, vegetables, shrimp and pork, chicken with chives, vegetables with chives, cheese and chicken, and cheese and vegetables. There are also the similar

Steamed Pork Purse and a Steamed Crab Meat and Pork Purse. These are really dumplings that are slightly smaller and folded in a different manner. Available either steamed or pan-fried, the dumplings are served in orders of six or ten. The drill is to create your own dipping sauce with soy sauce and a mixture of the contents of the other jars and bottles on the table: minced jalapeños and cilantro, minced garlic, oil and vinegar. These condiments are always in good condition, and plentiful for the table. Almost every type of dumpling is worth ordering. Unlike some other places where the pan-fried dumplings can be overly doughy and bland, both versions are consistently very good here. The only quibble, and a minor one, might be that the cheese and the crab meat are not very evident in those dumplings. The latter is not surprising given the very low price.

Though dumplings might get all of the attention from many patrons, Dumpling King also serves a large number of Chinese and Chinese-American dishes for very reasonable prices. These items seem to be popular with many customers, even the fairly numerous Asian patrons. With at least several items under each heading, the menu is divided among Soups, Noodle Soups, Crispy Pan-Fried Noodles, *Lo Mein*, Fried Rice, Bean Curd, Vegetables, Poultry, Shrimp, Pork, and Beef. The bean curd and vegetable dishes are parenthetically called "diet dishes" in case you are looking. There are also several other dishes listed under the "Chef's Specials" such as Seafood Noodle Soup, Beijing Style Toasted Shrimp, Mongolian Beef, and the curiously named Chinese Taco. Lunch specials come with fried rice, an egg roll, and a choice between hot and sour and egg drop soup, and are generously served six days a week until 4PM. The more than two dozen items include dishes such as Sweet and Sour Pork, Almond Chicken, Hot and Sour Chicken, the peanut-laden Kung Po Shrimp (called *Gong Bao* here), Pepper Steak, and, of course, General Joe's Chicken. These are a great value as they are all priced under four-and-a-half dollars.

This easy-to-miss restaurant shares a tiny strip center with a cigar shop and an erotic wear store on busy Westheimer near Voss and Hillcroft. The restaurant itself is fairly small and unassuming. The seating capacity is around fifty patrons, and all fourteen tables fit within the one dining room. These are often full during the lunchtime hours during the week. It's a pleasant room, though slightly shabby. A half-dozen Chinese watercolors adorn the wall along with a large, slightly kitschy framed woodcut of a scene of the Great Wall. It actually has more décor than most Chinatown Chinese restaurants even as the food is comparable to most of them. And, in further contrast, the service is generally attentive.

Edloe Street Delicatessen $9

6119 Edloe (between Rice and University) 77005, (713) 666-4302

Cuisine - American
Hours - Mon-Tue 11AM to 2:30PM; Wed-Fri 11AM to 2:30PM, 5 to 9PM; Sat 8AM to 3PM
Credit Cards - Amex, Discover, MC, Visa
Service - Table Service
Alcohol - Beer & Wine

Entrée Prices - $5 to $12 ($9 average)
Entrées $12 and less - 100%

Atmosphere & Décor - Pleasant
Appeal - A comfortable neighborhood restaurant for West University
Useful to Note - They serve breakfast on Saturday morning.
Menu Suggestions - French Dip Sandwich; Chicken Enchiladas; Chicken Salad Sandwich

Edloe Street Deli is not really a deli in most senses of the word; a neighborhood restaurant is a better description. And, it is a comfortable American neighborhood restaurant at that. Located in an older commercial building nestled in the heart of prosperous West University Place, the restaurant is fairly small, but cozy. The dining is done on well-worn wooden tables and chairs. The service is usually friendly and sometimes attentive. But, charm and quaintness would not have sustained the popularity for so many years unless the kitchen did a good job. Those well prepared dishes are familiar, and representative of the Houston area. It serves the types of regionally familiar food that is popular with most in the neighborhood. The restaurant is opened for lunch Monday through Saturday; and dinner for only three nights, Wednesdays through Fridays. The lunch menu consists of hamburgers, cold and some hot sandwiches, a couple of soups, quiche, a wide array of salads, and plates with sandwich or burrito, and soup or salad. The sandwiches and stuffed pita breads are well-made. A slice of cake or a brownie can serve as fitting, if not fit, end to lunch. For dinner, the range of offerings is much larger. In addition to what is served at lunch, there are pastas with a choice of several toppings, and "Grilled Specials" such as grilled shrimp, several chicken preparations and a couple different steaks. These can be a good value, as these are served with a salad, vegetable and twice-baked potato. Reflecting the kitchen staff, there are a number of Tex-Mex dishes including several types of enchiladas, *quesadillas*, *chalupas*, nachos, a Tex-Mex soup and a grilled chicken breast. Beer and wine are available, as is freshly made lemonade. The cooking is solid, if not spectacular. This is not a destination restaurant, but it is certainly popular, as it's often crowded during the day and evenings.

Catering and bulk take-away are very popular. In a large, sprawling city, Edloe Street Deli is a pleasant anomaly, a true neighborhood place.

El Hidalguense $10

6917 Long Point (between Silber and Antoine) 77055, (713) 680-1071
3631 Hillcroft (between Westpark and Richmond) 77057, (713) 781-6656

Cuisine - Mexican (taqueria)
Hours - Daily 7AM to 11PM
Credit Cards - Discover, MC, Visa
Service - Table Service
Alcohol - Beer

Entrée Prices - Dinner & Lunch - $5 to $18 ($10 average); Breakfast - $4 to $6
Entrées at Dinner $12 and less - 90%

Atmosphere & Décor - Spartan, at best
Appeal - Excellent and authentic regional Mexican food
Useful to Note - If you're just a casual Mexican food fan, you might not like this.
Menu Suggestions - Barbacoa de Borrego Estilo Hidalgo (lamb slowly cooked in maguey leaves in the style of Hidalgo); Torta de Fajita (Mexican-style sandwich with fajita); Enchiladas de Pollo (chicken enchiladas)

The appearance of the original El Hidalguense fits perfectly at the end of a forlorn, scruffy small strip center with other Hispanic businesses on Long Point will probably deter many potential customers. The second location on Hillcroft is nearly as unattractive. But, serving well-made, nearly authentic food from Hidalgo in central Mexico, its looks certainly does not dissuade the patrons from central Mexico who make up most of the clientele.

The food is more authentically Mexican than most area Mexican restaurants. For one, chips and salsa are not served here. Once you finish the rolled and deep-fried tortillas presented on a small plate with a bowl of smoky-tasting salsa that's it. No more fried goodness will be brought to the table. You will likely have to order in Spanish, too. The menu is divided among appetizers, smaller items such as tacos, *tortas,* and *quesadillas,* and dinner specials. Non-adventurous diners weaned on Tex-Mex might have difficulty in finding menu items to their liking. The stars of the open-air kitchen and the specialties of the restaurant are the grilled young goat and lamb slowly cooked with maguey leaves (*barbacoa*) in the manner of Hidalgo. The resulting meat is moist, tender and tasty. Scooping this meat into one of the tortillas, either flour or corn, made on-site and in sight in the kitchen is the way to consume this. For those who are wary of lamb, its flavor could easily pass for beef here. A light consommé of lamb with onions and chiles is included with the order of *barbacoa.* There are also fajitas, grilled chicken, and a couple chicken breasts, including one with the dark *mole* poblano available. The enchiladas can be filled with steamed and shredded chicken, fajita or even scrambled eggs. This last one comes with a piece of spicy cured beef (*cesina*).

The interiors might be even less appealing than the exteriors. It is tacky, but functional. Gazing at the hard-working staff preparing the interesting food in the open air kitchen might be the only saving grace. A stage takes up some of the dining room. There is live music many nights of the week, and possibly at other times, too. Service is often indifferent, and English is rarely spoken. The exception is during evenings when the owner is present. Non-Hispanic customers might be given several complimentary shots of low quality tequila. But, it's the thought that counts. For lunch, the daily specials are the way to go. These usually consist of a choice of one of two or three entrées plus a drink of *horchata* (a refreshing rice-based drink) and *arroz con leche* (rice pudding) for a relative pittance. The *barbacoa* is often offered as a lunch special, either in green salsa or red. Both versions are very good, but the red is slightly spicier and slightly more flavorful. Enchiladas can also appear as a special. And, if one of the specials does not appeal, there are plenty of inexpensive tacos and *tortas* from which to select. Breakfast is served daily from 8AM to 11AM.

El Paraiso $8

2320 Crocker (at Fairview, two blocks east of Montrose) 77006, (713) 524-0309

Cuisine - Mexican
Hours - Mon-Thu, Sun 7AM to 10PM; Fri-Sat 7AM to 11PM
Credit Cards - Amex, Discover, MC, Visa
Service - Table Service
Alcohol - Beer & Wine

Entrée Prices - Dinner & Lunch - $6 to $11 ($8 average); Breakfast - $5 to $7
Entrées at Dinner $12 and less - 100%

Atmosphere & Décor - Functional, but pleasant enough
Appeal - Comfortable neighborhood Mexican restaurant
Useful to Note - There's plenty of nearby street parking.
Menu Suggestions - Nachos Supremos; Queadillas with chicken; Entomatadas (enchiladas with a tomato sauce); Huevos con Chorizo; Migas (eggs scrambled with tortilla chops and onions)

Situated in an old house and tucked into the heart of Montrose, with its interiors painted a soothing yellow and the staff's low key and inviting demeanor, El Paraiso is a comfortable and very relaxed place to enjoy some unpretentious Mexican food. Open since 1978 in what once was almost a completely Hispanic neighborhood, El Paraiso is still popular with Mexican families, young couples and Montrose denizens. The food is solid and home-style; enjoyable, if not spectacular. The expanded house that the restaurant occupies is a nice complement for this. There is no waiting area and no bar area. There are only tables, chairs and booths among a couple of rooms. People come here to eat, not to hang out.

The menu contains traditional Mexican home cooking and Tex-Mex favorites, and the kitchen is proficient with most everything. That proficiency is evident right away with the basket of very thick and tasty tortilla chips cooked to golden brown. These help provide the base for some far-better-than-usual nachos. The traditional accompaniments, the moist short grain Spanish rice and noticeably flavorful refried beans are both exceptional. The appetizers begin with the Texas favorite, nachos that are served in several guises. There is also *Queso Flameado,* melted white cheese with *chorizo,* and, of course, *Chile con Queso,* which is made with the much tastier real cheese here. This necessitates much quicker action, as congealing becomes a problem after a few minutes. There are a couple of hearty soups, one with chicken (*Caldo de Pollo*), the other with beef (*Caldo de Res). Menudo* is also on the daily menu for those that need it. There are several types of enchilada dishes. These include one with *mole* that is available in a choice of fillings among shredded chicken, beef and a Mexican white cheese. One of the better enchilada dishes is the *Entomatadas,* which feature a light tomato sauce. Among the mostly traditional meat dishes are *Asado de Puerco* (pork tips cooked in a red sauce), *Carne Guisada* (stewed beef), *Mole Poblano* (chicken in the locally popular dark *mole* sauce), *Milanesa* (breaded and fried veal cutlet here), *Chuleta* (two pork chops in either *ranchero* sauce or the spicy *a la mexicana*), *Pechuga de Pollo* (grilled chicken breast), and a few steak dishes including *Carne Asada* (grilled skirt steak). El Paraiso has almost everything that you might expect at a local Mexican restaurant. They also serve *flautas, tortas,* tacos, excellent Tex-Mex-style *quesadillas,* tamales, *chile rellenos,* burritos and even *sopes* (thick flat tortillas topped with beans and choice of meats or avocado), and Tex-Mex combination plates. Seafood is an afterthought here with only two seafood dishes, the fried shrimp and fried fish fillet. El Paraiso is conveniently open for breakfast every day. The breakfasts served here are the popular Mexican egg-based breakfast plates such as *Huevos Rancheros, Huevos con Chorizo* (eggs scrambled with Mexican sausage), *Huevos a la Mexicana* (with tomatoes, onions and jalapeños), *Migas, Machacado con Huevo a la Mexicana* (with dried beef) and *Chuleta con Huevo* (two fried eggs with a pork chop topped with *ranchero* salsa). There are also breakfast tacos in several variations.

El Patio $11

6444 Westheimer (between Fountain View and Voss) 77057, (713) 780-0410
2416 Brazos (between Gray and McGowen) 77002, (713) 523-8181
www.elpatio.com

Cuisine - Tex-Mex
Hours - Mon-Wed 11AM to 11PM; Thu-Sat 11AM to 12 AM; Sun 11AM to 10PM
Credit Cards - Amex, Diners, Discover, MC, Visa
Service - Counter Service
Alcohol - Full Bar

Entrée Prices - Dinner - $7 to $19 ($11 average); Lunch - $7 to $12
Entrées at Dinner $12 and less - 80%

Atmosphere & Décor - Nice, even stylish at the Midtown location
Appeal - Good Tex-Mex in a nice and imbibing-friendly atmosphere
Useful to Note - Parking is limited at both locations; valet might be necessary.
Menu Suggestions - Enchiladas Suizas; Enchiladas Verdes; Sunrise Enchiladas (cheese enchiladas topped with fried eggs); Tamale Dinner; fajitas; Parilla Platter featuring fajitas, four bacon-wrapped shrimp and a half-rack of baby back ribs)

For quite a while El Patio was known almost solely for the separated bar area with a posted warning on the door that became its name in the original, long-standing Westheimer location, "Club - No Minors". That bar has long been extremely popular among twenty-somethings (and initially much younger) for very sweet but potent margaritas, and a knack for seemingly always overcharging groups for those. The food in the restaurant area was an afterthought, even before the margaritas. El Patio turned a new leaf, which became evident in 2006, and the food and overall quality increased markedly. It had to. The newer and nicer Midtown location had already witnessed two Tex-Mex restaurants come and go in a fairly brief time. El Patio has reacted to the considerable competition and ascribed to the notion that Tex-Mex restaurants can be nice restaurants provided the food quality matched the décor. White tablecloths cover the tables, which are set close together, and the settings are attractive, yet comfortable. But, most importantly, the kitchen improved considerably. And, the drinks still flow. The new location is probably the more proficient of the two locations.

The menu is not very lengthy, but it has a very high rate of dishes that will appeal to discerning Tex-Mex patrons. It contains most items from the familiar, local Tex-Mex repertoire, and these are conceived with a heavy-hand. That's meant as a compliment. Dishes are satisfyingly hearty here. An order of two enchiladas will satiate most appetites. Orders with three are also available. There are plenty of appetizers, soups and salads, soft and crispy tacos, *flautas*, enchiladas, *chile relleno*, *carne guisada* (beef tips stewed in a chile sauce), tasty fajitas available with several meats, seafood and ten or so Tex-Mex combination platters. In addition to the expected items, there are some twists: appetizers including fried shrimp and squid served with marinara sauce, the Acapulco Salad with spinach, mango, pineapple, red onions, bacon and tortilla chips, crawfish tacos in between two corn tortillas, fish tacos with mahi mahi, cheese enchiladas topped with fried eggs, bacon-wrapped quail legs, and seafood enchiladas made with flour tortillas and filled with red snapper, shrimp and crab. One very good dish for two hungry adults is their *Parilla* Platter featuring fajitas, four bacon-wrapped shrimp and a half-rack of baby back ribs served with guacamole and *pico de gallo.* The old timey combination plates are done well here such as surprisingly good tamales, a dish that is rather forgettable at too many restaurants. If you somehow have room for dessert, El Patio still serves *sopaipillas* (puffy deep-fried pastries drizzled with honey in case you have forgotten), plus flan, which can be topped with Kahlua or Bailey's, and the expected *tres leches.* To note, especially convenient for Briargrove and surrounding neighborhoods are the fajita packs to go that feed from two to a dozen, and El Patio does an especially good catering events.

El Pueblito $11

1423 Richmond (east of Dunlavy) 77006, (713) 520-6635
www.elpueblitopatio.com

Cuisine - Mexican (with Central American accents)
Hours - Mon-Thu 11AM to 9:30PM; Fri 11AM to 10:30PM; Sat 9AM to 10:30PM; Sun 9AM to 9:30PM
Credit Cards - Amex, Diners, MC, Visa
Service - Table Service
Alcohol - Beer & Wine

Entrée Prices - Dinner - $7 to $20 ($11 average); Lunch - $6 to $9
Entrées at Dinner $12 and less - 90%

Atmosphere & Décor - Comfortable; patio
Appeal - Very good Mexican food with tropical influence
Useful to Note - Live music Wed through Sat nights; nearly valet parking only.
Menu Suggestions - El Costeño Plate (carne asada); Quesadilla Del Norte (with chicken and Chihuahua and cheddar cheese); Tacos Marinos (tacos with grilled snapper); Huevos con Chilaso (eggs scrambled with poblano pepper); Migas Tejanas (eggs scrambled with tortilla strips); Chilaquiles (eggs scrambled with tortilla strips, chicken and melted cheese)

In a small, low-slung building on Richmond not too far west of Montrose , tough to overlook with its bright yellow exterior, El Pueblito has long been a convenient stop for Mexican food with a twist. The restaurant might not be as consistent as it once was, but it is still worth the visit. There is a great patio, at the very least. The owners are from Guatemala, so while the food at El Pueblito is mostly familiar Mexican food, it has a Central American accent. This translates into tropical flavors in many of the dishes, black beans often in place of refried beans, and plantains and yucca as sides. Another difference is that the food presentation is better than at most local Mexican restaurants. Some of the items actually look comely, often a tough thing for Mexican dishes, no matter how delicious.

The menu has grown over the years and offers many popular Mexican dishes plus several fairly imaginative seafood entrées. The seafood at El Pueblito includes shrimp sautéed in lemon and garlic, a spicy, marinated seafood cocktail, and fillets of red snapper, salmon and rainbow trout. The Snappper Santa Monica is a snapper fillet marinated in lemon and butter then grilled and served with a fruit relish. *Pez de Dioses* is marinated and grilled rainbow trout that is served with roasted almonds and guacamole. There are flavorful *carne asada* (grilled skirt steak), *carne guisada* (stewed beef), chicken breast dishes, tacos and *quesadillas*. The soft taco dishes come stuffed with red snapper, or grilled chicken or beef fajitas. The *Quesadillas del Norte* are made with two large flour tortillas sandwiching grilled chicken breast or beef fajitas, and a couple cheeses. Other *quesadillas* feature shrimp, and spinach and mushrooms. One minor quibble is that the sides of beans can be a little runny. This is undoubtedly due to the fact the restaurant states that it uses corn oil in all of the dishes instead of the tastier, artery-clogging *manteca de cerdo*. The two complimentary salsas are very good. One is a standard tomato-based salsa, spiked with cilantro, which is spicy and tasty. The other is unusual. It's yellow since it is made primarily with pineapples that are mixed with chopped serrano peppers, garlic, cilantro and lime. The resulting taste is both sweet with a noticeable piquant edge. It's very flavorful, though it might take a couple of scoops with the thick corn tortilla chips to get used to the unique taste. Unfortunately, there is a charge for extra chips and the tasty salsas here.

Lunch specials, with many of the same dishes for dinner, but a little cheaper, can be a good deal. The weekend breakfasts are also an honest value. These weekend mornings are good time to visit, especially when nursing a hangover, as it usually not very crowded, and the decibel level is manageable. And, the popular Mexican breakfasts, and some others, are all very reliable here such as the *Huevos con Chilaso* (eggs scrambled with poblano pepper), the *Migas Tejanas* (with tortillas strips), and *Huevos con Chorizo* (with *chorizo*) and *Huevoes Rancheros* (poached eggs in a tomato sauce). Their version of *chilaquiles* is also excellent. It is almost bright orange in color, featuring chunks of chicken, corn tortillas strips in scrambled eggs topped with white and cheddar cheese. Most breakfasts are served with some combination of refried beans, yucca, and roasted, cubed potatoes. An added attraction is the patio in back, which is lit at night with tiki torches and stringed lights for a Mexican resort feel. One of the enclosed cabanas there can be reserved for a more romantic dinner. To note, though there only is a small parking lot in front of the restaurant, there are additional spaces about a half-block east on Richmond. And, valets, of course.

El Pupusodromo $6

6817 Bissonnet (at Beechnut) 77074, (713) 270-5030
12325 Veterans Memorial (between Antoine and Richey) 77014, (281) 587-2800
5902 Renwick (between Southwest Freeway and Gulfton) 77081, (713) 661-4334

Cuisine - Salvadoran
Hours - Daily 10AM to 10PM
Credit Cards - MC, Visa
Service - Table Service
Alcohol - Beer

Entrée Prices - $5 to $100 ($6 average)
Entrées $12 and less - 100%

Atmosphere & Décor - Spartan
Appeal - Good Salvadoran food
Menu Suggestions - pupusas (stuffed corn meal); Combinado B (one tamal, two pupusas, sautéed sweet plantains)

The staple, and namesake of long-standing El Pupusodromo, *pupusas,* are described in the English verbiage on El Pupusodromo's menu as being one of El Salvador's typical meals that can "satisfy anyone's hunger,…[of] the several types of *pupusas*…the most popular ones are made out of handmade corn dough and stuffed with either cheese, pork, beans, or a mixture of all three ingrediants. You can find a *pupuseria* in every small town of El Salvador, as well as in the large cities". With the fairly large number of immigrants in the area from El Salvador, there are a number of *pupuserias* here, if you haven't noticed. The handful of El Pupusodromo locations, though fairly humble establishments, each seem to be a bit tidier, and run more efficiently than most other *pupuserias,* the very informal Salvadoran eateries that feature the *pupusas*. These are the Salvadoran versions of the similar Mexican *taquerias*.

Pupusas are somewhat similar to the more familiar Mexican *gorditas,* the stuffed corn dough pockets. The difference is that the entire *pupusa* is cooked, where the *gordita's* corn pocket and filling are cooked separately. A better description of a *pupusa* might be that it is a thick, circular corn dough pancake, stuffed with ground chicken, pork skin (*chicharron*) or cheese. The *pupuas* are served with a large plastic container, used communally, that is filled with a relish made primarily with pickled cabbage, carrots, and some peppers. This is to be scooped onto the *pupusas*. There is also a thin, tomato-based vinegary salsa for the *pupusas*, and other dishes. It has a decent flavor though it's not very hot. Most of the Salvadoran dishes are much less spicy than Mexican cuisine. Taking a cue from the Salvadorn patrons, the *pupusas* are meant to be folded and eaten with the hands like a taco. But, the *pupusas* retain heat very well and can be difficult to enjoy like this. These are also a little greasy, though the ones at El Pupusodromo are less so than other places. You might have to eat *pupusas* with the pathetically small plastic fork that is given as the only serving utensil. It works, though. And, the food is certainly worth the travail. One of the choices for *pupusas* here and at other *pupuserias*, is something called *loroco*. Chopped *loroco*, either dried or fresh, is a native Central American plant, often used to flavor *pupusas*. It is green and crunchy, and though its taste is somewhat tough to characterize, it seems to help the *pupusas*, as the ones ordered with *loroco* are very appetizing. The section of "*Antojitos*", or "small specialties" lists other palatable Salvadoran appetizers in addition to the *pupusas*. One way to sample them is one of the two combination plates. *Combinado B* consists of a couple of *pupusas* with a choice of fillings, a heavy corn tamale (or properly a *tamal*) stuffed with either shredded pork or chicken and sweet plantains served with sour cream. The first bite combining the plantain with the cream might seem too contrasting, but from the second bite on, the two very different flavors of sweet and sour make for a complementary and pleasing sensation. The other combination plate, *Combinado A*, substitutes fried yucca for the plantains. These are both a fair-sized amount of very good food for only six bucks. Other appetizers and small bites include tacos and *tortas* (sandwiches) with either grilled beef or chicken, the thick tamales, and *empanadas*, interestingly described here as deep-fried plantain puffs stuffed with custard cream.

Many of the main dishes, especially the seafood and plate dishes (*Platos Especiales)* are quite similar to Mexican dishes. Seafood is popular here; El Salvador has a coastline on the Pacific, after all. El Pupusodromo has three marinated seafood cocktails including the popular *Vuelve a la Vida* that features several types of seafood. The seafood platters, under the heading *Mariscos*, feature an entire fried tilapia fish, a more manageable fish fillet, shrimp either grilled, sautéed or battered and fried, a couple of rice dishes one with shrimp, the other with a mixture of seafood, shrimp, fish fillet, crab and mussels, and a combination dish with a fish fillet, grilled shrimp and fried calamari. The seafood platters are each served with rice or fries, a small lettuce salad and thick tortillas that are made in-house. The meat dishes offer the familiar-sounding *Carne Asada* (grilled skirt steak) *Carne Guisada* (stewed beef), *Chuletas de Puerco* (pan-fried pork chops), *Chiles Rellenos* (stuffed peppers, these are bell peppers instead of poblano peppers). There is also *Salpicon,* described as diced beef garnished with mint and onions, *Medio Pollo Encebollado,* half of a chicken fried and served with sautéed onions and sauce. The meat plates are accompanied by rice or refried beans, salad and tortillas. The restaurants are functional, converted old Grandy's or the like, very similar to a *taqueria,* but with a lot of blue paint, the most prominent color of the flag of El Salvador, and a jukebox that actually plays music at non-deafening levels and with some bass. Though the restaurants are clean, and at least slightly assimilated and well run, it helps to speak Spanish, as most of the waitress do not speak much English.

El Rey Taqueria $7

910 Shepherd (at Washington) 77007, (713) 802-9145
3330 Ella (at 34th) 77008, (713) 263-0659
233 Main (at Congress) 77002, (713) 225-1895

Cuisine - Mexican (with a handful of Cuban dishes)
Hours - Mon-Thu, 7AM to 9:30PM; Fri-Sat 7AM to 10PM; Sun 8AM to 4PM
Credit Cards - NONE
Service - Counter Service; Drive Thru
Alcohol - NONE

Entrée Prices - Dinner & Lunch - $6 to $9 ($7 average); Breakfast - $4 to $6
Entrées at Dinner $12 and less - 100%

Atmosphere & Décor - Spartan
Appeal - Generally decent tacos and tortas served via a drive-thru
Useful to Note - The breakfast tacos are small, get more than usual.
Menu Suggestions - Tempura Shrimp Taco; California Torta; Diablo Torta; Torta al Pastor; Chicken Tortilla Soup; rotisserie chicken; Chicken Enchiladas

The original El Rey Taqueria at Washington and Shepherd is one of the few places in Houston that serves pretty good food from a takeout window. At this location there is a decent chance you will get pan-handled while idling, but it's a small price to pay. There is also a small, plain interior with a nearly full view of the Shepherd and Washington intersection, if you choose not to use the drive-thru. The offerings on the slowly expanding menu board are mostly common Mexican items: tacos, *tortas,* burritos, *gorditas,* nachos and stuffed jalapeños. But, there is also a very good chicken tortilla soup that features their moist and flavorful rotisserie chicken, which can also be ordered as a meal, either as a half or whole chicken. If "rotisserie" is in the name, almost every dish featuring chicken is worth ordering. Be warned, though tasty, you are apt to find small pieces of cartilage in these dishes. Another winner is the lightly breaded and deep-fried shrimp tacos served with plenty of shredded lettuce and a complementary white sauce. These are much better with the corn tortillas. Avoid the non-fried version.

Tortas, the Mexican-style sandwiches, are usually also good to order and are probably the biggest sellers here. At around five bucks these are basically a good value, but are somewhat pricey in the warped economic world of *taquerias*. El Rey offers a wide range of choices of these *tortas* served on a decent, though not exemplary, *bolillo* bun. The available fillings include beef fajita, chicken fajita, *Ranchera Fajita* (beef cooked in a tomato sauce), rotisserie chicken, pork, grilled fish, grilled shrimp and *milanesa* (breaded, thin beef steak). There are also some specialty sandwiches such as the Hot Acapulco, *Diablo* and the California that are filled with a variety of other ingredients such as sliced avocados, jalapeños and the like. Some can be quite good, especially the California *Torta.* The Cuban sandwiches, very similar to the *tortas* here, mentioned prominently on the outside walls, are decent, but not as good as the other sandwiches. To help enliven the sandwiches and tacos, El Rey provides a very spicy and flavorful thin green salsa. The red salsa is also very fiery, though maybe a little less flavorful. These are great additions to most sandwiches if you like things on the spicy side. The tacos, available with many of the basic fillings as the sandwiches, are generally quite good. With the exception of the fried shrimp taco, the meats are better than the seafood. For example, the very basic marinated seafood *ceviche* is oddly served in a green salad. The *gorditas* and enchiladas are usually good bets. The menu has a few Cuban and Cuban-inspired dishes including *Ropa Vieja* (stewed shredded beef), rotisserie chicken with white rice and black beans, Cuban-style flan, and the surprisingly tasty Cuban Tacos. These are flour tortillas filled with grilled beef or chicken, black beans and plantains. These are even tastier with some of the decidedly non-Cuban spicy salsas. In the morning, their breakfast tacos, served on fresh flour tortillas, are quite small, but pretty decent, certainly far better than your other drive-thru breakfast taco options. Also in the morning, or possibly in the evening, you can get what the marquee has often advertised as the best coffee in town. The often very bitter espresso-like coffee does not live up to that billing. El Rey is a worthy stop for generally good Mexican dishes. Though not top-notch, most everything is well prepared. Plus, there are not too many other places where you can get decent Mexican food without getting out of your car.

El Tapatio $10

4550 N. Shepherd (just north of Crosstimbers / W. 43rd) 77018, (713) 695-9423

Cuisine - Mexican (taqueria)
Hours - Mon-Thu, Sun 6AM to 12AM; Fri-Sat 6AM to 2AM
Credit Cards - Amex, Discover, MC, Visa
Service - Table Service
Alcohol - Beer

Entrée Prices - Dinner & Lunch - $4 to $17 ($10 average); Breakfast - $4 to $8
Entrées at Dinner $12 and less - 80%

Atmosphere & Décor - Functional
Appeal - A taqueria that is trying harder than most
Menu Suggestions - Shrimp Ceviche; Enchiladas Verdes; grilled shrimp

---

Though its exterior, and its interior for that matter, might not suggest it, El Tapatio is more inviting and accommodating than most area *taquerias*. Though slightly more expensive than most similar establishments, with its large portions, it's still quite a value. Because of its Houston-friendly menu of beef, shrimp, seafood cocktails and hearty Mexican and Tex-Mex dishes served in large portions, it has made itself a welcome stop on busy North Shepherd since the early 1990s for both Anglos and Hispanics alike. As with all *taquerias*, breakfast is a popular meal, and El Tapatio obliges with very inexpensive breakfast tacos and plates in all of the familiar local combinations plus some more. Scrambled eggs are also featured in plates like *huevos con* pancakes, with beef ribs, *barbacoa* (sautéed beef cheeks here) and a tamale.

El Tapatio specializes in beef dishes, which the restaurant is quick to recommend. A key portion of the menu is dedicated to "*bistecks*". The signature El Tapatio is a grilled sirloin steak served with *nopalito* cactus strips. The Fajita Mix is a plentiful mix of fajita, grilled chicken, pork sausage with grilled onions, zesty guacamole, *pico de gallo* and charro beans for well under ten bucks. The fajitas are probably more flavorful than the steaks. Grilled pork and chicken aren't neglected. The *Chuleton*, unique to local menus, is a pork steak served with grilled onions. *Milanesas*, flattened, breaded and pan-fried cutlets, are made with a choice of beef, chicken and pork. This and similar sizzling platters are also available with grilled shrimp that are butterflied and cooked with the shell. These might even be tastier than the fajitas. El Tapatio also serves jumbo shrimp in several other ways: *empanizado* (breaded and deep-fried), *rancheros* (sautéed in a tomato sauce), *a la diabla* (sautéed in a fiery sauce), *a la plancha* (cooked on a flat grill), *al mojo de ajo* (with oil and garlic), *a la veracruzana* (with tomato sauce and pepper, onions, olives), and *al vapor* (steamed). The kitchen does a fine job serving the smaller shrimp, too, and the shrimp cocktail or *ceviche* is a good way to begin a meal here. El Tapatio is noticeably friendly. With a low ceiling and one long dining room, and televisions at either end providing a constant buzz from *telenovelas,* variety shows or *futbol* matches, it's fairly intimate. Décor is *taqueria*-like, but more inviting than most.

El Taquito Rico $5

3701 N. Main (just west of I-45 N.) 77009, (713) 426-4243

Cuisine - Mexican (taqueria)
Hours - Daily 6AM to 6PM
Credit Cards - Amex, Diners, Discover, MC, Visa
Service - Counter Service
Alcohol - NONE

Entrée Prices - Dinner & Lunch - $3 to $8 ($5 average); Breakfast - $3 to $6
Entrées at Dinner $12 and less - 100%

Atmosphere & Décor - Not really
Appeal - Very good, cheap tacos on freshly made flour and corn tortillas
Menu Suggestions - tacos de deshebrada (roasted and shredded beef); tacos de carnitas (stewed pork); tacos al pastor (roasted pork) breakfast tacos

Suitably unimpressive from the street, tiny El Taquito Rico is probably the best of the local taco stands. The usually amiable staff serves plump tacos with top-notch fillings and tortillas. It not only makes its own flour tortillas, which is fairly common at local *taquerias,* but, somewhat uniquely, also makes their corn tortillas. Each is warmed on the grill before assembly, and adds a lot to the quality. The tacos, past breakfast time, are dressed, perfectly complementary, in the traditional Mexican fashion, just chopped raw onions and cilantro. The grill, rotisserie and steam table are put to use here. They might run out the steam table contents, but that's a good thing, as the items do not seem to spend an overly long time there, as at some lesser places. For the breakfast tacos, whose fillings are usually made in some quantity, the bacon is thick and remains crisp. For the afternoon tacos, El Taquito Rico offers most of the near north side neighborhood favorites: fajita, chicken, *pastor* (roasted pork), *deshebrada* (shredded, slowly cooked beef), *chicharron* (pork skin), *barbacoa* (beef cheek), *carnitas* (pork), *lengua* (beef tongue) and *tripas* (pork intestines). It's tough to go wrong, though the roasted chicken can often be too dry and bland. The beef *deshebrada* is excellent, moist and very flavorful. The *carnitas* is prepared in a dry and stringy fashion; good, but different than most local versions. The other pork, the roasted *pastor,* is very good. Most of the tacos don't require it, but the two salsas are excellent: a viscous, fiery and slightly sweet green salsa, and a smoky reddish-orange one. These tacos are not only better here than at most places, but are cheaper, too. The tacos are the big draw, and the best items here, but there are also *tortas, quesadillas* in a couple of sizes, burritos, *gorditas, tostadas* and plates with the same meats. The *tortas* are usually served with avocado slices, but since the bread is not quite as fresh, nor as interesting as the tortillas, these are not quite as good. The *quesadillas* are good, though the larger size (medium here) can get a little doughy with the flour tortillas. *Menudo* is served daily and there are *hamburguesas al carbon estilo mexicana,* which comes with *papas* for under five bucks. The near complete lack of décor and the fact that there is only a half-dozen stools inside and a few forlorn tables outside, make quick consumption or takeaway a necessity here.

Empire Café $9

1732 Westheimer (west of Dunlavy) 77098, (713) 528-5282
www.empirecafe.net

Cuisine - American (with Italian accents)
Hours - Mon-Thu, Sun 7:30AM to 11PM; Fri-Sat 7:30AM to 12AM
Credit Cards - Amex, Diners, Discover, MC, Visa
Service - Counter Service
Alcohol - Full Bar

Entrée Prices - Dinner & Lunch - $6 to $13 ($9 average); Breakfast - $6 to $9
Entrées at Dinner $12 and less - 90%

Atmosphere & Décor - Cool, often lively; large patio
Appeal - Good food with a hip attitude and great people-watching
Useful to Note - It is very popular on weekend mornings.
Menu Suggestions - Focaccia Eggs; Irish Oatmeal; frittatas; cakes; coffee; latte

Empire Café is a both a laid-back, but often bustling, counter-service restaurant on Westheimer west of Montrose that has been serving students, self-styled bohemians, and a great many others since 1994 who want a good and good value meal. Though a big, cosmopolitan city, Houston is lacking in this type of comfortably hip, but worthy, informal restaurant. It is especially popular with many Inner Loopers, including a well-heeled older crowd, and Empire Café works well as a place for a full meal, or just a cup of coffee, a drink, and especially for dessert. Its hipness can sometimes be mistaken for attitude, but it is a friendly enough place. The scene is fairly cool and the patio is often very inviting, but the food is the main reason for the popularity, especially during the morning hours. The menu items are interesting, but unpretentious; basically Italian-inspired during the day, American in the morning. The food is generally well prepared and well presented.

The daytime menu is divided among appetizers, salads, soups, more than a half-dozen pastas, sandwiches on spongy *focaccia* bread, *frittatas* (Italian-style egg dishes), omelets, pizzas, and heartier entrées. Appetizers include *caponata* (a spread featuring eggplants and squash) with *focaccia* bread, stuffed mushrooms, phyllo pastry stuffed with spinach, cheese and onions, a medley of dips served with pita chips, and grilled chicken strips. With the exception of the largest pizzas, most of the dishes are around eight bucks. Pizzas with thick, doughy crusts are available with either the standard white flour or the whole-wheat crust in the individually sized 8″ and 12″ sizes. Called *panini,* the sandwiches are served on somewhat-fragrant *focaccia* bread. There are ones featuring roasted eggplant, chicken, turkey breast and Portobello mushrooms. Entrées include Chicken Parmesan, Chicken Florentine (chicken breast with spinach), a roasted half chicken, Chicken Parmesan, a braised pork chop, and grilled vegetables. Not really representative of these places, the pastas are mostly named after towns and cities in Italy plus the island of Corsica that was once part of greater Italy. But nicely, these are served with a small green salad or a cup of soup. If you need a cholesterol fix, both types of the egg-based dishes, the *frittatas* and omelets, are made with four eggs. Both are served throughout the day with herb-roasted potatoes plus another side dish which changes daily. All of the Italian espresso-based coffee drinks are offered plus a few drip coffees. Suitably, and conducive to continued lingering after the breakfast is finished, the house blend drip coffee is robust and very flavorful. In the morning, in addition to the omelets and *frittatas,* Empire Café serves most of the breakfast staples, tempered with some flair. These justifiably pack the place on weekend mornings. Their homemade desserts are also very popular, and some customers seem to visit just for these. The assorted and mostly tempting cakes and pies are usually served as a generous slice. If anything else, Empire Café is a great choice for dessert and a coffee at night.

Empire Turkish Grill $13

12448 Memorial (between Gessner and the Beltway) 77024, (713) 827-7475
www.theempireturkishgrill.com

Cuisine - Turkish
Hours - Daily 11AM to 11PM
Credit Cards - Amex, Diners, Discover, MC, Visa
Service - Table Service; delivery nearby
Alcohol - Beer & Wine

Entrée Prices - Dinner - $9 to $21 ($13 average); Lunch - $8
Entrées at Dinner $12 and less - 50%

Atmosphere & Décor - Pleasant
Appeal - Tasty Turkish food in pleasant surroundings
Useful to Note - Lunchtime specials provide a good introduction to the cuisine.

Menu Suggestions - Adana Kebab (ground beef kabob); Tavuk Adana (ground chicken kabob); Sis Kebab (lamb kabob); Doner Kebab (thin slices of grilled lamb)

Empire Turkish Café has been a welcome addition to the west Memorial dining scene. This is a friendly and inviting place, and a nice restaurant with white linen tablecloths that serves an interesting cuisine and does it very well. The Turkish cooking highlighted at Empire features straightforward grilled meats and contrastingly, zesty cold appetizers. There are a number of different grilled entrées with chicken, beef, and lamb prepared in various ways. It is tough to go wrong with one of these grilled items. All of the meat served here is *halal*, and that ensures a certain level of quality. The *Tavuk Kebab* (char-grilled cubes of marinated chicken) and the *Tavuk Adana* (kabob with ground chicken) shows that chicken can still be interesting. The similar preparations with beef are very good, also. The traditional *Sis Kebab* (or shish kabob) with char-grilled cubes of marinated lamb, and the *Doner Kebab* (thin slices of grilled lamb) are equally well prepared. If you find it difficult to choose among chicken, beef and lamb, there are nearly a dozen dishes with two or more of the meats. These are served with rice and grilled vegetables. Fitting complements to the meats hot off the grill can be one of the cold vegetable appetizers. There are the familiar items served all over the Middle East, *hummus, tabouli,* and *baba ganoush,* plus some enticing, more unique Turkish dishes. Some of these are fried eggplant with tomato, peppers and yogurt, *cacik,* diced cucumber in yogurt with garlic, and artichoke hearts with vegetables with olive oil and lemon. The two lunch specials help provide a fine and inexpensive introduction to the restaurant, both for around eight bucks. One offers a choice between a salad and lentil soup, and choice among four kabobs or stuffed cabbage, and a soda or coffee, which could be Turkish coffee. The second is vegetarian with a choice of two cold vegetable dishes instead of the meat, and the soup or salad. For those nearby, delivery is also an option, which is unusual for a restaurant this nice, but it gives an indication that Empire is trying hard to please its customers.

Emporio $13

12288 Westheimer (between Kirkwood and Dairy Ashford) 77077, (281) 293-7442
www.brazilian-cafe.com

Cuisine - Brazilian
Hours - Mon 11AM to 4PM; Tue-Thu 11AM to 4PM, 5 to 9PM; Fri-Sat 11AM to 4PM, 5 to 11PM; Sun 12 to 6PM
Credit Cards - Amex, Diners, Discover, MC, Visa
Service - Table Service
Alcohol - Beer & Wine; BYOB

Entrée Prices - Dinner - $9 to $16 ($13 average); Lunch - $7 to $14
Entrées at Dinner $12 and less - 30%

Atmosphere & Décor - Pleasant
Appeal - Well prepared Brazilian food on the west side
Useful to Note - This is not a churrascaria.
Menu Suggestions - Chicken Sandwich; Shrimp Risotto; Feijoada (Brazilian bean stew with black beans, bacon, pork sausage, cured beef, and pork ribs); coconut flan

There is more to Brazilian cuisine than the showy *churrascarias,* which focus on the bountiful ranch cooking of southern Brazil, where patrons eat grilled steaks and other meats to excess. Emporio is a quiet, small restaurant tucked into a shopping center on the western expanse of Westheimer that serves the more basic, and homestyle bill of fare of less meat-abundant Brazil. Several of the dishes are denoted to be from Bahia, the more tropical, more African-influenced portion of the country. Though the Portuguese-named dishes might be unusual for many, the straightforward flavors and several of the dishes will be quite familiar. Most of the patrons seem to be Brazilian, which is a testament to some level of authenticity. The American headquarters of Petrobas, the Brazilian state oil company, is just a mile or so down the road, and you're likely to see their yellow and green of the badges among fellow patrons, at least during lunchtime.

The menu has a manageable number of dishes, though this has been expanded over the years to include more seafood and beef dishes. Many items will be familiar. There are number of small appetizers such as Brazilian versions of chicken pot pie (*empadinha de frango*), shrimp pot pie (*empadinha de camarao*), chicken croquette, and puff pastries (*pastels*) with shrimp, meat, cheese or even salt cod, which are an inexpensive way to start a meal. Plus there are fried yucca, fried Brazilian sausage (*linguica frita*), and fried chicken for a little more. Sandwiches make for a popular lunch for around seven bucks, and a little more with a cup of soup. The sandwiches use a crusty small baguette, lettuce, tomato slices, and tart mustard, with steak, chicken or shrimp. The steak is not the highest quality, but it makes for a satisfying enough sandwich. The thin, crisp fries are a fitting accompaniment for the sandwiches. There are soup and sandwich combinations with the soup of the day, which could be a hearty potato and mushroom. Soup and salad is another lunchtime pairing. The salads include the ubiquitous Caesar, Caesar with seasoned shrimp, one featuring hearts of palm, and another with grilled sliced chicken breast on top of vegetables. The entrées, or "Daily Specials" and "House Daily Specials" include a number of more interesting dishes. These include baked fillet of salmon, fish stew (*peixada*), sautéed chicken breast with onions and garlic,

Beef Stroganoff, *feijoada* (the hearty bean-based stew that is the national dish of Brazil), two steak offerings, and *bacalhua* (salt cod that is shredded and sautéed in olive oil with garlic, onions and more). There are also a couple rice-based dishes, called risottos here. These rice dishes can be decent, but are not risottos in the Italian sense of the dish, which feature slowly cooked thick grain rice, but are probably more similar to jambalayas. The shrimp in the shrimp version can be quite small and doesn't add as much to the dish as these should, though. With the exception of the *bacalhua,* all of the entrées are under fifteen dollars. Emporio is a pleasant stop for lunch, especially if you are not in a rush. Dishes are cooked to order, and service can be South American in tempo (i.e. a little slow), but this is a friendly, comfortable place, even with the concrete floors. The complementary puffy cheese bread can be addictive when waiting for the meal. Just a lunchtime destination for many, Emporio is open for dinner on Thursday through Saturday when you are encouraged to bring your own beer or wine.

Erawan $12

5161 San Felipe (at Sage) 77056, (713) 961-5161

Cuisine - Thai
Hours - Mon-Sat 11AM to 3PM; 5 to 9:30PM
Credit Cards - Discover, MC, Visa
Service - Table Service
Alcohol - Beer & Wine; BYOB

Entrée Prices - Dinner - $8 to $17 ($12 average); Lunch - $7 to $10
Entrées at Dinner $12 and less - 60%

Atmosphere & Décor - Pleasant
Appeal - Tasty Thai in a quaint setting on Richmond near Gessner
Menu Suggestions - Panaeng with Chicken; Panaeng with Beef; Vegetable Curry; Thai Ginger with Chicken (stir-fried ginger and vegetables with a choice of meats); Green Curry with Chicken

In its second location in fairly nice digs on San Felipe near well-heeled neighborhoods and Galleria-area office towers, Erawan aims to satisfy these constituents with pleasant and recognizable Thai food in a comfortable setting. And, the meals are satisfying here, and done so in proper fashion: ingredients are fresh; the items taste as they should, and without any MSG; prices are fair; décor is nice; and service is solicitous. One drawback is that the spicing is usually toned down, but that can probably be easily remedied with the kitchen. The relatively small menu, with English names for many of the items, is divided among appetizers, soups, salads, noodle dishes, fried rice dishes, vegetarian items, entrées (served with the soup of the day and steamed jasmine rice), and the House Specials. Erawan serves most of the local Thai favorites with a steady-enough hand: soft spring rolls, *satays, tom ka gai* (chicken soup with coconut milk and kaffir lime), Pad Thai, red curry, green curry, yellow curry, *Panaeng*, Pineapple Fried Rice, and Tiger Cried (charcoal-grilled steak with a chili sauce). Each of the noodle dishes and entrées are served with a choice of chicken, beef, pork, or shrimp. The *Panaeng* dishes, with a viscous, flavorful brown sauce and strips of peeled red pepper and crisp green beans, are quite good. The curries, red, green and yellow are also satisfying, as is the Thai Ginger, which is stir-fried ginger, vegetables and a choice of meat. Lunchtime is a good time to visit with nearly a dozen different entrées that are served with fried spring rolls and a cup of the soup of the day for only eight bucks or so. Though a limited selection of beer and wine is offered, BYOB is encouraged with a small $5 corkage fee per bottle or six-pack.

Fadi's Mediterranean Grill $9

8383 Westheimer (at Dunvale) 77063, (713) 532-0666
4738 Beechnut (just west of Loop 610) 77096, (713) 666-4644
www.fadiscuisine.com

Cuisine - Middle Eastern
Hours - Mon-Thu 11AM to 10PM; Fri-Sat 11AM to 11PM; Sun 12 to 8PM
Credit Cards - Amex, Discover, MC, Visa
Service - Counter Service
Alcohol - NONE

Entrée Prices - Dinner - $8 to $12 ($9 average); Lunch - $7 to $10
Entrées at Dinner $12 and less - 100%

Atmosphere & Décor - Comfortable
Appeal - Generous servings of flavorful Middle Eastern food at low prices
Menu Suggestions - baba ganoush; hummus; Lamb Shank; baked chicken

With customers moving through a cafeteria-like procession to create a meal from an array of appetizing Middle Eastern foods from across a counter, Fadi's Mediterranean Grill is somewhat similar in concept to Dimassi's. That should not be a surprise, since the proprietor and namesake is Fadi Dimassi. He has certainly done nothing to diminish the family name, and Fadi's is actually probably the best of the user-friendly local Middle Eastern cafeteria-style restaurants. The original location on Westheimer in west Houston opened in 1996. Tucked into a strip center near Dunvale, it's a nice place, though often hectic during the lunch hours. The food is always fresh, usually very tasty, and healthier than most of our typical meals. With the right cuisine, ingredients and cooking techniques, it's true that you don't have to sacrifice flavor to eat healthy with cooking that features olive oil, whole grains, fresh vegetables and grilled meats. No butter lard or margarine, nor even dairy, is used in Fadi's cooking. The servings here are good-sized. This generosity with the serving is notably impressive because the combination platters are served on such large plates. Most meals manage to fill much of the substantial dishware. No effort is made to hide small portions on small plates at Fadi's.

With all of the freshly prepared items on display in front of you while in line, the best option is one of the bountiful combination platters which run between nine and twelve dollars during dinnertime, and cheaper at lunch. These include a Vegetarian Sampler, the Special with a choice among one salad, one vegetable, rice and a meat entrée, and the Ultimate Sampler with an entrée and a sample portion of all of the dips, salads and vegetables. The offerings change often at Fadi's because they aim to use only the freshest ingredients. The sides can include a number of things, salads, appetizers, and vegetables and vegetarian dips: a yogurt cucumber salad, *tabouli* (cracked wheat, tomato, cucumber, mint, lemon and olive oil), a Greek salad, *fatoosh* (lettuce, cucumber, tomatoes, parsley, mint and pita) an eggplant salad, *hummus, baba ganoush, kibbe* balls, stuffed grape leaves, okra, mashed potatoes, potatoes sautéed with tomatoes, squash, cauliflower, eggplant with *tahini* sauce, and green beans. These feature kabobs, a lamb shank, fish fillets, and *shawarma*s, and include a salad, rice, an appetizer, and pita bread. If you don't have the appetite for a large plate of food, you can also order well crafted sandwiches like *shawarma*s, *falafel,* or others with chicken, a choice of kabobs and Lebanese sausages. If you do have a big appetite or just need something sweet to finish the meal, there is a selection of a dozen Middle Eastern pastries. Notably, these and the breads are freshly baked in brick ovens in the restaurants. Though the line in front of the buffet choices during peak hours might seem intimidating to those not familiar with Middle Eastern foods, the staff is friendly and does a nice job of explaining the dishes if you need help.

Fiesta en Guadalajara $11

3522 Irvington (between Fulton and Patton) 77009, (713) 227-1800

Cuisine - Mexican
Hours - Mon-Wed 11AM to 10:30PM; Thu 11AM to 12AM; Fri-Sat 11AM to 2:30AM; Sun 11AM to 12AM
Credit Cards - Amex, Diners, Discover, MC, Visa
Service - Table Service
Alcohol - Full Bar

Entrée Prices - Dinner - $8 to $19 ($11 average); Lunch - $6 to $9
Entrées at Dinner $12 and less - 80%

Atmosphere & Décor - Comfortable, lively
Appeal - Good Mexican food in a festive environment
Menu Suggestions - Camarón Brocheta; Jalapos (shrimp stuffed with a jalapeño and cheese, marinated, breaded then deep-fried); Tampiqueña; fajitas; Mole Enchiladas; Enchiladas Verdes

---

Fiesta en Guadalajara is one of the most fun and most aptly named restaurants in the city. Nearly every night, especially on the weekends, it does seem like a fiesta, if not in Guadalajara, at least somewhere in Mexico. Though it is very popular with its neighbors in the near north side, it is somewhat neglected by folks from other areas. This is a shame, because Fiesta en Guadalajara is always a very enjoyable and interesting stop for anyone with even a passing interest in Mexican food. The restaurant offers more than just a meal. Mariachi bands play every night, and a second band wielding guitars, keyboards and amplifiers plays at fairly high volume on Friday and Saturday nights in the other half of the restaurant. Peddlers might be moving from table to table trying to sell flowers, cheap gifts, and the like. There might even be a clown entertaining the children among the breaks in the meal. Because of this atmosphere, and some often very good food, Fiesta en Guadalajara is packed on weekend nights. In the large parking lot, which is in view of the skyscrapers a couple miles to the south, it can be tough to find a space during Friday and Saturday nights.

The large, rambling menu at Fiesta en Guadalajara has continued to evolve in recent years and probably now appeals to a larger audience than ever before. It lists over fifty Mexican and Tex-Mex plates. Though the entrées are hearty, there are several interesting appetizers that will work as starters, or for sustenance with the after work drinks. There are well prepared nachos, *quesadillas,* a couple *queso flameado* preparations, and two more unusual, but appealing dishes. The *Jalapos* are large jumbo shrimp stuffed with jalapeño slices and cheese, marinated, then breaded and deep-fried. Another great companion for cold beer is the Papa Nachos, a choice of beef or chicken fajitas served over slices of deep-fried potatoes that are covered with gravy and cheeses. For entrées, there are fajitas, Mexican-style steaks, chicken breast dishes, quail, tacos, shrimp preparations, a number of different enchiladas, *flautas, gorditas,* pork chops, and several mixed grills, and Tex-Mex-style combination plates. The star of the entrées is the *Camarón Brocheta,* four jumbo shrimp that have each been stuffed with Monterey Jack cheese and a jalapeño slice, wrapped in an impossibly long slice of bacon and then cooked. It is one of the best shrimp dishes in the city. Unfortunately, the several other entrées featuring shrimp have not been nearly as successful in the past. The steak dishes can be very good, fitting for a city that loves beef. The *Tampiqueña,* especially, can be excellent. It is an 8-ounce cut of fajita steak that has been marinated, then grilled. It comes with a cheese enchilada, plus rice, beans and guacamole and *pico de gallo,* which accompany all of the steak dishes. The Carne Asada is a 10-ounce skirt steak that has been grilled then covered with Monterey Jack cheese. There is also a 12-ounce T-Bone that is broiled and topped with a choice of sauces. The enchiladas are generally quite good, especially the *Enchiladas Verdes* and the *Enchiladas Mexicanas.* The *mole* dishes, enchiladas and one with a chicken quarter, can be good, but have been inconsistent. Sometimes the dark brown *mole poblano* is balanced and quite flavorful, other times it is too sweet and lacking the expected complexity. For the biggest appetites, there are a couple of mixed grill platters, *parrillas,* for two or four people. These generous orders can include beef, chicken, quail, bacon, poblano peppers, and shrimp.

The restaurant is divided into two wings and has a stated capacity of 220. The wing to the left of the entrance is where the bar is located and has a couple of dining rooms. The area to the right of the entrance is the larger dining room, and is more popular with Hispanic families. This one is generally more spacious and comfortable than the other wing, but it can get very loud, rather than just loud, like on the other side, when a band is playing on the small stage in this room at night. Also, the waitstaff is more likely to speak only Spanish on this side. Wherever you sit, the food will be good and the atmosphere lively. There is also a small patio by the entrance that is a nice place to sit during those temperate evenings. Drinks, especially the margaritas, are usually a part of the dining experience at Fiesta en Guadalajara. Given its proximity to downtown and that it is an especially great value during happy hour, the restaurant is a first stopping point for some attorneys and other office workers who have cut the work day short. Their basic frozen margarita is surprisingly good, better than what you usually find, and quite inexpensive. And, unless specified otherwise, the margarita is served in a good-sized goblet making it a great value. These are easy to drink, and whose volume will help lead you into a more festive mood in case you have not already picked up that vibe, which pulsates throughout the restaurant most evenings.

Fiesta Loma Linda $8

2111 Telephone (east of I-45 S.) 77023, (713) 924-6074

Cuisine - Tex-Mex
Hours - Sun - Thu 10AM to 10PM; Fri-Sat 10AM to 11PM
Credit Cards - Amex, Diners, Discover, MC, Visa
Service - Table Service
Alcohol - Full Bar

Entrée Prices - Dinner - $4 to $19 ($8 avg.); Lunch - $6 to $8; Breakfast - $5 to $6

Entrées at Dinner $12 and less - 90%

Atmosphere & Décor - Pleasant
Appeal - Solid Tex-Mex from a long-time neighborhood restaurant
Menu Suggestions - Enchiladas Suizas; Alambres (beef or chicken shish kabobs); Deluxe Dinner (guacamole salad, chile con queso, beef taco, cheese enchilada, tamale, rice and refried beans)

Fiesta Loma Linda is a long time neighborhood favorite located close to the main campus of the University of Houston. Located on Telephone Road east of I-45, the proprietors have been serving the east side for roughly forty years. The nearby residents and students keep coming back to enjoy the satisfying and good-value Tex-Mex and Mexican fare. Blending easily into an area dotted with industrial buildings, Fiesta Loma Linda resides in a functional building. The setting and décor is similarly functional with formica-topped tables, vinyl-covered tall booths and kitchy folk art, but, it's often filled with lively large groups and families. The draw is that the food is generally good, freshly prepared and reasonably priced. As with most area Tex-Mex restaurants, you will undoubtedly leave with an increased waist size, but with the size of the wallet pretty much intact.

The food is more familiar and comfortable for local diners rather than trendy or innovative. Though it might not be the most exciting Mexican food around, it can be pleasantly surprising, and usually quite satisfying. Fiesta Loma Linda does well serving versions of the locally popular dishes like fajitas, enchiladas, Tex-Mex-style *quesadillas*, etc. A telling sign is that the complementary chips are always fresh, and the table sauces are above average. Though not initially compelling, the red salsa has a nice, long, spicy taste, and is certainly better than it looks. The green salsa is flavorful, slighly sweet and almost refreshing. The appetizers feature nachos with several different toppings. There is also *chile con queso* and the real cheese, *Queso Flameado* made with melted Monterey Jack with green onions and a choice of sausage, or grilled beef or chicken. Soups include *Caldo de Res* (a beef broth and vegetable soup), chicken soup and *menudo* on Friday and the weekends. Most of these are available as an appetizer or full meal. As with most Houston area Mexican restaurants, enchiladas dishes play a prominent role on the menu. There are the basic Tex-Mex versions with chicken, beef, and fajitas with either grilled beef or chicken. Fiesta Loma Linda's *Enchiladas Suizas* with a slightly sweet tomatillo-based green sauce and topped with sour cream is good, as are their enchiladas topped with a satisfying, but not terribly interesting, dark brown *mole poblano* sauce. Listed along with the enchiladas are the deep-fried *flautas* and *chimichanga,* plus the old-line Tex-Mex favorite, tamales with chile gravy. Other long-time popular menu items include the several combination dinners featuring tacos, enchiladas, *chalupas, chile con queso,* guacamole salad, and a taco salad. As an added touch, the salads come with a choice among housemade dressings like "Kickin' *Chipotle*" and "Sweet Poppyseed". The fajitas, and similar grilled items like the pre-assembled version, *Tacos al Carbon,* and the *Alambres* (a beef or chicken shish kabob), are popular and often leave an appetizing aroma in the air. Other dinners include platters with more Mexican-style *quesadillas* (though made with flour tortillas), the stewed beef *Carne Asada, Chile Relleno,* the interesting *Chile Dulce* (bell peppers with seasoned ground beef, raisins, rice and chopped pecans), and several chicken breast preparations. A couple of additional reasons to visit are the lunch specials during the week that includes the chance to save a couple of dollars on tacos al carbon, and breakfast is served on weekend mornings.

Fiesta Tacos $6

4620 W. 34th (at Mangum) 77092, (713) 686-6927

Cuisine - Tex-Mex
Hours - Mon-Fri 6AM to 3PM; Sat 7AM to 2PM; Sun 7:30AM to 2PM
Credit Cards - Discover, MC, Visa
Alcohol - NONE
Service - Counter Service

Entrée Prices - $4 to $9 ($6 average)
Entrées $12 and less - 100%

Atmosphere & Décor - Not much, but friendly and comfortable
Appeal - Enjoyable Tex-Mex for cheap
Menu Suggestions - Fiesta Mexicana Plate (2 cheese enchiladas topped with ranchero sauce, 2 crispy ground beef tacos refried beans, guacamole); Chicken Enchiladas; Tamale Plate (3 tamales topped with beef & cheese); breakfast tacos

A visit to this very friendly, very informal and welcoming neighborhood breakfast and lunch place ensures a satisfying Tex-Mex meal for a pittance. Importantly, the kitchen is very consistent, the portions are large, the orders are quickly turned around, but there is more. Fiesta aptly cooks all of the Tex-Mex favorites, often topped with plenty of shredded cheddar cheese: nachos, *chile con queso,* tacos, crispy tacos, burritos, tamales, *tostadas, flautas,* fajitas, enchiladas and plenty of combination plates. The nearly requisite red salsa that's brought to your table with the chips is flavorful with an inevitable chile bite, much better than most. Sturdy, homemade flour tortillas add to the taste of most of the dishes. Tamales are made in-house, as is the *chorizo,* which is rather unusual, especially for a modest place. The large enchiladas, especially those filled with the seasoned ground beef or shredded chicken, are very good. The big draw early is the bounteous breakfast tacos, which are made to order. Breakfast tacos, eggs in a dozen combinations and plates such as *huevos rancheros* and *chilaquiles* are served early and throughout the afternoon, until close at 3PM. There are also Super Tacos, both with breakfast and lunch items, which consists of a stuffed sturdy 8-inch flour tortilla. These are in the one's a meal category. In addition to the expected items, there are a number of extras that are not typically found on the suburban Tex-Mex palaces. There are tacos filled with *tripas* (beef tripe), *lengua* (beef tongue) and *barbacoa,* and *menudo* and the hearty *caldos* are served daily.

Fonda Doña Maria $10

120 Tidwell (between Airline and Bauman) 77022, (713) 695-5540

Cuisine - Mexican
Hours - Mon-Thu, Sun 8AM to 3AM; Fri-Sat 8AM to 4AM
Credit Cards - Amex, Discover, MC, Visa
Service - Table Service
Alcohol - Full Bar

Entrée Prices - $6 to $17 ($10 average)
Entrées $12 and less - 90%

Atmosphere & Décor - Pleasant
Appeal - Good quality Mexican food open most of the time
Useful to Note - Some Spanish language ability is helpful.
Menu Suggestions - Enchiladas Suizas; Fajita Enchiladas; Entomatada de Queso (a type of enchilada filled with white unmelted cheese); Bisteck a la Mexicana (steak sautéed with tomato, onions and jalapeños); alambres (beef kabobs)

What began as a very humble place years ago, Fonda Doña Maria is now nicer than most local Mexican restaurants. It is festooned with attractive tile, bright yellow walls, large jars filled with *aguas frescas,* Mexican pottery and knick-knacks. It has a more authentic feel than most area Mexican restaurants, and certainly all Tex-Mex palaces. This is reinforced by the fact that the staff and nearly all of the patrons are chatting solely in Spanish. Open until very early in the morning, Fonda Doña Maria might be nearly deserted at 8:30PM, but then crowded a couple hours later. The offerings are geared toward their primarily Mexican clientele who pack the place at these later hours, so there is not much in the way of Tex-Mex at Fonda Doña Maria. But, don't worry, there are margaritas and chips and salsa. The chips are plentiful, and fiery green salsa is a better bet than the usually bland watery red salsa. The menu sports *gorditas,* the shaped corn *masa* carriages *huaraches* and *sopes,* enchiladas, *almabres* (grilled kabobs), steaks, and an entire page of seafood dishes. The owner is from Guadalajara, and so several dishes from that region are offered, including the interesting beef that is cooked in its own sauce (*Carne en su Sugo*). You can point on the menu to order, but a minimal amount of Spanish is helpful, as most of the waitstaff does not seem to speak English. The enchiladas, in several guises, are done well here. Most of these are much more like the more traditional *entomatadas,* which is also an explicit menu item. One concession to Tex-Mex, the fajita enchiladas, is very good. It is a gooey cheddar cheese-laden mess filled with moist and tender pieces of flavorful beef. The steaks and beef *alambres* are also some of the better items. Guadalajara, situated away from the coast, is beef country. Breakfast is served daily, which is good to know if you are on or near the north side. It is not too far from I-45 North. Something of debatable interest, though more authentic than most, the restaurant's jukebox actually has some discernible bass.

Fountain View Café $7

1842 Fountain View (south of San Felipe) 77057, (713) 785-7060

Cuisine - Diner
Hours - Mon-Fri 7AM to 3PM; Sat-Sun 8AM to 3PM
Credit Cards - MC, Visa
Service - Counter Service
Alcohol - NONE

Entrée Prices - Lunch - $3 to $8 ($8 average); Breakfast - $4 to $11
Entrées at Lunch $12 and less - 100%

Atmosphere & Décor - Pleasant, especially for a diner
Appeal - Well prepared breakfasts near Tanglewood
Menu Suggestions - French toast; waffles; bacon; hash browns; Pastrami Melt sandwich

The Fountain View Café serves a near-necessary function for residents of the well-heeled Galleria neighborhoods: well-run diner food in a nice setting. That the dining room, heavy with dark wood, is usually nearly full of regulars attests to the fact that the Fountain View Café is serving its purpose well. It provides good diner-style breakfasts and basic lunches in a very pleasant, but informal environment. The menu covers the expected basics for breakfast: eggs, omelets, pancakes, French toast, bagels, biscuits and gravy, cereal; and for the health-conscious, oatmeal, fresh fruit, and yogurt. The former are served in very tasty fashion, but without quite the sheen of grease that less refined diners would usually have. As an added bonus, in fine diner fashion, breakfast is served from morning through the afternoon hours each day. Lunches are of the basic soup, salad, sandwich and one-third pound hamburger variety; most done in satisfying fashion. The menu is fairly large and there are many choices. For sandwiches the choices include a decent pastrami melt, peanut and butter, and even a bacon and egg sandwich. There are also daily specials that are available on a rotating monthly basis. These consist of an entrée, with sides and a couple soups during the week, and an egg dish on Saturday and Sunday. The specials during the week include many hearty regional favorites such as chicken fried steak, smothered pork chops, red beans and rice, chicken jambalaya, fried catfish, chicken and dumplings, and smothered steak. To note, orders are placed with the cashier at the counter, you take a ticket, find a table, and soon afterwards a friendly server delivers your food.

Fountainview Fish Market $6

2912 Fountain View (a block south of Westheimer) 77057, (713) 977-1436

Cuisine - Seafood
Hours - Mon-Sat 11AM to 7PM
Credit Cards - Amex, Discover, MC, Visa
Service - Counter Service
Alcohol - NONE

Entrée Prices - $4 to $8 ($6 average)
Entrées $12 and less - 100%

Atmosphere & Décor - Very Spartan
Appeal - Fresh fried seafood in a friendly, neighborhood fish market
Useful to Note - It can get packed during peak lunch hours.
Menu Suggestions - Shrimp Sandwich; Crab Meat Sandwich; Combination Plate (3 deep-fried pieces of fish, 3 shrimp, 3 oysters)

The Fountainview Fish Market is just that: a fish market located in a small strip center on Fountain View (both spellings of the street seem to work). It's a fish market that doubles as a small, unpretentious and laudable restaurant that serves an array of fried seafood such as shrimp, oysters, cod and catfish. It's all deep-fried here. The differences between this one and most fried food specialists are that frying is done with a noticeably lighter touch, the dishes are cooked to order, and, most importantly, as a fish market, the fish is generally fresher and of better quality. And, a great value. This is a friendly, family-owned and -operated venture. The father might be in the area behind the counter cleaning fish or assembling fresh seafood orders while the mother operates the dual fryer that is almost next to the cash register. There is neither much to hide nor much room to hide it in at this small-scale operation. The spartan, but clean, dining area in front of the seafood counter and cashier's stand consists of about a half-dozen tables. There is room for just under twenty people among the seven or so tables in its single, small dining room. The place fills up quickly during lunchtime with a diverse group of office workers and nearby residents who want to indulge in well prepared and freshly fried seafood. Each of the tables is replete with ketchup and tartar sauce in plastic squeeze bottles plus bottled Louisiana hot sauce. As the tables are often apt to be filled, takeout is a popular option. Fountianview Fish Market serves sandwiches and plates. Sandwiches are made with cod, oysters, crab meat and shrimp. The great value daily shrimp sandwich special consists of a few fried shrimp and a couple of fried onion rings between small hamburger buns with lettuce, tomato and tartar sauce plus an order of pretty decent fries. The similar crab meat sandwich features noticeable pieces of blue crab. Though these are tasty, big appetites will need to order two of these sandwiches plus a side. Plates come with shrimp, oyster, cod fillets, egg rolls and combinations thereof, plus a choice of two sides among fries, onion rings and cole slaw. The portions are small, but the prices are low. The most expensive plate is one with three pieces each of fish, oysters and shrimp, plus two sides, all for less than eight bucks. In addition to the popularity of its ready-to-eat foods, Fountainview Fish Market works well as a neighborhood fish purveyor. The fresh seafood display is well stocked. Among the choices on ice that day might be red snapper, redfish, flounder, speckled trout, catfish, shrimp of several sizes, lobster tail, frog legs, scallops, salmon, ocean perch, crab meat, and even soft shell crabs, Dungeness crabs, King crab legs and seafood gumbo.

Frank's Grill $6

1915 Mangum (between Hempstead Highway and 290) 77092, (713) 682-8221
4702 Telephone (just south of 610, near Gulfgate Mall) 77087, (713) 649-3296
5901 Clinton Drive (between Lockwood and Wayside) 77020, (713) 674-4571

Cuisine - Diner
Hours - Telephone - Mon-Sat 5AM to 3PM; Sun 7AM to 3PM; Other Locations - Mon-Sat 5:30AM to 3PM; Sun 7AM to 3PM
Credit Cards - NONE
Service - Table Service
Alcohol - NONE

Entrée Prices - Lunch - $4 to $8 ($6 average); Breakfast - $3 to $8
Entrées at Lunch $12 and less - 100%

Atmosphere & Décor - Kind of dumpy
Appeal - A more-than proficient greasy spoon with very good breakfasts
Menu Suggestions - eggs dishes; breakfast tacos; Belgian waffle; omelets; chicken fried steak

Situated on Mangum across from the gray Delmar Stadium complex, one location of Frank's Grill occupies the site of a former fast food restaurant. It doesn't look like much from the outside, nor does it look like much once entering. But, it has a mostly open kitchen turning out very good and better-than-expected meals to a usually crowded dining room. Frank's Grills are very proficient greasy spoons that serve high quality diner-style food very quickly, and usually with a smile. With the low prices and all-American fare, yet very humble setting, it's the type of the place, you will readily expect to see a parked patrol car in the parking and both police and thieves enjoying the food (well, maybe, not the latter).

Opened early in the morning, and closed by mid-afternoon, breakfast is the main draw for most folks here. Cooking across from a counter filled with patrons at the Mangum Frank's, the kitchen staff wears shirts proclaiming that Frank's has the best breakfast in Texas. Maybe not, but it sure is good at Frank's. The breakfast offerings here are the basic American diner breakfast items. The only concesion to the region are the biscuits and gravy with biscuits made on-site. (The S.O.S. on the menu is actually the biscuits and sausage-inflected gravy). There are egg combinations, omelets, pancakes, waffles, French toast, bacon, sausage patties, oatmeal and cold cereal. That is pretty much it. But, if you like the type of breakfasts that help make this country great, this a place for you. The egg breakfasts are probably the most satisfying dishes at Frank's. The eggs are large and perfectly cooked in several styles. The accompaniments are far better than what can be expected. The Steak & Eggs meal features a six-ounce sirloin that is actually tender and tasty. Other egg dishes, each of which includes two large eggs cooked to your order, includes ones with chopped steak, two pork chops, a hamburger patty, and chicken fried steak, plus ones with the usual bacon, sausage patties and ham sides. It is all done well at Frank's. A side of toast will be buttered for you. The bacon slices are thick, generous and not dried out, a problem that plagues some other local diners. The coffee will be promptly and regularly refilled with more of the piping hot liquid. An order of hash browns will give you a large amount of tasty potatoes that might be closer in consistency to mashed potatoes than the familiar crispy version at other places. But, no matter, these will still be satisfying. The omelets are large and fluffy. The pancakes are good, lighter than usual. The Belgian Waffles are popular. Even the plump breakfast tacos with flour tortillas are very good, too. It's difficult to go wrong at Frank's for breakfast.

The lunch items include hot and cold sandwiches, burgers, salads, and heartier items. The burgers are of the basic variety cooked on the grill, fitted with mayonaise, lettuce, tomatoes, onions, and pickles on toasted buns, and usually satisfying. A cheeseburger and fries will set you back only four bucks. For a big appetite there is the Frank's Burger that has a two-third pound patty topped with American cheese for a little more. The sandwiches are mostly cold, like a BLT, several types of the club sandwich, and a ham and cheese. There are grilled cheese sandwiches, patty melt, grilled chicken, and a tasty chicken fried steak and chicken sandwiches. The plate lunches include a six-ounce sirloin steak, chicken fried steak, Frank's Chopped Steak (a one-pound patty smothered with grilled onions and a brown gravy), fried chicken, pork chops, liver and onions, and battered then deep-fried catfish. The plates come "a la carte" with a choice of mashed potatoes or fries, plus fresh rolls or biscuits. The "Dinner" also includes a green salad or tomato juice and the vegetable of the day. These are quite a value, under ten dollars for the "Dinner" versions.

Fratelli's $13

10989 Northwest Freeway (on west side of 290, south of 34th) 77092, (713) 957-1150
www.fratellishouston.com

Cuisine - Italian
Hours - Mon-Fri 11AM to 12:30PM, 5 to 9:30PM; Sat 5 to 10PM
Credit Cards - Amex, Discover, MC, Visa
Service - Table Service
Alcohol - Full Bar

Entrée Prices - Dinner - $9 to $22 ($13 average); Lunch - $6 to $14
Entrées at Dinner $12 and less - 50%

Atmosphere & Décor - Comfortable
Appeal - Fairly authentic and well prepared Italian food that's a fair value
Useful to Note - Kitchen really does al dente, according to one Italian native.
Menu Suggestions - Saltimbocca alla Romana; Vitello Marsala; pizzas; Pennette Fratelli (small tube-shaped pasta topped with a special house sauce); Lasagna Bolognese

As with most Houston restaurants, Fratelli's is unassumingly located in a strip center. The fairly bland setting and the name, which means "brother" in Italian, gives no indication that the food is much better, and more ambitously authentic than what you might expect. The food is much more Italian than Italian-American (though not to imply that Italian-American is bad) with a pan-Italian menu favoring the rich region of Emilia-Romagna. This area favors freshly made pastas, butter and plenty of Parmigiano-Reggiano. The dishes at Fratelli's usually have the vibrancy and clarity of flavors that is evident when dining anywhere in Italy. There has to be a good amount of authenticity, not to mention quality, to entice the local Italy-America Chamber of Commerce to host dinners here, as it's done in the past. The owners would like to make it even more traditionally Italian, but are limited by the expectations of the customers they are able to attract. An Olive Garden sits crowded almost directly across the freeway, for example.

Just as with the cooking being more Italian, the size of the entrée portions are smaller than what most people might expect; though a little larger than the portion sizes in restaurants in Italy. Not too small, though an appetizer or salad might be ordered for dinner in addition to the entrée, which can easily be a pasta here. What can work as a casual entrée for one here, the pizzas, are usually very good. They are cooked in a modern, but proper, brick oven. The pizzas are made in the slightly more artful manner of those in northern Italy, rather than the original Naples-style, which reflects the influence of one the owners, who is from the northern region of Emilia-Romagna. Savory and light, thin crusts hold the judiciously administered, fresh ingredients. The pastas, in a fair number of variations, stuffed and flat, fresh and dried are also well prepared. For the latter, Fratelli's actually does *al dente,* which is really very rare in this country despite the considerable lip service given to it. Even the simple, side pastas during lunch are likely *al dente.* Some of the pasta attractions are cheese-filled ravioli topped with a properly crafted, tasty and meaty Bolognese-stye *ragù,* Lasagna Bolognese made with homemade pasta, and *Tagliatelle alla Boscaiola* in a hearty, creamy sauce of mushrooms, meat and peas. For the non-pasta and pizza entrées, there are chicken and veal dishes, which are reliably good such as the Veal Marsala, *Saltimbocca alla Romana,* rolled with prosciutto and plenty of fresh sage. A slight splurge might be the marinated, grilled jumbo shrimp served with a walnut-inflected pesto on top of risotto, *Speidini di Gamberi con Pesto.*

The small wine list is well chosen and thankfully affordable. It's easy to find an enjoyable and complementary bottle of wine for $30 and under. Italian food needs wine, after all. There are a number of wines, many of them somewhat unique, from the excellent and affordable producer Marcato in the Veneto. For whites, there are several well-made Soaves and Luganas, one of the best expressions of the Trebbiano grape in a table wine. The reds include food-friendly Barberas and others in addition to the expected Chiantis. There is also the fizzy and uncomplicated Lambrusco, the most popular wine in the Emilia-Romagnan region, from where most of the dishes are inspired, plus affordable New World wines. To complement lunchtime there is both a drinkable white and red sold for just a few dollars per glass.

Some well-stocked and fun wine bars

Though wine is a staple for a great many with an evening meal, wine bars work well for a before-restaurant drink and after dinner drinks; or, probably even more so, just as a bar that has a fine selection of wines in a pleasant setting. These are some of the best and most enjoyable of the wine bars that have exploded on the scene during the second half of the decade:

- **Boom Boom Room** - 2518 Yale

- **Corkscrew** - 1919 Washington
- **Cova** - 5600 Kirby & 5555 Washington - well-regarded food, too
- **Cru** - 9595 Six Pines Drive, The Woodlands
- **Max's Wine Dive** - 4720 Washington - primarily a restaurant
- **Sonoma Retail Wine Bar & Boutique** - 2720 Richmond
- **Tasting Room** - 114 Gray, 1101 Uptown Park & 2409 W. Alabama
- **13 Celsius** - 3000 Caroline
- **Wine Vine Room** - 12410 Memorial
- **Vineyard on the Square** - 16135 City Walk, Sugar Land
- **Wine Bucket** - 2311 W. Alabama

French Riviera Bakery & Café $8

3032 Chimney Rock (between Westheimer and Richmond) 77056, (713) 783-3264

Cuisine - Café / Bakery
Hours - Mon-Sat 7AM to 5:30PM
Credit Cards - MC, Visa
Service - Counter Service
Alcohol - NONE

Entrée Prices - $5 to $8 ($8 average)
Entrées $12 and less - 100%

Atmosphere & Décor - Comfortable; patio
Appeal - A good stop in the Galleria area for baked goods and sandwiches
Menu Suggestions - croissants; sandwiches with croissants; Danishes; pastries

Opened since 1977 the French Riviera Bakery & Café is a more-than-capable bakery located in an uglier-than-usual strip center in the Galleria area that works wells as a stop for breakfast pastries and coffee, a sandwich or salad during lunchtime, or just the daily bread. The joyous aromas of freshly baked bread and pastries always fills the small café. The staff, especially the Vietnamese owners, is always friendly, and though the seating is somewhat cramped, it's a warm and inviting place, befitting the café portion of the name. There is often a good number of patrons during the weekday lunchtimes, and it is usually crowded on Saturday mornings with people enjoying one of the popular espresso-based coffees drinks or *café au lait* with their oven-fresh baked goods. For breakfast, and into the day, while they last, there is a choice among a dozen types of flaky croissants, a couple brioches, several Danishes, some quiches and a few beautiful pastries, all of which are baked on site. The large, flavorful and buttery croissants are excellent and come in several variations to suit your mood: plain, slathered with almond paste or chocolate, or filled with ham and cheese. The design-it-yourself sandwiches ask for several choices, though it's tough to misstep, as the components are all quite good. The available fillings are ham and cheese, roast beef, turkey breast, egg salad, tuna salad, chicken salad, *mortadella,* Swiss cheese, and what's described as a French-style hot dog. The breads are white, wheat, a baguette, semolina, *focaccia* and croissant. The dressings are mayonnaise, Dijon mustard, lettuce, juicy, red tomato slices and pickle. Most can be served hot or cold, and in small and large sizes. The large size will be necessary for most diners for lunch. There are also the hot and melted-cheese-laden *croque monsieur* and *croque madame* sandwiches. Several entrée-style salads are also served for the midday meal including chicken salad, tuna salad, and a Niçoise salad with tuna substited for classic anchovies. These are accompanied with the house vinaigrette and a small loaf of bread. For bread for the meal at home, French Riviera also does an very good job with a number of mostly French varieties: *petit pain,* baguette, flute, *boule,* farm loaf, semolina, wheat, and on the weekends also *epi, etoile* and *petit pale.*

Frenchy's Chicken $6

3919 Scott (at Wheeler, between Elgin and Southmore) 77004, (713) 748-2233
6102 Scott (at Old Spanish Trail, in the HEB) 77021, (713) 741-2700
11631 Southwest Freeway (west of the Beltway) 77031, (281) 495-4415
5588 I-45 N. (at Tidwell) 77022, (713) 694-7060
7046 West Fuqua (at Blue Ridge, south of the Beltway) 77489, (281) 835-8009
www.frenchyschicken.com

Cuisine - Fried Chicken; Cajun
Hours - 3919 Scott- Mon-Thu, Sun 10:30AM to 1AM; Fri-Sat 10:30AM to 3AM; 6102 Scott - Mon-Thu, Sun 10:30AM to 8PM; Fri-Sat 10:30AM to 8PM; Other Locations - Mon-Thu, Sun 10AM to 10PM; Fri-Sat 10AM to 12AM
Credit Cards - NONE
Service - Counter Service; Drive Thru (all but the 6102 Scott locations)
Alcohol - NONE

Entrée Prices - $5 to $7 ($6 average)
Entrées $12 and less - 100%

Atmosphere & Décor - These are takeout fried chicken stands
Appeal - Some of the best fried chicken in town, for cheap
Useful to Note - Takeaway is a near necessity.
Menu Suggestions - fried chicken; red beans and rice; Sweet Potato Pie; Triple Chocolate Cake

The popular original location is well-situated in the Third Ward just off the University of Houston, a few blocks from Texas Southern University, and in front of the large Wheeler Avenue Baptist Church. Frenchy's has been a very well-liked standby for Louisiana-influenced fried chicken and other regional dishes for residents of the neighborhood and nearby students since opening in 1969. Thankfully, there are now a few more locations to make the tasty fare from this Houston landmark more easily accessible for most. The ones beyond Scott Street are franchised, but the food tastes the same, and matriarch Sally Cruezot is still overseeing the baking of the cakes, pies and cobblers served at all the stores. The fried chicken is the big draw, locally renowned, and exceptional, especially for the price and convenience. The fried chicken is generally salty and slightly spicy with a great taste overall. The skin is crisp, though not crunchy, and the chicken is always moist. A big reason why the chicken here is better than most is that the birds have never been frozen. The result is that the fried chicken at Frenchy's is some of the best around, especially for a place that is essentially a fast food operation. "Fast food" in the best sense, though. It's a great value. And, you get you order quickly, as the chickens are fried in small batches. For less than four bucks, you can get a very satisfying meal consisting of a couple of fried chicken thighs, a roll and the choice of French fries ("Frenchy Fries", of course) or rice. Another great deal is the "Campus Special", three pieces of fried chicken, a biscuit and a jalapeño pepper for around five dollars. Though the fried chicken is the most popular, Frenchy's also serves several of the southern Louisiana favorites such as red beans and rice featuring nearly whole beans, jambalaya, gumbo and dirty rice. As with the fried chicken, these dishes are not for calorie-conscious, and are usually delicious. Many patrons visit Frenchy's just for these. Also good bets are the steam table specials at the HEB location. The daily special changes each day of the week and includes Baked Chicken with Dressing, Smothered Chicken over Rice, Fried Catfish Fillets, Pork Chop over Rice, Oxtails and Gravy, and Creole Hot Sausage and Spicy Chicken over Spaghetti. The key ingredient to the last special is made by Frenchy's Sausage Co. in the Heights, "specializing in Frenchy's Creole Hot Sausage (*Chaurice*)". And, if you have room for dessert, or for an event at home, there are a handful of scrumptious, often sugary sweet cakes and pies. The Sweet Potato Pie is probably the most popular and is made at each location. The Triple Chocolate Cake might be the heaviest cake of its size in town. It's quite rich.

Most of Frenchy's business is from takeout customers. There are only a handful of tables at each location, anyway, and décor is pretty much an afterthought. Another big drawback, at least at the original Scott Street location, is the lack of air conditioning, or lack of well-functioning air conditioning. Thankfully, there is a drive-thru there and at other locations. This can move slowly during peak times, such as early Sunday afternoon after church services, but the food is certainly worth the wait. A great thing about Frenchy's is that it is open late night; until one in the morning during the week, and three in the morning on the weekends.

Giannotti's $7

6539 Bissonnet (between Hillcroft and Beechnut) 77074, (713) 270-4444

Cuisine - Italian-American; Sandwiches; Argentine
Hours - Mon-Fri 10AM to 5PM; Sat 10AM to 4PM
Credit Cards - Amex, MC, Visa
Service - Counter Service
Alcohol - NONE

Entrée Prices - $5 to $9 ($7 average)
Entrées $12 and less - 100%

Atmosphere & Décor - Spartan
Appeal - Excellent Italian-influenced sandwiches; freshly made pastas
Useful to Note - It's not open in the evenings and at night.
Menu Suggestions - Prosciutto Sandwich; Hot Capiccola sandwich; Beef Cannelloni; Spinach Manicotti

Giannotti's, subtitled "Italian-Argentinean Café", is a casual daytime eatery, a pasta factory, and a small Argentine specialty food shop. It seems to succeed in each capacity. There is not a lot of atmosphere at Giannotti's, but in a working class section of Bissonnet, it is more than functional. It feels like a store in a similar type of neighborhood in Argentina that has relocated to this section of Bissonnet. Most patrons seem to be workers of nearby businesses and South Americans originally from around the River Plate, *porteños* and otherwise.

For lunch or an early dinner, Giannotti's offers a selection of pastas and top-notch sandwiches. The pastas are all made in-house such as the stuffed ravioli, cannelloni, and manicotti, and the baked lasagna. All are in the Southern Italian strain, and topped with a tomato sauce. You cannot find a place in town that serves hand-made pasta more inexpensively. The Beef Cannelloni features four rolls of fresh pasta each enclosing a purée of primarily ground beef. Some of the other choices include manicotti stuffed with spinach, and ravioli filled with chicken. Served with a house salad featuring fresh greens and side of garlic bread, these pasta dishes can make for a very satisfying, if not quite sublime meal. The fact that the food is served on paper plates with plastic utensils probably takes away somewhat from the overall dining experience; that, and the lack of attractive décor, too. Of the twenty or so Italian-style sandwiches include ones featuring prosciutto, *mortadella* and *milanesas*, flattened, breaded and fried beef or chicken cutlets. One of the best sandwiches is the Hot *Cappiccola* (or *capocallo*) featuring the spicy, cured Italian-style ham often referred elsewhere by its name in Calabrian dialect, "cob-i-call". (*Sopranos* fans will recognize an even different term for it in their Neapolitan dialect). It's a very tasty, warmed sandwich that is sure to help raise your cholesterol. The similar one with prosciutto is also very good. All of the sandwiches begin with a fairly crusty, tasty loaf that is baked in-house. Similar in appearance to short baguettes, these are a big reason that the sandwiches are so good. The Hot *Cappiccola* and some of the other sandwiches feature thinly sliced and quickly sautéed onions, slices of black olives and slices of melted provolone cheese that greatly help to round out the tastes. A sandwich by itself at Giannotti's can make for an enjoyable meal. The large size is very large here, and most likely you won't need a side. The smaller version will be more manageable for most.

Giannotti's also sells frozen, house-made stuffed pastas and lasagna to re-heat at home. This includes the ravioli, manicotti, cannelloni and lasagna. Necessary for an Argentine *pastaria*, there are also frozen *empanadas*. In addition to the Italian and Argentine specialties made on premise, Giannotti's also carries some Argentine packaged food items such as several brands of *yerba maté* (a type of tea popular in Argentina and Uruguay), wine, and the Argentine beer Quilmes, which has actually improved after being purchased in recent years by Annheuser Busch, the brewers of Budweiser.

Givral Hoang Sandwich $4

9308 Bellaire (between Ranchester and Corporate) 77036, (713) 988-7275

Cuisine - Vietnamese; Sandwiches
Hours - Daily 8AM to 8PM
Credit Cards - NONE
Service - Counter Service
Alcohol - NONE

Entrée Prices - $3 to $5 ($4 average)
Entrées $12 and less - 100%

Atmosphere & Décor - Spartan
Appeal - Good and cheap Vietnamese sandwiches
Useful to Note - It is not related to the similar Les Givral's restaurants.
Menu Suggestions - Banh Mi Thit Nuong (char-grilled pork sandwich); Banh Mi Pâté, Banh Mi Thit (roast pork sandwich)

This small, cramped restaurant with just ten small tables, one of three Vietnamese sandwich shops within thirty yards of each other, is usually packed to the gills during the peak lunchtime hours as most diners wait in line to get to the counter to order one or more of the tasty and cheap Vietnamese sandwiches. Though lunchtime is often chaotic, the sandwiches are quick to arrive, and the tables turn over at a rapid rate, making it a quick stop. Givral posts around ten versions of the standard Vietnamese sandwiches. These begin with a crusty, fresh, suitably crisp, short baguette ladled with mayonnaise, marinated and thinly julienned carrots, sprigs of cilantro, cucumber slices and a slice of fresh jalapeño and topped with a variety of meats. The sandwiches listed include barbecued pork, chicken, pâté, beef curry, pork meatballs, and ham. The char-grilled pork is the most appealing of the sandwich options, at least for the non-Vietnamese patrons. It has to be specially requested from the counter staff whose English is usually limited. This can entail several shouts of "char-grill pork" or "*thit nuong*" (pronounced something like "tit nu-wong" in case you're wondering). The regular barbecue pork sandwich, actually made with roasted pork, is also quite good, as is the Special sandwich made with pâté and some kind of oddly colored ham-like substance. It is best not to look between the buns on this one, however. A selling point for Givral is that the sandwiches seem to have more meat than many of its competitors. Though inexpensive sandwiches make up most of their business, and apparently all of the non-Asian business, their soup and noodle dishes are popular with the Asian patrons. Near the cashier, Givral also has pre-wrapped rice dishes, spring rolls and sweets ready for quick takeout. For beverages, they have the potent and flavorful Vietnamese coffee drinks, a drink from freshly processed sugar cane, and the canned drinks utilizining a variety of tropical ingredients from Southeast Asia.

Golden Palace $10

8520 Bellaire (east of Gessner) 77036, (713) 776-8808

Cuisine - Chinese
Hours - Mon-Thu 10AM to 10PM; Fri-Sun 10AM to 11PM
Credit Cards - Amex, MC, Visa
Service - Table Service
Alcohol - Beer & Wine

Entrée Prices - Dinner - $7 to $20 ($10 average); Lunch - $5 to $8
Entrées at Dinner $12 and less - 90%

Atmosphere & Décor - Pleasant
Appeal - A nice place, one is of the best places in the area for dim sum
Useful to Note - Just ignore the scruffy parking lot and surroundings.
Menu Suggestions - most dim sum offerings - Char Siu Pao (steamed barbecued pork bun); Siu My (steamed pork dumplings); Deep Fried Shrimp Ball; Sui Loon Bao (steamed beef dumpling); Lemon Chicken; General Tao Chicken

Dim sum purveyors in New Chinatown seem to rise and fall in fairly quick succession. Golden Palace has managed to keep its reputation for a good weekend dim sum destination for years now. The dining room has remained packed each Saturdays and Sundays during the late morning and early afternoon hours. And, it seems to do a brisk lunchtime business during the week.

Dim sum is served daily from 10AM to 3PM. During the week, it is via a menu. On the weekends, the dim sum dishes are dispensed from the carts rolling through the large dining rooms. The weekends are very popular with the local Chinese families, especially on Sundays. It's best to arrive before 11AM on Saturday or Sunday, otherwise there is a high probability that you will have to wait for a while for a table. When the carts are used during the weekend, pushed by recent arrivals from China, like many other dim sum places, it's good to know the Chinese names of the dishes you would like to order. Otherwise, ordering can be somewhat of a chore. Though the dim sum is probably better and the offerings more diverse during the weekends (often including preparations of beef kidney, steamed mussels and clams, which you have to amble to in the back to get, in case you were wondering), it is easier for those who do not speak any Chinese during the week when the bilingual menus are used. And, this is one the best places for dim sum along with Fung's Kitchen and the Kim Son in Stafford. The nearly seventy-five items on the menu provide a wide range of choices. The English side of the menu gives a helpful description for each dish. Many of the readily enjoyable dishes are especially tasty, such as the steamed shrimp dumplings, fried sticky bun with barbecued pork, the steamed barbecued pork bun, shrimp pot stickers, and the deep-fried shrimp ball. If these are not enough, there is also much else from which to select, including dishes described as duck feet with oyster sauce, chicken feet with bean sauce, turnip pudding, sautéed chicken feet, jelly fish strips with vegetables, and pork feet with walnuts.

Though the prime draw is dim sum, the Chinese-American lunch specials are also quite good, in addition to being inexpensive. The twenty offerings are familiar: Hunan Chicken; Sweet and Sour Pork; Chicken Chow Mein; Lemon Chicken; Beef and Broccoli; General Tao (Joe's) Chicken; Peking Style Chicken, etc. For a pittance you get an entrée, fried rice, an egg roll, and the soup of the day. When available, the hot and sour soup is noticeably good. The deep-fried egg roll is better than most Chinese restaurants. The fried rice is moist, and flavorful. The main dishes at lunch can also be very good, such as the orange-color Lemon Chicken and the spicy, deep-fried General Tao Chicken. Though the lunch hours feature dim sum and the great-value lunch specials, the dinner menu provides many incentives to visit later in the day. The large number of entrées includes many of the familiar Chinese and Chinese-American ones, and all are well prepared. For starters there are several appetizers such as egg rolls and fried wontons, and the popular soups (hot and sour, egg drop and wonton). Under the heading, "Authentic

Chinese Cuisine", are roughly twenty dishes inspired from several regions in China such as Beef and Scallops, *Sung Chow Say Hai* (a spicy dish of sliced chicken, shrimp, beef, barbecue pork sautéed with carrots, bell peppers, bamboo shoots and bean sprouts), Mongolian Beef (sliced beef sautéed with thick hoisin sauce), Cantonese Chow Mein (pan-fried noodles with chicken, shrimp, barbecue pork and vegetables), and Hunan Shrimp (shrimp served with peppers and green onions in a spicy sauce).

Golden Room $12

1209 Montrose (between West Gray and W. Dallas) 77019, (713) 524-9614
www.goldenroomrestaurant.com

Cuisine - Thai
Hours - Mon-Thu 11AM to 2:30PM, 5 to 9:30PM; Fri 11AM to 2:30PM, 5 to 10:30PM; Sat 5 to 10:30PM
Credit Cards - Amex, Diners, Discover, MC, Visa
Service - Table Service
Alcohol - Beer & Wine

Entrée Prices - $7 to $19 ($12 average)
Entrées $12 and less - 80%

Atmosphere & Décor - Pleasant, tranquil
Appeal - Satisfying Thai food in an always-pleasant atmosphere
Useful to Note - There is plenty of nearby street parking, if the small lot is full.
Menu Suggestions - Garlic Beef; Garlic Chicken; fried rice; Shrimp Jackson (shrimp in red chili sauce with cashew nuts and peas)

Though the long-standing Golden Room has often been rated among the top Thai restaurants in the area by local publications in the past, it is ostensibly always sparsely filled. As a patron that's not a bad thing when planning a visit on short notice. You can be assured of getting a table and to be eating quickly. This pleasant restaurant is located in an old house, painted red, on Montrose, just north of West Gray. Golden Room works very well as a capable neighborhood restaurant, and is also worthy of a trip. The service is proficient and friendly. The quaint interior is nicely decorated red, of course, but plenty of muted gold. Without a packed dining room, it's usually quiet, and the dining experience is tranquil. Most importantly, the food is of good quality, often interesting, and fairly priced. The somewhat large menu contains many dishes, and is neatly divided among Appetizers, Soups, Salads, Pork, Poultry, Beef, Seafood, Thai Curry, Noodles, Vegetarian, Chef's Specials, and a Chinese section. It's easy to find a description that fits your current gustatory desire. Most of the Thai favorites are here: spring rolls, *satays, tom ka gai* soup, and a number of curry dishes. Many of the dishes can be ordered in different spice levels, from mild through medium to hot. The Poultry section contains solely chicken dishes, but under its own heading is the interesting Golden Duck. It consists of an entire duck breast that has been marinated, battered and deep-fried in peanut oil goodness. The seafood choices are from the nearby Gulf, shrimp and a red snapper fillet. Interesting are the handful of entrées described as Chef's Specials. There is Shrimp Jackson (jumbo shrimp stir-fried with red chili sauce and cashew nuts and snow peas), Spicy Mint Beef (or Chicken) that is cooked with garlic and jalapeños and basil, and a Clay Pot with Jumbo Shrimp. The Garlic Beef is a deservedly popular choice. This dish consists of thin slices of beef, trimmed of all fat and marinated in soy sauce, garlic and pepper then stir-fried, resulting in pieces of extremely tender, very flavorful meat. As with the best Thai beef dishes, it's filling without being heavy. Other worthy options are the curry dishes. And, Golden Room has more than a dozen vegetarian dishes should satisfy anyone not in the mood for much protein. Though the primary draw is the Thai food, the menu also has a Chinese section sporting familiar Americanized Chinese items such as the sweet and sour dishes, pepper steak, egg rolls, fried wontons, fried rice, *chow mein* (crisp noodles) and even chop suey.

* Goode Co. Barbecue $8

5109 Kirby (between Bissonnet and Westpark) 77098, (713) 522-2530
8911 Katy Freeway (east of Campbell, south side of I-10) 77024, (713) 464-1901
www.goodecompany.com

Cuisine - Barbecue
Hours - Daily 11AM to 10PM
Credit Cards - Amex, Diners, Discover, MC, Visa
Service - Counter Service
Alcohol - Beer & Wine

Entrée Prices - $5 to $12 ($8 average)
Entrées $12 and less - 100%

Atmosphere & Décor - Nice, appropriate; patio (Kirby)
Appeal - The best barbecue restaurant in the area
Useful to Note - The line always moves quickly.
Menu Suggestions - brisket; Czech Sausage; Jalapeño Pork Sausage; Turkey Breast; Turkey Sausage; Spicy Pork; Sweet Water Duck (half); Chicken (half); potato salad; Austin Baked Beans; cole slaw; potato salad; Jalapeño cheese bread; Stuffed Baked Potato; pecan pie

The overwhelming popularity of the informal, attractive Goode Co. Barbecue restaurants is exceedingly well deserved. These are the best overall barbecue restaurants in the area. The brisket, which in Texas *is* barbecue, is fantastic. Only strict barbecue purists would find any significant point for which to quibble. The brisket is green-mesquite-smoked for eighteen hours and exceedingly moist, tender, and delicious. As with any excellent brisket, knives are rarely required to cut it, and sauce is not really required. In addition to brisket, the house-made Czech and Jalapeño Pork Sausages, the spicy pork, and the turkey are especially flavorful. They also serve beef ribs, chicken and duck. These are also delicious. Unlike some lesser barbecue places, the fowl, turkey, chicken and even duck, are always very moist and tender. Well, pretty much everything is very good here. In addition to the plates, the sandwiches are also a great choice. The high quality, fresh bun makes for the best brisket sandwich around. Sandwiches are also available with their wonderful jalapeño cheese bread, and in the slightly larger po boy size that also features a bun freshly made for the task. The sauce, slightly spicy with a medium consistency, though a fine complement, can probably stand a slight improvement. It's probably the only real demerit, and a minor one at that. The meats are exemplary, especially given the broad range that are cooked. Another difference between Goode Co. and all of the other quality barbecue joints around is the very high quality of their side dishes. These are definitely not the scooped-from-the-can beans and potato salad that you typically find at other barbecue places. There are terrific Austin Baked Beans (baked beans cooked with chunks of apple for a slightly sweet taste); excellent potato salad; flavorful jambalaya; and the aforementioned house-made jalapeño cheese bread that is a far cry from the super-processed and tasteless white bread that usually serves sopping duty at the other places. And for dessert, there is their legendary pecan pie.

The rustic barn that is the Kirby location seems like an anomaly just off the very busy street and near well-to-do neighborhoods, but the antiquated atmosphere works well. This feels like a barbecue joint. Maybe it is part marketing expertise as the proprietor, Jim Goode, ran a successful sign company before becoming a restaurateur, but Goode Co. would be very popular no matter what the restaurant looked like. The quality of the food is undeniable. The service is cafeteria-style. The lines are usually long during the long lunch and dinner peak times, but the proficient staff makes sure things move very quickly. This is another hallmark of the Goode Co. restaurants, professional and prompt service. Seating inside is limited, but there is usually room at the picnic tables outside under the covered patio. The décor is a bit nicer at the larger location off the Katy Freeway, but the atmosphere is similar and comfortable. These are places to grab a longneck and enjoy the best in barbecue. They have all of the bases covered for a great, inexpensive restaurant: excellent food, professional service, a pleasant atmosphere, and an exceptional value.

* Goode Co. Taqueria $11

4902 Kirby (at Westpark) 77098, (713) 520-9153
www.goodecompany.com

Cuisine - Tex-Mex; American (regional)
Hours - Mon-Thu 11AM to 10PM; Fri 10:30AM to 10PM; Sat-Sun 7:30AM to 10PM
Credit Cards - Amex, Diners, Discover, MC, Visa
Service - Counter Service
Alcohol - Beer & Wine, plus margaritas and vodka-based morning drinks

Entrée Prices - Dinner & Lunch - $6 to $20 ($11 average); Breakfast - $8 to $12
Entrées at Dinner $12 and less - 70%

Atmosphere & Décor - Functional, bustling
Appeal - Fantastic breakfasts; very good hamburgers and Tex-Mex
Useful to Note - There is additional parking at Goode Co. Seafood.
Menu Suggestions - American Breakfast (eggs, hash browns and choices of meat and bread); Pork Chops and Eggs; Huevos con Tocino (eggs scrambled with bacon); Huevos con Nopalitos (eggs scrambled with cactus); Huevos Venado (eggs with venison sausage); Huevos Rancheros; Pecan Waffles; Chicken Enchiladas; Mesquite Grilled Burgers; Mesquite Chicken Burger; fries; crispy tacos; pecan pie; freshly squeezed juices, aguas frescas - watermelon

It might be not an understatement to write that Goode Co. Taqueria serves the best breakfasts in the city; the state; the country; etc. Proprietor Jim Goode has a restaurant that creates gustatory masterpieces with eggs, potatoes, mesquite-grilled meats, butter, and the ancillary grease, cholesterol and fat every weekend morning. The huge crowds are well aware of this. The breakfasts are Texan and Tex-Mex in nature. These have the influences of Mexico and south Texas ranch cooking, and are consistently exceptional and hearty. There is the basic American Breakfast that consists of two jumbo-sized eggs, a choice between house-made sausage and thick, smoked bacon, hash browns, and either soft, house-baked bread or an English muffin. Though similar dishes are served at virtually all other breakfast places, Goode Co. stands head-and-shoulders above the rest with its great flavors. The fresh, house-made bread with a little bit of butter is especially good. Another breakfast combination offers venison sausage instead of the more mundane meat choices. Some of the other combinations with eggs are one with pork chops, another with steak, another with fajitas, and then one with catfish. Though fried catfish and eggs may not sound appetizing to that many people, if it is offered here, it's probably as good as it gets. Other breakfast dishes are different Tex-Mex combinations featuring eggs scrambled with a choice of items: *tocino* (bacon) and egg; *chorizo* and egg; *nopalito* (nopalito cactus leaves). All are excellent. There are also the other

Tex-Mex breakfast dishes: *migas, huevos rancheros; huevos a la mexicana;* and a Mexican omelet. Pecan-topped waffles are also very popular and delicious.

In addition to the Tex-Mex offerings for breakfast, those served at lunch and dinner also are often excellent. The chicken enchiladas filled with thick strips of grilled and slightly smoky chicken breast are very good, as are the cheese versions. The expected sides, beans and rice, are first-rate as expected. Along with the Tex-Mex, Goode Co. Taqueria also does hamburgers and hot dogs quite well. The hamburgers usually rank among the best in town in local polls, and are available in one-third and two-third pound sizes. Actually, there is not an unappealing choice on the short menu. As with the other Goode Co. restaurants, there is their renowned pecan pie, if you have room for dessert. For both breakfast and afterwards, there is an excellent complementary and complimentary condiment bar. Freshly prepared red salsa, spicy *pico de gallo,* ripe, thinly sliced tomatoes, chopped onions, and sliced pickled jalapeños are some of the attractions. Though the restaurant is often crowded, especially for the weekend breakfasts, the lines move quickly. Once you get to the cashier and order, you won't wait long for your food. Typical of all the Goode Co. restaurants the service is proficient and the kitchen works quickly and never seems to miss a beat. It is an excellent informal restaurant that would do any neighborhood proud.

Gorditas Aguascalientes $7

6102 Bissonnet (between Renwick and Hillcroft) 77081, (713) 541-4560
3810 Irvington (south of Patton) 77009, (713) 697-7888
4721 N. Main (west of Airline) 77009, (713) 863-9915

Cuisine - Mexican (taqueria)
Hours - Daily 7AM to 3AM
Credit Cards - NONE
Alcohol - Beer

Entrée Prices - Dinner & Lunch - $4 to $12 ($7 average); Breakfast - $4 to $7
Entrées at Dinner $12 and less - 100%

Appeal - Excellent, inexpensive, regional Mexican food
Atmosphere & Décor - Functional if pleasant enough
Useful to Note - Some Spanish language ability is helpful.
Menu Suggestions - Huevos a al Mexicana (eggs scrambled with jalapeños, onions and tomato); Huevos Rancheros; Guisado de Puerco (stewed pork); Gordita de Deshebrada (corn pocket stuffed with shredded beef); Gordita de Queso y Rajas (corn pocket stuffed with white cheese and roasted strips of pepper); Quesadilla de Fajita (sautéed taco with marinated fajita meat); aguas frescas (sweetened fruit drinks)

Unlike other *taquerias* who at least give it slight mention, the menu at the noticeably well-run Gorditas Aguascalientes almost entirely avoids any Tex-Mex-style dishes. The fajitas, on the very bottom on one of the menu pages, is the lone exception. Gorditas Aguascalientes offers almost solely the nearly authentic, regional Mexican dishes. Not to worry, the casual Mexican and Tex-Mex connoisseur will be able to find enough familiar items that are common to both cuisines in addition to the fajitas: *enchiladas; quesadillas; burritos;* and *tostadas*. And, just about everything is very good, in any case.

But there are many more interesting items such as *Atole Champurrado,* made with the corn *masa* dough and chocolate, which has existed since well before Cortez visited Tenochtitlan. There are almost a dozen different types of the restaurant's namesake, *gorditas,* corn *masa* pockets filled with a variety a different items such as chicken, *rajas* (poblano pepper strips), mushroom, pork skins and *deshebrada* (shredded beef). There are also *sopes,* corn dough topped with different items and cheese. *Huaraches,* an item that is very seldom seen on any *taqueria* menus, are also served here. These are a regional item named after a sandal that it somewhat resembles. It consists of a long flat corn *masa* cradle for the toppings of beans, lettuce and *queso fresco* (cheese that does not melt). Some more interesting items are *Pozole Jaliciense,* a pork soup with hominy, shredded cabbage, onions, lime, tomatoes, and flavored with coriander. There are *Enchiladas Cordiniz, enchiladas* filled with quail and topped with *queso fresco,* carrots, potatoes, lettuce and tomatoes. Many of these items are very inexpensive; for instance, the *gorditas* are around a couple of dollars each, as are the *sopes*. The breakfast plates are more expensive than at most *taquerias,* but are still quite inexpensive and often excellent. Each of the breakfast plates featuring eggs, *Huevos a al mexicana, Huevos Rancheros, Huevos con Jamon,* etc., come with ample array of side portions of gloriously lard-laden refried beans, *chilaquiles* (without eggs), cubed and sautéed potatoes, and a dollop of fresh cream. *Queso fresco,* the white, crumbly Mexican cheese, is sprinkled on the beans and *chilaquiles* for a pleasant and tasty complementary touch.

The presentation, even for the breakfast dishes, is surprisingly attractive and generally much nicer than that of any other *taqueria* and most Mexican restaurants, fitting the tastiness of the dishes. The environs, maybe excepting the N. Main location, are also nicer than most *taquerias*. As in just about every *taqueria,* they have a jukebox, which at any given moment can start blaring very loudly Mexican pop music. It's a small price to pay for such savory and authentic, regional Mexican food. Because of their authenticity and quality in reproducing the best dishes of central Mexico, these restaurants are especially popular with recently arrived immigrants.

In addition to the food, the house-made *aguas frescas,* the Mexican fresh fruit drinks, are excellent, possibly the best in town. Among the several flavors, the *melon* (cantaloupe) and *horchata* (rice water) are especially tasty. These are places to try some excellent, and proudly, central Mexican cuisine.

Gourmet India $12

13155 Westheimer (between Dairy Ashford and Eldridge) 77077, (281) 493-5435
www.gourmetindiahouston.com

Cuisine - Indian
Hours - Mon-Thu, Sun 11AM to 2:30PM, 5:30 to 10PM; Fri-Sat 11AM to 3PM, 5:30 to 11PM
Credit Cards - Amex, Discover, MC, Visa
Service - Buffet at Lunch; Table Service at Dinner
Alcohol - Beer & Wine

Entrée Prices - Dinner - $9 to $23 ($12 average); Lunch - $9 - Mon-Sat; $10 - Sun
Entrées at Dinner $12 and less - 70%

Atmosphere & Décor - Functional
Appeal - Competent Indian on Westheimer
Useful to Note - The buffet might be better on the weekends.
Menu Suggestions - samosa (fried pastry filled with vegetables); Chicken Tikka Masala; Saag Paneer (creamed spinach); Chicken Tandoor (marinated, grilled chicken)

Even after changing ownership in recent years, the dining room at Gourmet India on the western expanse of Westheimer is still often at near capacity during lunchtime. You will find both Indians and non-Indians who have been attracted by the well prepared and reasonably priced buffet filled with appealing and locally familiar, mostly northern Indian dishes. This restaurant in a large and somewhat empty shopping center with plenty of nearby parking is a wise and usually convenient choice for a hearty lunch. Part of Gourmet India's appeal for casual fans of Indian food is found on the buffet here, and done well, too: Chicken *Tikka Masala* (boneless chicken cooked in a tandoor and served in a creamy and zesty sauce featuring plenty of clarified butter, *ghee*); and the desserts *kheer* (rice pudding) and the more expensive *gulab jamen* (sweet and syrup pastry balls scented with rose water). The kitchen seems to have a good hand with most dishes. It has no pretensions of being the best or most ambitious local Indian restaurant, but the fare is usually quite satisfying, and a fine value. The dinner menu is fairly extensive with roughly fifty entrées, plus a couple special multi-course dinners. There are several savory appetizers including the deep-fried and tasty *pakoras*, soups, plenty of vegetarian specialties, *tandoori* dishes (cooked in the hot cylindrical clay oven) with chicken, lamb and shrimp, several of the freshly baked breads, curries with shrimp, chicken and lamb, the rice-centric *biriyanis* and a handful of desserts. Among the entrées cooked in the tandoor oven is one touted as being from the mountains of Afghanistan enticingly featuring ginger-and-spice-marinated lamb chops.

The Grill of the Andes $10

12719 Westheimer (between Dairy Ashford and Eldridge) 77079, (281) 759-7778
www.thegrilloftheandes.com

Cuisine - Bolivian
Hours - Tue 11:30AM to 4PM; Wed-Sat 11:30AM to 10PM; Sun 11:30AM to 4PM
Credit Cards - Amex, Discover, MC, Visa
Service - Counter Service
Alcohol - Full Bar

Entrée Prices - $6 to $14 ($10 average)
Entrées $12 and less - 90%

Atmosphere & Décor - Pleasant
Appeal - Good hearty food with a Bolivian twist
Useful to Note - There is live music on the weekends and some other nights.
Menu Suggestions - salteñas (baked empanadas filled with beef); Rocotto Relleno (poblano peppers stuffed with a light cheese and baked with a tomato sauce); Brochetas (skewered and grilled pieces of beef or chicken breast); Salpicha (thin pan-fried steak topped with a fried egg)

The sign on the nondescript strip center on the western stretches of Westheimer reading "The Grill of the Andes" will likely be neither descriptive nor enticing enough to warrant a visit. But, it bears note that the restaurant underneath proficiently serves readily enjoyable, hearty food from Bolivia's mountain ranges and beyond for very fair prices. With much of the cooking here featuring meat, mostly in the form of beef, and potatoes, one of the great Incan gifts to the world, it's the type of fare that can easily fit in the category of "comfort food" for a great many in the area, regardless of heritage. Plus, there are even hamburgers, albeit with a slight twist. The flavors are straightforward, honest you might say, and robust in the better dishes. The occasional spice comes from the *salsa cruda,* a simple *pico de gallo*-like mixture that is ladled onto several entrées, and a small tub of puréed fresh jalapeños, which make for a tasty accompaniment to even the complimentary bread. Though of doubtful interest to most non-Bolivian patrons, the food here is authentically Bolivian according to some émigrés.

The moderately sized menu with entrées featuring beef, pork, chicken breasts and a handful of seafood items, sports useful, if not entirely accurate, descriptions for each dish and for several of the sauces. Sometimes "breaded" does not translate into breading on the dish, and "sautéed" could mean that the beef is actually stewed or boiled. No matter, the food is usually good. Though the portions are healthy, it's enjoyable to start with *empanadas* with a cheese or cheese with spices or ham, or the similar *salteñas,* which are baked rather than fried. There are also Bolivian takes on fried potato skins and chicken wings. There are several soups including *crema de choclo,* a thick and creamy sweet corn chowder that is topped with mild *queso fresco*. The nearly half-dozen salads are unique with tuna salad supporting a half of tomato and the *Papas a la Huancaina,* which is described as a traditional Andean dish with boiled new potatoes, lettuce, a hard boiled egg with a spicy peanut sauce. Even the side salads, featuring suitably fresh and crisp greens and quality complementary vegetables and dressings, that come with many of the entrées are quite good here. The main dishes are mostly divided between "The Andes Specials", about fifteen fairly authentic Bolivian dishes, and "Chef's Choice", a half-dozen items that use that part of the world as inspiration. The beef in the nearly ten beef entrées is suitably moist and tender. Thin slices are favored here, as in much of Latin America. The traditional *Silpancho* is an enjoyable entrée into Bolivian cuisine. It is a large flattened piece of tasty steak that has been pan-fried and placed atop fried potatoes and rice with a fried egg atop of it. The *Bistec Urubamba* is a stew of beef with an interesting and savory broth filled with onions, large pieces of tomatoes, slices of bell pepper and pieces of pineapple that is marred with bland chunks of steak that tastes like they have been plucked from a pot of boiling water. Dessert includes *flan,* a couple of sweetened *empanadas* and the Houston Latin restaurant requisite, *tres leches*. The dining area, served by an amiable staff, consists of a single room with almost twenty tables and booths that is more comfortable than sparse. There is live music most weekends and sometimes during the weekday evenings.

Guatemala $7

3330 Hillcroft (between Richmond and Westpark) 77057, (713) 789-4330

Cuisine - Guatemalan
Hours - Daily 9AM to 10PM
Credit Cards - NONE
Service - Table Service
Alcohol - NONE

Entrée Prices - Dinner & Lunch - $4 to $8 ($7 average); Breakfast - $3 to $7
Entrées at Dinner $12 and less - 100%

Atmosphere & Décor - Spartan at best
Appeal - Tasty, hearty and surprisingly familiar food with a sometime deft touch
Useful to Note - They serve several interesting cold and hot tropical drinks.

Menu Suggestions - Milanesa Empanizada (breaded and pan-fried beef steak); Pepian de Pollo (stewed chicken in a flavorful brown sauce); Carne Asada (grilled skirt steak); Pollo en Amarillo (stewed chicken in a piquant sauce)

The food at the Guatemala Restaurant should be recognizable and quite satisfying to most people in Houston. The restaurant is a great value, and many of the dishes are fairly similar to popular Mexican ones. For many, the food might be described as Mexican in style, but seemingly fewer ingredients and influences, and cheese is noticeably absent in the dishes. The food here has much more of the indigenous, Mayan influence; hearty, with the emphasis on meats, primarily beef and chicken, and vegetables, especially corn. It's flavorful, if not often spicy, and there are some tropical hints, mostly from the frequent use of plantains. The surroundings here are sparse but clean in the single dining room with just twenty tables, befitting the small restaurant's setting in an older shopping center on multicultural Hillcroft. Service is efficient and atmosphere is relatively negligible. The patrons are typically working folk, mostly immigrants and migrants from Guatemala and elsewhere in Central America, usually intent on enjoying a taste of home without much fuss.

In recent years, at least the menu has become better organized and easier for non-natives and non-Spanish speakers to navigate. The food on the menu is divided among *Antijitos* (appetizers), and entrées, which are listed under both *Desayunos* (breakfast) and *Almuerzos* (lunch), plus a handful of sides. The appetizers consist of a tempting and inexpensive array such as the Guatemalan version of tamales, small enchiladas, *tostadas,* fried plantains, plantains with cream, and something called *Chuchitos* of corn. The *garnachas,* small corn tortillas filled with shredded meat and cabbage, are probably the most popular and filling. The tamales feature heavy corn *masa,* and really need the accompanying spicy red salsa; otherwise these will be dry and bland for most palates. The half-dozen of dishes termed breakfast dishes, though which are available all day, include three featuring fried egg dishes, fried plantains with cream and refried beans, and *carne asada* (grilled beef) and *milanesa* (breaded and pan-fried beef cutlet). The latter two are also listed under the *Almuerzo* heading; the difference is that refried beans and rice come with the dish as a breakfast, and a salad replaces the beans for lunch. Go figure. Either as lunch or dinner choice the *carne asada* is very good. It's not the most promising slice of beef upon initial inspection, but it's moist and flavorful, especially with the accompanying piquant green salsa. One of the best entrées is the unusually named *Pepian de Pollo,* stewed chicken in slightly spicy, tangy brown gravy. There is also roast chicken, *chile relleno,* shredded beef, beef stew, beef tongue, and a few hearty soups, one featuring beef, a couple with chicken, and the *Kaq-ik de Pavo con Arroz,* described as a traditional turkey soup. One unexpected item, reflecting the

Chinese immigration to Guatemala, is the *Chaomein*, a Central American take on the fried noodle dish, *chow mein*. In addition to the pleasing entrées, the sides are quite good, and fairly interesting. The very moist rice, speckled with peas, is one of the best rice sides around. The salad (*ensalada rusa*) is a vegetable mix with bits of red pepper, carrot slices, green beans and peas in a mayonnaise-based dressing. Though possibly unusual, it can be quite satisfying, and a nice textural and temperature contrast with the meat entrées. Drinks are helpfully listed as either cold or hot. The former include *licuados* (fruit shakes), lemonade, and a couple *aguas frescas*, which are made in the restaurant, the rice milk *horchata* and one with tamarind fruit. The hot drinks, popular whenever there is a chill in the air, are coffee, *arroz con leche* (rice with milk), and a couple ancient thick sweetened *masa* concoctions, *atol de platano* and *atol de elote*. It helps to speak some Spanish here as the waitstaff's English might be limited, but it is usually accommodating. And, the menu is bilingual.

Guy's Meat Market $5

3106 Old Spanish Trail (between Highway 288 and Almeda) 77054, (713) 747-6800
www.guysseasoning.com

Cuisine - Barbecue; Hamburgers
Hours - Tue-Fri 8:30AM to 5:30PM; Sat 8:30 to 4PM
Credit Cards - Amex, MC, Visa
Service - Counter Service; it's takeout only
Alcohol - Beer

Entrée Prices - $4 to $9 ($5 average)
Entrées $12 and less - 100%

Atmosphere & Décor - Bare-bones; takeout only
Appeal - Very good hamburgers and solid barbecue for cheap
Useful to Note - Hamburgers often sell out quickly, sometimes before noon.
Menu Suggestions - hamburgers; Link Sausage Sandwich; Slice Beef Sandwich

Around since 1938 and in its present location since 1958, Guy's Meat Market is primarily that, a meat market. It's a meat market, or butcher shop, with a small grocery section that serves casual, meat-centric foods. It's strictly a bare-bones takeout operation; there are no tables, chairs, nor any place to sit in the place. Located not too far from the Astrodome, Medical Center and the Third Ward, Guy's also sells many of the popular Southern cuts of beef, pork and chicken and, additionally, several types of wood for barbecuing. Guy's menu, set above the counter, is straightforward and small, and humorously (and intentionally) misspelled. Guy's serves barbecue plates, a limited variety of cold po boys, barbecue sandwiches, and hamburgers. The plates feature beef brisket, sausage, chicken and ribs and a choice of two sides among the very dependable baked beans, potato salad and cole slaw. As with everything else here, these plates can be a great deal. The brisket and sausage are notably delicious. The sausage, called "link" at Guy's is similar to kielbasa, and different than either the locally popular barbecue standbys of Czech-style sausage or the crumbly beef links at the nearby Third Ward establishments. The barbecue sandwiches are a variety of different barbecued meats on a hamburger bun with a small amount of barbecue sauce and chopped onions and, or relish. For the sandwich meats, you can get chopped beef, sliced beef, sliced sausage, ham, and ham and cheese. But, Guy's is deservedly best known for their hamburgers. These are available only Tuesday through Friday from 11AM to possibly 1PM, and only 200 are made. The juicy half-pound patties feature a ground beef with a suitable 10% or so amount of fat, and, in very unusual fashion, are finished in a hickory-stoked smoker resulting in evident smoke rings and a great, slightly unique flavor. These burgers come fully dressed with mustard, mayonnaise, lettuce, onion, tomatoes, pickles and jalapeños unless otherwise noted, and are excellent. Those are even better if you can find a place to eat them within fifteen minutes or so. Also suitable for takeout, Guy's also has several brands of beers in tall boy format to help complement the barbecue or hamburger.

Henderson's Chicken Shack $6

3811 Ennis (just west of Alabama) 77004, (713) 533-0033

Cuisine - Fried Chicken
Hours - Mon-Wed 11AM to 10PM; Thu 11AM to 11PM; Fri-Sat 11AM to 12 PM
Credit Cards - MC, Visa
Service - Takeout; Counter Service
Alcohol - NONE

Entrée Prices - $4 to $10 ($6 average)
Entrées $12 and less - 100%

Atmosphere & Décor - Functional; it is mostly a takeout operation
Appeal - Excellent fried chicken near TSU and U of H
Useful to Note - It's all cooked to order, so call ahead when picking up.
Menu Suggestions - fried chicken

Not too far from the campus of TSU, Henderson's Chicken Shack makes some of the best fried chicken in Houston. Featuring large pieces of chicken crusted in a batter tasting of cornmeal then deep-fried, the result is nearly as good as it gets for fried chicken. The skin is golden and delicious, and the meat is moist and flavorful throughout with a hint of saltiness. The chicken here is not spicy like its very proficient Third Ward neighbor, the Creoletinged Frenchy's, but it might be just as good. Part of the reason that it is so good is that unlike nearly all fast food restaurants, and certainly other fried chicken establishments, the food at Henderson's is not cooked until ordered.

As with most places that specialize in fried chicken, the food is a very good value here, especially so since the pieces are noticeably very good-sized. A usually filling three-piece order with two thighs, a leg or thigh and a wing, served with fries and slices of processed white bread is only four bucks. The four-piece order is another dollar. Fifteen pieces, easily enough for a family of four or five, is priced at roughly a dollar per piece. And the pieces of fried chicken at Henderson's seem larger than at other places. In fact, the three-piece dinner here probably has two-and-a-half times as much food, which is also far superior, to a Central American fried chicken place that opened in Houston with great fanfare several years ago. Though the fare is undoubtedly much tastier, Henderson's is even a better price performer than the national fried chicken chains. With the exception of the red beans, which are generally flavorful and spicy, everything else is fried here. Fries come with all chicken orders. Unfortunately, these are pre-cut and become limp quickly. But, topped with a Tony Chachere's-like seasoning, these can be appetizing. There are also chicken gizzards and livers, catfish fillets, chicken tenders, and pork chops. The pork chops are somewhat thin and dry, and the pricing makes it not much of a deal, especially in contrast to the fried chicken. Henderson's is a sparse, but friendly operation that serves mostly takeout, and there are only a handful of places to sit inside. As the food is cooked to order, and will take at least twenty minutes, it is a good idea to phone beforehand. Near Alabama, Henderson's is quickly accessible from Midtown, Montrose, and the Museum District.

Hickory Hollow $8

101 Heights Boulevard (north of Washington) 77007, (713) 869-6300
8038 Fallbrook Drive (just east of Sam Houston Race Park) 77064, (281) 469-5323
18537 FM 1488 (north of FM 1774, in Magnolia) 77354, (281) 356-7885
www.hickoryhollowrestaurant.com

Cuisine - American (regional); Barbecue
Hours - Daily, 11AM to 9PM
Credit Cards - Amex, Discover, MC, Visa
Service - Counter Service
Alcohol - Beer & Wine

Entrée Prices - $6 to $15 ($8 average)
Entrées $12 and less - 90%

Atmosphere & Décor - Pleasant, casual and fitting
Appeal - Good chicken fried steak in a fittingly informal, rustic atmosphere

Useful to Note - The Heights and Magnolia locations have live music.
Menu Suggestions - Chicken Fried Steak; Sausage Sandwich; Chicken Fried Chicken; baked potatoes

Hickory Hollow is the type of place that many outside the state probably think is how Texans usually eat: huge plates of chicken fried steak or barbecue in rustic, Western settings. Hickory Hollow does this type of cooking well, and it's a great value here. The restaurants are informal, counter-service places with friendly staffs that have hit the right notes since 1977. The chicken fried steak is the biggest draw, and a great indulgence. It comes in three sizes. The medium-sized portion, advertised as "Big enuf fer a Texan", is served on a thin metal plate that is the diameter of a hubcap. The plate is large, nearly the breadth of a saddle blanket. It seems most male patrons are challenged into ordering this size (they can't get the small or the Cowgirl's Meal, can they?). As large as these are, it is surprisingly easy to finish; a testament to the quality. The chicken fried steak is tasty and tender, such that it can be cut with a fork. It's not heavy as most other versions, nor is the accompanying gravy. Chicken fried steaks come with a baked potato, or well prepared mashed potatoes and a trip to the salad bin. The salad is nothing special, iceberg lettuce with several add-ins and dressings, but everything is very fresh. In addition to the chicken fried steak dinners, Hickory Hollow also serves steaks, hamburgers, fried catfish, barbecue, and even an entrée salad and vegetables for those seeking to eat more lightly. Hickory Hollow barbecues beef brisket, sausage, ribs and chicken. The brisket is a tad dry and usually just passable at best for the Houston area. But, the sausage, similar in style to kielbasa, is very juicy and flavorful with a hint of smoke. There are pork ribs and barbecued chicken. Barbecue is available as plates or sandwiches. The plates come with a couple sides from the fairly long list among: baked beans, green beans, potato salad, cole slaw, mashed potatoes, fries, and okra. Though value is pervasive throughout the menu, there are also several family-style dinners for four adults that might be even a better deal. Another attraction is that the Heights and Magnolia locations have live old-line country and Western music on the weekends.

* Himalaya $9

6652 Southwest Freeway (northwest corner at Hillcroft) 77074, (713) 532-2837

Cuisine - Pakistani
Hours - Mon-Thu 11.30AM to 11PM; Fri-Sun 11AM to 12AM
Credit Cards - MC, Visa
Service - Counter Service
Alcohol - NONE; BYOB

Entrée Prices - Dinner - $7 to $13 ($9 average); Lunch - $9
Entrées at Dinner $12 and less - 90%

Atmosphere & Décor - Functional and informal, but inviting
Appeal - Excellent, spicy meat-laden Pakistani food
Useful to Note - The ever-changing lunch special is a great value.
Menu Suggestions - samosa (potato and spice filled turnover); Chicken Karhai (boneless chicken in a spicy tomato sauce); Gola Kabab (beef kabobs); Karachi Kabab Masala (beef kabobs topped with masala gravy): Hunter's Beef Plate (cured, diced beef cooked in butter and chiles); Behari Steak Tikka (marinated and grilled pieces of steak); Haleem (shredded stewed beef with lentils, chiles and ginger); Chicken Biryani (chicken in rice); Dal Fry (lentil curry); kheer (rice pudding)

The small sign that can be seen from the west-bound feeder road reading, "Kaiser's Himalaya / Restaurant", announces the chef and his restaurant, not a culinary legacy of some Bismarck-era colonialism. Opened since 2004, Himalaya has been a smart stop for a tasty, spicy, robust and a great value meal, even if you are not familiar with Pakistani food. The oft-present owner is welcoming and quick to explain the cuisine and offer suggestions, which are probably necessary. Conveniently located at Hillcroft and the Southwest Freeway, Himalaya is a quick trip for many Inner Loop neighborhoods and also the communities further southwest. Though the food is excellent, there is not much else to draw patrons to this storefront restaurant. The dozen or so tables are arranged for large groups and a desk with a computer is set in front of the cashier station above which there is the menu written on a dry-erase board. A television is tuned to news of the region, but it's usually in English.

The cooking here and at other Pakistani restaurants is quite similar, if differently termed, to the much more common Indian restaurants, most of which feature dishes from northern India, which shares a border with Pakistan. The most noticeable differences are that the Pakistani offerings are much more meat-centric, and the oil-quotient is more evident. The former is certainly true at Himalaya, though the latter much less here. Visiting during lunchtime, you will probably be quickly offered the lunch special, a few meat items including a curry and kabob and long-grain rice served in a cafeteria tray, possibly a soup and freshly baked *naan*. Get it. It's a great value way to sample several of the restaurant's highlights, though it might be too much food for many. The robust lamb curry is excellent. On cooler days, you might be served a good-sized soup bowl filled with small pieces of chicken, lentils and thin cuts of ginger topped with parsley. Hearty and zesty, it's especially well-suited for those occasionally brisk winter temperatures. It's also enjoyable with brisk air conditioning, too.

The menu is divided among grilled items, chicken, goat, curries, seafood, rice plates, sandwiches and a few vegetables. The various meat, chicken, lamb, goat and beef, are cooked to a very flavorful and properly moist conclusion. The owner is quick to recommend the grilled steak *tikka* that is marinated in a very flavorful mixture of garlic, ginger, chiles, papaya and yogurt. Actually, it's wise to get suggestions for almost everything since a menu with descriptions seems elusive, and the dishes on the whiteboard might be difficult to discern unless you are intimately familiar with the cuisine. But, the owner is more than helpful, and it doesn't seem that the kitchen makes any missteps. The vegetables offerings are limited to excellent, stewed preparations of lentils, eggplants, potatoes and the buffet staple, the creamed spinach *saag paneer*. Himalaya is seemingly well known locally for its *biryanis*, bountiful and fragrant rice plates topped with slowly cooked meats and spices, and about which the owner is quite proud. Among the limited number of desserts, the *kheer* (rice pudding) is excellent, thicker and tastier than other local versions, and one of a half-dozen sweet ways to finish a meal, provided you have some room.

Hoang Son $4

1005 St. Emmanuel (at McKinney, in the Kim Hung Market) 77003, (713) 225-2608

Cuisine - Vietnamese
Hours - Daily 10AM to 8PM
Credit Cards - NONE
Service - Counter Service
Alcohol - NONE

Entrée Prices - $2 to $6 ($4 average)
Entrées $12 and less - 100%

Atmosphere & Décor - Small shopping center food court
Appeal - Possibly the best Vietnamese sandwiches in town
Menu Suggestions - Banh Mi Thit Nuong (Vietnamese sandwich with char-grilled pork); Banh Mi Ga (Vietnamese sandwich with char-grilled chicken); Banh Mi Dau Hu (Vietnamese sandwich with tofu); Banh Mi Xiu (Vietnamese sandwich with a Vietnamese-style lunch meat - you might not want to know any more)

Located in the open area in the small, enclosed Kim Hung mall east of downtown, Hoang Son is a great stop for a Vietnamese sandwich or another casual Vietnamese dish for hardly a song. Open daily, it never appears to be crowded, but there is nearly always a patron or two sitting at one of the tables set in front of the food counter and the adjoining grocery store. Most of the customers are working class Vietnamese and Mexican folks from companies near the Ship Channel, and students from nearby apartments or colleges. The attraction for most of the non-Vietnamese patrons is the *banh mi,* the Vietnamese sandwiches. These sandwiches take longer to prepare than at any other local or Vietnamese sandwich shops, but these are certainly worth the wait. The sandwiches are carefully assembled to order with ingredients as good as you will find at any sandwich shop. Hoang Son then toasts each sandwich for a minute or so. The sandwiches arrive very warm, which is unusual for most local *banh mi.* The ingredients and fillings are all very good from the mayonnaise slathered in a thin coating on each of the sandwiches, to the homemade pâté, sprigs of fresh cilantro, marinated and shredded carrots, the meats, and especially the crusty standard-sized *banh mi* baguette. These things make these some of the very best Vietnamese sandwiches around. They go light on the fresh jalapeño here, but additional spice is easy to come by with a squirt of *sriracha.* Each of the sandwiches is worth ordering. The popular char-grilled pork is excellent. Nearly as good is the char-grilled chicken. These two will cost you an extra fifty cents more than the other sandwiches at $2. This is a great place if you've got a job, but it doesn't pay, or if it does. The versions with tofu, and a strange ham-like meat and pâté are also good, and even cheaper. Though tasty, and better than at most other *banh mi* purveyors, it's not an attractive mélange, and one which might upset the squeamish. Other sandwich fillings are pâté solo, shredded steamed chicken and pork meatballs. Depending upon which family member is behind the counter, if you do not speak or read some Vietnamese, it might be difficult to order anything other than the excellent sandwiches, or the sixteen dishes whose photos are shown behind the counter. On the far tableau there are *banh mi* (Vietnamese sandwiches), *pho* (beef noodle soups), *banh cuon* (rice rolls), *bun* (vermicelli dishes), and *com dia* (rice dishes) plus *che* (puddings) and *ghia khat* (drinks). The rice dishes look quite good. Another marquee reiterates the sandwich choices, which lists a half-dozen fried rice dishes for around $5.

Hobbit Café $9

2243 Richmond (between Kirby and Greenbriar) 77098, (713) 526-5460

Cuisine - American; Vegetarian
Hours - Mon-Fri 11AM to 9:30PM; Sat 10:30AM to 10:30PM; Sun 10:30AM to 9PM
Credit Cards - Amex, Discover, MC, Visa
Service - Table Service
Alcohol - Beer & Wine

Entrée Prices - $7 to $13 ($9 average)
Entrées $12 and less - 90%

Atmosphere & Décor - Comfortable and relaxed; patio
Appeal - Healthy and well prepared food in a pleasant, low-key setting
Useful to Note - Non-health conscious diners can also visit without trepidation.

Menu Suggestions - Wild Salmon Burger; Portobello fajitas; Spinach Mushroom Enchiladas; Gandalf sandwich (with avocado and mushrooms with melted cheese); Smaugs Delight sandwich (smoked turkey, avocado, tomato and melted cheese)

Quietly occupying a charming, low-slung Tudor-style building, you might envision that Hobbit Café is set in a shire. The expanse of the asphalt parking lot and house that is just a half-block from a busy street might quickly dissuade you from that thought, though. But, it takes nothing from the attraction of this friendly and comfortable vegetarian-leaning restaurant with an array of informal dishes that has been popular for a long time. As the name suggests, Hobbit Café has a connection to the Tolkien series, but it's not trying to capitalize on the blockbuster *Lord of the Rings* movies, which it predates by quite a few years; its predecessor opened in 1972. A number of dishes, mainly the popular vegetarian sandwiches and drinks, are named after characters in the book.

A key attraction for many customers is that there are well over a dozen vegetarian dishes, more than just soups and salads, which range from Tex-Mex to sandwiches to soy and black bean burgers. And, most of the other preparations strive to be healthier than is the norm, with the sandwiches and burgers are served between whole wheat bread and buns, but the carnivore should visit without trepidation. There are a number of juicy and tasty burgers, fajitas, enchiladas, meat-laden sandwiches on the good-sized menu, and the tasty and fat-laden avocados can make it into many dishes. Plus, everyone seems to like smoothies, of which there are several flavors, made here with fresh fruit, honey and ice. The kitchen is very proficient with apparently everything, regardless of the featured protein. One of the better dishes is the Wild Salmon Burger that features a hand-formed salmon patty with plentiful mixed greens and a dill-accented light cream sauce that is a welcome array of flavors. Interestingly, the standard side for the numerous sandwiches is shredded raw carrots, which is a hard-to-miss bright orange portion to many diners' plates. Black beans, wild rice and fresh fruit or the less heart-friendly, if possibly more enjoyable fries, chips or onion chips also available. Seating is divided between a couple rooms in the house, and there are tables on the good-sized porch. It's a quaint and relaxed place. Service is friendly and usually quite efficient, and an inviting selection of beers and wine are offered that can make the visit even more enjoyable.

Hollywood $11

2409 Montrose (just south of Fairview) 77006, (713) 523-8802

Cuisine - Vietnamese; Chinese
Hours - Mon-Thu, Sun 11AM to 2AM; Fri-Sat 11AM to 4AM

Credit Cards - Amex, Discover, MC, Visa
Service - Table Service
Alcohol - Beer & Wine

Entrée Prices - Dinner - $7 to $17 ($11 average); Lunch - $7 to $8
Entrées at Dinner $12 and less - 70%

Atmosphere & Décor - Very nice; patio
Appeal - Often excellent, wide-ranging Vietnamese fare; opened very late
Useful to Note - It's near the heart of the Montrose club district.
Menu Suggestions - Steamed rice with char-grilled pork and an egg roll (com dia thit nuong, etc.); Black Pepper Scallops; Black Pepper Soft Shell Crab; Chao Tom (shrimp paste on sugar cane skewers)

Now housed in the prime former space of the past favorite Café Noche on Montrose, Hollywood is one of the most attractive Vietnamese restaurants in town. Don't be dismayed by the fact that it shares the same name with several convenience stores (which are seemingly owned by the same family) and other nearby businesses, the food here can be excellent. Not only that, the décor and often the atmosphere are both very nice, and not just by local Vietnamese restaurant standards. Artistic etched-glass decorates dark wood partitions to help divide the dining areas into manageable sections and attractive plating, help give Hollywood a somewhat sophisticated, intimate while still lively feel. There are no plastic bottles of *sriracha* set on the tables. Service is usually earnest, if not terribly polished; very late at night, it certainly doesn't matter. In a city with a deficiency in quality late night eateries, Hollywood answers the call, as it's open until two each morning, and four on the weekends. It's very close to the center of the Montrose gay club action, which can make for some interesting late-night people watching. The large patio that faces Montrose is a popular attraction, as it has been with its predecessor restaurants. There is even a second patio to accommodate a large number of diners and drinkers. There are over twenty appetizers and a number of desserts that might provide a fine accompaniment to the imbiber.

In addition to the appetizers and desserts, Hollywood features an extremely lengthy menu, true to the local Vietnamese restaurant tradition, though English predominates, and some of the most exotic items are not represented. No tendon or tripe in the *pho* or eel clay pots. And, its also different in that it has a section dedicated to entrée-size green salads, all topped with some sort of tasty protein and available with a choice from among ten dressings. It also has a section of Vietnamese fajitas, not just with beef, but any of several char-grilled items served with the thin rice paper that is the substitute for tortillas. Additionally, there are some Chinese dishes, American and some French-inspired dishes, too. The numerous

Vietnamese dishes are probably the best bets here. The large menu is neatly divided among soups such as *pho*, rice noodle soups, egg noodle soups and the Chinese restaurant soups, stir-fried rice noodles, stir-fried egg noodles, salads, rice platter (*com dia*), vermicelli (*bun*), Vietnamese fajitas, pork, beef, chicken, seafood, vegetables, French and American dishes. Along with beef and chicken, there are plenty of seafood entrées. More than shrimp, there are crabs, squid, mussels, scallops, salmon and snapper. The black pepper creations with scallops and soft shell crabs are two favorites here, and there are similar dishes featuring other seafood and also chicken. For the value conscious, Hollywood does a very good job with the more humble *bun* and rice plates. The popular char-grilled pork is very flavorful, even the steamed white rice is noticeably better than at most other places. Some of these are available as lunch specials for a dollar less, along with about a dozen Chinese-American favorites. The latter is not a prime reason to visit, since here you'll get Bellaire Boulevard quality Vietnamese fare served attractively, in nice digs, and a neighborhood-friendly atmosphere and a couple of large patios. If you have room or desire for dessert, or just need some late night sugar, Hollywood serves nearly twenty cakes, tarts and mousses.

Houston Barbecue Company $8

1127 Eldridge Parkway (south of Memorial) 77077, (281) 531-6800
www.houstonbarbecue.com

Cuisine - Barbecue
Hours - Mon-Sat 11AM to 9PM; Sun 11AM to 8PM
Credit Cards - Amex, Diners, Discover, MC, Visa
Service - Counter Service
Alcohol - Full Bar

Entrée Prices - $6 to $14 ($8 average)
Entrées $12 and less - 90%

Atmosphere & Décor - Functional
Appeal - Good Texas-style barbecue on the west side
Menu Suggestions - sliced brisket sandwich; chopped brisket sandwich

Located in a small, not unattractive strip center built near the beginning of the millenium, Houston Barbecue Company aptly fills a need for quality Central Texas-style barbecue in this part of town. Situated near several office buildings, and a short drive from many more, this was bound to be a hit if the food was good. And, it is. Crowds have been filling this place during lunchtime for a while now. Many will notice a similarity with Luling City Market on Richmond, including service on butcher paper. This is no coincidence, as the owner of Houston Barbecue Company is also a part of the family that owns that long-standing Inner Loop favorite; certainly not a bad model to follow. It might not quite live up to the original, but Houston Barbecue Company still serves good barbecue. While the food might not be quite as flavorful, the service is friendlier and more proficient. This is an inviting place, one where lines move quickly, and there always seems to be a space to sit, even during the peak lunchtime rush. The minimal menu is just like that at Luling City Market. The choices of meats from the oak-fired cooking pit are brisket, pork ribs, turkey, chicken and beef sausage. The properly charred and attractive brisket, sliced in front of you, is reliably moist and tasty. The beef sausage, made on premise, is also worth ordering. Everything is better here with at least a few drops of the excellent mustard-inflected barbecue sauce, just like at Luling City Market. The smoked meats also are available as plates. The beef and turkey are also served as sandwiches on onion rolls. Both the sandwiches featuring the brisket, the sliced beef, and the pre-minced, chopped beef from the steam tray, which has a slightly different taste in addition to the different texture, are good here. In fact, all of the meats are worth ordering. The basic barbecue sides, potato salad and beans, are made in-house, but are rather forgettable. The similarly homemade desserts, however are much better. Both the chocolate chip brownies, and the tiny, invidual pecan pies are a nice way to finish a meal, if you have room.

Houston Tamale Company $8

1050 Studewood (at E. 11th) 77008, (713) 802-1800

Cuisine - Mexican (taqueria)
Hours - Mon-Fri 8AM to 6PM; Sat 8AM to 4PM; Sun 9AM to 2PM
Credit Cards - Amex, Discover, MC, Visa
Service - Counter Service
Alcohol - NONE

Entrée Prices - $4 to $9 ($8 average)
Entrées $12 and less - 100%

Atmosphere & Décor - Quite sparse, but noticeably friendly
Appeal - Top-notch tamales and hearty breakfast tacos
Menu Suggestions - carne guisada taco (stewed beef); breakfast tacos; pork tamales; beef tamales

Tasty, large breakfast tacos, suitably beefy *carne guisada* and some of the very best commercially made tamales in Houston are probably the best reasons to visit this low-key and friendly Heights eatery. The family that owns the place is originally from Monterrey in northern Mexico, and the small menu hits most of the casual local Mexican favorites from there, in addition to the breakfast tacos and tamales: burritos, fajitas, tacos, *flautas* and large *quesadillas*. There is also *barbacoa* and *menudo* on the weekends. The very satisfying tacos are available in a limited, but appealing array of fajita, grilled chicken, *carne guisada* (beef stew), *milanesa* (breaded beef cutlet) and the combination *norteño*. There is also *menudo* and *barbacoa* on the weekends. The *carne guisada* features flavorful, tender dark brown cubes of meat with some mild spicing. The thick homemade flour tortillas provide a properly tasty basis for these and other tacos and burritos. Each is served with cross-border combination of raw onions, cilantro, shredded lettuce and chopped tomatoes. The tamales are recognizably thin and served in corn husks. The beef and pork are possibly the best of the choices, which also includes the blander chicken, mixed meat, and by special request on a day's notice, vegetarian, and jalapeño and cheese. With items convenient for travel, takeout is popular. Probably, too, since décor and atmosphere are rather limited, and may discourage lingering. No matter, the food is very tasty and a good value. Plus, the restaurant is very convenient for residents in the greater Heights.

Hunan Plus $6

9124 Bellaire (between Gessner and Ranchester) 77036, (713) 995-8825

Cuisine - Chinese
Hours - Mon, Wed - Sun 11AM to 10PM
Credit Cards - MC, Visa
Service - Table Service
Alcohol - NONE

Entrée Prices - Dinner - $4 to $8 ($6 average); Lunch - $3 to $4
Entrées at Dinner $12 and less - 100%

Atmosphere & Décor - Spartan
Appeal - Very good, very cheap Chinese food, especially for lunch
Useful to Note - It is closed on Tuesdays.
Menu Suggestions - Tung Tin Shrimp; Shrimp in Lobster Sauce; Shrimp Fried Rice; Kung Pao Chicken

Hunan Plus is one of the many unassuming, relatively small, Chinese restaurants that are packed like sardines in strip centers on Bellaire in New Chinatown. Unlike many of its competitors, and in concert with its proficient neighbors Sichuan Cuisine and Shanghai, Hunan Plus stands out in that it provides one of the better combinations of usually delicious, familiar and freshly prepared Chinese food with prompt and mostly efficient service and very low prices. It is also one of the very few Chinese restaurants on Bellaire that gets an overflow crowd at lunch, both with the

Chinese and non-Chinese patrons. Though the service cannot be described as polished, unlike many other neighboring places, it seems to earnest and friendly, at least. And unlike many of those places, the turnaround from the kitchen (for all of the dishes) is usually quite fast, even with a full dining room. Décor in the one relatively small dining room is functional, if not as nice as some of its neighbors, but not dumpy, either. Your fellow patrons ensure that there is buzz to the place.

Lunchtime, daily from 11AM to 3PM, is a smart time to visit, as there are ten satisfying lunch specials available for the ridiculously low price of $3.25 or so. These include the Amercanized dishes such as Sweet and Sour Chicken, Sweet and Sour Pork, Beef Broccoli, Cashew Chicken, Scallion Beef and the very appetizing Kung Pao Chicken. Though maybe not authentic and popular with the non-Chinese crowd, these are nontheless prepared such that the dishes are flavorful, and not heavy or gooey, as many of these are sometimes served at other Chinese restaurants. For an additional dollar at lunch you can get several other dishes including the surprisingly very good Tung Tin Shrimp featuring loads of fresh broccoli and some green beans, and the Shrimp in Lobster Sauce, both served with plenty of very fresh, expertly cooked, decent-sized shrimp. All of these inexpensive lunch specials feature fairly large entrées and come with a choice of soup, an egg roll and moist fried rice. These accompianments are quite satisfactory. The hot and sour soup can be very good, viscous and full of flavor. It is one of the better starter soups in the area. The sides of fried rice, moist white rice tossed lightly with egg whites, are very reliable. Even the egg rolls, that are definitely an afterthought at most Chinese restaurants, are decent. It's amazing how much fairly high quality food you can get for lunch for under $4 (before drink, tax and tip). To be noted, even though the cuisine of the namesake Hunan region has a reputation for spicy cuisine, the dishes listed as hot and spicy are not so by Houston standards. There is plenty of hot chili sauce available upon request, though.

Though the lunch hours might be the most cost effective time to visit, almost any time is a fine time to visit Hunan Plus. There are appealing, and still very inexpensive dishes available beyond the hours of the lunch specials. The menu is divided among several appetizers, soups, and entrées featuring noodles, fried rice, vegetables, chicken, pork, beef, bean curd, fish, other seafood, and clay pots. There are over seventy entrées on the main menu. The Chinese patrons are usually enjoying dishes that do not seem to appear on the menu, though maybe it just is that the English description does not do them justice. Without fail, they also look very appealing when brought to the waiting tables. With the exception of the handful of hot pot dishes, all of the non-seafood dishes are under five dollars. Even most of the seafood entrées are well under $10. If the shrimp are any indication, these prices are an incredible bargin for fresh, well prepared seafood. The fried rice with shrimp is an amazingly large mound of perfectly cooked rice with scrambled egg scattered with very palatable, fresh shrimp for a song. Also available for those who speak or read Chinese, like its neighbors, Hunan Plus offers a small number of dim sum offerings such as steamed and pan-fried dumplings that seem quite appetizing.

Istanbul Grill $9

5613 Morningside (just north of University) 77005, (713) 526-2800
www.istanbulgrill.com

Cuisine - Turkish
Hours - Tue-Sun 10AM to 10PM
Credit Cards - Amex, MC, Visa
Service - Table Service
Alcohol - Beer & Wine

Entrée Prices - $7 to $14 ($9 average)
Entrées $12 and less - 90%

Atmosphere & Décor - Nice, inviting; patio
Appeal - Very good, inexpensive Turkish food in quaint, yet lively setting
Useful to Note - The Ginger Man is essentially next door, barely a stumble away.
Menu Suggestions - hummus; Karsuk Pide (cheese, eggs on meat stuffed in a thick pide bread); Kofte Kabab (ground lamb kabob); Adana Kabab (lamb seasoned with spicy, red peppers and broiled); Tavuk Adana Sandwich (chopped chicken breast with spicy peppers in pide bread); Doner Kabob (marinated slices of beef and lamb); Lahmacun (chopped tomatoes, parsley, green peppers, eggplant dip and garlic on a flat bread and baked); Turkish coffee

Istanbul Grill is another reason to brave the traffic and parking travails in the Village with its interesting, well prepared Turkish food in a pleasant, informal setting, often lively atmosphere, and noticeably friendly and eager service. With its comfortable décor of white walls, Turkish ornaments and travel posters, and somewhat open kitchen, this can be a nice place to linger and chat after dinner. There are also a few tables in front of the dining room and a small patio in the rear.

The Turkish fare here won't be unfamiliar to those who occasionally visit the more casual Greek and Middle Eastern restaurants. Many of the ingredients and dishes, in fact, are the same. Olive oil, cucumbers, eggplants, parsley, lemon juice and lamb are used in many of the dishes. From the broad Mediterranean and Middle Eastern traditions, Istanbul Grill features clean flavors, moist, grilled meats, and freshly baked breads. For appetizers, there are stuffed grape leaves, *hummus* and *tabouli*; for entrées, there are various juicy shish kabobs with marinated beef, lamb and chicken, and the fairly well-known Turkish dish, *Doner Kebab,* made with lamb and beef that is similar to gyro meat, though tastier than most local renditions of that; and there is the phyllo pastry *baklava* for dessert. In addition to these, Istanbul Grill offers a fair number of other Turkish specialties. Many are baked in a traditional brick oven that is evident in the somewhat open kitchen. The kabob platters are a great value here. The portions are generous and served with a large amount of moist rice and grilled tomatoes and bell peppers. Warm, house-made thin *pide* bread is on every table. This becomes difficult not to eat readily, especially when dipped into the nearly addictive olive oil and sesame seed mixture that accompanies it. This bread is prominent in one of the best entrées, the *Karadeniz Pide* that seems something like a pizza. It is hand-rolled *pide* bread, with a choice of two toppings among a mozzarella-like cheese, sausage, pastrami and eggs. It's especially good when topped with mozzarella and sausage. The *Lahmacun* Platter will make for an enjoyable and surprisingly familiar meal for most. It is of a small green salad and two *lahmacuns,* which consist of chopped tomatoes, parsley, green peppers, garlic and an eggplant dip that are wrapped in flat bread then baked. The result is something like large Turkish burritos. At under six bucks, the *pide*-filled sandwiches can make for a very satisfying and inexpensive lunch. These are half a loaf of the fresh *pide* bread with tomatoes, onions, red cabbage and a choice of any of the seven different kabobs. For beverages, Istanbul Grill offers several Turkish specialties including the very thick and strong Turkish coffee. It has a fairly large amount of flavor and caffeine in the half-dozen sips of liquid that are in the small cup. They serve the Turkish tea, *cay,* in small handleless glass cups that are a nice touch. There is also orange juice, a popular accompaniment in Turkey, and *ayran,* described as a creamy yogurt drink. Istanbul Grill serves beer and wine, much to the enjoyment of the patrons who wish to further complement the meal. Located at the edge of the Rice Village, the Istanbul Grill fits well with the myriad of other small ethnic eateries in the Village. Since it is in the Village and the restaurant has just a handful of spaces, parking can be bit tough at night. The restaurant is certainly worth a little effort to park. While there, you should plan to stay for a while, as the Ginger Man is conveniently located next door for a relaxing pre- or post-dinner beer.

Jade Village $10

5858 S. Gessner (southwest corner at Harwin) 77036, (713) 774-3800

Cuisine - Chinese
Hours - Daily 11AM to 10PM

Credit Cards - Amex, Diners, Discover, MC, Visa
Service - Table Service
Alcohol - Beer & Wine

Entrée Prices - Dinner - $5 to $20 ($10 average); Lunch - $4 to $5
Entrées at Dinner $12 and less - 90%

Atmosphere & Décor - Spartan
Appeal - Very well prepared Cantonese and Cantonese-inspired food for cheap
Menu Suggestions - hot and sour soup; Szechuan Chicken; Garlic Chicken; Szechuan Shrimp

On the northern edge of the New Chinatown area at Gessner and Harwin, Jade Village serves up good Cantonese food, and the familiar Cantonese-inspired food for very reasonable prices. It's popular both with the local Chinese community and a diverse group of local non-Asian office workers. This is another Chinese restaurant that aptly serves two distinct clienteles with nearly two completely different bills of fare. The restaurant is large, and décor is a bit lacking, as is often the service though the kitchen quickly turns around orders. But, most importantly, the food is consistently flavorful, even at its least ambitious. And, cheap. The quality-to-value factor is quite high here, especially during lunchtime.

For a fairly large restaurant in New Chinatown, it almost goes without stating that the menu will be tri-lingual and huge. The assimilated dishes that mostly appeal to non-Chinese are segregated in a small section of the menu. These include appetizers like egg rolls and crab puffs, egg drop and wonton soup, fried rice dishes and *chow mein* (fried noodles), *lo mein* (boiled noodles) and chop suey. The nearly thirty lunch specials fall into another similar section. No matter. These dishes are ridiculously cheap and still quite good, with the exception of the lame egg rolls. It is a testament to the kitchen that they do a commendable job with these more mundane dishes. OK, these can be gloppy at times, but for less than five bucks you can get a choice of an egg roll or fried chicken wing, fried rice or steamed rice, egg drop or hot and sour soup, and an entrée. It is a more-than-fair amount of food, especially for the price. The lunch special entrées include most of the Chinese-American favorites such as Moo Goo Gai Pan, Kung Pao Chicken, Lemon Chicken, Szechuan Beef, Shrimp with Broccoli and Sweet and Sour Pork. The Szechuan-named dishes (chicken, beef and shrimp) are reliably good, whether or not these are authentically re-created, it doesn't seem to matter much. Though not spicy, as indicated on the menu, these are quickly cooked with plenty of crisp scallions and a fair amount of good quality meat or shrimp. These lunch specials are generously served seven days a week from 11AM to 3PM. The usually large number of Chinese patrons certainly eschew the lunch specials and enjoy items from the main menu. The rest of this menu contains over 200 items, about two-thirds of which is seafood. The menu is divided among Soup, Abalone-Sea Cucumber (which can be excellent, by the way), Lobster, Clam, Oyster, Crab, Scallop, Fish, Seafood (shrimp dishes), Sizzling Plate, Squid, Beef, Duck - Squab, Chicken, Bean Curd, Clay Pot, Pork, Vegetable, Fried Rice and Noodle. There are a large number of enticingly listed dishes, so any craving for southern Chinese cooking could probably be satiated here. With the exception of some of the more exotic seafood such as the lobster, abalone and lobster, most dishes are around $10 But, during the day, with the lunch specials priced so low, these are tough to pass. Though the value-priced lunch specials might be a big attraction for the non-Chinese patrons, Jade Village also does very good business with the Chinese community in the evening.

Jarro Café $8

1521 Gessner (between Long Point and Hammerly) 77080, (713) 827-0373

Cuisine - Mexican (taqueria)
Hours - Mon-Thu, Sun 9AM to 10PM; Fri-Sat 9AM to 12AM
Credit Cards - Amex, Discover, MC, Visa
Service - Counter Service
Alcohol - NONE

Entrée Prices - Dinner & Lunch - $6 to $13 ($8 average); Breakfast - $4 to $6
Entrées at Dinner $12 and less - 100%

Atmosphere & Décor - Pleasant and comfortable; family-friendly
Appeal - Well-made Mexico City-style tacos and more
Useful to Note - The salsas can be incredibly hot, really; taco truck is good, too.
Menu Suggestions - taco saudero (with a lemon-tinged sirloin beef); bifsteak taco (tacos with sirloin); taco al pastor (with roasted pork); taco conchinita pibil (Yucatan-style stewed pork); breakfast tacos; Chilaquiles con Carne Asada; flautas

In a scruffy stretch of Gessner in Spring Branch, Jarro Café has grown from a taco truck to a pleasant, clean, family-friendly restaurant residing in a nicely refurbished old Pizza Inn. The restaurant is well-lit, bright and comfortable. Posters of the Beatles and old movies decorate a couple of the walls, much unlike restaurants that serve similar, authentic Mexican food. And, the air is often filled with Beatles music and covers to remind you that Beatlemania hasn't bitten the dust. The now very sleek and modern taco truck is still there. One sits in the parking lot in front of the restaurant and does a very brisk business with the more casual items from the restaurants menu. Another truck might be parked in back. The dishes, both outside and in, are inspired by Mexico City street fare with tacos predominately featured. Jarro Café is part of a small cross-border chain that actually began in Mexico. The fillings for the tacos are somewhat different than at many other local *taquerias* with *tinga* (spicy beef), *pastor* (pork roasted with pineapple), *carnitas* (pork), *bistek* (grilled beef steak), beef and mushroom, beef and *chorizo*, and *saudero* (lemon-tinged beef) comprising several of the choices. These are somewhat unusual, but even the Tex-Mex food lover should find an item or several that will satisfy. The beef is noticeably of better quality and is better tasting, both in the tacos and as the thinly sliced *carne asada*, than at most local Mexican eateries. It will probably take a moment with the menu, though now no longer confusingly multi-colored, as it contains many tempting and probably new choices for most customers. That is coupled with the fact that the service can be a bit clumsy, and the queue behind the order taker / cashier to place an order moves very slowly. Some Spanish is helpful. This doesn't deter the non-Mexican Spring Branch clientele who also frequent this place.

Once you order, you should find the tidy self-service area near the cashier that contains five salsas of bright and unusual hues, and flavors that are somewhat unique among local *taquerias*, yet quite enjoyable. The salsas used to carry the very accurate admonishment, "*salsas muy picosos* / salsas are very hot". In general order (that could change) from mild to exceedingly hot: dark maroon that has an enjoyable sweet taste with a hint of molasses; dull, deep green with a slight sweetness; brown with a strong flavor of oregano; very bright green, which is also fiery; and orange, seemingly made from the incendiary habanero whose taste pauses briefly, like a fist being pulled back, before delivering a scorching blow. In addition to these are a very different topping of coarsely chopped dark pink onions with large flecks of oregano, a bowl of chopped cilantro, and two others, one with white onion slices, and the other with noticeably fresh and ripe lime quarters. Unfortunately, the warmed orange salsa served with the chips is unusual-tasting with strong hints of oregano, though rather uninteresting. The tacos, in their many forms, are served with a choice of tasty flour or corn tortillas, are probably the best thing to order here. With a business that began as a taco truck, you would expect that they do these quite well; and, these rarely disappoint. The enchiladas, though tasty and plentiful, might contain steamed chicken that has not been fully drained for a too-watery result. The breakfast tacos are also different than the ones familiar to most Houstonians. Corn tortillas substitute for flour and pieces of what seems to be an omelet replaces the scrambled egg. No matter, the result is still delicious. Among the other choices is a bountiful version of *chilaquiles* that is served not only with eggs, but also beef. Fairly similar, though slicker, than most local *taquerias*, the biggest difference might be that there is no beer, much less *aguas frescas* or the smoothie-like *licuados*. No matter. It's a very good place to visit, if not to linger, and the lack of beer probably encourages more families to visit.

Jasmine Asian Cuisine $12

9938 Bellaire (between Corporate and the Beltway) 77036, (713) 272-8188
www.jasmineasiancuisine.com

Cuisine - Vietnamese; Chinese
Hours - Daily 11AM to 11PM
Credit Cards - Amex, Discover, MC, Visa
Service - Table Service
Alcohol - Beer & Wine

Entrée Prices - Dinner - $5 to $25 ($12 average); Lunch - $4 to $7
Entrées at Dinner $12 and less - 70%

Atmosphere & Décor - Very Pleasant
Appeal - Often excellent Vietnamese and Chinese food; very cheap lunch specials
Menu Suggestions - Cha Gio (Vietnamese egg rolls); Goi Bo (alphabet noodle soup in a beef broth); Chao Bo (beef salad); Bo Xao Lan (sliced beef in a curry sauce); Bo Luc Lac (broiled pieces of beef served with rice); Bo Nuong Xa (char-grilled beef with lemongrass): Shrimp with Honey Walnuts (lightly breaded and fried shrimp with honey-glazed walnuts in a mayonnaise sauce); Muc Rang Muoi (Salted Toasted Shrimp); whole grilled catfish

Located in an attractive spot near the Beltway that once housed Ba Ky, Jasmine, like its sister restaurant Saigon Pagaloc a few blocks east on Bellaire, is one of the best Vietnamese restaurants in New Chinatown. This means in the entire Houston area, too. In a smart and very appealing setting with over 200 seats, it offers a seamless blend of not only top quality Vietnamese, but also Southern Chinese dishes. In fact, it has been called both one of the best Vietnamese and Chinese restaurants by different sources. The dinner menu is amazingly large, and seems to contain almost everything from the Vietnamese restaurant repertoire and a good number from the Chinese. Most of the menu headings are: appetizers, soup (*canh*), hot pot, seafood (*do bien*), fish (*ca*), beef, chicken, pork, vegetables, House Specialties (*nuong vi* - "cook on a griddle at your table"), Grilled Specialties (*do nuong*), Fondue Style (*nhung dam*), vermicelli dishes (*bun*), rice platters (*com dia*), fried rice, *lo mein* (boiled noodles), pan-fried noodles (*mi xao din*), pan-fried thick noodles (*hu tieu xao*), rice noodle soups (*pho, mi* and *hiu*), desserts, and ice cream, even in homemade coconut and durian flavors. Plus, there are the seven courses of beef and seven and five courses of fish, and yet another page of twenty or so (non-griddle-cooked) House Specialties. The former of the House Specialties includes some very unique surf and turf combinations.

One of the several signs above the restaurant advertises "Beef / Fish / Seven Courses". The more familiar, if familiar is the correct phrase, refers to beef prepared seven different ways. It also offers fish in different preparations with grouper standing in for the beef. Without describing it in elaborate detail or doing it much justice, the courses of beef here consist of a manageable array that begins with slices of raw beef that you cook yourself in a hot water broth (the bowl with the sterno can below; the other is for soaking the rice paper wrappers), several sausage-like creations, meatballs, a salad with ground beef, and a bowl of alphabet (really) noodle soup in a beefy broth. The salad and soup are especially good. A bounteous plate of ridiculously large and fresh herbs accompanies the first course. Also, served with other entrées like the *pho* and the Imperial rolls, it can include basil, purple basil, mint and others that enhance the enjoyment of many of the main items. In addition to beef, seafood is a specialty here, as can be inferred by offering fish seven and five ways as entrées. One example is the Hong Kong-style Shrimp with Honey Walnuts featuring plump large shrimp in a light mayonnaise sauce, which is an excellent dish. The entire grilled catfish has drawn raves, and grouper, in its many guises, is also popular.

One of the best reasons to visit is not found on the voluminous dinner menu; it's the great value lunches. There is a long list of nearly fifty $4 lunch specials that are fantastic deals. These feature many of the beef, pork, chicken, vegetables and seafood entrées with steamed rice that are served at dinner, including Pepper Steak (*bo xao ot xanh*) and the savory Beef with Coconut and Curry Sauce (*bo xao lan*). In addition to these is a number of others that are just a dollar or two more such as char-grilled beef with lemongrass (*bo nuong xa*) and grilled shrimp (*tom nuong*). For the timid, there are some recognizable items such as Kung Pao Chicken, General Joe's Chicken and Moo Goo Gai Pan. Given the dexterity of the kitchen, even these draw patrons.

Java Java Café $8

911 W. 11th (east of Shepherd) 77008, (713) 880-5282

Cuisine - American
Hours - Mon-Fri 7:30AM to 3PM; Sat-Sun 8:30AM to 3PM
Credit Cards - Amex, MC, Visa
Service - Table Service
Alcohol - NONE; BYOB

Entrée Prices - Lunch - $5 to $12 ($8 average); Breakfast - $4 to $9
Entrées at Lunch $12 and less - 90%

Atmosphere & Décor - Comfortable
Appeal - Very good breakfasts at a colorful spot in the Heights

Menu Suggestions - Big Breakfast (three eggs cooked to order with meat, potatoes or grits and a croissant): Breakfast Combo (half of a Belgian waffle, three eggs and a choice of meat); Eggs Benedict; Chicken Salad Sandwich; Chicken Salad Platter

---

Near the western edge of the Heights, Java Java Café is bustling with a diverse crowd on most weekend mornings; deservedly so, as this is one of the better breakfast stops in Houston. Breakfast is also served daily during the week at this capable breakfast-and-lunch spot. Java Java sports a nice, urbane but breezy décor. It's a fairly hip place, but thankfully lacking any pretension. Excellent breakfasts and quick, friendly and usually efficient service are the hallmarks of Java Java. And, with a name like theirs, the coffee, that necessary morning beverage, should be rich and flavorful, and it is. They pour some of the best drip coffee in the area.

Java Java serves most of the standard American breakfasts, and breakfast tacos during the week, most with a bit more flair than is expected. Prices for most of the breakfasts seem slightly higher here than many casual restaurants, but portions are good-sized. Most of the egg dishes are made with three very large eggs, for example. A good basic, hearty breakfast is the aptly named Big Breakfast. It consists of three eggs cooked to order, a choice among bacon, ham or sausage, diced potatoes with scallions or grits, and a croissant. The side of bacon is properly cooked and plentiful. The kitchen does an admirable job with the eggs in most of its guises. Other regular egg dishes are the three-egg omelet with a choice of two or more ingredients and *Huevos Rancheros* (here, eggs any style over corn tortillas and salsa). The French toast is done differently here; house-baked croissants replace slices of bread for a very enjoyable revision. The waffles are served with toasted pecans and topped with an orange butter glaze. The malty Belgian waffle is proclaimed as being the best in town. It might be. This waffle is served plain, with fresh fruit, pecans, a fruit compote (a chilled syrupy concoction), or with three eggs, as part of the Breakfast Combo. Available just on the weekend is their version of Eggs Benedict with a croissant base, and another version that substitutes avocado and tomato slices for the ham. The more traditional version is especially tasty, even if the eggs have the tendency to be overcooked. There is also Eggs Florentine, a dish of spinach, artichoke bottoms (these are essentially the same as the artichoke hearts), poached eggs and covered with a hollandaise sauce.

In addition to breakfast, Java Java serves lunch fare until 3PM. The eclectic, but familiar menu, well-suited for the Heights, consists of soups, salad, a quiche of the day, sandwiches, burgers, pastas and Tex-Mex, most with a healthy bent; the burgers, maybe less so. The salads include the Java Chef with feta cheese, a Caesar with chicken or salmon, and the unusual Tropical salad. This is a pineapple stuffed with a choice among chicken, tuna or shrimp salad. There is a similar one that substitutes avocado for the pineapple. The sandwiches are a recognizable lineup such as roast beef, baked ham, roasted turkey, chicken, tuna and shrimp salads, BLT, a club, and the Java Sunrise, which is bacon or ham with two eggs and cheese (not to be confused with the similar Java Surprise omelet). The chicken salad served on a croissant is a winner. There are also pasta dishes, several of the basic Southern Italian-American choices such as lasagna, pasta with marinara sauce, Alfredo sauce with either chicken or shrimp and one with vegetables and a garlic-butter sauce. The Tex-Mex dishes are *quesadillas* with grilled chicken or beef, *chalupas*, nachos, fajitas, a vegetable sauté and the Waffelupa. This is a crisp stack of cornbread waffles topped with sautéed onions, peppers and beef or chicken, black beans and finished with melted cheese. Rounding out the offerings are the heartier Chef Specialties served during the week, which can include Beef Stroganoff, Shrimp Scampi, Fried Shrimp and chicken breast sautéed in a wine sauce.

Jax Grill $9

1613 Shepherd (between I-10 and Washington) 77007, (713) 861-5529
6510 S. Rice (near Bellaire) 77401, (713) 668-3606

Cuisine - Texan
Hours - Shepherd - Mon-Thu 11AM to 10PM; Fri-Sat 11AM to 11PM; S. Rice - Daily 11AM to 11PM
Credit Cards - Amex, Discover, MC, Visa
Service - Counter Service
Alcohol - Shepherd - Full Bar; 6510 S. Rice - Beer & Wine

Entrée Prices - $5 to $18 ($9 average)
Entrées $12 and less - 80%

Atmosphere & Décor - Pleasant
Appeal - Satisfying and familiar food in informal neighborhood restaurants
Useful to Note - There is live zydeco on the weekends at the Shepherd location.
Menu Suggestions - Fried Shrimp Po Boy; Jax Burger; West Texas Burger (with bacon and cheese); Mesquite Grilled Fajitas; Mesquite Fajita Salad (mixed greens topped with tomatoes, onions, cheese, pico de gallo, guacamole, sour cream with grilled fajita meat or chicken breast); Shrimp on a Skewer (mesquite-grilled jumbo shrimp)

In two well-attended, fun, neighborhood eateries, the appeal of Jax Grill is apparent: well prepared and very affordable, freshly made, regional favorites served in an informal, but often lively, atmosphere. Where else but Houston would fried shrimp po boys, catfish, steaks, salads, good quality hamburgers, and even better mesquite-grilled fajitas be at home on a menu, especially like at the Shepherd location where live zydeco music is a feature on a weekly basis. The Bellaire location, close to a prosperous residential area, is much more of a family establishment; popular as an after-game stop for youth baseball and soccer teams. The original Shepherd location has a more adult crowd, and one that is maybe a bit more diverse, not to mention loud, possibly encouraged by the popularity of the cold beer. The fare is familiar and unpretentious. There should be something fried, grilled or tossed for everyone in your family or group. Jax is fairly priced across the board. The steaks can approach twenty dollars at the upper end, but these come with a salad and a baked potato or fries. As can probably be expected in casual settings like these, brisk business is done with hamburgers. Those, and most everything else, is pretty decent, although the somewhat bland "The Best Smoked Corn and Chicken Chowder" is hardly that. An order of the tender, mesquite-grilled fajitas for under ten bucks is a very good value, as it is tasty, as well as filling. The quality of the meat easily compensates for the obviously store-bought tortillas. Though the food, with the exception of the salads, might not be the most heart healthy around, Jax does try to help in some way with the assertion on the menu that they cook with peanut oil rather than delicious, but artery-clogging, lard or butter. The French fries are crisp, and better than average. These extras help improve the dining experience. All of the vegetables are very fresh: sliced red onions, romaine lettuce, and ripe, juicy, sliced roma tomatoes. The eight or so salad dressings are made in-house. Things like this help make the two Jax locations worthy stops for a burger or something else that will go well with a longneck, or something even more ambitious. Very important for a neighborhood and family types of places, Jax offers a short children's menu.

Only in Houston - 10 unique eateries

Beyond Tex-Mex and barbecue, below is short list of ten very good restaurants too expensive to be profiled for the guide that seem natural for Houston, but would be difficult to imagine in another city.

- **Café Red Onion Seafood & Mas** - Seafood - 12041 Northwest Freeway – Peru is the influence for his "Latino Sushi" and other dishes well-suited for the Houston climate and temperament.
- **Churrasco's** - Pan Latin - 2055 Westheimer & 9705 Westheimer – The signature churrasco steak, a very flavorful cut from the tenderloin, takes only its name from Argentina, but is perfect for a city that loves beef and vibrant pan-Latin flavors.
- **El Tiempo** - Tex-Mex - 3130 Richmond & 5602 Washington – Where else in the country would anyone flock to restaurants to pay so much for what is unabashedly Tex-Mex.

- **Goode Co. Seafood** - Seafood - 2621 Westpark & 10211 Katy Freeway – Excellent mesquite-grilled flounder, redfish and red snapper filets are worthy options along with the southern Louisiana and Mexican-influenced dishes. Seafood cocktail Campechana is locally renowned.
- **Joyce's** - Seafood - 6415 San Felipe & 3736 Westheimer - Easily blends culinary traditions of the Gulf Coast, Cajun Louisiana and Mexico in tasty dishes such as Blackened Catfish Enchiladas, and a place to show that Texas Gulf Coast seafood cooking extends well past deep-fried shrimp.
- **Ouisie's Table** - Texan / Southern - 3939 San Felipe - Upscale Gulf Coast fare with plenty of Southern charm and very good seafood and meats, including regional favorites such as venison and quail.
- **Rio Ranch** – Texan - 9999 Westheimer - This is a very attractive, airy and expansive, yet comfortable, restaurant reeking with Texana that complements the fairly sophisticated Texas-inspired cuisine.
- **State Grille** - American - 2925 Weslayan - Gulf Coast, Central Texas, southern Louisiana, Mexican and Southern Italian-American influences and dishes populate this menu that would seem overly eclectic and unfocused outside of Houston.
- **t'afia** - American - 3701 Travis - Fairly representative of much of what's good about Houston: modern, more than proficient, interesting, relaxed, forward-looking and friendly. It goes out the way to incorporate local and regional ingredients in an eclectic array of flavorful preparations.
- **Tony Mandola's Gulf Coast Kitchen** – Seafood - 1962 West Gray - Manages a near seamless blending of Southern Italian-American, Creole, Cajun, Mexican, and native Gulf Coast influences to create wonderful seafood dishes that are representative of the area.

Jenni's Noodle House $8

2130 Jefferson (at Hutchins, east of 59, just north of I-45) 77002, (713) 228-3400
www.noodlesrule.com

Cuisine - Vietnamese
Hours - Mon-Thu 11AM to 10PM; Fri 11AM to 2AM; Sat 5PM to 2AM
Credit Cards - Amex, MC, Visa
Service - Table Service
Alcohol - Beer & Wine

Entrée Prices - $6 to $10 ($8 average)
Entrées $12 and less - 100%

Atmosphere & Décor - Comfortable, and sometimes fairly funky
Appeal - Fun, casual Vietnamese near downtown
Menu Suggestions - Super Fried Rice (Vietnamese-style fried rice with bean sprouts, chives and char-grilled chicken and roasted pork); Infernal Chicken

(chicken in a coconut curry sauce); Ginger Chicken (sliced chicken breast sautéed with red onions, fresh jalapeño slices, and minced ginger)

Jenni's Noodle House is a fun, casual and gregarious Vietnamese restaurant that aims to serve the general public, or a fairly with-it subset of the general public, at least. This is unlike most Vietnamese restaurants, which are still geared primarily toward Vietnamese patrons. But, like most capable Vietnamese eateries it does a good job in serving a lot of tasty food for a comparably small price. Unlike many inexpensive places, Jenni's, though, has a personality, and a quirky, fun one at that. This is somewhat evidenced by their T-shirts for sale above the counter emblazoned with "My Noodle is Bigger than Your Noodle" and "Madonna Eats Here". Jenni's has an attitude, but it's endearing rather than off-putting. This, plus the resulting scene, is an attraction for many, in addition to the food. The small setting is minimalist, but fairly attractive. Located among the Asian businesses near the intersection of I-45 and Highway 59, Jenni's is easy to get to for lunch if working downtown. In addition to the office workers in the center of town, who frequent during the weekday lunch hours, it is popular with an artsy crowd, including many folks driving their Art Cars. Weekends are a time for more fun at Jenni's with "Boa Friday" and "Celebrity Saturday" each week.

The number of offerings at Jenni's is roughly a manageable forty-plus rather than the usual 200 or so at most area Vietnamese restaurants. The dishes here are a mix of Vietnamese favorites with some Thai and Japanese ideas and influences. For example, that Japanese and student favorite, ramen, is featured in several dishes. Although the fare does not reach the level of some of the best local Vietnamese restaurants, Jenni's is a lot more fun than most. Each dish has a cute or descriptive name in addition to its Vietnamese moniker plus a detailed description, which can be very helpful. These dishes are divided among $3-5 Dollar Steals (appetizers), $6-7 Deals, and $9 Meals. The appetizers are an eclectic array that includes a couple types of spring rolls, the popular deep-fried Vietnamese egg rolls, Chinese-style dumplings either steamed or pan-fried, a seaweed salad, crispy tofu, and the Japanese *edamame,* steamed green soybeans. The Vietnamese egg rolls are thinner than most in the area, but still good. Among the Deals are two versions of wonton soup, ramen noodles with roasted pork, *pho,* several of the locally popular *bun* (rice noodle) dishes topped with a choice of egg rolls, tofu, char-grilled pork or chicken, a *soba* noodle dish, the Sexy Salad with peanut dressing and fried tofu or grilled chicken, and a commendable fried rice with bean sprouts, chicken and roasted pork. As would be expected, the more expensive Meals are heartier than the Steals. These include the spicy and sour Mama Tran Shrimp Soup, a steak salad featuring pan-seared tenderloin, a couple curries, ramen with shrimp, a steak salad, Salt-n-Pepper

Shrimp (just like it sounds), stir-fry with a choice of meats or tofu, *udon* with shrimp, and Ginger Chicken. Of the curries, there is the vegan Art Car Curry with tofu, and the Infernal Chicken with chicken, named after two eclectic and acclaimed local cultural institutions. Both are almost soups, and are served in a savory coconut-based curry sauce with potatoes and a small side of jasmine rice. Flecked with red pepper flakes, these can be spicy and satisfying. One of the most interesting is the Ginger Chicken that is sliced chicken breast sautéed with red onions, fresh jalapeño slices, and minced ginger.

The kitchen is amenable to most suggestions; just don't ask for half-orders. There are a number of vegetarian and vegan offerings. Spicing can be adjusted on most dishes. Shrimp can be added or substituted on virtually any item for an additional charge. And, you might have room for desserts. These can include *tres leches* and other cakes. Drinks are more important here than most other Vietnamese restaurants. There is bottled beer, even good beer, wine, and saké. The wine is very reasonably priced. Even though it is an inexpensive restaurant, one quibble is that solely bottled water is served. It is only a pittance, but then again, you can always pick up a boa to wear any time when dining at Jenni's.

Jerusalem Halal Deli $8

3330 Hillcroft (between Richmond and Westpark) 77057, (713) 782-2525

Cuisine - Middle Eastern
Hours - Mon-Sat 10AM to 9PM; Sun 10AM to 6PM (closed daytime in Ramadan)
Credit Cards - NONE
Service - Counter Service
Alcohol - NONE

Entrée Prices - $4 to $10 ($8 average)
Entrées $12 and less - 100%

Atmosphere & Décor - Just remember that you're there for the food
Appeal - Tough to find better local hummus, shawarmas, kabobs and falafel
Useful to Note - Restaurant is in the back of the grocery; don't be too skittish.
Menu Suggestions - hummus; Chicken Shawarma Sandwich; Beef Shawarma Sandwich; Falafel Sandwich; Lamb Kafta Sandwich; Beef Kabob Sandwich; Chicken Kabob Sandwich

With the exception of being completely inside and air-conditioned, the scene at the counter of Jerusalem Halal Deli is probably similar to that of a storefront deli in the Muslim section of Jerusalem or in Amman, Jordan. There are skewers of beef, chicken, and seasoned ground lamb displayed behind glass, prior to cooking in a charcoal-burning oven; spinners with sheets of chicken and beef await trimming; trays of rice-laden dishes, stews, vegetables and salads are in the steam table. And, as what might be expected of those locales, the scene is generally chaotic. In the midst of the lunchtime rush, there can be a number of hungry patrons milling around the deli counter and around the adjoining steam table bantering, or yelling, in Arabic with the cooks. The drill here is to wait in line, if there is one, and then hang about the cash register amidst the shouts in Arabic until one of the cooks notices you and asks for an order. There is no menu, nothing on a chalkboard, so you will likely need to call out the name of a casual Middle Eastern dish or say that you will have a plate from the steam table and then pick out the items on display on the steam table. After the order is placed, pick out a table from the small collection of mismatched ones and then select a bottled or canned drink from one of the half-dozen stand-up coolers that adorn a couple walls. The sandwiches are freshly prepared and take five minutes, or so, to make. At peak lunchtimes, the total time to get food can be lengthy.

The wait is usually always worth it. In a city with many worthy options for Middle Eastern sandwiches (various items wrapped within pita bread), such as *shawarma* sandwiches, ones filled with kabobs, and *falafel* sandwiches, the versions at Jerusalem Halal Deli are the best in the city. The pre-cooked kabobs, resting on skewers in the refrigerated glass cases, look fantastic, especially the beef. These kabobs, beef, chicken and ground lamb (*kafta*), are cooked in an actual charcoal-burning brick oven that is prominently displayed in the kitchen behind the counters. The lamb *kafta* kabob consists of marinated and spiced ground lamb that is patted together, assembled around a skewer and then grilled. The fillings are put into fresh pita bread along with a generous amount of pickles, onions and a little bit of lettuce and tomatoes. The optional, spicy and very flavorful, chile-based hot sauce makes these sandwiches taste even that much better. The somewhat more mundane, if amazingly flavorful, *shawarmas* with either chicken or beef slowly cooked and sliced from vertical spinners, and *falafel* sandwiches are also excellent. If you are in a hurry, it is to be noted that you will receive a *shawarma* or *falafel* more quickly than a kabob, as the kabobs are cooked upon order. There is more than just the excellent sandwiches. One great side and complement to those sandwiches is the exemplary *hummus*. This expert mix of mashed chickpeas, sesame seed oil, lemon juice and garlic is served with a decent amount of olive oil on top along with a sprinkling of fresh chives and paprika, and then presented with a fresh large piece of pita bread for scooping. It is especially creamy and flavorful, and one of the best versions in the area. If you desire something more substantial than a sandwich, one the choices from the steam table will be sure to satisfy. The dishes change daily, but the entrée usually consists of a preparation of juicy roast chicken served over rice, or possibly fish fillets or lamb. The accompanying vegetables and salads always are amazingly fresh and well prepared. The small kitchen is very adept with all of its offerings. Shareef would certainly like it.

Jerusalem Halal Deli is located in the back of a somewhat dumpy Arab grocery store in an older, and dumpy, strip center on Hillcroft, near many other ethnic restaurants. The front part of the establishment is the grocery store specializing in Islamic products. Directly in back is the *halal* butcher shop that prepares meat according to Islamic dietary laws. And to the right in back, is the deli. It's good to note that as a proper Islamic place, Jerusalem Halal Deli is not open during the daylight hours of Ramadan when observant Muslims do not eat during daylight hours.

Kahn's Deli $8

2429 Rice (at Kelvin, east of Kirby) 77005, (713) 529-2891
www.kahnsdeli.com

Cuisine - Deli
Hours - Mon-Fri 10AM to 6PM; Sat 10AM to 4PM
Credit Cards - NONE
Service - Counter Service
Alcohol - Beer & Wine

Entrée Prices - $5 to $13 ($8 average)
Entrées $12 and less - 90%

Atmosphere & Décor - Spartan, but with a personality; space can be tight
Appeal - Excellent deli sandwiches
Useful to Note - Dining space can be tight during peak lunch hours.
Menu Suggestions - Olajuwon Special (grilled knockwurst, hot corned beef, mustard, melted cheese, Russian Dressing, sauerkraut on rye); Reuben; Bratwurst Reuben; Hot Pastrami Sandwich; Sam's Special (roast beef and turkey with cheddar and Russian dressing on an egg roll)

Kahn's, with a somewhat small and cluttered storefront among many specialty retail shops on Rice Boulevard, fits in very well with the surroundings. This is not surprising, as the father of the owner ran a deli in the area for many years. All told, father and son have operated delis in the Village since 1948. Currently Kahn's, a mainstay in the Village since the mid-1980s, serves some of the best deli sandwiches around. Owner Mike Kahn would certainly dispute the qualification, "some". The pride in the sandwiches translates to excellent, freshly made-to-order sandwiches. Kahn's is a very good neighborood deli. For any neighborhood.

It all starts with the top quality ingredients: the deli meats come from Chicago; the sausages are from top quality producer Usinger's in Wisconsin; and the breads are fresh and flavorful. A good reason to visit is one of the several varieties of Reuben sandwiches. Each version is very good. There is the Knackwurst Reuben, Bratwurst Reuben, Alpine Reuben (with smoked turkey), and, of course, the basic Reuben. These sandwiches just vary with the type of meat. The basic Reuben, a juxtaposition of corned beef (or pastrami, if you prefer), sauerkraut, Russian dressing and cheese, might be the best barometer on which to judge delis. Kahn's uses top quality rye bread that is baked daily. The Russian dressing is also made daily. One of the best sandwiches, and equal to its moniker, is the Olajuwon Special which is named after former Rocket Hakeem Olajuwon, the greatest center of his generation. This is a warm and messy sandwich consisting of grilled knockwurst with hot corned beef, mustard, melted cheese, Russian dressing and sauerkraut on rye. Essentially, it is the Reuben with the addition of some flavorful sausage. It's not really clear if the sandwich is similar to the sandwiches that Hakeem grew up with in his native Lagos, Nigeria, or if he eats them at all, but it sure is delicious. Hopefuly Yao Ming will have similar carreer success to warant an eponymous tasty creation of salted and cured meats in Ashkanasi culinary tradition. In addition to the variety of Reubens, you can get almost any type of deli-style sandwich at Kahn's. Some of the other speciality sandwiches include a Tuna Melt that consists of tuna salad, melted Swiss cheese with lettuce and tomato on rye bread. There are a handful of appealing sandwiches featuring cole slaw and Russian dressing on rye bread: the New Yorker (with corned beef); the Slaw Dog (with knockwurst); the Slaw Bird (with smoked turkey) and the Texan (with roast beef). Kahn's also has a version of the popular cold po boy. This one mates prosciutto, Swiss cheese and spicy mustard on a baguette. If one of the specialty sandwiches is not desired, you can create your own with a choice of meats and breads. The sandwich fillings include chopped liver, tongue and liverwurst in addition to the more popular choices. Then there is the choice among the different breads and rolls: rye, wheat, onion roll, egg, French bread, kaiser roll or a bagel. Corned beef and pastrami, which always tastes better when warmed, are available for a slight additional charge. The Hot Pastrami Sandwich, with Swiss on rye, is very good. A deli cannot be complete without that Jewish-American favorite, lox. Kahn's takes pride in that their lox is flown in daily, and is never frozen. The sandwiches, and most of the other items, are truly made to order, so be prepared to wait a bit for the sandwiches even when the place is empty. It's not empty often during the peak lunch hours, nor is there usually much free space at all then, so takeout is often the best way to go. One drawback is that Kahn's closes early, 6PM during the week and a couple of hours earlier on Saturday.

Kam's Fine Chinese Cuisine $12

4500 Montrose (just north of the Southwest Freeway) 77006, (713) 529-5057

Cuisine - Chinese
Credit Cards - Amex, Discover, MC, Visa
Hours - Mon-Thu 11AM to 10PM; Fri 11AM to 11PM; Sat 5 to 11PM; Sun 5 to 10PM
Alcohol - Beer & Wine
Service - Table Service

Entrée Prices - Dinner - $7 to $18 ($12 average); Lunch - $6 to $11
Entrées at Dinner $12 and less - 80%

Atmosphere & Décor - Pleasant, fairly attractive
Appeal - Well prepared and reasonably priced neighborhood Chinese stop
Menu Suggestions - dumplings; Jade Dragon Fantasy (stir-fried jumbo shrimp with bok choy, mushrooms in a jalapeño sauce): Sesame Chicken; Manchurian Birdnest Beef (leeks and shredded beef on a "nest" of fried noodles); Garlic Beans; Cha Shiu Deluxe (barbecued pork with snow peas and water chestnuts)

Located on lower Montrose, just north of the smart bridge over the Southwest Freeway, Kam's Fine Chinese Cuisine has been popular with folks in Montrose and other nearby Inner Loop neighborhoods since it opened in 1988. The pleasant restaurant with its generally solicitous and efficient service is conducive for a nice dinner with soft lighting, a pleasing décor with plenty of dark wood and large windows looking out to an attractive stretch of Montrose just north of the museums. Takeout is also popular. Most of the menu is made up of the Cantonese-American dishes that have been popular for years, along with some influences from other regions including Vietnam and Singapore. Though many of the items will be similar to most area Chinese restaurants, at Kam's most dishes seem lighter, and the flavors seem more properly distinct than those in many of the others, plus the presentation is usually better, too. The appetizers are more appealing than similar Chinese restaurants. There are steamed dumplings with several fillings: pork, chicken, seafood and vegetables. The pork version is also served pan-fried. These dumplings come with bottles and jars containing soy sauce, vinegar and condiments to create your own dipping sauce. Other appetizers include spring and summer rolls, shrimp toast, and the Crabmeat Cream Cheese Rolls. One of the half-dozen different soups can also work as a starter: the familiar Hot and Sour; or somewhat more exotic, Seaweed and Tofu; or Wintermelon. The entrées consist of Chinese pasta that features several stir-fried and soft noodle dishes, and other dishes featuring chicken, beef, pork, seafood and fried rice. There is also a section of Kam's Specialties which lists some of the most artistic dishes. These include the Jade Dragon Fantasy (stir-fried jumbo shrimp with bok choy and mushrooms in a jalapeño sauce), Sesame Chicken made with marinated chicken, and Manchurian Birdnest Beef (leeks and shredded beef atop a "nest" of fried noodles). At lunch there are nearly twenty choices around $8, which includes soup, fried rice and a spring roll.

* Kanomwan $11

736 ½ Telephone (at Lockwood, in the Tlaquepaque center) 77023, (713) 923-4236

Cuisine - Thai
Hours - Mon 11:30AM to 1:45PM; Tue-Fri 11:30AM to 1:45PM, 5:30 to 9PM; Sat 5:30 to 9PM
Credit Cards - Amex, MC, Visa
Service - Table Service
Alcohol - NONE; BYOB

Entrée Prices - $8 to $18 ($11 average)
Entrées $12 and less - 80%

Atmosphere & Décor - More than functional; patio
Appeal - Arguably the best Thai food in Houston; BYOB, too
Useful to Note - Usually closed in December when the owners travel to Thailand.
Menu Suggestions - egg rolls (A4); salads (S6-S9); Tom Ka Gai (soup of coconut milk with lemon grass and chicken - S3); Pad Panaeng with Beef (curry with coconut milk - H5); Gang Ped (red curry with coconut milk and bamboo shoots and chicken or beef - S10); Gang Kyo Wan Gai (green curry with chicken, coconut milk and bamboo shoots - S11); Gang Garee Gai (curry with chicken and potatoes - S12); Goong Lard Prig (deep-fried jumbo shrimp with chili paste - H15); Pla Lard Prig (entire fried snapper topped with a chili sauce - H11); Pad Thai (N1); Pad Khuen Chay Pla (red snapper fillet with ginger, onion, scallions, Thai celery and a bean sauce - PK)

Kanomwan has long been popular with serious Thai food enthusiasts. Now in its third and nicest location, the decent-sized, nearly windowless no-frills dining room is often packed with diners who have made the drive down to Telephone Road. Even though it's an out of the way trip for most, but it's certainly worth the diversion. Though there are many worthy Thai restaurants in Houston, the food at Kanomwan is, in comparison, amazingly flavorful. There is a complexity and subtlety in tastes that is not evident in most other restaurants, Thai or otherwise. With ample reason, many believe that it is the best Thai food in the area. But, as exceptional as the food can be, the prices are very reasonable. Helping to keep the costs low in the evening is that Kanomwan is strictly a BYOB operation. It's easy to have an excellent and filling meal for two with beverages for under $20. Before heading to the restaurant it is a good idea to pick up some clean-tasting lager beer or a Gewurztraminer or Riesling to complement the usually spicy fare. And, maybe bring some extra for an especially enjoyable meal. With this relaxed policy and relaxed atmosphere, it's easy for you to empty a bottle and feel a bit free here. But, there is a sign stating, "BYOB not allowed after 8:30PM".

The menu offerings are probably more authentic, and the flavors less assimilated than most other area Thai restaurants. Try the stir-fried ground meat with garlic, onions, basil and peppers (*Pad Ka Pao*) if you have any doubts. Denoted as being very hot, this dish is unbelievably spicy, yet flavorful. There will also be something even for the most casual Thai food fan. It's tough to go wrong with almost anything on the menu. The curry dishes in their various forms are excellent, and the popular coconut milk-based soup with lemongrass and chicken (*tom ka gai*) might be addictive. The ingredients, especially the seafood, are notably fresh. Kanomwan is the place to try an entire deep-fried red snapper. They seem to have red snapper even when it might be tough for other places to procure it. This fish is especially good when topped with Kanomwan's special chili sauce (*Pla Lard Prig*). The deep-fried jumbo shrimp with a chili paste makes a compelling argument for being the best shrimp dish in the city, regardless of cuisine. Large and succulent shrimp are lightly breaded and deep-fried with the chili paste helping to impart a very complementary restrained spiciness. Some of the other specialties include *Gang Kyo Wan Gai* (sliced chicken breast with green curry and coconut milk), *Gang Ped* (red curry with bamboo shoots and coconut milk and either sliced chicken breast or beef), and *Pad Panaeng* (a choice of meat stir-fried with a curry with coconut milk). Many of the curry dishes are rubbed with a curry paste rather than a sauce.

The excellent food is certainly the biggest allure. Being easy on the wallets is another strong draw. But, an additional attraction, if slightly perverse, is that the owner of Kanomwan has the reputation for being somewhat stern; the area Thai version of the *Seinfeld* show's Soup Nazi. That reputation has more than a certain amount of truth, and though the service is never bad, the gruffness, which extends to much of the waitstaff, helps to add to the charm of the place. It's probably the least friendly Thai restaurant you'll find, but possibly the most enjoyable. When you are told that the kitchen closes at 9PM, believe that there will be nothing cooked past 9PM. The restaurant closes near the end of each year for a few weeks when the owners head back to Thailand, presumably after making enough money for the year. This can be tough, it is easy to get hooked by the great food here, and other Thai restaurants don't seem as good in comparison.

Kasra Persian Grill $11

9741 Westheimer (at the southwest corner with Gessner) 77042, (713) 975-1810

Cuisine - Persian

Hours - Mon-Thu 11AM to 10PM; Fri-Sat 11AM to 11PM; Sun 12 to 10PM
Credit Cards - Amex, Diners, Discover, MC, Visa
Service - Table Service
Alcohol - Wine & Beer

Entrée Prices - Dinner - \$7 to \$15 (\$11 average); Lunch - \$6 to \$13
Entrées at Dinner \$12 and less - 70%

Atmosphere & Décor - Nice
Appeal - Tasty Persian food in a pleasant setting, and a good dining value
Menu Suggestions - Chelo Kabob Kubideh (skewers of charbroiled beef that has been mixed with grated onion and spices); Chicken Kabob (with boneless chicken thighs); Chenjeh (skewer of chunks of filet mignon)

Tucked into a corner of the Westchase shopping center behind Churrascos, Yao Ming's grand palace, and a Benihana's, Kasra Persian Grill can easily be overlooked. And, if noticed, the moniker "Persian Grill" might deter other new patrons. This is a shame because the Persian food here includes very savory grilled meats, which are well-suited for most local palates. The portions are large, and the kitchen is very proficient at turning out these clean-tasting, flavorful dishes. Though not as attractive or lively as its neighbors sharing the parking lot, Kasra is nonetheless a fairly nice place and certainly a better value.

A significant portion of the entrées and a big part of the attraction at Kasra are the different types of kabobs, featuring mostly beef and chicken, but also shrimp and salmon, each well-prepared. The least expensive of the kabobs, and possibly the easiest introduction to the fare, is the *Kubideh.* This is two skewers of ground beef that have been seasoned with spices and grated onions, and two grilled tomato halves. The long rolls of beef are moist and flavorful, especially when eaten with part of the grilled tomato. The dish is a lot of food, and is an especially good bargin during lunch. It's not a bad deal at dinner, either. The other beef kabob entrées offer better cuts of beef, and combinations, and are slightly more expensive. The *Chenjah* is ribeye. The *Barg* is made filet mignon. The moist chicken kabobs are nearly as good as the beef ones. Kasra reminds you that chicken can be something other than the tasteless white chunks of protein that it is in many other restaurants. The Chicken *Kubideh* features ground chicken. The Chicken Kabob is an excellent skewer of boneless, marinated chicken thighs. The *Jujeh Kabob* is an entire Cornish hen that has been marinated, skewered and grilled. The kabob entrées are served with a large amount of basmati rice colored on top with a bit of yellow saffron. For a little more, you can get dill rice, fava bean rice or rice inflected with the red and tart barberries, or one with sour cherries and pistachios. These specialty rices, especially the ones with fruit can provide another contrasting, yet complementary level of flavor to the broiled meats. The Shrimp Kabob features a half-dozen jumbo shrimp. The salmon version has good-sized pieces of marinated salmon. Both are served with perfectly complementary, garlic-butter.

Another facet of the cuisine served at Kasra, and most of the rest of the entrées, is the stew-like dishes listed under Specialties. The most familiar and probably the most flavorful is the slowly braised and tender lamb shank. Most of the other half-dozen items cook beef or chicken with ingredients such as yellow split peas, ground walnuts and pomegranate juice and interesting spices to create different and uniquely Persian flavors. All meals begin with usually warm, flat *taftoon* bread (an airy bread somewhat like the Indian *naan*) and a plate of mint, basil, parsley, cilantro, scallions and a feta-like cheese, or some combination thereof that is brought to your table. The bread is wrapped with the herbs and some feta, and makes for a fine starter. Though the entrées are hearty, and the first large piece of bread is complimentary, you might want to start with one of several appetizers that is right for the Houston weather. There is *hummus*, warm and cold dips made with roasted eggplants, and a couple of yogurt-based dips, a plate with walnuts and minced herbs, pickled vegetables, and a savory lentil and onion soup. There are also salads like the Greek Salad, a version of the ubitiquitous Caesar Salad and the Persian Salad, which is made with diced cucumbers, tomatoes, red onions and herbs with a special dressing. The salads can be made into a meal with addition of the grilled chicken *Barg*. To note, wine and desserts are an afterthought here, but are available.

Katz's $11

616 Westheimer (two blocks east of Montrose) 77006, (713) 521-3838
19075 I-45 N. (in the Portofino Center) The Woodlands, 77385, (936) 321-1880
www.ilovekatzs.com

Cuisine - Deli
Hours - Westheimer - Daily 24 Hours; Woodlands - Mon-Thu, Sun 11Am to 11PM; Fri-Sat 11AM to 1 AM
Credit Cards - Amex, Discover, MC, Visa
Service - Table Service
Alcohol - Full Bar

Entrée Prices - Dinner - $5 to $15 ($11 average); Lunch - $8 to $10; Breakfast - $6
Entrées at Dinner $12 and less - 70%

Atmosphere & Décor - Nice, often lively
Appeal - A bustling New York-style deli serving very good food at all hours
Useful to Note - Parking is on both sides of Westheimer; good people-watching.

Menu Suggestions - Grilled 3 Cheese Supreme with Tomato and Fire Dog Sandwich; Reuben Sandwich; Mixed Deli Omelet; Yankee Pot Roast; "East Meets West" Sandwich (grilled salami and jalapeño cheese); Hot Pastrami Sandwich; Grilled Pastrami Hero (with sautéed onions, mushrooms, cheese and Russian dressing); bagels; Stuffed Cabbage (with ground beef and rice); Matzo Ball soup; chocolate milkshake

---

Though not related to the famous Katz's Deli in Manhattan, the progenitor of this restaurant has been one of the most popular restaurants in Austin since opening in 1979. The original Houston outpost is a hopping place much of the time. Some of that is due to the colorful lower Montrose address. That and its nonstop hours ensure some interesting people watching very late or very early. A second area location, the smaller Katz's Express, opened in the second half of 2006 in the amazingly garish take on Seville's Alcazar and inappropriately named Portofino strip shopping center on I-45 North near The Woodlands. The initial restaurant is in a very attractive two-story structure topped with a pressed tin ceiling. The downstairs contains a dining room and a bar area. Upstairs is another dining room. The décor, as with the menu, is a tribute to the isle of Manhattan. The walls are crowded with photos and artifacts of New York. Though a large restaurant, Katz's is a comfortable place. This is partially due to the fact that it is crowded during any of the even somewhat popular dining hours.

The menu at the Montrose location is very large. Slickly assembled, it has some heft to it, too. The Woodlands location has a more limited menu that is somewhat less deli-esque, less ethnic. But, from either menu, there should be something, actually, there should be many things, that meet your taste. The proficient kitchen is very adept with nearly all of them. The menu features all of the popular Jewish-American dishes of eastern European origin: blintzes (a crêpe folded over a choice of fillings and then topped with sour cream), warm deli sandwiches, freshly baked bagels, potato pancakes, knishes (a pastry that has usually been baked, stuffed with cheese, potato or chopped liver), matzo ball soup, and lox. The bagels are always very good here; and even better when toasted. That's just a start. There are daily soup specials ranging from split pea to New England clam chowder to French onion soup. There are salads, hamburgers, and a large number of cold sandwiches with a half-pound of deli meat on a choice of breads. The "Classic Deli Sandwiches" are some of the best around. It's tough to go wrong with any of these nearly twenty hot sandwiches. As you might expect from Katz's, the Reuben sandwich, made either with pastrami or the traditional corned beef, is excellent. It's a great blend of choice cold cuts, melted Swiss cheese, sauerkraut and Russian dressing on a light rye bread served warm from the flat grill. Another highlight is the Grilled 3 Cheese

Supreme with Tomatoes and a Firedog. It's a grilled cheese sandwich with three types of cheese, a ripe tomato slice and two halves of a grilled, spicy all-beef hot dog. Though the restaurant recommends sourdough, it's even better on rye. The Yankee Pot Roast is very good. It is tender, juicy roast beef piled on grilled light rye bread with melted Muenster cheese and sautéed onions. Hamburgers are well prepared at Katz's, and there are many things that you can add to spruce it up. Lest you think that Katz's serves only mundane, casual food, there are several daily specials and "Chef Barry's Dinner Suggestions". The rotating daily specials include a Penne Pasta Alfredo with Grilled Chicken Breast, Spinach *Frittata,* and meatloaf. The dinners that are available each day include roast turkey breast, potato pancakes, corned beef and cabbage, roast sirloin, and Links-n-Beans, a choice of two sausages among knockwurst, beef fire dog or beef frankfurter topped with sauerkraut and served with beans. The sides include a large list of American and Jewish-American favorites among which are: potato knish, cole slaw, apple sauce, fries, potato salad, sauerkraut, rice pilaf, creamed spinach, cheese stuffed potato, baked beans, etc.

Breakfasts are excellent at Katz's. These are mostly the traditional deli-style breakfasts. From 5 to 10AM every day, many are an excellent value for $6 or so. There are two egg combinations served with a potato pancake, a bagel, toast or muffin, and a variety of meats: beef bacon, a beef hot dog, grilled turkey ham, pastrami, sirloin steak, grilled salami, and lox and onions. The three egg omelets, filled with a wide range of cheeses, meats and vegetables, are very good. The best of which, or maybe worst depending on your cholesterol level, is the Mixed Deli omelet with salami, a beef fire dog, corned beef, peppers, onions, and the relatively healthy turkey ham. Though there are no *huevos rancheros* or the like, that many non-Mexican restaurants include for breakfast, in a nod to the region are Kosher-style breakfast tacos, flour tortillas filled with scrambled eggs, kosher salami and a beef fire dog. They have pancakes, poached eggs, corned beef hash, French toast on the light *challah* bread. Of course, they have the Jewish-American breakfast staples: bagels, lox and blintzes.

The desserts are another draw. With its roots in New York, you would expect that the cheesecake must be good. Diet-busting like the regular cheesecake, the Cheesecake Shake was advertised too gleefully on the radio as being, "a heart attack in a glass". It's a large slice of cheesecake blended with a choice of vanilla, chocolate or strawberry ice cream. The other shakes, especially the basic chocolate shake, are very rich and very good. There is a wide range of ice cream-based desserts plus and an assortment of pies and cakes. In addition to the cheesecake, there is a key lime pie, apple pie and carrot cake, and three extremely rich chocolate-based cakes. Katz's also has dessert blintzes and malts. All of the items on this large menu are available all the time; 24/7. Not only can you get one of their great cholesterol-laden egg dishes at all hours, they are even serving chicken soup for breakfast. And, of course, the Reuben can't fail.

* Kenneally's Irish Pub $8

2119 S. Shepherd (between Westheimer and Fairview) 77019, (713) 630-0486

Cuisine - Pizza; Hamburgers
Hours - Mon-Fri 3PM to 2AM; Sat 5PM to 2AM; Sun 4PM to 2AM
Credit Cards - Amex, MC, Visa
Service - Table Service
Alcohol - Full Bar

Entrée Prices - $6 to $11 ($8 average)
Entrées $12 and less - 100%

Atmosphere & Décor - A comfortable neighborhood bar
Appeal - Top-notch thin crust pizza, burgers, sandwiches and even potato chips
Useful to Note - There's some street parking around the corner, north of the bar.
Menu Suggestions - Any of the pizzas, especially the Shamrock Special; potato chips; fries; Reuben Sandwich (corned beef and sauerkraut here); hamburgers

It should be well known by now that Kenneally's serves some of the best pizza in the area, though this might be surprising to the uninitiated, given the setting. Pizzas move out of the kitchen at a rapid rate on a typical night at this convivial neighborhood bar on Shepherd, not too far north of Westheimer. The bar is adorned with items from many of the Chicago sports teams, since the owner is from the Chicago area and the pizza makers, in fact, were trained at a pizza joint in Chicago. Kenneally's pizza is the style that was once popular in Chicago when Neapolitans ran the first generation of pizzerias there before the advent of deep dish. Kenneally's pizza sports a very thin crust with minimal amount of toppings. It's interestingly cut into smallish squares; this allows you to eat without letting go of the pint glass. The quality of the pizza begins with the crust, which is thin, crisp and tasty. The cheese and toppings are of high quality, and are not overdone, as these are often so at other pizza places. The toppings include the usual suspects, with at least one twist that is found on the most popular pizza, the Shamrock Special. This is topped with mushrooms, onions, bell peppers and corned beef. As different as it sounds, it works very well. This is the most popular pizza at Kenneally's. The hamburgers are excellent. A few souls even believe that these are the real stars of the kitchen. The burgers made with a hand-crafted patty that remains juicy underneath the outer crust, it's then beautifully assembled. The well-made cold sandwiches include a club, honey baked ham that is baked in-house, turkey, corned beef and a Reuben with corned beef and sauerkraut. The house-made potato chips are also excellent. These are served very fresh, hot, crunchy and with enough grease to be noticeable in the Ship Channel. The potato chips are a nice complement to the burgers and sandwiches and even just a cold Harp lager. Unusual for most eateries, the fries at Kenneally's are not pre-cut and frozen, but made on-site. The difference is noticeable, as the fries are quite tasty. The food is very good all around. By the way, the bar is a worthy stop even if you are not planning to stay for dinner, even if the drinks are on the small side. The food will be a welcome treat if you happen to linger long enough to need to eat. Kenneally's is representative of two things that the city could use in a greater quantity: excellent pizza and good neighborhood bars (even if the pours could be heartier here).

Kenny & Ziggy's $13

2327 Post Oak Blvd. (between Westheimer and San Felipe) 77056, (713) 871-8883
www.kennyandziggys.com

Cuisine - Deli
Hours - Mon-Fri 7AM to 9PM; Sat-Sun 8AM to 9PM
Credit Cards - Amex, Discover, MC, Visa
Service - Table Service
Alcohol - Beer & Wine

Entrée Prices - Dinner & Lunch - $6 to $26 ($13 average); Breakfast - $6 to $11
Entrées at Dinner $12 and less - 40%

Atmosphere & Décor - Very Pleasant
Appeal - Slick deli-style restaurant near the Galleria
Useful to Note - It sports a very large menu; should be something for everyone.
Menu Suggestions - Grilled Knockwurst Platter; Hungarian Goulash; Grilled Cheese Sandwich with bacon; Reuben Sandwich; Swiss & Shout Sandwich (open face sandwich with turkey pastrami, melted Swiss, cole slaw and Russian dressing); Challah French Toast

Kenny & Ziggy's is a spiffy restaurant just north of the Galleria that serves slick renditions of Jewish-American deli food and sports a multi-generational deli legacy. The restaurant seems to work hard: the corned beef is cured in-house; the pickles are flown in regularly from Manhattan; the smoked fish is sliced by hand at the restaurant; both Kenny's and Ziggy's business cards are proudly displayed at the counter for takeaway; and most notably service is usually very efficient. The cheeky menu is very lengthy, and there should be something for everyone, deli aficionados and otherwise.

There are many large-sized Jewish-American starters, soups, smoked fish, grilled chicken sandwiches, deli sandwiches, meat plates, dinners, salads, hamburgers, knishes, knockwurst and frankfurters, numerous sides, and desserts. In true American style, abundance takes precedent over finesse here. The starters might not have a broad appeal with items like chopped liver, sweet and sour tongue, and pickled herring, but nearly all of the entrées are fairly quite hefty. The more familiar soups are served in pint- and quart-size portions. There is chicken soup with matzoh ball, rice, noodles, or *kreplach* (small stuffed dumplings); cold beet borscht; and a soup of the day. Kenny & Ziggy's probably has the biggest array of smoked fish in town: Nova Lox (brine-cured that's less salty), sturgeon, sable, baked salmon and several more. These are served with lettuce, tomato, onions, cream cheese and a toasted bagel. There are nearly fifty types of sandwiches filled with the full range of deli meats and other American favorites. The sandwiches are served in several styles: hot and cold, open-faced and triple-decker. Though none of these is cheap for a sandwich, these are overly stuffed, and should satiate all but the most voracious appetites. Be forewarned that the triple decker sandwiches are nearly impossible to eat as a sandwich unless some deconstruction is undertaken. If none of the many sandwiches look appealing, or too daunting, you can always create your own. Each of these comes with a crisp cole slaw, and some also come with freshly made fries. The two dozen hearty dinners include stuffed cabbage, Braised Short Ribs, grilled liver and onions, fish and chips, roast turkey, Chopped Steak, and a half of Roasted Spring Chicken. Either as dinners or starters there are also several eastern European dishes like potato-filled dough pockets, *pierogies*, goulash, potato pancakes and stuffed cabbage. The *pierogies*, a treat elsewhere, are nothing special here. Better are the grilled knockwurst served with sauerkraut and baked beans. These dinners are served with a small salad and a couple of side dishes. There's even more: deli salad platters, knishes, hot dogs, about fifty sides, and ten or so more heart-healthy salads. Most patrons seem to forget cholesterol concerns here, at least subconsciously, and desserts are a big draw. Their proper New York cheesecake is well done, and huge; it easily satisfies two. Other sweet finishes include a Chocolate 7 Layer Cake, Boston cream cake, apple pie, carrot cake and Ebinger's Style Blackout Cake. Shakes, floats and egg creams are also popular.

This is a nice setting in which to enjoy overindulgence. The pleasing décor screams New York, New York, 42nd Street…. The walls are covered with framed playbills of Broadway productions, posters of movies set in New York, and caricatures of New York area celebrities. Though maybe not the caliber of the celebrities whose images line walls, popular *Houston Chronicle* columnist and native New Yorker Ken Hoffman has proclaimed Kenny & Ziggy's his favorite deli.

Kim Son $11

2001 Jefferson (at Chartres, east of Highway 59) 77003, (713) 222-2461
12759 Southwest Freeway (in the Fountains Center) 77477, (281) 242-3500
10603 Bellaire (between the Beltway and Boone) 77072 (281) 598-1777
www.kimson.com

Cuisine - Vietnamese; Chinese
Hours - Jefferson - Mon-Thu, Sun 11AM to 12AM; Fri-Sat 11AM to 3AM; Southwest Freeway - Mon-Thu, Sun 11AM to 11PM; Fri-Sat 11AM to 12AM; Bellaire - Mon-Fri 11AM to 3PM, 5 to 10PM; Sat-Sun 11AM to 12AM
Credit Cards - Amex, Diners, Discover, MC, Visa
Service - Table Service
Alcohol - Full Bar

Entrée Prices - $4 to $27 ($11 average); Bellaire - Dinner buffet - $13, Friday night and weekend buffet -$15, lunch buffet - $8
Entrées at Dinner $12 and less - 70%

Atmosphere & Décor - Pleasant
Appeal - Very good Vietnamese food; great dim sum at Stafford location
Useful to Note - The Bellaire location is not quite as good as the others.
Some Menu Highlights - steamed dumplings; Black Pepper Crabs; Tamarind Crabs; Bo Nuong Xa ("Vietnamese Fajitas"); Black Pepper Chicken; dim sum (Southwest Freeway and Bellaire) - Steamed Shrimp & Pork Dumpling; Steamed B.B.Q. Pork Bun; Peking Style Pan Fried Dumplings; Fried Shrimp with seaweed; Sweet Creamery Cake

Kim Son is probably the best known Vietnamese restaurant in the Houston area, both by locals and nationally, as *Bon Appetit*, *Esquire*, and *Food & Wine* have all sung its praises. Through openings and closings over the years, there are now three sprawling and usually quite proficient restaurants in Old Chinatown, Stafford and once again in New Chinatown, plus several small counter-service operations in food courts with limited menus.

Matriarch "Mama La" arrived in Houston with her husband and their seven children in 1980 from Vietnam armed with a plentitude of recipes. This has translated into a voluminous menu with over 250 items packed with tempting Vietnamese and Chinese dishes. Amazingly, the menu used to be even longer. It's easy to get overwhelmed with the number of very appealing choices that hover around the ten dollar mark. To begin the meal there are about twenty appetizers, including excellent Vietnamese Egg Rolls, and a dozen different soups. The sheer number of tempting entrées is staggering. To start, and perfect for sharing are the *Do Nuong* or Grilled Section; grilled meat and seafood dishes that are served with a plate of fresh mint, cilantro, lettuce, pickled carrots, cucumbers, pineapple and bean sprouts. Among these is the well-loved *Bo Nuong Xa*, sliced beef that has been marinated in minced lemon grass that is char-grilled and served with rice paper for eating. Its popularity is partially a testament to the fact that it has been cleverly described as "Vietnamese Fajitas". Another popular item is the black pepper crabs, a very messy dish featuring whole crabs slathered in a savory sauce. There are scores of Vietnamese dishes served with steamed rice that are meant for communal dining, each in separate sections that feature beef, chicken, duck, pork, fish, shrimp, and hot pots. Then there are similar dishes with other seafood items such as scallops, oysters, squid and frog legs, vegetarian dishes, thin soups (*canh*) and hot pots. In addition to these Vietnamese entrées, there are a number of Chinese dishes such as those with sweet and sour sauces, the Chinese-American Egg Foo Young, *chow mein* (fried noodles), *lo mein* (boiled noodles), fried rice, and pan-fried noodles. Somewhat hidden near the end of the menu, there are some unpretentious Vietnamese dishes that are especially good price performers, listed under *abon* (rice noodle entrées or *bun*) rice platters (*com dia*), and the noodle soups, *pho* and the like. The popular *bun* dishes, entrées with a meat or seafood in a single bowl of rice vermicelli with bean sprouts, lettuce, cucumbers and mint with fish sauce are always well prepared here. Even more inexpensive are the *com dia* dishes consisting of meat over crushed rice. These can be adjusted to your tastes with choice of egg cakes, fried eggs, marinated and char-grilled pork (*thit nuong*) and thin pork chops. The very tasty version with just the char-grilled pork is an especially good value.

As an added reason to visit, the location on the Southwest Freeway in Stafford serves one of the best dim sums in town, certainly the best outside of Fung's Kitchen. Though not nearly as competently, the grand site in New Chinatown also serves dim sum, which is Cantonese for "heart's delight". It is composed of a variety of small mouth-watering dishes selected by the diners. The throngs of Chinese families that crowd the restaurant during the late morning and early afternoon on the weekends are indicative of the quality of its dim sum offerings. Some of the chefs are very experienced dim sum chefs from south China. Though it might seem unusual for a well-known Vietnamese to have the Cantonese dim sum, much less excellent dim sum, the La family that owns these restaurants are ethnic Chinese, and supposedly dim sum was popular among the Chinese who had settled in neighboring Vietnam. It is also one of the few restaurants that serves dim sum during the week in addition to the weekend. The Stafford location serves dim sum via a menu during the week; the carts roll on the weekend. For the uninitiated, the week might be a better time to visit, as the handy dim sum ordering sheet is well laid out, with each of the dishes briefly described in English, and these can be matched to a full color dim sum menu with color photos of the dishes. Unlike some of the other places that offer dim sum daily, the quality is still exceptional during the week. The paper ordering sheet lists almost sixty dishes with notations listing them as small-, medium- and large-sized, among four categories: Steamed; Pan-Fried & Deep-Fried; Cheung Fun & Congee, those dishes featuring a stuffed rice noodle somewhat like large ravioli and *congee,* the rice-based porridge; and Baked & Dessert. There are worthy dishes within each section. The dishes under the Baked & Dessert header are not sweet, and work well as intermittent palate cleansers. The shrimp dishes are especially well prepared. Some of the shrimp dishes are the better-than-usual steamed shrimp dumplings, a large steamed rice noodle filled with shrimp, and a fried roll stuffed with seaweed and shrimp. The barbecued pork dishes, filled steamed buns and rice noodles, are less numerous, but also very good. Though they are presented on the menu in a more approachable fashion than other restaurants that offer dim sum, Kim Son does serve many of the dishes that will appeal almost solely to the Chinese clientele such as dishes with chicken feet, beef tripe and taro root.

To note, the most recent addition, the grand palace on Bellaire, does not quite live up to the quality of the other locations. Though it's a fine value, most of the quickly cooked dishes don't shine sitting in trays in a buffet. Also, the dim sum operation here is not nearly as well run as the one at the Stafford location.

Kojak's Timberbrook Café $9

1912 W. 18th (west of Ella) 77008, (713) 426-1800
www.kojakscafe.com

Cuisine - American (with a Middle Eastern influence)
Hours - Mon 7AM to 10AM, 11AM to 3PM; Tue-Fri 7AM to 10AM, 11AM to 3PM, 5 to 8PM
Credit Cards - Amex, Discover, MC, Visa
Service - Counter Service
Alcohol - Beer & Wine; BYOB

Entrée Prices - Dinner - $6 to $13 ($9 avg.); Lunch - $5 to $9; Breakfast - $3 to $7
Entrées at Dinner $12 and less - 80%

Atmosphere & Décor - Spartan, but welcoming
Appeal - A very satisfying stop for a sandwich, salad and heartier items
Menu Suggestions - Muffaletta; Original Po Boy; Avocado BLT Sandwich; Greek Salad (with romaine, tomato, cucumber, pepperoncini, olives and feta); breakfast taco with eggs, spinach, mushrooms and feta; Parmesan Crusted Chicken Breast

Kojak's is not only a place to stop for a casual meal, dine-in or takeaway, but also to purchase some high quality ingredients to make a meal at home. The well prepared dishes at Kojak's are an eclectic array of mostly American items with some Tex-Mex, Italian-American and Lebanese influences and dishes, perfect for Houston. This is a smartly operated, inviting and interesting informal eatery with a good kitchen; a welcome part of the near northwest side of town. It aptly seems to serve at least a couple distinct clienteles. Opened early for breakfast during the week, Kojak's serves several types of the convenient breakfast finger foods that are easily consumed in the car or left in bulk in a break room in the office; and, not just breakfast tacos, but also stuffed biscuits and muffins. The breakfast tacos with flour tortillas are filled with several familiar choices such as scrambled egg and cheese and potato, egg and cheese, and also spinach, feta and mushrooms, and another with egg whites and turkey. There are freshly made biscuits and muffins filled with combinations of scrambled egg, cheese and bacon or sausage. Kojak's also has a homemade coffee cake with walnuts, steel-cut oatmeal, and, for those with more time or a greater appetite, several big breakfast plates featuring two or three eggs and several sides, *migas,* French toast and omelets filled with a choice among ten ingredients.

Though work or family demands will preclude most people from enjoying Kojak's for breakfast, the dining room is usually crowded during the lunch hours. The several hot and cold sandwiches are part of the attraction. There are unique and satiating takes on the muffaletta, Reuben, cheesesteak, BLT (that includes avocado), tuna melt meatball sandwich, Chicken Club, *falafel,* and even a black bean burger. Their muffaletta is quite different from the hard original Central Grocery version, and certainly smaller, but still enjoyable. It's made with a long spongy bun topped with a flavorful and unique olive relish with noticeable strands of carrot for a slightly sweet edge. The cheesesteak features strands of roasted peppers and melted provolone. The excellent cold sandwiches are ready-made in the deli case for a quick takeout. These are served on crusty, long rolls in the style that was popularized by Antone's, and are certainly in that league. There is the Original with salami, ham and cheese, larger Super Original, turkey, roast beef, tuna salad, and chicken salad. If something healthier is desired, there are several good-sized salads, Cobb, Greek, Caesar and Spinach. Each can be upgraded with chicken, chicken salad or tuna salad. There is also a sampler plate with *baba ganoush, tabouli* and *hummus,* plus small meat or spinach pies that make for a fitting complement to a sandwich. These are all pretty decent here, if not as good as many of the strictly Middle Eastern restaurants in the area. Kojak's has some baked desserts such as brownies, pecan pie, various cookies, and *baklava* that can be a tempting finish to lunch.

If something more filling is desired during lunch or in the evening, Kojak's has a half-dozen pastas, mostly made with linguini, with several popular toppings such as Alfredo sauce, marinara, pesto, *bolognese* (meat gravy), and, differently, one with the cold Sicilian eggplant spread *caponata*. These dishes are seven bucks and under, and chicken or a side salad can be added for an additional charge. At dinner, the salads are included and the pasta choices include crab-filled ravioli with pesto and topped with shrimp. During lunchtime there is at a couple plates, including a usually popular daily special that might be a Tex-Mex dish like enchiladas. In the evening, the plates are the biggest draw. These include veal scaloppini with mushrooms and artichoke hearts, salmon in mango sauce, fried shrimp cakes and the Parmesan Crusted Chicken Breast served with a side of pasta and vegetables.

Kraftsmen Baking $8

4100 Montrose (between Southwest Fwy. and Richmond) 77006, (713) 524-3737
www.kraftsmenbaking.com

Cuisine - Café / Bakery
Hours - Mon-Fri 7AM to 7PM; Sat 8AM to 7PM; Sun 8:30AM to 3PM
Credit Cards - Amex, Diners, Discover, MC, Visa
Service - Counter Service
Alcohol - NONE

Entrée Prices - Dinner & Lunch - $6 to $11 ($8 average); Breakfast - $3 to $6
Entrées at Dinner $12 and less - 100%

Atmosphere & Décor - A comfortable café; small patio
Appeal - Excellent bakery and attractive café in a great setting on Montrose
Useful to Note - There is parking on the street and in the garage in back.
Menu Suggestions - bread, sandwiches, Danish; Croissant Sandwich

Kraftsmen Baking has had an ambitious mission: "The goal…is to offer Houston top-notch artisanal bread…." And, it "represents true artisan style baking and an absolute commitment to quality…Kraftsmen products are handmade from high quality, often organic, ingredients". Since opening in late 2002, it has mostly lived up to that missive. Not only successful as an excellent bakery, Kraftsmen is also an adept and attractive café. Situated on lower Montrose in a very handsome, small red brick-laden center, Kraftsmen is adjacent to both a library and the Black Labrador pub. It's a great place in which to relax with a coffee or tea and one of the delicious baked items. Its attractive, comfortable modernist interior and the handful of tables outside make it conducive for lingering. The menu features breakfast items, pastries, salads and sandwiches atop their artisan breads. Its culinary attraction begins with the baked goods. Mostly because of these excellent breads, the sandwiches can be especially good. Each comes with numerous complementary high quality ingredients, including cheese with each meat sandwich, and plenty of greens. These sandwiches are not overly stuffed, but rather artfully constructed. One of the best of the ten or so creative sandwiches on the menu includes the turkey, brie, crisp bacon and slices of avocado and on a crusty small baguette that is buttered and toasted. Each sandwich has a recommended bread, but assuredly you can switch it to one of your choice among sourdough, whole wheat, baguette, an organic loaf, honey baguette and a brioche hoagie. Though very tasty, the sandwiches are somewhat slight. In addition to the baked goods and sandwiches, the eclectic soups have drawn rave reviews. Some examples of the single soup of the day might be French onion, cream of cauliflower, a bisque with butternut squash, and one featuring *cous cous*. It helps that acclaimed chef-owner Scott Tycer of Aries and Gravitas fame is also an owner of Kraftsmen. To wash down, or rather accompany the food, Kraftsmen serves good quality espresso and other coffees, plus high quality bottled teas, juices and waters. Breakfast is served until 11AM each day, and all day Sunday. The small number of offerings includes hefty breakfast tacos, ham or bacon and eggs, omelets, and an excellent croissant sandwich with eggs, cheese and bacon, if you'd like. Kraftsmen is a great place to stop for a baguette or another bread for the meal at home.

La Escondida $11

7270 Highway 6 S. (south of Lake Olympia) Missouri City, 77459, (281) 403-3306
www.laescondidagrill.com

Cuisine - Tex-Mex
Hours - Mon-Thu, Sun 11AM to 10PM; Fri-Sat 11AM to 11PM
Credit Cards - Amex, Discover, MC, Visa
Service - Table Service
Alcohol - Full Bar

Entrée Prices - Dinner - $7 to $15 ($10 average); Lunch - $4 to $9
Entrées at Dinner $12 and less - 70%

Atmosphere & Décor - Pleasant, reminiscent of a faded palacio
Appeal - Many interesting and well prepared Mexican items in Stafford
Menu Suggestions - Fajitas; Chipotle Carne Asada a la Escondida (skirt steak marinated in a spicy chipotle sauce and topped with pico de gallo and a blend of cheeses); La Escondida Strip (10-ounce strip steak seasoned with jalapeños and poblanos); Mole Enchiladas (chicken enchiladas topped with mole poblano and cheese); Carnitas a la Escondida (chunks of pork cooked in a copper pot)

In 2006 La Escondida made the move to much nicer, brighter and more fitting digs on Highway 6 from its previously depressing location. La

Escondida continues to be more capable than most area Mexican restaurants in terms of food, and more evidently, in terms of service, especially on the far southwest side. There seems to be more waitstaff per customer than most area restaurants, certainly at this price range. This ensures that service is usually attentive. It's also personable and efficient. Noteworthy for even most local Mexican restaurants, not just the flour tortillas, but the corn tortillas and tamales are made at the restaurant. The tomato-based salsa is very good, and the chips are always very fresh. The guacamole is freshly made tableside. An unusual side that makes it onto many plates is the very tasty cubed potatoes, which are sautéed with *chipotle* peppers.

The majority of the menu is divided among appetizers, soups and salads, tacos, enchiladas, fajitas, Authentic Platters, *De la Parrilla* (grilled items), and Tex-Mex combination dinners. Though the entrées are large, if you need to start there are nachos, *chile con queso*, Spinach Dip *Mexicana* (made with jalapeños), *quesadillas*, the freshly prepared guacamole, Jumbo Shrimp Stuffed Jalapeños, and a seafood cocktail with shrimp. The soups include the popular tortilla, and a vegetable soup with shredded chicken. The salads are greens with chicken, either grilled or fried, and a salad topped with shrimp. La Escondida serves taco dinners with tacos that have several types of filling, a choice between corn or flour tortillas, and soft or the increasingly locally endangered Tex-Mex crispy taco. There are several enchilada dishes from which to choose: cheese with chili gravy, shredded chicken, ground beef with chili gravy, chicken with a dark brown *mole poblano* sauce, *Verdes*, spinach, pork, grilled chicken, fajita, and shrimp.

The restaurant is subtitled "Mexican Grill", and actually with good reason. The fajitas and other grilled items are stars on the menu. La Escondida makes it a point to advertise that they use Certified Angus Beef in their beef dishes. Though it's not the top-quality USDA Prime, this certainly makes the beef offerings tastier than most area Mexican restaurants (where Select grade might be best you'll find). The good quality ingredients are coupled with skillful hands attending the grill. The fajitas are flavorful and very tender; it's easy to cut these with a fork. The *Fajitas a la Escondida* have the meat topped with *pico de gallo*, guacamole and blend of melted cheeses. There are also versions with chicken, shrimp and even vegetables. Similar to the regular fajitas are the well prepared *Carne Asada* and the *Carne Asada a la Escondida* that are meant to be eaten as steaks. Possibly even better is the La Escondida Strip, a ten-ounce strip steak that has been seasoned with jalapeño and poblano peppers then cooked to order. Some of the best dishes are listed under the heading of "Authentic Platters" such as the *Empanadas de Picadillo* (corn flour *empanadas* filled with ground beef and then deep-fried), a chicken breast in the *mole* sauce, homemade tamales with chili gravy, *carne guisada*, and *carnitas* (pork chunks) that are cooked in copper pots to "ensure its juiciness and rich flavor". For those seeking some more comforting items from times past or are having a difficult time choosing just one main dish, there are a half-dozen combination dinners featuring a number of plates with enchiladas, tamales, guacamole, fajitas and tacos. This is a restaurant that seems to try much harder than most, and it succeeds most of the time, even if they might have too much of an affinity for processed cheese.

La Fogata $9

11630 Southwest Freeway (north of freeway, at Wilcrest) 77036, (281) 575-8736

Cuisine - Colombian
Hours - Mon, Fri-Sun 11AM to 8:30PM, Tue-Wed 11AM to 5PM
Credit Cards - Amex, MC, Visa
Service - Table Service
Alcohol - Beer & Wine

Entrée Prices - Dinner - $7 to $14 ($9 average); Lunch - $6
Entrées at Dinner $12 and less - 90%

Atmosphere & Décor - Spartan, but friendly
Appeal - Well prepared and hearty food in a friendly, family-run restaurant
Menu Suggestions - Bistec a la Mexicana (steak strips that have been cooked with onions and tomatoes); Chuleta de Cerdo (thin, breaded pork cutlet); Milanesa (thin, breaded beef steak)

La Fogata is foremost a small, friendly, unpretentious, family-run restaurant serving well prepared and hearty portions of Colombian fare. Though Colombian food might seem exotic to many, La Fogata can serve as a capable and easy introduction to the often hearty cuisine that will be somewhat familiar, or at least readily approachable, for most diners. The use of tropical foodstuffs, especially plantains, and the ubiquity of steamed rice as an accompaniment are a couple of the hallmarks of Colombian cooking that is shared with the other Latin countries on the Gulf such as Cuba, Puerto Rico, Venezuela and most of the Central American countries. The more extraneous parts of the animals (tongue, liver and intestines) make it into the dishes more frequently than many people like, though. The food is prepared relatively simply, and while it is far less spicy than Mexican cooking, it can be flavorful. Don't let its unappealing location in a strip center on a feeder road deter you from visiting, as the kitchen here does a good job.

The weekday lunch hours are a good time to visit, as La Fogata has several value-priced specials. The *Bistec a la Mexicana* is strips of steak that have been cooked with onions and tomatoes. While it is not the best cut of steak, it is tender enough and flavorful, especially with the vinegary salsa that adorns each table. A staple of the Latin regions of the Caribbean, *Arroz con Pollo,* stewed chicken served over rice, is another lunch special. One of the lunch specials worth recommending is the *Chuleta de Cerdo.* It's not the more familiar pork chop served at Mexican restaurants, rather it's a cutlet of pork that has been pounded thin, breaded then pan-fried. It's essentially a pork *milanesa,* and more tender than most pork dishes. The regular *milanesa,* though not available as a lunch special, is a very good and similar dish made with beef. It is a huge, breaded steak that has been flattened such that it covers most of the plate. The *Bandeja Montañera* (Mountain Platter) is a hearty plate featuring a small steak, *chicharrones* (mostly pork skin with some fat), rice and a plantain. It is a decent dish, though maybe not as good as other versions in the area. In addition to the lunch specials, there are also daily specials. One is the traditional *Mondongo,* a thick stew of beef tripe, tomatoes, potatoes, pumpkin, chickpeas and other tropical vegetables. On Friday and the weekends, there are a couple of *Sancocho* dishes, vegetable stews made with potatoes, tomatoes and other vegetables. One features chicken (*Sancocho de Gallina*), the other with fish (*Sanchoco de Pescado*). The rice and kidney beans that are served with nearly every meal are a fitting and flavorful complement. The rice is always moist and the kidney beans are very flavorful. Mixed together, these are especially good.

The seafood dishes consist mostly of shrimp and Gulf fish that are fried or sautéed in a variety of ways. There is also a Colombian version of paella, seafood mixed among rice, here called *Arroz a la Valenciana.* Like many of the other Colombian restaurants, La Fogata serves a variety of interesting, mostly fruit drinks under the menu heading of *Jugo Naturales,* Natural Juices. These include *mora* (blackberry), *guanabana, maracuya* (passion fruits), mango, banana, *limonada* (lemonade), *milo* (chocolate), *avena* (oatmeal is how it is described here), and several others. These are very popular with the mostly Latin clientele of the restaurant. There are several other interesting non-alcoholic beverages plus a handful of different beers and wine. The small number of desserts includes *tres leches,* of course.

La Guadalupana Bakery & Café $7

2100 Dunlavy (between Fairview and West Gray) 77019, (713) 522-2301

Cuisine - Mexican (taqueria)
Hours - Mon-Sat 7AM to 9PM; Sun 7AM to 3PM
Credit Cards - Amex, Discover, MC, Visa
Service - Counter Service
Alcohol - NONE

Entrée Prices - Dinner & Lunch - $5 to $9 ($7 average); Breakfast - $2 to $6
Entrées at Dinner $12 and less - 100%

Atmosphere & Décor - Spartan
Appeal - Very good, unpretentious Mexican food and pastries in a quaint spot
Useful to Note - Small parking lot, but additional parking is nearby on Dunlavy.
Menu Suggestions - breakfast tacos; Huevos Rancheros; Migas; Mexican pastries; Torta de Pollo Picante (sandwich with spicy chicken); Torta de Pierna (sandwich with roast pork leg); Taco de Carnitas (with fried pork, especially good with the green salsa); Pechuga Poblana (a chicken breast covered in a cream sauce with poblano peppers, onions, and mushrooms); Mole Poblano (over a chicken breast); licuados (Mexican-style milkshakes)

Though not much to look at, and really not much at all in terms of size, La Guadalupana Bakery & Café is nonetheless an excellent neighborhood place for a pleasing Mexican meal, or to grab some attractive and scrumptious Mexican pastries (*garnachas, orejas,* Florentines, *conchas y mas*). As the name indicates, La Guadalupana is both a Mexican bakery (a *panaderia* in Spanish, whose storefront signs are popular sights in Mexican neighborhoods), and a restaurant. It's not really a café, though you can get coffee and the pastries. It's rather a small restaurant that serves familiar, and slightly more complicated Mexican fare, in addition to the pastries. The unpretentious and familiar items include the expected tacos and *tortas,* and some more grandiose dishes. Though the kitchen is reliable for all meals, breakfast might be the best. The breakfast tacos served in the mornings can be excellent, and are among the best in town, in fact. A lot of care is taken to construct these tacos. A judicious amount of fillings (eggs, bacon, etc.) are ladled into either a thin flour or corn tortilla. The tortillas are then rolled fairly tightly around the fillings. Indicative of the high standards of this small place, for takeout, each taco is wrapped carefully in wax paper. This wrapping helps heighten the anticipation of the food, and with the cheese invariably sticking to that wrapping, makes the taco a little messy even before the first bite. This wrapping does keep the tacos piping hot in transit. The salsas, a nice complement to these and most dishes, are fiery and packed with flavor. The other breakfast dishes such as *Huevos Rancheros* and *Huevos a la Mexicana* are also commendable. For lunch and dinner the *tortas* are well prepared, though maybe slightly smaller than some other *torta* purveyors. Served on the typical Mexican *bolillo* sandwich bread with refried beans, slices of avocado, pickled jalapeños, onions and tomatoes, the meats available are: beef fajita, *pierna* (pork leg), *milanesa* (breaded beef), chicken, *carnitas* (fried pork), and the unusual *cesina* (cured, thinly sliced beef). The more ambitious dishes can be a nice departure from familiar Mexican and Tex-Mex dishes. These include *Mojarra al Vapor* (a steamed fish fillet), *Pescado a la Veracruzana* (a whole fish served with tomato sauce and pepper, onions, olives), *Pechuga Poblano* (a chicken breast served with poblano peppers, onions, and mushrooms in a cream sauce), *Chile Relleno, Tacos al Carbon* (tacos filled with beef fajita meat) and *caldos* (broth-heavy soups) with chicken, beef or a mix of seafood.

There are only about ten tables at La Guadalupana, and only a handful of spaces in the parking lot, although there is plenty of space on the street on Dunlavy. Sparse decoration consists of a few paintings of Aztec gods or warriors and the Virgin of Guadalupe. Service is always very friendly, and unless the cashier has momentarily stepped away from the register, it's easy to order in English. As it is a small place, and all of the dishes are cooked to order, it can sometimes take a few minutes longer than you might expect to arrive. This is not a bad sign, as the food is consistently worth the wait.

La Hacienda $9

14759 Memorial (west of Dairy Ashford) 77079, (281) 493-2252
12503 Telge (between Highway 290 and Jarvis) 77429, (281) 373-0300

Cuisine - Tex-Mex
Hours - Mon-Thu, Sun 11AM to 10PM; Fri-Sat 11AM to 11PM
Credit Cards - Amex, Diners, Discover, MC, Visa
Service - Table Service
Alcohol - Full Bar

Entrée Prices - $6 to $13 ($9 average)
Entrées $12 and less - 90%

Atmosphere & Décor - Comfortable
Appeal - Solid, good value Tex-Mex in a family-friendly environment
Menu Suggestions - Enchiladas Suizas; Tacos al Carbon; fajitas

At the original spot, located on Memorial, just west of Dairy Ashford, La Hacienda has been a comforting presence for Tex-Mex since the 1970s to the folks who live and work on the suburban west side. This is primarily a family-oriented restaurant that really strives to please its customers. And, it seems to do so: service is friendly; the kitchen is proficient; helped by the low ceiling, the atmosphere is comfortable, and often somewhat festive. Most everything at La Hacienda is well prepared. One example that is noticed immediately is that the chips are thin, crisp, and usually very fresh. The salsas are freshly made and enjoyable, if not terribly spicy. The fairly large menu lists most of the Tex-Mex favorites, plus some more adventurous dishes. For appetizers, there are the expected nachos, *chile con queso*, Tex-Mex *quesadillas* made with large flour tortillas, but also *queso flameado*, melted cheese with beef fajita, *chorizo* or shrimp. La Hacienda serves almost twenty different old-fashioned Tex-Mex combination plates listed as such and as "La Hacienda Dinners". These include combinations with tacos, enchiladas, guacamole, tamales, *chile con queso* and the like. There are dishes with tacos made with flour tortillas, taco salad, *chalupas,* tamales and a number of enchiladas. These are decent, and include enchiladas filled with char-grilled beef, char-grilled chicken, spinach, ground beef, shredded chicken and cheese. There is also *Enchiladas Verdes,* chicken enchiladas topped with a tomatillo sauce and sour cream, the similar *Enchiladas Suizas* and Seafood Enchiladas filled with shrimp and fish then topped with a flavorful cascabel chile and sour cream sauce. There are fajitas and the similar *tacos al carbon.* The fajita and *tacos al carbon* dishes provide a choice among beef, chicken and even char-grilled pork. The most interesting part of the menu is listed under the title, "*Especialidades Del Chef*". These dozen or so dishes include *Pollo Loco,* a half-chicken that has been marinated then grilled until crispy and lightly charred; a quail dish with three of the small birds that is also marinated then grilled; Shrimp Vallarta, shrimp stuffed with the white *Chihuahua* cheese and jalapeño, wrapped in bacon then broiled; Shrimp Inferno, spicy butterflied shrimp served in a cilantro butter; and the La Hacienda *Chile Relleno,* a fried stuffed poblano chile pepper. The quick turnaround from the kitchen and the fine value make lunchtime popular at the original location with workers from the nearby Energy Corridor. La Hacienda might not be special, but it's comfortable, and the food is usually quite satisfying.

La Madeleine $9

6205 Kirby (north of University) 77005, (713) 942-7081
2047 West Gray (at S. Shepherd) 77019, (713) 526-9666
5015 Westheimer (in the Galleria) 77056, (713) 993-0287
10001 Westheimer (between Gessner and the Beltway) 77042, (713) 266-7686
6500 Woodway (east of Voss) 77057, (713) 722-8449
5505 FM 1960 W. (east of Champions Forest) 77069, (281) 893-0723
4700 Beechnut (in Meyerland Plaza) 77096, (713) 218-8075
4570 Kingwood (east of Lake Houston Parkway) Kingwood, 77345, (281) 360-1681
2675 Town Center (south of Southwest Fwy.) Sugar Land, 77479, (281) 494-4401
700 W. Sam Houston Parkway N. (in Town and Country) 77024, (713) 465-7370
929 West Bay Area Blvd. (Highway 3 and El Camino Real) 77598, (281) 316-6135
19710 Northwest Freeway (at FM 1960) 77065, (281) 720-1000
9595 Six Pines (at Research Forest) The Woodlands, 77380, (281) 419-5826
www.lamadeleine.com

Cuisine - Café / Bakery
Hours - Kirby - Mon-Thu, Sun 6:30AM to 10PM; Fri-Sat 6:30AM to 11PM; West Gray - Mon-Thu 6:30AM to 10PM; Fri-Sat 6:30AM to 11PM; Sun 7AM to 9PM; 5015 Westheimer - Mon-Sat 8AM to 9PM; Sun 10AM to 7PM; 10001 Westheimer - Mon-Thu 6:30AM to 10PM; Fri-Sat 6:30AM to 11PM; Sun 7AM to 10PM; Woodway - Daily 6:30AM to 10PM; FM 1960 W - Daily 6:30AM to 10PM; Beechnut - Mon-Thu, Sun 7AM to 9:30PM; Fri-Sat 6:30AM to 11PM; Kingwood - Daily 6:30AM to 9:30PM; First Colony - Mon-Thu 7AM to 10PM; Fri-Sat 7AM to 10:30PM; Sun 7AM to 9PM; Town & Country - Daily 6:30AM to 10PM; Bay Area Boulevard - Daily

7AM to 10PM; Northwest Freeway - Daily 6:30AM to 10PM; The Woodlands - Daily 6:30AM to 10PM
Credit Cards - Amex, Diners, Discover, MC, Visa
Service - Counter Service
Alcohol - Beer & Wine

Entrée Prices - Dinner & Lunch - $7 to $13 ($11 average); Breakfast - $4 to $7
Entrées at Dinner $12 and less - 90%

Atmosphere & Décor - Comfortable; outdoor seating (except in the Galleria)
Appeal - Satisfying, informal French-inspired fare, and tempting pastries
Menu Suggestions - Tomato Basil Soup; Ham Monsieur (hearty bread layered with béchamel, ham and melted Swiss); Chicken Friand (puff pastry with chicken, mushrooms, béchamel and mushroom sauce); Caesar Salad; Caesar Salad with grilled chicken; Quiche Lorraine; Spinach Quiche; chocolate croissant; French Country Breakfast (scrambled eggs, bacon, croissant and a potato patty)

Though a multi-state chain, La Madeleine holds its own against virtually all of the other informal, French-inspired cafés in town (which you can readily verify in the Village). La Madeleine is a reliable, and popular, quick stop for pastries, soups, salads, French sandwiches, pizzas and heartier fare. The restaurants feature counter service, and inviting faux-French country interiors. Not incidentally, almost all of the locations have a bakery. The quality of these baked goods is evident in most of the offerings. At the very least, La Madeleine is a reliable source for which to pick up a fresh baguette or another loaf of bread for the dinner at home.

The chain was created by a Frenchman originally from the Loire Valley, and it serves the everyday French specialties, but you won't find a place like this in Paris or Lyons. This is a good thing, at least in regards to the fact that the usually friendly staff will still be helpful when a patron mangles the French pronunciation of a dish. The menu is not completely French nor French-inspired, though. The Caesar Salad, of which La Madeleine does very brisk business, was created by an Italian restaurateur in Tijuana, Mexico during the 1920s, but is now quintesentially American. Soup and salad is the key attraction for many patrons. La Madeleine is well known for its strongly flavored Caesar Salad. It is available with chicken or salmon for a filling meal, or a small size that makes a fitting accompaniment to a sandwich or quiche. As with the other items that are availble for inspection through the glass counter, all of the half-dozen plus salads use noticeably fresh greens, vegetables and fruits. Possibly the most popular item is the Tomato Basil Soup. Creamy and robust, as the menu states, it is redolant of pureed tomatoes, cream and butter, topped with shreds of fresh basil. It can be nearly addictive, especially with some freshly ground black pepper and some of their good bread. The other soup offered daily, the French Onion, is pretty much what you would expect, and also very flavorful. The additional soups that rotate (potato, cream of mushroom, and vegetable) are also quite appetizing. Nearly as popular as the soups and salads, the Hot Sandwiches are generally very appealing, even if these have been sitting on warming griddle for some time. Quality, fresh bread and melted cheese goes a long way. Among the best of the "small" dishes are the French sandwiches, *friands* and *monsieurs*. The Chicken *Friand* is a flaky puff pastry filled with shredded chicken, mushrooms and bechamel sauce, then topped with a mushroom sauce. A bit awkward to eat, it is nonetheless very tasty. The Ham *Monsieur* is bread layered with bechamel sauce, thin slices of ham and Swiss cheese, then baked. More mundane sandwiches featuring turkey, ham, and chicken salad are also available, but they are better than usual because they are on very good, freshly baked breads or croissants. The sandwiches are a good value, as these come with a choice among a small Caesar salad, a mixed green salad, a pasta salad with pesto, or the utensil-free option, packaged potato chips.

Much more than just a soup, salad and sandwich place, La Madeleine serves many satisfying French and French-style dishes. The quiches are usally very good, especially the classic Quiche Lorraine. La Madeleine has over a dozen hearty entrées including several pastas with a French-American or Provençal touch, savory crêpes with beef, chicken, pork and shrimp, Beef *Bourguignon* and the long-time favorite, the moist Rosemary Rotisserie Chicken. Many of these dishes are not available at some of the smaller locations. In the morning, full French-inspired and American-style breakfasts are served. La Madeleine does a very commendable job with these, especially the ones with moist and fluffy scrambled eggs and their flavorful croissants. This is further evidenced by the usually good crowds on the weekend mornings. Though the authenticity of most of the entrees might be questioned by ex-pats from France, many seem to enjoy the results of the bakery and pastry cooks. The pastry display cases can be very tempting, both for a quick breakfast or a post-meal reward. The assorted pastries and desserts are beautiful, if nothing else. But, these usually taste as good as they look, and they are baked in-house. Among the vast array of choices, there are croissants in several varieties, a caramel pecan roll, *palmier*, scones, turnovers, muffins, a cinnamon twist, cakes, éclair, Napoleon, cheesecake, the Viennese *Sacher Torte*, Tiramisu, tarts, and cookies. To go with these, La Madeleine has better than average coffee, plus the espresso-based drinks and freshly squeezed fruit juices. Beer and wine are suitably available.

La Mexicana $12

1018 Fairview (at Montrose) 77006, (713) 521-0963
www.lamexicanarestaurant.com

Cuisine - Mexican
Hours - Daily 7AM to 11PM
Credit Cards - Amex, Diners, Discover, MC, Visa
Service - Table Service
Alcohol - Full Bar

Entrée Prices - Dinner & Lunch - $9 to $18 ($12 average); Breakfast - $5 to $9
Entrées at Dinner $12 and less - 60%

Atmosphere & Décor - Comfortable; patio
Appeal - Solid and unpretentious Mexican food in a relaxed atmosphere
Useful to Note - It can be a great place for Mexican breakfast.
Menu Suggestions - Guisado de Puerco (marinated and stewed pork tips); Fajitas a la Mexicana (Carne Guisada - marinated and stewed beef skirt tips); Sopes (thick hand made corn masa tortillas topped with refried beans and ground beef or chicken); Sopa Azteca (a soup with corn tortillas, chipotle peppers, Panela cheese, diced tomatoes and sliced avocados)

Though it is a worthy and often lively place for Mexican food and drinks, La Mexicana is more than just that. An outgrowth of its long ago life as a neighborhood grocery, La Mexicana also has a bakery, and does a brisk takeout business from a separate cafeteria section. The large menu has many familiar items and begins with appetizers such as nachos, *chile con queso* and a couple of the melted cheese dishes, *Queso Flameado* and *Queso Guisado* (the white *panela* cheese cooked in the tomato-based *ranchero* sauce). La Mexicana does a good job with enchiladas. Some of the choices of fillings are ground beef, chicken, *ranchero* cheese, *mole,* beef fajitas, shrimp and spinach. The entrées are headlined by their *Fajitas a la Mexicana.* Subtitled *carne guisada,* these are not really fajitas, as they are stewed beef rather than grilled. No matter, these are still satisfying. *Guisado de Puerco* is a similar dish with pork. Other enticing entrées include *flautas, chile relleno, Mole Poblano* (two boneless chicken breasts in a dark brown *mole* sauce), *milanesas* with beef or chicken, soups and a couple more unusual items. There is *Chicharron en Salsa Verde* (pork rinds cooked in a green sauce), and *Nopalitos en Salsa Chipotle* (cactus strips in a *chipotle* sauce). Other interesting entrées are listed under "Seafood" and "Grill". These include different reasonably priced steaks, grilled fajitas, and a mixed grill. For seafood, there is a seafood soup, *ceviche,* a catfish fillet and several shrimp dishes. The most appealing might be the *Camarones al Queso con Pimientos y Cebollas* (jumbo shrimp cooked in a sauce of onions and roasted red and bell peppers that is topped with melted white *Chihuahua* cheese). If one of the entrées is not enough, the a la carte items include tacos, *flautas, tostadas, quesadillas* (pan fried tacos, here), *sopes* (thick corn *masa* tortillas covered with beans, ground beef or chicken, topped with lettuce, cheese and guacamole), and a burrito. La Mexicana claims not to use tasty lard in their cooking. But, most dishes are pretty flavorful, anyway. La Mexicana is opened at 7AM each day for breakfast. The breakfasts are very good, and draw a crowd during the weekends. The offerings cover most of the popular Mexican breakfast items. These are maybe a little more expensive than other Mexican restaurants, but still a decent value. There are a different *migas* (scrambled eggs and strips of soft tortillas and topped with plentiful shredded cheese), *chilaquiles* (baked dish of corn tortilla chips, cheese and scrambled eggs), *Machacado con Huevo* (dried beef with scrambled eggs) and *huevos rancheros,* alone or served with ham, bacon, fajitas or tamales. *Menudo,* along with tacos with *barbacoa* are served on weekends.

La Sani $8

9621 Bissonnet (just north of the Southwest Freeway) 77036, (713) 270-5040

Cuisine - Pakistani
Hours - Daily 11AM to 12AM
Credit Cards - Amex, Diners, Discover, MC, Visa
Service - Table Service; Buffet at Lunch
Alcohol - NONE

Entrée Prices - Dinner - $5 to $11 ($8 average); Lunch Buffet - $10
Entrées at Dinner $12 and less - 100%

Atmosphere & Décor - Pleasant
Appeal - Very good, very spicy Pakistani cuisine in a comfortable setting
Menu Suggestions - Chicken Kahari (chicken cooked in a metal skillet); Chicken Tikka Breast (tandoori baked chicken); Aloo Bhindi (potatoes and okra); Butter Paneer Masala (cheese cooked in a curry sauce with plenty of butter); Haleem (shredded stewed beef with lentils, chiles and ginger); Kheer Shahi (thick rice pudding topped with crushed pistachios)

La Sani might be the only Pakistani restaurant in the area that offers a lunchtime buffet, something that is commonplace among the local Indian restaurants, which proffer a similar cuisine. This is a great way to sample this possibly unfamiliar food without having to negotiate a menu with many new dishes and exotic names. But, situated in a scruffy strip shopping center across from the underutilized Westwood Technology Center along with other businesses run by recent immigrants, the patrons here are mostly Pakistani and Muslim. The menu proclaims that La Sani is "The Ambassador of Taste & Hospitality". With often excellent food, an attractive dining room that belies the location, and solicitous service, it is tough to dispute that.

The flavors at La Sani are intense, which means in large part that many dishes are very spicy. Entire heat-bearing seeds are noticeable in many of the dishes, and you might notice entire pods with twenty or so seeds of the intense spicy-sweet cardamom. The buffet items change daily, and the choices are somewhat limited, but a high percentage of these should be enticing. The Chicken *Kahari,* chicken cooked in a metal skillet, features moist chicken parsed in large sections and served in a flavorful, spicy and complex sauce. Other items might be lamb meatballs in a pleasant curry, Chicken *Tikka* from the tandoor, Mutton *Biriyani* (stewed mutton atop a bed of fragrant basmati rice) and the like. As wonderfully greasy as the food is here, the menu states that canola and corn oil is used in the cooking. So, maybe it is not as unhealthy as it seems, though trying to control portion size here can be difficult, as it is very flavorful and all-you-can-eat. And, the creamy, delectable rice-based dessert, *kheer,* is quite possibly the best version in the area. It is a perfect, cooling end to a spicy feast. Very flavorful, it is thicker than most local versions, and nicely topped with crushed pistachios. If you are lucky, their excellent, plump rose-water infused sweet donuts, *gulab jamen,* might also make it to the buffet. Every day, La Sani offers plenty of delectable calories for only ten bucks. This is from 11AM to 3:30PM during the week, and from 11AM to 4PM on the weekends. As an added bonus, service is attentive, even during the lunchtime buffet hours. Water glasses are promptly refilled, and the necessary *naan* is freshly baked and frequently offered to the table.

The dinner menu at La Sani is straightforward, but no descriptions accompany the items. The vast majority of patrons don't need help with the names. But, if needed, the waitstaff is usually helpful in answering any necessary queries. The menu is meat-heavy, beginning with beef and chicken dishes cooked in the *tandoor* oven. There are shrimp and fish items, rice dishes, both the rice platters (*biryanis*) and those originated from China, stewed beef and goat preparations, various chicken dishes, and several vegetable sides. There are thirty-five meat and seafood preparations that are grilled, stewed and baked. Most are under ten dollars. Though the meat dishes are at the center of La Sani's offerings, as with all Pakistani restaurants, the vegetables can be very good here. These are also very tasty when picked from the buffet. Especially tasty are the deep-fried potato patties that are the size of a hockey puck, and the runny, but flavorful lentils (*dal*). Save room for dessert, if you can.

La Tapatia Taqueria $7

1749 Richmond (east of Dunlavy) 77098, (713) 521-3144
5551 Richmond (just east of Chimney Rock) 77056, (713) 787-9680
3965 S. Gessner (at Westpark) 77063, (713) 266-4756
6413 Hillcroft (south of Southwest Freeway) 77081, (713) 995-9191
4610 FM 1960 W. (at Veterans Memorial) 77069, (281) 537-7220
14025 Westheimer (east of Highway 6) 77077, (281) 531-1115
9902 I-45 S. (between Airport and Edgebrook) 77034, (713) 910-3410
www.latapatiamexcafe.com

Cuisine - Mexican (taqueria)
Hours - Mon-Fri 8AM to 2:30AM; Sat-Sun 8AM to 5AM
Credit Cards - Amex, Discover, MC, Visa
Service - Table Service
Alcohol - Beer

Entrée Prices - Dinner & Lunch - $4 to $12 ($7 average); Breakfast - $4
Entrées at Dinner $12 and less - 100%

Atmosphere & Décor - Spartan
Appeal - Decent Mexican food for cheap, and open late into the night
Menu Suggestions - barbacoa tacos; tacos al pastor (with roasted pork); tortas (Mexican-style sandwiches); menudo (tripe and hominy soup); Enchiladas de Queso (cheese enchiladas); Quesadilla Tapatia con Pastor (Tex-Mex-style quesadilla filled with roasted pork)

The original La Tapatia Taqueria in a scruffy old stip center west of the Montrose area on lower Richmond near Rice and the University of St. Thomas is many people's only experience with *taquerias*. And, that experience has become better in recent years. That restaurant was once as scruffy as the strip center, but it has been remodeled into a very nice space, especially for a *taqueria*. As the settings have moved more upscale and inviting, the food has improved, the quality control is better, and the dishes are probably more flavorful now. Service has seemingly become better, too. All of this is apparent even very late at night when the restaurant is crowded with boisterous patrons. With these improvements, the restaurants still provide great values. The fairly large menu is similar to most *taquerias* with both finger foods and larger plates, though with probably more Tex-Mex items than the others: nachos, salads, *queso flameados* (melted cheese dishes), fajitas, soups, enchiladas, burritos, shrimp, fish, seafood cocktails, burritos, tacos, *tostadas*, Tex-Mex *quesadillas*, *gorditas*, and *tortas*. The tripe-filled *menudo* is served only on the weekend. Reflecting the influence of central Mexico, they offer *sincronizadas* (essentially beans and melted cheese sandwiched between two tortillas) and *birria* (baby goat) as a filling for the tacos, *tortas* and *gorditas*. In addition to beer for libations, there are a handful of *aguas frescas* and *licuados* (the milk shakes). The menu is large enough so that everyone should find something appealing; either among the familiar items like nachos or enchiladas, or some of the Mexican food that can be considered an acquired taste. The *pastor* (roasted pork) is probably the best of the meat choices, and the flour tortillas are freshly made and warm. The complimentary chips are usually fresh and crisp, and the red and green salsas on the table are pretty tasty. The jarred, pickled vegetables are a nice touch, and something else to munch on while waiting for your order. One complaint, and one that won't effect the vast majority of patrons, is that the *machacado,* dried and salted beef that is scrambled with eggs for breakfast, which can be excellent at other places, can be tough here.

Lankford Grocery $7

88 Dennis (near Midtown, north of Brazos) 77006, (713) 522-9555

Cuisine - Hamburgers
Hours - Mon-Sat 7AM to 3PM
Credit Cards - NONE
Service - Counter Service
Alcohol - Beer

Entrée Prices - Lunch - $6 to $10 ($7 average); Breakfast - $4 to $7
Entrées at Lunch $12 and less - 100%

Atmosphere & Décor - Spartan
Appeal - Excellent hamburgers and hearty breakfasts in an anachronistic setting
Menu Suggestions - hamburger; cheeseburger; breakfast; Biscuits and Gravy and Sausages

Lankford Café 'N Ice House, or Lankford Grocery, as the sign outside reads, is a charming, somewhat anachronistic, place. It's a friendly, homey neighborhood eatery that seems oddly located very near to downtown. The modern, cosmopolitan Houston epitomized by the shining skyscrapers that are less than a mile away seem to have left this place behind, along with the recent urban housing boom that has crept to directly across the street with the uninspiringly designed townhomes. Located in an old house that functioned as a small grocery store until 1977, the Lankford is a small restaurant. It is somewhat quaint, sporting a warped floor, unmatched furniture, and adorned with a lot of old knick-knacks, and about a dozen booths and picnic tables in the small dining room. The biggest draw here is the excellent hamburgers. These are quite tasty; properly juicy and unpretentious. Not the designer-style hamburgers, these are the basic, very flavorful burgers that you wish you could consistently make on the backyard grill. Lankford begins with large handmade patties about a third-pound in size or so that are grilled to order, and are served with a slice of tomato, sliced white onions, and an ample-sized leaf of crisp iceberg lettuce on large toasted hamburger buns. Their versions are really among the very best hamburgers in town. You can get these fitted with cheese and bacon and with a second patty. The accompanying fries are freshly made, and are crisp and very satisfying. Tater tots are another option. There are other lunchtime offerings on the limited menu. Sandwiches include turkey, ham and tuna, and a deep-fried chicken strip sandwich. Salads come in the garden or chef variety, large and small sizes. They also have daily specials that can include those long-time Houston favorites such as an enchiladas, chicken fried steak and a taco dinner. If you have room for dessert, there is banana pudding and flan, which are made in-house and quite tasty. Offered during each morning from Monday through Saturday are the basic American breakfasts plus, requisite for this city, a few Mexican items: three eggs and toast with bacon or sausage and sautéed potatoes or grits; French toast; biscuits and gravy and sausage; omelets; oatmeal; *Chilaquiles* (fried tortilla strips, red salsa and cheese, served with eggs) and breakfast tacos on flour tortillas. These are all generally quite fulfilling, filling and good values. The biscuits and gravy, which are served with a couple of good breakfast sausage patties, might be the best in town. Fresh, butter-laden biscuits and thick flavorful gravy complement each other very well, if not your arteries. Only on Saturday mornings, though. Service is always very friendly here, as are the regulars.

Laredo Taqueria $6

915 Snover (on Washington between Heights and Shepherd) 77007, (713) 861-7279
311 Patton (east of I-45 N. between N. Main & Calvalcade) 77009, (713) 695-0504

Cuisine - Mexican (taqueria)
Hours - Mon-Sat 6AM to 10PM; Sun 7AM to 3PM
Credit Cards - MC, Visa
Service - Counter Service
Alcohol - Beer

Entrée Prices - Dinner & Lunch - $4 to $8 ($6 average); Breakfast -$4 to $8
Entrées at Dinner $12 and less - 100%

Atmosphere & Décor - Not a lot at either location, but it's functional
Appeal - Tasty tacos for cheap
Menu Suggestions - spicy fajita taco; fajita taco; asado de puerco taco; barbacoa taco

Reliably tasty, quick and cheap tacos are the reasons for the continued popularity of these two steam-tabled-oriented taco-centric restaurants. There's not much else, as atmosphere and décor are rather neglected here, though the Patton location is not unattractive. The cluttered interiors, a small gravel parking lot at the Washington one, and a not-terribly-inviting staff aren't deterrents to the patrons who flock to these humble taco purveyors. Though the area around it is continually gentrifying, the Washington location is now better than it's ever been after its kitchen was expanded several years ago. Freshly made flour tortillas provide the proper base for most of the tacos, at least for most of the non-Hispanic patrons. Corn is also an option, and these need to be ordered before stepping up to the counter. A smattering of runny refried beans is slathered on each of the tacos unless requested otherwise. Though there is seemingly always a queue at the Washington branch, the operation is very efficient, and you might have your tacos before you pay the cashier. The spicy fajita, cubes of seasoned beef and chopped bell peppers, jalapeños, and onions, and which occupies a large flat grill and a significant portion of the serving area, is reliably good, and probably the best filling to order of the dozen or so choices. The similar fajita is also good, as is the moist *asado de puerco* (roast pork here). The unusual *fideo* filling is short spaghetti-like noodles mixed with pieces of chicken and bell peppers, just like the soup. It can be tasty, though the tortilla quickly becomes soggy. The same goes for the chicken in the generally pleasing dark *mole* sauce. The *barbacoa* itself can be quite tasty, when you can taste it. Too often it is served with a lot of potatoes mixed in and hardly noticed. The breakfast tacos are popular during the morning, and are satisfying and inexpensive, if hardly the best around. Each of the tacos, three of which will be a sufficient order for most, is well complemented by the hot salsas, the red one, especially. There are also several larger plates, but the tacos are the real draws. To drink, the *aguas frescas* in several flavors are machine-made and nothing special. But, beer has been added.

Las Llardas $7

2400 Gessner (north of Hammerly at Emnora) 77080, (713) 461-2028

Cuisine - Mexican (taqueria)
Hours - Mon-Thu, Sun 7AM to 10PM; Fri-Sat Open 24 Hours
Credit Cards - MC, Visa
Service - Table Service
Alcohol - Beer & Margaritas

Entrée Prices - Dinner & Lunch - $4 to $10 ($7 average); Breakfast - $3 to $4
Entrées at Dinner $12 and less - 100%

Atmosphere & Décor - Functional
Appeal - Well-made and inexpensive renditions of the food of Mexico City
Useful to Note - Some Spanish is helpful here.

Menu Suggestions - Chilaquiles con Milanesa (thin breaded steak atop baked corn chips and green salsa); Milanesa; Pechuga de Pollo Empanizada (breaded chicken breast); Enchiladas Verdes con Pollo; Carne Asada (grilled skirt steak); Torta Chilanga (sandwich with ham, steak, chorizo and melted cheese); Torta Pierna (sandwich with roasted pork leg); Torta Chilanga (sandwich filled with thinly sliced ham, beefsteak, chorizo, melted cheese, chopped tomatoes and avocado slices)

Las Llardas is busy serving the immigrant and migrant Mexican population of Spring Branch, not with their inexpensive and pleasing Mexico City-style food, but also with a money order operation. This and its dumpy setting shouldn't dissuade you, though. You are not visiting for the atmosphere and décor, you're here for the interesting and usually very well-made food that is an excellent value. There are *tllacoyos* (masa around a filling like mushrooms and grilled), *pambazos* (dough filled with potato and *chorizo* and fried), *tostadas de pata* (topped with meat from a pig's foot) and *quesadillas* with *huitlacoche* (savory corn fungus) that you won't find on too many other local menus, though there should be several dishes to interest even the most casual fan of Mexican food. Plus, the menu is bi-lingual, and virtually all of the dishes are described in English. For lunch and dinner the offerings consist of tacos, *tortas*, specialty dishes (*Antojitos Mexicanos*), and plates. The tacos can be made with either corn or flour tortillas and can be filled with *milanesa* (breaded and fried steak), *carne asada* (grilled skirt steak), chicken, *chicharron* (pork skin) that are commonly found at local taquerias and some items that are not: *higado enceballado con rajas* (beef liver with onions and strips of pepper) and *saudero* (lemon-tinged beef). The *tortas* make for a bargain meal for around five bucks. Featuring bread that is more dense than is used at other *taquerias*, but well suited for the large sandwiches, these *tortas* are very good. The best may be the *Torta Chilanga* that is filled with ham, steak, chorizo and melted light cheese (*quesillo*). Among the several other varieties include a few with meat and scrambled eggs, and the *Cubanas* that can be filled with ham, frankfurters (*salchicha*), roasted pork leg (*pierna*), or *milanesa*. The *Anitojitos Mexicanos* include the familiar *quesadillas*, essentially warmed tacos with melted cheese in the Mexican style, with a choice among chicken, spicy brisket, pork skin and shredded beef, and *tostadas* with fairly similar toppings. The *gordita* is only available with pork skin filling. The less familiar items are the *sopes* and *huaraches*. The former is corn *masa* in the shape of a cup topped with beans. The *huarache*, which means "sandal" in Spanish, is a central Mexican dish, similar to the *sope*, but larger and looking, yes, somewhat like a sandal. These are available just with the beans and lettuce or with a choice of several meat toppings for an additional dollar.

There are heftier plates, too. One of those is the *Chilaquiles con Milanesa*. It is a long cut of beef strip steak pounded very thin and breaded, thinner than most *milanesas,* and sits atop fried triangles of corn tortillas doused with a tomatillo-rich *salsa verde.* The *milanesa* is large and tender. This is one of the better *milanesa* versions around, and a great value. The same *salsa verde* is used for the *Enchiladas Verdes,* the only enchilada dish that is served daily. Slightly different than the standard *enchiladas verdes,* these are completely covered with shredded lettuce and sit amidst of liberal dose of the green salsa. Other plates are the solo *Milanesa,* grilled skirt steak (*carne asada*), Mexican-style strip steak, grilled chicken (*Pollo a la Plancha*), a breaded and fried chicken breast, *flautas,* and an order of *tlacoyos,* a remnant of the Aztecs, served in the *salsa verde.* Most of the plates are served with rice, refried beans and a small shredded lettuce salad. Available only on the weekends are *menudo, posole,* enchiladas with *mole, birria* (a thick soup featuring baby goat), and a couple other specialties. There is *Costillas Garibaldi,* beef ribs served with nopalito cactus, avocado, *pico de gallo* and beans. The *Carne Asada* is not like fajitas, as in most of the other places, but marinated, thinly sliced cuts of beef that are then grilled. These are especially flavorful when sprinkled with the juice of the accompanying lemon and lime slices and wrapped in a hot tortilla and topped with fresh avocado and the excellent spicy yet slightly sweet complimentary green salsa. As with most *taquerias,* in the morning, Las Llardas does a nice job of providing often delicious and spicy breakfasts for just a few bucks: eggs scrambled with ham, *chorizo,* or frankfurters, plus *Huevos a la Mexicana* and *Huevos Rancheros.* Along with most *taqueria*-style restaurants service is perfunctory and décor is not at a premium. This might be an understatement for Las Llardas, as it is dumpier than most.

Le Viet $10

11328 Westheimer (between Hayes and Kirkwood) 77077, (281) 509-6666
www.le-viet.com

Cuisine - Vietnamese
Hours - Mon-Thu, Sun 11AM to 10PM; Fri-Sat 11AM to 11PM
Credit Cards - Amex, Discover, MC, Visa
Service - Table Service
Alcohol - Beer & Wine

Entrée Prices - Dinner - $6 to $25 ($10 average); Lunch - $6 to $10
Entrées at Dinner $12 and less - 70%

Atmosphere & Décor - Pleasant
Appeal - A nice restaurant serving a wide range of well-made Vietnamese food
Menu Suggestions - Bo Luc Lac (flame broiled pieces of filet mignon served on macaroni or rice); Bun Le Viet (vermicelli with a choice of toppings); Shrimp Volcano (shrimp with hot chili peppers and lemon grass); Le Viet's Honey-Braised Chicken (sautéed chicken with onions)

Le Viet is a fairly ambitious restaurant that serves mostly traditional Vietnamese dishes, while doing it in a more accessible big city fashion. The interior is much more attractive than most Vietnamese places, and less noticeably Asian, even if the fare is nearly entirely Vietnamese. Service is generally good, and the kitchen is efficient. The menu is wide-ranging and covers most of the local Vietnamese favorites plus some more creative and authentic dishes. Welcome to many, each dish has an English and helpful description. There are appetizers, soups, salads, pan-seared noodles, rice dishes, vermicelli dishes, nearly ten vegetarian dishes, chicken, seafood, beef and pork, hot pots, and Chef's Special, five different preparations of lobster. Le Viet does a credible job with most of the popular inexpensive Vietnamese dishes like the vermicelli bowls and rice dishes, though not as good as at places like Saigon Pagolac and Taydo. In addition to the lobster dishes, some of the more interesting items at Le Viet include Spicy Tamarind Chicken, Le French Soft Shell Crabs (lightly battered crabs with a French butter sauce), Le Viet's Grilled Mussels that are topped with an onion sauce, Shrimp Volcano featuring chili peppers and lemon grass, Mouth Watering Goat Hot Pot, and Spicy Wild Alligator. The fifteen lunch specials served during the week help fill the restaurant, and provide a wide range of choices. These include tasty, tender and soy-tinged Flame-Broiled Filet Mignon Chunks (*Bo Luc Lac*), Fried Rice, Grilled Catfish Filets, vermicelli (*bun*) topped with several choices, crushed rice (*com dia*) with toppings, beef stew, jumbo shrimp, and Crispy Honey Braised Lemon Grass Chicken. Le Viet has long offered a wine night on Mondays, when bottled wine prices are slashed in half. Unfortunately, the choice of wines can stand some improvement. There are the same wines and labels that are at most restaurants where wine is an afterthought. They would be well served to also offer more wines that complement the often spicy food such as Gerwurztraminers, Rieslings and the like.

Lee's Sandwiches $5

11210 Bellaire (at Boone) 77072, (281) 933-9988
8338 W. San Houston Parkway (at Beechnut) 77072, (281) 988-5788
www.leesandwiches.com

Cuisine - Sandwiches; Vietnamese
Hours - 24 Hours Daily
Credit Cards - Amex, Diners, Discover, MC, Visa
Service - Counter Service; Drive-Thru
Alcohol - Full Bar

Entrée Prices - $3 to $6 ($5 average)
Entrées $12 and less - 100%

Atmosphere & Décor - Functional, but nice
Appeal - Good Vietnamese and croissant sandwiches for cheap
Useful to Note - Have patience with the drive-thru.
Menu Suggestions - banh mi sandwiches; croissant sandwiches

The first local location, a spacious and airy 10,000 square foot restaurant in the heart of New Chinatown that seemingly became a hangout overnight for many nearby Vietnamese is the first Texas location of this California-based Vietnamese sandwich chain. It's not only the largest Lee's Sandwiches location, but it's many times larger than any Vietnamese sandwich shop in the Houston (the second Lee's location is next). If there are doubts about the quality of the fare at this West Coast transplant, it might quickly be allayed with the mouth-watering aroma of freshly baked French bread that fills the interior. The choices of sandwiches are much larger than the home-grown *banh mi* operations. And, Lee's northern Californian-Vietnamese sandwich is quite good and certainly recognizable, but slightly different than what is common here. It starts with the longer 10-inch French-style baguette that is a little unlike the local Vietnamese bakeries produce. This baguette is filled with a similar choice of meats, a house-made mayonnaise, pickled daikon, pickled juliened carrot that is more thickly cut, jalapeños, cilantro, sliced onions, salt, pepper, and somewhat uncommonly for here, soy sauce. For 75¢ more you can get additional meat; 50¢ for pâté and about a dollar for avocado. In addition to the *banh mi*, there are also sandwiches made with croissants in a wide-array of fillings, which began with top-notch, large, light and buttery croissants, and are quite tasty. All of the sandwiches seem to have a long shelf-life, or more accurately, refrigerator life, and taste very good several hours later, perfect for take-away. Lee's makes that easy with a drive-thru; a true stroke of genius. Lee's also serves iced coffee, and a wide array of smoothies like pineapple, mango, raspberry, passion fruit, papaya and cantaloupe plus many of which will appeal to the already converted, such as avocado, durian, soursop, jack fruit, taro, sapodilla, green bean, mocha and lychee. The French bread is baked by a large Rube Goldberg-like contraption behind a glass in the back of the store. A smaller, but similarly automated machine makes cream cakes behind a counter up front. You can buy chocolates and other candies and snacks plus there are over a dozen bins filled with dried fruit, dried beef and at least a couple types of squid jerky. If a perfect fit for New Chinatown and nearby, Lee's might not quite be ready for Main Street.

Leibman's Wine & Fine Foods $9

14529 Memorial (east of Dairy Ashford) 77079, (281) 493-3663
www.leibmans.com

Cuisine - Sandwiches
Hours - Mon-Fri 10AM to 7PM; Sat 11AM to 5PM
Credit Cards - Amex, Discover, MC, Visa
Service - Counter Service
Alcohol - Beer & Wine

Entrée Prices - $6 to $12 ($9 average)
Entrées $12 and less - 100%

Atmosphere & Décor - Pleasant
Appeal - Well-made sandwiches on the west side
Useful to Note - It's worth of visit also for their numerous food-related gifts.
Menu Suggestions - Rinke's Reuben Sandwich; Chicken Salad Afrique Sandwich; Big Apple Sandwich (pastrami with Swiss cheese, etc.); Muffaletta

---

Moving a little further west down Memorial after a fire destroyed their original location, Leibman's Wine & Fine Foods is again a fixture on the west side; since 1979, in fact. Though, primarily an upscale food and gift store, the deli portion of the business is far more than an afterthought. Around lunchtime, the bounteous and attractive deli area is busy and most of the tables are occupied with women from the nearby west Memorial residential areas and office workers from the Energy Corridor buildings. They come to enjoy the freshly prepared sandwiches, soups and salads. The deli cases display a big array of prepared salads, spreads, cheeses and lunch meats. The sandwiches are all made to order and come both cold and warm. The warm sandwiches and specialty sandwiches come in over three dozen interesting combinations made with a wide range of quality components. These range from a triple decker Reuben, a club sandwich, a meatball sub, a BLT, a Greek-influenced BLT (The Great Greek, which is bacon, lettuce, tomato, basil, mayonnaise with feta cheese), a grilled cheese, a few vegetarian options, a Houston-style soft loaf muffaletta, grilled chicken with pesto, and a salami and blue cheese creation (International Bounty). About a dozen are grilled or *panini*-style available with either *focaccia* or *ciabatta* bread. For the child in tow, there is even the peanut butter and jelly sandwich. One of the more familiar ones, the Reuben, is very good. If the menu-listed sandwiches don't seem interesting, you can always request one to be made to your specifications. There are several soups available each day and entrée-size salads, also. Along with hearty versions of the Greek, Chef, Caesar and Cobb salads, Leibman's offers nearly ten different housemade dressings including Southwestern Buttermilk, Honey Balsamic and Vidalia Onion & Peppercorn. A number of freshly baked desserts is available for the sweet tooth. Leibman's is also a great stop for prepared foods for home, a food-related gift or just a gourmet treat, with a selection of items including high quality chocolates, bulk candies, preserves, chutneys, plates, glassware and much more. Just be sure to check the expiration date on the more obscure food products here.

Lemon Tree $12

12591 Whittington (south of Briar Forest, at Dairy Ashford) 77077, (281) 556-0690

Cuisine - Peruvian
Hours - Tue-Sat 11AM to 3PM, 6 to 9PM; Sun 11AM to 4PM
Credit Cards - Amex, MC, Visa
Service - Table Service
Alcohol - NONE; BYOB

Entrée Prices - $7 to $15
Entrées $12 and less - 90%

Atmosphere & Décor - Pleasant, Homey
Appeal - Well prepared and approachable food
Useful to Note - The restaurant is closed on Mondays.
Menu Suggestions - Ceviche de Pescado; Ceviche Mixto; Tiradito de Pescado (marinated fish served with a creamy sauce); Pescado a la Menier (pan-fried fish fillet in a butter sauce); Tuca Tuca Lemon Tree (grilled steak, rice and onions topped with fried eggs and served with fries); Pollo a la Brasa (rotisserie chicken)

Occupying a small space in a small and unattractive strip center facing a side street in west Houston, Lemon Tree will come as a very pleasant surprise to most diners. Visiting this unassuming, sparsely decorated and obviously family-run restaurant on a random Saturday afternoon you could very well have to wait for a table since the restaurant is packed with members of the local Peruvian community, many drinking from large plastic bottles of distinctly flavored and urine-colored Inca Cola. This is some testament to both the authenticity and quality of the cooking here. For those that didn't know, Peru has a well-deserved culinary reputation that has begun to get some international attention in recent years as the country has become more politically stable. There is a wondrous seafood tradition in the coastal cities including the largest city, Lima, that features cold water Pacific fish and a strong influence from Japanese immigration that helped contribute to the raw fish culture, exemplified by the extremely popular local *ceviche*. This is coupled with an array of indigenous ingredients such as hundreds of varieties of potatoes and dishes that are being discovered by urban Peru. The coastal Peruvian cuisine featured at Lemon Tree will not be very exotic or unfamiliar with most Houston diners. The most unique items might be *ceviche* and yucca, which are hardly unusual for most these days. The spicing throughout is mild. Chile peppers are absent and there's not even salt and pepper on the table.

There are about thirty or so bountiful entrées, plates featuring cured fish, fish and shrimp, chicken and mixed platters. One of the handful of tart, refreshing *ceviches* is a tempting way to start, and you might begin to understand how Peruvian *ceviches* have garnered such acclaim throughout the Latin world. Though very tasty, these might work better as a shared starter as the cumulative acidity in the large dish will likely become noticeable when eaten alone. An appetizer won't be necessary when ordering the *Tuca Tuca* Lemon Tree, which should satiate most hungry carnivores. It consists of marinated and grilled, tender steak, moist fried rice, plenty of sautéed onions topped with two large, perfectly fried eggs and served with a side of sufficiently thick fries. Each of the components is very good, and these meld very well under the warm yolks of the eggs. The *Lomo Salteado* is another enjoyable dish for the beef-eaters. An entire rotisserie chicken is beautifully presented; butterflied and resplendent with attractive moist skin. It is also offered in half- and quarter-size portions. The strictly Peruvian *Aji de Gallina,* chicken in cream and yellow pepper sauce, can be very tasty. There are a number of fairly straightforward fish dishes, many pan-fried and properly clean-tasting. These cream sauces can overwhelm the light-breading and delicacy of the pan-fried versions, though. In addition to the Latin *Arroz con Mariscos,* seafood-studded rice, Lemon Tree includes several Chinese fried rice dishes. These are quite similar to what you will find in many local Chinese restaurants: rice with eggs scrambled in, chopped scallions that provide a proper textural contrast, and a hint of soy sauce. The difference might be that Lemon Tree is more generous in terms of entrée size, egg and certainly shrimp. The shrimp might be 15-20 count in size rather than the tiny ones that populate most Chinese restaurant versions.

With white tablecloth-draped tables topped with sometimes chipped IKEA-brand plates and crowded in the moderately sized dining room that seats around seventy, Lemon Tree is rather humble, far from a slickly run place. But, service is friendly, if uneven, and turnaround from the kitchen is surprisingly quick, even when the restaurant is packed. Though Peru is known for its *pisco,* a spirit distilled from grapes, and probably the best of the South American liquors, you won't find it at Lemon Tree. They don't have a liquor license, but you are welcome to bring in beer and wine.

Les Givral's $6

2704 Milam (between McGowan and Tuam) 77006, (713) 529-0462
801 Congress (between Travis and Milam) 77002, (713) 547-0444
www.lesgivrals.com

Cuisine - Vietnamese

Hours - Milam - Daily 8AM to 8PM; Congress - Mon-Thu 9AM to 6PM; Fri 9AM to 10PM; Sat 11AM to 10PM
Credit Cards - NONE
Service - Counter Service
Alcohol - NONE

Entrée Prices - $3 to $8 ($6 average)
Entrées $12 and less - 100%

Atmosphere & Décor - Functional, but comfortable
Appeal - Good and cheap Vietnamese sandwiches
Menu Suggestions - Cha Gio (deep-fried rolls); Bo Bia (summer rolls); Banh Mi Thit Nuong (char-grilled pork sandwich); Banh Mi Thit Nuong Pâté (char-grilled pork and pâté sandwich); Banh Mi Thit (roast pork sandwich); Banh Mi Ga Cha Bong (shredded chicken sandwich); Bun Bo Xao (vermicelli with stir-fried beef)

Not related to the Givral's that was the first Vietnamese sandwich shop on this site or the Givral in New Chinatown, these two small restaurants are still a popular and worthy stops for inexpensive fare. The food is still good, if not what some long-time patrons remember. It is undeniably much nicer and more inviting than it once was before the change in ownership, and nice, as far as Vietnamese sandwich shops go. Givral's posts eight or nine versions of the Vietnamese take on the sandwich. These begin with a crusty, fresh, familiar local Vietnamese baguette ladled with mayonnaise, marinated and thinly julienned carrots, cilantro, cucumber slices and a slice of fresh jalapeño and topped with a variety of meats. The types of sandwiches include barbecue pork, chicken, pâté, pork meatballs, and ham. The char-grilled pork is the best of the sandwich options. The regular barbecue pork sandwich, actually made with roasted pork, is also quite good, as is the Special sandwich made with pâté and some kind of ham-like substance that is much tastier than it appears. One selling point for Les Givral's is that the sandwiches seem to have a tad more meat than many of its competitors. Though inexpensive sandwiches seem to make up most of their business, and most all of the non-Asian business, their soup and noodle dishes are popular with the numerous Vietnamese patrons. The downtown location does an especially good job with some of the rice dishes (*com dia*). To wash down or complement the meal, Les Givral's serves the potent Vietnamese coffee, freshly made sugar cane drink and a variety of canned Southeast Asian drinks. As with most Vietnamese sandwich shops, Les Givral's also has pre-wrapped rice dishes, spring rolls and sweets, near the cashier ready for ready takeout for eating at home or back at the office.

Lila's $6

2704 S. Main (south of FM 518) Pearland, 77581, (281) 997-1288

Cuisine - Mexican
Hours - Mon 7AM to 3PM; Tue-Thu 7AM to 9PM; Fri 7AM to 10PM; Sat-Sun 7AM to 9PM
Credit Cards - Amex, Discover, MC, Visa
Service - Table Service
Alcohol - NONE

Entrée Prices - Dinner & Lunch - $4 to $8 ($6 average); Breakfast - $4 to $6
Entrées at Dinner $12 and less - 100%

Atmosphere & Décor - Rundown
Appeal - Inexpensive and homey Mexican food for cheap in Pearland
Menu Suggestions - barbacoa tacos; Chicken Flautas; Beef Enchiladas; Enchiladas Rancheras (chicken filled and topped with ranchero sauce); Eggs Celosos (eggs over easy topped with red and green salsas); Mexican Plate with barbacoa (barbacoa, rice, refried beans and tortillas)

Lila's is a popular stop for a primarily working class crowd, both Anglo and Hispanic, that enjoys well-made Tex-Mex and Mexican favorites for a pittance, in a casual and friendly environment near the heart of old Pearland. It's a hard-working and honest place where the food quality belies the very low prices. The most expensive plates are still well under ten bucks. Most of the familiar Tex-Mex dishes are available from Lila's fairly small menu: nachos, *flautas, quesadillas,* tacos, fajitas, *carne guisada,* chicken breast dishes, and combination plates. There are also hamburgers, even a double meat one with jalapeños and cheese for less than six bucks. The cooking is a cut above the typical Tex-Mex or Mexican restaurant, especially for Pearland. The tasty flour tortillas are properly made at the restaurant. The salsas are flavorful, especially the mild red one. Lila's is a cozy, functional place. You are coming here solely for the food. There is not much atmosphere, and no alcohol. Lila's is set in an open double-wide trailer with limited décor: Christmas lights, cheesy framed artwork, family photos, a small television in one corner usually tuned to a *telenovela,* and near the door, candy dispensers and an ice cream cooler below well-worn acoustic ceiling tiles.

An apparently significant attraction of Lila's is that it serves a number of the popular Mexican breakfast and several American egg-based breakfast dishes all day. These include Eggs *Celosos,* which are two very large eggs cooked over easy and each is topped separately with a green and red salsa and served with cubed potatoes and runny refried beans that taste of more than a hint of bacon. These flavorful beans are served with most dishes. There are also omelets and that regional necessity, breakfast tacos, on the fresh and sturdy flour tortillas. Primarily for the Mexican patrons, Lila's serves *menudo* and *caldos* on the weekends and a moist and piquant *asado de puerco* (stewed pork with red salsa) and "Mexican tacos and tortas" all of the time. The tacos are properly served with corn tortillas and simply dressed with chopped raw, white onions and cilantro leaves. These include an excellent *barbacoa,* which is necessarily a bit greasy, but whose flavor and texture and wonderfully complemented by the crunchy onions in a taco, plus *lengua* (beef tongue), *chicharron* (pork skin) and pastor (which here is a mixture of pork and beef). There is no alcohol, but *horchata* (rice and cinnamon water) and pineapple *aguas frescas* are made each day.

Lo Nuestro $10

9679 Bissonnet (between Southwest Freeway and Beltway) 77036, (713) 271-5593

Cuisine - Guatemalan
Hours - Mon-Thu, Sun 11AM to 10PM; Fri-Sat 11AM to 12AM
Credit Cards - Amex, Discover, MC, Visa
Service - Table Service
Alcohol - Beer

Entrée Prices - $4 to $17 ($10 average)
Entrées $12 and less - 80%

Atmosphere & Décor - Rundown, but clean
Appeal - Interesting and hearty food for cheap
Useful to Note - The other half of the restaurant is a pool hall.
Menu Suggestions - pork tamales; garnachas (small fried tortillas topped with seasoned beef, onions, cheese and salsa); Carne Adobada (marinated and sautéed pork); churrasco steak; El Plato Tipico con Carne Asadatwo eggs over-easy, a bowl of black beans, sautéed plantains, crema fresca, and queso fresca); Combination Chapinlandia (pork-filled tamale, tostada with beef and marinated cabbage, deep-fried plantains, and three garnachas - bite-sized tortillas topped with sautéed beef, etc.)

Lo Nuestro's location might be off-putting to some. And, the décor, too, for that matter. It is located in an older and somewhat derelict strip center, one of the many across the street from the former Westwood Mall. The décor in the small space consists of about ten mismatched Formica-heavy tables and chairs. Separated by a wall, half of it is dedicated to pool tables and televisions. This is certainly not a place in which to impress a date or a client. Those negatives are easily overcome with the satisfying, hearty and often interesting food for a very fair price.

Guatemalan cooking might seem to be unfamiliar to most in the area, but it should not be so. This cooking can be likened to Mexican food with a much more prominent indigenous, Mayan influence and use of more tropical ingredients, and somewhat less spiciness. This indigenous influence is evidenced, in part, by the use of the heavy corn *masa* in many of the dishes. Lo Nuestro's tamales consist of this *masa* and fillings wrapped in corn husks. These are a bit bland until dowsed with some of the salsa. The tropical bent is shown with plantains, yucca and black beans that are served as sides. As with the local Mexican restaurants, a basket of chips begin the meal. These are thick, slightly coarse chips served with a spicy tomato broth and sprinkled with white cheese. The menu, which has grown slightly over the years, provides appetizers, small plates (*antojitos*), entrées, sides, and a few desserts. Appetizers and small plates include *tortas, chuchitos* (pork-filled thick tamales), soft tacos with fajita or grilled chicken, and *garnachas*. The latter are small fried tortillas that are topped with seasoned beef, onions, tomato sauce and cheese, and a very enjoyable way to begin a meal. A side of the spicy cabbage salad, or slaw, provides additional flavor. *Vuelve a la Vida,* a seafood cocktail with shrimp, oysters, calamari and tilapia, *pico de gallo* and tomato sauce, and another with black clams are especially good on hot days or with a cold beer. The appetizers can entice, but the size of the entrées might discourage too much pre-entrée indulgence, at least after the first visit. The mixed appetizer plate, Combination *Chapinlandia,* with a tamale, *tostada,* fried plantains and *garnachas,* works well as a main dish, too, and a way to experience some more of the cuisine. Lo Nuestro serves a tender *churrasco* steak, one of a half-dozen beef entrées. These are accompanied with black beans, potato salad (*ensalada rusa*) and a small lettuce salad. The chicken dishes include *Pollo Encebollado* (grilled chicken breast covered with sautéed onions and a tomato salsa) and *Pollo a la Chula* (thin, sautéed chicken breast that is served with plenty of fresh cilantro in a heavy cream sauce). The *Carne Adobada* is a marinated, sautéed slice of pork that remains juicy and flavorful. As with some other entrées, it's served with a moist, almost creamy yellow rice smattered with peas, cubed carrots and an occasional lima bean. *El Plato Tipico* is a Central American version of *huevos rancheros* served with thick black beans. You have to apply the piquant salsa to the eggs yourself, though. That plate is even better when served with their moist and flavorful version of *carne asada*. Lo Nuestro does a commendable job with fish. The fried whole clean-tasting tilapia is well-complemented with grilled bell peppers and onions. The combination plate, consisting of a slice of the pork *adobado,* a tamal, *tostada* and several other items, is a lot of food, and the way to sample several of the specialties of the restaurant and Guatemala. This expertly made, rustic food is well matched with lager beer, which you can do quite inexpensively at Lo Nuestro.

"Welcome Stranger to this Humble Neighborhood"

This passage from the great song *Bhindi Bhagee* by the late legendary Joe Strummer and his band the Mescaleros about eating in London's eclectic, ethnic neighborhoods is easily relatable to Houston (though maybe more so, and certainly more enjoyable, when sung by the band):

Well, I was walking down the highroad,
And this guy stops me,
He'd just got in from New Zealand,
And he was looking for ***mushy peas***
I said, "no, we hadn't really got them 'round here
I said, but we do got…
Balti, Bhindi*, strictly* ***Hindi****,*
Dal, halal*, and I'm walking down the road,*
We got ***rocksoul, okra, Bombay duck-ra****,*
Shrimp bean sprout*, comes with or without,*
Bagels *soft, or simply harder,*
Exotic ***avocado*** *or toxic* ***empanada****,*
We got ***ackee, lassi****, Somali* ***waccy baccy****,*
I'm sure back home you know what ***tikka****'s all about…*
Welcome stranger…to the humble neighborhoods,
You can get inspiration on the highroad,
Hommus, cous cous*, in the* ***jus of octopus****,*
Pastrami *and* ***salami*** *and* ***lasagne*** *on the go,*
Welcome stranger, there's no danger
Welcome to this humble neighborhood…" *

Not that we have any highroads in Houston, nor hills, much less too many pedestrians or mushy peas on menus, though there are some New Zealanders (and an Humble). But, as fun as it is to dine in and around London, I'm pretty sure that we have it better here in Houston.

Lopez $8

11606 Wilcrest (north of Southwest Freeway) 77099, (281) 495-2436
www.lopezmexicanrestaurant.com

Cuisine - Tex-Mex
Hours - Mon-Sat 11AM to 9:45PM
Credit Cards - Amex, Diners, Discover, MC, Visa
Service - Table Service
Alcohol - Full Bar

Entrée Prices - $6 to $13 ($8 average)
Entrées $12 and less - 90%

* Reprinted courtesy of Epitaph Europe

Atmosphere & Décor - Nice, usually boisterous
Appeal - A solid, suburban, family-run Tex-Mex restaurant
Useful to Note - Plan on it being very crowded during peak hours.
Menu Suggestions - Chicken Enchiladas; Cheese Enchiladas; Hidalgo Dinner (beef taco and cheese enchiladas)

Lopez or, more properly, Lopez Mexican Restaurant has long been a very popular place in Alief. It's usually packed during the weekday lunchtime hours, and evenings on the weekend. The current location in a fairly large, stand-alone building on Wilcrest, north of the Southwest Freeway with an expansive parking lot, is much larger than their previous location. It provides a contrast from its former home, which is just a half-block away, in the middle of a long strip center. This upgrade is an indication that Lopez has been doing a more-than-proficient job of satisfying customers over the years. That satisfaction is also expressed with small tiles that decorate the entranceway with the names and platitudes of loyal customers.

The compendium of quality, familiarity, service, décor, location and price makes Lopez a pleasant value dining option. The menu is basic Tex-Mex; comfort food for a great many in the area and well-suited for suburban southwest Houston. You will be disappointed if you are looking for "authentic" or regional Mexican food. The food here is nothing spectacular, but it is usually quite satisfying. There are a fair number of combination plates, denoted "Dinners" and "Special Plates". These are a good value, inexpensive, and consisting of a fairly large amount of food. For example, the Hidalgo Dinner consists of a taco, crispy bowl-like tortillas containing a lot of ground beef with shredded lettuce, and then a plate with two large cheese enchiladas, refried beans and Spanish rice. In addition to these combination plates, there are individual orders of enchiladas, tacos, burritos, *chalupas* and nachos. *Chile rellenos* come in two versions, the American version that is made with bell peppers, and the Mexican version for a couple of dollars more that substitutes for those with the tastier poblano peppers. There are some more interesting dishes, too. *Carnitas, carne guisada,* pork chops, steaks, and even a couple egg dishes: *huevos rancheros* and *huevos con chorizo* for that post-morning cholesterol fix.

Lopez's popularity is due in large part to the execution of those familiar items. The basic tomato-based salsa is tastier than average, and better than what might be expected at a place like this. It's flavorful and spicy, with the pepper seeds very evident. The chips are consistently fresh. The cheese in the enchiladas is cheddar cheese. The refried beans are thick and heavy, as those used to be at most Mexican restaurants in years past. The one noticeable pitfall here is the fajitas, which are a far cry from those at the well-known fajita palaces. In addition to providing satisfying food, Lopez also provides a pleasant setting and proficient service. The spacious restaurant is done in the hacienda-style that is popular for Mexican restaurants. The restaurant is bright and airy. The walls are painted in a light beige color and a skylight provides an ample amount of natural light in the middle of the dining area. Three large paintings of attractive, tropical Mexican landscapes decorate a far wall. There are no teenage kids here, as in many similar suburban restaurants. The waiters seem to be all Mexican born, and adults, too. The service is better than at comparable establishments, and it is always friendly. The kitchen turns the orders around quickly even during the lunchtime or weekend bustle. If you live in far southwest Houston and like Tex-Mex, and do not mind a crowded restaurant, Lopez is a place to visit. Chances are good that you will become yet another regular patron.

Los Dos Amigos $7

5729 Washington (at Birdsall, east of Wescott) 77007, (713) 862-0462

Cuisine - Mexican (taqueria)
Hours - Mon-Sat 6AM to 11PM; Sun 7AM to 10PM
Credit Cards - MC, Visa
Service - Table Service
Alcohol - NONE

Entrée Prices - Dinner - $4 to $10 ($7 avg.); Lunch - $6; Breakfast - $3 to $4
Entrées at Dinner $12 and less - 100%

Atmosphere & Décor - Functional
Useful to Note - Breakfast is very cheap before 10AM.
Appeal - Well prepared, satisfying Mexican food for cheap, especially breakfasts
Menu Suggestions - Huevos Rancheros; Chilaquiles; Huevos a la Mexicana

A small, humble and generally friendly family-run place, Los Amigos has long been a popular stop for tasty and inexpensive Mexican meals in a no-frills setting with ten tables and some counter space cramped into a single dining room. Situated at the edge of what was once a working class Mexican neighborhood that has become gentrified, Los Dos Amigos is still appealing to a continually changing clientele. The dishes arrive quickly after ordering, and are generally well prepared, familiar, informal and inexpensive. Weekend breakfasts are a big draw here; always satisfying and served throughout the day.

In close proximity to Memorial Park, Los Dos Amigos is quickly accessible after exercise for some tasty caloric replacement. And, as a benefit to many patrons, English is readily spoken here. All of the popular Mexican breakfast dishes are served and done quite well: *Huevos Rancheros; Huevos a la Mexicana; Huevos Divorciados* (two eggs over-easy, one topped with red salsa, the other with a green salsa), *Chilaquiles* (two eggs scrambled with crispy tortilla chips, tomatoes, onions and fresh jalapeños), plus eggs scrambled with a variety of mostly meats. These include potato, *chorizo, chorizo* and egg, ham, bacon, pork sausage, and *machacado* (dried beef). These are served with refried beans, pan-fried potatoes, which are sometimes better than at other times, and fresh, hot tortillas. Also, fairly plump breakfast tacos cost a buck in the morning, and just a quarter more for ones filled with *carne guisada* (stewed beef tips) and *carnitas* (grilled pork here). After 10AM, all of these tacos are an additional fifty cents, and still quite a deal. Beyond the breakfast offerings, the crux of the meat-heavy menu, which is grown a little longer over the years, is divided among straightforward appetizers and a la carte items, soups, Tex-Mex dinners, and specials. To start, or to snack, there are nachos, *chile con queso, chalupas,* and a *sincronazada* (basically a ham and cheese sandwich with tortillas). The soups appeal mostly to the Mexican patrons such as the hearty beef soup (*Caldo de Res*), *menudo* (that is served daily), and the only seafood items served here, a fish soup, shrimp soup, and a combination of fish and shrimp soup. There are a number of enchilada dishes, several Tex-Mex combination dinners, *flautas*, burritos, and grilled items. These include fajitas, grilled chicken, *quesadillas* filled with fajitas, *tacos al carbon*, and *carnitas*, which is grilled pork rather than the traditional fried pork. Their *Carnitas Rancheras* is cooked with a tomato-based salsa. The most expensive item on the menu is the *Fogonero*, moist and tender fajitas topped with melted Monterey Jack cheese and *pico de gallo*, for only around ten dollars.

Los Gallitos $10

12030 Murphy (south of the Southwest Freeway) 77031, (281) 988-9705

Cuisine - Mexican
Hours - Mon-Thu, Sun 11AM to 10PM; Fri-Sat 11AM to 11PM
Credit Cards - Amex, Discover, MC, Visa
Service - Table Service
Alcohol - Full Bar

Entrée Prices - Dinner - $6 to $17 ($10 average); Lunch - $6 to $9
Entrées at Dinner $12 and less - 80%

Atmosphere & Décor - Functional
Appeal - Good value, well prepared Mexican food
Menu Suggestions - Carne Guisada (stewed beef); Shrimp Stuffed Avocado (a deep-fried avocado stuffed with shrimp and cheese); Shrimp Poblano (shrimp sautéed in a cream sauce with poblano pepper, onions, mushrooms, cilantro and Parmesan cheese); fajitas

Los Gallitos is situated in a fairly large stand-alone building meant to look like a hacienda on industrial Murphy Road not too far south of the Southwest Freeway in Stafford. Los Gallitos' parking lot is usually well populated during the lunch and dinner hours, a testament to the fact that Los Gallitos serves well prepared Mexican and Tex-Mex dishes in a comfortable environment for fair prices. It certainly gives the impression of a place working hard to please: service is generally attentive; orders arrive quickly from the kitchen; and about all of the local Tex-Mex and Mexican favorites appear on their large menu, and then some; and are prepared better than at most. To start there are several types of nachos, several *queso fundidos* (melted cheese), *chile con queso, ceviche,* shrimp cocktail, *quesadillas,* soups, and stuffed jalapeños. For entrées, there are salads, nearly a dozen types of enchiladas, *chalupas,* grilled platters (with pork ribs, beef short ribs, shrimp and fajitas), fajitas in several other guises, Tex-Mex combination dinners ("Mixed Plates" here), stuffed avocados, burritos, nearly ten dishes featuring chicken breasts, *flautas,* tacos, *carnitas, chile rellenos,* and seafood plates. The fajitas and seafood dishes are fairly highly regarded here. Jumbo shrimp, and the red snapper fillets are prepared in several ways. Two of the better ones are the Shrimp Poblano (shrimp sautéed in a cream sauce with poblano pepper, onions, mushrooms, cilantro and Parmesan cheese), and bacon-wrapped shrimp that is grilled and served with a lemon-butter sauce. The excellent *carne guisada* consists of juicy stewed beef tips served with bell pepper, red onions, wedges of tomatoes, and slices of fresh jalapeños served in a small casserole dish. The beef for this seems to be grilled or sautéed prior to stewing, and the sauce hints of wine. The enchiladas are enjoyable, though the ones filled with chicken might be slightly watery, since the chicken might not be fully drained after cooking, prior to assembly. But, most everything is good here, if not great, and with good-sized portions, a fine value. The salsa could be more interesting, and some dishes could stand some improvements. Los Gallitos might not be one of the best Mexican restaurants in the area, but it's one that is well worth a stop when on the southwest side.

Los Ranchitos $6

7687 Clarewood (east of Fondren, west of Sharpstown Mall) 77036, (713) 777-5703

Cuisine - Salvadoran
Hours - Mon-Fri 10AM to 9:30PM; Sat-Sun 10AM to 11:30PM
Credit Cards - NONE
Service - Table Service
Alcohol - Full Bar

Entrée Prices - $4 to $8 ($6 average)
Entrées $12 and less - 100%

Atmosphere & Décor - Functional
Appeal - Excellent Salvadoran food featuring very tasty grilled meats
Useful to Note - Try not to be scared off by the neighborhood, setting, etc.
Menu Suggestions - Carne Asada; pupusas (sautéed corn pockets stuffed with a variety of items); Pollo Encellado (roasted chicken half served with grilled onions in a tomato sauce); Combinado A (two pupusas, tamale, sautéed plantains and fresh cream); Combinado B (two pupusas, fried chicharron, sautéed plantains and fresh cream)

Try not to let the unexceptional location, façade, décor, unusual menu item names, and limited English ability of much of the waitstaff deter you from visiting Los Ranchitos. It is regarded by many from El Salvador as being the best Salvadoran restaurant in Houston. That might not be incentive enough for most to make a trip here, but it should be known that the food is usually amazingly tasty and inexpensive. And, the dishes will probably not be that unfamiliar, after all. In a city with a proliferation of popular Mexican eateries, Los Ranchitos serves food that should be fairly recognizable. Among these items are hearty beef soups, grilled steaks, *carne asada, ceviche,* seafood cocktails, tamales, and grilled and fried seafood. Though Los Ranchitos has a small menu there will be something that should interest everyone, especially since nearly everything on it is very good. Everything is also very inexpensive, especially for the quality. The dishes with grilled meats here can be excellent. The *carne asada* plate is served with a choice among beef, pork and chicken. The beef is recommended by the waitstaff, and is excellent. Featuring moist and flavorful grilled beef and freshly made thick flour tortillas, it would be difficult to imagine a similar dish that would be any better for such a small tariff. There is also the somewhat similar *lomito de puerco,* at least as it's described as pork fajitas. If chicken is desired, there is grilled chicken breast, and a half of roast chicken that can be served with sautéed onions and a mild salsa. For seafood, there are grilled jumbo shrimp, shrimp with tomato sauce, fried shrimp, and interesting shrimp with cream and a Salvadoran sauce (*"pruebélos estan deliciosos!"* the menu once stated). There is also fried tilapia, seafood cocktails, one with shrimp, the other with the somewhat unique black clam, shrimp *ceviche,* and a hearty Salvadoran-style seafood soup with carp, shrimp, eggs and cream. The national dish of El Salvador, the *pupusa,* is very good here, and less greasy than at most other local Salvadoran places. *Pupusas* are sautéed corn pockets that have been stuffed with a variety of items. These come filled with pork, cheese, pork and cheese, and cheese and *loroco,* a type of spice native to El Salvador. *Loroco* has a distinctive taste that works well in a *pupusa,* but might not be to everyone's liking. The ones filled with pork are probably the best. The large plastic jar at each table filled with pickled cabbage and peppers is a type of zesty relish that is meant to be ladled on the *pupusas.* It can be a good complement, as can a few splashes of hot sauce. Served with the *pupusas* in the *Combinado A* and *B* plates are wonderful sautéed plantains with a side of fresh cream that is fitting complement. Yucca and *chicharron* (fried pork skin) are also tasty sides to many of the plates. Other Salvadoran items served are the plump *tamales de elote* (sweet corn tamales), tamales with chicken and pork, and *empanadas de platano*.

You should, or you will, visit Los Ranchitos solely for the well prepared, interesting, and value-laden cooking. The setting is functional, as the restaurant is geared toward serving immigrants of modest means. The location in an older strip center close to Sharpstown Mall is not the best. Service is friendly, though some Spanish is probably helpful. Dishes are prepared once ordered, and it might take a short while for the more complicated dishes or larger parties. To note, beer is limited to three per person, total.

Lucky Pot $8

9888 Bellaire (between Corporate and the Beltway) 77036, (713) 995-9982

Cuisine - Chinese
Hours - Daily 11AM to 9:30PM
Credit Cards - NONE
Service - Table Service
Alcohol - Full Bar

Entrée Prices - $4 to $11 ($8 average)
Entrées $12 and less - 100%

Atmosphere & Décor - Functional
Appeal - Northern Chinese noodle shop with tasty soups and pan cakes for cheap
Useful to Note - Don't expect General Tso's Chicken here.
Menu Suggestions - lamb dumplings; House Special Noodle Soup (hearty soup with noodles, mushrooms and some pork); Pork Noodle with Brown Sauce (thick noodles topped with roasted pork, shredded lettuce, shredded carrots and hoisin); Pork Round Cake (pan-fried flat dumpling with pork); Beef Round Cake (pan-fried flat dumpling with beef); Special Cake (pan-fried dough); Green Onion Pan Cake (pan-fried cake with scallions)

In a clean, small storefront restaurant with only about a dozen tables covered in white tablecloths, in a pleasant strip center set amidst a number of other Asian businesses, Lucky Pot aptly fills a niche for straightforward, inexpensive northern Chinese fare. The restaurant is usually packed around noon most days during the week. Virtually all of the clientele is Chinese, a good sign, indicating a certain level of authenticity and quality. It's a great stop on the west side for large soups, noodle dishes and tasty pan-fried sides, all noticeably freshly prepared and featuring clean, approachable and enjoyable flavors, which has earned praise. For anyone who likes Chinese food, this is a worthy stop for another type of cuisine that is uncommon in this country, especially here.

The menu, in English, is divided among noodle dishes, "Pan Cake", and the entrées. For most non-Chinese the handful of noodle dishes, similar soups, and the pan-fried sides will probably be of most interest. You likely won't be able to order everything here anyway unless you can read Chinese. Two noodle dishes are the House Special Pork Noodle with Brown Sauce and the Sesame Sauce Noodle. The first features thick noodles with a rice-like consistency topped with roasted pork, shredded lettuce, shredded carrots and hoisin (a thick, slightly sweet and spicy sauce). The dish is served with the crisp lettuce, carrots and hoisin each covering a third of the bowl. Mixed together with the pork and noodles underneath, this combination makes for a very satisfying, and courtesy of the hoisin, slightly sweet entrée. The somewhat similar Sesame Sauce Noodle substitutes a sesame seed-based sauce for the hoisin. The soups are Beef Noodle, Lamb Noodle and the House Special Noodle, the best of the three. This features the same thick noodles used in the other dishes, plenty of black mushrooms and some pieces of pork. It is a very flavorful, if not spicy soup. It might be even better with the addition of the some of the chile-based hot sauce on the table. The pork used for the soups is of generally higher quality than the beef.

The soups and the noodle dishes will not be enough for those with large appetites. A very fitting complement, both in terms of additional food, and texture to the soft noodles is listed somewhat descriptively under "Pan Cake". These are small thin "cakes" consisting of pan-fried dough that are filled with a variety of meats and vegetables. There are the "Round Cakes" with lamb, beef, pork and vegetables. The beef and pork versions are especially good. These are even better when topped with some soy sauce, vinegar and chile sauce, which are set on each table. For a small tariff the Special Cake is just fried dough with an interesting flavor, and also well worth ordering, as is the Green Onion Pan Cake. It will still be an inexpensive meal when ordered with a noodle-based dish, which are all under five bucks. Also readily enjoyable and approachable are the handful of fried rice dishes. Most of the rest of the menu is geared to the Chinese patrons it's safe to assume. The "Cold Dishes" include Soy Sauce Pork Feet, Spicy Pork Stomach, Spicy Beef Stomach, Hong's Pig Ear, and Garlic Sea Weed. The list of twenty-plus entrées is headed with title only in Chinese, and only half of the dishes listed even have English translations for the items. Certainly there are some good ones, and there are several that are even recognizable and seem appetizing like the Moo Shu Pork, Sautéed Shredded Pork, Sautéed Shrimp, Ginger and Green Onion Beef, and Bell

Pepper Shredded Potato. Most of these will probably appear in an enticing fashion on a nearby table, ordered in Chinese. Lucky Pot is reputed to serve some of the best hot pot dishes in town, especially so the Beijing-style hot pot with lamb.

Luling City Market Bar-B-Q $9

4726 Richmond (east of Loop 610) 77027, (713) 871-1903
www.lulingcitymarket.com

Cuisine - Barbecue
Hours - Mon-Sat 11AM to 9PM; Sun 12PM to 7PM
Credit Cards - Amex, Diners, Discover, MC, Visa
Service - Counter Service
Alcohol - Full Bar

Entrée Prices - $7 to $13 ($9 average)
Entrées $12 and less - 80%

Atmosphere & Décor - Spartan, but fitting
Appeal - Excellent Texas barbecue with a small-town Central Texas feel
Useful to Note - The meats are served on butcher paper, not plates.
Menu Suggestions - Brisket; Sliced Brisket Sandwich; Beef Link; Barbecue Chicken Half; potato salad; barbecue sauce

Though residing in a strip center near the West Loop on Richmond since the early 1980s, with a rough wood interior, Luling City Market does have a feel of an authentic barbecue joint that you might find in a small town in central Texas. Luling always seems a bit smoky, probably both from the barbecue pit and the crusty regulars feeding their nicotine habit at the small bar viewing one of the several suspended televisions. Along with the genuine feel, you will also probably find better barbecue at Luling than you would find in the average central Texas town, much less around Houston. Among the limited, but very sufficient, number of offerings, the beef brisket, sausage and chicken are among the best in the area.

The post oak-smoked brisket is excellent. The proper slow cooking is evident, and the beef is tender, smoky and delicious. A testament to the worthiness of the brisket is that Luling's is quite satisfying alone, without any accompanying barbecue sauce. But, the sauce makes it that much better. This sauce might be Luling's real claim to fame among Houston area barbecue purveyors. Even though unique, it's simply great. With a faint mustard taste, it is distinctive, tangy, with a slow-working spiciness. It helps to make everything it touches taste better. The excellent brisket and sauce makes for superb chopped or sliced beef sandwiches that are served on a fresh onion roll. Turkey is also available on sandwiches. In addition to the brisket, the beef link sausages are exemplary, as is the half chicken. Plates are served featuring the beef link sausage, brisket, pork ribs, turkey and chicken. These come with a couple sides, of which there are only three: pinto beans, potato salad, and cole slaw. The sides, especially the beans and potato salad, are quite tasty, and well above average. If you have room for dessert, there is a brownie and a scrumptious individually sized pecan pie. There is counter service, as with all other barbecue places, but at Luling you can order your meats by weight like a half-pound of chopped brisket, a pound of ribs, or a couple links of sausage. Like in many barbecue joints in rural Central Texas, the meat is served on butcher paper. (The sides are on the plates.) Luling City Market does its namesake town proud.

Lupe Tortilla's $12

318 Stafford (just east of Highway 6, south of I-10) 77079, (281) 496-7580
2414 Southwest Freeway (just east of Kirby) 77098, (713) 522-4420
15315 I-45 N. (between Airtex and Richey) 77090, (281) 873-6220
891 W. Bay Area Boulevard (Highway 3 and El Camino Real) 77058, (281) 338-2711
15801 Southwest Freeway (just north of Hwy. 6) Sugar Land, 77478, (281) 265-7500
22465 Highway 249 (between Jones and Spring-Cypress) 77070, (832) 843-0004
19437 I-45 S. (south of Research Forest) The Woodlands, 77385, (281) 298-5274
www.lupetortillas.com

Cuisine - Tex-Mex
Credit Cards - Amex, Diners, Discover, MC, Visa
Hours - Stafford - Mon-Thu 11AM to 2PM, 5:30 to 9PM; Fri 11AM to 2PM, 5:30 to 9PM; Sat 11:30AM to 10PM; Sun 11:30AM to 9PM; Other Locations - Mon-Thu, Sun 11AM to 9PM; Fri-Sat 11AM to 10PM
Service - Table Service
Alcohol - Full Bar

Entrée Prices - $7 to $16 ($12 average)
Entrées $12 and less - 70%

Atmosphere & Décor - Nice, usually lively
Appeal - Excellent fajitas and Tex-Mex standards
Useful to Note - Very popular so the wait can be long after dark; kid-friendly.
Menu Suggestions - fajitas; Tacos al Carbon; Chicken Flautas; Tamales; Soft Chicken Tacos; Three Pepper Steak (fajita-style skirt steak topped with sliced jalapeño, Serrano and habanero peppers and melted cheese); "Cheeken" Lupe (marinated chicken breasts covered with tomato, onion, cilantro, Serrano peppers and melted cheese); Steak Lupe; Poblano Chicken (poblano pepper stuffed with shredded chicken and Monterey Jack and grilled); margaritas

In the mid-1990s, before the second location near Kirby was opened, it was fashionable for many Inner Loopers to drive out to Highway 6 for fajitas at the original location. That was high praise given that there were many very deserving Mexican restaurants, and noted fajita purveyors, much closer.

That sentiment has fueled the growth for expansion, and that high quality has been retained. The original restaurant has grown from just the small wooden house that served as the restaurant when it opened in 1983. With many expansions, it is now a sprawling establishment that seats around 150 people in several different dining rooms. Though a fairly large restaurant now, with the low ceilings and the smallish rooms, and also because it is usually crowded, it still retains somewhat of an intimate feeling. The new locations are similar in design, but more functional, and still family-friendly. For dinner at any of the locations, it's best to arrive early and be prepared to wait. Lupe Tortilla's do not take reservations. A margarita can help ease the pain from waiting, but be careful; the margaritas are very strong.

The food might be described as loud and brash Tex-Mex. The fajitas and fajita-like dishes are the main draw for many at Lupe Tortilla. Available by the pound with beef, chicken or a combination, the fajitas are served with guacamole, *pico de gallo,* char-grilled green onions and very thin, tasty fresh flour tortillas. The beef is moist and exceptionally flavorful. Unless you are very hungry, the individual-sized choices for fajitas, which are listed as *Tacos al Carbon* and *Carne Asada,* will suffice. The pre-assembled version of fajitas, the *Tacos al Carbon,* is two large tacos made with flour tortillas. The *Carne Asada* is an excellent, if unadorned, half-pound fajita steak. The other, similar steak dishes are also excellent. One of them is the spicy Three Pepper Steak, a half-pound fajita steak topped with a trio of fresh, sliced peppers (jalapeños, serranos and habaneros) and covered with melted Monterey Jack cheese. The chicken fajitas are also quite good, juicy and flavorful, some of the best in town. The appetizing "Cheeken Lupe" is two chicken breasts that have been marinated, then cooked and served with chopped tomatoes, onions, serrano peppers, cilantro and melted Monterey Jack cheese. There is a similarly good version with a fajita steak. Another favorite is the "Cheeken Leetle", a moist chicken breast marinated with lime and pepper that is placed on a corn tortilla, covered with their light, tomato-based *ranchera* sauce and roasted poblano peppers, then topped with Monterey Jack cheese and baked. Other enticing dishes feature chicken breasts with jalapeños and cilantro, and roasted poblano peppers.

In addition to the fajita, steak and chicken dishes, the rambling, ever-expanding menu covers most of the rest of the Tex-Mex favorites. The kitchens seem to do most things well. For starters, there are nachos with a number of different toppings from which to choose, *chile con queso,* the real cheese *Queso Flameado con Chorizo* (melted cheese with the Mexican sausage), and guacamole salad. For entrées, there are *chalupas,* the deep-fried *flautas* with chicken or beef, several varieties of enchiladas, tamales, a couple versions of *chile rellenos,* two taco salads, and tacos several ways. The tacos come with either corn or flour tortillas, soft or crispy, and with beef, chicken or cheese (in the No Meat Tacos). The Soft "Cheeken" Tacos are especially good; two tacos made with flour tortillas, shredded chicken, *ranchera* sauce and Monterey Jack cheese then heated in the oven to melt the cheese. For the indecisive, there are several combination dinners that feature choices among tacos, *chalupas*, enchiladas, tamales, and guacamole salad. The *flautas* and tamales are very good; noteworthy since it has become somewhat rare to find high quality tamales in restaurants these days. Also noticeable, and complementary to most dishes, is that both the corn and flour tortillas are freshly made at the restaurants. The chips are always crisp and fresh, although the companion salsas are nothing special. Not everything is exemplary at Lupe Tortilla's, though. Off-putting to some is the restaurant's mimicking of a Mexican immigrant's poor English. The menu is peppered with phrases like "es preety good", chicken is spelled "cheeken", with is "weeth", and the like. Also somewhat annoying is the too-often smug and too-often mediocre service. But, the quality of the food, aided by the strong margaritas, usually more than compensates.

Lyndon's Pit Bar-B-Q $9

13165 Northwest Freeway (west of 290, south of Tidwell) 77040, (713) 690-2112

Cuisine - Barbecue
Hours - Mon-Thu 11AM to 8PM; Fri-Sat 11AM to 9PM; Sun 11AM to 7PM
Credit Cards - Amex, Diners, Discover, MC, Visa
Service - Counter Service
Alcohol - Beer & Wine

Entrée Prices - $5 to $24 ($9 average)
Entrées $12 and less - 90%

Atmosphere & Décor - Pleasant
Appeal - Good barbecue in northwest Houston
Menu Suggestions - pulled pork sandwich; beef brisket

Lyndon's is a place that seems to care about being a prime stop for barbecue: for starters, pride in the restaurant is evident in the fact that caricatures of the owners grace the cover of the menu; the setting is comfortable, probably better than most for barbecue; service at the counter is friendly and proficient; and, most importantly, the food is good. The turnaround time is appropriately quick; near the counter you can easily see the staff frying or assembling your order. The menu states that all of their items are made from scratch daily, and suitable freshness and care in cooking are easily noticeable. Lyndon's serves the basic local barbecue fare, plus a little more. Beef brisket, pork spareribs, sausage, half chickens, pulled pork, fried catfish and hamburgers are the featured items. The requisite brisket is smoked for at least twelve hours and features very evident and attractive deep smoke rings, and is well worth ordering. The pulled pork, popular in the Southeast, is slowly cooked pork butt (shoulder, if you didn't know) that is pulled apart prior to serving. Lyndon's version is tender, slightly sweet and flavorful, and makes for a very enjoyable sandwich, complemented with fresh buns, buttered and toasted on the grill. The house-made barbecue sauce is excellent. A testament to its quality is that it is even available for purchase. Tomato-based with somewhat of a vinegary taste, it is served warm, a welcome complement. The barbecue can be quite good, but it is a little disconcerting that the barbecue, both the beef and pork, need the sauce to fully complete the meal. With the sauce, these are excellent, but the meats can taste a little dry and naked without it. No worry, the sauce is always nearby to make everything all right. And, Lyndon's does an admirable job with the side dishes. On a good day, these are some of the best ones outside of Goode Co. Barbecue. The beans have the barbecue taste and are further flavored with onions, garlic, tomatoes and cilantro. The Spicy Corn Casserole is another savory side dish. Spicy rather than hot, it's similar to a lighter version of creamed corn made with bits of bell pepper and fresh jalapeños. The strongly flavored potato salad with noticeable specks of skin is also worth ordering. The very large onion rings are served straight from the deep fryer, but can be a bland.

Lyndon's is accessibly located in a strip center off Highway 290 with about twenty other businesses, each with their own individually designed sign above their slot, instead of uniform signage. This makes for somewhat of a visual feast, though not necessarily a pleasant one. Anyway, that is not at all important, as Lyndon's has done a decent job of replicating a rustic setting inside the restaurant especially with a corrugated tin roof and lots of Texana adorning the walls. Unfortunately, this décor is fading rather than aging gracefully. Above all, the food is quite satisfying, and the restaurant is worth a visit.

Madras Pavilion $10

3910 Kirby (between Richmond and Southwest Freeway) 77098, (713) 521-2617
16260 Kensington (west of 6, north of Southwest Freeway) 77479, (281) 491-3672
www.madraspavilion.us

Cuisine - Indian; Vegetarian
Hours - Mon-Thu 11:30AM to 3PM, 5:30 to 10PM; Fri 11:30AM to 3PM, 5:30 to 10PM; Sat-Sat 11:30AM to 10PM
Credit Cards - Amex, Diners, Discover, MC, Visa
Service - Lunch - Buffet; Dinner - Table Service
Alcohol - Beer & Wine

Entrée Prices - Dinner - $7 to $15 ($10 avg.); Lunch - Mon-Fri - $8, Sat-Sun - $10
Entrées at Dinner $12 and less - 90%

Atmosphere & Décor - Comfortable
Appeal - Some of the best southern Indian food in the area
Useful to Note - There is buffet during lunch; Sugar Land location is not kosher.
Menu Suggestions - Vegetable Samosa (crispy pastry stuffed with potato, onions and peas); Masala Dosa (thin crêpes filled with potatoes and onions); Channa Masala Curry (stewed chickpeas); Paneer Butter Masala (cheese in a curry); Kadi Paneer (cheese with sautéed bell pepper and onions in a spicy curry); Batura (large puffy bread); Paratha (pan-fried whole-wheat bread); Carrot Halwa (a dessert of grated carrots cooked in honey and butter); Mango Lassi (a smoothie-like mango drink)

Madras Pavilion serves the spicy vegetarian fare of southern India. This is different than the food that is typically available at most Indian restaurants in this country, and also locally, that primarily serve the *tandoori* cooking of northern India, the popular grilled meats and curries. At Madras Pavilion you can discover the unique dishes from the regions in southern India. The fact that all of the dishes are vegetarian, and that the restaurant is advertised as such, will immediately deter many potential patrons. But, it's useful to know that there are a great many dishes that will satisfy most committed carnivores. For them, there should be enough fat, spicing and deep-frying, plus tasty, freshly baked breads to keep things interesting. Though the food is entirely vegetarian, it's hearty, filling and can be very flavorful. Many of the dishes are cooked with *ghee* (clarified butter) and contain cheese. It's vegetarian, but not vegan.

The easiest introduction for many will probably be the popular lunch buffet. But, the best way to enjoy the interesting flavors at Madras Pavilion is to come with a group and order several dishes from the full dinner menu. It's well laid-out, and most items are coupled with an explanatory description. If you are not familiar with southern Indian cooking, for two people, you might want to try a crispy *samosa* (a turnover filled with potato, onions and peas), a *dosa* (a large thinly sheathed crêpe) an order of rice, a bread, and a couple curry dishes. Pieces of the *dosa* are to be broken off and used to scoop up the curry sauce or dipped in a chutney. The *dosas* taste great alone, too. The menu is filled with explanatory descriptions and is divided among a dozen appetizers, a handful of soups, a dozen types of those *dosas*, several *uthappams* (described as an Indian pizza), a number of curries, several rice dishes, a half-dozen freshly baked breads, plus sides, fruit juices, other beverages, and desserts. The term "curry" in this sense refers to the style of cooking. For appetizers, in addition to the *samosa*, there are several *vadas* (lentil doughnuts) and a few deep-fried items. Most of the *dosas* are made with rice and lentils. These come plain or filled with a variety of items such as the Butter *Masala* Dosa that is filled with potatoes and onions and cooked in butter. The *uthappam* is made with the same dough as used for the *dosas* and topped with various combinations of onions, chiles, tomatoes and peas. The curries can be excellent, especially with bread like the *batura* (large and puffy), to scoop up the sauce. Several are fairly creamy. The tasty *Channa Masala* Curry features chickpeas. The *Paneer* Butter *Masala* is cheese in a creamy, flavorful sauce. There are other curries with lentils, okra, bell peppers and other vegetables. Of the nearly ten rice dishes, there are no *biriyanis*, but there are ones like the descriptively named Coconut Rice and Tamarind Rice. *Naan*, requisite in most local Indian restaurants, is not one of the breads on the menu, but there are several *parathas*, a thick multi-layered wheat bread. The desserts include the familiar *gulab jaman* (very sweet deep-fried balls of cheese) and pistachio ice cream, and also a scrumptious Carrot *Halwa* and *Badam Halwa* (shredded carrots and ground almonds, respectively, that are cooked in honey and butter). For a fitting complement, there are a number squeezed fresh fruit juices and excellent mango drinks.

The lunch buffet is just eight dollars during the week and ten on the weekends. With the buffet you can just select whatever looks interesting. The choices change daily. Madras Pavilion serves a choice of *dosas* that are free with the lunch price. The buffet is usually well attended. As a popular restaurant it is often crowded with folks from southern India, Indian food aficionados, and observant Orthodox Jews. Unusual among Indian restaurants, the Madras Pavilion location on Kirby is a kosher restaurant. There is another location in Sugar Land to serve the large Indian population in that area, but it's not kosher.

Mai Thai $10

3819 Kirby (between Richmond and Southwest Freeway) 77098, (713) 522-6707
www.maithaihouston.com

Cuisine - Thai
Hours - Mon-Thu 11AM to 2:30PM, 5 to 10PM; Fri 11AM to 2:30PM, 5PM to 11PM; Sat 12PM to 11PM
Credit Cards - Amex, Diners, MC, Visa
Service - Table Service
Alcohol - Beer & Wine

Entrée Prices - Dinner - $6 to $16 ($10 average); Lunch - $6 to $9
Entrées at Dinner $12 and less - 90%

Atmosphere & Décor - Pleasant, low-key
Appeal - Solid Thai on Kirby

Menu Suggestions - Thom Yum Goong (lime, lemon grass soup); Shrimp Delight (crispy fried shrimp sautéed with pineapple, tomato, onion and bell peppers); Gang Musamun (beef with potato and sweet potatoes in a brown curry sauce with peanuts); Chicken with Peanut Sauce; coconut ice cream

---

Since 1989 Mai Thai has been serving pleasing Thai food in a convenient location just north of the Southwest Freeway on Kirby. Though set in a small building, it's tough to miss this restaurant, as it's painted in an eye-catching, but fairly unattractive, pink and fuchsia. As is often said, it is what is on the inside that counts the most. Mai Thai is a deserving stop for reliably good Thai food in a decent, if quite dated and boring, setting. This is a relatively quaint restaurant with white tablecloths (and white wooden chairs) usually resulting in a tranquil dining experience, even with busy Kirby and the Southwest Freeway just outside of the restaurant's front door.

The dinner menu is fairly wide-ranging from a number of appetizers, soups, salads, curries, seafood, House Specials, vegetable dishes, fried rice, Thai noodle and special diet dishes (which are now low-calorie), plus desserts. The food here is possibly a little sweeter and less spicy than at some of the less assimilated local Thai restaurants. But, you can order the properly incendiary "Thai Hot" if need be. The soups are available in cups and also in pots for the table. There are over a dozen appetizers, along with the soups, to get you started at Mai Thai. They have the familiar *satays* with beef or chicken, *mee krob* (crispy fried noodles) and mostly deep-fried rolls. There is also *Tod Mun Pla (*deep-fried curried fish cake served with peanut and cucumber sauce), and *Nam Sod* (chopped chicken stir-fried with stock then blended with lime, pepper, chili, onions, peanuts and sliced fresh ginger). There are six or so commonly seen entrée-sized Thai salads that feature dried shrimp, grilled shrimp, char-grilled beef tenderloin, ground pork and boiled squid. The ample-sized curry dishes are ten bucks and less, and feature several choices. There is the red curry with coconut milk, green curry with coconut milk, *musaman* with curry and coconut milk, potatoes, sweet potatoes, onions and peanuts, a duck curry with red curry, coconut milk and pineapples, and yellow curry. With the exception of the Duck Curry, most of the curries are available with a choice of beef, chicken or shrimp. The noodle dish is the *Pad Thai* with either chicken or shrimp. There are fewer seafood items here than at most local Thai restaurants. Other seafood entrées include shrimp deep-fried or sautéed, a shrimp curry, a deep-fried red snapper, either a fillet or the entire fish, topped with a chili sauce, and deep-fried soft shell crabs and sole (or flounder). There are the less seldom seen dishes cooked and served in clay pots. There is one with shrimp and mussels, another with an array of seafood, and one with just vegetables. There is also an unusual hot pot dish with salmon and chile peppers. The lunch menu, available weekdays, offers nearly fifteen Thai dishes including *pad Thai* and green curry. The preparations with beef and chicken are around $7, a dollar more those with shrimp. If you are not craving Thai, there are also several Vietnamese rice noodle (*bun*) dishes for lunch. To note, not unusual for a Thai restaurant, the wine list is heavy on commonly seen red and varietals that are not terribly flattering to the food.

Mai's $10

3493 Milam (between Elgin and Alabama) 77002, (713) 520-7684
www.maisrestauranttx.com

Cuisine - Vietnamese
Hours - Mon-Thu, Sun 10AM to 3AM; Fri-Sat 10AM to 4AM
Credit Cards - Amex, Diners, Discover, MC, Visa
Service - Table Service
Alcohol - Beer & Wine

Entrée Prices - $5 to $20 ($10 average)
Entrées $12 and less - 70%

Atmosphere & Décor - Comfortable; often noisy late at night
Appeal - For that Vietnamese fix just about any time
Menu Suggestions - spring rolls; Bun Thit Nuong (vermicelli with char-grilled pork); But Ga Nuong (vermicelli with char-grilled chicken); Bo Luc Lac (pieces of steak with tomatoes and lettuce)

Opened since 1978, Mai's has long been a popular spot in Midtown, and it's often bustling late at night. Indeed, that is part of the draw, the fact that it is open for capable Vietnamese food until 4AM on weekends, and 3AM, otherwise. At that time it certainly beats the many alternatives especially in this city which has long been lacking in appealing late night options. Because of its hours, reasonable prices and its Midtown location relatively close to the University of Houston, Saint Thomas, Rice and the Medical Center, Mai's draws a steady stream of students. Close to downtown, it is also popular with office workers for lunch during the week. As one of the first Vietnamese restaurants in town, it has served as the introduction to this cuisine for many, and it still draws a loyal following after all these years.

The signature lengthy menu has nearly 200 choices. It is divided among Appetizers, Noodle Soups (*pho, hu, tiu* and *mi*), Vermicelli (*bun*), Combination Rice Platters (*com dia*), Family Dinners, Specials, Vegetables, Beef, Chicken, Pork and Seafood. The Specials section contains probably the most interesting, and certainly the most unique and expensive items on the menu with numerous beef, seafood and hot pot creations. A popular way to start any meal here is with an order of their well prepared rolls. Each is nicely complemented with a very tasty peanut dipping sauce. The spring rolls are soft rice paper filled with shrimp, pork, vegetables and rice noodles. Mai's even has versions with char-grilled pork or chicken. The summer rolls are similar, but made without the shrimp. For the meal, it is easy to find a reasonably priced entrée from the noodle soups, vermicelli dishes or rice platters. The noodle soups have several beef noodle soups, *pho,* but without the versions with tripe or tendon. There are plenty of other similar noodle soups with different broths and ingredients. The vermicelli and rice platter offerings provide entrées with the char-grilled chicken, pork and shrimp plus several other toppings, most for around six bucks. A useful measure for comparison with other Vietnamese restaurants for inexpensive dining, the marinated, char-grilled pork (*thit nuong*) is reliable at Mai's, but not quite as tender nor flavorful as at other top places. For grander dishes, better for community dining than a soup, vermicelli dish or rice plate, Mai's has a number of potentially enticing choices. These include: Stir-Fried Chicken with Hot Chili and Lemon Grass; Charcoal Broiled Beef Wrapped with Hawaiian Leaf; Garlic Chicken; and Mai's Special Spicy Garlic Shrimp. There are probably both more beef and vegetarian entrées than at most local Vietnamese restaurants, with roughly twenty of each. Mai's does a very good rendition of the *Bo Luc Lac,* an often-enjoyed dish of chunks of tender steak with lettuce and tomatoes served with rice. With generally low prices, good food, and a kitchen open well into the night, the service can sometimes be a little ragged. Mai's may not the best Vietnamese restaurant in town nor does it particularly stand out from many of the others, but the food is generally well prepared, and there should be something for everyone. And, it can be very convenient, too, when in Midtown or downtown.

Mak Chin's $11

1511 Shepherd (between Washington and I-10) 77007, (713) 861-9888

Cuisine - Pan Asian; Chinese
Hours - Mon-Thu, Sun 11AM to 10PM; Fri-Sat 11AM to 12AM
Credit Cards - Amex, MC, Visa
Service - Counter Service
Alcohol - Full Bar

Entrée Prices - Dinner - $6 to $15 ($10 average); Lunch - $7 to $9
Entrées at Dinner $12 and less - 100%

Atmosphere & Décor - Comfortable yet hip; patio
Appeal - Chinatown quality fare with a cool atmosphere, bar and still low prices
Useful to Note - Takeout is convenient; lunch specials are good on the weekends.
Menu Suggestions - Crab and Cream Cheese Wonton; Bacon-Wrapped Egg Rolls; Salt and Pepper Chicken (strips of chicken battered and fried with a salty and spicy finish); Wok Seared Rice Noodles (with Chinese broccoli and bean sprouts); Mango Sweet 'n Sour Chicken (with mango and red onions); Shanghai

Shrimp (battered and fried with a spicy and salty garnish); Special Fried Rice (with beef, chicken and shrimp)

When first approaching the counter at the very appealing, fast-casual Mak Chin's, which opened during the summer of 2006, some diners might be initially think of Pei Wei. That notion will be dispelled quickly, as the only similarities are that both offer Asian fare via counter service. Mak Chin's serves far better and more authentic food, has unexpectedly attractive presentation, a fairly cool décor, some atmosphere, a bar, a nice patio, and, all things considered, is a better value, too. This is counter service done right. This is Asian, mainly Chinese, food done right, too. Though the cooking is very good, and quite interesting, Mak Chin's also has plenty of space dedicated to its lounge and patio, which are also attractions. The restaurant is airy and cleanly designed with large swaths of red and black, somewhat hip and inviting. Cheeky, post-empire, pre-war Chinese pin-up posters decorate some of the walls.

Mak Chin's serves mostly Cantonese-style cooking with a deft touch in recognizable and appealing ways. With nearly everything cooked quickly in a wok in the open kitchen, the very fresh and well-chosen ingredients are allowed to shine through nearly every dish, even the fried ones. Most dishes feature a wonderful combination of textures, colors and flavors. The expected gooey sauces that are found at too many Chinese restaurants are thankfully absent. The short and well-chosen menu will certainly have a number of enticing choices for even the most casual of Chinese food fans. There are soups, noodles, fried rice and heartier entrées. There are plenty of robust flavors in each, and local favorites such as shrimp and beef are each served in several ways. There are several very familiar dishes, often with a twist: fried rice; beef and Chinese broccoli; hot-and-sour soup is made with miso; and the lighter sweet-and-sour has mango and red bell peppers. Properly plump shrimp are featured fried in a zesty sauce that is both salty and spicy. It is also wok-served with garlic mushrooms and vegetables and chili peppers. In true South Chinese fashion, even the dishes marked as spicy are not at all fiery. If you need to spice things up, Mak Chin's has an excellent condiments bar to provide it. With a dozen items set in small containers, its bounty is similar to that at Café Express, even if its flavor is different. Minced fresh jalapeños, chopped garlic, Chinese hot mustard, a bright garlic-chile sauce and others can be tempting additions to any dish.

Well-suited for a place with a large lounge and fairly spacious patio, the starters are quite appealing here. Among these are the familiar, though upgraded versions of egg rolls, potstickers, steamed dumplings, hot-and-sour soup and wontons. It's tough to go wrong with the wontons. Here these are stuffed with cream cheese and noticeable crabmeat, and, though fried to a crispy texture, are noticeably light and immensely flavorful, especially with the accompanying sweet-and-sour sauce. The egg rolls are wrapped in tasty bacon and properly seared, the spicy Thai Chicken Wings should go with most of the beers, and the lightly fried, finger-friendly Salt and Pepper Chicken is easily tasty and plentiful enough to order as an entrée. Some of the main dish highlights include Wok Seared Rice Noodles, Flaming Beef made with seared tenderloin, Tender Pork in Garlic Sauce with mushrooms, jicama and bamboo shoots. Vegetarians are well represented with the Japanese Chicken Mango Salad, versions of fried rice, seared rice noodles, tofu, and the Fresh Vegetable Medley. The only dud on the menu might be the non-Chinese Thai Curry. To note, Mak Chin's features a festive, drink-inducive brunch on Sundays with bottomless Asian- or rather Trader Vic-style frozen bellinis flowing readily from machines for just fifteen bucks.

Mama's Café $9

6019 Westheimer (between Fountain View and Voss) 77057, (713) 266-8514
www.mamascafe.net

Cuisine - Diner
Hours - Mon-Wed 6:30AM to 1AM; Thu-Fri 6:30AM to 4AM; Sat 8AM to 4AM; Sun 8AM to 1AM
Credit Cards - Amex, Diners, Discover, MC, Visa
Service - Table Service
Alcohol - Full Bar

Entrée Prices - Dinner & Lunch - $7 to $16 ($9 average); Breakfast - $5 to $8
Entrées at Dinner $12 and less - 90%

Atmosphere & Décor - Comfortable, lively
Appeal - High quality diner food in nicer-than-usual surroundings
Menu Suggestions - Huevos Hofbrau (eggs scrambled with tortilla chips, pico de gallo, onions and topped with queso); chicken fried steak; French toast; Combo Mexican Platter (cheese enchiladas, bean and cheese tostada, refried beans and Spanish rice); Sizzlin' Chicken Melt (grilled chicken breast with sautéed onions and mushrooms under melted provolone); fried okra

Long a favorite for late night meals, San Antonio-based Mama's is worth visiting even before midnight. The crowds during the weekday lunchtime attest to that. Mama's is popular because it provides commendable versions of the comfortable regional dishes in a pleasant setting for a reasonable price. The restaurant is nice; generally more so than a typical diner, but certainly casual. The service is always cheerful and efficient. The food is honest and hearty and on target for much of Houston. It's Tex-Mex-tinged with a heavy Central Texas accent with a clear lineage from its Central

European antecedents; at least the food is reliably heavy. The fact that it's part of a small chain, other than the efficiency, is not really in evidence. Even on a busy part of Westheimer, it manages to be a friendly, almost homey place.

The lunch and evening menu contains many of the familiar local favorites. There are soups, salads, half-pound hamburgers with several variations, sandwiches, ribs, a half-dozen flat-grilled steaks, Texas home-style cooking, several fish and shrimp dishes, and Tex-Mex. The small Tex-Mex section has fajitas, a tomato-y King Ranch casserole served in an individual-sized skillet, an enchilada dish, *chalupas*, and something called "Sancho Panza". Though of doubtful healthiness, this is a potentially mouth-watering combination of chopped sirloin stuffed with sliced pickled jalapeños and cheddar cheese then topped with chili and more melted cheese. The Texas diner dishes, listed under the heading, "Mama's Specialties", include liver and onions, meatloaf, a handful of chicken breast dishes, and a fine version of the requisite chicken fried steak. All of the dinner plates come with a choice of two vegetables and bread. If you need some more food than these hearty plates, Mama's has appetizers like Buffalo wings and fried mushrooms to start the meal. The breakfast offerings are probably the most popular ones at Mama's. This is a very popular spot for weekend breakfasts, and the signature morning dish is the *Huevos* Hofbrau: two very large scrambled eggs with onions, fresh chili peppers, *pico de gallo* and crushed tortilla chips topped with *chile con queso* that is served with refried beans, hash browns and flour tortillas. Other unique egg-based dishes are termed "skillet breakfasts;" two eggs any style, hash browns and biscuit served in a sizzling skillet with a choice of three toppings. There is the San Antonio with *chorizo* and *chile con queso*, the Country with a chicken fried steak, onions and white gravy, and the Works (smoked, diced ham with sautéed mushrooms, tomatoes, diced bell peppers, onions and melted cheddar cheese). Mama's also does a nice job with the more traditional American breakfasts. The eggs, pancakes and French toast are all reliably tasty. Pancakes are available with fruit toppings, or filled with blueberries. Reflecting this area, there are also biscuits and gravy, and Eggs Benedict *Mexicana*. This consists of toasted English muffins topped with Canadian bacon, poached eggs and *chile con queso*, and served with hash browns, refried beans and salsa. Continuing with that theme, there are also breakfast tacos. Described as "Texas-sized", these are good-sized flour tortillas filled with different combinations including potato and eggs, bacon and eggs, *chorizo* and eggs, and sausage, potato and eggs. Mama's has all of the extra sides and beverages, so it is easy to have a very pleasing, filling and usually cholesterol-laden breakfast that hits the spot either in the morning or late at night.

Mambo Parilla $9

6890 Harrisburg (at 78th) 77011, (713) 921-4100
www.mamboparrilla.com

Cuisine - Mexican (taqueria)
Hours - Mon-Thu, Sun 11AM to 10PM; Fri-Sat 11AM to 11PM
Credit Cards - Amex, MC, Visa
Service - Table Service
Alcohol - Beer, Margaritas

Entrée Prices - $6 to $14 ($9 average)
Entrées $12 and less - 90%

Atmosphere & Décor - Functional, but well-designed
Appeal - A slick taqueria featuring well prepared grilled beef dishes
Useful to Note - A little Spanish language ability is helpful here.
Menu Suggestions - Tacos de fajitas al carbon; Fajita Torta; fajitas; Beef Enchiladas al Carbon; Camarones Cozumel (butterflied shrimp topped with ranchero sauce and panela cheese)

When driving past Mambo Parrilla in the East End, or maybe even just hearing the name, you might quickly assume that it is quite like the Mambo Seafood. And, you'd be right. If you like its similarly named predecessor, you should like this. The menu is not terribly dissimilar, and the efficient kitchen, friendly service, atmosphere and crowds are almost identical. The interiors are just like those of the newer Mambo Seafood locations, airy, well-designed, pleasant and inviting for the whole family; even more so, if you speak a little Spanish. Mambo Parrilla serves several of the Mexican seafood cocktails that are popular at Mambo Seafood, oysters on the half shell, and about a dozen seafood entrées, plus a number of beef and chicken dishes, often grilled, to warrant the "*Parilla*" in the name. It's best to stick with the grilled beef dishes, mostly fajitas, and those seafood cocktails and seafood that Mambo Parrilla's sister restaurants have done so well. The aromatic, moist and very flavorful cubes of beef make it into a number of dishes: fajitas in several guises, enchiladas, tacos, *tortas* on sturdy *telera* bread, nachos, *tostadas, chimichangas,* and the mixed grill, *parrillas.* The less flavorful, if healthier in some eyes, grilled chicken can be substituted in most of these dishes. There are also several grander preparations such as a *milanesa* with chicken (breaded and pan-fried thin chicken breast) and topped with a *chipotle*-tinged cream sauce and grilled chicken topped with their spicy *diabla* sauce. For seafood entrées one of the highlights is the *Camarones* Cozumel that features battered and fried butterflied shrimp topped with the tomato-y *ranchero* sauce and melted white *panela* cheese. Grilled bacon-wrapped jumbo shrimp is also a winner on the *parrilla,* which might also include fajita, grilled chicken, pork ribs and sausage. These can make for a very enjoyable meal for one, two or four. Many dishes are supplemented with thick refried beans, moist rice, actually brightly colored *pico de gallo* and freshly made flour tortillas or corn tortillas. Mambo doesn't do everything right. Not so good is the listless pork in a green *mole* sauce served on the weekends, for one.

Mambo Seafood $10

6697 Hillcroft (north of Bellaire) 77081, (713) 541-3666
6101 Airline (between Tidwell and Parker) 77076, (713) 691-9700
10810 I-45 N. (south of the Beltway) 77037, (281) 820-3300
13485 Northwest Freeway (near Tidwell) 77040, (713) 462-0777
10002 Long Point (between Blalock and Gessner) 77055, (713) 465-5009
www.mamboseafood.com

Cuisine - Mexican; Seafood
Hours - Mon-Thu, Sun 11AM to 11PM (Airline - 10:30PM); Fri-Sat 11AM to 12AM
Credit Cards - Amex, MC, Visa
Service - Table Service
Alcohol - Beer, Margaritas

Entrée Prices - $4 to $21 ($10 average)
Entrées $12 and less - 80%

Atmosphere & Décor - Functional, but well-designed
Appeal - Fresh, inexpensive Mexican seafood
Menu Suggestions - Fried Shrimp; Mambo Rice; ceviche; Vuelve a la Vida (seafood cocktail with shrimp, oyster, fish and octopus)

A mambo might not be Mexican, nor are the owners for that matter, but the food here is Mexican, by way of the Gulf. Mambo Seafood provides satisfying, unpretentious, mostly Mexican-style seafood in several locations. With table service, a prominent display of fresh seafood that offers a view of what the kitchen is working with, and reliably well prepared food for a more-than-fair price, there is no wonder these places are usually always bustling. These are slickly run operations: service is prompt, the orders are quickly turned around, the menu is broad, and décor is inviting and appropriate. Some minimal Spanish language ability might be helpful when ordering from the waitstaff, though. Indicative of the quality and value of Mambo Seafood is the fact that it is often crowded, both during lunchtime and in the evenings, with Hispanic couples, families and workers enjoying various Mexican preparations of fresh seafood often with a *michelada* that the restaurant pushes. If you're not a Mambo or *taqueria* regular, it's a spicy beer and tomato juice cocktail. The restaurant even sells its own mix for it.

Surveying the tables, you'll notice that a popular way to start a meal here is with one of the appealing, raw seafood cocktails. There are tomato-based Mexican seafood cocktails with fish, shrimp, octopus, oyster, a combination, and the supposedly restorative *Vuelve a la Vida* with all four. A small order of their excellent *ceviche* (without the tomatoes) can work well as a starter for three or four people. Raw Gulf oysters on the half shell are also another popular appetizer, and cheaper than most places. The soups can be either a starter or a meal. These are the locally requisite Seafood Gumbo, which is, unfortunately, rather inconsistent, and the Seafood Soup made with fish and shrimp. The former, though laden with seafood, has a slightly different taste from the local Louisiana-accented restaurants, and is not as consistently balanced nor flavorful as it should be. Beyond the cocktails and soups, cooking methods for the fish and shellfish are more than just frying, which is often just about the only way served in many other inexpensive Mexican seafood restaurants. Mambo also sautés with butter (described as scampi, or *a la mantaquilla*), grills, boils, steams and stews in a light tomato sauce (*a la ranchera*). Jumbo shrimp, squid and octopus are offered sautéed in butter. There is also a combination dish with all three of these. Grilled platters feature either jumbo shrimp or a fish fillet (probably tilapia). Many more items make their way into the deep fryer: jumbo shrimp, fish (tilapia) fillets, red snapper fillets, stuffed blue crabs, oysters, scallops, and combinations. There is also a steamed fillet with garlic, and fish fillets, shrimp and the *Vuelve a la Vida* cocktail combination (shrimp, squid and octopus) prepared *a la ranchera*. Even if these are not very large, the fried shrimp are especially flavorful; butterflied before being breaded then deep-fried. If one of the standard dishes does not satisfy a particular craving, you can also order many of the shellfish and fish by the pound or half-pound and specify the cooking method. The range of choices is shrimp in different sizes, scallops, squid, octopus, oysters, lobster and fish that could be red snapper, catfish, tilapia, flounder or redfish. So, if you are in the mood for boiled shrimp, grilled oysters or octopus in *ranchero* sauce, and it is not specifically on the menu, you can get that. Just about all of the entrées are served with a choice between fries and the Mambo Rice. With some influence from Chinese restaurants, this is a satisfying dish of fried rice with small shrimp and small pieces of pork and chicken. Different versions of this fried rice are also available as an entrée.

Working well for lunch, there are about ten reasonably priced combination dishes featuring fried seafood such as fish fillets and shrimp, shrimp and Mambo Rice, fish fillets and Mambo Rice, shrimp and fries, whole tilapia, grilled catfish fillet, and fried gar (yes, gar). Seafood is in the name for a reason. For those not inclined to seafood there are only a handful of options: Grilled Chicken Salad; Grilled Chicken [Breast] Dinner; Grilled Chicken

Sandwich; a hamburger; and fried rice with either chicken or pork. You come here for the seafood, though.

Mandola's Deli $8

4105 Leeland (at Cullen, east of I-45 S.) 77023, (713) 223-5186

Cuisine - Sandwiches; Italian-American
Hours - Mon-Fri 9AM to 3PM; Sat 10AM to 2PM
Credit Cards - Amex, MC, Visa
Service - Counter Service
Alcohol - Beer & Wine

Entrée Prices - $5 to $9 ($8 average)
Entrées $12 and less - 100%

Atmosphere & Décor - Spartan
Appeal - Honest Southern Italian-American sandwiches and pastas
Useful to Note - They also specialize in catering and party foods.
Menu Suggestions - Deluxe Paisano Po Boy; Italian Beef Po Boy; Meatball Po Boy; Eggplant Parmesan; fries; Meat Lasagna

One of the many restaurants run by the extended Mandola clan in the Houston area, Mandola's Deli serves casual fare in a family-run place with some character near the University of Houston. The setting is not much and the décor is functional, both in tune with the industrial neighborhood. The walls of the dining room are mostly covered with old and new posters from University of Houston sports teams and photos of the amazingly numerous Mandola clan. The menu consists of sandwiches, po boys (sandwiches on po boy bread), half-pound burgers, salads and pastas. The pasta dishes are spaghetti with meatballs, Italian sausage in red gravy, spaghetti with grilled chicken, another one with mushrooms, spaghetti with a cream sauce, and a pesto-cream sauce. The highlight is probably the very good lasagna, served in the expected Southern Italian-American fashion with plenty of tomato sauce, ricotta and ground meat. Hidden in under the Pasta header are worthwhile eggplant Parmesan and a familiar tasting Sicilian-American chicken dish; both of these are served with a side of spaghetti. The po boys and sandwiches on sufficiently fresh bread are probably the biggest draws. Sandwiches are served on a choice of white, wheat or rye. The po boys and sandwich fillings include the traditional cold cuts, turkey, tuna, meatball, sausage, Chicago-style Italian beef (grilled sliced sirloin), roast beef, shrimp, chicken, Chicken Parmesan, Reuben, a turkey Reuben, corned beef, pastrami, ham, grilled chicken breast, and chicken salad. The kitchen is heavy on the pickles for some. One of the best sandwiches is the Paisano Po Boy, their version of the muffaletta. It contains all of the muffaletta fillings (green olive spread, ham, salami, and provolone cheese) on a po boy bun rather than the traditional large round loaf. The meatball sandwich is also quite good. The fresh Italian sausages, which are also featured in a sandwich, though made in-house, are lacking in fennel, and some flavor. The fries provide a fine accompaniment to the sandwiches and burgers: thin, crisp, and greasy enough. Thinking of the burgers, these can be, nicely adorned in feast day fashion with sautéed peppers, mushrooms or grilled onions for a small additional charge. Mandola's has house-made desserts, which are generally more satisfying: cheesecakes, brownies, a carrot cake, chocolate cake and Italian cookies. Alas, though Mandola originated in Sicily, there is no cannoli. They also provide a number of items for parties and office events: sandwich trays, lasagna and the other pastas, sandwiches, etc. The most interesting dishes, and one of the most popular during the holidays, is the *Faccia Di Vecchia* ("old women's face"), a version of the Sicilian baked pizza.

Manena's Pastry Shop & Deli $8

11018 Westheimer (at Wilcrest) 77042, (713) 278-7139

Cuisine - Argentine; Café / Bakery
Hours - Mon-Sat - 8:30AM to 8PM
Credit Cards - Amex, Discover, MC, Visa
Service - Counter Service
Alcohol - NONE

Entrée Prices - $6 to $8 ($8 average)
Entrées $12 and less - 100%

Atmosphere & Décor - Pleasant
Appeal - Tasty casual Argentine fare and pastries
Useful to Note - This is a low-volume place; food is served in a measured pace.
Menu Suggestions - sandwich de miga with prosciutto (thin toasted sandwiches on a good white bread); spinach empanadas; ground beef empanadas; milanesa napolitana; pastries

Tucked behind a large drugstore in a dull strip center on Westheimer and Wilcrest, Manena's is easy to overlook. It's is a quaint café and Argentine bakery with just a handful of tables creating pleasingly fragrant freshly baked pastries and desserts in many styles. These might have unfamiliar names, but recognizable tastes. Charmingly chaotic at times this low volume restaurant with just a half-dozen tables or so is also a good stop for a light lunch with sandwiches made with noticeably freshly baked bread, *empanadas*, or some other casual Argentine fare. Highlighted here in the savory, inexpensive and straightforward dishes are quality ingredients, especially the bread baked in-house, and some basic, but well-loved Italian flavors. These are some of the enticements to Argentine fare rather than their country's famous steaks. The golden-hued *empanadas* are very good here, as you would expect from any competent Argentine bakery. Fillings include piquant ground beef, chicken, spinach, corn and *queso y cebolla* (cheese, onion, tomato and basil). The listing for the *sandwiches de miga* might not initially register with non-Argentine customers. These are rather small, simple sandwiches on toasted, freshly made white bread available with a choice of fillings such as ham and cheese, hearts of palm, anchovies, blue cheese, celery and walnuts and prosciutto. It might not be *prosciutto di San Daniele*, but it will be satisfying enough, especially for the price. Two orders of these sandwiches will be needed for most. The Argentine staple, *milanesas*, the flattened, breaded and pan-fried beef cutlets, are done well here. These are nicely complemented by the baguette sandwiches that use freshly baked bread. The nearly ten variations include roast beef, vegetarian with eggplant, and even the time-consuming-to-make *matambre*, the sliced cold beef roll and a favorite from the pampas that is an interpretation of the Italian *braciole*. Manena's also offers a wide variety of Argentine food products, several brands of *yerba maté* with their equipment, *bombillas* and gourds, *dulce de leche* (the well-loved caramelized milk and sugar mixture), a whole slew of Argentine sweets including *alfajores* (cookies made with corn starch and filled with *dulce de leche*), and more.

Manny's Café $10

8475 Highway 6 N. (at West) 77095, (281) 856-9075

Cuisine - Greek
Hours - Tue-Fri 11AM to 7PM; Sat 10AM to 4PM
Credit Cards - Amex, Discover, MC, Visa
Service - Counter Service
Alcohol - NONE

Entrée Prices - $6 to $15 ($10 average)
Entrées $12 and less - 80%

Atmosphere & Décor - Pleasant
Appeal - Good Greek food in a charming little café
Menu Suggestions - gyro sandwich; Manny's Gyro Steak sandwich (gyro with sautéed bell peppers, onions, mushrooms and melted Swiss cheese); Gyro Platter; Manny's Cheese Steak sandwich (served on pita bread); coffee

Gyros, in one fashion or another, are a big part of the attraction for most customers at Manny's, a charming, well-lit, and mostly tidy little restaurant in Copperfield. The standard gyro sandwich is quite good; flavorful without being cloying, as lesser versions sometimes are. It features the tasty lamb and beef mixture, chopped, and mixed with slices of onions and tomatoes with a house-made *tzatiki* sauce on a noticeably soft, heated pita bread. The version done with sautéed, nearly caramelized onions, bell peppers and melted Swiss cheese is also very satisfying, as is the Gyro Platter and the Gyro Club, which is the most expensive item on the menu. This draws inspiration from the Club sandwich with pitas substituting for the white bread, and gyro meat, tomatoes, onions, lettuce and *tzatziki* sauce providing the two levels of filling. That other Greek restaurant favorite, the Greek salad is also done nicely here. Even as a side salad it is served in a good-sized chilled bowl with a plentiful amount of thickly chopped cucumbers and tomatoes along with shredded non-iceberg lettuce, Kalamata olives, feta cheese and pepperoncini. There are other salads here, too, and with a choice of dressings made in-house such as 1000 Island, Lemon Olive Oil, Ranch and Creamy Lemon Caesar. There are several appetizers, the expected foursome of *spanakopita* (spinach and feta cheese baked in phyllo dough), *tiropita* (feta cheese in phyllo dough), stuffed grape leaves, and meatballs, plus *hummus* and *tzatziki* for dipping. There are several Greek-tinged pastas and a small number of baked desserts including cakes and Greek pastries; much more than just *baklava*. Some of these can make a tempting finish to a visit or just as an accompaniment to one of Manny's coffees.

Unlike many other restaurants, "café" is actually appropriately included in the name, as coffee is an integral part of the place. Coffee-related signage and artwork make up much of the décor, and this friendly place with less than a dozen booths and tables is well-suited to some coffee-related lingering. Even more significantly, Manny's uses the Illy brand coffee, which is probably Italy's best, and certainly the most expensive to purchase here, for its espresso-based drinks, which you'll find at many of the tables. In addition to the coffee drinks, they also serve several flavors of frozen frappes and smoothies that are very well suited for our many warmer months.

Maria Selma's $13

1617 Richmond (between Mandell and Dunlavy) 77006, (713) 528-4920
www.mariaselma.com

Cuisine - Mexican
Hours - Mon-Thu 8AM to 11PM; Fri-Sat 9AM to 12AM; Sun 9AM to 10PM
Credit Cards - Amex, Diners, Discover, MC, Visa
Service - Table Service
Alcohol - Full Bar

Entrée Prices - Dinner & Lunch - $7 to $19 ($13 average); Breakfast - $5 to $9
Entrées at Dinner $12 and less - 60%

Atmosphere & Décor - Pleasant; patio
Appeal - Usually tasty and sometimes very interesting Mexican food
Useful to Note - There is mostly just valet parking here.
Menu Suggestions - Aguacate Relleno de Jaiba (stuffed avocado with crab meat); Enchiladas Poblanas (with mole sauce, red onions, sesame seeds, fresh cheese and filled with shredded chicken); Enchiladas Suizas; La Gringa (marinated and roasted pork with grilled pineapples, onions and melted cheese); El Zarape (a platter of pieces of carne asada, bell pepper and topped with melted cheese); Cubana Torta (a sandwich on fresh telera bread and filled with ham, pork and melted cheese)

In a city with no shortage of Mexican restaurants, Maria Selma's strives to be something somewhat a little different. It's more ambitious, and more authentic than most area Mexican restaurants. Though it might not succeed for all it strives, and the kitchen has been somewhat inconsistent in the past, it's still an interesting and worthwhile place to visit. And, importantly, the meals are a fine value. With the exception of the complimentary and necessary chips and salsa and the fajitas, Maria Selma's tries to avoid Tex-Mex and sticks to Mexico City-style cooking, even as the menu has evolved to align more closely with local tastes. It's divided among appetizers, soups, salads, *quesos,* seafood, meat and poultry, tacos, *tortas,* enchiladas, and several house specials. Though many items might be unfamiliar to many whom usually frequent the large suburban Mexican restaurants, there should be enough familiar and certainly appealing dishes from which to choose.

The starters and small plates might get your attention. The appetizers include *flautas* filled with shredded duck, *empanadas,* and an avocado stuffed with crab meat in addition to artful nachos and *chile con queso.* There are several soups including a tortilla soup, a hearty chicken soup and an enticing Cream of Poblano Pepper. Melted cheese dishes listed under "*Quesos*" get more attention at Maria Selma than most other local Mexican restaurants. There is the popular dish of cheese melted with *chorizo, Queso a la Plancha,* which here is a thin layer of crispy *panela* cheese with jalapeños cheese that has been cooked on the grill. The meat dishes listed under the headers Meat and Poultry and Specialties seem to include most of the best of the entrées. There *milanesas* with beef and chicken, pork loin served in either a rich *adobo* or an earthy green *mole* sauce, pork chops, *Papas con Rajas* (potatoes with strips of poblano pepper), a potato cake, and a marinated, grilled steak with *nopalito* cactus. Their specialty dishes are platters of meat such as *carne asada, puerco al pastor, chorizo,* and pork loin sometimes mixed with chopped onions and pepper, and topped with melted cheese. Served with fresh tortillas, each of these five choices is usually quite satisfying: quality meat prepared in zesty and interesting combinations. Similar mixed grills (*el comal*) can be cooked for two or four. Maria Selma's does a very good job with the variety of enchiladas, which the menu states are made as in Mexico City. These will be quite recognizable, in addition to being quite enjoyable. The seafood dishes are both familiar and fairly unique. There is poblano pepper stuffed with seafood, fried shrimp served with a *chipotle*-studded mayonnaise plus snapper *a la Verucruzana* and snapper *ceviche*. Unfortunately, the quality of the seafood, especially the fish fillets dishes, is variable. The aforementioned meat items are much more reliable. Though most of the dinner plates are not pricey, the casual finger foods are even a better value. The *tortas*, the Mexican versions of the sandwiches, are an especially good deal. These are served on *telera* bread, which is slightly different, maybe more dense here, than the *bolillo* bread that most local places employ for their *tortas*. The taco choices are the pork *al pastor*, served with a pineapple topping, *carne asada* with grilled onions and cactus, chicken in a tomato sauce, marinated shrimp, and breaded and fried fish with the *chipotle* mayonnaise. Among the nice touches is that unlike most Mexican restaurants in town, the corn tortillas in addition to the flour tortillas are made on site. These are delivered to the table in a small cloth pouch to keep them warm. To help wash down the food are the *aguas frescas* in a half-dozen different flavors that are made in-house, Mexican sodas, and the other usual suspects. The margaritas could be better, but can get expensive near the higher end, which are pushed, of course. Maria Selma carries a huge range of tequilas. It might be a better idea to drink one of these top quality tequilas neat, rather than in a margarita. The weekend breakfasts are worthy of a visit; some of the prettiest Mexican morning fare in town. There are even a couple dishes that would be difficult to find at most *taquerias*.

The setting is pleasant and comfortable, and there is a good-sized patio in front that is usually crowded on weather-amendable evenings. The pressed tin ceiling inside is a nice try, though the final result is a bit clumsy. But, this is another indication that the restaurant seems very keen in providing a better-than-usual dining experience, as is the often attentive and always friendly service. It usually hits its marks.

Marine's Empanadas & Bakery $7

3227 Hillcroft (between Richmond and Westpark) 77057, (713) 789-2950
www.marinesempanadas.com

Cuisine - Colombian
Hours - Mon-Thu 7:30AM to 8PM; Fri-Sat 7:30AM to 9PM; Sun 10AM to 9PM
Credit Cards - Amex, Discover, MC, Visa
Service - Counter Service
Alcohol - NONE

Entrée Prices - Dinner - $5 to $9 ($7 average); Lunch - $5 to $8

Entrées at Dinner $12 and less - 100%

Atmosphere & Décor - Spartan
Appeal - Very tasty empanadas; a couple empanadas make for a cheap meal
Useful to Note - Some Spanish is probably helpful here.
Menu Suggestions - Pancho Villa empanada (mozzarella, cheddar cheese and jalapeños); Hot Tia Maria empanada (stewed beef with jalapeños, tomatoes and onions); Dulce de Leche empanada (a sweet empanada with caramel)

Empanadas by Marini, a long-time institution that served excellent Argentine-style *empanadas,* turnovers filled with a variety of meats, cheeses and fruits, closed its doors early in 2000 (later resurrected in Katy, see next profile). Thankfully, most of its recipes live on in the similarly named Marine's, a small storefront restaurant on Hillcroft, and another Marini's way out west in Katy (see next entry). Though Marine's proclaims itself a Colombian restaurant and does serve Colombian specialties, its *empandas* are what you might find in Buenos Aires and Córdoba rather than Bogata or Cartegena. For a takeout order, the cashier might be overheard saying on the phone, *"si, empanadas argentinas"*. Maybe these are not exactly like the Argentines consume, as there is the locally prevalent Mexican influence on some of the *empandas.* But, in this culinary melting pot, this is certainly not a bad thing.

The menu is divided among beef *empandas,* chicken *empandas,* cheese *empandas,* vegetable *empandas,* fruit *empandas,* dessert *empandas,* double-size dessert *empandas,* and *Antijitos Columbianos* (Columbian favorites) such as *chorizo con arepa* (cornmeal stuffed with sausage), tamales, *buñuelos* (deep-fried pastries), Colombian *empandas.* The Argentine-style *empanadas,* the attraction for most of the non-Colombian patrons, are freshly crafted, deep-fried pockets of white dough nicely folded to enclose a variety of fillings. The twenty-five or so non-dessert (beef, chicken, cheese and vegetarian) ones are complemented very nicely by the traditional *chimi-churri* sauce of olive oil, vinegar, parsley and garlic that comes with each order. There are quite a number of different fillings, so there should be a few that fits your mood. Of those non-dessert items, several of the beef and cheese *empanadas* are the best of the lot. The Beef Gaucho is a traditional Argentine *empanada* filled with chopped beef, fried onions and a boiled egg. The Pancho Villa, described on the menu as "Mexican hot", though not overly spicy, is made with mozzarella and cheddar cheese and jalapeños. Other combinations such as chicken with *mole* sauce; avocado with mozzarella; refried beans with cheddar and jalapeños; and shrimp with Chinese vegetables. The *empanadas* at Marine's are larger than most that are served as appetizers at other restaurants. Most people can make a meal out of two *empanadas,* three if you are hungry. With *empanadas* costing $2.25, a few pennies more with the addition of cheese, it is possible to feed yourself for under $5, if you're not that hungry. Double-sized dessert *empanadas* are quite large, and just an additional dollar. The dessert *empanadas*, or "Special Empanadas" as they are noted on the menu, feature fillings of fruits with cream and sugars. As with the non-dessert ones, there should be enough choices among the dessert and fruit ones, including *dulce de leche* (hot caramel cream), fig with cheese and walnuts, and apple with cheese, cinnamon, sugar and walnuts. The fruit *empanadas* include banana, apple, pineapple, peach, cherry, strawberry, apricot, blueberry, raspberry, and the tropical guava and mango. These are also available with cheese.

Popular with many regular customers, Marine's menu also offers full Colombian meals (with English descriptions) such as *Bandeja paisa* (grilled steak, rice, pork skin, sweet plantain, an *arepa* and a fried egg), *Bistec a la criolla* (grilled steak with onion), *Arroz con pollo, Chuleta Empanizada* (breaded and pan-fried pork chop), *Sobrebarriga* (grilled flank steak with sautéed onions), *Carne Asada*, and *Higado* (liver) There are also lunch specials that feature a Colombian dish that changes daily and can include *Ajiaco* (potato and chicken stew that is the national dish) *Sancocho de Gallina* (a hearty chicken soup), *Consomé y arroz con pollo* (a light soup with chicken and rice) and *Mondongo* (beef tripe stew). Marine's also offers fresh fruit juices in the Colombian fashion with a variety of tropical flavors, which can be quite exotic, that include: banana, *guayaba* (guava), mango, strawberry, *guanabana* (custard apple or soursoup), peach, *lulo* (a sour-tasting tropical fruit), *maracuya* (passion fruits), *mora* (blackberry), a combation of banana, *tomate y arbol* (tree tomato that has a flavor somewhat of mild tomato), pineapple and *curbua* (*¿que?*). These are available mixed with water or milk. The décor is much befitting a place in an older strip center, but, the décor is fitting for the flavorful, but unprentious Latin fare.

Marini's Empanada House $7

3522 S. Mason (north of Westheimer Parkway) Katy, 77450, (281) 391-4273
www.theoriginalmarinisempanadahouse.com

Cuisine - Argentine
Hours - Tue-Thu 11AM to 9PM; Fri-Sat 11AM to 10PM; Sun 11AM to 9PM
Credit Cards - Amex, Discover, MC, Visa
Service - Counter Service
Alcohol - Full Bar

Entrée Prices - $6 to $9 ($7 average)
Entrées $12 and less - 100%

Atmosphere & Décor - Comfortable; patio

Appeal - Top-notch Argentine-style empanadas made to satisfy local tastes
Useful to Note - Their empanadas are great for take-away.
Menu Suggestions - Hot "Tia Maria" empanada (with sliced beef brisket, onions, jalapeños and tomato sauce); Beef "Gaucho" (with ground beef, olives, onions and a hard-boiled egg); Texas BBQ (with chopped brisket and barbecue sauce); Italian "Marcello" (with sausage, mozzarella, provolone and tomato sauce); Apple empanada

Marini's Empanada House, or more properly, The Original Marini's Empanada House has been around the Houston area off-and-on since 1971. The first restaurant was on lower Westheimer in Montrose, and then later further down Westheimer, west of the Galleria. Today it's operated by the offspring of the founding couple. Though its comfortable, well-scrubbed location in suburban Katy might not have the funkiness of its previous settings, the *empanadas* haven't changed, and are still very good, plus the small counter-service restaurant still exudes a friendly feel.

The *empanadas* here are made in the Argentine-style with wheat flour dough attractively rolled around any number of ingredients and baked until the sturdy, flavorful crust is golden. The fillings are more American, or more properly, Houstonian in nature, than Argentine. Of the nearly twenty savory *empanadas* and about the same number of dessert ones, there are ones filled with beef brisket and barbecue sauce, brisket and pickled jalapeños, avocado, broccoli and cheeses, refried beans, apples and cinnamon, and raspberry with cream cheese. Befitting the name Marini, there are a number with identifiably Italian ingredients such as mozzarella, provolone, Italian sausage, pepperoni, basil, tomato and oregano. These are typically all quite tasty. The savory *empanadas* are divided among those primarily filled with meat, vegetable or cheese, and are served with a side of *chimi-churri* sauce, which seems to complement each of these. Three of the decent-sized *empanadas* should be more than sufficient for most; or, a couple of *empanadas* and an order of curly fries or a side salad. The dessert *empanadas* feature fruit, homemade fruit preserves, fruit and cream cheese and *dulce de leche,* the gooey caramel syrup that is a Latin favorite. A couple of double-sized versions with bananas or apples with *dulce de leche,* spices, cheese and whipped cream are also offered. No matter which versions are ordered, it's wise to note that the fillings are often surprisingly hot, temperature-wise. In addition to *empanadas,* Marini's has a few sandwiches on a small baguette such as beef marinated in *chimi-churri* and another with *milanesa.* Beer and wine are served by the glass, plus sangria and several smoothie-like *licuados.*

* Market Square Bar & Grill $8

311 Travis (across from the Market Square Park) 77002, (713) 224-6133
www.marketsquarehouston.com

Cuisine - Hamburgers
Hours - Mon-Thu 11AM to 10PM; Fri-Sat 11AM to 12AM
Credit Cards - Amex, MC, Visa
Service - Table Service
Alcohol - Full Bar

Entrée Prices - $6 to $11 ($8 average)
Entrées $12 and less - 100%

Atmosphere & Décor - Comfortable, pub-like
Appeal - Excellent hamburgers and far-above-average pub fare
Useful to Note - It's a great stop before an Astros game.
Menu Suggestions - Market Square Burger; Bacon Cheese Burger; Blue Burger (burger with crumbled blue cheese and sautéed mushrooms); Jalapeño Burger; Cheese Steak Sandwich; Hummus; Chipotle Chicken Jalapeños; Grilled Chicken and Mandarins Salad; French fries; BLT&A (bacon, lettuce, tomato and avocado sandwich); Beef Fajita Salad (fajita strips on mixed greens with a cilantro-lime vinaigrette)

Market Square Bar & Grill, located on Travis in an old building on Market Square, is a friendly, quiet place just off the Main Street club scene. It has a long narrow interior with a nice bar, across from which are several tables and booths against the exposed brick wall, and the high ceiling has pressed tin decorations. This is what a bar should look like. It's surprising that the food is so well prepared. At the end of the lengthy interior space is a small and very cool courtyard reminiscent of a small courtyard in the French Quarter. Its brick walls, at least two stories high at each turn, are covered in ivy, somewhat similar to the outfield walls during the summer at Wrigley Field. A more conscious likeness with the Cubs Park is that during baseball season, the standings in each league are shown with team-logoed license plates substituting for the flags in center field that overlook Waveland Avenue on the north side of Chicago. Not incidentally, the owner grew up rooting for the Cubs. And, he still continues in that painful passion. Mentioning baseball, Market Square is a good place to stop before or after a game, as it is an easy ten-minute walk to and from the ballpark. It's wise to grab some food here rather than the wretched and overpriced fare that is served there. Not only is a filling meal far tastier at Market Square, it's also much cheaper.

The menu items are somewhat typical, but somewhat more refined pub fare: finger foods for appetizers, burgers, sandwiches, other grilled items, salads, and even *hummus*. The difference is that everything at the Market Square is made to order, and there is more attention paid to detail. So much so, it's been a fairly crowded stop for lunch for years. To start or to munch on over beers, there are wings, stuffed jalapeños, the even better *Chipoltle* Chicken

Jalapeños, *quesadillas* and Chicken and Sausage *Alambres* (chicken tenders wrapped around Monterey Jack cheese, jalapeños and then skewered and grilled with smoked sausage). The sides are quite pleasing; nicely roasted potatoes, fresh fruit, and potato salad, and the most popular, the thin, crisp fries, are consistently excellent. These are a fitting complement to the burgers, which are among the best in town. All of the burgers are made with seven ounces of high quality ground chuck, properly cooked to juicy goodness and served on a fresh sesame seed bun with very fresh romaine lettuce, ripe roma tomatoes and slices of red onions. Fitting one of the very best burgers around, Market Square's toppings and condiments are top-notch, and a differentiator from most other places. Unlike many purveyors of hamburgers, where the lettuce and tomatoes are barely green and red, respectively, Market Square's lettuce is resplendently verdant, the tomato slice is juicy and flavorful. The buns are higher-than-usual quality, always fresh, and nicely toasted. All of the burger variations are very good, especially the ones with plentiful and sturdy bacon, and another with blue cheese. The turkey burger is actually more than quite palatable, too. They also serve an excellent version of the (Philly) cheese steak sandwich with plenty of tasty sliced beef, cheese on a fresh sandwich roll, a crusty Vietnamese baguette in this case. It's even more flavorful when you request the addition of blue cheese, and sliced and quickly sautéed fresh jalapeños; Pete's Philly on the menu. These additions make it one the best hot sandwiches in town. Though there are more authentic South Philly style cheesesteaks in town, there is not one nearly as tasty as this. Their version of the BLT, the BLT&A, with slices of avocado added, is very good. Fresh slices of sourdough bread, roma tomatoes and romaine lettuce, the additional tasty fat of the avocado, and most importantly, very thick slices of bacon, make this one of the best versions of this sandwich in town. For those hoping to eat healthier, or slightly healthier, the kitchen can oblige with several very good entrée-sized salads including one with grilled chicken breast, lettuce, tomato, onion, avocado and mandarin orange slices and a side of ranch dressing. The Beef Fajita Salad featuring tasty strips of beef and an excellent cilantro-lime vinaigrette is especially satisfying.

As primarily a bar, Market Square has over a dozen fresh beers on tap and a full selection of liquor. For the martini drinker, they, along with their sister bar, T.K. Bitterman's on West Alabama, are often rated as pouring the top martinis in town. Stop in for lunch, and then return for a drink in the evening. Or, drink at lunch and make the day more enjoyable.

Take me out to the ballpark...but not to eat

Professional baseball, with its comfortable pace, has long been associated with food, "buy me some peanuts and Cracker Jacks" has been sung at every professional ballgame since well before Dizzy Dean pitched for the Houston Buffs. Visiting the home of the San Francisco Giants, I was amazed to find an incredible array of concessions and found it a far cry from our hometown MinuteMaid Park. In the City by the Bay, major league baseball and garlic fries have gone hand-in-hand for many years, and whose aroma is tough to ignore, there are also attractive, sizzling sausage sandwiches and freshly made soft pretzels. There is even an enticingly prepared seafood chowder served in a sourdough bread bowl. The quality choices extend to the beer, where it is even somewhat tough to find the nearly tasteless bulk-produced *schlager lager*, which is pretty much all that's served at MinuteMaid. Instead there is tap after tap of tasty Anchor Steam, Sierra Nevada Pale Ale, Lagunitas IPA, Gordon Biersch Marzen, and even at least one stand pouring Guinness. Guinness at a ballpark? It may not be a match like "Galway Bay" and the NYPD choir, but it works better than some listless industrial swill. Just like the food, the service was much more efficient and far friendlier than at MinuteMaid, where lines seem always move in often agonizing slow-motion, especially the ones for beer. Still all too appropriate are the choice descriptions used in *Dodger Dogs to Fenway Franks* to describe the Dome's "sleepwalking vendors" in 1988: "absolutely lifeless", "bumbling", and "extras practicing for another sequel to *Night of the Living Dead*."

If far more abundant in more-than-palatable food and drink, San Francisco is not alone: Chicago's ballparks have much better fare, especially the depressing and sometimes violent Sox Park; the overly dark and foreboding ballpark in Phoenix has a great array of tasty ballpark-friendly food and good beer; St. Louis has bad beer, but tasty, hearty food to satisfy the best of America's baseball fans, plus some of the flabbiest and most pasty; Coors Field, named after a certain large brewer, even has a great array of Colorado micro-brews that's easy to find and good ballpark fare; Milwaukee baseball has long been more well-known for their bratwurst than their ballclubs; San Diego and Los Angeles have served sushi since the 1990s; the new Philadelphia park has a great selection of regional micro-brewed beers, one less thing for their fans to boo; and, though the venerable Fenway Franks are really nothing special, the array of carts serving hot Italian sausages and peppers before or after a Red Sox game always provide satisfaction. Wait. Every ballpark, with the possible exception of our in-state neighbor in suburban Arlington, has at least passable food coupled with the friendly and prompt service. As a season ticket-holder since the inception of the ballpark downtown, I'm very happy that MinuteMaid is a terrifically designed place to watch baseball. But, **in a city with great, inexpensive restaurants, possibly the best in the country, the food is generally terrible, and the service is amazingly slow.** I've eaten in the Club section several times, too;

at least the service is better there. I always eat, and almost always drink before and after the game; not during.

Why not have good and interesting local restaurants at the ballpark? Wouldn't **Goode Co. Barbecue**, **tacos** from one of the better *taquerias* or the fish tacos from **Berryhill**, **Kim Son** (spring rolls and Imperial rolls are easy to eat and go well with beer, and they already operate in several food courts), **Ragin Cajun** (at least for their po boys), and several others be a nice addition to the ballpark? **Vietnamese sandwiches**, like the po boys from **Antone's Import Co.** are easy to make in bulk, inexpensive, tasty with crusty French-style baguettes and, most importantly, great with beer. How about *empanadas* and *shawarmas*, both tasty finger foods? At the very least, how about having the beer from hometown Saint Arnold far more accessible? If these suggestions prove too much, how about serving much better hot dogs and soft pretzels, serving margaritas in something other than nearly fluorescent colors in beer-bong-esque plastic contraptions, encouraging more food stands outside of the ballparks, and, most easily, how about more beer stands and beer vendors?

Mary'z $11

5825 Richmond (between Chimney Rock & Fountain View) 77057, (832) 251-1955
www.maryzcuisine.com

Cuisine - Middle Eastern
Hours - Mon-Thu, Sun 11AM-10:30PM; Fri-Sat 11AM-11PM
Credit Cards - Amex, Discover, MC, Visa
Service - Table Service
Alcohol - Beer & Wine

Entrée Prices - $8 to $17 ($11 average)
Entrées $12 and less - 70%

Atmosphere & Décor - Friendly; popular with a young, hookah-smoker at night
Appeal - Homey Lebanese food
Useful to Note - Valet parking is available in the evening.
Menu Suggestions - kibbe ball; Ternderloin Kabab; Mixed Grill Platter (a kabob with tenderloin, chicken kabob, and kafta kabob)

Distinctively named Mary'z is a popular, earnest and friendly Lebanese restaurant west of the Galleria. The portions are large, the kitchen is competent, and the value is quickly evident. And, it has a couple patios that are draws for a club-hopping younger crowd at night to smoke hookahs (filled with tobacco, of course), and most everyone else on nice days and evenings. There's a very good chance that you won't be wowed here, but it's tough not to appreciate at least some of its charms. Well-suited for groups and, or lingering, Mary'z has nearly two dozen different appetizers. A combination *mezze* plate with eight different items might be a good way to start with a table of several people. There are all of the expected Middle Eastern appetizers plus the Armenian stuffed cabbage and local favorites, oysters and quail, boiled and sautéed, respectively. The *hummus* and *baba ganoush* are decent, though not helped much by store-bought pita bread that might be a little gummy. The best thing about each is that these are served in good-sized portions. The half-portion might be enough to split for a couple. The deep-fried *kibbe* balls filled with ground beef, and the flaky stuffed pies (*empanadas* from the Levant) are probably more reliably done. One of the nearly ten salads can also help start a meal; *tabouli, fatoush* (pita bread with parsley, tomato, onions and cucumber), leafy spinach, Greek and Caesar salads, and a refreshing one with yogurt, cucumber and mint. Somewhat unusual for a Middle Eastern restaurant, Mary'z doesn't serve lamb at dinner, just chicken and beef, though that might change. Snapper is the only other protein that makes it as an entrée. The kabobs, with moist and slightly charred beef or chicken, might be things to order here. These are also available as large pita-wrapped sandwiches. The *shawarmas* are decent, if not quite ready for Hillcroft. These can feature meat that is little dry, and not helped by the lack of much juice from the somewhat underripe tomato slices. These can also be under-seasoned, even with the lauded garlic sauce that, at times, is not applied liberally enough. Service is seemingly unfailingly cheerful, if not terribly polished. You are often greeted by one of the family when entering and leaving, which helps to make you feel some more at home, and root for this place to grow.

Masala Wok $8

10001 Westheimer (between Gessner and the Beltway) 77042, (713) 784-8811
www.masalawok.com

Cuisine - Indian
Hours - Mon-Thu, Sun 11AM-10PM; Fri-Sat 11AM-11PM
Credit Cards - Amex, Discover, MC, Visa
Service - Table Service
Alcohol - NONE

Entrée Prices - $7 to $9 ($8 average)
Entrées $12 and less - 100%

Atmosphere & Décor - Comfortable
Appeal - Good value Indian food with an Indo-Chinese twist done quickly
Useful to Note - This concept has already been replicated in the Dallas area.
Menu Suggestions - Karahi Chicken (chicken sautéed with a mild curry sauce); Chicken Tikka Masala (marinated and grilled chicken cubes served in a creamy tomato sauce); Paneer Butter Masala (cubes of cheese served in a creamy tomato

sauce); Stir Fry (a mix of stir-fried vegetables served in a light, ginger-based sauce); Chole Masala (garbanzo beans stewed in a curry sauce with cilantro)

Masala Wok is an aptly named, slickly designed and well-run fast-casual restaurant that began in 2006 that is well-suited for the numerous Westchase area office workers with roots in the Subcontinent, and anyone who enjoys generally well prepared food with some *masala*-tinged flavor. It's a bright and genuinely cheery place, at least during the lunch hours. Masala Wok serves many familiar Indian dishes and Chinese-Indian items that are popular in large Indian cities such as Bangalore, if not yet Houston. The latter are served with rice or noodles and described as a "blend of Chinese wok cooking and traditional Indian spices". Part of the appeal here is that all of the food is prepared to order, quality ingredients and freshly ground spices are noticeably employed, and the breads are freshly baked. Plus, there is a choice among vegetables, *paneer* (fresh cheese), chicken, lamb or shrimp for the protein for many of the dishes (in ascending order of price), and the food is served more quickly and conveniently. The concept seems to be working, as the dining room is packed during most weekday lunchtimes. It should be easy to find some desirable options among the roughly thirty entrées. With the choice of main item, this leads to almost 150 possible combinations. Casual Indian food fans will enjoy the fact that the spiciness can be ordered mild, medium, or (fairly) spicy, and quickly recognize dishes like Chicken *Tikka Masala* (marinated and grilled chicken served in a creamy tomato-based sauce), curry with lamb, and *biriyani* (long-grain rice cooked with meats or vegetables). There are also soups, starters, a couple of wraps made with fresh *naan*, and desserts, including Houston's favorite, *tres leches*. The menu is well-explained, and the friendly staff is quick to provide explanations. The flavors here are toned down somewhat, and less complex than in many local Indian restaurants (which is very noticeable in their simple *korma* items), but the dishes are usually clean-tasting, and possibly healthier. That, but mostly because it is not an all-you-can-eat buffet for lunch, you will likely feel far less stuffed than coming from most other Indian restaurants. The rice is always properly cooked and the *naan*, which accompanies the *masala* entrees, is always warm from the oven and tasty. There are even numerous enticing vegetarian choices and even some appealing low carb items. Most of the crowd is Indian or Pakistani, which might allay some concerns about the authenticity of the dishes or the proficiency of the kitchen. The meats are *halal*, too.

Maxey's Cajun Patio & Grill $6

14507 S. Post Oak (between W. Orem and Fuqua) 77045, (713) 434-1100

Cuisine - Cajun; Hamburgers
Hours - Mon-Thu 11AM to 10PM; Fri-Sat 11AM to 12AM; Sun 12 to 8PM

Credit Cards - NONE
Service - Counter Service
Alcohol - NONE

Entrée Prices - $3 to $9 ($6 average)
Entrées $12 and less - 100%

Atmosphere & Décor - Not much; only three outside tables for seating
Appeal - Excellent South Louisiana-style food, hamburgers and fried catfish
Useful to Note - Good source for bulk orders of boudin and Cajun fried turkeys.
Menu Suggestions - hamburgers; boudin; boudin balls; Creole Hot Sausage Sandwich; Whole Catfish Dinner; Seafood Gumbo; fries; onion rings

For over twenty-five years, Maxey's Cajun Patio & Grill (formerly Cajun's Patio & Grill) has flown under the radar screen for the vast majority of local diners, even though it's only one of a very small handful of area restaurants that have been profiled on a show on the Food Network. No telling how it caught their attention as the local press had missed it other than one brief visit from a *Chronicle* reporter at the end of the 1990s that resulted in a short article. It's not surprising, as it is an extremely modest, relatively low volume establishment that is located on what has long been a forlorn section of South Post Oak; just a few miles down the road from Meyerland, but a world away. But, it's worthy of notice, as Maxey's does a great job with a small menu of South Louisiana and other locally popular informal items, including one of the top hamburgers in town. Before venturing out to it, you'll need to note that it's mostly a takeaway operation, and it might be good to call ahead with your order. There are only three concrete tables with benches in front for seating. Not much atmosphere and no air conditioning. You're here entirely for the food, though.

A very experienced and more-than-competent hand in the kitchen and a lot of pride with what comes out are a couple of the reasons why the food is so good here. With the exception of the necessarily long-simmered dishes such as chili and chitterlings, it is all cooked to order from the spacious and suitably very clean kitchen. Turnaround is not very quick, and often it is quite slow, but it's definitely worth the wait for the hearty fare. The fryer is used to good effect. Fries, onion rings, boudin, pork chops, shrimp, trout, catfish and even whole turkeys emerge with properly golden-hued, intact battering, covering succulent, perfectly cooked flesh. The top-notch hamburgers begin with a hand-formed patty that is usually charred to blackness on the outside, but retains proper juiciness inside. Served with a buttered and toasted buns, these patties are a quarter-pound in size. A second patty is just a buck and a quarter more. The sandwiches, featuring fried items or otherwise, are also very good. These are served on thick slices of Texas Toast. The one with Creole Hot Sausage is very good, though the sausage is not terribly spicy, but rather mostly garlicky and quite flavorful. This and the other sandwiches are served "all-the-way" with plenty of mayonnaise, pickles, lettuce and tomatoes. The crisp onion rings are some of the best in the area. The fries are quite tasty when eating at the restaurant, but don't have the necessary crispness to last for much of a journey.

Maxey's might make the best boudin in the Houston area. If you are hankering for the taste of those Acadiana convenience stores that invariably sell the best boudin, and haven't been satisfied with the different-tasting local versions, Maxey's excellent non-smoked creations might just satisfy. These might taste even better deep-fried as boudin balls. The swampy, homey gumbo sports a tasty, dark roux and possibly the most abundant amount of shrimp, crab, sausage and chicken that can possibly fit into pint-size soup container. The crab will slide easily from the small claws as the gumbo is cooked for such a long time. Ordering it on a Saturday afternoon you might be eating gumbo that has stewed since Wednesday. In addition to its lunch and dinner dishes, Maxey's is a great idea for bulk orders of boudin and the Cajun fried turkeys. The friendly and accommodating owner seems to have a genuine affection for folks who like good food. And his food certainly is.

Mayuri $12

5857 Westheimer (just west of Fountain View) 77057, (713) 975-6565
www.mayuri.com

Cuisine - Indian
Hours - Daily 11AM to 2:30PM, 5:30 to 10PM
Credit Cards - Amex, Discover, MC, Visa
Service - Table Service
Alcohol - Beer & Wine

Entrée Prices - Dinner - $9 to $16 ($12 average); Lunch Buffet - $10
Entrées at Dinner $12 and less - 80%

Atmosphere & Décor - Pleasant
Appeal - Bounteous buffet at lunch including dosas; large menu at dinner
Useful to Note - During lunch you get fresh dosas from the guy in the booth.
Menu Suggestions - Tandoori Chicken (yogurt marinated chicken legs and baked in a tandoor oven); Chicken Kandhari Kabob (marinated and baked chicken in a thick, spicy sauce); Mayuri Special Chicken; Mayuri Lamb Special (stewed lamb in a thick sauce)

Named after the national bird of India, which is not the chicken *tikka masala,* by the way, Mayuri is a large and attractive spot for well-made northern and southern Indian food plus the popular-in-Mumbai Chinese-Indian dishes.

The menu is very lengthy and expansive by local Indian restaurant standards, but the prime attraction for most is the menu-free lunchtime buffet. Though the other restaurants in the shopping center might be empty during the extended lunchtime hours, there is a good chance that Mayuri will be packed for its buffet, mostly with Indian patrons. Don't be surprised if you have to wait a few minutes for a table around noon. The requisite Indian restaurant all-you-can-eat lunch spread is plentiful and changes daily. There might be an array of curry dishes with goat, chicken, or vegetables, tandoor chicken, and a slew of chutneys, soups and *sambals* (accompaniments to the rice and curries) and fresh fruits. *Naan* and the light crêpe-like *dosas* are continuously made during the lunchtime hours by a man in a small windowed room adjacent to the buffet and these are laid on the counter when finished. The sauces in the dishes are noticeably thinner, and maybe lighter, than at other local places, but are still very flavorful. That American and British favorite Butter Chicken is very good; especially tasty since the buttery, if not heavy sauce, is studded with pieces of the extremely tasty tandoor chicken, which is somewhat unusual. This bright red chicken is moist, and more flavorful than at most area restaurants, especially on a buffet. The *kheer* and *gulab jamen* (rosewater-scented donut balls) are not quite as viscous and tasty, respectively, as at most other places. But, these are offered daily, as is soft-serve ice cream, which seems to be a favorite on at least a couple of continents.

There might be something for nearly everyone during dinner time. In case you need time to peruse the menu, Mayuri offers over forty appetizers and about twenty-five soups, each listed as either vegetarian or non-vegetarian. The menu also designates a number of side dishes like *dosas* in a variety of styles and *parathas* (stuffed flat wheat bread) as specifically northern or southern for your edification. For entrées, there are plenty of vegetarian dishes, chicken and lamb and a lesser number of seafood, which is either shrimp or some kind of fish fillet. Each of these can be served as part of multi-course *thali*. All of the expected dishes are offered, and more. There are several dishes baked in the *tandoor* oven, for which Mayuri seems to have a very good hand, *biryanis* (fragrant long-grain rice cooked with a choice of toppings), and a number of different types of breads. Plus, there are about fifty Indo-Chinese dishes.

McGonigel's Mucky Duck $10

2425 Norfolk (a block east of Kirby) 77098, (713) 528-5999
www.mcgonigels.com

Cuisine - Irish; American
Hours - Mon-Sat 11AM to 2AM (kitchen closes earlier)

Credit Cards - Amex, Diners, MC, Visa
Service - Table Service
Alcohol - Full Bar

Entrée Prices - $7 to $13 ($10 average)
Entrées $12 and less - 90%

Atmosphere & Décor - Nice
Appeal - Very good pub fare and hearty sandwiches; and, great bands, too
Useful to Note - This is primarily a live music venue at night.
Menu Suggestions - Fish & Chips; Shepherd's Pie (ground beef and mushrooms topped with mashed potatoes and cheddar cheese then baked); The Mark Portugal Sandwich (sliced turkey, avocado and bacon with melted cheese on a French roll); Texas BLT (bacon, lettuce, tomato, avocado and jalapeños)

McGonigel's Mucky Duck, or simply the Mucky Duck, is first and foremost an excellent small showcase club for live music. It is an intimate spot to catch top regional and national acts such as Jack Ingram, Okkervill River, Kelly Willis, and the legendary Texas troubadour Alejandro Escovedo, who long ago bummed a ride on the rock 'n' roller coaster. But, the adept kitchen makes the Mucky Duck a worthy stop even when there are no performers. The food is far better than it has to be. The kitchen does a great job with food well-suited for the setting and the liquid offerings. This is pub fare of the quality that would be difficult to find in the less food-friendly cities on the other side of the Atlantic.

The generally hearty offerings are divided among Irish and British specialties and basic American dishes such as hamburgers, hot sandwiches and soups and salads. The Fish & Chips, made with beer-battered cod, and served with fries and cole slaw is very good, and always worth ordering, as is the similar Fish & Mash (with mashed potatoes). Another traditional pub dish that's well prepared here is the waistline-expanding Shepherd's Pie, ground beef and mushrooms that are topped with mashed potatoes and sprinkled with shredded cheddar cheese then baked. Among the other similar dishes are a Scotch Egg, Welsh Rarebit (aged sharp English cheddar and ale baked over toast and topped with bacon and sautéed mushrooms), wild Smoked Scottish Salmon, beef stew made with Guinness, and the Ploughman's Lunch (English cheeses, French bread and a pickle). The Mucky Duck even serves the real kidney pie. Actually, Steak, Kidney and Mushroom Pie, so there are more familiar meat pieces in the mix. If traditional pub fare does not entice, there are salads and very good sandwiches. One of the best sandwiches is The Mark Portugal, sliced turkey with avocado slices and topped with melted Muenster cheese and a large strip of bacon on a crusty French roll that is served warm. It's named after the former beer-loving Astros pitcher who was a regular at the Mucky Duck while he pitched here in the 1990s. The other sandwiches include a Roast Turkey, Veggie Melt, Grilled Chicken, Philly Cheese Steak, Sirloin Steak, a couple burgers, BLT, and the Texas BLT (which adds avocado and jalapeños). The salads can be hearty such as the Grilled Steak Salad and the McGonigel's Salad, each with crumbled blue cheese and a walnut-based vinaigrette, with strips of grilled ribeye and roast turkey, respectively. There is also the Grilled Chicken Salad and the Greek Salad for a somewhat lighter meal.

The setting is quaint. A small stage sits at one corner to your left when entering. An attractive bar that holds a good number of beer taps flanks the far wall, a line of tables sitting on a slightly raised platform on the near wall, and in the center of this main room tables are set closely together. It's a comfortable place. The cheesy bookcase wallpaper and the white acoustic ceiling tiles are easy to ignore, and the often-unfriendly person at the door is usually quick to forget once you've settled in at night. The Mucky Duck works well for lunch, dinner, or just a drink, before or after a show in the evening. There are nearly 30 beers on tap (served in proper 20-ounce Imperial pint glasses), plus a good selection in bottles, and an interesting, well-chosen, and well-explained small wine list. There are several sparklers to help with any celebration. Mucky Duck is ready with the Cristal in case 50 Cent or Jay-Z makes an acoustic appearance.

The Memorial Grill $10

14510 Memorial (between Kirkwood and Dairy Ashford) 77079, (281) 496-1780

Cuisine - American
Hours - Mon-Thu, Sun 11AM-9PM; Fri-Sat 11AM-10PM
Credit Cards - Amex, Discover, MC, Visa
Service - Table Service
Alcohol - Beer & Wine

Entrée Prices - $7 to $18 ($10 average)
Entrées $12 and less - 90%

Atmosphere & Décor - Friendly and functional; can get loud when crowded
Appeal - Generally well-made familiar food
Menu Suggestions - The Fat Frank (all-beef foot long hot dog topped with chili); Roasted Poblano Cheeseburger; Black and Bleu Bacon Burger

Located directly across the street from Leibman's Wine & Fine Foods, with a capable kitchen and friendly, earnest service, Memorial Grill has become another comfortable addition to this west Memorial neighborhood and seems to have patrons whenever the doors are open. The fare here is what most of the world would quickly term, "American". Among the roughly sixty entrées are a number of half-pound hamburgers, salads including Caesar and Cobb, cold sandwiches, several grilled chicken breast dishes, and steaks. It's also the type of cooking that readily appeals to most long-time west side Houstonians. Memorial Grill also serves pastas including regionally attuned fettuccine Alfredo with shrimp and a cream sauce flavored with jalapeños and cilantro. In American fashion, you can create your own combination with a choice among four dried pastas, eight sauces and four meats or shrimp. For all the dishes, the spicing is relatively light here, and the several types of cheeses that can accompany the hamburgers, sandwiches and salads are strictly industrially made, as at most local restaurants in this price range. But, this small place does other things to try to stand out: the nearly ten sides can be quite good, including the nicely chunky, tasty skin-on mashed potatoes, and the crisp fries sprinkled with seasoned salt; the burgers and sandwiches are served on good quality whole wheat buns and bread; the five salad dressings are made in-house; and the choice for the fish fillets extends well beyond the ubiquitous grilled salmon to include swordfish with barbecue sauce, tuna and sole with the classically inspired *meunière* sauce. Set in what was once a fast food restaurant, the single dining room is cramped with about twenty tables and booths in utilitarian fashion. The closeness of the tables and tiled floors can make for some loud dining when the restaurant is crowded, but it's quite comfortable at most times. Ice tea and water come in large, thick glasses and a plump slice of lemon. To finish, Memorial Grill has about a dozen cakes and pies. All look good in the display. The apple and pecan pies, maybe more so, since these are made at the restaurant.

Mexico's Deli $5

2374 Dairy Ashford (between Westheimer and Briar Forest) 77077, (281) 679-7790

Cuisine - Mexican (taqueria)
Hours - Mon-Thu 9AM to 10PM; Fri-Sat 9AM to 11PM; Sun 9AM to 9PM
Credit Cards - MC, Visa
Service - Counter Service
Alcohol - NONE; BYOB

Entrée Prices - Dinner & Lunch - \$3 to \$6 (\$5 average); Breakfast - \$4 to \$5
Entrées at Dinner \$12 and less - 100%

Atmosphere & Décor - Casual, appropriate and inviting
Appeal - Quite possibly the best tortas in the area, and for cheap
Useful to Note - One sandwich might be enough for two small appetites.
Menu Suggestions - Torta with oven roasted pork loin; Torta al pastor; Torta with chorizo, mozzarella and mushrooms; Torta with shredded chicken and mole poblano; Torta with milanesa and mozzarella; Tacos al pastor; Eggs in Mole Sauce

Excellent, hot Mexican-style sandwiches, which are not only delicious, but a great value is the simple reason to visit here. There are over twenty *tortas*, plus soups, tacos, burritos, grilled items (*alambres*), *pambazos* (tasty, but very messy *guajillo* chile-dipped stuffed sandwiches), and breakfast, all prepared to order on the flat grills and a meat-laden spinner in the open kitchen. This comfortable, low-key and informal small eatery with muted brass and copper hues has a proper modern Mexican feel for its *torta*-centric menu. These large sandwiches are served on airy *telera* bread, which is light, relatively thin and quite flavorful, if barely containing the bounteous filling. It might take a while to properly digest the wide array of tempting sandwiches on this small menu. The primary fillings include steak in the nutty and piquant cascabel chile sauce, fajitas, chicken fajitas, *chorizo*, sirloin, shredded chicken, roasted pork (*al pastor*) cut from a spinner, shredded pork or chicken with the dark, piquant *adobo* sauce, and *milanesas* (breaded cutlets) with beef, chicken and even veal. Many are served with melted cheese, usually mild *Chihuahua* or mozzarella, or for some reason, American cheese-food. Most come with sliced avocados, raw onion, tomatoes, jalapeños and refried beans, plus a choice of smoky or sweet-and-spicy salsas to further enliven the sandwiches that can be brought to your table in large canisters. This might take a special request when they are very busy. For frequent *taqueria* patrons, the Spanish and English descriptions don't always exactly jive, but no matter, the results will be satisfying. These are some of the best *tortas* and hot sandwiches around. It's almost impossible to make a misstep when ordering any one of the *tortas*. The meats are reliably moist and flavorful, the other ingredients are tasty and complementary, and the combinations always work. These are also some of the most attractive *tortas* around, though generously filled, these can quickly become messy. Mexico's Deli is subtitled, "Tortas & Tacos", and there are several taco plates with three tacos with a choice among a handful of meats, including pork chop (*chuleta*) and a cup of charro beans. The larger burritos come with an even greater choice of fillings. The couple salads include that Tijuana-created Italian-American classic, Caesar salad, made entrée-size with grilled chicken. The ten or so breakfast dishes are meant for dine-in, including the breakfast tacos, which come in orders of three. There are also a couple omelets, *huevos rancheros, huevos a la mexicana, chilaquiles* without eggs, and the locally unusual eggs cooked over easy with the dark brown *mole poblano*. There's no beer here, but there are the Mexican sodas, coffee, juices and a small handful of *aguas frescas*, which are made in house.

Miguelito's $9

5506 Richmond (between Rice and Chimney Rock) 77056, (713) 783-8644
www.miguelitos.net

Cuisine - Venezuelan
Hours - Mon-Thu, Sun 11AM to 9PM; Fri 11AM to 12AM; Sat 11AM to 3AM
Credit Cards - MC, Visa
Service - Table Service; Delivery within 3 miles
Alcohol - NONE; BYOB

Entrée Prices - $6 to $10 ($9 average)
Entrées $12 and less - 100%

Atmosphere & Décor - Quaint and comfortable
Appeal - Tasty and inexpensive tropical fare in a homey setting
Useful to Note - Some Spanish might be helpful.
Menu Suggestions - Milanesa de Carne (breaded beef cutlet); Pabellón Criollo (mixed plate with shredded beef, black beans, rice and fried sweet plantains); Asado Negro (pot roast served with semi-sweet rice)

The small, homey restaurant is decorated with Venezuelan folk art, photos, and Venezuelan television is usually on the air here. Most of the patrons seem to be Venezuelan, but Miguelitos has its charms for more than for Venezuelans desiring a taste of home. The kitchen turns out usually flavorful and often hearty fare in seemingly consistent fashion. It's a friendly, relaxed place, as service can often lag, but the food and value make this easy to overlook. The Venezuelan cuisine here is quite similar to many of those restaurants whose homelands share the Gulf of Mexico: Colombia, Cuba, Puerto Rico, Dominican Republic and the countries of Central America. The flavors are straightforward, sometimes sweet, but not spicy, and the dishes are usually filling. White rice, sweet and green plantains, yucca, stewed beef and chicken, the breaded *milanesas* and *empanadas* make up much of the menu. *Arepas,* corn pockets, are available plain or with a variety of fillings such as cheese, shredded beef, chicken, cheese, ham, black beans, pork and more unique items. These and the somewhat similar *empanadas* along with a couple unique soups are popular ways to preface the nearly twenty entrées. Beef and chicken predominate, but there are also pork chops and shrimp and fish. But, there's no *capybara,* the retriever-sized rodent that's a delicacy in Venezuela. The *milanesa* with tender beef is much better than the bland chicken version. The beef dishes are generally the best ones to order here. The mixed plate *Pabellón Criollo* that features a flavorful, moist shredded beef along with white rice, stewed black beans and fried sweet plantains is an enjoyable way to sample the cuisine. To finish, there is *tres leches,* of course, plus flan, cheesecake and *arroz con leche* (rice pudding) that are each complemented by the fine *café con leche*. You'll notice brightly colored fruit drinks on many of the tables. There are ten or so tropical flavors that can also be blended with milk. Miguelito's doesn't serve alcohol, as it's located across from a school, but it has a welcoming BYOB policy that can make the visit even more pleasurable.

Mint Café $11

2800 Sage (at W. Alabama) 77056, (713) 622-3434
www.mintcafehouston.com

Cuisine - Middle Eastern
Hours - Mon-Thu 11AM to 11PM; Sun 12 to 9PM
Credit Cards - Amex, Discover, MC, Visa
Service - Counter Service; Delivery with a three-mile radius
Alcohol - Beer & Wine

Entrée Prices - $7 to $17 ($11 average)
Entrées $12 and less - 80%

Atmosphere & Décor - Cool
Appeal - Hip and friendly café with attractive Middle Eastern fare
Menu Suggestions - Makanek Sandwich (sautéed sausages wrapped in pita bread with tomatoes and pickles); Chicken Shawarma Sandwich; namoura (yogurt-based cake)

Mint Café is certainly the sleekest and most attractive local Middle Eastern restaurant. The one dining room that might be able to squeeze in 40 patrons features modern, mostly minimalist design employing warm tones of various shades of browns in attractive, alternating-colored square tiles with sleek dark chairs, tables, a half dozen low banquettes, and a counter for single diners. The effect is both cool and comfortable. The shaded sidewalk patio is often in use with smokers and conversationalists, often enjoying tea or one of the several freshly squeezed fruit juices. The counter area at the opposite end of the restaurant from the entrance is set with a few tempting trays of salads and dips situated in front of the grills and spinners of chicken and beef, and just below the flat-panel display of the menu. A readily available paper menu or the welcoming and friendly staff will be quick to provide help with explanations of the dishes. Whatever you choose will be very attractively presented on oversized plates and interestingly designed serving bowls, which will be nicely prefaced by pita chips and a dark olive paste.

The offerings here are similar to other local Middle Eastern restaurants with a few surprises. Among the dozen appetizers are artichoke hearts with garlic, cilantro and olive oil (*ardishawki*), and fava beans with garlic, tomatoes and olive oil (*fool*). The *hummus* is rather bland, as is the *baba ganoush,* which can also have an unwelcome stringy consistency. There are soups and verdant and vibrant salads including *tabouli* and Caesar salad.

The grill and the spinner are in use for the most of the pita-wrapped sandwiches and similar entrées. The expected *shawarmas* and kabobs are a big part of the menu. These are presented somewhat differently, additionally warmed and cut into thirds for a nice effect. The ground meat *kafta* kabob features ground beef, and maybe conscious of its Galleria location, lamb's only appearance on the menu is as part of a gyro. The sandwiches are generally pretty good, even better with some bright red hot sauce, with the sausage *makanek* and moist chicken probably the best two. The daily specials, which are more elaborate dishes, are the favorites of regular patrons. Though the kitchen has not been as consistent or as proficient as some other Middle Eastern restaurants, the décor, and genuine warmth and evident hard work of the staff help to compensate for this. You get the impression that this place will continue to improve. And, the setting is cool, in any case.

Miss Saigon Café $13

5503 Kelvin (at Times) 77005, (713) 942-0108

Cuisine - Vietnamese
Hours - Mon-Thu 11AM to 3PM, 5 to 9PM; Fri 11AM to 3PM, 5 to 9:30PM; Sat 11AM to 9:30PM
Credit Cards - MC, Visa
Service - Counter Service
Alcohol - Beer & Wine

Entrée Prices - Dinner - $8 to $18 ($13 average); Lunch - $7 to $15
Entrées at Dinner $12 and less - 40%

Atmosphere & Décor - Charming and comfortable
Appeal - A good Vietnamese option in the Rice Village
Useful to Note - Pho is only served from Thursday through Saturday.
Menu Suggestions - Spicy Lemongrass Chicken; Beef Ginger; Vietnamese Crêpe (rice flour crêpe with pork, shrimp and bean sprouts)

Miss Saigon Café is an inviting small restaurant located in the heart of the Rice Village shopping area. It is a nice fit in the panoply of ethnic eateries in the neighborhood. A big part of the charm is Miss Saigon's very pleasant ambiance, something missing from most small restaurants in Houston, and most Vietnamese eateries of almost every stripe. This restaurant features an attractive, small and comfortable dining area, and large curtained windows facing the retail shops in the Rice Village. One wall features a large, nicely executed mural of a pre-war Saigon street scene. A nice wood bar sits at the rear of the one small dining room with about a dozen tables.

The menu items are certainly Vietnamese, but the selections and to a lesser extent, the preparations are both more assimilated and approachable than most. The presentations are nicer, too. This is a restaurant that has to compete with the wide array of quality restaurants in the Village, rather than focusing mostly on the Vietnamese community, as most its brethren do. The menu has more than enough inviting selections, but compared to many local Vietnamese restaurants with hundreds of choices, this one is downright puny with less than forty, including desserts. But, most of the Vietnamese favorites are here, and nearly all of the choices seem appealing. For appetizers, there are four types of spring rolls and the fried spring rolls, the popular Imperial rolls, just called egg rolls here. The fried calamari with a dip of aïoli, ancho pepper and jalapeños is a comfortable, if somewhat unexpected, choice for an appetizer. Entrées run from $8 on the low end to $18 for salmon cooked with Vietnamese flair. One of the highlights is the Spicy Lemongrass Chicken. There are a couple dishes cooked in small clay pots. One features caramelized salmon, the other mixed seafood. Among the other plate selections are a couple curry dishes, a vegetarian stir-fry, a Vietnamese crêpe with either shrimp or pork, and a steamed fish fillet with mushroom, scallions, ginger and cilantro. There are several traditional *bun* dishes made with vermicelli rice noodles, bean sprouts, shredded lettuce, cucumbers, carrots, crushed peanuts, cilantro and the fish sauce. These come with several toppings: char-grilled pork, Vietnamese egg rolls, char-grilled tofu, grilled shrimp, char-grilled chicken and combinations thereof. As with all of the other places, the marinated, thinly sliced char-grilled pork, either alone or with the Vietnamese egg rolls, is the best of these dishes.

For the expense-conscious, and lunchtime patrons, Miss Saigon offers a couple Vietnamese sandwiches, one with char-grilled pork, and the other with the somewhat unusual shredded rotisserie chicken. These feature a toasted French baguette with mayonnaise, cucumbers, marinated carrots, cilantro and jalapeño slices. Though quite satisfying, for around seven bucks, these sandwiches are more than triple the price of similar sandwiches at Vietnamese sandwich shops in the Chinatowns. It's a deal in any other sense of comparison, though. The hearty beef broth soup, *pho,* is similarly expensive, and, unfortunately only available from Thursdays through Saturday. It's a good restaurant, and fairly priced for the quality in relationship with non-Vietnamese restaurants. But, especially for value, it suffers somewhat in comparison with the Vietnamese places in Midtown and New Chinatown. It is far more charming, attractive and service-oriented than those places, and Miss Saigon Café certainly provides enough value for the Rice Village area with its quality and quantity.

Mission Burritos $8

2245 W. Alabama (between Greenbriar and Kirby) 77098, (713) 529-0535
1609 Durham (south of I-10) 77007, (713) 426-6003
www.missionburritos.com

Cuisine - Tex-Mex
Hours - Mon-Fri 11AM to 10PM; Sat 11AM to 10PM; Sun 11AM to 9PM
Credit Cards - Amex, Discover, MC, Visa
Service - Counter Service
Alcohol - W. Alabama - Beer, Wine & Margaritas; Durham - Beer & Wine

Entrée Prices - $6 to $12 ($8 average)
Entrées $12 and less - 100%

Atmosphere & Décor - Comfortable, cool; patio
Appeal - Good, freshly made burritos - lots of tasty calories for cheap
Useful to Note - Possibly the best place in town for a lot of calories quickly.
Menu Suggestions - burritos; fish tacos

Mission Burritos was the local response to the national wrap fad that began in the 1990s. Given the ubiquity of very good Tex-Mex and Mexican restaurants in the area, it is no surprise that the burritos here are much better than the ones from any of the imports. Each of the Mission Burritos spots is stylish, featuring Catholic (hence, "Mission") iconography throughout the restaurants, and are a worthwhile stop for a quick, informal meal. It's fresh food fast, as is subtitled on the menu. Turnaround time is quick. The food is very good, and a great value. The calorie-dollar ratio is quite high at Mission Burritos.

The drill is to join the queue in the cafeteria-like assembly line. For the namesake burritos, it begins with your selection of a fresh large tortilla, either flour or wheat; then the meat, seafood or grilled vegetables; and then the rest of ingredients which are chosen one-by-one until it is wrapped up. The array of roughly two dozen different and high quality ingredients that will be part of your customized burrito includes rice, beans (black or pinto), guacamole, grated cheese, cilantro, avocado, onions, jalapeños, fresh or pickled, roasted red peppers and various salsas. Both the beef and chicken are quite good, though the nod might go to the beef version that features cubes of steak that are always moist and flavorful with proper hints of the grill. There is also a vegetarian version (sautéed spinach, mushrooms or the roasted red peppers), and, for an additional charge, ones with citrus-marinated grilled shrimp or clean-tasting tilapia, or breaded and fried catfish. The regular size burrito is enough, or more than enough for most people. It's a great value, too. The super size, for just about twice the price, is for small families or those in training for morbid obesity. Though burritos are the biggest draw, Mission Burritos also serves chicken and a vegetarian tortilla soup, salad with a choice of toppings and house-made dressings, *gordita*-like grilled cheese, stuffed jalapeños, and tacos made with a choice among corn, flour or crispy tortillas. The manageably sized tacos filled with fried catfish pieces, grated cheese, cilantro, onions, lettuce and tomatillo salsa in corn tortillas are especially satisfying.

Morningside Thai $11

6710 Morningside (just north of Holcombe) 77030, (713) 661-4400

Cuisine - Thai
Hours - Mon-Fri 11AM to 2:30PM, 5 to 10PM; Sat 11:30AM to 10PM; Sun 5 to 10PM
Credit Cards - Amex, Diners, Discover, MC, Visa
Service - Table Service; Delivery
Alcohol - Beer & Wine

Entrée Prices - $7 to $18 ($11 average)
Entrées $12 and less - 90%

Atmosphere & Décor - Pleasant
Appeal - Reliable Thai near the Medical Center
Menu Suggestions - Tom Ka Gai (soup with coconut milk and lemongrass); Red Curry (chicken simmered in red chili paste, coconut milk and kaffir lime leaves); Gai Lard Prik (a fried chicken breast covered in chili sauce and served with grilled plantains); Beef Panang

Located in a somewhat ramshackle house on Morningside, just north of Holcombe, Morningside Thai, or the Original Morningside Thai, as it was formerly known, has been providing reliable Thai food for the nearby Medical Center workers, and residents of the nearby Southampton and West University since 1982. This is almost ancient by Houston restaurant standards. It's a friendly, neighborhood place that provides proficient Thai food for dine-in, takeout or delivery, but for some reason, it appears to be empty quite often. Most of the popular Thai items are offered at Morningside Thai and the menu will be familiar to most infrequent Thai restaurant-goers. The well-focused menu is conveniently organized with the following sections: appetizers, soup, Thai-style salad, curry, poultry, seafood, beef, pork, vegetables, fried rice, and noodles. There are red, yellow and green curry dishes made with coconut milk along with a dry curry dish. The beef dishes are a nice value, as most of the beef dishes feature a half-pound of beef, and the menu states that it serves only certified Angus beef. Their version of the curry Beef Panang is especially good. There are almost a dozen vegetarian dishes. In user-friendly fashion, they can also substitute tofu in most of the other preparations. Something to note for those who take home the leftovers, or who order too much food for takeout, the food from Morningside Thai seems to last longer than those from other restaurants. This seems due to the proclivity of the kitchen to use a lot of lime in many of the dishes, and this acts as a preservative.

Mucho Mexico $11

1310 N. Wayside (south of I-10) 77020, (713) 673-4598
www.muchomexicorestaurant.com

Cuisine - Mexican
Hours - Mon-Thu 9AM to 11AM; Fri-Sat 8AM to 1:30AM; Sun 8AM to 11AM
Credit Cards - Amex, Diners, Discover, MC, Visa
Service - Table Service
Alcohol - Full Bar

Entrée Prices - Dinner - $5 to $19 ($11 avg.); Lunch - $5 to $8; Breakfast - $5 to $8
Entrées at Dinner $12 and less - 70%

Atmosphere & Décor - Comfortable
Appeal - Usually very good hearty Mexican cooking
Useful to Note - Live music nightly; there is an adjoining bakery.
Menu Suggestions - Carne Huasteca (marinated, thinly sliced steak); Chiles Rellenos; Chicken fajitas; molcajeteada salsa (a spicy salsa); Migas Mucho Mexico; Huevos Mucho Loco (eggs scrambled with potatoes, bacon and salsa)

The menu at the solo Mucho Mexico is less *mucho* than it used to be. It's more focused with regional, northern Mexico-inspired meat-laden specialties, several combination plates, and Gulf seafood dishes comprising most of the current offerings. Opened in 1971, Mucho Mexico is a family operated restaurant that strives to offer authentic home-style Mexican cooking. It seems to have succeeded, as it's still often crowded with Hispanic families from the nearby east side neighborhoods. But, this location is fairly accessible for those not on the east side, as it is only a few minutes east of downtown on I-10. It's easy for those working downtown to enjoy one of Mucho Mexico's nearly twenty value-priced lunch specials.

There should be something for everyone at Mucho Mexico, as there is much on the menu. Very thick chips with salsa precede the meal. Though the salsas placed on the table are sufficient, ask for the house special fiery, yet very flavorful *molcajeteada* salsa if you want some added spice. If the chips are not enough, you can start with nachos with a choice of toppings, jalapeños stuffed with cheese and crab meat, *queso flameado,* mostly melted white cheese here, Tex-Mex-style *quesadillas* or *chile con queso*. There are a number of salads and soups. The brothy soups-as-meals, *caldos*, include soups of beef, chicken, fish, shrimp and mixed seafood, and are popular with its East End clientele. Mucho Mexico also serves *Caldo Tlalpeño*, a soup initially from Mexico City that is made with shredded chicken breast, slice of avocado, tortilla strips and *chipotle* chiles. *Menudo* (described as "the best for hung-overs and breakfast") is served daily. Many of the most appealing dishes are listed under the headings of *Platillos Mexicanos* and *Especialidades*. These include *Carnitas Estilo Mexico* (slices of pork), *Steak a la Mexicana* (chopped sirloin steak sautéed with onions, tomatoes, hot peppers in a fresh tomato sauce), *Carne Guisada* (stewed beef), *Carne Huasteca* (thin sirloin cooked with *adobo* sauce), the dark brown *Mole Poblano*, *Milanesa Cordon Azul* (breaded beef cutlet filled with ham and a couple cheeses), *Filete con Championones* (a grilled rib-eye topped with mushrooms), and probably a fitting number of enchilada choices. There are several interesting items from the grill like the *Carne Asadas* on the menu, which are first marinated, then grilled. In addition to the popular fajitas, there are *Costillas de Res* (beef short ribs), *Alambres* (shish kabobs with beef), a couple steaks, and *parrilladas*, the mixed grills featuring several items. Among the highlights is the chicken fajitas dish served as one large slice of grilled chicken breast. On the more inexpensive end, Mucho Mexico serves *tortas* (the Mexican-style sandwiches), tacos and *tostadas*. The tacos are only available as plates, and one order features several tacos, which should satiate most appetites. Though meat is probably the biggest draw, Mucho Mexico is subtitled with, "Seafood Bar", so the seafood offerings are more than incidental. In addition to the seafood soups, there are sections featuring cooked seafood dishes (*Mariscos*), and another for marinated, raw seafood dishes (*Del Oyster Bar*). Each is "made fresh when ordered" according to the menu, in case you had any concerns. There are many different preparations of Gulf shrimp and other bounty of the Gulf. For the true fisherman, as the menu states, or maybe a couple, is the *Huachinango Frito*, an entire fried red snapper.

Opened each day at nine in the morning they offer most of the popular Mexican breakfast plates among the nearly ten selections (and listed under *Almuerzos* instead of *Desayunos*). Each is well prepared and expectedly robust. These include *Huevos Rancheros, Migas, Machacado con Huevo* (scrambled eggs with dried beef), *Huevos con Chorizo*, and *Chilaquiles Michoacon* (pieces of tortilla, green onions and cilantro cooked in cascabel chile salsa then topped with *queso fresco*, though no eggs), *Chicharron con Huevo en Salsa* (pork rinds and scrambled eggs cooked in salsa), *Huevos Mucho Mex* (two jumbo eggs scrambled with potatoes, bacon and salsa) and the *Migas Mucho Mex* (with crisp tortilla pieces, *chorizo* and cactus strips. And, like most of the other breakfast plates, enough food to fill four tortillas. Not just for breakfast, the setting at the original location is appropriate for all meals. It cannot be described as especially nice, but it is perfectly fine for a group in search of good Mexican or Tex-Mex food.

Nam $11

2727 Fondren (at Westheimer) 77063, (713) 789-6688
www.namcuisine.com

Cuisine - Vietnamese
Hours - Mon-Thu 11AM to 10PM; Fri-Sat 11AM to 11PM; Sun 5 to 10PM
Credit Cards - Amex, Diners, MC, Visa
Service - Table Service
Alcohol - Beer & Wine

Entrée Prices - Dinner - $5 to $21 ($11 average); Lunch - $5 to $7
Entrées at Dinner $12 and less - 80%

Atmosphere & Décor - Nice
Appeal - Good food in a setting nicer than most Vietnamese restaurants
Menu Suggestions - Vietnamese Smoked Beef (marinated and sautéed flank steak topped with crushed peanuts); Vietnamese Duck (a half-duck, marinated in white wine, steamed and then deep-fried); Chicken with French Butter Sauce

With pleasing, butter-rich aromas wafting into the parking lot, you quickly assume that this is a worthwhile restaurant. Aside from some Asian decorative items, the pleasant, if not quite cutting edge, setting could be that of any number of cuisines. And, Nam is also more assimilated than most Vietnamese restaurants in town; the menu is completely in English and chop sticks will likely have to be requested, for example. But, the food is still well prepared, and service is noticeably friendly and generally proficient.

The food here is heavier and sweeter, and more sauce-laden, which will make it more appealing to many patrons. Plus, the portions are large and the flavors are generally agreeable. In that vein, the menu offers a great number of tempting items. It's large by almost any standard, other than that set by many of the local Vietnamese and Chinese restaurants. If the roughest edges might not be present, the preparations really don't shy away from its roots, as there are several clay pot dishes, whole fish in several guises and duck. The dinner menu is neatly partitioned among appetizers, soup, salads, specialties, chicken, duck, beef, pork, seafood, fried rice, *bun* (rice noodle dishes), vegetarian and desserts. A good way to start is with the deep-fried Vietnamese Egg rolls that are served with a suitably fresh array of lettuce and herbs. There are also the soft spring rolls and *satays* with beef, chicken or shrimp. The soup offerings include Asparagus and Crab, Duck and egg noodles, and Shrimp Wonton, but no *pho* or its similar brethren. Among the four score of entrées some appealing ones are Vietnamese Smoked Beef (marinated and sautéed flank steak topped with crushed peanuts), Special Crunchy Noodle (pan-fried noodles with shrimp, scallops, chicken, beef, vegetables in a spicy sauce), Grilled Lemongrass Beef, and

Spicy Shrimp (jumbo shrimp sautéed with garlic, butter and chiles). There are a total of a dozen or so shrimp entrées, including a couple in which these are paired with scallops. Seafood is also present in several snapper presentations and a couple crab dishes. Some of the best values are the locally popular Vietnamese dishes like the meal-in-a-bowl *bun* dishes for around eight bucks. These are bowls of thin rice noodles plentifully topped with one of several marinated, charcoal-broiled meats and shrimp, and egg rolls. The twenty or so Combination Plates are also nice values at well under ten bucks, and offer a variety of meats mostly served with steamed rice. Some of the dishes feature Grilled Chicken, Spicy Shrimp, Smoked Beef, Curry Chicken, and Grilled Scallop Salad, all with steamed rice and fish sauce. Unusual for a Vietnamese restaurant, many items are available with a choice of level of spiciness. For dessert, Nam serves several sweet Vietnamese specialties such as a fried banana and Sweet Rice with Mango. The lunch specials are a fine value. They serve over twenty items that feature different Vietnamese preparations of chicken, roasted duck, beef, pork, and tofu, plus some interestingly described ones like Shrimp and Walnuts and Fried Chicken and sticky rice. Most of these are served with soup (opt for the silky chicken and rice), an egg roll and fried rice. It is not the best the restaurant can offer, but the food is usually quite satisfying and plentiful.

New York Coffee Shop $6

9720 Hillcroft (south of S. Braeswood) 77096, (713) 723-5879

Cuisine - Deli
Hours - Mon 6AM to 3PM; Tue-Sun 6AM to 3:30PM
Credit Cards - NONE
Service - Table Service
Alcohol - NONE

Entrée Prices - $4 to $10 ($6 average)
Entrées $12 and less - 100%

Atmosphere & Décor - Functional
Appeal - Good breakfasts and deli food in well-run diner in Meyerland
Useful to Note - You can purchase top-notch bagels at the adjoining shop.
Menu Suggestions - Pastrami Omelet; Salami Omelet; Reuben Sandwich; bagels

Really two businesses in one, a bagel shop and deli, New York Coffee Shop is a long-time fixture in Meyerland. Almost always bustling, clean and efficiently run, it aptly fills the neighborhood need for a Jewish-American deli and breakfast spot. A Jewish-American diner is probably the best description for this. On the restaurant side, the menu is filled with all-

American breakfast items, including Corned Beef Hash, and the expected Jewish-American luncheon dishes. The grits, and the jalapeño bagel are the only regional concessions among the breakfast offerings. The egg dishes might be cooked a little dry for some tastes, but the three-egg omelets are usually very good here. There are a good number of deli-style sandwiches, plus hamburgers, hot plates, and cold plates. The sandwiches are not the monster creations found in some Jewish-American eateries. Actually, they might be a tad on the small side for Houston, but you will usually be satisfied when ordering a Reuben or the similar Hot Pastrami, Corned Beef or even Dinty Moore (corned beef, tomato, lettuce with Russian dressing) sandwiches. Each is served with an excellent small cup of cole slaw and a crisp dill pickle. If a sandwich will not be enough for lunch, you might want to try a hot platter of chopped sirloin steak, roast beef or broiled or boiled knockwurst and beans. For the deli aficionados, New York Coffee Shop also has cold platters that feature chopped liver, chopped herring, pickled herring, gelfilte fish, canned tuna, chicken salad, seafood salad, tuna salad, and several other choices. In addition to the more common fare described above, the "Fish Box", unusual for Houston, but apt here, is an array of cured fish: lox, Nova, chub, smoked sable, and kippered salmon. Their natural frequent accompaniment, excellent, suitably hard bagels are made in the adjoining shop, and might be the best bagels to be found in the Houston area. Available for eating at the restaurant, or take-away at the shop, the array of choices should please nearly any type of bagel lover. In addition to the tasty basic bagel there are: poppy seed, sesame seed, onion; garlic, pumpernickel, rye, bialy, salt, cinnamon raisin, whole wheat, oat bran, banana nut, blueberry, sun-dried tomato, chocolate, etc.

The Nickel Grill $7

5601 Lyons (at Lockwood, just north of I-10) 77020, (713) 674-8020

Cuisine - American; Barbecue
Hours - Mon-Fri 10AM to 7PM; Sat 11AM to 5PM
Credit Cards - Amex, Discover, MC, Visa
Service - Counter Service
Alcohol - NONE

Entrée Prices - $4 to $10 ($7 average)
Entrées $12 and less - 100%

Atmosphere & Décor - Very little; the only seating is in an enclosed patio
Appeal - Tasty burgers, sandwiches and barbecue that is a great value
Useful to Note - Ordering and dining are done in two separate areas.
Menu Suggestions - Nickel Burger; fries; Beef Sandwich; Beef Plate (beef brisket with two sides); Catfish Po Boy; Smoked Cajun Turkey Sandwich; 2 BBQ Leg Quarters (two leg-and-thigh pieces with two sides)

The tidy, but unassuming Nickel Grill in the Fifth Ward has a small, but diverse menu that's fairly common among local restaurants located in predominately African-American neighborhoods. There is barbecue, plenty of deep-fried dishes, seafood, a juicy grilled hamburger, and Cajun items. And, it's all very tasty here, and a very good value. Portions are large and prices are low, and the kitchen here is much better than most similar type of neighborhood places. The barbecue here is an electic array of beef brisket, meaty pork ribs, house-made beef sausages (links), chicken, smoked boudin, smoked Cajun turkey, and brisket filled baked potatoes. The brisket is properly smoky, sufficiently fatty and quite flavorful, and served in bountiful portions. Just about as good is the meaty chicken. This is served as two leg-and-thigh combinations with a couple sides, which is an amazing deal for under five bucks. The sides are limited but satisfying, just a cheese-laden potato salad, beans, and especially the dirty rice. The smoked boudin might disappoint a Cajun purist, but the flavor will please most locals weaned on slowly cooked barbecue. The fryer stays busy with several other items, such as chicken tenders, pork chops, clean-tasting trout and catfish fillets and shrimp. Many of these, plus the output of the smoker, makes it into sandwiches or po boys, too. The sandwiches, even the burger, are served on thick slices of buttered toast that work quite well. The po boys are served on a small, crusty baguette-like roll. The one burger features a half-pound juicy patty cooked with a desired redness in the middle and served with verdant non-iceberg lettuce and ripe tomato slices. The fries, a recommended accompaniment, are cut by hand, fried crisp enough and tasty.

Though inexpensive, The Nickel isn't fast food. There will certainly be a short wait for your food, but it's certainly worth it. You walk inside and order. You have to walk back outside and into the enclosed patio if you plan to eat there. It can be a little confusing to select a dish when inside, if a paper menu, the only type of menu here, is not readily available, as the lists of items posted in several places are rather incomplete. But, no matter, you can always ask the accomodating person at the cashier station for help. It's good to note that everything is cooked or assembled to order, and it might take a few minutes. Condiments are dispensed solely in the small plastic bags. The Nickel seems to do a brisk take-away, catering, and custom cooking businesses. The restaurant is easy to get to from downtown; it's located on Lyons, near Lockwood, just north of I-10.

Nidda $11

1226 Westheimer (west of Montrose) 77006, (713) 522-8895

Cuisine - Thai
Hours - Mon-Fri 11AM to 2:30PM, 5 to 9:30PM; Sat. 12 to 10PM; Sun 12 to 9:30PM
Credit Cards - Amex, Diners, Discover, MC, Visa
Service - Table Service
Alcohol - Beer & Wine

Entrée Prices - Dinner - $6 to $13 (11 average); Lunch - $7
Entrées at Dinner $12 and less - 80%

Atmosphere & Décor - Comfortable
Appeal - Friendly and good value Thai in Montrose
Menu Suggestions - Steamed Dumplings (with minced chicken and water chestnuts); Green Curry; Panang Curry (made with coconut milk, carrots and kaffir lime leaves); Spicy Lemongrass Chicken

Noticeably friendly and inviting, even by gracious Thai standards, Nidda is an outpost of enjoyable and good value Thai food in the heart of Montrose. The fare here might not be quite as flavorful or as complex as the top Thai places in town, but most of the most popular Thai dishes are served in consistently satisfying fashion. The kitchen is steady and the service is affable and mature. The accompanying steamed rice will quickly be replenished when necessary. The restaurant itself is comfortable, consisting of one quaint dining room that is made somewhat more intimate by its relatively low ceiling. The menu is divided among appetizers, soups, salads, fried rice, curries, seafood, noodles, vegetarian dishes, and ten or so "Chef Recommendations", which, surprisingly, are not the most expensive items on the menu. There are seven curries, including the ones you'll find on most local menus: red, yellow, green, *massaman* (brown) and *panang* (and deep orange-ish, to continue the color scheme). The peanut-laden *massaman* is also served with pieces of sweet potatoes. Vegetables are well treated here. Even as supporting parts of a dish, the thick green beans, and red and green peppers will be properly very fresh and crisp, and plentiful. Sliced white chicken and beef provide most of the meat choices, but pork is available in about a dozen of the dishes. Shrimp is, by far, the most common of the seafood choices, and there are a couple of squid dishes, and several with the clean-tasting, and price-friendly tilapia. There are nearly a dozen good-sized lunch specials that are served with soft rolls and either a soup or salad, depending on the day of the week.

Nielsen's Delicatessen $10

4500 Richmond (east of Weslayan) 77027, (713) 963-8005
26830 I-45 N. (near Woodlands Parkway) The Woodlands, 77386, (281) 363-3354

Cuisine - Sandwiches

Hours - Richmond - Daily 8AM to 4PM; The Woodlands - Tue-Fri 8:30AM to 5:30PM; Sat 8:30AM to 12PM
Credit Cards - Amex, MC, Visa
Service - Counter Service
Alcohol - NONE

Entrée Prices - $8 to $12 ($10 average)
Entrées $12 and less - 100%

Atmosphere & Décor - Spartan, functional
Appeal - Good cold sandwiches for takeout
Useful to Note - Not just cheese, but lettuce and tomato are extra.
Menu Suggestions - Turkey Sandwich; Pastrami with Swiss Cheese Sandwich; Chicken Salad Sandwich; Roast Beef Sandwich on Rye; Cheesecake

---

Originally opened in the 1950s by Danish immigrants, and located since the 1980s in the Afton Oaks subdivision west of Greenway Plaza, Nielsen's is a very popular purveyor of cold sandwiches. The lunchtime crowd is evidence of that. After fifty years or so, it opened a second restaurant, this one in The Woodlands. There is a small amount of counter space at the original location, room for maybe a dozen or so, but those spots are usually hard to obtain during the crowded and long, peak lunch hours. Your best bet is to order something for takeout, as most customers do.

The choices are fairly basic; familiar sandwiches and more than a handful of sides, and some sweets. High quality ingredients are the cornerstones of their straightforward sandwiches. The meats, along with the breads are also sold individually, in a testament to their quality. The options for filling the cold sandwiches include: turkey, roast beef, chicken salad, tuna, corned beef, ham, pastrami, liverpaste, salami, and cheese. Most sandwiches are avialable in two sizes. The larger of the two, the regular, is an average-sized sandwich for an adult. The turkey sandwiches are one of the biggest sellers, and is due, in part, to the fact that Nielsen's roasts their own turkeys. For the less publicly health-conscious, the pastrami is also of noticeably high quality. The choices of bread for these are wheat, white, a very light but flavoful rye, pumpernickle, and an herb toast. They taste the best when ordered with some of Nielsen's housemade mayonnaise; a special treat in this era of packaged Lite Mayonnaise and Miracle Whip. The list of sides, available in dixie cups (quite small), half-pint, pint, and quart sizes, are: potato salad, fruit salad, chicken salad, tuna salad, coleslaw, beans, beets, red cabbage, crab salad, and pasta salad. Hard-boiled eggs are prominent in their potato salad. Though the food is quite good, Nielsen's has become fairly pricey in recent years for what it is; a cold, small sandwich, small side salad, and small drink will cost you over $10. Other items include soups and housemade desserts. For a sweet end to lunch, there are cheesecakes, cookies and brownies, all made in the store. For many, cheesecakes are what Nielsen's does the best. In addition to slices, you can get a half, or an entire cake. To take home, of course. Nielsen's can provide sandwich trays and the like for your next event, which will certainly more than satisfy, or just lunch meat, bread and cheese to make the sandwiches at home.

Niko Niko's $10

2520 Montrose (between Westheimer and Fairview) 77006, (713) 528-1308
www.nikonikos.com

Cuisine - Greek; American
Hours - Mon-Thu 10AM to 10PM; Fri-Sat 10AM to 11PM; Sun 11AM to 9PM
Credit Cards - Amex, Diners, Discover, MC, Visa
Service - Counter Service
Alcohol - Beer & Wine

Entrée Prices - $6 to $16 ($10 average)
Entrées $12 and less - 80%

Atmosphere & Décor - Casual and pleasant; patio
Appeal - Unpretentious Greek food in a friendly and comfortable setting
Useful to Note - Teas, coffees, iced drinks and desserts entice lingering.
Menu Suggestions - Chicken Avgolemono Soup (with rice, vegetables and lemon); Greek Salad; Gyros Sandwich; Chicken Kabob Sandwich; Falafel Sandwich; Gyro Plate; Souvlaki Plate (marinated cubes of grilled beef); fries; Spanakopita; Athenian Mushroom Burger (with sautéed onions, bell pepper and feta); Char Grilled Pork Chops

Since 1977 Niko Niko's has been a well-loved fixture in the heart of Montrose for inexpensive, satisfying and unpretentious Greek and Gulf Coast favorites. Comfortable and rather nice after re-modeling in recent years, it's more fashionable than ever and usually crowded, even well beyond regular lunch and dinner hours. The large number of regular patrons greatly appreciates this friendly, hard-working eatery that serves well prepared, zesty and reasonably priced fare. That you will find all of the well-known Greek dishes and more on the expansive menu is a big part of the draw.

Niko Niko's is accurately subtitled, a "Greek and American Café". The large menu consists mainly of Greek specialties, which are aptly explained, and a number of other homey, but well prepared dishes, one of which will certainly satisfy any craving. There are numerous appetizing beef, lamb, seafood and vegetarian items; plus seafood po boys and hamburgers. It's easy to satiate at different levels of healthiness and price. At the more affordable end of the menu are about twenty sandwiches, which come with a choice of roasted potatoes, rice or fries. There are po boys, hamburgers including the top-notch Athenian Mushroom Burger, a juicy half-pound burger complemented with mushrooms, sautéed onions, bell peppers and feta cheese, and very reliable versions of the expected pita-wrapped sandwiches such as gyros and *souvlaki* (moist, marinated and grilled chunks of beef). Possibly more interesting to the health-conscious are entrée-sized salads in either the familiar or the more traditional Greek versions that can be served with shrimp, meat or even *falafel* patties.

Niko Niko's also has a large number of generously proportioned Greek plates. These plates include gyros, *souvlaki*, chicken kabob, lamb kabob, lamb shanks roasted with olive oil, garlic, oregano and lemon, *mousaka* (layered eggplant with ground beef and cream), *pastichio* (the Greek lasagna-like dish), *keftedes* (Greek meatballs), *kreatopia* (phyllo pastry stuffed with ground beef, garlic, onion, carrots, peas and cheese), *souzoukakia* (seasoned beef with tomato sauce) and *domathes* (grape leaves stuffed with ground beef and rice). The rest of the plates are less noticeably Greek, but still popular, such as Niko's Honey Chicken Wings (a dozen chicken wings in a spicy honey sauce), Oven Roasted Chicken, Vegetable Lasagna and Char-Grilled Pork Chops. In addition to the seafood po boys, Niko Niko's also serves seafood. It comes both broiled and fried. Among the more interesting of the seafood dishes are the Seafood Kabob, and the Grilled Rainbow Trout cooked in olive oil with garlic, rosemary and lemon. For those desiring to eat in less healthy fashion, their version of fish and chips is very good. This along with most everything at Niko Niko's is satisfying, and fairly priced. To finish up the meal, or, more likely, for those not dining, the breadth of teas, coffees and desserts has increased in recent years to encourage further lingering.

* Ninfa's (Original) $12

2704 Navigation (between Jensen and Sampson) 77003, (713) 228-1178
www.mamaninfas.com

Cuisine - Tex-Mex
Hours - Mon-Thu, Sun 11:30AM to 10PM; Fri 11AM to 11PM; Sat 11:30AM to 11PM
Credit Cards - Amex, Diners, Discover, MC, Visa
Service - Table Service
Alcohol - Full Bar

Entrée Prices - $7 to $22 ($12 average)
Entrées $12 and less - 70%

Atmosphere & Décor - Festive
Appeal - Some of the best Tex-Mex around in fun and festive environment

Useful to Note - This is a great place to take out-of-town visitors.
Menu Suggestions - Queso Flameado (melted Jack with chorizo); Tacos a la Ninfa (beef fajita tacos); Carne Asada; beef fajitas; Carnitas (tender stewed pieces of pork); Enchiladas Verdes (filled with carnitas and topped with a tomatillo salsa); Enchiladas Suizas with chicken; Enchiladas al Carbon (filled with beef fajita); Mexican Style Charbroiled Barbecue Pork Ribs; El Dannie (crispy tacos with ground beef or chicken); margaritas or Ninfaritas (by the pitcher is best)

Tasting the various dishes featuring the beef fajita in the warm, fun, and still often crowded setting on the east side of downtown, you can understand how this one, initially quite humble restaurant greatly helped to popularize Tex-Mex in the area, even nationally. *Original* needs to be emphasized here, as everyone in town should know. The other restaurants in the Ninfa's chain do not come close to measuring up to the original location. In local parlance, this restaurant is "Original Ninfa's", or "Ninfa's on Navigation". The old sign still hanging above this location features an image of a relatively youthful, though now deceased, matriarch, Mama Ninfa over the phrase, "*Tacos a la Ninfa*". The restaurant is still fairly unreconstructed, and that is part of its charm. It shows signs of its former life as a small taco stand that grew into a restaurant, and then many restaurants. Also aiding in the appeal is the friendly and very solicitous service, fun atmosphere. And, not least, the excellent Tex-Mex, both food and drink.

From the 1970s Ninfa's has helped to popularize the grilled skirt steak from its humble beginnings in the border areas into part of the national menu. "Fajitas" properly refer to the somewhat lowly skirt steak that has been grilled and cut in strips, and these do not come much tastier than at the Original Ninfa's. Using marinated, high quality outside skirt steak, these are extremely flavorful and juicy, and are found in various guises here. The fajitas are the meat unadorned in sizes from a quarter-pound, half-pound and one pound accompanied with *pico de gallo*, guacamole and sour cream on the side. For an additional charge, there is a choice of toppings, *a la Mexicana* (sautéed jalapeños, tomatoes and onions), *Chihuahua* (bacon, poblanos and Monterey Jack cheese), and *Tratinada* (sautéed mushrooms, onions and bell pepper). Then there are the *Tacos a la Ninfa* (called *tacos al carbon* elsewhere), where the meat is already placed inside a large flour tortilla. And, the Enchiladas *al Carbon*, stuffed with the tasty fajita, makes for very good enchiladas. Other enchilada dishes are good here, as are the pork ribs, which is something unusual for a Tex-Mex restaurant. Actually, most everything is very well prepared here on their fairly extensive menu, and the portions are the size of what most patrons in the area have come to expect. It's tough to go wrong at the Original Ninfa's if you are in the mood for Tex-Mex, and it's tough not to be in a good mood while you are here. Though it is easy to spend money here with the allure of *chile con queso*, a bountiful and plenty of *Ninfaritas* (the margaritas), the prices here are really not much different than other popular Tex-Mex establishments. The food will generally be better, too, and you will have a very enjoyable and filling dining experience.

Nippon $13

4463 Montrose (just north of the Southwest Freeway) 77006, (713) 523-3939

Cuisine - Japanese
Hours - Daily 11AM to 10:30PM
Credit Cards - Amex, Diners, Discover, MC, Visa
Service - Table Service
Alcohol - Beer & Wine

Entrée Prices - Dinner - $7 to $28 ($13 average); Lunch - $7 to $14
Entrées at Dinner $12 and less - 50%

Atmosphere & Décor - Pleasant, inviting; patio
Appeal - Well prepared Japanese food, and good sushi in a pleasant setting
Useful to Note - Parking lot driveway is one lane; nearby street parking is wise.
Menu Suggestions - nigiri sushi, especially the flounder (hirame), snapper (tai) and yellowtail (hamachi); Tempura Udon (tempura shrimp on top of a noodle soup); Katsu Don (fried pork cutlets served over rice with egg); Tempura Don

Nippon is a pleasant, small restaurant on a similarly pleasant stretch of lower Montrose just north of the artful bridge over the Southwest Freeway. One of a diverse group of commendable spots within a couple of blocks, Nippon serves some of the very best Japanese food inside the Loop. Unlike the vast majority of area Japanese restaurants, Nippon is Japanese-owned and -staffed. And, the comfortable dining room is usually peppered with ex-pat Japanese clientele, a sure sign of its authenticity and quality. It's also one of the best value Japanese restaurants in the city. Separated from the main dining room, the sushi bar of soothing, light wood and the small tables that flank it, provide an enjoyable place to enjoy some of the better sushi in Houston, for which Nippon has long been known. The sushi is reliably very good and expertly prepared by a friendly Japanese sushi chef; the senior one is a certified master. Nippon features a similar array of fish in the sashimi, *nigiri sushi* (the popular version with fresh fish sitting atop vinegared rice and wasabi) and the related rolls that is found in most area Japanese restaurants. You can order without hesitation, as almost every sushi item will be sufficiently savory. Some of the seafood used in the sushi is ostensibly from the Gulf, such as the snapper (*tai*) and flounder (*hirame*). Usually one or the other is featured, and both can be excellent. The sushi is reasonably priced, certainly in relationship to its quality. For much better sushi, the prices are mostly competitive with the sushi happy hour places.

The commonly seen Spicy Tuna Rolls are tasty, and actually fairly spicy. Representative of the city (possibly), there is even a Houston Roll with yellowtail tuna, green onion and cucumber.

The offerings at Nippon extend well beyond sushi. And, these other dishes seem to be more popular with the numerous Japanese customers. The wide-ranging menu is slightly larger than that of many other local Japanese restaurants. There are the tempura and teriyaki dishes, but also some less familiar ones, mostly featuring seafood. These are most evident in the two dozen appetizers and soups. Along with the *yakitori* (grilled chicken) and *edamame,* there are dishes such as broiled eggplant with ginger sauce, grilled smelt, cooked scallop with mushrooms, *Takosu* (a salad of vinegared octopus and Japanese cucubmer), and another salad with seaweed and Japanese cucumber. The main courses begin with the several *nabemono* dinners that you cook at the table including beef dishes such as *sukiyaki* and *shabu shabu,* plus ones featuring seafood. There are combination dinners primarily with different tempura and teriyaki dishes. These can be ordered separately, along with other ones with red snapper and scallops. There several good-value *donburi* dishes, which are meals in a bowl, or an attractive box, actually, with meats or seafood served over rice, including *Katsu Don* (pork cutlets and egg) and *Una Ju* (broiled eel fillet). For noodle lovers, and also lighter on the wallet, Nippon obliges with a number of *udon* and *soba* noodle dishes. The dish of *udon* with chicken is superb. During lunchtime, Nippon has a number of bento boxes, and it's tough to go wrong with any of these or really anything on the lunch menu. Along with providing well prepared food and a generally relaxed mood for dining, the service is usually quite solicitous, as with most Japanese restaurants. All and all, Nippon is an interesting and capable neighborhood restaurant.

Some reliable stops for sushi

Though sushi is not one of the most inexpensive meals around, knowing where to find good sushi is usually more satisfying than knowing where you can scarf all you can eat for $1 or so a piece at where the quality is of secondary concern at best. Probably more so than most food, it pays to pay for quality with sushi. Excepting atmosphere, décor and the attractiveness of the patrons as factors for consideration, some of the places for the most reliably good sushi are listed below. Some are even Japanese-owned.

- **Aka Japanese Cuisine** - 1460 Eldridge Parkway
- **Azuma** - 909 Texas & 5600 Kirby - also features *robata* cooking
- **400 Sage** - 400 Sage - fun and stylish place in the Galleria area
- **Ginza** - 5868 San Felipe
- **Kubo's** - 2414 University - some of the best sushi around
- **Nippon** - 4463 Montrose

- **Oishi** - 3674 Richmond
- **Osaka** - 515 Westheimer & 3147 W. Holcombe
- **Rickshaw** - 2810 Westheimer
- **Sasaki** - 8779 Westheimer - popular with a Japanese clientele
- **Teppay** - 6516 Westheimer - the best Japanese restaurant in the area
- **Uptown Sushi** - 1131 Uptown Park Boulevard - the scene is a big draw

Nit Noi $12

2462 Bolsover (west of Morningside) 77005, (713) 524-8114
6395 Woodway (east of Voss) 77057, (713) 789-1711
850 1960 W. (west of I-45 N.) 77090, (281) 444-7650
11807 Westheimer (southeast corner at Kirkwood) 77077, (281) 597-8200
6700 Woodlands Parkway (at Kuykendahl) The Woodlands, 77381, (281) 367-3355
www.nitnoithai.com

Cuisine - Thai
Hours - Mon-Fri 11AM to 3PM, 5 to 10PM; Sat 11AM to 10PM; Sun 5 to 9PM
Credit Cards - Amex, Diners, Discover, MC, Visa
Service - Table Service
Alcohol - Full Bar

Entrée Prices - $8 to $16 ($12 average)
Entrées $12 and less - 70%

Atmosphere & Décor - Very Nice
Appeal - Pleasing Thai in attractive and often festive surroundings
Menu Suggestions - Crispy Spring Rolls; Pad Thai with chicken (stir-fried rice noodles, eggs and bean sprouts); Chicken Curry; C-R-S (crispy red snapper)

From its somewhat humble beginnings in an older building in the Rice Village that first opened in June of 1987 and from which it has long since moved, Nit Noi has grown considerably to several locations around the area. Nit Noi might mean "a little bit" in Thai, but there is nothing diminutive about the ambitions of these restaurants to provide a very enjoyable dining experience, much more than just what is on the plate. These are very stylish and atmospheric restaurants that are justifiably crowded on most weekend nights.

The offerings are pretty standard for local Thai restaurants, though the number of entrées might be a little larger than usual. The portions are also larger than usual among the area Thai restaurants. Many can plan on leftovers after dinner. Nit Noi is far from the best Thai food in town, but the combination of décor, serving size and plating are probably the best among local Thai restaurants. With those plentiful dishes, Nit Noi provides a good value. Thai food aficionados will find many appealing dishes. The kitchen does an excellent job in quickly processing the orders, even during the very busy weekend nights. With a group you might want to begin the meal with an appetizer such as the Crispy Spring Rolls served with peanut sauce, an order of *satay,* or a cup of soup from several Chinese-influenced hot and sour, egg-drop or vegetable. Nit Noi serves the hot and spicy Thai-style salads that are served with steamed rice. There are salads that feature chicken, beef, shrimp, squid and one with assorted meats. Entrée-sized soups include the zesty *Tom Gum* and several other soups. The *Pad Thai,* stir-fried rice noodles with eggs and vegetables, is available with beef, chicken, pork and shrimp. In addition to the *Pad Thai,* there are several other noodle-based dishes that feature noodles that have been steamed, stir-fried or deep-fried. The rest of the menu is divided among entrées featuring rice, chicken, pork, beef, seafood and vegetables, plus the House Specials that feature dishes with all of the above. There is not a separate section for curry preparations. This might be a good thing, as curries here are less exciting than at other Thai places. The Beef Panang, for example, is a bland and mostly forgettable dish with beef that is seemingly not the highest quality. Compared to other local Thai restaurants, there are a large number of seafood and vegetarian entrées; over a dozen seafood dishes and nearly two dozen vegetarian dishes, which are among the most interesting offerings. Among the House Specials are Sautéed Chicken (or Shrimp) with Peanut Sauce, C-R-S (crispy red snapper with a house special sauce), a favorite among some of the most discerning patrons, and Stir Fried Mussels with Chili Sauce, Garlic and Sweet Basil. To be noted, there are also smaller versions of the restaurant, called Nit Noi Café, but its offerings are not the quality of its larger brethren.

* Noemi's Tacos $6

8010 Park Place (just west of I-45 South) 77087, (713) 645-7907

Cuisine - Mexican (taqueria)
Hours - Mon-Sat 8AM to 4PM
Credit Cards - NONE
Service - Table Service
Alcohol - NONE

Entrée Prices - $4 to $8 ($6 average)
Entrées $12 and less - 100%

Atmosphere & Décor - Spartan, but very friendly
Appeal - Tasty barbacoa, carne guisada and wonderful tacos made to order
Useful to Note - Be prepared to wait; it's always worth it; not much room.
Menu Suggestions - Carne Guisada Special (with rice, beans, guacamole and flour tortillas); carne guisada tacos; breakfast tacos; barbacoa

Noemi's Tacos is a very small, very unpretentious eatery just off the Gulf Freeway near Hobby Airport serving excellent home-style Mexican food. There is not much to this restaurant. The interior consists of seating for only eleven, maybe twelve people, plus a couple long picnic tables in the covered outdoor area in front of the store, facing the street. The menu is as humble as the setting though maybe slightly larger. There are tacos, burritos, tamales, breakfast plates, two soups, and a small number of "Deluxe Mexican Dinners" featuring familiar Tex-Mex and more traditionally Mexican dishes.

The tacos alone are worth a visit. Made with a choice of either house-made flour or corn tortillas, it's tough to go wrong among any of the fillings for the breakfast and afternoon tacos. Each of these well crafted tacos is a pittance, around $1.50. An order of three should be filling for most. You can get the breakfast tacos and breakfast dishes at all hours. Well, from 8AM to 4PM when they are open. . The more standard breakfast tacos choices are potato and egg, *chorizo* and egg, bacon and egg, and beans and eggs. There are also beans unadorned, guacamole, *barbacoa,* hamburger, chicken, fajita, grilled chicken and the excellent *carne guisada* (stewed beef tips). Succulent and flavorful, it is almost orange in color. Though maybe a bit unusual in appearance, their *carne guisada* is one of the best versions in town, especially among taco stands and other small restaurants. Another treat for many, especially in the East End, is that the *barbacoa* is made daily. Here, it is also somewhat unique in appearance. A very dark brown, almost black, it is served with no juice, but the meat is moist and very tasty. In a taco it is well complemented with the fresh cilantro and chopped fresh white onions in properly Mexican fashion, and the viscous, spicy green salsa. The *barbacoa* is available as a plate with rice and beans, and by the pound for takeout. Also ready for takeout in family-size portions are the tamales, freshly made flour tortillas, beans, guacamole, and the soups, the *menudo* (beef tripe and hominy soup) and *fideo* (small pasta and tomato soup). It's run by a very friendly husband and wife team who have been at it for a while. Turnaround time from the kitchen at this very small and often crowded place can sometimes be very slow. The dishes are cooked when the order is placed, with the exception of the soups, of course. The food at Noemi's is certainly worth the wait, though. Given its quality, along with the genuine affability and warmth of the owners, you don't often feel like the wait is much of an imposition.

Nonmacher's Bar-B-Que $9

606 S. Mason (at Kingsland, south of I-10) Katy, 77450, (281) 392-7666

Cuisine - Barbecue
Hours - Mon - Sat 11AM to 8PM
Credit Cards - NONE
Service - Counter Service
Alcohol - NONE

Entrée Prices - $6 to $12 ($9 average)
Entrées $12 and less - 100%

Atmosphere & Décor - Dumpy, but appropriate
Appeal - Very good brisket
Useful to Note - The menu is very limited.
Menu Suggestions - sliced brisket sandwich; chopped brisket sandwich

Like the preceeding Noemi's, there is not much at all to long-standing Nonmacher's, either in terms of the size of the restaurant or the size of the menu. It's just smoked beef brisket, pork ribs and sausage served as plates (or rather in Styrofoam containers with plastic utensils) or in sandwiches and a small handful of sides. There is something to be said about focus, as the limited array of meats is very good, especially the requisite brisket, which is moist, flavorful and properly exhibits deep smoke rings. Though it might be a little pricey for what it is, the barbecue is very good, and very good brisket is what a great many in the area really enjoy. Served on basic buns with sliced onions and pickles, both of the brisket sandwiches are quite good, though surprisingly different. The chopped beef, is cut finely, and is served from a container where it develops a fairly unique taste; the onions and pickles can provide an especially noticeable textural contrast, and a taste complement. The meaty ribs have their fans, as do the central Texas-style smoked sausage. The sides are average, at best. It's probably wise to choose the beans or cole slaw rather than the chunky, thin and bland potato salad. The small resturant resides in a small, nondescript shopping center with a relativey small parking lot. There are just five or so tables, one of which might be occupied with the owner or his laptop. Décor consists of faded posters and photos, mostly from the 1980s and a collection of foam-billed caps, probably also from that decade. There is really no atmosphere, but it's fitting for a barbecue joint. And, you're strictly here for the high quality Texas-style barbecue, or more than likely, here to pick up it, as much of the business seems to be takeout.

Nundini Deli $7

500 N. Shepherd (just north of I-10) 77007, (713) 861-6331
www.nundini.com

Cuisine - Italian; Sandwiches
Hours - Mon-Fri 10AM to 6PM; Sat 10AM to 5PM

Credit Cards - Amex, Discover, MC, Visa
Service - Counter Service
Alcohol - Beer & Wine

Entrée Prices - $6 to $8 ($7 average)
Entrées $12 and less - 100%

Atmosphere & Décor - Spartan, it's primarily a retail shop
Appeal - Very good Italian-style sandwiches, and freshly made gelato
Useful to Note - Turnaround time is quite slow.
Menu Suggestions - Parma Sandwich (prosciutto and mozzarella); Caprese Sandwich (mozzarella, tomato and basil); New Orleans Sandwich (mortadella, ham, salami, provolone and an olive mix); gelato; sorbetto; tiramisu

---

Nundini Deli or Nundini Food Store is a small retail food store, *gelato* factory and sandwich shop. Nundini specializes in Italian and Mediterranean food products and is a good stop if you are looking for dried pastas, olive oils, canned tomatoes, vinegars, spices, sauces, spreads, and excellent Italian and Italian-style lunch meats and cheeses. Nundini offers very good prices for *prosciutto di Parma, prosciutto di San Daniele, jamon serrano* and other Italian meats such as *capicallo* and even speck, the smoked, spiced and cured ham from the Alpine regions of Italy that is usually tough to find. On the wall near the deli section is a short menu of a half-dozen or so salads and nearly twice as many sandwiches. Most are Italian or American with Italian sensibilities rather than Italian-American: judicious use of a simple combination of meats and cheeses on fresh roll rather than large, zesty and abundant creations with plenty of fillings. The listed sandwiches include the imported prosciutto and mozzarella, *mortadella* and mozzarella, tomatoes and mozzarella, tuna salad, chicken salad, roast beef, turkey, and smoked salmon with cream cheese and capers served on a bagel. The ingredients are good quality; Italian cured meats, fresh sandwich rolls, the mozzarella is freshly made and white, the tomatoes are ripe and juicy. If one of the menu board selections is not exactly what you want, you can have the always amiable person behind the counter make one to your specifications from the meats, cheeses and other items that are on display. The sandwiches are assembled to order and some are run through an Italian sandwich press, and served with a bag of chips. Care is taken to create a sandwich, so it's best not to be in a hurry when visiting. It will take a few minutes or more. For salads there are *Insalata Caprese* (tomatoes, fresh mozzarella and olive oil) and the ubiquitous American favorite Caesar. To dine in, there are several tables placed among the shelves and refrigerators. Dining is low-key.

Most interesting for many is that Nundini makes and sells *gelato* at this location. *Gelato* is the creamy, dense Italian-style of ice cream that is made with egg custard, sugar and flavorings. Nundini actually makes *gelato* and the similar *sorbetto* (sorbet) for most of the restaurants in town that serve this Italian take on ice cream. These are distributed to more than Italian and Italian-American restaurants, so they have been willing to expand the boundries of traditional flavors for local restaurant, corporate or individual customers. What you will find at the store will be several basic flavors, all very tasty, and a scoop is a good complement to a lunchtime sandwich or salad. You can also take home larger portions.

Ocean Palace $13

11215 Bellaire (west fo Boone, in the Hong Kong City Mall) 77072, (281) 988-8898

Cuisine - Chinese
Hours - Mon-Thu 10AM to 10PM; Fri 10AM to 11PM; Sat 9AM to 11PM; Sun 9AM to 10PM
Credit Cards - Amex, Discover, MC, Visa
Service - Table Service
Alcohol - Beer & Wine

Entrée Prices - Dinner - $6 to $40 ($13 average); Lunch - $5 to $11
Entrées at Dinner $12 and less - 50%

Atmosphere & Décor - Nice, if cavernous
Appeal - Daily dim sum and unusual Chinese specialties
Useful to Note - The seafood menu can be expensive; dim sum is cheap.
Menu Suggestions - dim sum: steamed pork dumplings; sticky rolls filled with barbecued pork; coconut sticky roll; shrimp with noodles

Anchoring one end of the Hong Kong City Mall on Bellaire, Ocean Palace is a huge space in which to enjoy dim sum daily, exotic Chinese specialties, or reliable, more recognizable Chinese fare. Featuring an immense main dining room, the scale immediately makes an impression. The restaurant must be able to seat at least 500 in that space. There are also private rooms and an upstairs ballroom. In fact, Ocean Palace is alleged to be the largest American restaurant west of the Mississippi.

To the mostly Asian clientele, and value-conscious diners, the big draw is daily dim sum. For the uninitiated, often bustling, immense Ocean Palace is the place to try it. Dim sum translates to "heart's delight" in English, which probably doesn't help, but this is the Hong Kong and southern Chinese way of serving a variety of small dishes that fall into four general categories: fried; steamed; interesting; and sweets. A number of these dishes will make up the meal. These are ordered intermittently from women pushing small carts full of one or two items. Just point to what you want when the appropriate cart arrives (though it seems to be easier to order if you know Cantonese). Unless your table is well-situated among the push cart routes, it can take some effort to attract the attention of the women with the carts of desired items. During the week, Ocean Palace is one of the very few places that is large enough to be able to provide the push carts instead of having customers order the dim sum items from a menu. The array of dishes during the week is impressive, even much more so on the weekends. During the weekends, the very large dining room is packed with a cast of hundreds for dim sum. It makes for a neat spectacle to watch the numerous carts snake through the boisterous, crowded circular tables. The patrons are seemingly mostly Chinese, but there is also a diverse array of non-Chinese. This might be the most popular, and fun, place for non-Chinese to enjoy dim sum. And, it is a great value, too. It's very possible to leave full, spending less than $10 per person. As with most other restaurants that offer dim sum, it is helpful to speak a little Cantonese or Mandarin, at least the names of the dishes, since the waitstaff speaks nearly no English. Service can be trying at times. Ocean Palace does a very capable job with the more easily enjoyable dim sum offerings such as the dumplings, steamed buns, sticky buns and noodle dishes. The pork and barbecued pork buns are usually better than the corresponding ones with shrimp. The popular and tough to miss chicken feet are also reputed to be well prepared.

If dim sum is not for you, there are the lunch specials with familiar Chinese-American dishes, and a very large dinner menu. These are much easier to negotiate without the knowledge of Chinese than the dim sum offerings. Even in New Chinatown, it would be surprising to find a restaurant with a greater number of unusual Chinese dishes than Ocean Palace. This can be a cause of concern for the squeamish. The extensive English language menu is heavy on seafood, and can be quite expensive in the more exotic sections of the menu such as those that feature shark fin or abalone. But, most entrées are roughly twelve bucks. The menu is divided into a number of helpful sections: Appetizers; Shark Fin; Double Boiled Soup; Soup; Abalone and Sea Cucumber; Fresh Live Seafood; Crab; Scallop; Lobster; Shrimp; Poultry; Fish and Squid; Beef; Pork; Vegetable; Frog; Hot Pot; Bean Curd; Noodle in Soup; Noodles and Rice Plate. Under each of those headings, is a number of interesting items. Maybe too interesting. For example, for an appetizer you can order something called Pickled Crystalled Chicken Paws or Chilled Jelly Fish. The poultry is not limited to chicken and ducks; there are a couple of pigeon dishes (at least according to the menu). There are scores of other dishes that are less unusual and more generally appealing with recognizable Cantonese flavors. The seafood dishes are usually well prepared.

* 100% Taquito $7

3245 Southwest Freeway (west of Buffalo Speedway) 77027, (713) 665-2900
www.100taquito.com

Cuisine - Mexican (taqueria)
Hours - Mon-Thu, Sun 11AM to 10PM; Fri-Sat 11AM to 3PM
Credit Cards - Amex, Discover, MC, Visa
Service - Counter Service
Alcohol - Full Bar (limited)

Entrée Prices - $4 to $11 ($7 average)
Entrées $12 and less - 100%

Atmosphere & Décor - Spartan
Appeal - Very good Mexican fast food
Menu Suggestions - Torta de Tinga (sandwich with spicy, shredded barbecued beef); Taquito al pastor (taco with pork and pineapples); Quesadilla de Tinga; Tres Leches (moist white cake made with three types of milk)

The now fair-sized 100% Taquito sits in a strip center on the south side of the Southwest Freeway amidst a cluster of other small restaurants. In a city with an excess of obnoxious billboards, the one that creeps above the rooftop right near 100% Taquito is particularly obtrusive. However, it does signal motorists on the freeway and feeder road the location of some of the best tacos and *tortas* in the city, as the many Mexican and non-Mexican patrons alike have discovered. The fare at 100% Taquito is the street food of Mexico City: tacos, *quesadillas, tortas, sopes, molletes, banderillas*, etc., though done in a slightly more upscale and air-conditioned fashion. The tacos here are *taquitos* (small tacos in Spanish). An order consists of three small tacos filled with a choice of excellent ingredients: chicken, regular brisket (*barbacoa de brisket*), spicy brisket cooked with *chipotle* peppers (*tinga*), and pork (*al pastor*). You can get these with either small fresh corn or flour tortillas. These seem to taste a tad better with the more authentically Mexican corn tortillas. All *taquitos* are garnished with just cilantro and onions, as they are in Mexico. The complimentary salsas, red and green, are excellent. The *pico de gallo*, suitably vibrant and zesty, is also a very nice complement to the dishes. The best bets are the spicy brisket and the pork served with pineapple cubes. *Quesadillas* here are prepared in the Mexican fashion. These are very similar to tacos, but with the addition of cheese, and then warmed on the grill. Most are excellent, too. The pork with pineapple tastes better as a taco than a *quesadilla*. The average person will need to order at least two orders of tacos or *quesadillas* to be satisfied. Three, if you are a little hungry, or just large.

Along with the *taquitos* and *quesadillas*, the *tortas* are excellent. These are the Mexican versions of the sub sandwich, with toasted good-quality French-style *bolillo* bread, a choice of similar fillings for the tacos and *quesadillas* (fajita, pork, spicy brisket, regular brisket, chicken, or vegetarian) topped with sour cream, onions, lettuce, tomato, avocado and either *chipotle* salsa or spicy carrots. For an extra nominal charge, you can add some mild *Chihuahua* cheese. The *torta de tinga* (with spicy brisket), is one of the best hot sandwiches in town. The *sopes* consist of two flat corn tortillas with a border pinched around them and topped with beans, onions, cilantro and white cheese and the typical variety of fillings. *Molletes* are toasted French bread topped with black beans and melted cheese. *Banderillas, flautas* on many other Mexican restaurant menus, are three tiny brisket-filled tacos rolled and fried and topped with cream, *fresco* cheese and the red and green salsa. These are not quite the quality of the *tacos* or *quesadillas*. There are plenty of non-meat fillings to keep a vegetarian happy. To wash it all down, they have the range of *aguas frescas,* fruit drinks that are made in the restaurant: *limon, melon, jamaica* (sweet and tart, made from the hibiscus plant), *horchata* (made with rice) and *tamarindo* (a fruit from a tropical tree of the bean family, by the way); and Mexican soft drinks. Beers are inexpensive, and a safer choice than the margaritas. And, there are also the *micheladas*, a possibly refreshing mixture of beer, lime, Tabasco sauce, soy sauce, Worcestershire sauce and salt and pepper.

After identifying what you want, and how much of that you need, you order at the counter. But, then comes the toughest part, waiting for the order. Though quickly prepared and informal, it's not really fast food. Each dish is prepared as it is ordered, so you will have to wait at least a few minutes for it. This really is necessary, as all dishes are freshly prepared. With the high quality of the food, and the friendly staff, you can easily overlook the cheekiness of the surroundings, and that the television is often tuned a little too loudly to a Mexican pop video station. Much of the interior is meant to resemble the taco trucks that you see in Mexico City (or Houston, for that matter) and their environs. With a seating capacity over 150, and liquor available, it's like a taco truck on steroids (and HGH, too). You might want to save room for dessert as 100% Taquito has a very good *tres leches* cake. So, maybe you should just have two orders of tacos or *quesadillas*.

Ostioneria Arandas $9

10601 I-10 E. (east of Loop 610) 77029, (713) 673-5522
5826 Airline (between Tidwell and Parker) 77076, (713) 699-3392
www.ostioneriaarandas.com

Cuisine - Mexican; Seafood
Hours - I-10 East - Mon-Fri 11AM to 11 PM; Sat-Sun 10AM to 11PM; Airline - Mon-Tue 11AM to 12PM; Wed-Sat 11AM to 2AM; Sun 10AM to 2AM
Credit Cards - Amex, Discover, MC, Visa
Service - Table Service
Alcohol - Beer

Entrée Prices - $4 to $16 ($9 average)
Entrées $12 and less - 90%

Atmosphere & Décor - Functional
Appeal - Well prepared, fresh Mexican seafood in a fairly nice place
Menu Suggestions - Tacos de Mariscos; Ceviche Natural; Campechana (tomato-laden seafood cocktail); Seafood Torta (with shrimp)

The Ostioneria Arandas restaurants are the seafood-oriented cousins of the very successful Taqueria Arandas chain. These, too, are very well run and serve consistently good food; central Mexican- and Gulf Coast Houston-influenced style seafood. Befitting the Arandas name, these are more reliable than other small *ostionerias* around town. The restaurants are clean, and service and the kitchen are efficient, and amply satisfy the predominately working class Hispanic clientele. The wide-ranging menu is similar to most local Mexican seafood restaurants and where soups and cured and fried Gulf seafood predominate. There are the tomato juice-laden seafood cocktails with small pieces of shrimp, oyster, and octopus with the popular *vuelve a la vida* and the *campechana,* a mix of octopus, oyster and shrimp. There are *tostadas* topped with *ceviches* made with shrimp, octopus and pieces of fish, probably tilapia. The *ceviche,* only served on the *tostadas,* is different than at most area versions; less citrus flavor and some tomato, which is absent elsewhere. There is also an unusual hot *tostada* with cooked shrimp or octopus. The soups are hearty varieties featuring shrimp, octopus and fish, plus the spicy, mixed seafood soup (*Caldo Picosos de Mariscos*). Working as appetizers and perfect accompaniments to a cold lager beer, there are raw oysters, fried oysters, peel-and-eat shrimp, and deep-fried jalapeños stuffed with seafood. Shrimp and tilapia are served fried, battered and deep-fried, grilled, and on a sizzling platter (*parrillada*). Shrimp also is prepared sautéed with a garlic sauce (*al mojo de ajo*) or in a spicy, tomato sauce (*a la diabla*). These plates usually come with rice, fries, and a somewhat green salad. For a few more dollars more you can order red snapper, either as a fillet or whole, which can be prepared in nearly ten different ways. Salmon even sneaks onto the menu for one dish. If you can't decide exactly what you want, there are a half-dozen combination dishes that will likely help.

Ostioneria Arandas offers attractive items even at the low price end. One of the best items is the seafood tacos. Served with sautéed shrimp or a choice of fish fillet and shrimp, these are excellent, different than the popular Baja-style seafood tacos like those at Berryhill and Cabo. These are more like traditional Tex-Mex tacos (on flour tortillas if you don't specify otherwise), but with noticeably fresh seafood. A dash or two from the bottle of Valentina hot sauce on the table helps to enhance the already good tastes.

Decent-sized tacos are less than five bucks for a pair. Other great values are the seafood enchiladas filled with grilled shrimp and fish, seafood-filled *flautas,* a *torta* with either grilled or breaded and fried shrimp or fish on French bread, or the Po Boy Mexican with deep-fried shrimp.

Ostioneria Puerto Vallarta $10

6827 Griggs (east of the Gulf Freeway) 77023, (713) 926-6344

Cuisine - Mexican; Seafood
Hours - Mon-Thu, Sun 9AM to 3AM; Fri-Sat 9AM to 4AM
Credit Cards - Amex, Diners, Discover, MC, Visa
Service - Table Service
Alcohol - Beer

Entrée Prices - Dinner - $4 to $17 ($10 average); Lunch - $5
Entrées at Dinner $12 and less - 90%

Atmosphere & Décor - Comfortable
Appeal - Well prepared, fresh Mexican seafood in a fairly nice place
Useful to Note - It shares ownership with the very good Fonda Doña Maria.
Menu Suggestions - raw oysters on the half-shell (served with limon); Tostadas de Ceviche; Queso Del Mar; Filete Empapelado (snapper wrapped in tin foil); Cazuela De Mariscos En Guajillo (seafood stew in a spicy chile-based sauce)

If you are looking for authentic, and well prepared, Mexican seafood in fairly nice surroundings, Ostioneria Puerto Vallarta on the south side is the place. Though its offerings are similar to those of many of the bare-bones *ostionerias* (the seafood equivalent of *taquerias*), the décor of this restaurant is more typical of the suburban Tex-Mex locations, though with a greater sheen of authenticity. It occupies a fairly large yellow hacienda-style building on a busy street, and is a nice place. So, Ostioneria Puerto Vallarta is somewhat the best of both worlds: satisfying, authentically prepared Mexican seafood in an attractive setting. As with other *ostionerias,* most of the waitstaff speaks only Spanish, so knowledge of restaurant Spanish, at least, is helpful. This fact does not deter the non-Hispanics, as many lovers of Gulf seafood have found this place.

Most of the offerings reflect the bounty of the Gulf: shrimp, oysters, red snapper, octopus and squid. And, many of the dishes are very appealing. The *ceviches,* and other marinated seafood cocktails are some the best around. The *Vuelve a la Vida,* with its famous restorative powers, is a cocktail mix of marinated raw shrimp, oyster, octopus and squid with tomato juice. The raw oysters are popular and are served with *limones,* limes rather than lemons in the Mexican parlance. Other reliable starters are the *Queso Del Mar,* melted cheese with shrimp, and the *Tostada Ceviche,* the delicious *ceviche* on top of a crispy tortilla. There are a number of popular Mexican shrimp preparations. Each dish is around $10 and includes rice and vegetables or fries: *Camarones Empanizados* (breaded and fried shrimp), *Camarones a la Diabla* (sautéed shrimp in a hot sauce), *Camarones a la Veracruzana* (shrimp cooked with tomato sauce and peppers, onions, olives), *Camarones a la Plancha* (grilled shrimp), and a shrimp-filled enchilada. Other dishes of special interest include the spicy *Cazuela De Mariscos En Guajillo* (a piquant seafood stew), and *Arroz Con Mariscos* (shrimp, oyster, octopus, squid and fish over rice). There are a couple of reasonably priced fish fillets that are quite good: the *Filete Empapelado* (fish fillet wrapped in foil and cooked with tomatoes, onion, bell pepper and cilantro), and the *Filete en Mojo De Ajo* (a fillet sautéed in garlic and butter). These are served with rice and vegetables. As with other restaurants, some of the preparations with Gulf red snapper are not inexpensive. These can be excellent, and given the quality, seem to be a fair value. Though primarily a seafood restaurant, Ostioneria Puerto Vallarta has enough dishes to satisfy any committed carnivore in the group. They serve fajitas with beef or chicken, beef short *ribs (Costillas de Res*), a T-bone steak, quail and *Alambres,* a shish kabob featuring either beef or chicken. Indicative of the quality of the restaurant, the *aguas frescas* are made by hand.

* Otilia's $11

7710 Long Point (between Antoine and Wirt) 77055, (713) 681-7203
www.otilias.com

Cuisine - Mexican
Hours - Mon-Thu 11AM to 9PM; Fri-Sat 11AM to 10PM; Sun 11AM to 3PM
Credit Cards - Amex, Diners, Discover, MC, Visa
Service - Table Service
Alcohol - Beer & Wine

Entrée Prices - Dinner & Lunch - $7 to $13 ($11 average); Breakfast - $5 to 7
Entrées at Dinner $12 and less - 80%

Atmosphere & Décor - Functional, but often lively; patio
Appeal - Some of the very best regional Mexican food in town
Useful to Note - Stick to more ambitious dishes; tacos can be an afterthought.
Menu Suggestions - Cream of Poblano Soup; Cochinita Pibil (pork cooked with red onions and banana leaves); Chile en Nogada (a stuffed pepper in a creamy white sauce); Plato Huasteco (a marinated, thinly sliced and piquant beef steak); Chile Relleno; Enchilada de Mole Poblano (an enchilada in a rich, dark mole sauce); Mexican Plate (tostada, taco and enchilada); Cebollas Oaxaqueñas (onions stuffed with ground beef pork, olive, caper and raisin mixture and deep-fried); aguas frescas

Otilia's proudly advertises that it serves "100% Mexican food - No Tex-Mex". The food is pan-Mexican with dishes from several regions throughout the country. With the exception of the complimentary chips and salsa on the tables, there is little concession to American mores or tastes. But local Americans definitely like this food, and make a big percentage of the clientele. The emphasis is on quality and authenticity. Indicative of a place situated in the A-frame shell of what was an old What-a-Burger with a covered car port that once served the drive-in customers, the décor and atmosphere are not much, even after expansion and remodeling. This lack of ambiance has not stopped Mexican food aficionados from finding this very friendly and efficient restaurant that is located on unfashionable Long Point in Spring Branch. This is the type of place where you come to savor the cuisine rather than swill margaritas. Further evidence of this is that Otilia's is often rated among the top Mexican restaurants in the area, and very deservedly so. They serve some of the very best Mexican food in town.

Just about every entrée at Otilia's is worthy of mention from the soups, the tortilla-centric dishes to meat and seafood entrées. There are soups that work as a meal, the brothy *Caldo de Res* made with beef and vegetables, and *Pozole Rojo,* a pork and hominy soup. Otilia's version of *menudo* is called *Pancita;* beef tripe soup without the hominy. Otilia's serves three types of enchiladas daily. There is the very satisfying basic dish filled with a choice of chicken, ground beef or white cheese. The *Enchiladas Verdes* are filled with chicken and topped with white melted cheese, a tomatillo-based salsa, sour cream and chopped onions. And, there are the unusual *Potosinos* that are described as a different type of enchiladas; corn tortillas sautéed in *guajillo* chiles, filled with crumbled, mild *Chihuahua* cheese and chopped onions, served on a bed of lettuce, and topped with sautéed carrots, potatoes, onions and more crumbled white cheese, though no sauce. There are *Chuletas de Puerco,* moist center cut pork chops in a zesty sauce. The *Flautas,* two long rolled and fried corn tortillas, are filled with a choice among ground beef, chicken, potatoes or *rajas con queso* (strips of marinated poblano peppers with cheese). Even without a menu item for fajitas, the beef dishes are especially good at Otilia's. Beef as a main dish is served as the *Milanesa,* a steak pounded thin, breaded and pan-fried, *Arracheras,* their version of fajitas, and the *Plato Huasteco.* The *Plato Huasteco* is a thin marinated steak (*cesina*) that is then grilled, and served with gilled onions, guacamole, tomato slices, a roasted jalapeño, and a side enchilada. This reddish-orange meat is tender and especially flavorful with a squeeze of lime. The excellent *Conchinita Pibil,* a dish from the Yucatan, consisting of pork and red onions stewed with banana leaves, arrives with an unnatural bright reddish color. Eaten with the house-made tortillas, the juicy pork has a slightly sweet taste. The *Chile en Nogada* consists of a large poblano chile stuffed with either chicken, ground beef or cheese that is served in a creamy white sauce made with tomatoes, onions, peppers and cilantro and then topped with walnuts, and sometimes pomegranate seeds. Not very spicy, but with a lot of taste, this is another excellent dish, if somewhat heavy. The similar more standard *chile relleno* is almost as good. This can be filled with a special version of *picadillo* consisting of ground beef, pork, olives, capers, almonds and raisins. There are other specials that are equally well prepared. Most of the entrées are served with either refried pinto beans or refried black beans. Soupy *charro* beans can be substituted for an additional charge.

The chocolate-based *mole* dishes, by way of Puebla, in southern Mexico, are exceptional: sweet, rich and complex; certainly some of the best *moles* in town. Unfortunately, they are only served Friday through Sunday. These include the *Mole con Pechuga,* a boneless, moist chicken breast topped with *mole,* and the excellent *Enchiladas de Mole Poblano,* chicken enchiladas covered with the same *mole.* Also, only at the end of the week is *Camerones en Nogada,* a similar dish to the *Chile en Nogada,* with sautéed shrimp substituted for the chile pepper. Another shrimp dish is the *Camarones Endiablados,* a spicy dish featuring shrimp sautéed with *chipotle* peppers, and served with grilled onions and bell peppers. If you are more in the mood for the familiarity of Tex-Mex, Otilia's does not quite acquiesce, but their Mexican Plate is similar enough to the popular Tex-Mex combination platters. It is a combination dish featuring a chicken *tostada,* a ground beef taco, and rice and beans, plus an optional enchilada in reddish, tomato-based sauce. It's far better than any similar plate you will find at the popular Tex-Mex stops.

On the more low key, and inexpensive, side, there are *tortas* (the Mexican sandwiches) that are better than most, and are an absolute steal for around 4 bucks; tacos; *tostadas; gorditas* (essentially a fried and stuffed corn pocket); and *sopes* (thick round tortillas topped with beans, *queso fresco,* onions and salsa). There are about a half-dozen fillings and toppings for each. These can vary slightly, but they include marinated and roasted pork (*al pastor*), baked pork (*pierna al horno*), spicy pork (*tinga veracruzana*), stewed chicken breast (*pollo guisado*), ground beef (*picadillo*), fajita beef (*carne asada*), and, for *tostadas,* even pickled pork skin (*cueritos*). Unfortunately, with nearly all of the patrons ordering the more ambitious (and expensive) plates, the tacos, though decent, are somewhat of an afterthought and somewhat pricey for what these are. The *aguas frescas,* the fresh fruit drinks, are made daily from scratch, and are very tasty. The *horchata* (made with rice and condensed milk) is especially notable. Breakfast is served daily until 1PM. Since the restaurant only opens at 11AM, this leaves only a couple of hours to sample it, usually as a substitute for the lunch offerings. Breakfast tacos are just a couple dollars, fairly pricey by local standards, but worth the additional cost. All of the breakfasts are egg-based, and some have added flair: *Huevos Rancheros; Chilaquiles* with scrambled eggs, and the option to add additional over easy eggs on top, an omelet; *Huevos a la Otilia's,* two eggs over easy, covered with salsa and served with rice and refried beans mixed together; and *Huevos Divorciados,* two eggs over easy, one covered with green salsa, the other with red salsa, separated by refried beans and topped with crumbled white cheese. There is also the Breakfast Plate and choice of eggs prepared *a la mexicana,* with potatoes, ham, *chorizo,* bacon or salsa.

Palazzo's $11

2620 Briar Ridge (north of Westheimer, east of Voss) 77057, (713) 784-8110
2300 Westheimer (between S. Shepherd and Kirby) 77098, (713) 522-6777
10455 Briar Forest (just west of the Beltway) 77042, (713) 784-8110
www.palazzoscafe.com

Cuisine - Italian-American; Pizza
Hours - Briar Ridge - Mon-Fri 11AM to 2PM, 5 to 10PM; Sat 5 to 10PM; Westheimer & Briar Forest - Daily 11AM to 10:30PM
Credit Cards - Amex, Diners, Discover, MC, Visa
Service - Table Service; Delivery
Alcohol - Briar Ridge - Beer & Wine, BYOB; Westheimer & Briar Forest - Full Bar

Entrée Prices - Dinner - $6 to $23 ($11 avg.); Lunch - $6 to $13; Brunch -$7 to $17
Entrées at Dinner $12 and less - 70%

Atmosphere & Décor - Pleasant, often lively; patio (Westheimer)
Appeal - Good, basic Southern Italian-American food reasonable prices
Useful to Note - The pizzas are the best reason to visit.
Menu Suggestions - pizzas; Athena Pizza; Chicken Cannelloni; Southwestern Chicken Lasagna (with chicken, black beans, poblanos and cheddar); Penne Stefano (Italian sausage in a creamy tomato sauce)

The original Palazzo's has been a favorite in the Briagrove area for over a decade, so be prepared for a short wait at the peak times for Friday and Saturday dinners. That popularity has spawned two other locations, first to the east, and then to the west (and the east again, as the second location moved to nicer digs in 2007, into the former Torcello-Armando's-Dish-Two Chef's Bistro-Beso spot). The attraction is very satisfying, basic Southern Italian-American in comfortable, casual settings for very reasonable prices. The pizzas, especially, are very good, and some of the best in the area. Their dough is made daily and is quite flavorful, and the ingredients are always good quality. The fairly thin crusts are always cooked to a proper crispness and feature a sometime artful and generous spread of toppings. Of the nearly ten specialty pizzas, especially good is the Athena that is topped with pepperoni, roma tomatoes, red onions, feta cheese and black olives. The range of available toppings is fairly comprehensive, including even roasted garlic and anchovies. Pizzas make for great value meals, and are popular for take-away. The rest of the menu, which has grown over the years, consists of salads, pastas and entrées with chicken, veal and seafood. In addition to an admirable house salad featuring romaine and feta, there is the ubiquitous Caesar salad and Tomatoes Caprese, that popular Southern Italian mix of slices of mozzarella and tomatoes with basil. For the pastas, the chicken cannelloni, stuffed with a mix of chicken, spinach, mushrooms and ricotta cheese, and topped with a nice marinara sauce, is very good. Possibly even better is the Southwestern Lasagna that is regionalized with poblanos, black beans, and cheddar, lathered with a creamy sauce. The dishes with commercial pasta, which are done to the expected level of firmness, include pasta Alfredo, pasta primavera, spaghetti and meatballs, lasagna, are all generally quite reliable. Of these, the Pasta Palazzo with bowtie pasta and chicken, sun-dried tomatoes, capers and artichoke hearts, and the Penne Stefano, with Italian sausage and a cream-laden marinara sauce are probably the most enticing. Most of the dozen or so entrées are out of the great Italian-American repertoire with expected preparations of chicken marsala, veal piccata, veal Parmesan and the like, but also a red snapper encrusted with thin pasta and the Italian-esque rainbow trout grilled and served with olive oil, garlic and lemon. The décor at the original, as fitting of a location in an older strip center just off Westheimer, is somewhat minimal. It's a relatively small place with a concrete floor, and it can get a bit loud, especially with the family with young children that is invariably a table or two away. The newer locations are nicer, but seem to work as well as the original, if without quite the decibel level at peak times. The service and restaurants are friendly and welcoming, even when packed. And, as a nice bonus the original location allows you to bring in your own wine for a very minimal corkage fee.

Panini $7

711 Louisiana - Tunnel (below the Pennzoil Building) 77002, (713) 223-2022

Cuisine - Sandwiches; Pizza
Hours - Mon-Fri 11AM to 3PM
Credit Cards - Amex, Diners, MC, Visa
Service - Counter Service
Alcohol - NONE

Entrée Prices - $6 to $8 ($7 average)
Entrées $12 and less - 100%

Atmosphere & Décor - Spartan; it's in the Tunnel, after all
Appeal - Excellent Italian-inspired sandwiches

Useful to Note - Not much seating; owner also runs Perbacco on street level
Menu Suggestions - Arcobaleno Sandwich (meatballs with red bell peppers on ciabatta roll); Roast Beef Sandwich (with provolone, lettuce and tomato) Mozzarella Pomodoro & Prosciutto Sandwich; Ciabatta Deliziosa (with mozzarella, mortadella and roasted red bell peppers); pizzas; Caprese Salad (mozzarella, tomatoes, basil and olive oil)

Where as the vast majority of lunch-only restaurants downtown rarely rise about the caloric needs of its nearly captive crowd, Panini does far more. Located in the tunnel beneath the Pennzoil Building since the 1990s, the aptly named Panini serves very good made-to-order sandwiches and individually sized pizzas to the hungry downtown office workers for lunch. These are not flat sandwiches run through a small toaster oven that are often called *panini* at many Italian restaurants or sandwich shops. Rather, at Panini's these are served on fresh, soft and crusty *ciabatta* rolls that provide for a flavorful distinction from average sandwiches, and *panini* for that matter. You can also order many of the sandwiches on white and wheat bread, but why bother. There are about two dozen versions of zesty, unfussy sandwiches, most of which are served warm, and many with those Southern Italian staples, provolone and mozzarella cheeses. The ones with an Italian bent are usually the best such as the excellent hot meatball sandwich, called the Arcobaleno, and the similar one with Italian sausage, the latter slathered in tomato sauce. Good quality cold cuts like *mortadella, sopressata* salami and prosciutto are featured in several versions. A non-Italian sandwich that is well worth ordering is the flavorful, if somewhat different, roast beef sandwich. Grilled chicken, grilled salmon, chicken salad and tuna salad are prepared here much better than most places. Half-sized versions are available for half-dozen or so of the sandwiches. As the owners are from Capri, across from Naples, you can expect that the pizzas will be worth ordering, and they are. As with the pizzas, the *Insalata Caprese,* the familiar mixture of mozzarella, ripe tomato, basil leaves and olive oil has to be done well here. There are also other salads, nearly a dozen from leafy to tuna salad. Panini also has a soup of the day. A sandwich and a bag of chips, or a small pizza, can make for a satisfying meal whether eaten in the tunnel or at your desk. There are only a handful of tables in the small restaurant, but others are in the tunnel beyond its doors. Takeout is necessarily very popular, and the sandwiches and salads travel especially well.

Pappas Bar-B-Q $8

1217 Pierce (at San Jacinto) 77002, (713) 659-1245
1100 Smith (at Lamar) 77002, (713) 759-0018
8777 S. Main (at McNee near OST) 77025, (713) 432-1107
4430 I-45 N. (at Crosstimbers) 77022, (713) 697-9533
9815 Bissonnet (between Southwest Freeway and Beltway) 77036, (713) 777-1661

7007 Southwest Freeway (between Hillcroft and Bellaire) 77074, (713) 772-4557
7050 I-45 S. (at Woodbridge, north of Loop 610 S.) 77087, (713) 649-7236
8560 I-45 S. (at Monroe / Winkler) 77017, (713) 947-9927
20794 I-45 S. (at NASA Road 1) 77598, (281) 332-1285
11311 Fondren (at W. Belfort) 77035, (713) 721-6360
9797 Westheimer (at Gessner) 77042, (713) 780-0081
703 FM 1960 W. (just west of I-45 N.) 77090, (281) 893-5571
7925 FM 1960 W. (at Highway 249) 77070, (281) 469-7166
12917 Northwest Freeway (between Bingle and Hollister) 77040, (713) 462-2550
3950 S. Terminal (at IAH - Terminal E) 77032, (281) 443-3487
3814 Little York (just west of Highway 59) 77093, (713) 697-4417
19713 Highway 59 (at FM 1960) 77338, (281) 446-0441
www.pappasbbq.com

Cuisine - Barbecue
Hours - Mon-Thu, Sun 11AM to 10PM; Fri-Sat 11AM to 11PM
Credit Cards - Amex, MC, Visa
Service - Counter Service
Alcohol - Beer

Entrée Prices - Dinner & Lunch - $6 to $11 ($8 average); Breakfast - $3 to $6
Entrées at Dinner $12 and less - 100%

Atmosphere & Décor - Nice (especially for barbecue restaurants)
Appeal - Pretty good barbecue in well-run and very convenient restaurants
Useful to Note - The chopped beef seems to taste better earlier in the day.
Menu Suggestions - Chopped Beef Sandwich; Sliced Beef Sandwich; Baked Potato with Chopped Beef; Baked Potato with Turkey; Pork Ribs

---

As with the other Pappas restaurants, which are not the best or most authentic purveyors in each of the several food genres (Mexican, Cajun, etc.), Pappas Bar-B-Q serves up good quality Texas-style barbecue in generously sized portions. This is even after the expansion to include the former Luther's locations. These are well-run, fairly attractive restaurants, which are often crowded, where you can count on getting a satisfying meal for a reasonable price with friendly and efficient service. Though local barbecue purists might argue that this is corporate, modern barbecue, these are very popular restaurants, and the food really is better than most.

The offerings at Pappas are typical of most barbecue restaurants in the area, though maybe a little more extensive. The standard barbecue plates, called Specials here, feature slowly cooked and mesquite-smoked meats and two sides. The meats served at Pappas are: beef brisket, pork, ham, sausage, beef ribs, pork ribs, turkey and chicken. The sides are fairly numerous and generally well prepared: spicy rice, ranch beans, lima beans, cole slaw, potato salad, yams, macaroni salad and cucumber salad. This is the odd barbecue purveyor where the vegetables are actually popular. In place of the standard sides, for slightly more, the meats are available with a baked potato or salad. All of the meats are also served in sandwiches, and some as the slightly larger po boys. As it is Texas, the beef brisket is probably the choice of meat to order. It hits the proper notes, and is tender and usually quite flavorful, like it must be for all worthwhile local barbecue restaurants. In a chopped beef sandwich, the brisket is almost minced and served with a lot of sauce so the sandwich is similar to a sloppy Joe. The sliced version is noticeably lean yet tender and tasty. In addition to the brisket sandwiches and plates, hamburgers, chicken burgers and stuffed baked potatoes with plenty of tangy barbecue sauce and shredded cheese are also popular. A few salads and a couple baked desserts are available for those who are watching their caloric intake and those who are not, respectively. Pappas strives to be convenient for families. The restaurants are fairly spacious for barbecue joints, and certainly nicer. There are plenty of tables and several televisions scattered about to help occupy the kids, or dad, as these are usually tuned to a sporting event. For takeout, Pappas offers a half-dozen Value Packs that can serve from six to twenty-five that can help make for an economical meal for a group. During the weekday mornings, some locations serve the convenient-for-takeout local favorite, breakfast tacos.

Pappas Burger $10

5815 Westheimer (west of Chimney Rock) 77057, (713) 975-6082
www.pappasburger.com

Cuisine - Hamburgers
Hours - Mon-Thu, Sun 11AM to 10PM; Fri-Sat 11AM to 11PM
Credit Cards - Amex, MC, Visa
Service - Counter Service
Alcohol - Beer & Wine

Entrée Prices - $7 to $15 ($10 average)
Entrées $12 and less - 90%

Atmosphere & Décor - Pleasant
Appeal - Very good hamburgers served with Pappas' efficiency
Useful to Note - Burger meat comes from Pappas Bros. Steakhouse next door.
Menu Suggestions - Pappas Burger; Bleu Cheeseburger; Buffalo Wings; Mary's BLT Salad (romaine, roma tomatoes, blue cheese and bacon); Oriental Chicken Salad (mixed greens, red cabbage, carrots, roasted peanuts and grilled chicken)

As a hamburger joint with Pappas in the name, Pappas Burger is pretty much what you would expect from the family. This is a good thing. Pappas Burger is a slicker-than-usual operation for a modestly priced restaurant that primarily serves hamburgers: service is much better; the setting is cleaner and more comfortable; the food is well prepared; the large portions provide a decent value; and the menu hits more accurately at its target patrons. Not unimportantly, the burgers are very good here, too.

The burgers are made with patties of around one-third pound. These are cooked to the properly charred exterior while retaining a juicy interior. The buns and the rest of the accompaniments are fresher, and better than at most burger places. For burgers, creations beyond the basic Pappas Burger, there are a cheeseburger, double cheeseburger, chili cheeseburger, and the Hickory Cheddar Bacon Burger. The similar hot sandwiches include a Grilled Portobello mushroom burger served with grilled onions and feta cheese, a grilled chicken sandwich, a fried chicken sandwich, and a Grilled Ahi Tuna steak "Burger". Each of the hamburgers and sandwiches comes with a large amount of suitably crisp, freshly cut fries. Though burgers are the primary attraction here, the well-planned menu is more than just burgers and hot sandwiches. In fact, it will probably appeal to those who never eat burgers. The lunchtime tables of office workers sporting a wide diversity of dishes is testament to this. There are a number of appealing, zesty dinner-sized salads including the popular Caesar and Greek Salads. Though "Burger" is in the name, the salads are also a reason for a visit. There is the Oriental Chicken Salad with grilled chicken, red cabbage and roasted peanuts with an Asian-style vinaigrette. Another is the BLT Salad made with romaine, crumbled blue cheese, ripe roma tomatoes and crispy thick bacon. Then there is a Niçoise salad with grilled ahi tuna instead of anchovies with mixed greens, new potatoes, green olives, capers and slices of a hard-boiled egg. For the less health conscious, there are also cheese fries, nachos, cheese bread, *quesadillas* with chicken, Buffalo wings and a half-dozen rich desserts. All of these are well done here, and more than sufficiently caloric. As proficient as Pappas Burgers is, the system of ordering is a little odd: you order at the counter; find a seat; your food is brought to the table; and you pay the wait staff when finished. No matter, Pappas Burger is well worth at least a short drive when you have the craving for a well made burger and fries, or the like.

Patu $11

2420 Rice (between Kelvin and Morningside) 77005, (713) 528-6998

Cuisine - Thai
Hours - Mon-Thu 11AM to 2PM, 5 to 9:30PM; Fri-Sat 11AM to 2PM, 5 to 10PM; Sun 11AM to 5PM
Credit Cards - Amex, MC, Visa
Service - Buffet at Lunch; Table Service at Dinner
Alcohol - Beer & Wine

Entrée Prices - Dinner - $7 to $16 ($11 avg.); Lunch - $9 (all-you-can-eat buffet)
Entrées at Dinner $12 and less - 70%

Atmosphere & Décor - Nice
Appeal - Good Thai lunch buffet; interesting entrées at dinner
Useful to Note - Not much parking in front, but plenty within a half-block.
Menu Suggestions - Gang Panaeng (curry with potato, peanut, coconut milk and beef or vegetables); Pineapple and Shrimp Curry (cooked with red curry and coconut milk); Gang Keiw Wan (green curry with coconut milk)

Situated in between two other buildings, Patu Thai Cuisine occupies a sliver of a space on Rice Boulevard in the heart of the Rice Village among many quaint shops and eateries. Patu is one of the several reliable Thai restaurants in the area. Thai Spice and Nit Noi are each just a couple of blocks away. Morningside Thai and Mai Thai are about a mile away. Patu is a charming small place that consists of one thin, long dining room with around a dozen tables. A long-time attraction is that Patu offers a buffet for lunch, which is available 11AM until 2PM from Monday through Saturday, and from 11AM until 5PM on Sundays. At nine bucks, the all-you-can-eat lunch buffet is a good value. It's both a bit more bountiful than most lunchtime buffets and the food is generally better. The well-labeled and well prepared dishes include an array of soups, *satay*, salads, spring rolls, curry dishes, *Pad Thai*, dishes with beef and chicken, fresh fruit, and a dessert. Especially good selections from the buffet are *Gang Musaman* (curry with potato, peanut and coconut milk) with chicken or pork, other curries, and the spicy Basil Chicken.

The fine value lunch buffet is the prime draw for many, but the full dinner menu has an even greater array of appealing choices. Most of the locally popular Thai dishes are represented, and the fairly large menu is divided among appetizers, soups, sides, salads, fried rice dishes, noodle-based dishes, curries, non-curry entrées, and House Specials. These are the Patu's most interesting, and most expensive, dishes. These dozen entrées include the House Special Duck, a boneless roast duck, which is battered then deep-fried and served with stir-fried vegetables. There are a couple of dishes featuring an entire fried fish, and a couple others with deep-fried soft shell crabs. There are several seafood curries including the Pineapple and Shrimp Curry cooked with red curry and coconut milk. There is also something called the Bangkok Love Boat. This is described as a spicy dish with stir-fried seafood with lemon grass, *kaffir* lime leaves and basil that is baked in an aluminum foil "boat" that is cut open at your table. Many of the dishes on the menu come with a choice of spiciness among mild, medium, hot, and the properly incendiary Thai hot.

Paulie's $10

1834 Westheimer (east of S. Shepherd) 77098, (713) 807-7271
2617 Holcombe (west of Kirby) 77025, (713) 660-7057
11550 Louetta (west of Highway 249 and Jones) 77070, (832) 717-5445
www.pauliescafe.com

Cuisine - Sandwiches; Italian-American
Hours - Mon-Sat 11AM to 8PM
Credit Cards - MC, Visa
Service - Counter Service
Alcohol - Beer & Wine

Entrée Prices - $7 to $17 ($10 average)
Entrées $12 and less - 80%

Atmosphere & Décor - Nice
Appeal - Top-notch Italian-inspired sandwiches in appealing, casual surroundings
Menu Suggestions - gazpacho; Principe Panino (sandwich with Italian sausage, mozzarella, grilled onions and bell peppers); Pizzitola Panino (sandwich with mozzarella, roma tomato slices, and pest); Torregrossa Panino (sandwich with Genoa salami, ham, Swiss cheese and olive relish); Pork Tenderloin with Cajun Mustard Sandwich; Meatball Sandwich; Grilled Shrimp BLT; cookies

Now with three locations, each Paulie's retains a stylish interior and well-presented, mostly informal Italian-inspired food. Although the Italian accents are clear and though Italian-themed sandwiches are the prime attraction, this is quite different than the typical Italian deli. Inexpensive and very satisfying, these help make Paulie's an excellent choice for a quick, delicious lunch or dinner. The interiors are modern and very attractive for what is primarily a sandwich shop. Actually, given the high quality in all respects, "good, informal neighborhood restaurant" is a more appropriate phrase. The fairly sleek decor at the original site is on lower Westheimer makes this space a very nice one to enjoy a relatively quick meal.

Artfully assembled with quality ingredients such as ripe roma tomatoes, noticeably fresh spinach, roasted red peppers and good, fresh bread, there are basically two types of sandwiches here. These are some of the very best in the area, and the best reasons to visit Paulie's, though some might argue for the cookies. The *panini*-denoted sandwiches are warm sandwiches served with a variety of Italian-type fillings on grilled hearty white bread that is often termed "country Italian". Though slightly greasy, these are great. The namesake *Petronella* consists of smoked turkey and bacon with Swiss cheese. The *Principe* is Italian sausage with mozzarella and grilled onions and peppers. The *Torregrossa* is Genoa salami, ham with Swiss cheese and a light brushing of an olive salad. There are a couple of vegetarian options: the *Pizzitola* with fresh mozzarella, roma tomatoes and pesto; and the *Yezzi*, spinach and roasted tomatoes with feta cheese. The unqualified sandwiches are also quite good. These are much better than your typical sandwiches, in part, because the sandwich grill is often in use. There are grilled shrimp BLT, grilled cheese, grilled chicken breast, grilled tuna, grilled Portobello mushroom and red pepper, moist pork tenderloin with a zesty Cajun mustard, a unique chicken salad, smoked salmon, the Shrimp Cake Burger featuring ground shrimp, and even pimento cheese, and peanut butter and jelly. The sandwiches come with sides of either a flavorful cold pasta salad with red peppers and artichoke hearts, or what is called Italian potato salad that includes olives.

Sandwiches are just part of the menu. There are also very appealing salads, pastas, pizzas and large entrées. Salads will work as a meal for most, and include an Italian Family Salad with romaine, cucumbers, tomatoes, olives, pepperoncini, mozzarella and salami; Spinach Salad with mushroom and egg; a Caesar Salad without egg; their version of *Insalata Caprese*, mozzarella, roma tomato slices and basil. Chicken, chicken salad, shrimp and salmon salad can be added to any of the salads for a few dollars more. The several pasta dishes are simple, yet imaginative. Though the pastas are generally light, an exception, and an enticing one, might be the Pasta Portobello that features fettuccine with Portobello mushrooms, and red pepper in a creamy sherry-based sauce. The soggy-crusted pizzas are best ignored. There are heartier plates, too, featuring a range of Italian-American dishes.

Pavani $11

10554 Southwest Freeway (inside the Beltway, on north side) 77074, (713) 272-8259

Cuisine - Indian
Hours - Tue-Sat 11AM to 2:30PM, 5 to 11PM
Credit Cards - Amex, Diners, Discover, MC, Visa
Service - Buffet at Lunch; Table Service at Dinner
Alcohol - Beer & Wine

Entrée Prices - Dinner - $11 (buffet); Lunch - $9 weekday, $10 weekends (buffet)
Entrées at Dinner $12 and less - 100%

Appeal - Savory southern Indian food; and a good value lunch buffet
Atmosphere & Décor - Pleasant
Useful to Note - All-you-can-eat buffet all of the time.
Menu Suggestions - Masala Dosa (a light crêpe filled with potato and curry); Chicken Tikka Masala; Chili Chicken (chicken in a brown sauce with chili peppers); chickpeas; spicy potatoes

Pavani Indian Cuisine is very nicely set in a former Steak & Ale (really) under the soaring overpass. Proficiently serving both northern and southern

Indian food, Pavani is a popular destination for both Indians and non-Indians looking for consistently flavorful and well prepared food. The expected lunch buffet for nine bucks with usually around twenty items is one of the better lunch deals in town. On the weekends and in the evenings, it's still buffet, and two or three bucks more, but certainly worth it.

The lunch buffet offerings are pretty much what you will find at most local Indian restaurants. There are mostly inspired from the northern area that feature grilled meats and buttery curry sauces. Though the lunch buffet items are fairly standard, the choices are more numerous, and the execution is better than most. Each meal comes with a *dosa,* a delicious, long, thin Indian-style crêpe, either plain or *masala* (with a potato and vegetable curry). Another southern Indian dish usually available during the day is the *sambar,* a thick soup made with lentils, coconut and spices. There are usually a fair number of items featuring chicken, goat, and vegetables, plus soups, chutneys and desserts. A favorite among non-Indians, the Chicken *Tikka Masala* is very good here; moist chicken grilled in a *tandoori* oven and served in a creamy, spicy reddish curry. Other curries can include lamb *masala,* chicken in a mild curry, lentil curry with spinach and tomatoes, and a goat curry in a mild sauce. There are plenty of vegetable dishes in addition to the standard *saag paneer,* which is less creamy than at most other places. Providing a very fine complement, the *naan* is freshly baked. The dinner buffet includes more southern Indian specialties. These are primarily vegetarian dishes, but there are still many, more familiar meat dishes. Actually, there are just meats and vegetables among the main items, no seafood. No Goan or other southern seafood specialties. At dinnertime you can experiment with some new dishes or enjoy a more familiar Indian meal. The southern Indian items might be new to many who just visit the buffets, and appetizers and small plate dishes might be the biggest relevation for those. These include a variety of *pankoras,* vegetables that are battered then deep-fried and served with a couple of chutneys, one hot tomato, and the other, a mild coconut. There might also be one of a variety of *vadas* (deep-fried lentil patties somewhat like doughnuts), *parathas* (a pan-fried wheat bread filled with potatoes), *pooris* (a puffy bread), *sambar, rasam* (a spicy tomato and tamarind soup), *raita* (yogurt with vegetables), and *papad* (lentil wafers). There is usually the delectable *gulab juman* (the very sweet, spongy pastry in syrup) among the desserts.

Paw Paw's $13

12151 Westheimer (between Kirkwood and Dairy Ashford) 77077, (281) 920-2730
www.pawpawgrill.com

Cuisine - Greek; Persian

Hours - Daily 11AM to 11PM
Credit Cards - Amex, Diners, Discover, MC, Visa
Service - Table Service
Alcohol - Full Bar

Entrée Prices - $8 to $30 ($13 average)
Entrées $12 and less - 70%

Atmosphere & Décor - Very nice, fun
Appeal - Stylish place serving well prepared Persian and Greek dishes
Useful to Note - The grill can get backed up with large parties; free appetizers.
Menu Suggestions - Paw Satay Treats (skewers of grilled chicken topped with a peanut sauce); Spring Rolls (fried phyllo pastry with vegetables and chicken or beef); Kubideh (two skewers of seasoned ground beef); Souvla (rotisserie cooked and sliced pork, chicken, beef or lamb); hamburgers

---

The stylized sign above the restaurant might be tough to read, and, though accurate, the subtitle, "Bar & Grill", gives no indication of the fare. Paw Paw's is a very good choice for a visit. Soon after being seated, a couple or so appetizers, more if your group is large, such as *hummus*, a Persian-style potato salad or a cucumber salad will be set on your table with bread. Dig in, these are complimentary (that's free), and a good introduction to the food and the level of accommodation here. The dishes are attractively presented on square- and rectangular-shaped shallow glossy black plates, and the service is earnest if not expert. The oft-present owner working the floor is quick to remedy any mistake or misunderstanding. Set just south of Westheimer behind long-standing Jimmy Wilson's Seafood & Chop House (the former Denis') and the Phoenicia Specialty Foods, Paw Paw's shares some good food neighbors. It features a single, long and very stylish dining room covered in plenty of bold, deep red mixed with black and with a bar running for much of the length of one side is an attractive and possibly fun place for both a meal and a drink. This personable restaurant also allows you to eat in a comparatively healthy fashion while being able to satisfy the most committed and hungry carnivore.

Half the menu is Persian and half the menu is Greek, which reflects the husband and wife team that own and run the restaurant. The friendly and gregarious Greek wife is often greeting and seating customers while her Persian husband is seen tending the visible grill set in back between sides of the expansive bar. The Greek and Persian cooking traditions are really not terribly dissimilar and the items meld well on the copious menu and on the plate. In addition to the Greek and Persian items that take most of the space on the menu, there are juicy half-pound burgers and several steaks, all-American classics. The grill gets a workout here. Odd for a Greek restaurant, there is not the expected compressed gyro meat here, just recognizably meaty pieces of beef, lamb, chicken and pork, plus, very interestingly, entrée-sized presentations with vegetables and tofu. There are chops, *souvlaki*, and Persian grilled items such as *kubideh* (ground beef skewers), *jujeh* (a marinated Cornish hen) and *barg* (filet mignon). The restaurant is quick to recommend the Chicken Souvla, which is said to be to the more traditional version of the better known *souvlaki*. This is available in each of the meats. For this, and other dishes, the portions are very large. One recommended tact is to select an appetizer and a small salad, which will make for a satiating meal for most. The list of appetizers (or "Paws Firsts (*Meze*) here) is lengthy, more than the handful that might be at your table while perusing the menu. These are mostly Greek in nature with *hummus*, *taramosalata* (a spread made with fish roe), stuffed grape leaves, *spanakopita* (flaky pastry filled with spinach and feta), grilled Cypriot-style cheese (*halloumi*), and feta cheese with olive oil and warm pita bread. But, there are a few decidedly not Greek nor Persian items that the kitchen does a surprisingly good, if slightly unique, takes on such as chicken wings, satay (grilled pieces of marinated chicken with a peanut sauce), *edamame* and spring rolls. These are good with any meal, but might be especially well-suited as accompaniments to the drinks. In addition to the mostly healthy appetizers, Paw Paw's serves nearly ten salads that are nicely available in two sizes, so that you can have salad either as an accompaniment or as a meal. These include a loaded Greek salad and a slightly modified traditional Caesar.

Peking Cuisine $10

8332 Southwest Freeway (at Gessner, northeast corner) 77074, (713) 988-5838

Cuisine - Chinese
Hours - Tue-Sun 11AM to 11PM
Credit Cards - MC, Visa
Service - Table Service
Alcohol - Beer & Wine

Entrée Prices - Dinner - $7 to $18 ($10 average); Lunch - $5 to $8
Entrées at Dinner $12 and less - 90%

Atmosphere & Décor - Functional
Appeal - Well prepared, familiar Americanized Chinese dishes; Peking Duck
Useful to Note - There are different menus for Chinese and non-Chinese patrons.
Menu Suggestions - Shredded Pork with Garlic Sauce; Kung Pao Chicken; Chicken with Garlic Sauce; hot and sour soup; egg rolls; Peking Duck (order in advance)

Located not too far from New Chinatown, Peking Cuisine is an interesting example of how a restaurant can satisfy two completely different clienteles at the same time with two separate menus and dishes (which only seems to happen at Chinese restaurants). During the lunch hours, if you are non-Chinese you will be seated at a table with knives and forks, and presented with a short menu listing a number of the familiar Cantonese-inspired dishes. Seated at a nearby table might be a group of Chinese patrons enjoying a plentitude of small dishes that are certainly not on your menu. But, the dishes from that menu are only available if you are proficient with the Chinese script.

No matter. The lunch specials, available from 11AM to 3PM Tuesday through Friday, are generally very well prepared, plentiful, and ridiculously cheap. Ingredients are noticeably good, the vegetables are crisp when they should be, and there is no discernible MSG. Peking Cuisine has fifteen lunchtime choices priced for around $5, plus a daily special for even less. Most of the familiar choices are here for lunch: Sweet and Sour Chicken, Sweet and Sour Pork, Moo Goo Gai Pan, Beef with Broccoli, General Tso's Chicken, Shrimp with Garlic Sauce, and Kung Pao Chicken. The only disappointment might be the General Tso's Chicken with its overly sweet and syrupy sauce. The sides for any Chinese-American lunch special, the soups and egg rolls are a cut above the norm. The hot and sour soup is noticeably more viscous and flavorful than most. The egg roll is large, sufficiently crisp and fairly tasty. It seems that some care is actually taken when preparing these, unlike many places, where the egg roll is an afterthought or began in the freezer. The large dinner menu is mostly bilingual, and a better chance to try the restaurant's specialties. The business card advertises (just in Chinese) that it features dishes from Peking and a neighboring province, and it boasts in English that it specializes in Peking Duck. The word is that they do a very good job with Peking Duck, possibly the best in the city. It should be ordered in advance of your visit, though. There are also a number of choices featuring pork, beef, poultry, seafood and vegetables, including the not-necessarily-appetizingly-named Three-Cup Chicken, Crispy Duck, Braised Pork Front Hock, Beef with Snow Peas, and Squid with Black Bean Sauce. Peking Cuisine draws a large Chinese clientele, and you are apt to find the place packed if you drop by for lunch on the weekends.

Pho Danh $6

11209 Bellaire (west of Boone, in Hong Kong City Mall) 77072, (281) 879-9940
13480 Veterans Memorial (just south of FM 1960) 77014, (281) 583-1417

Cuisine - Vietnamese (pho)
Hours - Mon-Thu 8AM to 8PM; Fri-Sun 9AM to 9PM
Credit Cards - NONE
Service - Table Service

Alcohol - NONE

Entrée Prices - $5 to $8 ($6 average)
Entrées $12 and less - 100%

Atmosphere & Décor - Spartan, but clean
Appeal - Possibly the best pho in town
Useful to Note - Hong Kong City Mall location can be crowded on weekends.
Menu Suggestions - pho in nearly every variety

There is nearby *pho*-flavored relief after finding yourself lost in the expansive supermarket in Hong Kong City Mall. Walking west down the long corridor, in a corner, there is Pho Danh #2. It's tough to miss because it is usually packed with mostly Vietnamese patrons during the extended lunchtime hours each day. Don't be surprised to find a wait during the weekend. This is because Pho Danh serves possibly the best *pho* in town in a couple of clean and well-lit locations. This is some praise because Houston is the *pho* capital of country with over fifty restaurants dedicated to this flavorful soup, about twice as many as Seattle, the city with the second most, according to a web site dedicated to *pho* (www.phoever.com, in case you're curious).

The popularity of Pho Danh properly begins with its broth which is agreeably rich, flavorful and more complex than typical. And, this great tasting base is noticeably laden with meat, more so than at most other places. Turnaround from the kitchen is quick. And, the plate of complementary herbs and other items is seemingly quite similar to what is done in Saigon. It is amazingly bountiful and fresh: mint, giant basil leaves, and maybe *ngo gai* leaves (the Vietnamese sawleaf herb), bean sprouts, sliced onions, sliced fresh jalapeños, and quartered limes. Bottles of hoisin sauce and *sriracha* are conveniently placed on each table to round out the necessary additions. All these help to make an already good soup even better. Because the *pho* is so good here, so flavorful, Pho Danh serves just *pho,* and similar soup dishes, unlike many other *pho* restaurants that serve other Vietnamese dishes. Or maybe, it is so good here because they serve only *pho* and its close cousins. The *pho* is available here with all of the popular and not-so popular meats and offal. The brisket is good quality. The meatballs, as at other restaurants, can be somewhat bland, but do not detract too much from the flavorful broth. As a bonus, Pho Danh is slightly larger, and certainly cleaner than most other *pho* spots. It is well worth a trip if you a fan of *pho,* or just hot soups.

Pho One $7

11148 Westheimer (at Wilcrest) 77042, (713) 917-0351

Cuisine - Vietnamese
Hours - Mon-Sat 10AM to 9PM
Credit Cards - MC, Visa
Service - Counter Service
Alcohol - NONE

Entrée Prices - $6 to $9 ($7 average)
Entrées $12 and less - 100%

Atmosphere & Décor - Functional
Appeal - Good Vietnamese in Westchase
Menu Suggestions - Pho Tai (beef noodle soup with medium rare beef slices); Pho Nam (beef noodle soup with well-done beef slices); Pho Ga (chicken noodle soup); Com Thit Nuong (char-grilled sliced pork over steamed rice)

Run by a family displaced from New Orleans, Pho One is friendly, airy, clean and clean-lined little Vietnamese restaurant at the busy intersection of Westheimer and Wilcrest, next door to a Japanese grocery store and sharing the parking lot with a capable French bistro. Lunchtime is crowded with Vietnamese and non-Vietnamese office workers from the nearby energy and technology companies to take advantage of inexpensive and tasty soups or other fare served quickly in a welcoming, almost cheery atmosphere. Dinnertime is quite a bit more tame. But, at any time, you'll find bowls of steaming *pho*, the beef broth and rice noodle soup, on most tables. And, given the name, this is what Pho One does best. Accompanied with a small plate of fragrant fresh herbs, bean sprouts, sliced jalapeños, and lime quarters, you can fill the basic broth with a choice of beef and offal. There is *tai* and *nam*, medium-rare and well-done slices of thin beef that are the most popular among the non-Vietnamese, plus fatty beef brisket, flank, and also beef tendon and tripe. They do a good job with the similar chicken soup (*pho ga*), and a vegetarian version with deep-fried tofu and assorted vegetables in a vegetable broth. Noodles can be added to the latter with a choice among, rice, egg, clear, bean, or tapioca noodles for a small extra charge. It can be made into a seafood and vegetable soup for a couple of bucks more. All of the soups are served in regular and "Extra large" sizes, both of which are very good values. In addition to *pho* and its chicken and vegetarian variations, the menu is divided among appetizers, Fried Rice Noodles (*pho ap chao*), Steamed vermicelli clusters with a choice of toppings (*banh hoi*) that are served with very thin, translucent rice papers for wrapping, Vietnamese sandwiches (*banh mi*), vermicelli bowls (*bun*), rice platters (*cac mon com,* listed as *com dia* elsewhere). A half-dozen of the appetizers are conveniently served in half-sized portions. These include thin deep-fried Imperial rolls, and spring rolls with several fillings beyond the typical vegetarian and shrimp and pork including char-grilled shrimp, char-grilled pork (*thit nuong*) and lemongrass beef.

The spicing is toned down compared to most local Vietnamese restaurants. This might be a legacy of New Orleans, where the food is noticeably less pepper-intensive than it is in Houston. The jalapeño slices are used less vigorously here, especially for the sandwiches. For that section and for the *pho*, the menu warns of "HOT!!! peppers". The fish sauce is also less robustly flavored than is typical here; it's much clearer, and less pungent. Also unusual for the area, is that several of the rice platters are served with honey mustard sauce on the side, substituting for the more traditional fish sauce. These rice platters are presented more artfully and more vertically than is common. These are quite good, and the nearly ten combinations can suit a variety tastes from marinated Cornish game hen, lemon grass beef, char-grilled pork chop to a seafood assortment that regrettably includes imitation crab. Each can be made more protein- and cholesterol-rich by adding a couple of fried eggs for just a buck more. One litmus test for Vietnamese eateries, the *thit nuong*, marinated and char-grilled thinly sliced pork is suitably tender and tasty. It is available atop rice noodles, in rice platters and in a sandwich. The sandwiches are decent, though not nearly ready for Midtown or Bellaire Boulevard. The bread is properly crusty, but not quite as flavorful. The latter might be an apt description for the rest of the sandwich, too. Spicy commercial *sriracha, hoisin* and soy sauce are on each table for ready accompaniment. And, the Vietnamese-style ham, *thit*, is served noticeably too cold for the room-temperature sandwiches. And, it's a bit gummier than most other local versions. Stick with the char-grilled pork or chicken. These sandwiches suffer in comparison to the *banh mi* specialtists, but are still a fine value for a light and cheap lunch, even when paired with a half-order of the rolls, which will be necessary for most appetites. It's a fine option in Westchase. There is no alcohol here, but plenty of Vietnamese drinks including freshly squeezed lime juice and iced coffee.

Pho Saigon $6

2808 Milam (between McGowan and Tuam) 77006, (713) 524-3734
11360 Bellaire (between Wilcrest and Kirkwood) 77074, (281) 564-9095
4645 Highway 6 S. (at Kirkwood) Sugar Land, 77478, (281) 491-2988
7400 W. Tidwell (just east of 290) 77040, (713) 462-4935
2553 Gessner (between Hammerly and Kempwood) 77080, (713) 329-9242
10910 Fuqua (west of I-45 South at Sabo) 77089, (281) 481-8929
890 S. Mason (between Kingsland and Highland Knolls) 77450, (281) 392-9022
15754 FM 529 (at Highway 6) 77095, (281) 463-6722
www.phosaigonnoodlehouse.com

Cuisine - Vietnamese (pho)
Hours - Milam - Daily 7:30AM to 8PM; Bellaire - Daily 7:30AM to 10:30PM; Gessner - Daily 9AM to 9PM; Other Locations - Daily 10AM to 10PM
Credit Cards - Amex, Diners, Discover, MC, Visa
Service - Table Service
Alcohol - NONE

Entrée Prices - $6 to $7 ($6 average)
Entrées $12 and less - 100%

Atmosphere & Décor - Spartan, but noticeably clean and inviting enough
Appeal - User-friendly, inexpensive Vietnamese dining
Menu Suggestions - French Beef Stew; bun (vermicelli) dishes; pho

---

Pho Saigon is a little different than most *pho* restaurants. In general, *pho* restaurants are small, spartan, and inexpensive eateries that specialize in the Vietnamese beef noodle soup, *pho*. The other non-*pho* or *pho*-like dishes are seemingly an afterthought. This is not the case at Pho Saigon. The fairly large number of dishes are usually all well prepared, and the restaurant is also more assimilated than most of the other *pho* places. Their menu is not exhaustive like many other full-service Vietnamese restaurants, yet it presents a fairly wide range of the standard Vietnamese dishes that have become familiar in the Houston area. As an added benefit to most, the menu is well organized and chock full of color photos and descriptions that make it very easy to navigate, and easier to be adventurous. This helps make Pho Saigon one of the more comfortable, inexpensive places for the non-Vietnamese to experience. It is also a tad cheaper than the average Vietnamese restaurant, so it is very easy on the wallet to explore the different options on the menu. More so than most other *pho* restaurants, which can fairly be called dives, the oft-crowded Pho Saigon locations are situated in slightly nicer strip centers and are clean and brightly lit, if sparse and functional in layout and décor. For the price of the food, you cannot expect much more. The variety, quality and inexpensiveness of the offerings, an explanatory menu, and somewhat inviting settings are why you will always see a number of non-Vietnamese patrons along with the throngs of Vietnamese who frequent their locations.

The menu includes appetizers, beef noodle soup (*Pho Bo*), chicken noodle soup (*Pho Ga*), egg noodle soup (*Mi*), steamed rice plates (*Com Dia*), vermicelli (*Bun*), and desserts. Each item is conveniently numbered for easy ordering. For appetizers there are the fried Vietnamese egg rolls and fresh spring rolls, either with shrimp and pork, or vegetarian. Befitting a *pho* place, there are nearly thirty variations on the basic soup of beef broth and rice noodles. There are also several versions with chicken, and one with seafood. All of the *pho* dishes are available in small bowls, or for about another buck, large bowls. Tucked among the *pho* dishes is a very satisfying French-style beef stew (*Banh Mi Bo Kho*) made with red wine, and served with a half of a baguette. The steamed rice dishes are generally reliable. The toppings include the common ones: char-broiled sliced pork, pork chop, chicken, egg rolls and sliced lemon grass beef. The popular marinated then char-broiled pork, *thit nuong*, is usually very pleasing. The vermicelli (*bun*) dishes are decent, if not as good as the rice dishes, nor similar items at other places. Pho Saigon has a large assortment of Vietnamese beverages including various coffee drinks and other southeast Asian specialties. Desserts seem to pre-date and post-date the French occupation: bean puddings, smoothie-type drinks, etc.

Phoenicia Deli $8

12116 Westheimer (west of Kirkwood) 77077, (281) 558-0416

Cuisine - Middle Eastern
Hours - Mon 8AM to 8PM; Tue-Fri 8:30AM to 8PM; Sat 8:30AM to 7PM
Credit Cards - NONE
Service - Counter Service
Alcohol - Beer & wine

Entrée Prices - $6 to $9 ($8 average)
Entrées $12 and less - 100%

Atmosphere & Décor - Functional
Appeal - Quick, inexpensive and satisfying Middle Eastern food
Useful to Note - It is across the street from the Phoenicia supermarket.
Menu Suggestions - hummus; Kibbe Ball Chicken Shawarma; Beef Shawarma Falafel; Chicken Shawarma Plate

On the western reaches of Westheimer, Phoenicia Deli is a very popular option for quick and well prepared Middle Eastern food especially for lunch during the week. The painting along a couple walls suitably evokes ancient Phoenicia, the forbearers of present-day Lebanon. That, and more so, the spinners with noticeably moist slices of beef and chicken set well behind the deli counter that is topped with attractive and tasty dips, soups, savory finger foods and well-made sweet pastries, should put you in the mood for Middle Eastern fare. Indicative of its popularity, the line for food can be a couple dozen people long during peak lunchtime hours, beyond the deli and the small grocery section, and it can be sometimes tough to snare one of the twenty or so small tables. Takeout is usually not a bad idea. As the small restaurant has become fairly nice over the years, if still quite casual, the food has correspondingly become tastier and more consistent. The menu has grown over the years, but is still quite manageable. The most popular items remain the pita-wrapped sandwiches with meats cooked on a spinner, usually moist beef and chicken *shawarmas,* and the vegetarian *falafel* that is made with ground chickpeas and tastily deep-fried. The sliced chicken *shawarma* is served with a tomato slice or two, a viscous garlic sauce and, unusual for the area, pieces of potato. The nearly as tasty beef *shawarma* substitutes onion and the more traditional *tahini* sauce for the potatoes and garlic sauce. Each of these sandwiches tastes better with the addition of the spicy, chili-based hot sauce that is available in a self-service station with the utensils. The *shawarmas* and *falafel* are available as a plate with a side of their very tasty *hummus* and either *tabouli* or a cooling cucumber salad, respectively. There are also a handful of interesting cold "sandwiches served on roll", *hummus, baba ganoush, muhammara* (roasted red pepper and walnut dip), stuffed grape leaves, and *kibbe* balls (deep-fried small balls of ground beef, bulghur wheat, onions, pine nuts and spices). A sandwich might not be enough for many, and *hummus*, a fried *kibbe* ball, small soup or one of the half-dozen side salads will be a necessary accompaniment. There are usually a couple flaky pastries such as at least one type of *baklava* to help finish a meal. The sister Phoenicia supermarket across Westheimer has a fantastic selection of Middle Eastern, other Mediterranean and European items.

Some interesting and useful ethnic groceries

For Mexican and other Latin fare, we assume that you already know about the Fiesta supermarkets and, for local produce and regionally produced artisanal items, are aware of the large commercial Farmers Market on Airline and the small, mostly weekend, farmers markets that have come to life in recent years. And, that Central Market and Spec's Liquor Warehouse have fine selections of ethnic foods of many stripes. But, listed below are some of the best markets for exotic food products where English is probably not the language of choice by the cashier or most customers.

- **Asia Market** - Thai, Laotian & Vietnamese - 1010 Calvalcade
- **Droubi's Bakery & Deli** - Middle Eastern - 7333 Hillcroft & 2721 Hillcroft
- **Golden Foods Supermarket** - Chinese - 9896 Bellaire
- **Hong Kong Market #4** - Chinese - 9968 Bellaire
- **Hong Kong Seafood City** - Chinese - 9896 Bellaire
- **India Grocers** - Indian - 6606 Southwest Freeway
- **Jerusalem Halal Meat Market** - Middle Eastern - 3330 Hillcroft
- **Jordan Imported Food & Bakery** - Arabic & Persian - 5922 Hillcroft
- **Komart Marketplace** - Korean - 1049 Gessner
- **Maru Ethiopian Grocery** - Ethiopian - 6065 Bissonnet
- **Moscow** - Russian - 1001 Dairy Ashford & 202 Sawdust, The Woodlands
- **Nippan Daido** - Japanese - 11138 Westheimer
- **Nundini Food Store** - Italian - 500 N. Shepherd

- **Patel Brothers** - Indian - 5815 Hillcroft
- **Phoenicia Specialty Foods** - European & Arabic - 12141 Westheimer
- **Polish Food Store** - Polish - 1900 Blalock
- **Viet Hoa** - Vietnamese - 8300 W. Sam Houston Parkway

Pizza Bella $10

1306 Pin Oak (south of I-10, west of the mall) Katy, 77494, (281) 693-3880

Cuisine - Pizza
Hours - Mon-Sat 11AM to 9PM
Credit Cards - Amex, Discover, MC, Visa
Service - Counter Service
Alcohol - Beer & Wine

Entrée Prices - $5 to $11 ($10 average)
Entrées $12 and less - 100%

Atmosphere & Décor - Functional
Appeal - Very good pizza near the Katy Mills Mall
Useful to Note - You can order their pizzas partially cooked to finish at home.
Menu Suggestions - pizzas

A small strip mall beyond the Grand Parkway near the Katy Mills Mall might seem to be an unlikely place for a top-notch pizzeria, but it is there. Pizza Bella does much more than you might expect given the location: the dough is suitably made each day and hand-tossed; the tomato sauce is made daily; top-notch toppings include roasted red bell peppers, gorgonzola, chevre and noticeably fresh herbs and vegetables; and, even the Italian sausage is made at the restaurant. This translates into well crafted pizzas with a solid, crispy and tasty crust properly supporting an array of enticing combinations. There are nearly two dozen specialty pizzas that are sure to tempt from traditional to not-so-traditional. Some of the more interesting ones include the Mushroom Provençal featuring a mix of fresh, wild mushrooms, chevre, red onions and roasted garlic; the Genovese with spinach, toasted walnuts and gorgonzola; the Thai with a spicy peanut sauce, sweet peppers, green onions, teriyaki-scented chicken and mint; and the *a la Greca* with feta, basil, red onions and a pesto of sundried tomatoes. One of the best is the Siciliano with excellent mild Italian sausage, onions, roasted peppers, tomato sauce and mozzarella. Though generous with the toppings, these do not overwhelm the pizzas, as too often happens at lesser pizza joints. If one of the specialty pizzas doesn't exactly strike a chord, you can create your own from almost forty different toppings.

Though the restaurant is small, it does a brisk lunch-time business, as the few tables inside and on the sidewalk are often filled. Well-suited for lunch, it serves pizza by the slice, several sandwiches, lasagna on Wednesdays and a half-dozen salads that can ordered with grilled chicken breast. Also an attraction, especially at lunchtime or post-shopping, is the number of desserts that are baked in-house including an Italian cream cake, brownies, tiramisu, *tres leches,* and some very large cookies. Very convenient for many, Pizza Bella also sells all of its pizzas par-baked, partially cooked, for you to take home and finish cooking in under ten minutes. These will most likely be tastier, and much easier, than your local delivery pizza option. To note, the restaurant believes that these par-baked pizzas can last in the refrigerator for up to three days before cooking.

Pizzitola's Bar B Cue $9

1703 Shepherd (south of I-10) 77007, (713) 227-2283

Cuisine - Barbecue
Hours - Mon-Fri 11AM to 8PM; Sat 11AM to 3PM
Credit Cards - Amex, Discover, MC, Visa
Service - Table Service
Alcohol - Beer

Entrée Prices - $6 to $12 ($9 average)
Entrées $12 and less - 100%

Atmosphere & Décor - Spartan
Appeal - Tasty Texas barbecue cooked in an old style barbecue pit
Menu Suggestions - beef brisket; ribs; Chicken Sandwich; Coconut Cake; Bread Pudding

Don't let the name fool you, there is nary a pasta, pizza or cannoli to be found at Pizzitola's. The functional metal building with its gravel parking lot does, however, boast a barbecue pit that has been in operation since the 1930s, probably the oldest commercial pit in use in the city. Shepherd Drive Barbecue was the name prior to Pizzitola's in the early 1980s. That pit is put to very good use, as Pizzitola's serves up excellent Texas-style barbecue. The large weekday lunch crowd, including many from downtown office towers a few miles away, is a testament to this.

The hickory-smoked and somewhat piquant brisket is delicious, as it should be for a top local barbecue place. Somewhat unusual though is that the chicken is also very moist and very flavorful. It is available as a half-chicken, a deboned half-chicken, skinless chicken breast and as Fajita Style Deboned Chicken; the last is served with pinto beans, cheese, *pico de gallo,* sour cream and flour tortillas. The central Texas-style sausage, made with ground pork and beef, is quite satisfying. The pork ribs, a popular draw, are pretty good, but seemingly less meaty than at some of the best stops for ribs, like Williams Smokehouse. The accompanying warmed sauce is excellent and a nice complement to all of the meats. Relatively thin, it is sweet with a hint of vinegar, and fairly spicy. As at other places, each of the meats can be ordered solo, in a sandwich, or as a dinner plate with a choice of two sides among pinto beans, potato salad, cole slaw, grilled vegetables and rice. Pizzitola's is a tad pricier than most barbecue places, but still a fine value. In addition to very good barbecue, Pizzitola's has a couple of other selling points, and things that you will not typically find at a barbecue joint: very good grilled vegetables, and a silky, top-notch homemade coconut cake. The bread pudding is no slouch, either; the desserts are made from scratch by the owner's mother. The sides are secondary to the meat and desserts. In addition to the vegetables, another reliable choice is the Pinto Beans with Pico & Cheese. This is a soup of pinto beans with shreds of melted cheese and fresh bits of jalapeños and onions. Unfortunately, the potato salad is a bit tasteless, and the bread is of the white, super-processed variety. The walls are cluttered with photos, complimentary articles and memorabilia of friends, food and fish. Overall, the interior is not much of an improvement over the metal exterior, but it's a comfortable and a personable place. Too nice, and it would be incongruous with the very commendable barbecue.

Poblanos $9

9865 South Post Oak (between Loop 610 S. and W. Belfort) 77096, (713) 723-8100
www.poblanosrestaurant.com

Cuisine - Tex-Mex
Hours - Mon-Thu 11AM to 2:30PM, 5 to 9PM; Fri 11AM to 10PM; Sat 11AM to 10PM; Sun 12 to 9PM
Credit Cards - Amex, Discover, MC, Visa
Service - Table Service
Alcohol - Full Bar

Entrée Prices - Dinner - $7 to $12 ($9 average); Lunch - $7
Entrées at Dinner $12 and less - 100%

Atmosphere & Décor - Pleasant
Appeal - Very good Tex-Mex near Meyerland
Useful to Note - They are also a good-value caterer.
Menu Suggestions - Queso Flameado (melted Monterey Jack Cheese with ground beef, chorizo or fajitas); Enchiladas Verdes; Chicken Enchiladas Verdes; Spinach Enchiladas; Chile Relleno; Tacos al Carbon; fajitas; Poblanos Steak (half-pound fajita steak topped with grilled poblanos and Monterey Jack cheese)

Poblanos is a comfortable and well run restaurant, and a very good neighborhood Tex-Mex spot. Given its easily accessible location just south of 610 near Meyerland, and its quality, it's worth a drive after traffic dies down. Though the offerings are not much different than a great number of area Mexican restaurants, the execution is better than most as is the value, considering the quality. There are appetizers, salads, burritos, tacos (soft and crispy), *tostadas*, *flautas*, enchiladas, tamales, fajitas, and slightly more ambitious Poblanos Specialties. And, more so than most, this family-operated restaurant gives the impression that it really aims to please. For starters there is an especially good *queso flameado*. A prime attraction for many regular customers is the top-notch fajitas. The fajita meat is likely higher quality than most, and noticeably moist, tender and very flavorful. The similar *tacos al carbon*, wrapped in fresh flour tortillas, makes for a very satisfying meal. One of the more interesting dishes is the Poblanos Steak, a half-pound fajita steak with grilled poblano peppers and topped with Monterey Jack cheese. Poblanos also does the enchiladas quite well. Each dish contains two large enchiladas with the requisite refried beans and Spanish rice. There is the Tex-Mex favorite cheese enchiladas with cheddar cheese and topped with chili gravy, plus similar ones with ground beef and fajitas. Topped with a tomatillo salsa and melted Monterey Jack cheese, there are versions with spinach, shredded chicken, and cheese. All of the basics are done well here, and the details are also well covered. For example, the refried beans seem properly laden with lard, and so, very tasty. The frozen margaritas are a bit frothy and noticeably much above average. The slightly sweet green tomatillo-based salsa is similar to that of Ninfa's, and is a fitting complement to the fresh chips. The tortillas and even the tamales are made on site. As mentioned on the menu even the rustic dark wood tables and chairs are handmade, making the setting even more fitting and relaxed. Poblanos is worth a visit for very capable, familiar Tex-Mex, and a little more.

Pollo Riko $5

7229 Fondren (north of the Southwest Freeway) 77036, (713) 271-4321
14443 Bellaire (east of Highway 6) 77083, (281) 498-4716
5532 Airline (just north of Tidwell, next to HEB) 77076 (713) 692-2822

Cuisine - Colombian
Hours - Daily 11AM to 10PM
Credit Cards - NONE
Service - Counter Service
Alcohol - NONE

Entrée Prices - Dinner - $3 to $6 ($5 average); Lunch - $4
Entrées at Dinner $12 and less - 100%

Atmosphere & Décor - Functional
Appeal - Very good and cheap rotisserie chicken and sides; and, good to go
Useful to Note - This can provide great take home for the family.
Menu Suggestions - Roast Chicken; mashed potatoes

Pollo Riko, which first opened in 1992, offers the Colombian version of fast food: a portion of a chicken that has been cooked on a constantly spinning rotisserie oven, rice and a small variety of side dishes. Though maybe not as fast as a typical fast food place, the food is certainly much fresher, much tastier than those, and possibly even cheaper. Rotisserie-cooked chickens are the only main dishes here. The variations in these are only in the choice of white or dark meat (or a combination thereof), and the size, a quarter, half or whole chicken. The chicken at Pollo Riko is a notable, and very welcome, departure from the ubiquitous, nearly tasteless meat that is served in many area restaurants under the name of chicken. At Pollo Riko, the chicken comes with the skin, under which, the chicken meat is juicy and tender. The skin itself is crispy, moist and slightly salty, and quite tasty, of course. The overall effect is surprisingly complex, and very flavorful. The owner has claimed that the chickens are marinated in a beer-based sauce with roughly thirty herbs and spices. It certainly tastes so. The chicken, and everything else, is even better with the complimentary zesty green sauce (*aji*) that is made with garlic, parsley and onions.

From the limited menu, the most popular orders are the Lunch Special and the Dinner Special, each with a choice of white or dark meat. The only difference between the two is that the lunch special is a dollar cheaper, and only available from 11AM to 2PM from Monday through Friday. These specials consist of a quarter chicken of either white or dark meat, a choice between an *arepa* or corn tortillas, choice of two sides, and a small soda. The *arepa* is the somewhat spongy and bland Colombian white corn bread disk. The sides that are available are white rice, red beans, mashed potatoes, salted new potatoes, potato salad, corn on the cob, cole slaw, a small house salad or Caesar salad. The mashed potatoes are especially good, very creamy and quite flavorful. Conversely, the red beans can be fairly dull. The Dinner Special with white meat is a great deal for less than $5. A quarter of a chicken with bread and the sides are enough for most people, but heartier appetites might opt for the Half Chicken Combo that comes with a couple sides. For the family, there are the Whole Roast Chicken Combo with two sides, and the Half and Whole Chicken Super Combos with five. Additional small dishes, available with these, are fries, fried yucca, fried plantains, and *tostones* (double-fried, flattened green plantains). The desserts, to help complement the meal, include rice pudding, flan, The Colombian specialties *arepa con queso* and *pandebono* on the weekends, and the popular and Latin-restaurant-requisite *tres leches*. It's not the best *tres leches* in town, by far, but it's better than no *tres leches* at all, plus it's reasonably priced. The Pollo Riko settings are appropriate for an inexpensive fast food restaurant where takeout is a very popular option. It's utilitarian (or proletarian?) at best. But, the food, and the value, more than compensate.

Polonia $12

1900 Blalock (at Campbell) 77080, (713) 464-9900
www.poloniarestaurant.com

Cuisine - Polish
Hours - Tue-Thu 11AM to 9PM; Fri 11AM to 10PM; Sat 11Am to 11PM; Sun 11AM to 8PM
Credit Cards - Amex, Diners, Discover, MC, Visa
Service - Table Service
Alcohol - Full Bar

Entrée Prices - $6 to $20 ($12 average)
Entrées $12 and less - 60%

Atmosphere & Décor - Pleasant, comfortable
Appeal - Flavorful, filling fare
Useful to Note - Have no fear, though duck is on the menu there's no czarnina.
Menu Suggestions - Sour Rye Soup with Sausage and Egg; Pierogi with potato and cheese; bigos (sausage and sauerkraut stew); Golabki (cabbage rolls filled with ground veal); Breaded Chicken Breast; Roasted Duck Legs; Breaded Pork Cutlet; Breaded Pork Cutlet stuffed with mushrooms and onions; Golonka (roasted pork shank)

Tucked in a corner in Spring Branch near the only Polish church in the diocese, Polonia offers very well prepared, great value food in a friendly, quite efficient, small, family-run restaurant. Its one dining room is comfortable and quaintly decorated with earnest, representative artwork that's a far cry from Bellotto or Da Vinci's *Lady with an Ermine*, but somehow charming and appropriate. The restaurant is nice in an ethnic neighborhood in Chicago or Cleveland type of way. With an owner and much of the staff from Poland, the fare is authentically Polish, hearty and flavorful. Bountiful plates are filled with dishes featuring readily enjoyable dishes of meats, potatoes, cabbage, often cured with vinegar and resulting in a frequent sour flavor, as in the pickles, house-made sauerkraut and zesty cucumber salads. For those not familiar with Polish food, it's rich in proteins and richer in starches, and similar to other Slavic fare such as Ukrainian, Slovak or Byelorussian, and not unlike German cooking. Maybe more recognizably very similar dishes are found on the plates found at more expansive Jewish delis, as most American Jews have roots in the former greater Poland (once "the two saddest nations on this earth").

The tables are soon set with tasty, sturdy bread, wonderfully complemented with a small cup of creamy lard with pieces of bacon (*smalec*). For starters there are several savory soups featuring chicken and dumplings, beets, mushroom, and beef tripe. Other starters include chicken or pork in aspic, marinated herrings in oil or sour cream and a crisp vegetable salad. Most diners won't find most of the rib-sticking entrées exotic, with many featuring tasty breaded and pan-fried pork cutlets, chicken breasts, and the light-tasting tilapia. There is also baked pork and beef dishes, roasted veal, pan-fried veal schnitzel, a pork meat loaf, and roasted duck legs. Most are served with boiled potatoes and often with house-made sauerkraut flecked with shreds of carrots. There are *pierogies,* of course, buttery stuffed packets of fresh dough that are favorites of dining room tables from Warsaw, over Kiev and down to the sea, all over the lands of the former Jagiellon realm. As everywhere else, the potato- and cheese-filled versions are the best. Not as good as my grandmother's, but very good for a restaurant. Other Polish staples, the stuffed cabbage are well-made, filled with ground veal, as are the potato pancakes. Probably the best value entrée is the *bigos,* made with stewed pieces of sausage mixed into a bed of sauerkraut. The heartiest meal is the large pork shank (*golonka*), literally the size of Chicago area-staple sixteen-inch softball, which is baked for hours in beer, carrots, onions and horseradish and served resplendent bone-in with soft and tasty fat and skin, and with sides of succulent sauerkraut (really) and thick mashed potatoes. For sharing or the unbelievably glutinous, Polonia also serves a combination plate featuring *pierogies,* stuffed cabbage, *bigos,* meat loaf, baked pork, and roasted duck legs, plus the salad. The only dishes to avoid are the veal ones, as both are lackluster, and too often tough. There are desserts, too, with cheesecake, apple pie and the Polish take on donuts (*paczki*), which seem to be an afterthought. Nearly necessary for a Slavic restaurant, there is a full bar, and for a western-leaning Polish one, good beer on tap in the form of the widely available great-tasting Czech lager Pilsner Urquell served in both half-liter and steel-worker-size one liter mugs. The latter is just a scant seven bucks. If you really like the food, Polonia operates a small Polish grocery store nearly adjacent to the restaurant.

Ponzo's $8

2515 Bagby (at McGowen) 77006, (713) 526-2426
www.ponzos.com

Cuisine - Sandwiches; Pizza
Hours - Tue-Thu, Sun 11AM to 10PM; Fri-Sat 11AM to 11PM (open on Mondays during football season)

Credit Cards - Amex, MC, Visa
Service - Counter Service; Delivery
Alcohol - NONE

Entrée Prices - $5 to $15 ($8 average)
Entrées $12 and less - 90%

Atmosphere & Décor - Spartan
Appeal - Very good Italian-American-style sub sandwiches and calzones
Useful to Note - There have delivery to the surrounding neighborhoods.
Menu Suggestions - Ponzo's Original Sub (hard salami, cotto salami, mortadella, provolone with pepperoncini and an olive relish); The Ham & Cheese po boy; Italian Roast Beef (hot po boy featuring spicy roast beef and roasted peppers); Roasted Turkey Sub; Sausage and Pepper Sub; calzones

---

A good fit amidst the bars and more upscale Midtown eateries, Ponzo's is a more-than-competent sandwich shop and pizzeria. It's a friendly, small storefront eatery with only a handful of tables inside, and on the covered sidewalk. So, it is primarily a takeout and delivery operation. But, it is conveniently and synergistically next door to the Dog House Tavern for when the hunger pangs begin to hit.

Ponzo's serves all the familiar casual Italian-American staples: hot and cold sandwiches, calzones, pizzas, several pastas, and a couple salads. The sandwiches and calzones are the best bets here. All of the cold sandwiches feature the diced pepperoncini, shredded lettuce, thin tomato slices, and the flavorful olive relish, or properly titled Ponzo's Original Vinaigrette Dressing. Each is made to order, and features high quality ingredients beginning with a fresh, slightly crusty toasted sandwich roll. The cold sandwich choices include the Original, The Ham & Cheese, Italian Tuna, honey-roasted turkey, Italian Roast Beef. The best sandwich is the Ponzo's Original Sub with origins stretching back to the mid-1950s. It includes hard salami, *cotto* salami, *mortadella* and provolone with diced pepperoncini, thin slices of tomato, shredded lettuce and an olive relish on a soft, fresh po boy bun. Another excellent cold sandwich is The Godfather, a 15-inch sandwich that is built for two, or Marlon Brando in his glutinous prime. It's an *abbodanza* of hard and *cotto* salami, ham, roast beef, honey roasted turkey, *mortadella*, provolone and Swiss. The well prepared hot sandwiches are just about as good and feature meatball, Italian sausage and peppers, a hot Italian roast beef, pastrami, and pepperoni and mozzarella. Of these it's tough to go wrong with the Italian Roast Beef that has spicy Italian roast beef (Chicago-style) with roasted bell peppers.

The calzones, essentially folded over pizzas that are then baked, are very good, and a great value. These begin with chopped garlic, mozzarella,

Romano, plenty of dough and are served with marinara sauce for dipping. One hot, savory and doughy calzone will make for a big meal for one. These are filled with a choice of fillings also available for the pizzas. Part of the list, which is longer than most pizzerias, is: pepperoni, sausage, meatball, ham, salami, olives, mushrooms, basil, fresh tomatoes, ricotta, feta and jalapeños. One or two additional fillings, maybe a meat and a cheese, can make the calzone even tastier and filling. Though the somewhat similar calzones are always top-notch, the quality of the pizza is maddeningly inconsistent. At some times it approaches some of the better places for thin crust New York-style pizza in the city. At other times, the same pizza is mediocre, at best, with a hard, bland crust and boring ingredients on board. Though maybe more suitable for the weekday lunch crowd, Ponzo's also serves pastas and salads. The handful of pastas include manicotti, lasagna and ravioli, which are made in-house, and served with garlic bread. The baked manicotti and lasagna dishes are filled with both ricotta and Italian sausage and topped with melted fresh mozzarella. Maybe not heart healthy, but satisfying, as is the cannoli for dessert.

Porras $4

6301 Market (at Kress) 77020, (713) 673-0727

Cuisine - Mexican (taqueria)
Hours - Mon-Sat 5AM to 8PM; Sun 6AM to 8PM
Credit Cards - NONE
Service - Counter Service
Alcohol - NONE

Entrée Prices - $2 to $7 ($4 average)
Entrées $12 and less - 100%

Atmosphere & Décor - Comfortably almost none
Appeal - Very good, very inexpensive home-style Mexican food
Useful to Note - You can park in the area across the street if necessary.
Menu Suggestions - Carne Guisada (stewed beef) Burrito; Carne Guisada Plate; Fajita Burritos; breakfast burritos; huevo and chorizo burrito; Ham & Cheese Burrito; Chorizo con Huevo Plate

Porras Prontito, or Porras Bakery, as it's known by in some Anglo circles, is a bakery serving area grocery stores and Mexican restaurants with tortillas and Mexican baked goods, a neighborhood food store and a great place for inexpensive, casual home-style Mexican food. It really is "the real burrito" as the marketing proclaims. There are not tacos here, but burritos, which are what most Houstonians will recognize as tacos, but put together on very large flour tortillas. A big reason why these are so good, are that as a bakery, the tortillas, the basis for any good taco or burrito, are freshly made and very tasty.

This is a very humble and long-standing counter service operation with a huge take-away business, and maybe eight tables set in the center of the store. Everything is prepared-to-order and arrives at a counter in a bag encased in aluminum foil or Styrofoam with plastic utensils. Porras serves the large tacos and *tortas* with nearly thirty choices for fillings, and breakfast and lunch plates. These plates are decidedly home-style: *carne guisada* (stewed beef with gravy), *papas con carne* (beef and potatoes), fajitas, chicken fajitas, *lengua* (stewed tongue), *barbacoa* (Mexican-style barbecue), and the most recent additions, cheese and chicken enchiladas. These plates feature a generous serving of the entrée plus rice, refried beans, guacamole and a couple slightly charred, thin, but sturdy, burrito-size flour tortillas. The moist, tender and very flavorful *carne guisada* has long been considered one of the very best in the area. The fajitas are almost as satisfying. The breakfast plates are as filling as those for lunch. There are just several simple, but healthy combinations of eggs scrambled with a choice among potatoes, ham, excellent *chorizo* that is clearly a cut above, and salsa, plus fried eggs and salsa. The eggs are almost fluffy and not overly dry as occurs at many *taquerias*. Each breakfast plate is served with suitably heavy refried beans, crisp thick bacon, pan-fried pieces of potatoes, a good-sized dollop of juicy, stewed onions and tomatoes, and the large tortillas. And, a couple of slices of oranges provide some vitamin C. Most of the lunch and breakfast entrées are available in burritos or *tortas* plus a number of simple and enticing combinations such as refried beans and bacon, *chicharron* (pork skin) with chiles, potato and refried beans and even a surprisingly good ham and cheese one. Though the bread for the *tortas* is baked in-house, the tortilla-clad burritos are a better option. The tortillas are much better than the bread here. For drinks, there are plenty of canned and bottled items including ones from Mexico on the shelves. Porras also sells a wide range of Mexican pastries throughout the day, as they do *menudo*; *barbacoa* is available only on the weekends.

Pronto Cucinino $9

1401 Montrose (between West Gray and W. Dallas) 77019 (713) 528-TOGO
3191 W. Holcombe (at Buffalo Speedway) 77025, (713) 867-5309
www.pronto-2-go.com

Cuisine - Italian-American
Hours - Daily 10:30AM to 9PM
Credit Cards - Amex, Diners, Discover, MC, Visa
Alcohol - Beer & Wine
Service - Counter Service

Entrée Prices - \$6 to \$12 (\$9 average)
Entrées \$12 and less - 100%

Atmosphere & Décor - Casual, but nice; patio
Appeal - Convenient and well prepared Southern Italian-American food
Menu Suggestions - Chopped Salad (mixed greens, artichoke hearts, roasted red peppers, candied walnuts, blue cheese and ceci); ravioli; rotisserie chicken; cannelloni (with rotisserie chicken, mushrooms, spinach and ricotta); Chicken Vincent (Parmesan-crusted chicken breast sautéed with artichoke hearts, lemon and butter)

From Vincent Mandola, whose very popular nearby restaurant complex on W. Dallas includes Vincent's, Nino's and Grappino, this is locally tuned, straightforward Southern Italian-American food meant to be taken home or eaten at the restaurant in typically quick American fashion. Popular and boisterous since opening in 2005, Pronto features friendly and efficient service, and seems to have hit most of the right notes for quick, convenient and inexpensive dining.

The focused menu includes a handful of appetizers, several salads that can be upgraded with grilled chicken, salmon or shrimp, pastas and about ten meat- or seafood-centric items. Many of the dishes are Southern Italian-American favorites such as fried mozzarella, fried calamari, *Insalata Caprese,* Caesar salad, chicken and eggplant Parmesan, chicken Marsala, sausage and peppers, lasagna with ground beef and tomato sauce, ravioli, and fettuccine Alfredo. These are done with a proficient hand, or hands, in the kitchen. The heartier entrées include grilled pork chops, grilled salmon, grilled steak with melted mozzarella *Pizzaiola*-style (with a seasoned tomato sauce), the delectable Chicken Vincent (Parmesan-crusted chicken breast sautéed with artichoke hearts, butter and lemon), and wood-roasted chicken. Unfortunately, no veal, though. But, these fairly priced entrées come with a choice of a side among mashed potatoes with roasted garlic, sautéed green beans and spinach, pasta with a tomato sauce, or fettuccine Alfredo. The rotisserie chicken, one of the specialties at Vincent's, has become very good. It's cooked over a wood fire and is juicy and redolent of lemon, garlic and black pepper. It can be carved with a leg and thigh, with a breast, or a half-chicken. An entire chicken, great for two, is available for takeout only. The pastas are decent, with the fresh and stuffed ravioli filled with ricotta and spinach, and cannelloni with the flavorful roasted chicken might be the highlights. These with a small Chopped Salad can make for a very satisfying meal. The lasagna might be somewhat under-seasoned, but there are several other hearty pastas with the tubular penne and rigatoni. The convenient food is the draw here, and though the layout is fairly attractive and there is even a patio facing Montrose, the restaurant is probably too loud and frenetic to encourage much lingering.

Ragin Cajun $11

4302 Richmond (west of Weslayan) 77027, (713) 623-6321
9600 Westheimer (Gessner at Westheimer) 77063, (832) 251-7171
930 Main (in the Tunnel) 77002, (713) 571- 2422
16100 Kensington (west of 6, north of Southwest Freeway) 77479, (281) 277-0704
www.ragin-cajun.com

Cuisine - Cajun
Hours - Richmond - Mon-Thu 11AM to 10PM; Fri-Sat 11AM to 11PM; Westheimer - Tue-Thu 11AM to 10PM; Fri-Sat 11AM to 11PM; Sun 11AM to 9PM; downtown - Mon-Fri 10:30AM to 3PM; Sugar Land - Tue-Thu 11AM to 10PM; Fri-Sat 11AM to 11PM; Sun 11AM to 9PM
Credit Cards - Amex, Diners, Discover, MC, Visa
Service - Counter Service
Alcohol - Main - NONE; Other Locations - Full Bar

Entrée Prices - $7 to $19 ($11 average)
Entrées $12 and less - 70%

Atmosphere & Décor - Spartan, but engaging; patio (Sugar Land)
Appeal - Popular, excellent Cajun eateries
Useful to Note - They do a good job with catering and large take-away orders.
Menu Suggestions - Shrimp Po Boy; Crawfish Po Boy; Shrimp Étouffée; Shrimp and Crab Gumbo; Chicken and Sausage Gumbo; Fried Crawfish Tails; Fried Oysters; raw oysters (in season); Grilled Cajun Catfish (marinated then grilled); boiled crawfish (in season)

The original location of Ragin Cajun on Richmond has been packing in the crowds for many years with its often excellent, unpretentious Cajun food. The food here makes one understand why folks become nostalgic for Lafayette and southern Louisiana. But, it's not just Cajuns and Coon Asses who frequent the Ragin Cajun. The multi-ethnic crowds from presumably nearly all walks of life that happily wait in line to order pack the tables, and certainly seem to like the food. Buckets and baskets quickly litter most tables, as the ample customers enjoy feasts of raw oysters, boiled crawfish, gumbo, fried baskets and the like. It's also a great for take-away with its hand-eaten fare. The long-standing success has translated into three other locations and an expanded menu.

The Ragin Cajun does a great job in replicating the tastes of South Louisiana, especially with its more humble, if not exactly heart-healthy fare. Most everything is true and flavorful. The po boys are excellent, and more than stand up against just about any po boy that were available in the French

Quarter, Central Business District (Mother's might be the exception), or even the blue-collar west bank of New Orleans, pre-Katrina. The shrimp po boy is especially good. It is made with properly battered and deep-fried, medium-sized shrimp inside a good-quality, crusty French roll with lettuce, tomato and tartar-like sauce. In addition to fried shrimp, there are a number of other possible fillings such as fried crawfish, fried oyster, fried catfish, fried soft shell crab, boiled shrimp, grilled catfish, seafood, roast beef with gravy, ham, boudin, chicken, smoked sausage, ham and cheese, and Big Daddy's Special (roast beef with gravy, ham and cheese). In addition to po boys, there are other sandwiches, including the New Orleans classic, muffaletta. For a filling meal, a side or soup is usually needed with a sandwich or po boy. The former can include fries, spicy fries, onion rings, a link of hot boudin sausage, crab nuggets (deep-fried small pieces of crabmeat), deep-fried, whole jalapeños stuffed with cream cheese, or the Hot Bites (deep-fried pieces of jalapeño and cream cheese). Even a better accompaniment is a cup of gumbo or red beans and rice. Ragin Cajun serves a seafood gumbo made with shrimp and crabmeat, the Bayou Style with chicken and shrimp, and an occasional special gumbo made with chicken and sausage. All versions feature a dark, rich broth studded with white rice, and are very good, especially the ones with chicken. Both versions of the étouffée, one with medium-sized shrimp and the other with crawfish, are very flavorful. The version with shrimp might be the better of the two. When in season, the Ragin Cajun has the reputation for serving some of the best boiled crawfish in town. A regular-sized order might be pound and three-quarters of crawfish boiled with new potatoes and corn, though there is also three-and-a-half pounds, a normal amount for many crawfish lovers. Other items from the Gulf and the bayous are also very popular. There are raw oysters, a dozen for seven dollars and a popular order, boiled spicy shrimp in the shell, and the fried seafood and crawfish baskets. Served with fries and bread, these include shrimp stuffed with crabmeat and fried, fried crawfish tails, fried shrimp, a dozen fried oysters, fried catfish, and the marinated Frank's BBQ Crabs when in season, a delicious, but messy meal, as you have to crack the crabs yourself. For dessert, there is the Louisiana specialty, Bread Pudding with Rum Sauce, plus pecan pie.

The long-standing original location is cluttered with photos and posters of sports celebrities, long-past Houston sports teams, and those of USL (or U La-La) and LSU. It is the most consistent of the four. The second location in Woodlake Square is more spacious, cleaner and nicer, as is the one in Sugar Land. Though it might not have the character or the consistency of the original location, dining there is certainly more comfortable. The menu also has a handful more items, more upscale grilled dishes featuring snapper, catfish, shrimp and chicken. The downtown tunnel branch is understandably more functional, suited for the office lunch rush; you'll have to be content with just the good food there.

Red Lion $12

2316 S. Shepherd (between San Felipe and Westheimer) 77019, (713) 782-3030
www.redlionhouston.com

Cuisine - British; American
Hours - Mon-Thu 3PM-2AM; Fri-Sun 11:30AM-2AM
Credit Cards - Amex, Diners, Discover, MC, Visa
Service - Counter Service
Alcohol - Full Bar

Entrée Prices - $8 to $24 ($12 average)
Entrées $12 and less - 40%

Atmosphere & Décor - Very comfortable British pub setting
Appeal - Excellent British-inflected pub fare; great pub atmosphere
Useful to Note - Is not related to the old Red Lion that was on Main years ago.
Menu Suggestions - Fish & Chips; Mini Burgers; Cheeseburger; Free Range Filet Mignon dinner; Indian Quesadillas (naan baked with mozzarella and beef tips)

Red Lion proudly sits nearly across Shepherd from the similarly adept and long time favorite, Kenneally's. Usually always crowded, and with good reason, as the Red Lion is not only a convivial, well-run British-style pub with an expansive array of appropriate and enticingly good draft beers served in properly sized Imperial pint glasses (20 ounces, which you'll pay for), whiskies, other spirits, and even a fair number of well-chosen wines, it also offers excellent pub fare. Most of this is British but some is local, all several notches above you would expect in the UK, and in this country, too. This proficiency in the kitchen alone makes Red Lion is worth a visit. And, it draws patrons that visit solely for their excellent British-inflected pub fare that is properly tuned to the local palates. The food here is much better than would be expected from its very English exterior.

The dishes are made to order and with fresh ingredients; there are supposedly no freezers or even canned items. Though the most expensive of the local pubs, the cooking is consistently very good, and the portions are very large. The Red Lion is well known and deservedly praised for its rendition of moist and crisp fish and chips, their Mini Burgers that are really a hearty meal, and their amazingly hot Beef Vindaloo. British dishes include a Scotch Egg Dinner, Banger and Mash, and Shepherds Pie. There are a handful of entrée-sized salads and plenty of enticing small plates, well crafted for sharing and complementary to imbibing. Some of these are baked brie, bites of tempura-battered and fried sushi grade tuna, chicken satay skewers, smoked salmon and cheese and crackers. The kitchen serves an interesting array of dishes, some of which is fairly ambitious for a pub kitchen. There is some fusion with local favorites, spring and Imperial (or egg) rolls and *quesadillas* imbued with Indian components and flavors. Most of these seem to work well with a lager beer and a good many white wines. The mini burgers ramp up nicely to a full-size Cheeseburger that is cooked to order. Other sandwiches include the Portobello Sandwich, a BLT with Irish black bacon, and an interesting take on the roast beef sandwich with a hoagie roll, mozzarella, sautéed onions and a horseradish and caper aïoli. There is even a Seared Duck Breast, and the very popular 8-ounce Free Range Filet Mignon. The latter plate is served for several dollars cheaper on Thursday nights, and its quality puts other local bar's steak nights to shame. There are specials other nights of the week so check the board at the restaurant or the website. Bolstered by songs from Hitsville, U.K., from the last quarter century, the pub itself is quite attractive, roomy and filled with dark wood, enough bar seating and upholstered octagonal booths. It's comfortable and well laid-out, certainly more so than an ancient tavern in London or the English countryside, and all for the better in modern-day Houston. Not incidentally, service is friendly and very efficient, though you might have to watch out for the cantankerous owner late at night.

Reggae Hut $10

4814 Almeda (south of Southmore, west of Highway 288) 77004, (713) 520-7171

Cuisine - Caribbean
Hours - Mon-Sat 11AM to 9PM
Credit Cards - Amex, Diners, Discover, MC, Visa
Service - Counter Service
Alcohol - NONE

Entrée Prices - $9 to $12 ($10 average)
Entrées $12 and less - 100%

Atmosphere & Décor - Comfortable, low-key and urbane
Appeal - A cool place with well prepared Caribbean food
Useful to Note - There's only street parking, but it's plentiful nearby.
Menu Suggestions - patties; cocoa bread; Jerk Chicken; Curry Goat; Oxtails; Curry Shrimp

Currently owned by the folks who run the very popular Breakfast Klub not too far away in Midtown, they have helped make the Reggae Hut more consistent, and better than its been in quite a while. The Reggae Hut is now again an inviting destination with an urbane, friendly and cool vibe amidst the storefronts on Almeda, almost adjacent to Spanish Village, near Hermann Park and the heart of the Third Ward. The restaurant is situated in two fairly small and sparse dining rooms seating around fifty people total in black-tableclothed tables and mix-and-match chairs that come alive in the evening with the chatter of other patrons off the surrounding hard surfaces, the flickering of the candles, and the reggae all around.

Though it is a cool place in and of itself, the real draw, of course, is the food that is very tasty and reasonably priced. Reggae Hut is quite proficient with the small list of Jamaican specialties that it serves, which includes a slight nod to locally popular ingredients, shrimp and snapper. It's tough to go wrong with anything on the well-focused, but very small menu. There are just ten entrées and a just a handful of appetizers. For the latter there are just patties with several different fillings, cocoa bread and plantains. The cocoa bread, a sweet, flavorful bread made with coconut milk that is baked fresh twice daily in the restaurant. The patties, a savory baked turnover like an *empanada* are made with a choice of chicken, beef or vegetables. The chicken dishes are made with large pieces of moist chicken and include a very good Jerk Chicken that has been marinated and slowly cooked such that the meat slides easily from the bones. The jerk sauce is flavorful and very spicy. It also works well complementing the Jerk Shrimp. The popular Brown Stew Chicken made with lightly fried chicken and is served with a thick, sweet gravy. To note, the chickens are served as most of the rest of the world eats chicken, roughly separated and resplendent with bones and cartridge. The Curry Goat featuring yellow curry and more than a hint of ginger is another winner, as are the similar curries with chicken and shrimp. A version with snapper is availably as a "seasonal" dish. The meaty oxtails are properly tender and served with a delicious sauce. Each of the entrées is served with moist coconut-soaked rice and peas (plump rice dotted with kidney beans) and a limp cabbage salad with zucchini, squash, corn and carrots to make a good-sized meal. For libations, there are smoothies, Caribbean sodas and the kid- and heat-friendly ginger beer.

Rita's Café $8

755 Dairy Ashford (between Memorial and I-10) 77079, (281) 493-9200

Cuisine - Middle Eastern; with some Armenian dishes
Hours - Mon-Fri 10:30AM to 8PM; Sat 11AM to 5PM
Credit Cards - Amex, Discover, MC, Visa
Service - Counter Service
Alcohol - NONE; BYOB

Entrée Prices - $6 to $11 ($8 average)
Entrées $12 and less - 100%

Atmosphere & Décor - Spartan

Appeal - Friendly informal stop for Middle Eastern food
Useful to Note - Bring some wine and visit for dinner.
Menu Suggestions - hummus; spicy hummus; olive hummus; cabbage rolls (filled with ground beef and rice); steamed potatoes with parsley; beef shawarma; kafta kabob (ground beef kabob); lamb kabob

---

Rita's Café is owned and run by a friendly and engaging older couple. The small, unpretentious restaurant is often populated by returning customers enjoying some of the many healthy daily dishes in the steam table, or from the grill or spinner. The affable owners seem to be nearly as much an attraction as the food. The array of choices at Rita's Café is generally similar to most local Middle Eastern restaurants, except that the steam table seems to contain a greater spread than most, over two dozen small trays, in fact.

Among these dips and salads that make up most of the items on display, there are a myriad of choices that change daily: *tabouli, hummus, baba ganoush, mouhammara* (a spread made with red peppers), corn salad, lima bean salad, steamed potatoes with parsley, lentil salad, cucumber and tomato salad, cucumber and yogurt salad, spinach, Greek salad, cabbage salad, fried *kibbe,* and stuffed grape leaves. Of these, the steamed potatoes are excellent and the *hummus* and *baba ganoush* are reliably good. The *hummus* here can come with a couple variations, with olives and a spicy version. The sandwiches are *shawarmas,* and kabob and *falafel* sandwiches. Each is wrapped in store bought pita bread, and accompanied with just tomato and lettuce. The beef *shawarma* might be tastiest of the lot, though the *kafta* kabob sandwich featuring seasoned ground beef is also good. These are also available as plates that are served with rice, pita bread and a couple side orders from the steam table. For less fat there is *Mezze* Sampler with *tabouli, kibbe* ball, *baba ganoush, hummus* and a spinach turnover, and the Vegetable Plate with several choices from the steam table. A few Armenian dishes make it to the steam table and the menu, as these do on the odd Lebanese restaurant here and there. These items are generally hearty, and similar to many popular eastern European dishes such as stuffed cabbage. These items actually fit in nicely among the more strictly Mediterranean fare. Their inclusion is because the owners are of Armenian descent whose family escaped to Lebanon during the Turkish genocide of the Armenian population early in the last century. Several desserts are available, including *baklava* with walnuts, pistachios and cashews, plus other sweet cookies. Rita's Café does not serve any alcoholic beverages. But, opened until 8PM during the week, they encourage patrons to bring in beer and wine, for an even healthier and more enjoyable dinner.

Romano's $10

1528 West Gray (west of Waugh) 77019, (713) 526-1182
14520 Memorial (just east of Dairy Ashford) 77079, (281) 589-7000

Cuisine - Pizza; Italian-American
Hours - Mon-Thu 11AM to 10PM; Fri-Sat 11AM to 11PM; Sun 12 to 9PM
Credit Cards - Amex, Discover, MC, Visa
Service - Counter Service
Alcohol - Beer & Wine

Entrée Prices - $6 to $16 ($10 average)
Entrées $12 and less - 70%

Atmosphere & Décor - Spartan
Appeal - Very good New York-style pizza
Menu Suggestions - pizzas; calzones; Chicken Marsala; Baked Ziti

Romano's Italian Restaurant, or "Romano's Flying Pizza - *Cucina Italiana*", as it's billed above the original location, is a very good place for those homesick New Yorkers to get a slice of home. Literally. Romano's pizza is the New York-style thin crust pizza with a properly thin, slightly malleable and tasty crust, good and judiciously used toppings, and that nearly perfect level of greasiness. It's the style of pizza you find all over the New York area and the northern portion of the Garden State, and Romano's would certainly make the grade in any neighborhood. Just the pizzas alone are certainly worth a trip here. Probably not incidentally, Romano is a common surname in Naples, the birthplace of pizza. The restaurants are deserving stops for a slice, a whole pie, or something heartier. Along with the authentic New York-style pizza and Italian comfort food, you get the gruff Italian-Americans from New York working the counter. The counter staff adds some neighborhood flavor to otherwise bland strip center locations.

This is a pizzeria that serves most of the common Southern Italian-American specialties. The difference is that it is done much better than most similar places in the area. In addition to the pizzas, they serve calzones, subs, pastas and more. The dinner plates include the most popular American translations of the *mezzogiorno* Sunday and feast day dishes with veal, chicken and eggplant such as Veal Francese, Chicken Piccatta, and Eggplant Parmigiana. At least one dish is more than one would expect at a place like this; the Chicken Rollantina, a chicken breast that is rolled and stuffed with ricotta, spinach and prosciutto, sautéed in garlic and white wine and served with a bit of tomato sauce. The pastas listed under "Homemade Pastas" include Fettuccine Alfredo, Lasagna, Manicotti, Ravioli and Linguini with a choice of red or white clam sauces. There is also a list under spaghetti and ziti where you can get either of those pastas with a choice of several varieties of Southern Italian-American sauces: meat sauce, marinara, and the like. Baked ziti is usually a winner. As a bonus for both the pocketbook and the palate, with an order of pasta or main courses, you receive zesty garlic bread, and a dinner salad, which is fairly large and more interesting than the typical side salad. Though made with iceberg lettuce, it comes with a tangy housemade Italian-style dressing and slices of red, ripe tomatoes, Genoa salami, and triangle-shaped pieces of provolone. With the dinner plates, you also get a generous side portion of ziti or spaghetti. As you would expect, red sauce predominates on the menu. Here it is relatively light, and freshly made, much like a true marinara more than a rich, deep Sunday gravy. Beer and wine are available, though, the house wines are rather forgettable. At least these are available in carafe sizes.

Romero's Las Brazas $10

15703 Longenbaugh (at Hwy 6 N., FM 529 and West) 77095, (281) 463-4661

Cuisine - Mexican
Hours - Mon-Thu 8AM to 10PM; Fri-Sat 8AM to 11PM; Sun 8AM to 9PM
Credit Cards - Amex, Discover, MC, Visa
Service - Table Service; Delivery (from 5 to 9PM, limited area, of course)
Alcohol - Full Bar

Entrée Prices - Dinner - $7 to $19 ($10 average); Lunch - $5 to $7; Breakfast - $5
Entrées at Dinner $12 and less - 80%

Atmosphere & Décor - Comfortable; patio
Appeal - Good regional Mexican food in a friendly suburban setting
Useful to Note - Breakfast is served daily.
Menu Suggestions - Chile Relleno; Enchiladas Verdes; Enchiladas de Mole

A treat for the Copperfield area, Romero's does a very good job both with the expected popular Tex-Mex dishes and some regional Mexican favorites. Unusual for a distant suburb, Romero's is a restaurant rather than a *taqueria* that serves some authentic Mexican dishes. Something from the large menu, which lists over seventy entrées, should satisfy most tastes. There are nachos, *chile con queso,* taco salad, cheese enchiladas, chimichangas and chicken breast plates, but also *caldos,* daily *menudo* and *pozole* (chicken and hominy soup), both the somewhat common dark *mole poblano* and the locally rare green *mole, chilaquiles* in a red salsa, *chicharron en salsa verda* (fried pork skin in a green salsa), *pambazos* (bread filled with potato, cheese, cream and *chorizo*), plus a section for *antijotos mexicanos,* more Mexican specialties, which include those *sopes* (fried corn *masa* rounds topped with beans and meat) and *huaraches* (*masa* shaped somewhat like a shoe and topped with meat and beans). And, it offers noticeable value with generously sized portions.

The kitchen seems to do a good job with most of the wide-ranging offerings at Romero's. It's not Hugo's or Otilia's, but it's good here. To start, the chips are always crisp and fresh, and the salsas are flavorful, and with a noticeable chile presence. Probably in deference to the area, the chicken used is the relatively bland white chicken breast. Tacos, *tortas, quesadillas,* burritos and more are available with a choice of meats: *picadillo* (ground beef), fajita, *pastor* (roasted pork), *barbacoa, milanesa* (breaded and pan-fried beef cutlet), *deshebrada* (shredded beef) and *chicharron* (stewed pork skin). There are a number of seafood preparations with most of the locally popular shrimp and snapper fillet dishes, plus a version of fajitas with shrimp. There is also Seafood Enchiladas filled with a combination of shrimp, crab and snapper. There are other interesting enchilada dishes in addition to the familiar ones. There are ones filled with spinach, another with mushrooms topped with a guacamole salsa, and another filled with chorizo and potatoes. Lunch specials are truly specials, as the entrées are a few dollars cheaper than at dinner, and portions are satiating. Residing in a small strip center with enough parking, Romero's is comfortable, if not a terribly attractive moderate-sized restaurant. The décor with exposed cooking ducts and a functional set up, is perfectly appropriate, if not that attractive. The adjacent bar area stocked, with over two dozen tequilas, tables and booths set close together and plenty of tile, make sure there is usually a buzz in the evening. The hard-working, friendly and plentiful staff ensures that it's comfortable all the time.

Royal $9

11919 Bissonnet (just west of Kirkwood) 77099, (281) 530-1100

Cuisine - Pakistani
Hours - Daily 12PM to 12AM
Credit Cards - Amex, Diners, Discover, MC, Visa
Service - Counter Service
Alcohol - NONE

Entrée Prices - $7 to $11 ($9 average)
Entrées $12 and less - 100%

Atmosphere & Décor - Spartan
Appeal - Excellent Pakistani food; very flavorful and spicy, stewed meat dishes
Useful to Note - It's mostly tasty meat dishes here, don't be scared.
Menu Suggestions - Beef Bihari (stewed ground beef); Kadahi Chicken (a chicken stew); Chicken Korma (another chicken stew); Sheekh Kabab (ground beef kabob); Royal Keema Masala; vegetable Samosa; meat Samosa; Chicken

Corn Soup; Khata Khat (a stew of dry chicken): Chicken Tikka Breast (chicken breast cooked in a tandoori oven); sweet lassi (a mango and yogurt drink)

Located in a scruffy, less-than-fully-utilized strip center in far southwest Houston among several other establishments that also have "Royal" in the name, Royal Restaurant & Supermarket is a very similar operation to that of the somewhat nearby Savoy, but slightly nicer. One part is a decent-sized grocery store featuring Pakistani and Indian grocery items and *halal* meats. The other part is a counter-service restaurant serving the zesty and well prepared Pakistani food. The restaurant itself is divided into two sections. The nicer side features large booths, and sports a sign stating that it is reserved for families. The other is more utilitarian, but nice enough for an informal meal. During lunchtime a large screen television blares documentaries and other programming in Arabic (or Urdu or Punjabi) that seems to capture the attention of many of the patrons.

You order at the counter from a menu that is located on the wall above the cashier. It is neatly divided among various Pakistani dishes with somewhat descriptive headers: Chicken Dishes; *Gosht*/Goat/Fish Dishes; Rice Dishes; Chinese Dishes; and General Varieties. There is really no written menu, other than the order slip that just mimics the menu board. The dishes are listed under each heading without an explanation. With menu items that have names such as Beef *Bihari, Khata Kat, Keema, Haleem* and *Zardha,* this could be intimidating to most non-Pakistani or non-Indian patrons. But, thankfully, almost everything at Royal is very good, especially if you like hearty, spicy, fairly complex, very flavorful and often very greasy, stew-like dishes of chicken, beef and lamb. As most of the entrées will take at least fifteen minutes to prepare, it is not a bad idea to start with an order or two of *samosas*. These are somewhat similar to the South American *empanadas,* if made with different spices; deep-fried pastry pockets, filled with either ground meat or potatoes served with both a mint-based, and tamarind sauces. Both the meat and vegetarian *samosas* are delicious, though the vegetarian is probably better, and larger. Just about all of the roughly twenty dishes listed under the headings of Pakistani and Indian Dishes and Chicken Dishes are very good. The *Sheekh* Kabab is a juicy, flavorful kabob of ground meat, and the Chicken *Korma* made with ground chicken are just two of the highlights. Visiting with a group can be a lot of fun in that you can sample several invariably very good and disparate dishes. The *Kadahi* Chicken is a flavorful chicken stew served in the metal pot in which it is cooked. Most of these other dishes are similar stews of chicken and ground beef with subtle variations of the spices. With delectable sauces, these dishes, along with most of the items at Royal, need to be accompanied by the freshly baked large flat bread, *nan* (the Indian *naan*) that is perfect for sopping. In addition to the chicken, beef and lamb dishes, there are also several dishes featuring goat and seafood, such as shrimp *masala* and fish *masala*. And, as at Savoy, you can satisfy your craving for Goat Brain *Masala* here. Though most dishes are meat-based, there are also some vegetarian dishes and sides like *Dal* (refried lentils here), *Palak Paneer* (creamed spinach), rice and a Vegetable *Pulaw* (rice with peas and other vegetables).

The dishes are reasonably priced, and with a group it is easy to enjoy a very interesting, filling and satisfying feast with several different dishes for maybe $10 per person. Service is friendly and efficient, but the dishware, unfortunately, is Styrofoam plates and small plastic utensils. If you have room after the copious amount of meat, bread and grease, a mango *lassi* (similar to a mango smoothie), mango shake or a *chirr* (rice pudding, *kir*) is a nice way to finish the meal. Each is excellent at Royal.

Rudyard's $8

2010 Waugh (between Fairview and West Gray) 77006, (713) 521-0521
www.rudyards.com

Cuisine - American
Hours - Mon-Thu, Sun 11AM to 12AM; Fri-Sat 11AM to 1AM
Credit Cards - Amex, Discover, MC, Visa
Service - Counter Service
Alcohol - Full Bar

Entrée Prices - $5 to $11 ($8 average)
Entrées $12 and less - 100%

Atmosphere & Décor - Pub
Appeal - Very good American pub fare in a amiable neighborhood bar
Useful to Note - Rudz is a bar, first and foremost.
Menu Suggestions - Rudz Burger; Cheese Steak; fries

This long-time Montrose neighborhood pub and live music venue with plenty of character has made its kitchen an attraction in its own right in recent years. This is casual, locally tuned pub fare done very well here. Rudyards, or Rudz, even opens during the day to meet the demand. The setting is strictly a pint-centered pub, so the quality of the food might come as a surprise. The food is well worth a visit for the food alone, though a beer or two from one of the nearly twenty tempting choices might make it even more enjoyable. And, there is almost nothing on the menu that won't be complemented with a beer. Though the menu might not seem much different from most area bar menus with hot and cold sandwiches, hamburgers, pizza, and a few Tex-Mex dishes, the difference is in the ingredients and execution. The fresh and noticeably top-notch breads and buns for the sandwiches are from Kraftsmen Baking, possibly the best of the local commercial bakeries. The hamburgers are where Rudyards' kitchen first gained some notice. These substantially sized and well crafted burgers on excellent, light buns are some of the best in town. Other hot sandwiches such as a ribeye, grilled chicken and pulled pork are also on those buns. Several others are on a crusty, tasty baguette, as their version of the now de rigueur cheesesteak, a shrimp po boy, another featuring cod, and the somewhat unique Shrimp Melt featuring grilled shrimp, bacon and melted cheddar. Each of these burgers and hot sandwiches is served with crispy, hand-cut fries or sautéed vegetables. The Tex-Mex offerings include fajitas, nachos with black beans, *quesadillas,* and fish tacos. For bigger appetites, there is a steak, fish and chips, chicken fried steak, and chicken fried chicken. For those looking past the fryer and grill and to eat something healthier, Rudyards obliges with The Big Salad, with is actually a choice among romaine and other greens, spinach and a Caesar. It is big, though. And, it can be made even bigger with the addition of fajita, grilled chicken or shrimp for a couple of extra bucks. As an added bonus and unusual for Houston, the kitchen stays open until midnight most nights and one in the morning on Fridays and Saturdays.

Ruggles Café Bakery $10

2365 Rice (between Greenbriar and Morningside) 77005, (713) 520-6662
www.rugglesgrill.com

Cuisine - American
Hours - Mon-Thu, Sun 10:30AM to 10PM; Fri-Sat 10:30AM to 11PM
Credit Cards - Amex, Discover, MC, Visa
Service - Counter Service
Alcohol - Beer & Wine; BYOB

Entrée Prices - $5 to $14 ($10 average)
Entrées $12 and less - 80%

Atmosphere & Décor - Pleasant
Appeal - Good food and excellent desserts
Useful to Note - There is also some street parking nearby.
Menu Suggestions - goat cheese salad with apples and toasted almonds with a sun-dried tomato vinaigrette; Cuban Black Bean Soup with Goat Cheese and Bacon; Blue Cheese Bacon Burger; cheeseburger; most desserts, especially the White Chocolate Bread Pudding

Ruggles Café Bakery is another example of an upscale restaurant having a fast-casual outlet that provides a good value with quality and interesting food in comfortable and approachable settings. Given the crowds, Ruggles Café is filling a necessary niche. For lunch, in the evening, or at night, it is an informal place in which to enjoy a salad, soup or sandwich, and, of course, the well-regarded Ruggles desserts. Similarly good muffins and other baked goods are available in the morning. Many come here to eat healthy, at least while they block thoughts of the dessert offerings and Ruggles obliges with a number of interesting entrée-sized salads such as Warm Baked Goat Cheese with Apples in a Sun-Dried Tomato Vinaigrette and a Spinach Cobb Salad with a roasted garlic dressing. There are also soups, sandwiches and pastas. Among the dozen artful and enticing sandwiches are Toasted Pecan White Albacore Tuna Salad on a croissant, roast pork loin with caramelized onions and mozzarella, and Grilled Ranch Chicken and Mozzarella and Bacon. Each is served with a pleasant choice among thickly cut fries, sweet potato fries, dill-rich potato salad, or fresh fruit salad topped with a poppyseed dressing. Ruggles Café also serves some excellent burgers, especially the Bleu Cheese Bacon Burger, each made with the better-than-average quality Angus beef in between much better-than-average accompaniments. The handful of pasta dishes feature chicken, shrimp or salmon in some kind of interesting creation. Bakery is in the name, and not incidentally, the daily baked breads are also reason enough for a visit. These are an integral part of the sandwiches, and are also available for purchase by the loaf. It's a wide array: sourdough, buttermilk currant, rustic potato, sourdough rye with caraway seeds, honey wheat bread with poppy seeds, sun-dried tomato, walnut, semolina sesame seed, country-style hearth loaf with cilantro and cinnamon raisin.

To a great many, Ruggles Café's chief attraction is that they offer the same highly popular and usually quite rich desserts that the original Ruggles offers. There are over thirty choices. For six dollars you get a number of tempting cakes, pies, muffins, scones and other pastries. The number of dessert items is staggering. There are Brownie Baked Alaska, Chocolate Pecan Torte, Oreo Cheesecake, Coconut Cake, Apple Spice Cake, Tres Leches, Chocolate Orange Mousse, White Chocolate Cheesecake, Apple Tart and Chocolate Truffle Cake with Grand Marnier Mousse. The White Chocolate Bread Pudding is especially delicious. If this is not enough, there is also a fine selection of hefty cookies and brownies for just a couple bucks. Nearly everything in the dessert cases looks great. Even well before dessert, Ruggles Café will provide more than enough to satisfy your palate.

Rustika Café $7

3237 Southwest Freeway (west of Buffalo Speedway) 77027, (713) 349-8000
www.rustikacafe.com

Cuisine - Café / Bakery; American; Tex-Mex
Hours - Mon-Sat 8AM to 7PM
Credit Cards - Amex, Discover, MC, Visa
Service - Counter Service

Alcohol - NONE

Entrée Prices - Dinner & Lunch - $4 to $10 ($7 average); Breakfast - $4 to $8
Entrées at Dinner $12 and less - 100%

Atmosphere & Décor - Pleasant
Appeal - An eclectic place with good breakfast, lunch and dessert items
Useful to Note - They are well-suited for bulk orders for meetings and parties.
Menu Suggestions - Empanada Platters; Migas Mexicana (scrambled eggs, caramelized onions, tomatoes, fresh jalapeños and fried tortilla strips); Chicken Salad Sandwich; Tuna Salad Sandwich; Mexicana Sandwich (open-faced sandwich with sautéed onion, tomatoes, melted cheese and chicken)

Rustika Café is now a casual restaurant that serves a number of dishes including Tex-Mex breakfasts, soups and sandwiches, and Argentine-style *empanadas*. The good-sized and wordy menu might seem daunting at first, but almost every dish is well-explained, even if it can be tough to make a choice among the tempting options. There is likely something for nearly every taste and appetite, and Rustika is a low-key, well-lit and inviting place for an informal meal. With Rustika opening at 7AM, breakfast is served daily, and it might be the best in the neighborhood. With something to satisfy a score of diverse tastes, the lengthy breakfast portion of the menu is divided among mostly Mexican scrambled and fried egg dishes, omelets, breakfast tacos served in a choice of flour or corn tortillas, breakfast sandwiches, sweet crêpes, fresh fruit, grits and French toast and pancakes. Among the egg-centric fare, there are a couple of versions of *migas, huevos a la mexicana, huevos rancheros*, Eggs Rustika (two fried eggs over ham, cheese and corn tortillas that are topped with salsa), a few Spanish-style egg dishes (called *tortillas*) including a few with decidedly Mexican flavors (*mole*, poblanos and salsa), and the opportunity to create your own omelet with a variety of ingredients. Even lox and cream cheese with scrambled eggs is part of the mix. The egg dishes are probably the best here, as the French toast and pancakes do not quite measure up. For lunch there is also a wide array of good options among the tacos, soups, hot and cold sandwiches, entrée-sized salads and *empanadas*. The *empanadas* are cased in a slightly different dough than are served in most other local restaurants. These can be filled with shredded chicken, ground beef, spinach, chicken in *mole*, plus apple and pumpkin. These are reliably enjoyable, the savory ones topped with the accompanying salsa, especially. The warm *empanadas* are served as a platter with tortilla chips and a very good small salad of mixed greens and a house-made red wine vinaigrette. The sandwiches are always a good choice because these feature high quality bread baked in-house. Interestingly, the Chicken Salad Sandwich might be the highlight, and is quite possibly the best version in the area. Other choices include grilled chicken, a hefty club, turkey and cheese, roast beef, pastrami, the Veggie (sautéed spinach, tomatoes, onion, mushrooms, celery and toasted almond slivers), and a couple of other salads, tuna and egg. Then there are soups and several salads to appeal to the less hearty or healthier appetites. The soups include Tortilla with Beef Broth, Creamy Potato, Poblano Pepper with corn, Chicken Vegetable, Matzo Ball, and suited for our long summertime, Gazpacho. There are soup and salad, and soup, salad and sandwich combinations, too. Its display case is filled with varieties of tempting cookies and sweets that can provide a reward for a healthy entrée choice, or just some more tasty fat.

* Saigon Pagolac $8

9600 Bellaire (in Dynasty Plaza, at Corporate) 77036, (713) 988-6106

Cuisine - Vietnamese
Hours - Tue-Sun 11AM to 11PM
Credit Cards - Amex, Diners, Discover, MC, Visa
Service - Table Service
Alcohol - Beer & Wine

Entrée Prices - Dinner - $5 to $20 ($8 average); Lunch - $3 to $7
Entrées at Dinner $12 and less - 90%

Atmosphere & Décor - Nice
Appeal - Excellent Vietnamese food; Seven Courses of Beef; lunch specials
Useful to Note - Your server's English might not be very good; closed on Monday.
Menu Suggestions - Vietnamese Egg Rolls; Bun Thit Nuong; Com Thit Nuong (sliced char-grilled pork with rice); Seven Courses of Beef (seven different preparations of beef); giant shrimp on vermicelli

For a number of years now, Saigon Pagolac has been one of several restaurants, some of them quite proficient, located in the Dynasty shopping center on Bellaire, just east of the Beltway. Tucked in a corner away from the busy street, it's the best of the lot serving often excellent and reasonably priced Vietnamese food. In fact, Saigon Pagolac is one of the very best restaurants in town in terms of the ratio of quality-to-value, regardless of cuisine. Impressively, it does so while offering a wide range of well prepared Vietnamese specialties with more décor and atmosphere than most area Vietnamese restaurants. Unfortunately, the service can be very uneven and even quite ragged at times, especially if you don't speak Vietnamese. No matter, the quality of the food and the corresponding price for such food always compensates for any lags in service.

Saigon Pagolac serves all of the locally popular Vietnamese dishes in addition to some specialties. On the cover of the menu, along with a drawing of cows in front of a farm, is the phrase "*Bo 7 Mon*; Seven Courses of Beef". These are seven different preparations of beef, which you can order as a meal. You'll need at least one other dining partner to do this, and it's more fun if the entire table partakes. You can also get larger, entrée-sized portions of each of the seven. Some are better than others. To begin the meal, it is tough to beat the excellent Vietnamese egg rolls, probably the best in town. These are quite unlike the soggy egg rolls served in Chinese restaurants. Instead, these are plump spring rolls filled with fresh vegetables and pork, fried to a crisp exterior and served with large lettuce leaves and an array of fresh herbs. A mild peanut sauce is also served to complement these. Among the more well-known entrées, the *Com Thit Nuong*, the marinated and char-grilled thinly sliced pork served with rice, shredded carrots, a large lettuce leaf and fish sauce is very good. The servings of pork are more generous than most places. The most inexpensive beef dish, the *Com Bo Lui* consists of char-grilled chunks of tender beef on a skewer along with thick slices of onion and green pepper. It's also excellent. Amazingly, both the *Com Thit Nuong* and the *Com Bo Lui* are just three bucks for lunch, and just a dollar more at dinner. If not the best meal deals in town, these are very close. The similar *bun* (rice vermicelli) dishes are well prepared and savory, as are the chicken, shrimp and egg roll version, both for the *bun* and the *com*. The char-grilled chicken available in rice and rice noodle dishes is very good. There is a large *pho* (beef noodle soup) selection. Among the seafood dishes, the prawns (real prawns, in fact) served with rice are worth ordering. This consists of three extremely large, shell-on prawns, which are quite flavorful. As an added bonus, the small number of wines offered is surprisingly good and inexpensive, especially for a Vietnamese restaurant. The restaurant, though in a bustling workaday shopping mall, is among the nicest of the unassimilated Vietnamese restaurants in the area. The walls are painted in a soothing yellow and adorned with framed cases of Vietnamese musical instruments. The patrons in this often-crowded restaurant are almost exclusively Vietnamese at night. During the day nearby office workers in the know join the Vietnamese patrons.

San Dong Noodle House $4

9938 Bellaire (between Corporate and the Beltway) 77036, (713) 271-3945

Cuisine - Chinese
Hours - Daily 11AM to 8PM
Credit Cards - NONE
Service - Counter Service
Alcohol - NONE

Entrée Prices - $3 to $5 ($4 average)
Entrées $12 and less - 100%

Atmosphere & Décor - Spartan
Appeal - Excellent Chinese dumplings and tasty soups for a pittance
Useful to Note - It's just dumplings and soup here.
Menu Suggestions - Pork Leek Dumplings (steamed dumplings filled with ground pork and leeks); Cabbage Pork Dumplings (steamed dumplings filled with ground pork and cabbage); Pan Fried Pork Dumplings; Beef Dumplings Soup (a rich soup filled with a dozen ground beef-filled dumplings)

San Dong Noodle House, formerly known in English as Santong Snacks moved to much nicer digs a little further west down Bellaire Boulevard. During the week it is a good idea to get to here before 11:30AM. For the next hour-and-a-half there is a decent chance that you will have to wait to be able to find a table among the two dozen at this small restaurant. San Dong is very popular for the straightforward informal Chinese fare such as dumplings, soups and noodle dishes. The flavors here are true, clean, and free of any of the cloying sweetness that is characteristic of the familiar Americanized Chinese food. Though it has received flattering reviews in the local (English-language) press, the clientele is still mostly Chinese.

The routine is somewhat straightforward here. Upon entering, you look up at the list of dishes on the small menu, approach the counter, order your food (it is easiest to do so by number), then hopefully find a seat. You can then get a glass of water and complimentary hot tea, and await your order. The dishes are prepared or assembled to order, and service is somewhat indifferent, so the food will come out when it is ready, if it has not been misplaced among the crush of patrons. The food is very much worth the occasional small hassle. Some of the twenty dishes that are listed in placard form on one wall are: Roast Beef Noodles, Roast Beef Soup Noodles, Mustard Green Noodles, Sour Mustard Green Noodles, Pork Rib Noodles, Beef Dumplings Soup, Pork Turnip Noodles, Simple Soup Noodles, steamed Pork Leek Dumplings, steamed Cabbage Pork Dumplings, and Pan Fried Pork Dumplings. The dumplings are the dishes that are the most popular with the non-Chinese patrons. Also, the menu names for the dumplings are the most accurately descriptive. These are probably the best Chinese dumplings in the city. Freshly steamed or pan-fried, these feature a thick, moist (though doubtfully Maoist) wrapping, around fresh ingredients like roasted pork, leek and cabbage. Very flavorful, these hold together well, and are even better when dipped in a mixture of the tabletop condiments: soy sauce, chili sauce and a dash of vinegar. The dumplings are smaller than at other local places, but there are fifteen to an order for the steamed versions, and a dozen for the fried. One order is usually sufficient for a meal. If hungry, the Simple Soup Noodles can be a good complement to an order of the dumplings. This soup is a tasty, simple broth with medium-thick noodles, seaweed, other greens, and some fresh scallions or chives.

Another similar, very flavorful dish is the similar Beef Dumplings Soup with a dozen of the beef dumplings in a brown broth. As popular as these are, San Dong also has packaged dumplings and several other items for sale.

Sandwich King $6

6615 Long Point (between Silber and Hempstead Highway) 77055, (713) 681-1265
5242 Hollister (between Hempstead and 290) 77040, (713) 688-4446
11611 W. Airport (north of the Southwest Freeway) 77477, (281) 313-0942

Cuisine - Sandwiches
Hours - Mon-Fri 7AM to 5PM; Sat 7AM to 4PM
Credit Cards - NONE
Service - Counter Service
Alcohol - NONE

Entrée Prices - Lunch - $5 to $7 ($6 average); Breakfast - $2 to $3
Entrées at Lunch $12 and less - 100%

Atmosphere & Décor - Not much
Appeal - Delicious and inexpensive cheese steak and other hot sandwiches
Useful to Note - Just overlook the scruffiness of the Long Point location.
Menu Suggestions - Cheese Steak Sandwich; Roast Beef Po Boy; Bacon Cheeseburger

The owners of the family-run Sandwich King Deli & Mesquite Grill at its original spot on Long Point have been happily serving top-notch hot sandwiches, most prefaced with "Giant" on the menu, and good-naturedly calling customers "boss" for over twenty years. The Sandwich King (it's not really a deli, though a grill, possibly mesquite-fueled, is used to good effect) offers good value with deals such as a very satisfying, freshly constructed cheese steak on a fresh, long French roll, crisp, hot fries and a soda for around five bucks. The bread for the po boys is baked daily, and especially for the Sandwich King. This helps make the sandwiches here much more than a typical sandwich. The most popular one is the excellent, if maybe not authentic, Philly cheese steak sandwich that is not only better than most local versions, it's much cheaper, too. It's even made with thinly sliced beef, melted cheese, grilled onions and a bit of pepperoncini. The trademark pepperoncini is included on all of the sandwiches. Though the hot sandwiches are the best items here, the variety of cold sandwiches includes roast beef, turkey, ham and cheese, a club, meatball and various cold cuts. They also have hamburgers and a chili dog, and a number of meats stuffed into pita bread. Many of the sandwiches and burgers are available as the Chef's Special. This includes fries and drink with the sandwich for just five bucks. It's a very nice price performer. The thin fries are cooked to order, and are sufficiently crisp and a very good complement to the sandwich.

Though every item is "Giant", these sandwiches are not overly large and most appetites will need the fries or chips to satiate. Sandwich King also serves breakfast in the similar long sandwich fashion: scrambled eggs, cheddar-like cheese and choice of sausage, bacon or ham on a French roll. These are a great value. There are a handful of salads, too, but only one, a Greek Salad, without meat. Don't come to the Sandwich King expecting heart-healthy fare or décor. These restaurants are conspicuously lacking in it, and the original location on Long Point is downright dumpy. About the only decoration there is a framed photo of the owner's hometown in Lebanon. But, do not be deterred by the dumpiness, or the accompanying surroundings, which can also be off-putting. There are great places to get a hot sandwich, and for a very reasonable price, which is why these are often crowded with folks who need to ingest tasty calories fairly quickly during the work day.

Sandy's Market $10

12171 Katy Freeway (between Kirkwood and Dairy Ashford) 77079, (281) 870-9999

Cuisine - American
Hours - Daily 6AM to 8PM
Credit Cards - Amex, Discover, MC, Visa
Service - Buffet
Alcohol - NONE

Entrée Prices - Dinner - $10; Lunch - $9; Breakfast - $7; Brunch - $9
Entrées at Dinner $12 and less - 100%

Atmosphere & Décor - Functional; an airy, large grocery with tables and chairs
Appeal - Wide-ranging healthy food in all-you-can-eat fashion
Useful to Note - You can call for reservations.
Menu Suggestions - salad bar; fresh fruit

Sandy's Market, or Sandy's Produce Market & Vitamins, is still somewhat of a health foods market, but the main reason for the vast majority of customers is their bounteous vegetable- and fruit-heavy all-you-can-eat buffet. In the spacious market just off the Katy Freeway there is much more room to dine than there is to shop. Tables and chairs seemingly gleamed from various closeout and fire sales are scattered among the aisles and buffet stations, ever taking more space as the prepared foods became more and more popular compared to the vitamins and other health food items. The prepared food here is not the best around, and the spicing and flavorings won't ever be described as robust, but there is a lot from which to choose, and you can satisfy your fruit and much of your vegetable cravings with ease here, and the breads are freshly baked. The salad selections are numerous with over forty items including a few types of lettuce, lots of shredded and chopped vegetables and some fresh fruits that are correctly colored. If available, the corn will be shorn from the cob, and the cut up fruit might include mangos and papayas. Other salads in the broad sense that you'll find here are chicken, tuna and even salmon. The hot buffet selections change daily depending on what's fresh and available. There are always a few soups, but just a handful of meat entrées, and none of these are on the heavy side. For example, there might be spaghetti with turkey meatballs, turkey and vegetarian chilies, fajitas, a "Mexican" chicken stew and the like. These can be nicely supplemented with chopped fresh jalapeños, garlic, cheddar, feta, mozzarella, Parmesan or cheddar cheeses. A choice of hot teas will be offered by a server who will visit your table soon after sitting down. Sandy's even serves that gaucho favorite, the strongly vegetal-flavored *yerbe maté,* but not the gourd or *bombilla.* Be sure to note that it's expected that you leave a tip on the table for the tea server. There is also iced tea, in a handful of unique flavors, available in a back corner of the store, and only in small ceramic cups. Breakfast is served from 6AM to 11AM from Monday through Friday and the popular and similar brunch is a couple of dollars more on the weekends from 6AM to 5PM. As an added attraction for some, there is live, pleasant acoustic music, which might be jazz, classical or Spanish, Friday through Sunday during the day, and Friday and Saturday at night.

Santa Fe Flats $9

21542 Highway 249 (between Louetta and Spring-Cypress) 77070, (281) 655-1400
www.santafeflats.net

Cuisine - New Mex-Mex
Hours - Mon-Thu - 11AM to 9PM; Fri-Sat - 11AM to 10PM; Sun 11AM to 8PM
Credit Cards - Amex, Diners, MC, Visa
Service - Table Service
Alcohol - Full Bar

Entrée Prices - Dinner - $6 to $15 ($9 average); Lunch - $6 to $8
Entrées at Dinner $12 and less - 90%

Atmosphere & Décor - Comfortable; patio; live music on patio Tue-Sat
Appeal - Good Mexican food for Willowbrook with a New Mexico accent
Useful to Note - It's pretty much Tex-Mex.
Menu Suggestions - Red Enchilada (filled with ground pork and cheddar and topped with red chile sauce); Santa Fe Burrito (filled with steak)

Santa Fe Flats specializes in good-value, mostly informal New Mexican-style Mexican food, New Mex Mex, if you will. For chauvinistic Texans, this is very similar and almost as good as our own Mexican food. The dishes here are very familiar with enchiladas, burritos, tacos, fajitas, *chile con queso* and the like. The chiles used here and the resulting flavors can be slightly unusual. But, chiles from high altitude New Mexico have a well-deserved reputation. The expected chips come with a boring red salsa and a unique and flavorful avocado-based one. There also the "salsa bar" that you can amble to for those two, plus a few additional salsas including a very tasty warmed one, flecked with red chiles that is not unlike a viscous tortilla soup. Favorite Mexican or Tex-Mex dishes might taste a little differently here, though enjoyable. For example, the enchiladas are topped with interesting and piquant smoked red or green chile sauces that are unique and flavorful. Each is available with a fried egg, and can be made with blue corn tortillas. The kitchen seems to do most things fairly well on the focused menu, though it might be quite as proficient as other places. The entrées on the menu are divided among the enchiladas, burritos, tacos, fajitas, *quesadillas*, salads, and specialties. These Santa Fe specialty dishes include a few chicken breast dishes and a half-pound hamburger topped with a green chile sauce. There is a slightly different version of *chile rellenos* with two chiles stuffed with *Chihuahua* cheese and topped with more cheese. The large burritos are of the knife-and-fork variety and can feature either flour or wheat tortillas and topped with a red or green chile sauce and cheese and filled with grilled beef or chicken. The tacos are served in either the flour or corn tortillas. There are even New Mexican-style grilled shrimp and fish tacos. The décor and service are attractive enough, if rather suburban: video arcade games occupy one small nook of a side room; there is a separate bar area, isolated from the dining room; and there is a decent chance that your waitress will be a teenager. The service is usually earnest, but far from polished. There is a user-friendly patio, which is obscured from much of the parking lot and nearby freeway. Family friendly, not just with the video games, there is also a small playground for kids. Do you like *sopaipillas*? Santa Fe Flats still serves these if you have room for dessert along with a few other items including a fried cheesecake.

Savoy $8

11246 Wilcrest (north of W. Belfort) 77031, (281) 568-6772

Cuisine - Pakistani
Hours - Daily 9AM to 11PM
Credit Cards - Amex, Diners, Discover, MC, Visa
Service - Counter Service
Alcohol - NONE

Entrée Prices - $6 to $9 ($8 average)
Entrées $12 and less - 100%

Atmosphere & Décor - Spartan
Appeal - Good, cheap and greasy (in the best sense) Pakistani food
Useful to Note - This is good for take-away.
Menu Suggestions - samosa; Special Karahi Chicken; Beef Bihari; naan; lassi

---

Savoy is both a restaurant and a grocery store that primarily serves the local Pakistani and Muslim community in far southwest Houston. The operation is divided neatly in half, the Spartan, but very proficient counter-service restaurant separated from the grocery section. The restaurant's dishes are those of Pakistan and the Muslim cooking of neighboring India, and it will be familiar to those who frequent local Indian restaurants. Many of the dishes might have different names, but there are also a *masala*, a *biriyani*, chicken *tikka*, *samosa* and *naan*. The person at the counter will be willing, and hopefully able, to explain the items, if necessary. Though there are lentils and a mixed vegetable dish, most of the items are meat-based. For those, Savoy features *halal* meat. This is meat that has been butchered according to Islamic law, similar to kosher meat. And, which ensures a certain level of quality. There are a number of different preparations of chicken, beef and goat as well.

Savoy's nearly twenty entrées are robust, often spicy, filling and laden with cooking oil. For a group of several, it is probably best to order a number of dishes and share among the group. A nice way to start the meal is with *samosas*, the Indian and Pakistani version of an *empanada*, large, deep-fried pockets of thick dough filled with either ground meat or potatoes that are very good with the mint-based chutney. Possibly the best dish is the Special *Karahi* Chicken, a chicken leg and thigh in a flavorful, red *garam masala*-like sauce. The kabobs, Beef *Seekh*, Beef *Boti* and *Shami* are all pretty good, as are the stew-like preparations that make up a good portion of the menu. The latter might taste even the next day, as leftovers. Pools of oil will decorate just about any finished dish, though the dishes themselves don't taste overly greasy. Alcohol consumption is not permitted by Islam, but most of these dishes must be great when hung over. The moist rice and the fresh bread, *naan*, are requisite companions to soak and sop up all of the tangy sauces that come with the entrées. When available, the sweet *lassi*, a yogurt-based drink with the consistency that is a little less thick than that of a smoothie, is delicious. It is a fitting end to a meal. Keeping with the minimalist setting, which is pretty much bereft of any atmosphere, the food is served on Styrofoam plates with small plastic utensils. It really does not seem to matter. The food is appetizing, filling and inexpensive.

Sawadee $12

6719 Weslayan (at Bellaire) 77005, (713) 666-7872

Cuisine - Thai
Hours - Mon-Fri 11AM to 3PM; 5 to 10PM; Sat 11AM to 10PM; Sun 5 to 11PM
Credit Cards - Amex, Discover, MC, Visa
Service - Table Service
Alcohol - Beer & Wine

Entrée Prices - Dinner - $7 to $16 ($12 average); Lunch - $6 to 9
Entrées at Dinner $12 and less - 80%

Atmosphere & Décor - Comfortable
Appeal - Good Thai food in West University
Menu Suggestions - Crispy Spring Rolls; papaya salad; Chicken Panaeng (chicken in curry sauce with coconut milk); Beef Panaeng; Shrimp Curry; Patt Thai with chicken (Pad Thai); Chicken Curry with green curry sauce; Sautéed Chicken with Snow Peas and Peanut Sauce

Though there is no shortage of enjoyable Thai restaurants in the surrounding area, Sawadee provides another good one even closer for the folks in West University and Southside Place. It's not a grand place, but it is a welcome, comfortable and unpretentious neighborhood fixture. Service is prompt and friendly. The setting is nothing special with its sparse décor featuring Columbia blue walls and industrial grade carpet. But, the attractions are the familiar, well prepared, not overly challenging and well-proportioned food, not the décor. Sawadee does have two large saltwater aquariums featuring a great number of very brightly colored fish, sea anemones, and other exotic sea creatures and even living coral that can make for a fun diversion while waiting for your food, especially if children are in tow. The offerings are similar to that of most local Thai restaurants, and the properly sized menu is easy to follow. There are the appetizers such as rolls, *satays* and *mee krob* (a dish of sweet crispy noodles), familiar soups and noodle dishes plus the seventy good-sized entrées. The crispy spring rolls work well as starters. Though fried, they still retain a fresh taste. The Sawadee Chicken Wings in gooey bland sauce should be avoided, however. Of the many dishes, there are several similar preparations with beef, chicken, pork, shrimp and vegetables such as the Garlic Curry (with chicken, pork or shrimp) where it makes sense. The chicken dishes are more prevalent than the others. Well-suited to vegetarians, Sawadee has over fifteen strictly vegetarian entrées. For the entrées, the Chicken *Panaeng* is a reliable dish with white chicken meat in a sauce of yellow curry and coconut milk with crisp green beans. Sautéed Chicken with Snow Peas and Peanut Sauce is also a winner, as is the Shrimp Curry. This dish consists of medium-sized shrimp in a moderately spicy, surprisingly complex and tasty curry sauce with tomato, chunks of pineapple, green beans and sweet basil. Though made with coconut milk, it is not heavy. The curry entrées are engaging, but the spices are restrained, as with most dishes here, which is not very surprising given the restaurant's location near West U. Many items are also on the slightly sweet side. In addition to shrimp, other featured seafood items are fillets of snapper and flounder, an entire snapper and mussels.

Seco's Latin Cuisine $11

2536 Nottingham (east of Kirby, south of Sunset) 77005, (713) 942-0001

Cuisine - Tex-Mex
Hours - Mon-Thu 11AM to 11PM; Fri-Sat 11AM to 12PM; Sun 10:30AM to 9PM
Credit Cards - Amex, Diners, MC, Visa
Service - Table Service
Alcohol - Beer & Wine

Entrée Prices - $7 to $13 ($11 average)
Entrées $12 and less - 80%

Atmosphere & Décor - Pleasant, low-key
Appeal - Favorites from departed Jalapeños in a quaint café-like setting
Useful to Note - Small parking lot; but street parking is within a half-block or so.
Menu Suggestions - Chupe de Camaron Chef Seco Style (a zesty shrimp soup); Milanese Napolitana (breaded, flattened round steak sautéed then baked with ham and mozzarella); The Real Spinach Enchiladas; Corn Enchiladas; Enchiladas Suizas; Pollo Jalisco (sautéed chicken breast served with tomatoes, scallions and jalapeños that is flambéed with tequila and lime)

Owned by the former chef at the long-time Upper Kirby favorite Jalapeños, which succumbed to development at the end of 2005, Seco's Latin Cuisine combines several Argentine café-style items from the previous tenant, Europa Café, with many unique Tex-Mex favorites from Jalapeños. It's a somewhat odd jumble of dishes, but maybe not for Houston. That the kitchen can handle most of the disparate offerings is the question, and it seems that it can.

There are still some *empanadas*, pastas, *milanesas*, *chimi-churri* sauce, and coffees. These are now joined with a wide array of Tex-Mex specialties: *quesadillas*, soups, enchiladas, *tacos al carbon*, fajitas with a choice of meats and shrimp, fish tacos, and Tex-Mex combination platters. There should be at least several items that will interest. And, the kitchen seems to be flexible, as many items are available with a choice of cooking methods. Given the chef / owner's pedigree, the Tex-Mex dishes are probably the best. The once popular corn and spinach enchilada dishes at Jalapeños are resurrected in very fine fashion. The Real Spinach Enchiladas are filled with cooked but still verdant spinach and topped with a cilantro cream sauce. There are also a commendable *Enchiladas Suizas* and one filled with shrimp and spinach that is covered in a tomatillo and *guajillo* chile cream sauce. Interestingly or strangely, the enchiladas can be made with a choice among the usual corn, and the sure-to-be-somewhat-gooey flour and wheat tortillas. The fish tacos are available with shrimp, blackened salmon, blackened tilapia, and even redfish. In addition to tacos, redfish, salmon, shrimp and tilapia appear on the menu in a number of other preparations. Each can be simply grilled or sautéed with garlic in olive oil. There is a section on the menu dedicated to sautéed chicken entrées, several of which are especially interesting. The most eclectic has been the *Aji de Gallina,* a dish from Peru, probably of Incan origin, made with shredded chicken mixed Parmesan cheese, condensed milk, bread, peppers, walnuts and almonds served over boiled potatoes. There is the former Jalapeños staple, quail, which is now served in a sauce made with pineapple, ginger and *chipotles*. The remaining pastas are slightly different, maybe just a little heavier, than the familiar preparations. The Argentine influence is further evident with the *empanadas* and *milanesas* (spelled *milanese* here). The *Milanese Napolitana* is a slice of round steak that has been pounded thin, breaded and sautéed then topped with a slice of ham and mozzarella and baked. It's served with a marinara sauce and some well-crafted fries that do very well without ketchup. There is also a heartier *milanesa* topped with a couple of fried eggs, in the South American fashion. For lighter fare, there are several entrée-size salads, an excellent shrimp soup, and several sandwiches, most served on a small baguette. On Sundays, there is a bountiful and good value brunch with over twenty items including an omelet station, waffles, and desserts.

Seco's is set in an old house with several small rooms. It has a comfortable feel, almost like a safe European home. That this is a fairly small place adds to this. Beer and wine are served, and the selection, like the restaurant is rather small. One drawback with Seco's is that there are very few parking spaces at the restaurant. However, it is usually easy to find parking on the street nearby.

Shanghai $9

9116 Bellaire (between Gessner and Ranchester) 77036, (713) 771-8082

Cuisine - Chinese
Hours - Mon-Fri 11AM to 10PM; Sat-Sun 9:30AM to 10PM
Credit Cards - Amex, Discover, MC, Visa
Service - Table Service
Alcohol - Beer & Wine

Entrée Prices - Dinner - $5 to $24 ($9 average); Lunch - $4 to $6
Entrées at Dinner $12 and less - 90%

Atmosphere & Décor - Pleasant
Appeal - Very good Chinese food for cheap, especially during lunchtime
Useful to Note - Shanghai is just the name, not the cuisine any more.
Menu Suggestions - Cashew Shrimp; Kung Pao Chicken; Roasted Duck

Shanghai is one of the many pleasant and inexpensive small Chinese eateries on Bellaire. Its tables are filled with mostly Chinese patrons, but the décor is nicer than most, and it seems more inviting, and possibly even more consistent than many similar establishments that crowd this part of Bellaire. There are many interesting dishes, and nearly everything seems to be well prepared here. The flavors and colors are distinct and vibrant within a dish, vegetables are properly crisp, and the dishes mostly clean-tasting, as these should be, and not heavy. Even the Sweet and Sour dishes, which avoids the gloppiness that affects most other versions. Like nearly all of its Chinese neighbors, the menu is extensive, and the lunch specials are amazing values. Until mid-decade Shanghai actually did serve Shanghai-style cuisine, and a special type of dumpling that was a treat to dumpling aficionados, but it seemed that this heavier and greasier fare was not as popular as the lighter Cantonese cooking, especially with the recent immigrants, many of whom prefer the food of their home region.

The appropriately lengthy menu is divided among soups, clay pots, seafood, beef, poultry, pork, tofu, vegetables, noodles, noodles in soup, *lo mein*, fried rice and *congee*. There should be something for everyone among these seemingly authentic southern Chinese offerings. For the Chinese seafood lover, befitting a good, local Cantonese restaurant the seafood specialties are extensive. Sea bass, sole, flying fish, scallop, shrimp, crab, sea cucumber, abalone, cuttlefish, oysters, clams, squid and lobster are all represented, at least in the English translation of the menu. The lunch specials are an especially good value, even by New Chinatown standards. Of the twenty choices there are dishes centered on beef, chicken, shrimp, pork and tofu. There is even roasted duck for just five bucks. Beef Brisket, Beef with the (really) Bitter Melon, and Pig's Feet are some of the other choices, but there is also more familiar peanut-laden Kung Pao dishes with a choice among chicken, shrimp and beef. Cashew Shrimp, featuring medium-sized shrimp, is one of the best choices. Shanghai sports a fairly nice interior, though its formerly very handsome dark red décor is now primarily white, and probably less attractive, and certainly less distinctive from many other nearby restaurants. But, it's no longer as unique menu-wise, either, and neither fact should be a deterent from visiting. Importantly, the fare is very good, and very fairly priced, amazingly so during lunchtime.

Shawarma King $8

3121 Hillcroft (between Westheimer and Richmond) 77057, (713) 784-8882
www.sharwarmakingonline.com

Cuisine - Middle Eastern
Credit Cards - Diners, Discover, MC, Visa
Hours - Mon-Thu 11AM to 10PM; Fri-Sat 11AM to 11PM; Sun 12 to 10PM
Service - Counter Service
Alcohol - NONE

Entrée Prices - Dinner - $5 to $12 ($8 average); Lunch - $5 to $9
Entrées at Dinner $12 and less - 100%

Atmosphere & Décor - Functional
Appeal - Very good, inexpensive casual Middle Eastern food
Useful to Note - They are good for take-out and catering.
Menu Suggestions - chicken shawarma sandwich; beef shawarma sandwich; falafel sandwich; chicken shawarma plate; beef shawarma plate; baba ganoush; cashew baklava; pistachio baklava; walnut baklava

Shawarma King's name might indeed be correct, as the *shawarmas* here are some of the very best in town. This is a great stop for some well prepared, casual Middle Eastern fare. The choices are somewhat limited, but there should be enough to satisfy most diners. There are mostly vegetarian appetizers and sides, mostly meaty sandwiches wrapped in pita bread, heartier plates, and some delicious Middle Eastern pastries. Shawarma King is a small, bare-bones, but inviting and efficiently run restaurant on Hillcroft, south of Westheimer that is easily reached from the Galleria and much of west Houston.

Serving is cafeteria-style, the appetizers are the ones that are found at most local Middle Eastern eateries such as *hummus, baba ganoush, tabouli,* stuffed grape leaves, spinach pies in phyllo, similar meat pieces, deep-fried balls of *falafel* and *kibbe,* and spicy potatoes. One of these makes for a fitting complement to one of the sandwiches, especially so the *baba ganoush* and *tabouli.* And, as the menu has stated, "appetizer is served with nice presentation". The sandwiches are generally excellent, especially the chicken and beef *shawarma.* These feature juicy, flavorful meat that has been slowly roasted then placed inside a large piece of pita bread and adorned with crisp shredded lettuce, tomato wedges, pickles, and a thin yogurt-type sauce, possibly *tahini.* These are even tastier with a few drops of the red chili-based hot sauce that is on the table. There are sandwiches with *falafel, kafta* (ground beef and lamb), *souvlaki* (marinated and skewered chunks of beef), *breemo* (ground beef), and a lamb kabob. Each is worth ordering. For the larger appetites, almost all of the sandwich choices are also served as plates, which consist of a generous portion of the meat or *falafel* balls, pita bread, and a choice of two of the appetizers. These are reasonably priced between five bucks for the plate with the vegetarian *falafel* to eight for the half-chicken to still under ten bucks for the generous mixed grill or the lamb. There are also various specials that change daily.

At Shawarma King you usually pay after finishing the meal. Situated by the cashier are some delectable-looking pastries: *baklava, namora,* ladyfingers, and the like. It is not a bad idea to give into temptation, as these are always very good. Unusual for Middle Eastern restaurants in Houston, Shawarma King makes *baklava* with cashews in addition to the more popular walnuts and pistachios. All three versions are very good, fresh, flaky gooey and tasty. The one with cashews might be the best. For a sweet tooth, these are reason enough to visit Shawarma King.

Sichuan Cuisine $10

9114 Bellaire (between Gessner and Ranchester) 77036, (713) 771-6868

Cuisine - Chinese
Hours - Daily 11AM to 10PM
Credit Cards - MC, Visa
Service - Table Service
Alcohol - NONE; BYOB

Entrée Prices - Dinner - $5 to $21 ($10 average); Lunch - $4 to $5
Entrées at Dinner $12 and less - 90%

Atmosphere & Décor - Functional
Appeal - Excellent, authentic Szechuan cooking
Useful to Note - The staff's English is limited, but are accommodating.
Menu Suggestions - Chengdu Dumplings; Ma Po Tofu; Crispy Chicken with Chili; Kung Pao Chicken; Kung Pao Shrimp; Kung Pao Chicken and Shrimp; Hot Pot

Sichuan Cuisine is located next door to two other very good inexpensive storefront restaurants, Shanghai and Hunan Plus. But, unlike those two restaurants, Sichuan actually serves mostly the authentic fare of its namesake region. "Szechuan" for the sake of consistency with other profiles, if inconsistent here; different English spellings of the same thing. Though the fare here can be exotic, it will be readily enjoyable by anyone with a passing interest in Chinese food. There are a decent number of the more Americanized dishes, though less numerous, and somewhat less gloppy than elsewhere. The cuisine of this fertile subtropical region features robust and often spicy flavors. A big part of the uniqueness of Szechuan cuisine is the namesake peppers that make it into some of the signature dishes, and which were illegal in this country until recent years. These give Szechuan cooking some of its unique taste. Looking somewhat like a black pepercorn, when eaten, it imparts a very apparent tingling sensation on the tongue, quite unlike any other pepper. It has a unique fragrance and flavor hints of herbs like rosemary and star anise. It is mildy hot. It might be difficult to learn from the staff actually which dishes have the peppers, but a couple are the Ma Po Tofu and the Kung Pao dishes.

The lengthy menu is divided among Sichuan Snacks, cold appetizers, and the entrées under the following headers: poultry, beef and lamb, seafood, tofu, vegetable, casserole, soup, noodles, fried rice, hot pots, and the House Specials. Conveniently for those not well versed in the cuisine, the restaurant has color photos in the window and on the menu of many of the dishes. Featuring primarily the cuisine of land-locked Szechuan province, there are fewer seafood dishes than at most New Chinatown restaurants, so that means only about two dozen or so. The southeast Texas favorite, shrimp makes it into make of a good of number these, including a worthwhile Kung Pao Shrimp. Then there is Chengdu Style Catfish with Hot Sauce, yellow eel, and sea cucumber. For starters, under Sichuan Snacks, there are wontons, steamed buns and several dumpling preparations that should be readily enjoyable for most. Near the other end of the spectrum, the Diced Rabbit Meat appetizers will have far too many small pieces of bone in each small piece of meat for all of the most dedicated cold rabbit lovers. This dish is rather bland, though. Other cold appetizers, excepting the pork kidney, might have broader appeal with various preparations of chicken, beef, salted duck and the Sichuan Fried Peanuts, which are certainly a match for a cold lager beer. For that you will have to bring yourself. Sichuan Cuisine doesn't sell alcohol, but they will quickly supply an opener if needed. The hot pots are quite popular here. Featuring a large metal bowl filled with steaming broth, an array of attractively presented items are brought to the table for your cooking: rolls of slices of marbled red beef, pieces of chicken, leaves of cabbage, etc. With a helpful staff (and maybe the larger bowl), these seem less intimindating than elsewhere on Belliare Boulevard, and are a good deal for $15 per person, cheaper with more participants.

With the amazingly cheap lunch specials at Hunan Plus a couple of doors down, Sichuan Cuisine obliges with around forty choices for four bucks at lunchtime. There are several choices for the less adventurous such as Cashew Chicken, Mongolian Beef, Chicken Fried Rice and General Tso's Chicken, though done in less-assimilated and tastier fashion than is common. There are many more selections such as the Ma Po Tofu served in a wonderful oil-laden sauce studded with Szechuan peppers, Double

Cooked Pork and Beef with Chinese Pickle. Though you'll usually find some non-Chinese patrons in attendance, the staff's English is rather limited. No matter, they are usually quite friendly and try be accomodating.

Sinh Sinh $11

9788 Bellaire (between Corporate and the Beltway) 77036, (713) 541-2888
www.sinhsinh.com

Cuisine - Chinese; Vietnamese
Hours - Mon-Thu, Sun 10AM to 2AM; Fri-Sat 10AM to 3AM
Credit Cards - Amex, Diners, Discover, MC, Visa
Service - Table Service
Alcohol - Beer & Wine

Entrée Prices - Dinner - $6 to $20 ($11 average); Lunch - $5 to $6
Entrées at Dinner $12 and less - 70%

Atmosphere & Décor - Spartan
Appeal - Inexpensive Chinese barbecue and fresh Cantonese-style seafood
Menu Suggestions - BBQ Pork with Rice; Roasted Duck and Pork with Rice; Roasted Duck and BBQ Pork with Rice; Wonton Soup; Chicken Corn Soup

Sinh Sinh is a fair-sized and fairly pleasant, efficiently run restaurant just inside the Beltway that continues to draw a steady crowd of area residents and office workers during the day, and a younger crowd late at night, to enjoy satisfying and inexpensive Southeast Asian cooking. The restaurant's marquee is subtitled with "Chinese BBQ". This refers to one segment of the house specialties that help differentiate Sinh Sinh from some of the other restaurants in New Chinatown. In the back on one side is a glassed-in section where hanging from hooks are whole roasted ducks, burnished red in color and racks of pork ribs. The barbecue advertised and served at Sinh Sinh is not barbecue in the Texas sense of the word, nor is it like the "BBQ" pork that is seen at most Vietnamese restaurants. Roasting is a more accurate term for the cooking described as Chinese barbecue, and here its barbecue pork, the similar "roasted pork", pork ribs and duck. This type of food is found in several other smaller restaurants and in many of the Chinese grocery stores, usually sold as fast food. It will likely not appeal to those whose meat consumption consists mainly of white chicken breast. After roasting, the meats are chopped in a somehwat indiscriminate fashion, then served. You will need to pick among the bones and cartilage, especially with the ducks. This can be a little annoying for those not used to it, but the meats are usually quite full of flavor and well worth the effort. From the section on the menu titled "From the BBQ Pit", these Chinese barbecue dishes are only served until 4PM each day. The half-dozen choices featuring the pork and duck are an excellent value; most are around five bucks.

The rest of the main menu has become streamlined (and solely English) in recent years. Instead of the over 200 items they served in the past you'll have to find something from the only sixty or so entrées. The rest of the fare is mostly stir-fried and deep-fried and is divided among appetizers, soups, vegetables, seafood, meat and poultry, the "Favorite Corner", and set family dinners for four, six, eight and ten. The basic soups, especially the wonton and egg drop soups might be better than most places, and are a good way to start a meal. Then there are many beef, pork and chicken entrées, and some recognizable items such as Kung Pao Chicken, Moo Goo Gai Pan, Sweet and Sour Chicken, Shrimp Fried Rice, and General Tso's Chicken. Possibly more interesting entrées include Creamy Walnut Shrimp (battered and deep-fried jumbo shrimp served in a cream sauce with honey-glazed walnuts), Oyster Sizzling (battered and deep-fried oysters with scallions and ginger on a sizzling platter), Orange Flavor Ribs, Curry Beef Fillet, and Steak Tips with French Fried Rice. A big attraction for many patrons, and something not on the regular menu, is the impressive array of seafood in numerous tanks on display that are scattered about the restaurant. These might be holding tilapia, a type of sole, various types of lobsters, Dungeness crab, blue crab, shrimp, prawns, giant geoduck clams, and some strange-looking denizens of the deep.

Southwell's Hamburger Grill $8

5860 San Felipe (west of Chimney Rock) 77057, (713) 789-4972
2252 Holcombe (near Greenbriar) 77030, (713) 664-4959
9410 Gaylord (at Bunker Hill, south of I-10) 77024, (713) 464-5268

Cuisine - Hamburgers
Hours - Mon-Wed 10:30AM to 9:30PM; Thu-Fri 10:30AM to 10PM; Sat-Sun 10:30AM to 9:30PM
Credit Cards - Amex, Diners, Discover, MC, Visa
Service - Counter Service
Alcohol - Beer

Entrée Prices - $5 to $11 ($8 average)
Entrées $12 and less - 100%

Atmosphere & Décor - Spartan, but comfortable
Appeal - Nice neighborhood hamburger joints
Menu Suggestions - Chili Cheese Fries; onion rings; hamburgers

The three Southwell's locations serve the function of the nice and safe, friendly local hamburger joint, and are the best local representation of the fast-casual hamburger concept. Especially popular with teenagers and young families, the hamburgers, after all, usually make the trip worthwhile for anyone. The ingredients are fresh, and everything is cooked to order with the flat grill and the deep-fryer getting a lot of use. The main attraction, the better-than-average hamburgers are juicy and generally quite flavorful. The staff is always friendly and pretty efficient. The restaurants are each in strip centers, as are most Houston restaurants. Though the settings are somewhat spartan, the restaurants are certainly inviting and have some character. Photos of Houston from the last century adorn the walls. These make for a nice diversion while waiting for your food. Seating consists of a number of small tables and low-back booths. The hamburgers are available in enough variations to satisfy most everyone: blue cheese, Swiss cheese, Monterey Jack cheese, cheddar cheese, hickory barbecue sauce, bacon, pickled jalapeños, ham, mushrooms and Swiss cheese, grilled onions, chili and cheese, avocados, and with two patties. There are also hot sandwiches and salads. For the former there is the Onion Patty Melt, grilled cheese, grilled ham and cheese, BLT on Texas Toast, Chili Cheese Hot Dog, and several grilled chicken sandwiches, including the appropriately named Chicken Supreme (peppercorns, and another with bacon, cheese, Thousand Island dressing and lettuce and tomato). As this is primarily a hamburger grill, the salad offerings consist of only a garden salad in a couple of sizes, but there is a surprisingly tasty vegetarian burger. The sides include fries, waffle fries, onion rings and stuffed jalapeños. Though the regular and waffle fries are not that great as solo items, the chili cheese fries versions are excellent. Lots of tasty chili, shredded cheese and onions atop the fries, transform them into something great, if not exactly heart healthy. As a healthier option, the onion rings are a much better bet than the non-chili-laden fries.

Spanish Flowers $10

4701 N. Main (about a mile west of I-45 N.) 77009, (713) 869-1706
www.spanish-flowers.com

Cuisine - Tex-Mex
Hours - Open 24 Hours (closed only Tue from 10PM to Wed 10AM)
Credit Cards - Amex, Diners, Discover, MC, Visa
Service - Table Service
Alcohol - Full Bar

Entrée Prices - $6 to $18 ($10 average)
Entrées $12 and less - 80%

Atmosphere & Décor - Comfortable, often lively
Appeal - Just about always open for the Tex-Mex fix; fresh flour tortillas
Useful to Note - They are nearly always open

Menu Suggestions - Queso Flameado; Caldo de Rez (beef and vegetable soup, served with rice); Chicken Flautas; Steak Chipotle (broiled T-bone topped with chipotle pepper sauce and Monterey Jack cheese); quail

---

Contributing to the long-running popularity of Spanish Flowers (or Flower depending on the signage) is that it is nearly always open to happily help satisfy the Mexican food fix of residents of the near north neighborhood, those of the nearby Heights, or late night revelers from elsewhere in town. In fact, it is only closed on Tuesday night at 10 PM until 10AM on Wednesday morning. Some other selling points include service that is usually quite solicitous and prompt. There are also some other welcome touches: all entrées come with a pleasant, complimentary light soup (*fideo*) and a slice of fresh fruit at the end of the menu from 10AM to 10PM; freshly made and very tasty, soft flour tortillas are brought to the table just after being baked throughout the meal, if needed; and, maybe most importantly for many, breakfast is always served. If *huevos* are not the answer, something on the fairly large menu should appeal to anyone. There are the Tex-Mex and Mexican basics and more among the items served: *nachos*; fajitas; *tacos al carbon*; Mexican-style steaks; quail, grilled, fried or stuffed; enchiladas; fish tacos; other seafood dishes; chicken *mole*; salads, soups; and even beef liver, tongue and *menudo* all the time. It's certainly not the best Mexican restaurant around, not even the best in its immediate neighborhood, but it is the most easily approachable for most, and it's nearly always open.

Spanish Village $9

4720 Almeda (south of Southmore, west of Highway 288) 77004, (713) 523-2861
www.spanishvillagerestaurant.com

Cuisine - Tex-Mex
Hours - Tue-Thu 11AM to 9:30PM; Fri-Sat 11AM to 10PM
Credit Cards - Amex, Diners, Discover, MC, Visa
Service - Table Service
Alcohol - Full Bar

Entrée Prices - $6 to $14 ($9 average)
Entrées $12 and less - 90%

Atmosphere & Décor - Comfortable, lively and often loud on the weekends
Appeal - Solid Tex-Mex in a festive atmosphere; tangy and potent margaritas
Useful to Note - "No beverage served without meal."
Menu Suggestions - Southern Fried Spring Chicken; Broiled Chicken; Tacos al Carbon; Fajita Steak with ranchero sauce; Pork Carnitas (sautéed chunks of pork); Devil Shrimp; margaritas

---

Not to be confused with the similarly named and more well known Spanish Flowers, Spanish Village is on Almeda, south of downtown and close to Rice University, Hermann Park and the Medical Center and the Third Ward. Spanish Village has been serving very pleasing Tex-Mex in a festive, old-timey Tex-Mex atmosphere for many years. The only thing Spanish about the restaurant is the language in which the dishes are named, and the native tongue of most of the staff.

Be sure to comb the fairly large menu before ordering, as many enticing dishes are to be found all over. It seems to have grown organically over the years, as cheese cake is listed between the diminishing old Texas classic *chili con carne* and the Stuffed Devil Crab Dinner. There are mostly Tex-Mex standards here: nachos, *chile con queso, quesadillas,* fajitas and *tacos al carbon,* tacos, burritos, enchiladas, the Tex-Mex combination dinners, a number of different *chalupas, chiles rellenos,* and *tamales.* And, there are also some interesting additions such as a couple paella dishes, a few steaks, including a rib-eye and strip sirloin, stuffed crabs, *carne guisada* (stewed beef), *carnitas* (sautéed chunks of pork), a shrimp brochette with white cheese and jalapeños (called "Devil Shrimp" on the menu), and *ceviche.* As a very nice touch, you can always get *huevos rancheros* and *menudo.* Most everything is done quite proficiently by the kitchen. One thing that turns out very well, and is a surprise from a Mexican restaurant, is the fried chicken (Southern Fried Spring Chicken on the menu). Given the proximity of the Third Ward, maybe it's not much of a surprise. Chicken is also served in several other ways, broiled, and as a breast of chicken topped with a choice of sauces. You can also call ahead and order a roasted chicken dinner, which can be superb.

During the often busy times, Spanish Village is not a restaurant for a quiet conversation. Adding to the noise, or the intimacy, is the fact that the ceiling in the main dining room is rather low and the floors are tiled. This can be a fun and boisterous place, as the noise level helps to indicate. Also attesting to this is that the walls of the entranceway are covered with Polaroids of patrons enjoying themselves. The décor fits in well with the atmosphere and the food, and the drinks. The margaritas are quite tasty and quite potent. Unlike most other places, Spanish Village does not use a mix for its house margarita, but rather fresh lime juice. Their margarita is just the long-chilled lime juice with triple sec and a decent tequila. Though the coldness of the juice seems to be Spanish Village invention, its spirit echoes the intent of the original crafters of the margarita (in Tijuana, Ensenada, San Antonio, Los Angeles, Juarez, or wherever exactly they might have been): a tasty cocktail meant to put you into the proper mood quickly. The ones at Spanish Village certainly do that, and are very easy to drink. Maybe too easy to drink. Early in the week is for recuperation, as Spanish Village is closed on Sundays and Mondays. Though the parking lot is small, there are usually spaces available on the street close to the restaurant.

Star Pizza $8

2111 Norfolk (at S. Shepherd) 77098, (713) 523-0800
3616 Washington (just east of Heights) 77007, (713) 869-1241
www.starpizza.net

Cuisine - Pizza
Hours - Norfolk - Mon-Thu, Sun 11AM to 11PM; Fri-Sat 11AM to 12AM; Washington - Mon-Thu, Sun 11AM to 10:30PM; Fri-Sat 11AM to 11:30PM
Credit Cards - Amex, Discover, MC, Visa
Service - Table Service
Alcohol - Beer & Wine

Entrée Prices - Dinner - $6 to $11 ($8 average); Lunch Buffet - $8
Entrées at Dinner $12 and less - 100%

Atmosphere & Décor - Comfortable, and appropriate for a pizza joint
Appeal - Some of the best pizza around in funky, laid-back settings
Useful to Note - Star does a good job with the lunchtime all-you-can-eat buffet.
Menu Suggestions - Starburst Deluxe (pizza with pepperoni, Italian sausage, ground beef, mushrooms, green pepper and onions); Joe's Pizza (with spinach and garlic); Hank's Pizza (Italian sausage, mushrooms and black olives)

The laid back, yet somewhat urbane Star Pizza restaurants have long been well-liked and well-awarded destinations for some of the better pizzas in town. The key for their deserved long-standing popularity is that Star knows how to combine top-notch and generously supplied ingredients in often interesting combinations on top of a suitable and savory base. It is evident in the first bite that the dough for the pizza crusts, the starting point for any worthwhile pizza, is made daily at the restaurants. Both the regular white crust and whole-wheat crust make for a tasty platform. In addition to the pizza dough, the tomato sauce is made from scratch, in-house. From these quality building blocks, they serve both thin-crust and the Chicago-style deep dish pizzas. Both styles are worth ordering, but the Chicago-style is especially good. Star does a nice job replicating the taste, if not the exact makeup, of some of the better pizza places in Chicago. These are a little thinner than most places there, but are nonetheless about a couple of inches thick, and loaded with tomato sauce, fresh toppings on a thick crust these make for a quickly satisfying experience, as two slices of the Chicago-style pizza might be enough for one person. The half-dozen or so specialty pizzas include the popular Starburst Deluxe that is loaded with ground beef, Italian sausage, pepperoni, onions, mushrooms and green peppers, and Joe's Pizza that features sautéed fresh spinach and garlic. If one of the specialty pizzas does not excite, you can show your creativity with a laundry list of toppings: anchovies, avocado, bacon, Canadian bacon, fresh garlic, ground beef, ham, green olives, pesto, feta cheese, Italian sausage, mushrooms, black olives, pineapple, salami, sautéed spinach and garlic, meatballs, red peppers, artichoke hearts, sun-dried tomatoes, goat cheese, gorgonzola cheese, broccoli, cauliflower, green peppers, onions, roma tomatoes, alfalfa sprouts, zucchini, fresh jalapeños, marinated jalapeños, carrots, potatoes and fresh basil. Various combinations make it to the all-you-can-eat lunchtime buffet, which is surprisingly good for what it is.

In addition to the pizzas, Star also serves a number of hearty Italian-American pastas and sandwiches that might be of interest with a group. The pasta dishes include both the stuffed pastas such as lasagna and cannelloni and dried pastas that are served with a variety of toppings. With a choice of pastas among angel hair, spaghetti, fettuccine or penne, the sauces are butter, olive oil, marinara, pesto, and spicy tomato-basil. Meat and other ingredients can be added to each of these to create whatever you are in the mood. These pastas are under $10 and include garlic bread and a choice between a garden and Caesar salad. The sandwiches are available on white, wheat or French bread and include a cheese sandwich made with four cheeses, Meatball, Italian Sausage, Pizza Grinder (sausage, pepperoni, onions, green peppers, melted cheese and tomato sauce) and a vegetarian sandwich. These are all around $6 and come with either potatoes or a pasta salad. There are several beers and inexpensive wines to help wash down the food. Along with the décor, the atmosphere is very informal, as is the service. You are likely to get a waiter sporting a combination of piercings, tattoos and beads who is invariably very friendly and helpful, if possibly a little slow. The turnaround time from the kitchen can often be lengthy, but usually does not detract from the dining experience. And, the pizza is usually very satisfying, so no matter. To note, for some reason the new Washington location seems to draw screaming children with oblivious parents on Sunday evenings.

Sunrise Taquitos $5

9545 Townpark (inside the Beltway at Corporate) 77036, (713) 771-1038
6855 Highway 6 S. (at Bellaire) 77036, (281) 776-9924
3425 FM 2920 (a couple miles west of I-45 N.) Spring, 77338, (281) 528-2181

Cuisine - Mexican (taqueria)
Hours - Townpark & Highway 6 - Mon-Fri 6AM to 3PM; Sat 6AM to 2PM; Sun 7AM to 2PM; Spring - Mon-Fri 5:30Am to 8PM, Sat 7AM to 8PM; Sun 8AM to 2PM
Credit Cards - NONE
Service - Counter Service

Alcohol - NONE

Entrée Prices - $4 to $6 ($5 average)
Entrees $12 and less - 100%

Atmosphere & Décor - More than functional, and almost quaint
Appeal - Tasty, casual Mexican food for cheap
Menu Suggestions - breakfast tacos; barbacoa taco; carne guisada taco; Barbacoa Plate (with two eggs over easy with a ranchera sauce)

One surprisingly attractive location, especially given its previous setting, in a small office park not too far north of Bellaire Boulevard is near the heart of New Chinatown. Sunrise Taquitos is now an even more than ever a reliable stop for basic, casual and amazingly cheap quality Mexican food than it has been in the past. Opened early in the morning through the early afternoon, Sunrise Taquitos specializes in the hearty and quick breakfasts and lunch items, mostly tacos. The menu is limited, but there will be plenty from which to choose. Takeout is popular during the morning hours. But, the comfortable interior encourages dine-in, too, a far cry from their previous location a mile or so away. There are a couple of probably even more approachable locations, one further west in Alief, and another in Spring, which is opened until 8PM during the week and Saturday.

There are about two dozen choices of tacos from which to choose, about two-thirds are geared more toward the breakfast time. Taquitos (small tacos) are in the name for a reason, even if their tacos are generally good-sized. The homemade flour tortillas provide a very good starting point for all of the tacos. These tortillas are not only fresh, but noticeably fluffy, more so than at any other *taqueria* that comes to mind. An added benefit is that the tacos are cheap; none are priced over $2, and average about a buck-and-a-half. It's tough to go wrong with any of the tacos, from the less-greasy-than-usual *huevos y chorizo*, to the *huevos a la mexicana*, bacon and egg, potato and egg, beans & cheese, *migas*, *al pastor*, and *picadillo* (ground beef with potatoes). The *barbacoa* is very good. Nearly black in color, it is stringy and slightly dry, but the fat and gristle are neatly trimmed away. It is quite flavorful by itself, and does not need the house tomatillo-based salsa, which is quite tasty, by the way. The Mexican-style beef stew, the *carne guisada*, which is served with a brown gravy, also features quality meat, and is very savory and enjoyable. In addition to the tacos, there are several breakfast plates, including ones with *machacado* (dried beef) and *barbacoa*, *migas*, with eggs in different guises that are served with refried beans, fried potatoes and tortillas. There are also about ten lunch plates such as crispy corn tacos, nachos with grilled chicken or fajitas, burritos, taco salad, *carne guisada*, *tostadas* and fajitas. But, you will have to wait for the weekends for their *menudo*.

Sylvia's Enchilada Kitchen $10

12637 Westheimer (just west of Dairy Ashford) 77077, (281) 679-8300
www.sylviasenchiladakitchen.com

Cuisine - Tex-Mex
Hours - Mon-Thu 11Am to 9PM; Fri 11AM to 10PM; Sat 8AM to 10PM; Sun 8AM to 3PM
Credit Cards - Amex, MC, Visa
Service - Table Service
Alcohol - Full Bar

Entrée Prices - Dinner - $8 to $12 ($10 avg.); Lunch - $6 to $8; Breakfast - $5 to $8
Entrées at Dinner $12 and less - 100%

Atmosphere & Décor - Comfortable
Appeal - Very well prepared Tex-Mex in far west Houston
Useful to Note - They have regular cooking classes, if you really like the food.
Menu Suggestions - McAllen Enchilada (chicken enchiladas topped with chili gravy); Mexico City Enchiladas (enchiladas verdes filled with chicken); Donna Enchiladas (ground beef enchiladas topped with chili gravy); San Miguel Enchiladas (enchiladas suizas filled with chicken)

Since it has moved to larger and nicer digs several years ago, Sylvia's Enchilada Kitchen has continued to serve better-than-usual Tex-Mex in a very friendly and family-friendly atmosphere. Service remains prompt and solicitous, and the setting is nice in a bustling suburban sense. The ingredients, preparation, and presentation are all better than most Tex-Mex restaurants. You'll first notice it with the flavorful, warm, tomato-based, cilantro-spiked salsa that comes with the thin, crisp chips. It deservedly remains a popular stop for Tex-Mex on the western stretches of Westheimer. The menu, which has grown as the restaurant has, sticks to most of the local Tex-Mex favorites, and it successfully provides what most people here deem as comfort food. There is a limited choice of starters and soups with all of the expected local favorites, but also including daily *menudo*. The entrées are meat and cheese-centric and divided among enchiladas, twenty or so Tex-Mex combination plates, a few fajita-type dishes with either beef or chicken, *quesadillas*, *chalupas* and a half-dozen specialties such as *chile rellenos*, *flautas* and *carne guisada*. From what you should be able to guess, the specialty is enchiladas, and they do the expected local versions of the enchilada quite well. There are almost twenty enchilada plates that are classed as "Tex-Mex Style", "New Tex-Mex", and "Mexican" that are named after towns in Texas or regions and cities in Mexico (for the "Mexican Style" enchiladas, of course). All of these are really all pretty much made in the same style, and just differ with the fillings and toppings. Some of the highlights are the McAllen, which is a basic chicken enchilada plate topped with Sylvia's Signature Chile Gravy, the similar Donna, but filled with ground beef, Crystal City, an especially good spinach-filled enchiladas topped with a slightly sweet tomatillo-based salsa, and the San Miguel, *enchiladas Suizas.* It's really tough to go wrong with any of the enchiladas here. Nicely, each of the enchilada plates is available with a choice of either two or three enchiladas. Though portions are generous at Sylvia's, bigger appetites will need to opt for three enchiladas.

Taco Milagro $8

2555 Kirby (at Westheimer) 77019, (713) 522-1999
7877 Willowchase (north of FM 1960, east of Highway 249) 77070, (281) 664-7070
19325 I-45 S. (east of freeway, at W. Bary Area Boulevardl) 77598, (281) 954-3070
1701 Lake Robbins (east of Six Pines) The Woodlands, 77380, (281) 602-7070
www.taco-milagro.com

Cuisine - Mexican
Hours - Mon-Tue, Sun 11AM to 10PM; Wed 11AM to 11PM; Thu 11AM to 1AM; Fri-Sat 11AM to 12PM
Credit Cards - Amex, Diners, Discover, MC, Visa
Service - Counter Service
Alcohol - Full Bar (over 50 tequilas)

Entrée Prices - $6 to $13 ($8 average)
Entrées $12 and less - 90%

Atmosphere & Décor - Very nice, if casual
Appeal - Interesting, fast-casual Mexican; bustling singles scene (or vice versa)
Useful to Note - Nice days, Thur-Sat, it's a bar first at the Kirby location.
Menu Suggestions - Pork Barbacoa Enchiladas in a mole sauce; Pork Barbacoa Plate (pork roasted in banana leaves with a mole sauce); Grilled Shrimp Plate (with poblanos, bacon and Chihuahua cheese); Spinach & Cheese Enchiladas; Traditional Tortilla Soup; Tacos with Grilled Shrimp and Bacon

Opened since 1998, and long more popular as a place to socialize, the food at the original Westheimer and Kirby location seems to have rebounded to its former quality. Taco Milagro is from the restaurant group of Robert Del Grande, the executive chef and proprietor of Café Annie. As with their first counter-service concept, Café Express, Taco Milagro is very well run and provides very fresh, interesting and flavorful food for adults in a nicely informal atmosphere. This place appeals to both the hard-core lovers of Mexican food, and, more so, singles needing a venue while ingesting some calories. This is a very capable place to get a quick meal, either to eat there or to take home. For those on the run, not incidentally, the packaging of the takeout orders is some of the best around.

The fare is better described as Mexican rather than Tex-Mex. The menu is well chosen, the presentation is much better than most area Mexican restaurants, and, more importantly, the ingredients are always very fresh. This is evidenced in part by the fact that the tamales are handmade at the restaurant daily. Sirloin steak is used in the beef dishes. The *aguas frescas* are made each day with freshly squeezed fruit juices. Typically, eight fresh salsas are provided at the salsa bar. These are made throughout the day. And, no processed cheese graces any item. Care is taken to use traditional Mexican ingredients such as *Chihuahua* and *cotija* cheeses, pumpkin seeds, and *crema fresca* in many dishes, including Tex-Mex ones. The dishes are familiar, but coming from the owners of Café Annie, the food is a bit more refined than typically priced Mexican dishes elsewhere. As with Robert Del Grande's missive on the menu to "approach [Mexican food] with the utmost dedication and respect", the selection of tequilas is excellent, especially for such an inexpensive restaurant. There is also a fairly long list of tangy tequila-based drinks including the unfairly locally neglected Paloma, truly a refreshing Mexican classic with good tequila, fresh lime juice and the grapefruit soda. The basic Milagro Margarita, served on the rocks, is very satisfying. For those not interested in alcohol, there are a couple of house-made fresh fruit drinks, *aguas frescas*, and mango-flavored iced tea.

There are popular appetizers such as *chile con queso*, made more interesting with smoky chile peppers, nachos, Tex-Mex *quesadillas* and Shrimp Campeche, a shrimp cocktail with avocado and a tomato-based cocktail sauce. The soups are meals by themselves. The tortilla soup, made with grilled chicken, tortilla strips, guacamole and *pico de gallo*, is very good. There are a handful of salads including a Caesar salad with tortilla strips, *cotija* cheese and a spicy *chipotle*-based dressing. There are also tamales and several enchiladas. With the exception of the one with sweet potato and Swiss chard, each of the enchilada dishes is well worth ordering. The pork *barbacoa* enchilada is covered in a flavorful, slightly sweet *mole* sauce with sesame seeds. The *mole* sauce is slightly thin and sweet, but with a nice taste. The other *mole* dish, the Pork *Barbacoa*, does not work as well since the pork steak does not retain enough of its moistness after cooking. This Pork *Barbacoa* is among several of the more elaborate dishes under the heading of "*Platitos Festivos*". The other ones include a grilled chicken breast with poblano peppers and onion strips, grilled beef fajitas also with poblano peppers and onion strips, and lastly, grilled shrimp with poblano peppers, bacon and the meltable *Chihuahua* cheese, the most expensive dish offered just $13. The stated house specialty is the *chile relleno* dish. It consists of two grilled (not fried, as is most common) poblano peppers filled with *Chihuahua* cheese, pecans, dried fruit and topped with their spicy *guajillo* chile salsa and another white cheese and fresh Mexican-style cream (*crema fresca*). There are also several burritos and tacos on the menu. The tacos are encased in two soft corn tortillas and filled with a spicy cabbage slaw. The best of the tacos is the grilled shrimp and bacon tacos; the shrimp and crispy bacon complement each other very well. The fish tacos are decent and pleasant. Because tilapia is used, these tacos often taste just a little bland.

The Kirby location is surrounded by the smart two-story shopping center, the River Oaks Garden Center across the street on the south, and another nice shopping center across the street to the west, there is a sprawling patio, or plaza, where, when the weather is nice, you can eat outside (or more likely, drink outside). Though the setting is similar, it's far removed from a sparse De Chirico piazza, as it's usually packed with a lively group of diners and drinkers. The other suburban addresses are more standard in appearance; pleasant and functional, if lacking the buzz of the original.

Tacos del Julio $6

8141 Long Point (between Wirt and Bingle) 77055, (832) 358-1500
6701 Spencer Highway (between 8 and Red Bluff) Pasadena, 77505, (281) 487-1114
10719 Airline (south of W Road, east of I-45 N.) 77037, (281) 260-0660

Cuisine - Mexican (taqueria)
Hours - Mon-Thu, Sun 9AM to 11PM; Fri-Sat 9AM to 12AM
Credit Cards - MC, Visa
Service - Table Service
Alcohol - Beer

Entrée Prices - $4 to $7 ($6 average)
Entrées $12 and less - 100%

Atmosphere & Décor - Functional
Appeal - Excellent, casual northern Mexican food
Useful to Note - Some Spanish is very helpful here.
Menu Suggestions - Tacos Tlaquepaque (small corn tortilla tacos filled with shredded beef and served with a spicy, savory salsa); Enchiladas Rojas (topped with a light tomato sauce and Chihuahua cheese); Monterrey 400 (platter of beef fajita, seasoned beef, avocoados)

"*No coma ansias coma tacos*" is their motto. This is a play on words that roughly translates to, "don't worry, eat tacos". And, tacos are what the aptly named Tacos del Julio specializes in. Actually, it's *taquitos,* the small corn tortilla tacos that are more popular in Mexico than the plus-sized versions that are more commonly served on this side of the border. The menu might be the smallest and most unique of any local *taqueria,* or any Mexican or Tex-Mex restaurant, for that matter. But, nearly everything is appealing, or interesting, and mostly unique for the Houston area. The dishes are seemingly all inspired by street fare from northern Mexico. Many are small tacos, dishes that resemble *chalupa* or maybe just a flat, overstuffed taco, an excellent enchilada dish, *flautas,* and a bounteous mixed platter, burritos and a *tortas.* As with the fare, the décor is a little different, too; nicer than a typical *taqueria,* if not exactly a grand restaurant.

The meat served here is limited to just shredded, moist beef (*carne deshebrada*), slowly roasted, seasoned beef (called *carne de trompo* here, and can be a bit tough), grilled steak, and shredded chicken (*pollo deshebrada*), but, no goat (*cabrito* or *birria*), though. The offerings are a little different, and sport some unusual names such as tacos and *tostadas* in *estilio Siberia. ¿Que?* Both of which feature large fried corn tortillas and sour cream. One of the specialties is a dish consisting of a flour tortilla topped with grilled beef, seasoned and shredded beef, mild *Chihuahua* cheese and avocado. This is also available without one or the other of the toppings. Big appetites might consider the Monterrey 400, which is a bounteous plate of the *carne de trompo,* grilled steak and several slices of avocado. Tortillas need to be ordered separately for this, though. Salsas are served in red and yellow plastic squeeze bottles (that were certainly marked as "ketchup" and "mustard" in the restaurant supply store). The slightly smoky red salsa is in the red bottle, the excellent, viscous and fiery green salsa is in the yellow bottle. One *molcajete* (a small bowl) brought to the table contains chopped cilantro and chopped raw onions, and another contains lime quarters, both to complement the tacos. These are for the soup and the dishes that you've ordered, as there are no chips, but you do get a complimentary and flavorful soup of *charro* beans. For breakfast, they do a fine job with the familiar breakfast tacos with either flour or corn tortillas, and plates including *machacado con huevo* (dried beef with scrambled eggs), create-it-yourself omelets, the American breakfast with pancakes, eggs and bacon and the unusual *tacos al vapor.* These are small tacos with corn tortillas and filled with a choice of beef, beans or potatoes and steamed. The preparation might be unique, but the result is rather bland. On the weekends, they serve *menudo, caldo tlalpeño* (a hearty soup with chicken, avocados and *chipotles*) and "*exquisita barbacoa*". At any time, there are a half-dozen beers from which to choose, which are a better bet than the machine-made *aguas frescas.*

Tampico $11

2115 Airline (between Cavalcade and Loop 610 N.) 77009, (713) 862-8425
www.tampicoseafood.com

Cuisine - Mexican; Seafood
Hours - Mon-Thu, Sun 10:30AM to 10PM; Fri 10:30AM to 12PM; Sat 11AM to 12AM
Credit Cards - Amex, Discover, MC, Visa
Service - Table Service
Alcohol - Full Bar

Entrée Prices - $5 to $17 ($11 average)
Entrées $12 and less - 80%

Atmosphere & Décor - Spartan
Appeal - Fresh Mexican seafood near the Farmers Market
Useful to Note - They are especially popular on Fridays during Lent.
Menu Suggestions - Queso Flameado with Shrimp; Red Snapper a la Plancha (grilled red snapper); Snapper a la Diabla (red snapper in a hot sauce)

Tampico is an unpretentious Mexican seafood restaurant and market on Airline near the large commercial farmers market. Located in a two-story building, the brightly lit, well-run restaurant is often crowded with patrons seven days a week enjoying Gulf seafood and other popular regional items. The phrase painted on the front of it is, "you buy, we fry". Fortunately, it's not terribly accurate as the kitchen shines beyond the fryer.

The quality and the freshness of its fish and seafood is the big attraction at Tampico. This is evident in a variety of preparations: cured, in soups, appetizers, and filleted and grilled, fried, etc. To begin the meal they offer the locally popular seafood cocktails: *ceviche,* oysters, octopus, shrimp, combination, and *vuelve a la vida.* There are also a number of appetizers such as nachos, nachos with shrimp, *queso flameado,* the melted cheese, with shrimp or *chorizo,* and stuffed jalapeños. There are soups: a seafood soup; a shrimp soup; and gumbo. The Fish Platters offer a half-dozen different preparations of fish fillets. The standard fish is a farm-raised catfish, but for just a buck-and-a-half more, the much tastier Gulf red snapper is also available. The cooking methods include deep frying, of course, but there are many more interesting preparations for the fish. These include steamed with butter, garlic and green onions; *Al Mojo,* a buttery garlic sauce with mushrooms, bell peppers, and onions; *A La Plancha,* grilled with onions and butter; *Ranchero,* a hot sauce with peppers, onion and tomato, and *A La Diabla,* a spicy sauce of *chipotle* peppers, tomatoes and onions. The restaurant's pride is the Red Snapper *a la Plancha* that is cooked with butter on a flat grill then topped with onions and bell peppers. These platters are served in a choice of three or a substantial four pieces. Appetizers are usually warranted with this dish, as it can take nearly thirty minutes to prepare. There are Shrimp Platters that are served with similar preparations as the fish. These platters are accompanied with a choice of fries or shrimp fried rice. There are fried platters and combination dishes featuring fried oysters, shrimp, catfish and tilapia. Among these are the Fried Family Platter with a pound of large shrimp, a pound of medium-sized shrimp and a half-dozen pieces of catfish, a value for the larger than average family at less than fifty dollars, and the Fried Shrimp Special featuring thirty medium-sized shrimp for less than fifty cents a shrimp. A grilled item of note is the *Brochettas*, a half-dozen jumbo shrimp that are stuffed with *Chihuahua* cheese and a jalapeño slice then wrapped in bacon and grilled. To complement your meal, Tampico offers several fried seafood items on the side: scallops, oysters, shrimp, catfish, red snapper, and stuffed crab. If one of the numerous menu items does not quite strike your fancy, Tampico sells different specialties by the pound at their market price and will cook them to your whim. These include red snapper, shrimp, squid, flounder, scallops, King Crab legs, frog legs, baby octopus and lobster tails.

Tampico is eager to satisfy everyone. For those not interested in seafood, they serve more than enough items to keep those customers satiated: fajitas, steaks, *tortas*, enchiladas, *quesadillas*, tacos, and *tostadas*. For drinks they offer a couple different *aguas frescas*, most of the popular Mexican beers including a *michelada* (here made with lime juice, hot sauce and salt added to the beer), frozen margaritas (regular, strawberry and the unique tamarind), daiquiris, sangria and a piña colada. With the exception of the case displaying the fresh seafood that provides an interesting quick diversion, the restaurant's décor is just functional, as Formica abounds. The atmosphere is often fairly lively. Since the restaurant usually has a good crowd, there will be a decent amount of background noise. If not crowded, that noise will come from one of the often blaring televisions. The service is notably attentive, especially for a fairly low-key restaurant. Tampico is almost always a smart stop for high quality local seafood prepared in the Mexican fashion.

Tan Tan $10

6816 Ranchester (at Bellaire) 77036, (713) 771-1268
www.tantanrestaurant.com

Cuisine - Vietnamese; Chinese
Hours - Mon-Thu 10AM to 2AM; Fri-Sat 10AM to 3AM
Credit Cards - NONE
Service - Table Service
Alcohol - Beer

Entrée Prices - $5 to $20 ($10 average)
Entrées $12 and less - 80%

Atmosphere & Décor - Spartan
Appeal - Good and cheap Vietnamese food late in the night in New Chinatown

Menu Suggestions - hot pots; rice cake; Shrimp Wonton with Egg Noodle Soup; BBQ Pork & Chinese Sausage Fried Rice; French Style Beef Fried Rice; French Style Diced Beef with Macaroni; BBQ Pork Lo Mein; Lemon Chicken; Garlic Spicy Chicken; Saté Beef

---

Tan Tan is a long popular restaurant serving Vietnamese and similar Chinese fare prepared quickly and very proficiently and served efficiently to hungry throngs at most hours during the day. Tan Tan has grown in size over the years, and beyond its former, odd "Fast Food" designation, but it remains as good as ever. Tan Tan is one of a number of value-oriented places in New Chinatown that serve a great many unassimilated dishes expertly cooked with fresh ingredients. Tan Tan just serves more of them. Many more, as the menu is huge. Really huge. It's almost overwhelming with over 350 different items. Among those are a number of dishes around eight bucks, and the portions are good-sized, so it is easy to get a flavorful, freshly cooked, and filling meal for very fair price.

The extensive menu printed in Chinese, Vietnamese and English has descriptively named sections such as: Appetizers, Vietnamese Dishes; Soup (*Canh*), Noodle Soup (*Mi*), Rice Soup (*Congee*), Fried Rice, Steamed Rice Platter, Tofu & Vegetables, Beef, Pork, Poultry, Pan Fried Noodles, Stir Fried Flat Rice Noodles, Stir Fried Macaroni & Vermicelli, Seafood, Sizzling Plates. There is nearly everything but *pho*, at least in name. The forty noodle soup dishes are each available with a choice among egg noodles (*mi*), wide egg noodles, flat rice noodles, thin rice noodles and vermicelli. Each of these sections typically lists fifteen or more dishes. With such a large menu you can play it safe with something fairly familiar, or you can be adventurous. There is a lot from which to choose. For the unadventurous, it's tough to go wrong with one of the fried rice dishes. The French Style Beef Fried Rice with pieces of moist beef and the barbecued Pork and Chinese Sausage Fried Rice are two reliable choices. Listed in the Beef, Pork, Chicken and Seafood sections are several familiar Americanized dishes. For example, there are Mongolian Beef, Sweet and Sour Pork, Szechuan Chicken, Sesame Chicken, General Tso's Chicken and Kung Pao Shrimp. The Lemon Chicken and Garlic Spicy Chicken are quite good. The hot pots with the table-top cookers require at least two people to order, and these are popular here. To be noted, these can be a lot of work for first-timers. Service can be somewhat chaotic, but dishes are typically served soon after they are ordered. It is easy to get in and out of the restaurant quickly during the lunchtime, even though the restaurant is usually fairly crowded. With its late hours, Tan Tan is very popular on weekend nights with young club-goers who pack the nearby clubs. Late at night on the weekends, it can be tough even to find a seat in this large restaurant, a testament to its quality and value.

Taqueria Arandas $7

4609 Irvington (north of Patton) 77009, (713) 699-2415
5826 Airline (between Tidwell and E. Little York) 77076, (713) 691-5364
920 N. Shepherd (just north of I-10) 77008, (713) 426-0804
1840 Wirt (south of Long Point) 77055, (713) 681-1019
2701 Mangum (south of 34th) 77092, (713) 688-3104
1826 Gessner (between Long Point and Hammerly) 77080, (713) 827-1565
1629 South Richey (south of W. Southmore) Pasadena, 77502, (713) 473-2808
8767 S. Gessner (south of Southwest Freeway) 77074, (713) 272-8236
10333 I-10 E. (east of Loop 610, near Mercury Drive) 77023, (713) 674-0855
190 I-45 S. (near FM 518) 77573, (281) 338-9764
10905 I-45 N. (between West and Aldine-Bender) 77037, (281) 591-1999
10403 I-45 S. (between College and Edgebrook) 77034, (713) 910-2905
6803 Highway 6 S. (near Alief-Clodine) 77083, (281) 495-8356
5931 I-45 S. (south of S. Wayside) 77023, (713) 923-1433
364 Uvalde (north of Woodforest) 77015, (713) 455-4774
2307 Garth (south of 146) Baytown, 77520, (281) 837-9300
4228 Highway 6 N. (south of Clay) 77084, (281) 463-0099
16822 Highway 290 (inside the Beltway) 77040, (832) 243-0873
22453 I-10 W. (between Mason and Grand Parkway) Katy, 77450, (281) 395-2755
335 FM 1960 W. (west of I-45 N.) 77090, (281) 440-3377
11929 Eastex Freeway (between Mt. Houston & Aldine Mail) 77037, (281) 442-9700
1837 North Main (north of FM 518) Pearland, 77581, (281) 412-4165
13703 Highway 249 (at N. Houston-Rosslyn) 77086, (281) 405-0544
19740 Highway 59 N. (just north of FM 1960) Humble, 77338, (281) 446-2500
9401 S. Main (between Fondren and 8) 77025, (713) 432-0212
25598 I-45 N. (north of Rayford / Sawdust) The Woodlands, 77386, (281) 419-3582
5560 Gulfton (just west of Chimney Rock) 77081, (713) 839-0090
www.taqueriasarandas.com

Cuisine - Mexican (taqueria)
Hours - Most are open at least from 7AM to 1AM daily, some at 6AM, and until 3AM and later on the weekends; the 190 and 5931 I-45 S., Baytown, Katy and Astrodome locations close earlier.
Credit Cards - Amex, Discover, MC, Visa
Service - Table Service
Alcohol - Beer

Entrée Prices - Dinner & Lunch - $3 to $13 ($7 average); Breakfast - $2 to $6
Entrées at Dinner $12 and less - 90%

Atmosphere & Décor - Spartan, but getting nicer
Appeal - Consistently very tasty and fresh Mexican food for very cheap
Useful to Note - Breakfasts are an especially good value here.
Menu Suggestions - Sinchronizada (a tortilla sandwich of cheese, ham and refried beans); Super Burrito California (a giant burrito); tacos; quesadillas; Quesadilla Grande (pastor is the best filling); Torta al Pastor (sandwich filled with pork from the spinner); Fajita Ranchera (grilled chopped beef skirt steak covered with a spicy tomato salsa and sautéed onions); Arandas Specials (choice of grilled beef skirt steak, chicken or pork); Entomatadas (enchiladas with chicken in a tomato sauce)

Now with over twenty locations in the Houston area, some fairly nice, newly constructed stand-alone structures, Taqueria Arandas is the largest local chain of *taquerias,* informal Mexican restaurants. It is easy to believe that the popularity resulting in the expansion is due to the fact that they offer some of the best food among the *taquerias*. Though some locations are nicer than others, and some kitchens are more consistent than others, these are each usually quite reliable places to have very good Mexican food for a low price. Fresh chips, fresh tortillas and breads, tender and flavorful meats, top-notch salsas coupled with efficient kitchens, prompt service and great values have long been key parts of the attraction. The cuisine is generally that of the namesake central Mexican town of Arandas, in the state of Jalisco. A photo of the town's attractive cathedral adorns the menu cover.

The dishes are the generally casual Mexican food common at local *taquerias*: tacos; *quesadillas*; *tortas* (sandwiches on a soft Mexican *bolillo* bun); burritos; enchiladas, and the like. There are a few meat-heavy combination platters that can be especially nice values. These are not the Tex-Mex combination dinners, but rather about a dozen of the somewhat more elaborate meat-based dishes that are served with rice and beans. The first one listed, the Arandas Special, can be very good. It consists of a choice or mixture of grilled meats, beef skirt steak, chicken or pork, served with lettuce, tomato, cactus strips, avocado and pinto beans that are topped with *Chihuahua* cheese then served with tortillas. This is a fair amount of flavorful food for seven dollars or so. The similar, *Fajita Ranchera* is also tasty; grilled, chopped beef skirt steak covered with a spicy tomato salsa and sautéed onions. Among the other house specials is a fajita plate, a *tampiqueña* (the outer cut of the skirt steak), an eight-ounce T-bone steak, *flautas*, enchiladas with a choice of fillings, a marinated chicken breast and the Super Burrito California. The Spanish language description of the Super Burrito California used to contain the phrase *GIGANTE* (gigantic) in bold letters. No more accurate statement has ever been made on a menu. This burrito is enormous. Even those with huge appetites will have trouble finishing it. Surprisingly, as large as it is, it is excellent. It features a very large, fresh flour tortilla filled with the aforementioned choice of meats and other things, such as rice, refried beans, avocado, sour cream, lettuce, tomato, and cheese. It is then briefly baked, unlike many other burritos that are just different ingredients wrapped in a large tortilla. One can understand how a burrito like this could inspire the wraps craze in recent years. There is also a version with shrimp.

The array of "meat choices", their term, available for stuffing tacos, *quesadillas*, burritos and *tortas* is more wide-ranging than about any other of the Mexican restaurants around, and should satisfy lovers of nearly all parts of the cow and a couple of the cows' farmhouse mates. The list goes: *pollo* (chicken); *pastor* (pork from the spinner); *lengua* (beef tongue); *cabeza* (the barbecued head of a cow that can be a bit greasy); *pierna* (pork leg); *sesos* (brains); *nopales* (cactus); *chorizo con huevo* (Mexican sausage and eggs); *jamon* (ham); fajitas; *milanesa* (breaded ground steak); and *birria* (steamed baby goat). These tacos and *quesadillas* made from this array of fillings and a choice of tortillas are consistently excellent, though some might be more appealing than others. Anything with the *pastor* is superb. The fresh flour tortillas made in the restaurants provide a flavorful shell for the tacos and *quesadillas*. The basic *quesadilla* here is the traditional Mexican version, which is essentially a warmed taco with melted *Chihuahua* cheese. The chicken and *pastor* versions are especially delicious. The *Quesadilla* Grande is one of the most flavorful values. It's done in the Tex-Mex fashion with two large flour tortillas sandwiching a choice of meats and served hot with melted cheese. As with all of the other *taquerias*, the *tortas* are an excellent deal at three bucks; a large sandwich with the choice of "meats" with avocado, lettuce, tomato and sour cream that is a meal in itself. Taqueria Arandas also sells *tostadas*, the crispy corn tortilla covered with refried beans and a choice of toppings with lettuce, tomato, cheese and sour cream, and *sincronizadas*. The *sincronizadas* here are two soft flour tortillas filled with refried beans, a slice of ham and melted cheese. These can be messy, but are quite satisfying. The seafood dishes can be more variable in quality than the meat-based ones. For example, the shrimp that are used for tacos, *quesadillas*, burritos, *tortas* and *chalupas* can often be small and tasteless.

Breakfasts are popular at Taqueria Arandas. These are well prepared and incredibly cheap. Most are less three bucks from 7AM to 11AM, and just four afterwards. These are the popular *Huevos Rancheros*, and several combinations of scrambled eggs and fillings such as *chorizo*, potato and ham. Each is served with sliced ham or bacon and refried beans and tortillas. For a dollar or two more you can get *Machacado con Huevo* (eggs scrambled with salty, dried beef) or *Chilaquiles* (fried tortilla strips with tomato salsa and white cheese; here, without eggs). And, here you won't be conspicuous if you are drinking brew with breakfast. Not insignificantly, the green salsa, offered complimentary with chips and now at apparently every Arandas location, is one of the best salsas in town. A purée with chiles of a thick consistency, it is both very spicy while remaining very tangy and savory. It seems to complement every dish offered, at least when used in moderation. Another nice thing with these restaurants is that the flour tortillas are made fresh at each location. These are consistently fresh and very tasty, and an integral part of many of the most enjoyable dishes; one of the many reasons why Taqueria Arandas is one of the best *taqueria* chains, and a solid bet for very good Mexican food.

Taqueria Cancun $7

8111 S. Gessner (between Beechnut and Southwest Freeway) 77036, (713) 773-1777
9957 Long Point (at Witte) 77055, (713) 932-6533
1725 Wirt (south of Long Point) 77055, (713) 932-8800
2227 Gessner (north of Hammerly) 77080, (713) 932-9566
1630 Gessner (between Long Point and Hammerly) 77080, (713) 932-1815

Cuisine - Mexican (taqueria)
Hours - Long Point - Open 24 hours; Other Locations - Mon-Thu 8AM to 2AM; Fri 8AM to 12AM; all weekend
Credit Cards - MC, Visa
Service - Table Service
Alcohol - Beer

Entrée Prices - Dinner - $4 to $12 ($7 average); Lunch - $6; Breakfast -$3
Entrées at Dinner $12 and less - 100%

Atmosphere & Décor - Spartan
Appeal - Very well prepared and inexpensive Mexican food; good seafood
Useful to Note - Just remember you're here for the food, not the décor.
Menu Suggestions - Beef Enchiladas; Chicken Enchiladas; Quesadillas al Pastor (flour tortillas filled with pork); Caldo de Camarones (shrimp soup); Taco al Pastor (seasoned pork and pineapple)

The location on Gessner near Hammerly, and the original Long Point locations of Taqueria Cancun are usually always crowded during the extended hours for lunch and dinner. The popularity stems from providing often excellent food at bargain basement prices (if not the bargain basement-like settings). Befitting the numerous brightly colored paintings and drawings of edible sea denisons including the mascot, a surprisingly happy shrimp festooned in a sombrero holding a beer and what looks like a shrimp taco, there is an emphasis on seafood (especially shrimp) at Taqueria Cancun. This emphasis is a difference between Taqueria Cancun and the other local *taqueria* chains. That, and the founder is a tall gentleman originally from Hong Kong, a Señor Wong.

Lunch is a good bargain at Taqueria Cancun, and about six bucks will get you a plentiful, usually hearty entrée from a nice range of choices served with rice and refried beans prefaced by soup. On top of that, sodas and ice tea are also included in the price. Lunch specials include entrées featuring the *Cancun Platillos* with a choice of grilled beef fajitas, chicken or shrimp or roasted pork (*al pastor*), enchilada plates with two large enchiladas, Tex-Mex-style *Quesadilla* and Nachos Plates, grilled beef short ribs, the Cancun

Bowl Salad that's topped with beef fajitas, chicken or shrimp, and a plate of three fairly large tacos with beef fajitas, chicken or shrimp. The soup that comes with the lunch special is a choice of either a chicken soup and the better bean soup. It's essentially their take on the locally familiar charro beans. Unless you don't mind a skin-on portion of a mostly identifiable and varying chicken part served along with quite large chunks of vegetables in your soup, choose the chicken, which does have a flavorful broth. The best of the lunch specials are the enchiladas and *quesadillas*. If the waitress thinks to ask, the enchiladas come with a choice of corn or flour tortillas. Choose the corn. Though the enchiladas made with the flour tortillas are still decent, these will become gummy with all of the cheese. And, there is a lot of cheese on the enchiladas, which is not necessarily a bad thing. These are heavy, though very satisfying dishes. Both the beef and chicken versions are usually quite good. The beef, made with marinated and grilled fajita meat is very moist and flavorful, especially for such a reasonable price. Though reliable in the soups, cocktails, and plates, the shrimp in the enchiladas and *torta*s is of variable quality. The *quesadillas* are served in the Mexican fashion, as warmed tacos. A plate comes with the Tex-Mex accompaniments of guacamole, sour cream and lettuce and tomatoes. The pork and beef *quesadillas* are especially worth ordering. The full menu contains some additional seafood specialties. Though shrimp is the most prominent seafood served at Taqueria Cancun and the only seafood served at lunch, in the evening there is also *mojarra* (tilapia) along with a greater selection of shrimp preparations. Listed under "*Cancun Especialidades*" are: Grilled Shrimp with Chile Ancho Sauce, grilled shrimp in a garlic sauce (*al mojo de ajo*), Lightly Battered Fried Shrimp, fried tilapia fish, either a fillet or the entire fish; a marinated shrimp cocktail with avocado and *pico de gallo*, and a large shrimp soup made with potatoes and carrots. For a dollar more you can get a combination order with shrimp and fish. Also for dinner, there is an expanded selection of the *Cancun Platillos*. In addition to the beef, chicken and pork, you can also get *barbacoa* (beef cheek here, the real thing), *milanesa* (breaded and flattened skirt steak) and beef ribs. With rice, a choice between charro and refried beans, lettuce, tomato and tortillas, it is a bargain for around seven bucks. Combination specials featuring several types of meats are also available. Served at all times, Taqueria Cancun does brisk business with its soups, the brothy *caldos*, soups made with beef, chicken or shrimp, and an acclaimed version of *menudo*, the hominy and beef tripe soup. Along with soft drinks and ice tea, beer, Mexican sodas and a small number of machine-made *aguas frescas* and *licuados* (fruit shakes) are offered.

Necessary of a *taqueria*, Taqueria Cancun serves the familiar Mexican food standards with a variety of toppings and fillings, such as tacos, *quesadillas*, *tortas*, *tostadas* and burritos that can be ordered individually. The meat choices for these are: beef fajitas, chicken, pork (*al pastor*), *lengua* (beef tongue), *barbacoa*, ham, *milanesa*, and *carnitas* (sautéed pork). The *tortas* are well crafted, and one of the best values for the cost-conscious. During the morning Taqueria Cancun serves most of the straightforward Mexican egg-based breakfasts and breakfast taco combinations such as *Huevos con Papas* (potatoes), *Huevos con Tocino* (bacon), etc. These are dirt cheap. The scrambled eggs can be on the dry side, but are still tasty. During the morning, the plates, served with rice, refried beans, potatoes and tortillas, are still less than three dollars. The breakfast tacos are just over a buck. The unique (though not for Cantonese cooking) egg and shrimp combinations are an additional quarter or so, though.

Taqueria Del Sol $5

8114 Park Place (at I-45 S., east side of the freeway) 77017, (713) 644-0535

Cuisine - Mexican (taqueria)
Hours - Mon-Thu, Sun 7AM to 12AM; Fr. - Sat 7AM to 3:30AM
Credit Cards - Amex, Diners, Discover, MC, Visa
Service - Table Service
Alcohol - NONE

Entrée Prices - Dinner & Lunch - $3 to $9 ($5 average); Breakfast - $4 to $5
Entrees at Dinner $12 and less - 100%

Atmosphere & Décor - Functional
Appeal - Popular family-oriented neighborhood taquerias
Useful to Note - There is plenty of parking at the adjacent banquet hall.
Menu Suggestions - gorditas; quesadillas; tortas

Taqueria Del Sol, just off the Gulf Freeway near Hobby Airport, is a popular neighborhood place. The well-lit restaurant seems to be always nearly filled with customers from the surrounding East End. The waitresses are conversant in both English and Spanish. That helps, along with its setting at an intersection, just off the freeway, to make this a mostly accessible *taqueria*. The food here is solid, if far from spectacular. Its attraction is that it's a well-run, fine value, and convenient family-oriented establishment.

Taqueria Del Sol offers many of the same informal dishes that are served at most area *taquerias*, though the menu is not nearly as extensive. For lunch and dinner there are tacos, *gorditas*, *tortas*, burritos, *tostadas*, Mexican-style *quesadillas*, several plates, and soups. The finger foods such as the tacos and *tortas* might be more popular than the plates here. The tacos are served with a choice of tortillas among freshly made flour, corn and even, in the old style Tex-Mex fashion, crispy corn. The fillings for the tacos are *carne asada*, chicken, *pierna* (pork leg), *barbacoa, lengua* (beef tongue) and *cabrito* (goat). The first three are served with lettuce and tomatoes; the others are served in the traditional Mexican fashion with cilantro and onions. The *tortas,* sandwiches with guacamole, lettuce, tomato, and sour cream on a soft *bolillo* bun, offer a similar array of fillings, plus *al pastor,* which here is described as marinated meat and pork. These are less than three bucks for all but the *milanesa* (breaded beef cutlet) that is slightly more. The *gorditas,* fairly thick homemade corn pockets filled with cheese, beans and several types of interesting, combination fillings, are probably more popular here than at other *taquerias.* The fillings include melted white cheese with shredded poblano peppers (*chile deshebrada con queso*), pork skins (*chicharron*) cooked in a spicy sauce, ground beef with potatoes (*picadillo*), cactus and eggs (*nopalitos*), grilled beef, chicken breast and *barbacoa.* Unlike the others, the burrito, *tostadas* and *quesadillas* come with only two choices for fillings or toppings; beef or chicken for the burrito and *tostadas,* and fajita meat and cheese, or cheese only for the *quesadillas.* The soups offered daily are the *caldo de res,* a brothy soup filled with a variety of chunky vegetables and beef, and the similar *caldo de pollo.* You'll have to wait for the weekends for the tripe and hominy *menudo,* though. This is a popular draw for the families packing the tables on the weekends (at least for the father). The small number of dinner plates includes enchiladas, *carne asada, alambres* (a shish kabob), *flautas,* the grilled skirt steak, *Tampiqueña,* and *milanesa.* The breaded and pan-fried *milanesa* is decent and a fair amount of food, though not terribly exciting. For breakfast Taqueria Del Sol serves most of the popular Mexican egg-based breakfasts including a couple of dishes with *machacado,* the dried, salted beef. Breakfast tacos are still well under a buck-and-a-half each. For all of the dishes, the complimentary tomato-based salsa is served warm and is pretty decent. With a stated intention of keeping it a family-oriented place, Taqueria Del Sol does not serve any alcoholic beverages. They do serve hand-made *licuados,* malted shakes with a choice of a handful of fruit flavorings, and a couple of the *aguas frescas, limonada* (lime) and *horchata* (made with rice and condensed milk). If you have room for sweets there is flan, cheesecake, *tres leches,* and an adjoining *panaderia.*

Taqueria El Herradero $7

5862 S. Gessner (between Harwin and Bellaire) 77036, (713) 541-3723
9521 Telephone (between Brannif and Almeda Genoa) 77075, (713) 991-1360

Cuisine - Mexican (taqueria)
Hours - Daily 7AM to 10PM
Credit Cards - Amex, Discover, MC, Visa
Service - Table Service
Alcohol - Beer

Entrée Prices - Dinner & Lunch - $3 to $10 ($7 average); Breakfast - $2 to $5
Entrées at Dinner $12 and less - 100%

Atmosphere & Décor - Functional, but pleasant
Appeal - Very good and convenient Mexican food
Useful to Note - You are limited to three beers here.
Menu Suggestions - Enchiladas Verdes (with chicken); Enchiladas Rojas (with chicken); taco de pierna (with pork leg)

The most recent location of Taqueria El Herradero on South Gessner, in a nicely re-done former fast food restaurant, is very comfortable as far as *taquerias* go. With good service, and a large menu, this is a fairly slick operation. Taqueria El Herradero offers a larger number of items than most *taquerias,* and most everything seems to be done well. As an indicator of its quality, the complimentary tomato-based red salsa is flavorful and sporting a pleasant, but eventually distinct chile presence. Its green counterpart is, in contrast, viscous, mild and slightly sweet. The chips are reliably fresh. Not just flour tortillas, but also the corn tortillas are made in-house. There are appetizers, *quesos flameados* (melted Monterey Jack cheese dishes), salads, grilled items, soups, seafood soups, seafood cocktails, shrimp dishes, *tortas,* burritos, *gorditas, sopes, quesadillas,* large Tex-Mex-style *quesadillas, sincronizadas* (flour tortillas sandwiching a ham slice and melted cheese), tacos and nearly twenty *Especialidades* (specialty plates). Most of the specialties feature grilled or pan-fried meat. These include grilled chicken breast, fried chicken, fried chicken breast, *carne asada* (grilled skirt steak), an eight-ounce t-bone, an eight-ounce sirloin (still only eight dollars with rice, beans and fries), *carne adobada* (seasoned pork), pork chops, fajitas, *milanesa,* and *Bistec Ranchero* and *Bistec a la Mexicana.* Each of these plates comes with at least rice and either *charro* beans or refried beans. As with most *taquerias,* the chicken used to fill the enchiladas and burritos is shredded. Both the light and the often tastier dark meat are used. Taqueria El Herradero seems to do a better job than most *taquerias* ensuring the bones have been removed from the meat in all dishes. Though at times they don't thoroughly drain the chicken after cooking, and the enchiladas become a little soggy. As with the rest of the menu, the number of choices of meats for the tacos, *tortas, quesadillas* and burritos is lengthier than most *taquerias* now, maybe too lengthy for some. Here, you can still get moist *pierna* (pork leg), *cabeza* (barbecued cow head), *lengua* (cow tongue), and *sesos* (cow brains), plus ones with fajita, chicken and ground beef. As expected, tacos are a great value, with most still under a buck-and-a-half.

Taqueria La Flor $6

4328 Washington (between Heights and Shepherd) 77007, (713) 880-1981

Cuisine - Mexican (taqueria)
Hours - Mon 6AM to 3PM; Tue-Sat 6AM to 10PM; Sun 7AM to 9PM
Credit Cards - Amex, Diners, Discover, MC, Visa
Service - Table Service
Alcohol - Full Bar

Entrée Prices - Dinner & Lunch - $3 to $9 ($6 average); Breakfast - $4 to $8
Entrées at Dinner $12 and less - 100%

Atmosphere & Décor - Functional, at best
Appeal - Very good Mexican food on Washington Avenue
Useful to Note - Some Spanish is usually helpful for ordering.
Menu Suggestions - Huevos a la Mexicana (eggs scrambled with onions, tomatoes and fresh jalapeños); Huevos con Chorizo; Chilaquiles (con huevos); Entomatadas de Pollo en Salsa Verde (enchiladas filled with chicken and topped with melted cheese and piquant tomatillo sauce); Caldo de Res (hearty soup with beef)

If you don't actually overlook it, try not to be put off by the scruffy men who often hang around the convenience store at the other end of the tiny strip center in which Taqueria La Flor is situated. They probably discourage a number of potential customers from what is some of the best, casual Mexican food on the near west side. It's too bad, as La Flor offers a more wide-ranging list of options, and often better prepared, than it's much more popular neighbor across the street, Laredo Taqueria. Though the exterior can be off-putting, the small, thin interior is actually fairly pleasant, if far from grand. With a nicer décor and a shorter menu, La Flor is more of a humble restaurant than a typical local *taqueria,* though the distinctions have long since blurred. Service here is relaxed if mostly competent. Like many restaurants in their price range, La Flor offers appetizers, soups, tacos, *tortas,* enchiladas, grander plates and excellent Mexican breakfasts. Breakfast tacos, which have won some acclaim, are still less than a buck during the week. La Flor seems to do most everything well. Indicative of the quality of its food, the sturdy flour tortillas are made in house, and the two salsas on the table are excellent, a thick, green fiery one, and another that is brick red with bits of chile pepper and seeds, but a comparatively mild, and interesting taste. One of the good choices on the menu is the *Entomatadas de Pollo en Salsa Verde*. These are basically four enchiladas filled with chicken and topped with melted cheese and a piquant tomatillo sauce. The chicken used is both white and dark meat, far more flavorful than the chicken breast that is used at some of places. With sides of moist Spanish rice and tasty refried beans, obviously made with a sufficient amount of lard, this is a large amount of food for a lot less than ten bucks. The other enchilada dishes are similarly very good, too. The *caldos,* the soups that are meals, are done well here. The *Caldo de Res,* with beef, is especially good. The more humble dishes are presumably a better bet than the more expensive ones like the steaks, where the skill in the kitchen cannot quite overcome the quality of the ingredients. Like all other *taquerias*, they aren't working with USDA Prime beef.

Breakfast is very good at La Flor. And, for what it is worth, the presentation of these is far nicer than most places. All of the familiar Mexican scrambled egg-based dishes are served here and done well: *huevos a la mexicana, huevos rancheros, migas, chilaquiles* (*sin huevos* unless specified otherwise), etc. The scrambled eggs are served moister than most places. The *migas* are made with hardened strips of tortillas, a component that is missing from an increasing number of versions in town. Most breakfasts are served with flavorful browned cubes of sautéed potatoes that contain some pieces of peppers. A couple of large fruity *aguas frescas*, made on-site, are available each day. These, like the cantaloupe (*melón*) with bits of fresh melon, can be a good companion to a breakfast for morning when lots of fluids are needed. To note, a minimal amount of Spanish is helpful.

Taqueria Mexico $7

3240 Fondren (at Richmond) 77063, (713) 334-8999
6219 Bellaire (east of Hillcroft) 77081, (713) 271-0251
401 Winkler (west of I-45 S., near Gulfgate Mall) 77087, (713) 645-3433

Cuisine - Mexican (taqueria)
Hours - Fondren - Daily 10AM to 4AM; Other Locations - Mon-Thu, Sun 8AM to 12AMs; Fri-Sat 7AM to 4AM
Credit Cards - MC, Visa
Service - Table Service
Alcohol - Full bar

Entrée Prices - Dinner - $4 to $12 ($7 avg.); Lunch - $4 to $6; Breakfast - $4 to $5
Entrées at Dinner $12 and less - 100%

Atmosphere & Décor - Functional, and maybe a little more
Appeal - Excellent Mexican food in places that are pleasant and gringo-friendly
Menu Suggestions - Huevos a la Mexicana (eggs scrambled with onions, tomatoes and fresh jalapeños); Huevos con Machacado (scrambled eggs with dried beef); Enchiladas Potisano (cheese enchiladas served with a small steak); Enchiladas Suizas; Pollo Guisado tacos and quesadillas; Tacos al Carbon; excellent tequilas

Taquerias by definition cater to a mostly Mexican immigrant and migrant worker crowd. Almost all have a stripped down, functional interior, though many have been growing nicer in recent years. The Taqueria Mexico location on Richmond and Fondren, however, is a fairly attractive place. It's the kind of interior that can help attract the type of people who typically shy from the thought of visiting a *taqueria*. The menu is even nicer and probably more compelling than most other *taquerias*. But it's certainly not the nicer-than-usual interior that should be the prime attraction; it's the usually excellent authentic Mexican food. The breakfasts, lunch and dinner items are typically very well prepared. For lunch and dinner, the inviting menu ranges from *Queso Fundido* (melted white cheese), salads, burritos, *tortas, flautas, tostadas,* nachos, seafood cocktails, *gorditas* (stuffed corn pockets), tacos, *menudo,* fajitas, enchiladas, *quesadillas,* a few combination dinners, and more than a dozen seafood dishes featuring shrimp, red snapper and catfish. The tacos and *quesadillas* are very good. An especially flavorful filling is the *pollo guisado* (stewed chicken). The enchiladas are good, too. Sometimes available as a lunch special is the *Enchiladas Positano,* an enchilada filled with *Chihuahua* cheese and topped with red salsa. It comes with a small, moist and surprisingly savory, skirt steak that has been marinated (possibly in red wine) and then grilled. This is something that is not expected in an inexpensive Mexican restaurant, much less in one billed as a *taqueria*. For another dollar or so, the *tacos al carbon* plate is similarly a steal. Filled with marinated fajita meat, these are excellent.

A reason to make the drive during the weekends is their morning fare. The breakfasts can be excellent, especially so, the *huevos con machacado,* scrambled eggs with dried and smoked beef. A plate includes the egg dish plus refried beans, cubed potatoes, and tortillas, which is more than the tariff for the other plates, but it is certainly justifiable, and quite reasonable. *Machacado* (dried beef) can sometimes be too salty, but here it is excellent, tender and very flavorful. Virtually everything is well prepared at Taqueria Mexico. It is tough to go wrong, no matter if it is breakfast, lunch or dinner. The ingredients are fresh, better than at most Mexican places, and the cooking is often exceptional. As with many other *taquerias,* Taqueria Mexico serves *aguas frescas* (fresh juice drinks) and *licuados* (shakes). Unlike most other *taquerias* though, they have a full bar, and one that includes high quality *reposado* and *añejo* tequilas such as *Cazadores Reposado, Herradura, Patron Añejo, Porfidio Cactus* and *El Tesoro*. The selection is very good, and the prices are certainly lower, too.

Upscale Tex-Mex – a fairly recent phenomena

In addition to nice restaurants that try to serve more authentic regional Mexican cuisine such as Hugo's and Las Alamedas, which might be classified as fine dining, there are several worthwhile, fairly upscale restaurants that are proudly Tex-Mex. With attractive décors, good service and valet parking, the prices are beyond the strictures of this book, but are worthy to visit, nonetheless. Though Armandos (reborn in 2007) pioneered the concept in the 1980s, these are really a somewhat recent phenomenon, and indicate that Tex-Mex as a cuisine, at least regionally, is reaching some sort of maturity. Some of the best are listed below.

- **Cantina Laredo** - 11129 Westheimer - This Dallas-based chain does a respectable job, especially for the west side.
- **Cyclone Anaya's** - 1710 Durham, 309 Gray & 5761 Woodway
- **El Tiempo** - 3130 Richmond, 5602 Washington - The best of the lot, and the most expensive; a great place to take out-of-towners.
- **Escalanate's** - 1281 Kimberly, 4053 Westheimer, 6582 Woodway & 590 Meyerland Plaza
- **Laurenzo's 1308 Cantina** - 1308 Montrose
- **Santos - The Taste of Mexico** - 10001 Westheimer
- **Tila's** - 1001 S. Shepherd

Tau Bay $6

8150 Southwest Freeway (on north side at Beechnut) 77074, (281) 771-8485

Cuisine - Vietnamese
Hours - Mon-Sat 10AM to 10PM
Credit Cards - MC, Visa
Service - Table Service
Alcohol - NONE

Entrée Prices - $5 to $11 ($6 average)
Entrées $12 and less - 100%

Atmosphere & Décor - Functional
Appeal - Very good Vietnamese food right off the Southwest Freeway
Useful to Note - It's not related to Pho Tau Bay on Bellaire.
Menu Suggestions - Com Chien Duong Chau (fried rice with shrimp and pork); Bun Thit Nuong (vermicelli with char-grilled pork); Com Thit Nuong Bi Cha (rice plate with char-grilled pork, egg cake and shredded pork); pho; pineapple shake; jackfruit shake

Since at least 1990, Tau Bay has been serving very good and great value Vietnamese fare. The focused menu contains roughly forty entrées, miniscule by local Vietnamese restaurant menu standards. But, it seems well-tuned for the steady stream of both the Vietnamese and non-Vietnamese customers that frequent their large, high-ceilinged, informal dining room. Its proficiency is marked in some sense that each table is readily stocked with soup spoons, chop sticks, jalapeños, chile sauce, hoisin and *sriracha,* and for the rolls, soups and *bun* (vermicelli) dishes, the accompanying mint, cilantro, sliced jalapeño, lettuce, bean sprouts and lime quarters are as resplendently green and as fresh and fragrant as anywhere else in town. The flavorful fish sauce is less pungent than at other places, too. The items that are offered are the more casual, and the less exotic, mostly soups, rice, and noodle dishes, and Tau Bay is appropriately subtitled, "Vietnamese Noodle House".

The menu is divided among a handful of appetizers, just rolls here, *pho* (beef noodle soup), *hu tieu* (rice noodle soup), *mi* (egg noodle soup), vermicelli soups, *com dia* (rice plates), *com chien* (fried rice), and *bun* (vermicelli dishes). The Imperial rolls, which can top a vermicelli dish or work as a starter, are on the small and thin side, but an order of an appetizer includes eight pieces. Big bowls of soup seem to be on nearly every other table, but nearly everything seems to be done well here. The rice plates, vermicelli, and fried rice dishes are as tasty as hoped. The popular vermicelli dishes are very good, especially with the char-grilled pork, as at other places. In addition to the expected versions of these there are a few twists such as *Com Bo Luc Lac* (red rice with pieces of steak), fried rice with diced chicken and salty fish, and vermicelli with crisp vegetables complementing the meat. The *pho* is good and a key reason for Tau Bay's long-time popularity; a tasty base that comes in ten versions with various soft parts from the cow. There is at least one misstep, the *bun bo hue*, a soup with beef and pork with thick rice noodles, a specialty of the central Vietnamese city of Hue, which is marred by far too much fat, and not enough spice. Though the number of dishes is less than most other full-service restaurants, the list of beverage offerings is lengthier with fresh fruit drinks, fruit shakes, hot and iced coffees, tea and some more unusual items. Many are easily enjoyable shakes like ones with familiar pineapple and strawberry, but, others like durian, nuts, red beans and avocados don't seem to make it on most local beverage lists, Vietnamese and otherwise. There's no sugar cane drink, though.

Taydo $11

11201 Bellaire (at Boone, in the Hong Kong City Mall) 77072, (281) 988-8939
2529 Highway 6 S. (at Westheimer) 77082, (281) 584-0097

Cuisine - Vietnamese
Hours - Bellaire - Mon-Thu 10:30AM to 10PM; Fri-Sat 10:30AM to 11PM; Sun 10:30AM to 10:30PM; Highway 6 S - Daily 10:30AM to 10PM
Credit Cards - Amex, Diners, Discover, MC, Visa
Service - Table Service
Alcohol - Beer & Wine

Entrée Prices - Dinner - $6 to $63 ($11 average); Lunch - $6 to $7
Entrées at Dinner $12 and less - 70%

Atmosphere & Décor - Pleasant

Appeal - Extensive range of well prepared Vietnamese food
Useful to Note - Skip the lunch menu; the main menu has many cheap items.
Menu Suggestions - Bun Thit Nuong Cha Gio (char-grilled pork and Vietnamese egg roll over vermicelli); Com Chien Bo (beef fried rice); Com Bi Cha Thit Nuong (rice served with char-grilled pork, shredded pork and an egg cake); Com Chien Ga (fried rice chicken) Cua Rang Muoi (stir-fried salty crab in a black pepper sauce); Tom Hum Rang Muoi (Stir-fried Maine lobster with black pepper, bell peppers and onions)

During lunchtime at the Bellaire location you will find multi-generational Asian families and at least a handful of non-Asian office workers enjoying a part of Taydo's wide range of offerings. Taydo is fairly similar to some other area Vietnamese restaurants, which is not a bad thing. These are owned by ethnic Chinese who have emigrated from Vietnam, and offer an amazingly extensive list of both Vietnamese and Chinese dishes. These are each fairly spacious and somewhat grand places. These well-appointed restaurants will seem much more approachable to non-Asians than the typical Chinatown restaurants, but these are also very popular with the local Chinese and Vietnamese communities. The location in the Hong Kong City Mall is one of the nicer Vietnamese restaurants on the west side.

The primarily Vietnamese menu is voluminous. There are over 200 different menu choices, including the Chinese dishes, so there should be something that fits the mood and the budget, from the exotic to the locally popular. Though the individual entrées can range over $60 (for soup featuring fresh shark fin), most are for under $10. Fortunately, the menu is well-organized and the dishes, listed also in Chinese and Vietnamese, are fairly well-described in English. There are over forty "House Specialties". These are arranged on the menu among Cold Dishes, including a version of steak tartar and another with crunchy jellyfish. Then there are a number of popular crab entrées, some with the Pacific Dungeness crab. As with other Vietnamese restaurants that serve these, the crab dishes can be well worth ordering. The fresh crabs usually arrive at the table cracked in half, covered with the selected sauce, with a nutcracker to finish the rest of the job. These can be delicious, but messy, dishes. The crab with a curry sauce, and the Stir Fried Salty Crab in Black Pepper, are both menu highlights. Similarly tasty, and necessary of a splurge is the stir-fried Maine lobster. There are several other dishes featuring the seasonally priced Maine Lobster. There are the oft-unusual items under the headings Fried Favorites, Duck/Goose/Clams, and Fish. These items are often unusual (Goose Intestine Stir Fried with Black Bean Sauce, for example) and whose appeal is presumably restricted to the local Asian community. The rest of the large menu is divided among the sections: Appetizers, including the Vietnamese egg rolls; Soup; Clay Pot & Hot Pot; Seafood; Beef; Chicken; Pork; Vegetable & Bean Curd; Grilled and Charcoal Broiled Favorites; Vermicelli (*Bun*) dishes; Rice Platters (*Com Dia*) and Fried Rice; Chow Mein (crisp noodles) and Rice Noodles; Beef, Pork & Shrimp Noodle Soups; and Desserts. There are usually a dozen or more dishes under each of these headings, many with very appetizing descriptions. Taydo has almost ten items featuring excellent grilled or charcoal broiled items, each served with a very fresh salad and a choice of fish sauce or peanut sauce for dipping the meat. Among these is the *Chao Tom,* the enticing creation of ground char-grilled shrimp wrapped around a sugar cane and served over steamed rice noodles. For the value-oriented diners, three sections of the many on the lengthy menu are noteworthy: Vermicelli; Rice Platters and Fried Rice; and Noodle Soup. For around six bucks, these locally popular dishes featuring bowls of rice noodles, or plates of rice with similar toppings, and the meal-sized soups are all well prepared, and great values. The vermicelli and rice dishes with char-grilled pork (*thit nuong*) are especially good. As with the other char-grilled items, Taydo does a very nice job preparing these thin strips of pork. They are fairly generous in the servings of this. Listed with the Vietnamese Rice Platters, the Chinese fried rice dishes are also very pleasing and inexpensive. Taydo serves a half-dozen preparations of *pho,* the soup made with a beef broth, rice noodles and different parts of the cow. There are similar soups featuring seafood, plus a few other interesting soups.

At night the clientele is almost exclusively Asian, and the restaurant on Bellaire in Chinatown is often packed. Probably not surprisingly, the Highway 6 location, in suburban far west Houston, is not nearly as consistent as the Chinatown location. With a pleasant décor and an incredible range of interesting and flavorful food that is reasonably priced, you should definitely consider making the drive to the Bellaire location.

Teotihuacan $9

1511 Airline (just north of N. Main, west of I-45 N.) 77009, (713) 426-4420
4624 Irvington (between Patton and Cavalcade) 77009, (713) 695-8757
6579 W. Bellfort (at Fondren) 77035, (713) 726-9858

Cuisine - Mexican
Hours - Daily 8AM to 10PM
Credit Cards - MC, Visa
Service - Table Service
Alcohol - Full Bar

Entrée Prices - Dinner - $5 to $15 ($9 avg.); Lunch - $5 to $7; Breakfast - $3 to $7
Entrées at Dinner $12 and less - 90%

Atmosphere & Décor - Pleasant; patio at the Airline location

Appeal - Consistently very good Mexican and Tex-Mex food; large portions
Useful to Note - It's good for the whole family.
Menu Suggestions - Tacos de Fajita (two large flour tortillas filled with fajitas); Enchiladas Rojas (enchiladas filled with fajita or grilled chicken and topped with chili gravy); Enchiladas Chilangas (enchiladas filled with shredded chicken or ground beef and topped with chili gravy); El Chon (enchiladas filled with scallops and crab meat, topped with a tomatillo sauce); El Jinete (an eight-ounce grilled sirloin topped with melted cheese and ranchera sauce); Machacado con Huevo (eggs scrambled with dried beef, jalapeños, onions and tomatoes)

Difficulty for non-Spanish speakers in pronouncing the name (tay-oh-TEEH-wah-kun), which comes from the famous Mayan ruins in the Yucatan, by the way, might help to keep these Mexican restaurants from being as popular as they should be with folks from beyond the near north side neighborhoods. These two are certainly more deserving of business than many of their more heavily trafficked brethren, especially the Teotihuacan on Airline near Main. The food is consistently very good. The portions are large. The checks are comparatively small. And, service is solicitous to help make these inviting and comfortable places for dinner, lunch and even breakfast.

The fairly long list of menu items here will contain something for everyone, and most of the area favorites for Mexican food. You might have to look somewhat closely at the descriptions as many of the dishes have cute names, which are seemingly named after friends and family. But, a great thing at Teotihuacan is that it is really tough to make a poor choice. The beef, in its various preparations, is moist and flavorful, the seafood is reliably fresh and savory, and the portions bounteous. There are nachos, *quesadillas, quesos fundidos* (melted cheese), salads, soups, tacos (soft and crispy), *tortas, flautas,* enchiladas, burritos, *tostadas,* char-grilled quail dishes, Tex-Mex combo plates, chicken breast dishes, kabobs (*alambres*), steaks, ribs, shrimp, fish, and the mixed grills (*parrilladas*), which contain fajitas. The *Tacos de Fajita* dish is a noteworthy value for only eight bucks. It consists of two large fresh flour-tortilla-wrapped *tacos al carbon,* with rice and refried beans. The taco's fajita filling is moist and flavorful. All of the grilled beef dishes are very good. For ten dollars you can get the moist and tasty *El Jinete,* which is an eight-ounce sirloin topped with melted cheese and the tomato-based *ranchera* sauce. Some of the more distinctive items at Teotihuacan include enchiladas filled with crab meat and scallops (*El Chon*), chicken breast sautéed with garlic, wine and served in a creamy mustard sauce (*Pollo a la Mostaza*), fajita steak lightly breaded and fried (*La Darinka,* not your typical *milanesa*), jumbo shrimp sautéed with garlic, wine, tequila, bell peppers, tomatoes, onions, jalapeños and served in *chipotle*-based sauce, and the Snapper Cilantro, which is a snapper fillet covered with egg then sautéed in garlic, wine, cilantro and served in a lemon-butter sauce. Served with rice, *charro* beans and guacamole, this last dish is only twelve bucks. Teotihuacan is good on many counts in addition to their hearty morning and daytime fare. The daily happy hour from 3PM to 7PM is an especially good deal when their pretty decent margaritas are still only two dollars. The fully stocked bar contains a few interesting tequilas, and are served for very reasonable prices. Not incidentally, the breakfasts are very good here, and very large. Teotihuacan uses three large eggs in each of their breakfast dishes; and when scrambled these are moist and almost fluffy. In their many guises, these are some of the best Mexican breakfasts around.

Terlingua $12

920 Studemont (between Memorial and Washington) 77007, (713) 864-3700
3801 Bellaire (at Braes) 77025, (713) 665-3900
www.terlinguabordercafe.com

Cuisine - Tex-Mex
Hours - Studemont - Mon-Thu 11AM to 10PM; Fri-Sat 11AM to 11PM; Sun 11AM to 9PM; Bellaire - Mon-Thu 11AM to 10PM; Fri-Sat 10AM to 11PM; Sun 10AM to 9PM
Credit Cards - Amex, Discover, MC, Visa
Service - Counter Service
Alcohol - Full Bar

Entrée Prices - Dinner - $6 to $25 ($12 average); Lunch - $6 to $10
Entrées at Dinner $12 and less - 90%

Atmosphere & Décor - Comfortable; Montrose location can be lively at night
Appeal - Family friendly Tex-Mex and more
Useful to Note - They serve brunch on Saturday and Sundays.
Menu Suggestions - chicken enchiladas verdes; cheese enchiladas; Smothered Burrito (with fajita); Super Burrito; Chicken Lajitas (broiled chicken breast topped with spinach, artichoke hearts and white cheeses)

Run by the same family that were the once and current owners of Cyclone Anaya's, Terlingua serves tasty Houston-focused Tex-Mex along with some other regional favorites in three attractively comfortable restaurants where most details seemed to have been attended to. This will be noticed right away with the suitably crisp and fresh chips and piquant salsas, both of which are better than most. It should be possible to satisfy most all local tastes at these family-friendly eateries with its lengthy, wide-ranging menu and healthy portions. Fajitas, enchiladas, burritos, *flautas, carne asada,* Steak *Ranchero* and *Camerones al Mojo de* Ajo (jumbo butterflied shrimp sautéed with garlic and butter), and shrimp brochette (jumbo shrimp stuffed with jalapeño and cheese, wrapped in bacon and grilled) make up the core of the menu. The Tex-Mex offerings include favorites old and new. The contemporary items include *ceviche,* which until recent years was found just at Mexican seafood restaurants and *taquerias,* a *torta* with grilled chicken, and Baja-style fish tacos. The plump enchiladas can be excellent, especially the chicken filled ones, which feature shredded white and dark meat. Properly rich, thick refried beans and moist Spanish rice accompany most of these plates. The items from the Cyclone Anaya heydays include the tamale pie ("Don't you know?" queries the menu), taco salad, chili, and *sopaipillas.* There are soups and salads with a Southwestern flair. The decidedly not Mexican, or Tex-Mex dishes are an integral part of the menu here, unlike at some other places, and these are well prepared, too. There are burgers, even a pound version for under $10, New Orleans-style po boys, a cheese steak, fried catfish, fried shrimp, hearty American-style steaks, pork ribs, Southwestern-influenced *chipotle*-rubbed pork chops, and chicken fried steak. The chicken fried steak is served in straight-up Central Texas fashion, though with a little better cut of meat than is typical, a skirt steak, and the result is a little better, too. To be noted, the lunch specials are a little skimpy here. An order of enchiladas contains a solo enchilada, for example.

Terlingua has more personality than some of its neighbors. The original location is in an art deco-esque strip center on Studemont right near a processed white bread factory and in front of an even much blander outcrop of recently built townhomes that sits like a banal Potemkin Village come to life. This location, north of Montrose, might turn into a quasi-disco late on the weekend nights, while the one in Braes Heights is much more geared toward families. With the comfortable settings, over a dozen tasty, if often fried, appetizers it's easy to visit just for munching and drinks, without or with kids in tow.

Tex Chick $8

712 1/2 Fairview (between Taft and Montrose) 77006, (713) 528-4708

Cuisine - Puerto Rican
Hours - Mon-Sat 11AM to 6PM
Credit Cards - NONE
Service - Table Service
Alcohol - NONE

Entrée Prices - $5 to $12 ($8 average)
Entrées $12 and less - 100%

Atmosphere & Décor - Spartan, tiny
Appeal - Home-style Puerto Rican food in a friendly and very quaint setting
Useful to Note - This restaurant is very small; takeout might be a good option.
Menu Suggestions - Carne Frita (pan-fried cubes of beef); Pollo Empanizado (breaded and pan-fried chicken breast); Pollo Guisado (stewed chicken) hamburgers; onion rings

The unusually named Tex Chick is a tiny restaurant situated deep in the heart of Montrose. Even driving on Fairview, east of Montrose, it is easy to overlook, as it is such a small place. Located in a stand-alone building, there are only three tables, space for just a dozen or so diners. Though they do serve chicken and the restaurant is located in Texas, the name is not terribly representative or explanatory; Tex Chick specializes in family style Puerto Rican food. You can be assured that the food is freshly prepared and home style, as you can easily peer across the counter into the small kitchen area where one or both of the affable, older Puerto Rican couple is preparing your food. The décor can be described as homey, and eating at Tex Chick is almost like eating at someone's house.

The small number of the restaurant's specialties is shown on the chalkboard that hangs at the counter. For those unfamiliar with it, Puerto Rican cooking is very similar to Cuban cooking and other nearby island cooking, and fairly comparable to that of most tropical Latin areas in Central America and Bolivar's homelands of the northern South America. There are beef and pork dishes with straightforward flavors, some fish, black beans, white rice, root vegetables and some tropical fruits. A slight smell of cooking onions that are used in many of the dishes pervades the place. The entrées include beef steak, *Carne Frita* (fried beef cubes), *Chuleta* (pork chop), *Carne Guisada* (stewed beef), *Pollo Guisado* (stewed chicken), *Pechuga Empanizada* (breaded and fried chicken breast) and the acquired taste that is *Bacalao,* the salted cod that has a very fishy taste. The *Carne Frita* featuring just fried crispy lean cubes of meat might be a nice entrée with which to start. The eight or so plates run around ten bucks. Rice and string beans (called *habichuelas*) come with some of the plates. Red beans are served in place of the string beans for some dishes. Each of the entrées is also served with *tostones y mofongo,* twice-fried mashed plantains and a small lettuce and tomato salad. The plantains are a bit bland themselves, and are much better with the accompanying spicy green salsa. The tiny lettuce and tomato salad is just a diversion. A handful of non-Puerto Rican items are listed on the back wall, tacos and hamburgers. The tacos can be overlooked, but Tex Chick does serve a well crafted hamburger. The properly sized patty and buns is assembled in front of your eyes with fresh ingredients that can include cheese and bacon. The crisp, thin fries and onion rings are nice accompaniments to the hamburgers. The small restaurant has unusual hours, Monday through Saturday, from 11AM until 6PM. It is often crowded, as four tables are easy to fill, with Spanish-speaking patrons, mostly from the Caribbean. To assuage the apprehensive, numerous awards from Marvin Zindler for a clean kitchen are displayed on the wall. Tex Chick is an interesting place to try.

Texas Cheesesteaks $8

12225 Westheimer (between Kirkwood and Dairy Ashford) 77077, (281) 493-0640

Cuisine - Sandwiches
Hours - Mon-Sat 11AM to 9PM
Credit Cards - Amex, Discover, MC, Visa
Service - Counter Service
Alcohol - NONE

Entrée Prices - $6 to $11 ($8 average)
Entrées $12 and less - 100%

Atmosphere & Décor - Functional and inviting
Appeal - High quality cheesesteaks and similar hot sandwiches
Useful to Note - There are more than just cheesesteaks here.
Menu Suggestions - Houston sandwich (cheesesteak sandwich); Austin sandwich (pulled-pork sandwich); San Antonio sandwich (fajita-filled po boy); Big Tex sandwich (large cheesesteak po boy); onion rings; chicken fajita cheesesteak with honey-mustard sauce

Reportedly inspired by fond memories of his student days on the beautiful west side of Philadelphia, restaurateur Donald Chang, who has run successful Japanese and sushi restaurant concepts such as Nara and Uptown Sushi, took a step in a much different direction in 2006, Texas Cheesesteaks. The foresight and knowledge of the local dining scene is evidenced here in many aspects. Of the local cheesesteak eateries, many of which have popped up in recent years, the very sleekly designed and thoughtfully constructed Texas Cheesesteaks is easily a cut above. It's modern, polished metal décor, complemented by the warm browns and beiges of the booths and walls is both somewhat hip and inviting, the latter helped by the friendliness of the staff. They serve not only very good cheesesteaks and other hot sandwiches with fajita, chicken breast, turkey breast and even "hand-pulled" pork and *quesadillas,* which is the Tex-Mex version of the cheesesteak sandwich, after all.

The difference starts with the ingredients. Rib-eye is used for the steak sandwiches, noticeably flavorful, and more tender than at other similar eateries. The bread used for the cheesesteaks are the 10-inch long Amoroso Philly Roll, the same used for most Philadelphia-area cheesesteak shops. These are the thaw-and-serve version and are fresh, and provide the solid basis for all of the sandwiches. Each is cooked and assembled to order in front of your eyes, if you wish, in the open kitchen; and each of the cheesesteak-style sandwiches is nicely complemented with minced onions that provide a subtle, slightly sweet taste to each of the meat and cheese combinations. Emulating the concept that Texadelphia started years ago, each of the build-it-yourself cheesesteaks is served with a choice of a couple complimentary toppings, cheeses and sauces. Served in separate small containers so you can add as you like, some of the choices include: banana peppers, minced onions, bell peppers, mushrooms, jalapeños, Pepper Jack, American, Mozzarella, Honey Mustard dressing, Red Tomatillo Sauce, Marinara, Ranch and Jalapeño-Avocado Sauce and Mayonnaise. And, Cheez Whiz, too, for the sake of South Philly authenticity, if not taste. The Honey Mustard makes for a great companion with either of the chicken fillings. Though complementary, it is not completely authentic, as the provolone is attractively melted on top instead of lining the roll. You'll eat it quickly enough anyway before it becomes too soggy. For sides, which are a necessary addition for most appetites, there are hand-cut French fries, sweet potato fries, beer-battered onion rings, and several flavors of potato chips. Even the potato chips are made on-site. The lightly battered onion rings are some of the lightest and tastiest onion rings around. For those understanding that beef and cheese might not make for the healthiest of daily lunch options, a cup of assorted fruit is also an option. There are several standard versions including the Big-Tex with a double amount of beef (around 10 ounces), cheddar, mozzarella, minced onions and jalapeños, which might be the best of the lot. Other ones feature chicken breast, fajita and a moist and flavorful pulled-pork. You can also create your own with those meats plus turkey breast and chicken fajita, and the various cheeses, vegetables and sauces. For the health-conscious from the office, there are also salads topped with grilled chicken or grilled turkey, or even a side wedge salad to have with your cheesesteak.

Thai Cottage $9

5124 Cedar (near Bissonnet and Bellaire) 77401, (713) 838-0707
4723 Sweetwater (just north of Lexington) Sugar Land, 77479, (281) 313-0707
3995 Richmond (on Weslayan, just south of Richmond) 77027, (713) 623-0707
565 W. Bay Area Boulevard (between I-45 S. & Highway 3) 77598, (281) 554-9999
www.thai-cottage.com

Cuisine - Thai
Hours - Mon-Thu 11AM to 3PM, 5 to 9:30PM; Fri-Sat 11AM to 3PM, 5 to 10PM
Credit Cards - Amex, Discover, MC, Visa
Service - Table Service
Alcohol - Beer & Wine

Entrée Prices - Dinner - $7 to $15 ($9 average); Lunch - $6 to $7
Entrées at Dinner $12 and less - 90%

Atmosphere & Décor - Pleasant
Appeal - Well-run, comfortable and inviting small Thai restaurants
Useful to Note - They are closed on Sundays.

Menu Suggestions - Red Curry (chicken with red curry, coconut milk and bamboo shoots - L10, C1); Yellow Curry (Garee Gai - sliced chicken in yellow curry with chunks of potato and carrots - L7, C2); Pineapple Curry (shrimp, chicken and pineapple with curry in coconut milk - C3); Crab Meat Fried Rice (F6)

Thai Cottage began in an unassuming, but very pleasant location in a strip center on Bellaire Boulevard, in Bellaire, which has been replicated three times over. These are proficiently operated with adept kitchens and service, very user-friendly and noticeably welcoming Thai restaurants that most Houstonians will find appealing. Appropriately fresh ingredients and flavorful curries describe a fair amount of the gustatory appeal of Thai Cottage, even if there are fewer curry dishes than at other area Thai restaurants. The still good-sized menu with about eighty items has most of the Thai dishes that are popular in the area. Each is helpfully accompanied by a descriptive sentence or two. The menu is divided among appetizers, soups, salads, curry dishes, seafood and rice, noodles, grilled items, fried rice, vegetarian dishes, "A La Carte and Rice", and "Chef's Specials". Some of the more intriguing items are under these last two headings with dishes such as the Cheese Roll appetizer (rice wrapper filled with cream cheese and raisins then deep-fried), Sizzling Beef (fresh spinach and slices of beef that has been marinated in peanut and cucumber sauces, served on a sizzling plate), Garlic and Pepper Lover (stir-fried choice of meat with plenty of garlic and a black pepper sauce), *Panaeng* Curry made with coconut milk and either beef or chicken, Triple Spicy Fish (a deep-fried redfish topped with chili sauce). Unusual for a local Thai restaurant, the grilled entrées are well suited for the area and, also maybe those in the group not entirely in the mood for Thai. Among these are grilled chicken breast with teriyaki sauce, marinated shrimp and marinated pork chops. To be noted, the level of spicing is generally low here, but can be adjusted as high as needed. There are nearly twenty lunch specials that include many of the more popular dinner entrées. These are all priced below seven dollars for a fair amount of food. Geared to the customer base, nearly all of these specials feature white meat chicken. Virtually all these lunch specials are served with steamed rice and a choice between fried wontons or a crispy vegetarian roll, and either a cup of the soup of the day, or a small green salad with a peanut dressing or vinaigrette.

Thai Gourmet $11

6324 Richmond (between Fountain View and Hillcroft) 77057, (713) 780-7955
www.thaigourmethouston.com

Cuisine - Thai
Hours - Mon-Thu 11:30AM to 2:30PM, 5 to 9:30PM; Fri 11:30AM to 2:30PM, 5 to 11PM; Sat 11AM to 11PM

Credit Cards - Amex, Diners, Discover, MC, Visa
Service - Table Service
Alcohol - Beer & Wine

Entrée Prices - Dinner - $8 to $22 ($11 average); Lunch - $7 to $9
Entrées at Dinner $12 and less - 70%

Atmosphere & Décor - Nice
Appeal - One of the best Thai restaurants in town
Menu Suggestions - Spicy Chicken Noodles (chopped chicken with fresh garlic, onions, tomatoes and yellow curry powder served over noodles and lettuce); Pad Thai; Green Curry Chicken (with coconut milk, basil and bamboo shoots); Yellow Curry Chicken (with coconut milk, red onions, potatoes); Mussamun Curry Beef (with coconut milk, peanuts, red onions and potatoes); Red Curry Duck; Pineapple Curry Shrimp (shrimp and pineapple chunks with red curry paste and coconut milk in a pineapple shell); Garlic Shrimp; Basil Beef; Pineapple Fried Rice (with chicken, pork, beef, cashews and pineapples); Drunken Noodles (rice noodles and a choice of meat stir-fried with garlic, tomatoes, onions, basil and mushrooms)

In business since 1995, Thai Gourmet is a more-than-worthwhile stop for a well prepared Thai meal in a fairly pleasant and surprisingly tranquil setting just off busy Richmond Avenue. In fact, Thai Gourmet serves some of the best Thai food in town. And, service is solicitous, efficient and friendly, as you would expect from most good Thai restaurants. Adding to the charm of this average-sized restaurant is a large and delicate chalk drawing of an idealized Thai scene occupying most of one wall of the dining room, as it has done for over a decade. Good karma? Its location and value-priced lunch specials make it popular with office workers from around the nearby Galleria area.

The large menu at Thai Gourmet is user-friendly, and the items, if more numerous will be readily recognizable to patrons who dine out for Thai, even occasionally. With the exception of the well-known dish names, all of the menu items are in English. These are coupled with short descriptions of the items. Most importantly, the kitchen seems to have a sure hand with pretty much the entire range. The menu is divided among appetizers, soups, Thai salads, fried rice, noodles, beef, chicken, duck, pork, vegetarian and seafood. The more than a dozen appetizers such as *satay* (with pork, shrimp and tofu in addition to chicken and beef), spring rolls, calamari, and Thai Gourmet Crispy Rice (crispy rice served with simmered ground chicken and shrimp, minced garlic, and red onions in coconut milk). One of the soups can also make for a nice starter. The well-known *Tom Yum Goong* is Hot and Sour Fisherman's Soup here. The hot and spicy entrée-sized salads have drawn rave reviews. There are salads featuring papaya and grilled eggplant. One of the better dishes, which is nicely also served as a lunch special, is the Spicy Chicken Noodles; chopped chicken with fresh garlic, onions, tomatoes and yellow curry powder with pan-fried noodles and lettuce. Thai Gourmet also does very well with the popular *Pad Thai,* stir-fried rice noodles and bean sprouts, tofu, egg and chicken. They serve a greater range of seafood than at most local Thai restaurants. In addition to shrimp, red snapper, scallops, squid, soft shell crabs, mussels, and even prawns, real prawns, not jumbo shrimp, all make it into dishes. You'll notice the difference with the prawns; you have to pay six or seven dollars more for their inclusion. Vegetarian versions of a good number of the dishes are available. Most of the dishes can be adjusted for level of spice (mild, medium, hot or Thai hot). Though the kitchen seems to hold back a tad with many preparations, the spicing can get fairly aggressive and authentic, if you so desire. Tempt them, if you are dare. Many of the favorite dishes are served as lunch specials mostly around eight dollars. The dozen offerings include dishes with chicken, beef, duck and seafood such as the *Pad Thai,* Curry Chicken, Beef with Oyster Sauce, and a sliced, boneless Roasted Duckling. The kitchen does a commendable job with these. Each is served with a small green salad and a couple small deep-fried spring rolls, which help make for a pleasing and filling meal.

Thai Pepper $11

2049 W. Alabama (just east of S. Shepherd) 77098, (713) 520-8225
www.tealas.com

Cuisine - Thai
Hours - Mon-Thu 11AM to 2:30PM, 5:30 to 10:30PM; Fri 11AM to 2:30PM, 5:30 to 11PM; Sat 5:30 to 11PM; Sun 5 to 10PM
Credit Cards - Amex, Diners, Discover, MC, Visa
Service - Counter Service
Alcohol - Full Bar

Entrée Prices - Dinner - $9 to $15 ($11 average); Lunch - $7 to $9
Entrées at Dinner $12 and less - 50%

Atmosphere & Décor - Very nice, even cool
Appeal - Good Thai in an attractive and vibrant, if not quite current, setting
Useful to Note - Parking can be somewhat limited.
Menu Suggestions - pad Thai; Golden Crispy Toast (deep-fried pieces of bread filled with spices, ground pork and shrimp); Pineapple Shrimp and Curry (shrimp and coconut milk curry served in a pineapple); basil duck; basil beef; garlic noodles

Thai Pepper is unobtrusively located on West Alabama, just east of Shepherd; maybe too unobtrusively, as Thai Pepper has undeservedly been off many diners' radar screens for quite a while. Festooned fairly handsomely, if for a number of years now, in a plentitude of very dark wood paneling and tiled floors complemented by vibrant greens on other surfaces, Thai Pepper is one of the more attractive and charming local Thai restaurants; plus, it's probably the most accessible. Those unfamiliar with the cuisine and just looking for a "good restaurant" will be made to feel at home, and should be able to negotiate the menu quite readily. At the same time, Thai food fans should also enjoy dining here. In business for twenty-plus years, Thai Pepper is one of the longest-lasting Thai restaurants. The inviting décor, affable and attentive service and consistently good Thai cooking are reasons for its long tenure.

The menu is entirely in English, which seems to be a legacy of the time, not too far passed, when Thai food was an unusual and exotic cuisine for most diners. With over sixty entrées, all of the now-familiar Thai dishes are served here, and there are more than a half-dozen sweet Thai desserts for the full meal experience. Though the ability to mix and match curries with meats is not done here, the somewhat limited number of curry dishes that are served are quite good. The best might be the Shrimp and Pineapple, which features a coconut milk-laden curry, pineapple and is attractively presented in a pineapple half. There are a good number of beef, chicken breast and pork dishes, but there are also several duck ones, which is somewhat unusual among local Thai restaurants. These are served boneless, in user-friendly fashion. That also extends to the several fish preparations, which are served as fillets rather than the entire fish, as is traditional. The understanding of the local tastes extends to the inclusion of Gulf shrimp into several dishes, mostly stir-fried, and even crawfish. Not local, nor Thai, but well-liked Alaskan King crab meat is the basis for another entrée. The dishes here might be tuned to American palates, but these are far from bland or uninteresting. Spicing for most entrées is available in mild, medium, and hot enough for nearly all palates.

Thai Racha $6

10085 Long Point (east of Gessner) 77055, (713) 464-7607

Cuisine - Thai
Hours - Mon-Sat 10AM to 10PM
Credit Cards - NONE
Service - Counter Service, Drive-Thru
Alcohol - NONE

Entrée Prices - $3 to $7 ($6 average)
Entrées $12 and less - 100%

Atmosphere & Décor - Rundown
Appeal - Generally solid, and inexpensive, Thai food served quickly

Useful to Note - Takeout is probably the best option here.
Menu Suggestions - Red Curry Chicken; Panaeng Curry Chicken; Beef Pad Thai

Beginning in the mid-1990s, Thai Racha has done its part to help improve the reputation of fast food in the area. It is possible to get a flavorful, often hearty, freshly prepared Thai meal for a little more than the cost of a burger and fries at most typical fast food places. This restaurant is in an untrendy part of Spring Branch, a surprising location for the first (and still only) Thai fast food restaurant in town. With a drive-thru, and in an older building that was once a Burger King or the like, it's not a fashionable place, or one with much in the way of seating. But, it serves satisfactory Thai food, quickly. Racha is "king" in Thai. Thai Racha is certainly the king of the Thai drive-thrus. Well, being the only one, maybe that moniker doesn't mean much, but given that the food is generally good, and priced so low, it still seems to work.

The menu is a good deal shorter than at most Thai restaurants, but there should be enough items of interest. The appetizers are a spring roll with marinated chicken, a deep-fried egg roll with ground pork and chicken, and Thai Toast, airy bread topped with marinated ground chicken, deep-fried and served with a slightly sweet, cucumber dipping sauce. The soups are *Tom Yum* Chicken, the hot and sour soup with chicken, mushrooms lemon grass and *kaffir* lime leaf, the southern Thai *Tom Ka* Chicken, sliced chicken in a coconut milk and lime sauce, and Vegetable Chicken, which is cabbage and chicken in a chicken broth. There are salads, heavy with lime; the Thai variations on chicken salad, garden salad, and the Thai Beef Salad. The noodle-based dishes are a decent version of *Pad Thai* with either beef or chicken, the beef being the better choice of the two, and *Pad See Ew*, stir-fried noodles with broccoli and either beef or chicken. The noodle dishes, along with the Rice Bowl and Fried Rice dishes come in two sizes, a small and a large, for an additional buck or two. The Rice Bowl dishes are a choice of meats served on top of steamed rice. The meats include Garlic Beef and Garlic Chicken, each stir-fried with soy sauce, garlic and pepper, Jalapeño Beef and Jalapeño Chicken, each stir-fried with jalapeños, onion and soy sauce, and *Kee Mow* Beef and *Kee Mow* Chicken, ground meat stir-fried with onion, meat and a Thai chili paste. The chicken seems to be more variable, as it is too often served a tad dry. The only curry served daily is the red curry, which is also one of the best items to order. Their version is made with red chili paste, plenty of coconut milk, bamboo shoots, and beef or white chicken breast, and served with steamed rice. For Thai food arriving in a couple of Styrofoam containers, it is exceptionally flavorful. Spicy, without being overly hot, it's a relatively straightforward interpretation that should satisfy nearly any curry lover. There are also fried rice dishes with beef, chicken, shrimp or a combination of these three. Each of the noodle, Rice Bowl and curry dishes can be made vegetarian with the substitution of tofu for the beef or chicken. This is fast food, but all of the food is prepared to order. So, do not expect the rapidity of service that you expect from the local Burger King, but the additional time is certainly worth it.

Thai Restaurant $11

5757 Westheimer (west of Chimney Rock) 77056, (713) 780-0888

Cuisine - Thai
Hours - Mon-Fri 11AM to 3PM, 5 to 10PM; Sat-Sun 11:30AM to 10PM
Credit Cards - Amex, Diners, Discover, MC, Visa
Service - Table Service
Alcohol - Beer & Wine

Entrée Prices - Dinner - $8 to $17 ($11 average); Lunch - $7 to $8
Entrées at Dinner $12 and less - 70%

Atmosphere & Décor - Nice
Appeal - For good Thai in the Galleria area; efficient value-priced lunch specials
Useful to Note - Also run Singha at 12102 Westheimer
Menu Suggestions - Gang Masaman (curry with peanuts and coconut milk); Pad Gra Pow (chicken sautéed with chili, basil and onions); Deep-Fried Jumbo Shrimp Topped with Tamarind Sauce

Thai Restaurant does not have the most imaginative name around. But, it is suitably descriptive. Located in the same small strip center as another fine inexpensive restaurant, Café Lili, it's a short drive west from the Galleria. With an interior adorned with dark wood, and a clean and airy design, it's a generally pleasant place for a meal. It's a gracious, fairly attractive, user-friendly place that is geared toward its mostly professional clientele. The spices might be slightly muted here, but the food is well prepared and flavorful. Thai Restaurant is a popular lunchtime spot for the nearby office workers in and around the Galleria. Deservedly so. Service is extremely efficient during the lunch hours, as your table will receive the complimentary roll and salad or soup very soon after being seated, and your order returns from the kitchen in rapid fashion. And, for just seven or eight bucks the lunch specials consist of many of the most popular Thai dishes. The fifteen or so entrées feature a choice among chicken, beef, pork, shrimp and tofu, in very customer-friendly fashion. Served with white rice, these include your choice of protein sautéed with chiles, basil, onions and vegetables; *masaman* curry, peanuts and avocado slices; green curry with green beans, green peas and carrots; *panang* curry with bell peppers, snow peas, carrots and basil; and *Pad Thai*. From Mondays through Wednesdays, these entrées come with soup and a soft spring roll with peanut sauce. On

Thursdays and Fridays, it is a thinly sheathed deep-fried spring roll, a salad comprised of cabbage, lettuce, shredded carrots and diced cucumbers and a slightly sweet and perfectly complementary dressing.

In the evening the well-presented dinner menu provides a nice array of choices, and a much greater emphasis on seafood than during lunchtime. There are many enticing choices found among appetizers, soup, a salad, fish, shrimp and squid, meats, vegetable dishes, noodles and rice dishes, house specialty dishes, and desserts heading. Appetizers are numerous and include *satays,* spring rolls, dumplings and also shrimp and squid salads and a deep-fried soft shell crab with a sweet chili sauce. Soups include the requisite spicy *Tom Yum Koong* with shrimp, chili, lemon grass, mushrooms and lime and the coconut milk *Tom Ka Gai.* There are many of the popular sautéed dishes such as *Pad King* (with ginger and onions), *Pad Pak* (with mixed vegetables), *Pad Gra Pow* (with chili, basil and onions) plus several curry-based dishes. These are made with a choice of beef, chicken or pork. There are a number of sautéed shrimp entrées, a couple with squid, and a handful of preparations of a deep-fried Gulf red snapper. The fish is served whole in the traditional manner or as a fillet for a couple of dollars more. The house specialties include crispy jumbo shrimps sautéed with chili, onion and basil; deep-fried soft shell crab topped with chile peppers, onion and basil; frog legs sautéed with garlic and white pepper; a deep-fried chicken breast, sliced and topped with a tamarind fruit sauce and served flambé-style; and crispy duck served with a sweet chili sauce. They serve several sweet Thai desserts that are attractively advertised at your table, beers including several interesting Belgian fruit-flavored *lambics,* and a less interesting selection of wines.

Thai Spice $10

5117 Kelvin (at Dunstan) 77005, (713) 522-5100
460 W. 19th (between Heights and N. Shepherd) 77008, (713) 880-9992
www.thaispice.com

Cuisine - Thai
Hours - Kelvin - Mon-Sat 11AM to 2:30PM, 5 to 10:30PM; Sun 12 to 3PM, 5 to 9PM; W. 19th - Tue-Fri 11AM to 2:30PM, 5 to 10:30PM; Sat-Sun 11AM to 11PM
Credit Cards - Amex, Diners, Discover, MC, Visa
Service - Table Service at Dinner; Kelvin - Buffet at lunch; W. 19th - Delivery
Alcohol - Kelvin - Beer & Wine; W. 19th - BYOB

Entrée Prices - Dinner - $7 to $12 ($10 average); Lunch - $6 to $9
Entrées at Dinner $12 and less - 80%

Atmosphere & Décor - Nice
Appeal - Pleasing and approachable Thai food in a pleasant setting

Useful to Note - There are also buffet restaurants, and the great value Express.
Menu Suggestions - Green Chicken Curry; Chicken Panang; Pineapple Fried Rice; Drunken Chicken (with bell pepper, onion, sweet chili sauce and wine)

Opened in 1996, Thai Spice holds its own with the several good Thai restaurants in and around the Village. Located on the second floor of an attractive refurbishment of a former bank at the edge of the Rice Village. This area is a fun, small eating and drinking nexus with benjy's, Antone's and the truly Scottish pub, Kelvin Arms sharing the handsome building. Thai Spice is more than just a pleasant setting in which to enjoy some satisfying food, as it also offers value-priced lunch buffets, dinner specials, convenient takeout service, large portions, all with friendly and proficient service.

The menu is divided among Appetizers, Soups, entrée-sized Salads, Fish and Seafood, Curry with Coconut Milk, Rice and Noodle Specialties, and Entrées or house specials. Each of the dishes is coupled with a description and peppers to indicate the relative level of spiciness. One is spicy. Two is hot. Three is "Madly Hot", which can be suitably spicy. The appetizers include a variety of rolls, soft and deep-fried and filled with crab meat, shrimp, vegetables or chicken. There is also chicken *satay*, fried calamari, crab cakes, rice dumplings and *Mee Krob* featuring crispy rice noodles. The curry dishes, all made with coconut milk, are very good. The flavorful curry sauces are populated with reliably fresh, crisp vegetables and quality, tender pieces of meat. There are yellow, green and red curries, with one to three chilis, respectively, plus *Panaeng* curry sauce and *Massamun* with peanuts. These are presented in a metal bowl accompanied by steamed rice. With the exception of the Yellow Curry, each of the curries is available with either chicken or beef. With these, and with most of the entrées at Thai Spice, the chicken version is better than the beef version. Unlike some other Thai restaurants, the seafood dishes feature only fillets, in typical customer-friendly fashion, not whole fish. Among these is Crispy Snapper (a red snapper fillet with herbs and a chili sauce) and the Sautéed Spicy Seafood (shrimp, squid and scallops that are stir-fried with onions, chiles, green beans and basil). The Pineapple Fried Rice is made with shrimp and shredded pork with pineapple, onions and raisins in the fried rice. Among the house special entrées are the Bangkok Treat (sweet and sour chicken or pork with pineapple, onions, cucumbers, tomatoes and bell peppers), Drunken Chicken (with onion, bell pepper, chili sauce and wine), and Crusted Ginger Sesame Beef Tenderloin with grilled onions and mushrooms. There is not much in the way of vegetarian dishes on this Texas carnivore-friendly menu. The Village location offers a daily lunch buffet from 11AM to 2:30 PM every day. Many of these dishes work well from the steam table. Though not as good as when cooked to order from the menu, the buffet here is an excellent value. For beverages, they serve the popular non-alcoholic Thai fruit drinks and iced coffee plus beers and wine. Unfortunately, too many of the wines offered are oakey chardonnays or tannic reds that do not complement the spicy food.

Thai Spice Express $6

8282 Bellaire (between Fondren and Gessner) 77036, (713) 777-4888
www.thaispice.com

Cuisine - Thai
Hours - Daily 11AM to 10PM
Credit Cards - Amex, Diners, Discover, MC, Visa
Service - Counter Service
Alcohol - Beer & Wine

Entrée Prices - Dinner - $5 to $7 ($6 average); Lunch - $4
Entrées at Dinner $12 and less - 100%

Atmosphere & Décor - Utilitarian
Appeal - Cheap and fast Thai food in New Chinatown
Useful to Note - The lunch specials are some of the very best deals in the area.
Menu Suggestions - Green Chicken Curry

Humble, functional Thai Spice Express, is set in the first Asian strip center on Bellaire you'll encounter when driving west from the Southwest Freeway. After parking, it's almost like you're standing at the gates of the East, and a portent of the exotic and tasty fare to come. Thai Spice Express is a mostly steam table operation that caters to the local Asian community for their value Thai fix. This is a bare-bones, often bustling place without the charm of its full service sister restaurants, Thai Spice, in the Rice Village and in the Heights. The food, though simpler, quicker, and with no effort made in presentation, is still quite satisfying. This is a place to quickly satiate your Thai fix, or pick up some good Thai food to go, for not a lot of money. The most expensive items at the restaurant are seafood including an entire fish, and these are just seven bucks. The daily specials on the steam table are even a better deal. For less than four bucks you get the choice of two items, among a half-dozen, served over white rice. Because of such value, this is what most patrons choose for lunch. This buffet typically consists of a choice of chicken curries plus various seafood dishes. The items change daily. When available, the red chicken curry is the spiciest, and tastiest of the buffet curries. Of the seafood choices, somewhat surpisingly, the mussels can be fresher than that local favorite, shrimp. Clean-tasting, farm-raised catfish seems to be appear frequently in a several guises. If the current steam table offerings don't seem suitably enticing, the menu has more than fifty entrées, mostly Thai, but with some Vietnamese dishes, from which to choose. Each dish is listed in four languages for your convinience: English, Chinese, Vietnamese and Thai. Among the numerous and varied menu items prepared- or assembled-to-order are *pho*, the Vietnamese beef noodle soup, *Pad Thai*, deep-fried spring rolls with minced shrimp, chicken and vegetables, Radish Rice Cake, the Vietnamese rice with thinly sliced, char-grilled pork, baked mussels, a Raw Papaya Salad, Squid Salad, Sticky Rice with Fried Chcken, Sautéed Catfish with Chili Sauce, Chicken with Peanut Sauce and the *Thai Prik* King. Each table is well stocked with enough condiments to complement your food: *sriracha* hot sauce, sliced jalapeños, crushed red pepper, and other, Thai condiments. For beverages, there are beers and wines in addition to the non-alcoholic drinks such as a tamarind fruit drink, lemonade, a coconut drink, plus Vietnamese coffees, Thai Ice Coffee and Thai Ice Tea. There should be enough choices to create a satisfying and inexpensive meal.

Thanh Noi Sandwich Shop $5

9284 Bellaire (between Ranchester and Corporate) 77036, (713) 779-1833

Cuisine - Vietnamese
Hours - Daily 8AM to 9PM
Credit Cards - NONE
Service - Counter Service
Alcohol - NONE

Entrée Prices - $2 to $6 ($5 average)
Entrées $12 and less - 100%

Atmosphere & Décor - Spartan
Appeal - Good and very cheap Vietnamese sandwiches
Useful to Note - Their sandwiches are great for take-away.
Menu Suggestions - Char-grilled pork sandwich

For a number of years it was only announced by its Vietnamese moniker, *"Banh Mi Thanh Noi"*. Thanh Noi Sandwich Shop carries on as probably the longest-running Vietnamese sandwich shop along Bellaire Boulevard with a seemingly loyal clientele, even as two other very good Vietnamese sandwich shops are located within yards of it. You've got to love New Chinatown. Thanh Noi has become slightly more assimilated this decade to take advantage of the more numerous non-Vietnamese patrons, but don't expect much ambiance. Though the average Vietnamese sandwich shop does not have much décor or atmosphere, this has even less so. A few tables are usually filled with several customers chattering away in Vietnamese while puffing tar-laden cigarettes. And, don't expect much English at the counter, either. In the past, the menu board above the counter was solely in

Vietnamese. But, then, as now, all most patrons need to know is "Char-grilled pork", for the char-grilled pork sandwich (*banh mi thit nuong*). The versions with "BBQ Pork", shredded pork, and chicken are also worth ordering. As with most other locally spawned Vietnamese sandwich shops, the sandwiches are served on a commonly found crusty, small French-style baguette and filled with shredded, marinated carrots, sprigs of cilantro, pâté, the meat of your choice, and a fairly large slice of fresh jalapeño. Thanh Noi dispenses jalapeños more liberally than other sandwich shops. If there still is not enough heat, there is plenty of fiery, oily house-made chili sauce available. Along with the spiciness, the sandwiches are consistently tasty, featuring quality ingredients, zesty flavors and nicely contrasting textures, as it should, all for a song. To boot, Thanh Noi seems to be a little more generous with the meat than most of the other Vietnamese sandwich shops. Heartier appetites will most likely require two sandwiches, but at prices around $2 and $2.50, it won't put much of a dent in the lunch budget. If not two sandwiches, others will probably need to order some packaged shrimp crackers, or the like, to make it a meal. Sandwiches are the big draw, but Thanh Noi also serves a few other hot Vietnamese dishes such as "Noodle Dishes", "Rice Dishes" and the well-made, crunchy deep-fried Imperial rolls. Thanh Noi is also one of the few places that still serves the sugar cane drink.

Thelma's Bar-B-Que $8

1020 Live Oak (at Lamar, east of the convention center) 77003, (713) 228-2262

Cuisine - Barbecue
Hours - Mon-Thu 11AM to 7PM; Fri-Sat 11AM to 7PM
Credit Cards - Amex, Discover, MC, Visa
Service - Counter Service
Alcohol - Beer

Entrée Prices - $6 to $12 ($8 average)
Entrées $12 and less - 100%

Atmosphere & Décor - Spartan; it not only looks, but feels like a barbecue shack
Appeal - Often very good East Texas-style barbecue
Useful to Note - Turnaround time is slow; you can call ahead; often closes early.
Menu Suggestions - Chopped Beef Sandwich; Ribs; Links (pork sausage); Fish Sandwich (catfish); Pecan Pie; Lemon Pie

Business justifiably boomed since being featured in a nationally aired special on PBS several years ago that aimed to highlight the best regional sandwiches throughout the country. This being Texas, and Thelma's being a barbecue joint, it was their tasty, very messy beef brisket sandwich that was so honored. Since then, Thelma has also been honored with a photo on the back cover of one of barbecue maven Steve Raichlen's cookbooks. Though it operates from a very unassuming old house east of downtown, patrons have long since found the friendly, homey Thelma's, even more so since the television program.

Thelma's uses both hickory and pecan to cook its meats. The pride of that fire and smoke is the brisket. The result is usually moist, tender and very flavorful. Thelma's brisket has a flavor that is slightly different than that of the more frequently found mesquite-cooked barbecue. Unfortunately, it's not as consistent as it should be as the place might be operating just above ideal capacity at times. The brisket is usually very good, but sometimes within an order there is a piece that is hard, unlike it should be, possibly overcooked. The meaty ribs are moist and messy, as expected, and the kielbasa-like sausage (called links here) is also worth ordering. Thelma's also serves ham and chicken, including an entire bird, for a couple additional meat choices. Each is served with a judicious amount of their distinctive sweet barbecue sauce that tastes of more than a hint of molasses. A dinner plate featuring one or two of the meats for less than eight and nine bucks, respectively, and a couple of plentiful side dishes and bread can be great values. The amount of food is amazingly large, even for super-size Houston. The choice of sides includes green beans, pinto beans, potato salad, cole slaw, dirty rice, okra, cabbage, yams and fries. With the exception of the sugary yams, most are just passable complements for the meats. The fries seem to have detoured in a freezer before reaching the deep-fryer, and are bland and can be avoided.

Be forewarned, with a couple of exceptions, the sandwiches are nearly impossible to eat as you would expect to eat these since they are stuffed with so much meat, especially for the comparatively flimsy bread. These are tasty, but often require a knife and fork for much of it. Be sure to ask for sauce on the brisket sandwiches, and on the side, if possible. Since Thelma's has become very crowded much of the time, the sauce provides a lot of aid towards the enjoyment of these sandwiches. The well prepared hamburger, and, unusual for a barbecue restaurant, a fish sandwich can be eaten solely with your hands. Thelma's Fish Sandwich features fresh, moist, firm, and nearly perfectly fried catfish fillets. Like the other sandwiches, it is simple, with large unadorned hamburger buns enclosing the meat or fish. It is especially good when spread with hollandaise sauce. Though probably not after a full dinner plate, you might have room for one of their rich, sweet, homemade pies or cakes that are arrayed on the counter where you place your order. The pecan pie is very good, and the Lemon Cake is quite tasty, too. Service is always noticeably friendly, though the kitchen can get bogged down when the restaurant becomes crowded, which has been often in the days since the first airing of the show. Be patient, as it usually is worth the wait. Thelma's can get packed quickly during the lunchtime hours. The scruffy, cramped dining room full of mismatched tables and chairs can only seat about forty-five patrons. Calling ahead and getting something to bring back to the desk is not usually a bad idea. You'll still likely smell like barbecue for the rest of the day, though.

This is It $8

207 Gray (west of Bagby) 77002, (713) 659-1608
www.thisisithouston.com

Cuisine - Soul Food
Hours - Mon-Fri 11AM to 8PM; Sat 6:30AM to 8PM; Sun 6:30AM to 6PM
Credit Cards - Amex, Discover, MC, Visa
Service - Counter Service
Alcohol - Beer & Wine

Entrée Prices - Dinner & Lunch - $8 ($8 average); Breakfast - $6
Entrées at Dinner $12 and less - 100%

Atmosphere & Décor - Spartan
Appeal - Convenient soul food near downtown
Useful to Note - Check their website for the day's offerings.
Menu Suggestions - oxtails; smothered chicken; mashed potatoes

Located in the Fourth Ward, just on the other side of the Pierce Elevated from the skyscrapers of downtown, at the edge of Midtown, This is It is the best known purveyor of soul food in town. It now sits in a cool pedestrian-friendly area with several other restaurants, bars and retail shops that's broken up at the southern end at Bagby by an incongruous and expansive drug store parking pot. It's popular at lunchtime with many casual soul food fans from the nearby office towers, while the soul food diehards are present at both lunch and dinner. It (not a contraction of the full name) has been around in the Fourth Ward since 1959, and the present location since 1982. Incredibly, the menu is almost unchanged since it opened (sans the prices, of course). The old adage, "if it ain't broke, don't fix it" certainly applies here.

For lunch and dinner there are typically seven different entrées and a half-dozen side dishes each day. Service is cafeteria style. For around eight bucks you get a choice of one entrée, three side dishes and cornbread. The portions are generous; the calories-per-cent value is quite high here. The selections for the main dishes include most of the soul food specialties.

These include oxtails, meatloaf, pepper steak, chitterlings (every day but Monday), baked and smothered chicken, meatballs, chicken and dumplings, pork chops, ham hocks, turkey wings, and barbecued rib ends. The oxtails, large and meaty, are especially satisfying (it's just beef, for the uninitiated). The smothered chicken is also appetizing. The menu is different each day of the week. Possibly in deference to the somewhat nearby Sacred Heart Cathedral, seafood gumbo and fried catfish are served on Fridays. The sides offered on a rotating basis are candied yams, rice, black-eyed peas, cabbage, pinto beans, string beans, mashed potatoes, mustard greens, macaroni and cheese. The mashed potatoes are good, very whipped and smooth. The candied yams are very candied. So much so, they are almost glistening with sugar. The green beans and the greens are expectedly cooked in the Southern fashion, to within almost an inch of their usefulness. After the hearty entrée and side, if you still have room, there are also some tempting desserts. These are baked on site and include a delicious peach cobbler and a choice of moist and rich cakes. Unlike lunch and dinner, breakfast is cooked to order. All of the fat and cholesterol-laden specialties that you might expect are offered. These are all usually quite pleasing, and a nice value, especially when you consider the amount of food. This is It also caters. Fried turkeys are among the popular catering options.

Thu Thu $9

5015 Antoine (between W. 43rd and Pinemont) 77092, (713) 956-4970

Cuisine - Vietnamese; Chinese
Hours - Mon-Thu 10AM to 9PM; Fri-Sat 10AM to 9:30PM
Credit Cards - Amex, Diners, Discover, MC, Visa
Service - Counter Service
Alcohol - Beer & Wine

Entrée Prices - Dinner - $5 to $19 ($9 average); Lunch - $4
Entrées at Dinner $12 and less - 90%

Atmosphere & Décor - Comfortable, if sparse, but inviting
Appeal - Very good, wide-ranging and consistently great value Vietnamese
Useful to Note - Though the Chinese menu can be good, stick to the Vietnamese.
Menu Suggestions - Cha Gio (fried egg rolls); spring roll; Com Ga Nuong (char-grilled chicken rice plate); Bun Ga Nuong (char-grilled chicken with vermicelli); Com Thit Nuong (char-grilled pork rice plate); Bun Thit Nuong (char-grilled pork with vermicelli); Bun Tom Nuong (char-broiled shrimp with vermicelli); Com Bo Nuong Xa (char-grilled beef rice plate); Com Chien Duong Chau (fried rice); pho (beef noodle soups); Bo Luc Lac (steak salad); Luon Xao Xa Ot (stir-fried eel with chiles and lemon grass)

Located somewhat anonymously on Antoine in near northwest Houston, Spartan, but spic-and-span and well air-conditioned-during-the-summer Thu Thu consistently serves often excellent Vietnamese food that would stand out on Bellaire Boulevard. And, it's a terrific bargain, to boot. The service is also friendly and accommodating for the preponderance of non-Vietnamese customers. The bilingual Vietnamese menu (there is another one with Chinese-oriented cuisine, too) has over 120 dishes, as is not unusual for local Vietnamese restaurants. While perusing the lengthy menu, it's a good idea to start with the savory, plump and well crafted, deep-fried Imperial rolls or the soft spring or summer rolls.

The great value vermicelli (*bun*) and combination rice plates (*com dia*) are very good. The char-grilled pork, beef, chicken, and even shrimp that top the noodles or rice are each excellent. Unusual for local Vietnamese restaurants, the char-grilled chicken served in thick pieces, maybe thighs, is still moist and very flavorful. The *pho*, in several versions, is good, suitably beefy and flavorful, and the complementary plate of herbs is bountiful and very fresh and fragrant. The one fried rice dish (*Com Chien Duong Chau*) on the menu is very satisfying and another very good value for seven bucks. Though Thu Thu does such an exemplary job with these more well-known and especially value-laden dishes, it's wise to look through the entire menu. One or more of the descriptions might entice. The rest of the Vietnamese entrées are divided among headers for pork and shrimp noodle soups, egg noodle soups, vermicelli soups, Specialties, beef, duck, chicken, pork, seafood, thin soup, and fried noodles. Plus, there are the acquired-taste Vietnamese desserts. There are thirty seafood entrées; shrimp, oysters, scallops, squid, seasonally fresh fish and snail and eel preparations, including hot pots and clay pots come into use for some of these. A couple of the house specialties include the black pepper crabs, served in messy fashion still in their shells (*Cua Rang Muoi*), and the char-grilled shrimp wrapped in sugar cane (*Chao Tom*). You should be visiting for the Vietnamese dishes, but Thu Thu also has the Chinese menu that has almost 90 items. This has all of the familiar Chinese-American dishes plus a couple seafood clay pots. During lunchtime, there are over thirty specials, all Chinese-oriented, but just for four dollars each. Given the kitchen's proficiency, these are bound to be decent.

Tony's Mexican $10

2222 Ella (south of Loop 610 N.) 77008, (713) 862-6516
870 S. Mason (at Cimarron) Katy, 77450, (281) 392-6681

Cuisine - Tex-Mex
Hours - Mon-Thu 11AM to 9:30PM; Fri-Sat 11AM to 10PM

Credit Cards - Amex, Discover, MC, Visa
Service - Table Service
Alcohol - Full Bar

Entrée Prices - Dinner - $6 to $16 ($10 average); Lunch - $5 to $11
Entrées at Dinner $12 and less - 80%

Atmosphere & Décor - Comfortable and festive
Appeal - Fun and popular Tex-Mex with good service and strong margaritas
Useful to Note - The Ella location is very crowded on Friday nights.
Menu Suggestions - Carne Asada (grilled skirt steak); Tacos al Carbon; Fajitas; Mole Enchiladas (filled with chicken and topped with mole and white cheese); Vegetarian Special (bean taco, guacamole, chile con queso, two cheese enchiladas with rice and beans); Cheese Enchiladas; Enchilada Combination (beef, chicken and cheese enchiladas covered with chili gravy)

For a good number of people, Tony's Mexican Restaurant is the best Mexican food restaurant in Houston. Some other folks don't understand the appeal at all, including many restaurant reviewers, who decry the food as unremarkable. But, it does draw a large and very loyal clientele, and the original restaurant, which has expanded significantly over the years and into a second location in Katy, is crowded most nights of the week, especially on the weekends. Tony's is filled with gay men on Friday nights; gay women the night before. Families and groups of singles mostly from the nearby Heights and Garden Oaks occupy most of the tables the rest of the week. Part of Tony's reputation is due to the very potent margaritas. A couple will usually ensure a very enjoyable visit. After all, alcohol numbs it all. Another key to its popularity is the fact that it is a well-run and inviting place. Service is always proficient, the turnaround is always quick from the kitchen even at peak times, and the staff is always helpful, even when the restaurant has a large wait, which is often. Most of the best dishes are the ones with grilled beef. The fajitas and the similar *Carne Asada* and *Tacos al Carbon* dishes are all worth ordering. The beef is tender, moist and generally quite flavorful. The *Mole* Enchiladas, filled with chicken and topped with a brown *mole* sauce and plenty of melted white cheese, are rich and tasty. Tony's dark brown *mole poblano* is not the most complex or flavorful, but it makes for an enjoyable topping to enchiladas. Also well-done is the basic Tex-Mex combo dinner called the Vegetarian Special with a bean taco, cheese enchiladas guacamole and a puffy crispy tortilla topped with *chile con queso*. That Tex-Mex favorite the cheese enchiladas are properly cheesy and comforting. There are pitfalls on the good-sized menu, but stick to the dishes with fajitas and some of the other basics, have a margarita or two, and soak up the atmosphere of fellow patrons enjoying themselves.

Tookie's $8

1202 Bayport Boulevard (south of NASA Road 1) Seabrook, 77586, (281) 474-3444

Cuisine - Hamburgers
Hours - Mon-Thu, Sun 11AM to 9PM; Fri-Sat 11AM to 10PM
Credit Cards - MC, Visa
Service - Counter Service
Alcohol - Beer

Entrée Prices - $7 to $9 ($8 average)
Entrées $12 and less - 100%

Atmosphere & Décor - Very casual
Appeal - Tasty grilled hamburgers
Useful to Note - Tookie's can be fun for the whole family.
Menu Suggestions - hamburgers

Tookie's has been a popular stop near the Kemah Boardwalk for locals and day-trippers since 1975. Relatively small but very tasty, charred, thin patties are the core of these very good burgers, and the heart of the attraction of Tookie's. These patties are small, smaller than most are used to, so get the double-meat for just an additional buck if you are at all hungry. With a choice between toasted wheat and sesame seed-topped white buns, the burgers are available in a variety of fashions. There are a handful of popular, unusual versions like the #99 Burger with a patty that has been marinated in wine, the Squealer with ground beef mixed with hickory-smoked bacon for a subtle and pleasant result, and the Bean Burger with refried beans, cheese, crushed Fritos and salsa. The Bean Burger and Stomp's Ice House Special are both tasty, as are all of the burgers, though neither are very spicy, and each would certainly be better if a homemade salsa was used instead of the jarred Pace Picante sauce. Fries and large-sized onions provide accompaniments for the burgers. There's probably too much décor in terms of old signs and the like for this sprawling, dumpy, but charming setting, which is very appropriate for a burger joint. It's also quite kid-friendly. To note, the only draft beers are Budweiser and Miller Lite.

Treebeards $7

315 Travis (at Preston - Market Square) 77002, (713) 228-2622
1117 Texas (at San Jacinto - in the Christ Church Cathedral) 77002, (713) 229-8248
1100 Louisiana - Tunnel (under the Wells Fargo Building) 77002, (713) 752-2601
700 Rusk - Tunnel (under the Pennzoil Building) 77002, (713) 224-6677
www.treebeards.com

Cuisine - Cajun; Southern
Hours - Mon-Fri 11AM to 2PM

Credit Cards - Amex, MC, Visa
Service - Counter Service
Alcohol - Tunnel locations - NONE; Other Locations - Beer & Wine

Entrée Prices - $4 to $9 ($7 average)
Entrées $12 and less - 100%

Atmosphere & Décor - Comfortable
Appeal - Popular Cajun and Southern lunches for downtown office workers
Useful to Note - They have a very informative web site; check the day's menu.
Menu Suggestions - Red Beans and Rice with Sausage; Chicken Fried Steak; Baked Chicken Breast; Shrimp Étouffée ; dirty rice; jambalaya; carrot cake; Yellow Cake; Buttercake

At least one of the Treebeards outlets is within a short walk down the tunnels for a good portion of the downtown workforce. Most would certainly agree that this convenience is very welcome, as Treebeards has long been a favorite lunch spot for satisfying Cajun and Southern cooking. Treebeards has four of these lunch-only spots in downtown Houston since its original restaurant opened in 1978. Two locations are street level, both in attractive nineteenth century buildings. One is in a handsome structure on Market Square that was built in the 1860s. The other location, the Cloisters, is interestingly set inside the Christ Church Cathedral, the first church in the city, Episcopal, at least. To get to that restaurant, you will need to go through the doors at the rear of the courtyard that faces Texas Street. The other two Treebeards are in various spots in the tunnels; maybe not nearly as engaging settings, but probably more convenient. These two locations, with much more room to dine, and probably to cook, serve food that seems more satisfying than the tunnel locations.

The food is served cafeteria-style from steam tables. A set array of familiar Cajun dishes is offered daily. The Southern and regional entrées (called Daily Specials) and vegetables vary each day. There are also soups and salads. Each location has a choice between two of the daily entrées plus two of the typical three vegetable choices. An entrée with two sides is around eight or nine dollars, depending on the entrée, and a little cheaper at the Rusk location. The offerings are slightly different at each location, and the larger Market Square and Cloisters locations have more selections than the ones in the tunnel, which are primarily, or solely, takeout operations. The Market Square and Louisiana locations feature baked, grilled and fried items; the Cloisters, backed and fried; and the Rusk location, just baked. The entrées can include: meatloaf; fried chicken; jerk chicken; pot roast; baked catfish; stuffed pork chop; chicken fried chicken; chicken fried steak; and baked chicken in a mushroom cream sauce. The daily vegetables showcase a wide range of regional favorites which can include: okra and tomatoes, black beans, dirty rice, mashed potatoes, roasted new potatoes, mustard greens, Hopping John (a Southern dish of cowpeas and rice), dirty rice fritters, *maque choux* (a Cajun mix of corn with onions and peppers, just served at the Cloisters location), green beans, squash casserole, and cornbread dressing. You can make a meal of three of these for just five bucks. One of the best of the daily specials is the chicken fried steak. Unfortunately, it is now served only at the Cloisters location on Mondays and Tuesdays. It's tender and covered in a dark brown gravy rather than standard white cream gravy. To stay up-to-date with the current daily specials, Treebeards has one of the best, most informative and accurate local restaurant web sites. The Cajun dishes feature several gumbos, jambalaya, étouffée and Red Beans and Rice. The filling Red Beans and Rice with Link Sausage is the most popular, and best, dish at Treebeards. While the gumbo and étouffée might not stack up that great against those from some other local Cajun places, the Red Beans and Rice more than hold their own. Featuring whole beans rather than the mushier, more cooked-down versions, this dish is flavorful, especially with shredded cheddar cheese and a link of sausage. Many of the most popular items are served at each location: the Red Beans and Rice, both with and without sausage; Beef and Bean Chili; Shrimp Étouffée; Vegetable and Chicken Soup; Chicken and Sausage Gumbo; Chicken Salad; Shrimp Salad; and the Green Garden Salad. For each of the locations, it is best to try to arrive before or after the prime time lunch rush around noon, or you will be waiting in a potentially lengthy line. For that sweet end to a meal, Treebeards has several cakes, including a carrot cake and an Italian cream cake, brownies and cookies.

Tubtim Siam $10

6488 FM 1960 W. (between Champion Forest and Cutten) 77069, (281) 474-3444

Cuisine - Thai
Hours - Mon-Thu 11AM to 2PM, 5 to 9PM; Fri 11AM to 2PM, 5 to 10PM; Sat 12 to 3PM, 5 to 10PM
Credit Cards - Amex, Discover, MC, Visa
Service - Table Service
Alcohol - Beer & Wine

Entrée Prices - Dinner - $7 to $16 ($10 average); Lunch - $6 to $7
Entrées at Dinner $12 and less - 100%

Atmosphere & Décor - Pleasant
Appeal - Good, homey Thai food in the Champions area
Menu Suggestions - Hot and Sour Soup; Tom Kha Seafood Soup (coconut milk-based soup with scallop, shrimp, squid and snapper); Green Curry Beef; Gang Paa (jungle-style red curry chicken cooked in a chicken stock with vegetables)

Tubtim Siam is a usually quiet, longstanding Thai restaurant that has been turning out homey and apparently fairly authentic Thai cuisine for well over a decade just off always-busy FM 1960 near Champions Golf Club. Service is often slow, especially during lunchtime, if quite pleasant and friendly. It's an earnest family-run place that is easy to like, especially with the quality and value of the fare. It's a nice choice for a quiet evening, and one with more interesting fare than you might expect. It's a small, truly quaint restaurant with just less than twenty tables in two sections divided by a shoulder-high partition. The fuchsia-colored walls, not unlike the exterior of Mai Thai on Kirby, emphasized with darker tone trim help give this strip center location a more noticeable and truly Thai flavor, as it's difficult to think of another reason for its, well, interesting, décor.

Though the presentation is quite nice, the cooking gives the impression that it's home-style fare, as will be readily confirmed by the owner, who is from northern Thailand. Served in sensibly sized portions, this is very good home-style cooking with plenty of subtlety, even if the spices are toned down here. Whole fish is an option for many of the fish entrées and there are several clay pot dishes. There also are several Thai beverages beyond Thai coffee such as the Golden Raisins Drink, and nearly ten Thai desserts, many featuring sweetened rice or fried bananas, and no Western desserts. The offerings can be slightly different than most local Thai restaurants (Fluffy Catfish Salad and Steamed Fish with Chinese Plum, for example), but most are readily identifiable for even infrequent Thai food consumers. The bulk of the menu is divided among appetizers, soups, salads, house specialties, chicken, beef, pork, seafood, curries, fried rice, noodles, clay pots and vegetarian. There are a dozen appetizers and roughly seventy-five entrées from which to choose. The tasty coconut milk broth *tom kha* seafood soup, served with a thin base like in Thailand and plenty of plump morsels of seafood, is a perfect starter.

Most of the colors of the curry rainbow are served here: red, green, yellow (*gang garee*) plus *massamun* and the seldom seen "fancy" *chuchee* that is mild and slightly sweet and a ready companion to delicate seafood. Red is the most prevalent curry, and is featured in a number of interesting dishes: Red Curry Roasted Duck cooked with coconut milk, pineapple and Thai eggplants; Spicy Green Shell Mussels sautéed with basil, asparagus in a red curry sauce; and a flavorful, light "Jungle Style Curry" that has red curry cooked in a chicken stock with a slew of vegetables. The green chicken curry is well done here, though it tastes slightly different than most versions in the area. This might be due to the addition of slices of the unique-tasting Thai eggplant. Without admonition otherwise, it is served mildly spicy, fairly flavorful, and almost complex. Beef might be a better choice for the curries, as the thinly sliced pieces of white chicken meat can be bland, like at many other local Thai eateries. One of the unique dishes worth investigating is the Volcano Chicken, which is a marinated whole chicken that is roasted then deep-fried and served with a sweet chili sauce and pickled vegetables. The deep fryer also does its magic another house specialty, Angel Wings with Curry Sauce, which is deep-fried stuffed chicken wings that are sautéed in the curry sauce and served with kaffir lime leaves. The deep fryer is also used for seafood, with shrimp, catfish and snapper preparations including ones with the entire fish. There are a dozen entrées listed under the seafood header, plus several others in other sections. During lunchtime, most of the same items are served, roughly twenty, in slightly smaller portions, but just for $5 to $7, and that includes a thin fried spring roll and a cup of soup. The latter might be a Thai version of the familiar hot and sour soup. This is not particularly hot or sour, but still wonderfully satisfying with a small range of tastes, including from the black mushrooms, and textures, which thankfully does not include overly spongy pieces of tofu that afflict too many local versions. It's just one indication of the pleasant surprises to be found here.

Van Loc $11

3010 Milam (between McGowen and Elgin) 77006, (713) 528-6441

Cuisine - Vietnamese
Hours - Mon-Thu, Sun 9AM to 11PM; Fri-Sat 9AM to 12AM
Credit Cards - Amex, MC, Visa
Service - Table Service
Alcohol - Beer & Wine

Entrée Prices - $6 to $20 ($11 average)
Entrées $12 and less - 80%

Atmosphere & Décor - Spartan
Appeal - Good Vietnamese food in Midtown
Useful to Note - Food trumps atmosphere by a wide margin here.
Menu Suggestions - Imperial rolls; char-grilled pork spring rolls; spring rolls; pho; crushed rice with shredded pork, charcoal broiled pork, egg cake and fried egg; Thit Kho To (clay pot pork)

Van Loc is probably the best of the less-numerous-than-before Vietnamese restaurants in Midtown, though it does have its off nights. The fairly spacious dining room is spartan, but inviting. Maybe that's just the aromas or anticipation. Service is usually decent enough. But, the décor and service are secondary to the food. The cooking is mostly unassimilated, but Van Loc appeals to both the local Vietnamese community and non-Asians alike. Van Loc provides more than commendable versions of most of the popular, and not-so-popular, Vietnamese dishes. If there is a Vietnamese dish that you like, Van Loc undoubtedly serves a version of it. Virtually all of the many menu items are under $10, and many of those are around six bucks.

The lengthy menu contains mostly Vietnamese dishes, along with some Chinese ones among the myriad of choices. The bilingual Vietnamese and English menu begins with Appetizers, then Soup, and on and on. The rest of the fairly descriptive menu headings are: Beef Noodle Soup (*Pho*), Rice Noodle Soup, Egg Noodle Soup, Vermicelli Soup, Vermicelli (*Bun*), Combination Rice Plate (*Com Dia*), Fried Rice, Pan Fried Noodles, Special Thin Vermicelli, Rice Paper Dishes, Chicken Dishes, Pork Dishes, Beef Dishes, Seafood (shrimp), Fish, Clay Pot Specials, Special Hot Pot Soup, Thin Soup, Specialties Dishes, Special Salads, and Vegetarian Dishes. A great way to start a meal is with one of the rolls. There are the soft spring and summer rolls and the deep-fried Vietnamese Egg Rolls. In addition to the familiar versions featuring shredded pork and a combination of the pork and shrimp, there are also versions with the delicious char-grilled chicken or pork. As with other Vietnamese restaurants, inexpensive meals can be made with *pho*, the beef noodle soups, the meal-in-a-bowl vermicelli dishes (*bun*), or the Rice Plates. The *pho* soups are very good, and feature only beef, beef meat balls and chicken, not the extraneous parts, as are served at the restaurants that specialize in *pho*. The similar, and similarly inexpensive, rice noodle soups (*hu tiu*) and egg noodle soups (*mi*), are not made with a beef broth (as is the *pho*) and feature other main ingredients such as shrimp. Popular toppings for the vermicelli and rice plates are the aforementioned moist and flavorful char-grilled pork and char-grilled chicken. About half of the rice plates are served with the Vietnamese-style crushed rice instead of the familiar, and seemingly less flavorful, steamed rice. The egg cakes in several of the rice dishes are quite tasty. At Van Loc these are yellow in color, as these should be, rather than brownish, as at some other places. The Chinese-style fried rice dishes (pork, beef, chicken and shrimp) are other excellent values.

The more expensive dishes under the various headings such as Chicken, Pork, Beef, Seafood, etc., also have their adherents. Chicken with Ginger, Spicy Chicken in Hot Chili and Lemon Grass, Short Spare Ribs (pork), Cooked in Fish Sauce, and Salted Fried Shrimp are among the choices. A couple of the beef dishes seem especially appealing: the beef with curry, coconut and peanut; and the filet mignon chunks that are sautéed with garlic and scallions, and served with fresh lettuce and tomatoes. The Clay Pot Specials are interesting and flavorful. Cooked in a small clay pot, they arrive at the table sizzling. The one with pork has a unique taste, but is more readily enjoyable for most than the one with fish (and a prominent fish head). On the rest of the large menu, there are many potentially gratifying choices. Eel, frog legs, quail, pigeon and soft shell crabs are among the other entrées. A strong Vietnamese iced coffee might be a fitting way to finish the meal. The desserts, unfortunately, do not have the French heritage, as does the coffee. The choices are mostly ones with beans and coconut milk, plus lychee and longan.

Victor's Delicatessen $9

4710 FM 1960 W. (just west of Veterans Memorial) 77069, (281) 583-7271

Cuisine - Deli
Hours - Mon-Sat 7AM to 9PM; Sun 7AM to 3PM
Credit Cards - Amex, Discover, MC, Visa
Service - Table Service
Alcohol - NONE

Entrée Prices - Dinner & Lunch - $5 to $14 ($9 average); Breakfast - $5 to $8
Entrées at Dinner $12 and less - 80%

Atmosphere & Décor - Pleasant
Appeal - Good deli and diner-style food on 1960; a slew of sandwich choices
Useful to Note - Breakfast is served all the time.
Menu Suggestions - Reuben Sandwich; Salami and Swiss Cheese Omelet; Delicatessen Omelet; Pastrami Omelet; hash browns

Victor's Delicatessen does a good job with the deli basics. Its proficiency is evidenced by the often- bustling business from those patrons who eschew the many chains that crowd it among the strip centers on 1960. Just ignore the display case near the entry that is filled with an uninspiring array of packaged bulk cheeses and meats. Victor's is a good-sized, comfortable place with a number of choices so that it is easy to find an enticing dish or two for everyone in the family here.

The menu here is extensive. But for many, the most important thing is that breakfast is served all of the time at Victor's. The breakfast options take up a page, one-third of the menu, and cover most of the basic diner favorites. There are not many ethnic or regional additions other than the lox, potato pancakes, a blintz, and biscuits and gravy. The egg dishes predominate. The omelets can be good here, and are a filling meal for around eight bucks. Made with three eggs, and probably a good amount of butter, these deli-oriented omelets are folded over the fillings and though cooked to a slightly dry finish have a rich taste, and even have a hint of mustard, which is actually quite complementary. If you desire hearty rather than heart-healthy, the omelets with pastrami, salami, corned beef and cheese in various combinations are for you. They are served with good, slightly greasy and properly made hash browns. These are certainly worth ordering as a side if it does not come with your breakfast. The rest of the dishes are an assembly of all-American favorites with a few deli items thrown in for good measure. There are several appetizers, salads and soups, including the requisite matzoh ball soup. The "Old Time Favorites" sandwiches include a grilled cheese, patty melt, BLT, a club, and hamburgers. The very thickly cut fries provide a fitting accompaniment. There are additional specialty and deli sandwiches. Excepting hamburgers, there are nearly forty different sandwiches from which choose here. And, Victor's does a good job with the Reuben. Though not the best in town, as proclaimed on the menu, it's certainly the best one in the Champions area. If breakfast or sandwiches do not appeal there are basic dishes such as meatloaf, hot turkey, hot roast beef, and even hearty dinners that are served after 5PM. There are also deli-style cold plates such as salmon, chopped liver and sardines. There should be something for nearly everyone here. For a small dash of panache, and a nice example of recycling, iced tea is served in 1.5 liter wine bottles. It's a good idea given how quickly most Houstonians go through iced tea. Service is usually attentive to filling your other needs, for example, extra ice for the tea is usually brought to your table without prompting, and turnaround from the kitchen is quick. But, with the comfortable booths, and friendly air, many patrons seem content to linger after the meal, which is a nice change from many of the nearby restaurants.

* Vieng Thai $8

6929 Long Point (between Antoine and Silber) 77055, (713) 688-9910
www.viengthai.com

Cuisine - Thai
Hours - Daily 11 AM to 10PM
Credit Cards - MC, Visa
Service - Table Service
Alcohol - NONE; BYOB

Entrée Prices - $6 to $13 ($8 average)
Entrées $12 and less - 90%

Atmosphere & Décor - Limited
Appeal - Excellent, authentic Thai food that is a great value
Useful to Note - The optional eggplants in the green curry aren't for everyone.
Menu Suggestions - Tom Yum (hot and sour soup with shrimp); Tom Kha Gai (coconut milk soup with chicken, lemongrass and lime); papaya salad; Gang Keaw Whan (green curry with coconut milk, basil and chicken or beef); Panaeng Curry (a curry with coconut milk, green beans and kaffir lime leaves); Gang Dang (red curry with coconut milk, bamboo shoots, bell pepper and basil); Pad Thai

with shrimp; Pad Prik Khing (pork sautéed in curry paste); Pad Prik Paow (beef or chicken sautéed with basil, bell pepper, onion and a sweet chile paste); Yum with squid (a spicy salad of cucumber, onion, mint, cilantro and dressing); Pa Ka Na (stir-fried Chinese broccoli with crispy pork); Thai Omelet; Plaa Pad Ped (crispy catfish with curry, herbs and basil)

Unassuming Vieng Thai serves some of the very best Thai food in town. This quickly became a favorite of diehard Thai food lovers in a few months after opening in 2004. You'll often notice Thai patrons, too. Though most local Thai restaurants do a commendable job, the food at Vieng Thai is in another league compared to almost all the others. The aromas and flavors in most of the dishes are amazingly vibrant, and there is evident, and often unexpected, complexity in many dishes. The large menu, the most extensive of local Thai restaurants, with its innumerable tempting choices, and its English descriptions, should be easily navigable by most visitors. It's divided among appetizers, soups, Thai-style salads, curries, a number of vegetarian entrées, rice dishes, noodle dishes, soups with noodles and the somewhat oddly named "Main Dishes". This last category features an array of Thai dishes unique to the area. Some under this heading includes what is described as fried pilot fish (*Plaa Sa-lid Tod*), fried mackerels, fish balls sautéed with chili paste, and *Nam Prik Krapi*, described as a "Thai chili paste" that is "only for the adventurers!" You are forewarned. It's certainly good, if fiery hot.

Among the appetizers are a couple of types of Thai sausages that don't make it to many local menus. The more familiar soft spring rolls, served with peanut sauce, are done well here. Among other popular items, the *Pad Thai* and green curry (*Gang Keaw When*) are both excellent, probably the best local versions of each, and two of the many highlights. The green curry with coconut milk and basil is probably best with chicken, at least that's what has been recommended by the restaurant staff. This dish is also served with Thai eggplants, which can be quite interesting in both taste and texture. Different, certainly, and authentic, but these additions might not appeal to a great many of the non-Thai diners. Fans of the Simpsons might be reminded of tomacco. The less complex red curry (*Gang Dang)* is also very good, and also presented in a bountiful-sized portion. These excellent curries are served with a choice between chicken and beef, and sometimes pork. There is even an intriguing version with shrimp with coconut milk in a hot-and-sour sauce (*Gang Soum Goong*). It's truly tough to go wrong here. The kitchen is usually very consistent and versatile. The one demerit that might be readily noticed is that the shrimp is not as reliably of the quality it should be. The rest of the dish usually more than compensates for any lower quality. They might run out of items, mostly during weekends. No matter, the menu is lengthy. Service is homey and friendly, though not terribly polished. English language ability varies among the wait staff. And, be prepared to open your own wine. You brought it, after all.

In concord with its location in a dumpy strip center on Long Point, there is not much to the décor, one dining room that is bisected by the entrance, a television set in one wall, a serving and cashier counter, and a table slightly elevated and set apart that is reserved for a favorite patron, a certain Mr. Keith. Though the service here is noticeably friendlier here, many diners notice the similarities between Vieng Thai and long-standing Kanomwan: both serve robust, intriguing Thai dishes, without many concessions to local palates; both are BYOB-only; both are almost completely lacking in atmosphere; both are wonderful, and some of the very best inexpensive restaurants in the Houston area, Thai or otherwise. These two restaurants give credence to the thought that in somewhat out-of-the-way, less-than-charming settings, it can be easier to serve very bold and more authentic flavors.

Vietnam Coast $9

2910 Hillcroft (between Westheimer and Richmond) 77057, (713) 266-0884

Cuisine - Vietnamese; Chinese
Hours - Mon-Thu, Sun 11AM to 11PM; Fri-Sat 11AM to 12AM
Credit Cards - Amex, Diners, Discover, MC, Visa
Service - Table Service
Alcohol - Beer & Wine

Entrée Prices - $5 to $17 ($9 average)
Entrées $12 and less - 90%

Atmosphere & Décor - Spartan
Appeal - Reliable and inexpensive Vietnamese food
Useful to Note - Vietnam Coast is also good for take-away.
Menu Suggestions - Spring Rolls; Vietnamese Egg Rolls; lemon grass beef; Pho Tai (with recognizable beef); Bo Nuong Banh Hoi (char-grilled lemon grass beef); Bun Thit Nuong (vermicelli with char-grilled pork); Bun Cha Goi (vermicelli with egg rolls); Curry Shrimp; Curry and Coconut Chicken

A testament to its dining quality and value, Vietnam Coast has been open for well over twenty-five years, ancient by Houston standards. The setting is functional, genial enough, and the service is reliably efficient. Vietnam Coast has the familiar menu of Vietnamese and Chinese dishes, around 150 in all, that are common in many primarily Vietnamese restaurants. The kitchen seems to do a good job with most everything, and the prices are a little lower than many Vietnamese restaurants. The large menu is divided among Appetizer, Soup, Duck, Crab, Fried Favorites, Grilled, Entrées,

Vegetarians, Fried Rice, Pan-Fried Noodles, Chow Mein (crispy noodles) and Lo Mein (soft noodles), Vermicelli, Rice Platters, Noodle Soups (Traditional Breakfast), and Combination Plates. Though maybe not the best Vietnamese food in the area, the kitchen does a commendable job with most everything. For example, the barometer for many at local Vietnamese restaurants, the marinated char-grilled pork (*thit nuong*) is quite satisfying here. Thicker than many places, it is nonetheless tender and very tasty. It even makes it into spring rolls along with the char-grilled chicken. The plump deep-fried Vietnamese egg rolls are also well prepared. Among the many choices is a number of appealing dishes in the Entrée section such as Vietnamese Fajitas (marinated and char-grilled strips of beef); boneless deep-fried half of duck; Hot Special Hot Pot with shrimp, scallops, squid, chicken, mushrooms and vegetables; ground shrimp wrapped around sugarcane; Clay Pot Pork; and Cornish Hen with a honey garlic sauce. Most of these dishes cost just around seven bucks. Interestingly, most of these preparations are available with a choice among beef, chicken, shrimp and squid. The vermicelli, rice plates (*com dia*) and rice noodle bowls (*bun*) make for a savory and amazingly affordable meal. The deserved long-time customer favorite char-grilled lemon grass beef is available as a stand-alone dish or topping a rice plate or bowl of noodles. The noodle soups have the non-Asian customer in mind, as none have any extraneous parts, as in the *pho* houses. The Entrée section includes many of the Chinese-influenced items such as Hunan Chicken, Curry Shrimp and Lemon Chicken. These and the Americanized Chinese dishes under the heading of Special Combination Plates are not the same level as the strictly Vietnamese offerings. The latter are available during all hours for a song with fried rice and an egg roll; you can choose from among twenty-five or so dishes such as Moo Gai Pan, Kung Pao Chicken, Beef and Broccoli, General Tso's Chicken, Garlic Beef and Sweet and Sour Pork.

Villa Arcos $6

3009 Navigation (east of Canal, a few blocks east of Ninfa's) 77003, (713) 227-1743

Cuisine - Mexican (taqueria)
Hours - Tue-Sat 5:30AM to 2PM; Sun 8AM to 1PM
Credit Cards - NONE
Service - Counter Service
Alcohol - NONE

Entrée Prices - Lunch - $4 to $7 ($6 average); Breakfast - $4 to $6
Entrées at Lunch $12 and less - 100%

Atmosphere & Décor - Spartan
Appeal - Excellent tacos, tamales and family-style Mexican dishes

Useful to Note - Opens very early for your breakfast taco needs; closes early, too.
Menu Suggestions - breakfast tacos - especially, bacon & egg, chicharrones & egg, and chorizo & egg; carne guisada (stewed beef) taco; Beef Plate (carne guisada served with beans, rice and salad); tamales

---

Located on Navigation a few blocks from the original Ninfa's, Villa Arcos has also been serving this east side neighborhood since in the 1970s. Fliers advertising community activities like the local chapter of the Knights of Columbus and events at the nearby Our Lady of Guadalupe are posted near the counter. It's a friendly, family-run, and very informal restaurant that works well for a quick casual meal eaten either in the small, nearly unadorned dining room, or, maybe even more common, taken home, or back to work. The food is straightforward, casual, locally popular Mexican fare such as tacos, tamales, and uncomplicated breakfast and dinner plates.

Breakfast tacos have helped make a name for Villa Arcos. These feature a tasty, housemade fresh flour tortilla of medium thickness sealed around a plentiful amount of moist scrambled eggs and whatever else is chosen as the filling. These are also a great value, and are larger than at most other places. Two tacos will suffice for most, where three might be necessary at other *taquerias*. Most breakfast tacos are around a buck-and-a-half or so. The larger specialty tacos are still less than three bucks. Shredded cheese, not a necessity with these flavorful handfuls, is an additional charge. The spicy green salsa provides very good complement for these and most dishes here. Also good for breakfast are the scrambled egg plates, *migas, a la mexicana, chorizo* and the *huevos rancheros*. In addition to the fabulous breakfast tacos and breakfasts, Villa Arcos has also earned its reputation with its top-notch tamales. These are thick, heavy, and filled with shredded pork, and some of the best commercially produced tamales in town. An order of a half-dozen for around $5 is a great deal. Prepare for a nap afterwards. The "Lunch Tacos" might be quite as tasty as the breakfast tacos, though with a more limited number of choices. The ones with *carne guisada* (stewed beef tips) are excellent. These beef tips are well trimmed and are served in a flavorful brown sauce. The *carne guisada* also comes as a lunch plate with beans, rice and a small salad. Other choices for lunchtime plates are hamburger meat (which sounds tastier as *picadillo*), beef enchiladas, cheese enchiladas, broiled chicken, crispy tacos, and tamales. There is also the Rice Basket, rice and whole beans covered with chili con carne for the *pobrecito* for just a few dollars. Villa Arcos serves *barbacoa* and *menudo* on the weekends. Important to note, you can call ahead, as many patrons do. Everything is prepared to order, otherwise and you might end up waiting for a short while.

* Williams Smokehouse $7

5903 Wheatley (north of Tidwell) 77091, (713) 680-8409

Cuisine - Barbecue
Hours - Tue-Thu 11AM to 8PM; Fri-Sat 11AM to 10PM
Credit Cards - NONE
Service - Counter Service
Alcohol - NONE

Entrée Prices - $6 to $11 ($7 average)
Entrées $12 and less - 100%

Atmosphere & Décor - Spartan, but almost quaint
Appeal - Probably the best ribs in town, plus other very good barbecue
Useful to Note - This is definitely worth the drive.
Menu Suggestions - pork ribs; beef brisket; beef sausage (links); pecan pie

Williams Smokehouse is located in a small, tidy building a bit off the beaten track in the heavily wooded, almost rural, Acres Homes area of north Houston. This is after Ella turns into Wheately just north of Tidwell, a few miles north of the 610 Loop. It is not the area that most would expect to travel for a meal, but it's well worth making the drive. Critics have long made the trip, as Williams Smokehouse is consistently and deservedly rated as one of the very top barbecue joints in the area in the local press. The properly succinct East Texas-style barbecue menu hits the mark, as it has since the 1980s. The pork ribs are probably the biggest claim to fame for Williams Smokehouse. These are fantastic, quite possibly the best in town. A dry rub is applied to the ribs, and then these are slowly cooked for four hours over an oak-fueled fire. This results in ribs that are moist, tender and encased in a crusty exterior. These are succulent, and especially good with the tangy and spicy barbecue sauce. The ribs are cooked so expertly that the meat usually slides easily off the bone. Unlike ribs at most other places, virtually no gnawing is required. The meat can be tougher at the ends, but it will be more tender than elsewhere. If you are rib aficionando, or just a barbecue lover, you owe it to yourself to make the trip to Williams Smokehouse (these are even the favorite ribs of the Chicago-based pop band OK Go, the treadmill video guys). But, ribs are not the only thing done well here. The crumbly beef sausage (or "links") is spicy and savory, as is the more mild-tasting brisket. The usually very tender and flavorful brisket makes for a great, somewhat messy sandwich. Pork sausage is another opton. As with the ribs, the excellent barbecue sauce helps to make all of the meats even tastier. For sides, the heavy and tangy baked beans, and the thin, crisp fries are two of the best sides. The potato salad, though house-made, is somewhat bland. Plates come with a couple of sides, and a couple slices of processed white bread. This makes for a lot of food, and a great value. Unless you are very hungry, it can be tough to finish all the rich, sufficiently smoke-scented and delicious food that comes with a plate. If you can, and you still have room, you should try the excellent and sugary sweet pecan pie. Williams Smokehouse has probably the cleanest dining room of any barbecue establishment in the area. Adorned with polished wood, it is small with less than ten tables inside. There are a few more tables outside when the weather is warm. No matter, much of the business is takeout anyway. But, if you have made the trip from another part of town, it will be difficult to drive very far with such mouth-watering, tempting food in the car.

Wunsche Bros. Cafe $9

103 Midway (in Old Town Spring) Spring, 77373, (281) 350-1902
www.wunschebroscafe.com

Cuisine - Texan
Hours - Mon 11AM to 3PM; Tue-Thu 11AM to 10PM; Fri-Sat 11AM to 11PM; Sun 11AM to 8PM
Credit Cards - Amex, Discover, MC, Visa
Service - Table Service
Alcohol - Beer

Entrée Prices - $7 to $10 ($9 average)
Entrées $12 and less - 100%

Atmosphere & Décor - Comfortable in an attractive old building; can be lively
Appeal - The most inviting restaurant in Old Town Spring
Useful to Note - There is a regular schedule of live music on the weekends.
Menu Suggestions - hamburgers; onion rings

When shopping in Old Town Spring, the most enjoyable stop for a meal, dessert or just a cold beer is at Wunsche Bros. Café. It serves hearty, satisfying and consistently well prepared regional American food in a charming and friendly environment. The attractive building that houses the place dates from 1902 and was originally constructed as a hotel and saloon. It's been in its present guise as a restaurant and a venue for live music since the early 1980s. Probably the best bet here is their tasty, basic, greasy, meaty, grilled burger. The even greasier beer-battered onion rings are a better side to the burgers than the fries. In addition to the burgers, Wunsche Bros. Café is known for its chicken fried steak. There might not be a more attractive chicken fried steak around. It consists of a beautiful dark golden-hued batter encompasing a large slab of beef. Unfortunately, it's not quite as flavorful as it looks, as the batter separated too easily from the meat, and some portions of it might take some effort to cut. Other entrées include a

German Sausage Sandwich, Chicken *Quesadillas*, grilled catfish, chicken tenders, a chicken salad sandwich, ham and turkey sandwiches, Caesar salad with grilled chicken, plus there are daily Blue Plate Specials. There are a couple of salads that might scare a dietician, but fit well on this menu. One features deep-fried chicken tenders on mixed greens, and another gooey, deep-fried pieces of cheese, sausage and sauerkraut that is "recommended with bleu cheese dressing". In additon to the big food, there are eight cakes and pies. There is a fudge cake, key lime pie, coconut cream pie, peach cobbler and several others. The touted Famous Chocolate Whiskey Cake is rich, but rather unremarkable. At Wunsche Bros. Café portions are large, prices are reasonable, and the service is friendly, the setting is interesting and comfortable. Another draw is live music each Tuesday through Saturday. Local boys made good, Lyle Lovett and Clint Black, played here while they were coming up.

Yia Yia Mary's $13

4747 San Felipe (just west of Loop 610) 77056, (713) 840-8665
www.yiayiamarys.com

Cuisine - Greek
Hours - Mon-Thu 11AM to 10PM; Fri-Sat 11AM to 11PM; Sun 11AM to 9PM
Credit Cards - Amex, Diners, Discover, MC, Visa
Service - Table Service
Alcohol - Beer & Wine

Entrée Prices - $7 to $19 ($13 average)
Entrées $12 and less - 50%

Atmosphere & Décor - Comfortable; patio
Appeal - Generally well-made and approachable Greek food; carafes of wine
Useful to Note - The front entrance faces Loop 610.
Menu Suggestions - spanikopita (phyllo pastry filled with feta and spinach); dolmades (grape leaves stuffed with a pork-currant stuffing); Baked Feta; Lamb Chop Appetizer (marinated and broiled lamb chops); Rotisserie-Carved Lamb Sandwich; Gryo Sandwich; Gyro Platter; Chicken Souvlaki; Niki Chocolata (chocolate mousse cake with raspberry and ouzo); baklava

This is the Pappas family's return to their Greek roots. Yia Yia Mary's, which means "Grandma Mary's" is unmistakably a Pappas establishment: large, loud, bold, affable and efficient. This is mostly casual Greek food done in large, gregarious, convenient and family- and group-friendly fashion. The sprawling, high-ceiling, often-buzzing and comfortable dining room is usually crowded during the long lunch hours and most weekend evenings. It's not a fine-dining restaurant, but it would probably work well for a pleasant family meal or a casual date. With many televisions tuned to the local sports teams, it's a good place to dine while not missing the game. The expected Greek dishes are served here suitably well, with robust flavors taking precedence over finesse, and in expected Pappas-size portions. Wine, an integral part of the Greek diet, is made easily available. There is a short wine list with two dozen Greek and New World wines ranging in general drinkability from *retsina* to one of California's better merlots, Shafer. A dozen are served by the glass and even more are served by the easily refillable carafe (750 ml, the same size of a bottle, but it's cheaper).

The grill gets a workout here, with its lamb, beef, chicken, and shrimp items. The fairly lengthy menu is divided among appetizers, salads and soups, pita sandwiches, *souvlaki,* rotisserie and *souvlaki* combinations, a handful of Greek specialties such as *moussaka,* seafood, sides and nearly ten desserts. There are over twenty appetizers, much more than just *domaldes* (stuffed grape leaves), *spanikopita* (phyllo pastry filled with spinach and feta), *keftedes* (meatballs in tomato sauce) and the flaming cheese. Though Yia Yia Mary's is not a cheap restaurant, a big appetizer, pita sandwich that's served with crisp fries, or a salad can make for a satisfying and affordable meal. The Greek Salad is decent, though the ingredients are probably too coarsely cut and chopped, and more so, the unexpected presence of briny capers can be distracting. The *souvlaki,* cubes of grilled beef are juicy and fairly tender, but not as seasoned and as flavorful as these should be. The lamb in its several guises is better. Though the local favorite shrimp gets the most various treatments, there are also entrées featuring salmon, redfish, mahi mahi and rainbow trout, often with fresh oregano, garlic, lemon and olive oil. If you have room, there is a rich and unique chocolate mousse cake and well-made baklava featuring walnuts. To note, for groups from three to ten and maybe more, Yia Yia Mary's has bountiful multi-course family dinners.

Yo' Mama's Soul Food $8

5332 Antoine (between Pinemont and Tidwell) 77091, (713) 680-8002

Cuisine - Soul Food; Barbecue
Hours - Mon, Sun 12 to 6PM; Tue-Sat 11AM to 9PM
Credit Cards - Amex, Diners, Discover, MC, Visa
Service - Counter Service
Alcohol - Beer & Wine

Entrée Prices - $5 to $10 ($8 average)
Entrées $12 and less - 100%

Atmosphere & Décor - Spartan
Appeal - Honest food for cheap; a lot of calories for the buck
Useful to Note - The Yo' Papa's Barbecue trailer is also worth visiting.

Menu Suggestions - meatloaf; smothered steak; steamed corn; seafood gumbo; beef brisket sandwich; German chocolate cake

---

"Yo' Mama's" might be the answer to this one, as this humble steam table operation serves up some of best soul food in town. Not only that, Yo' Mama's provides one of the best ratios for calories to the dollar on the Houston dining scene. Most people will be amply filled after finishing, or nearly finishing, one of the reasonably priced and very copious, plates served cafeteria-style. The tasty and value-laden food is combined with service that is always very friendly and efficient. Yo' Mama's is a fairly small and welcoming place. This might be the most accessible local soul food place.

The most popular orders begin as the Regular Meal and the Big Meal. The former includes a choice of one slice or piece of a meat dish plus three vegetables and cornbread muffins. The Big Meal is the same as the Regular Meal, but with two slices or pieces instead of one. Unless you are very hungry, or really huge, the Regular Meal will usually satisfy. The steam table items change daily and include most of the locally popular soul food and Creole offerings. Three of the highlights are the meatloaf, smothered steak, and the seafood-rich, hearty gumbo that will satisfy most Louisiana natives. The flavorful meatloaf is made with ground beef and served in a tomato-based sauce. The fried steak is sufficiently covered in a heavy dressing. Other worthwhile centerpieces include oxtails, smothered steaks, chitterlings (pig intestines), pig's feet, turkey necks, and smothered pork chops. The vegetable choices include black-eye peas, corn, white rice, pinto beans, and different greens. The steamed corn is especially good, surprisingly crisp and light. The rice is moist, and a perfect accompaniment to most of the entrées and the beans. The related operation, Yo' Papa's Barbecue that resides in a trailer in the parking lot, and serves in the restaurant during the week, does a very commendable job with East Texas-style barbecue. The brisket sandwich, featuring plenty of excellent, tender brisket barely fitting between two thick slices of toast, is worthy of a trip itself. If you have room for dessert, or just a big sweet tooth, Yo' Mama's is justifiably proud of their moist and mostly decadent cakes, served in generous-sized portions: raspberry; strawberry; Italian cream; coconut-pineapple; Sock-it-to-Me; chocolate; 7-Up; lemon; and German chocolate. The restaurant is situated in a somewhat forlorn strip center, which hopefully won't deter a visit. It walls are painted in a mauve color and are decorated with framed posters of several icons of the African-American community such as: Malcolm X, Billie Holiday, MLK, Earl "Fatha" Hines, JFK, Nelson Mandela and Buckwheat. Unless you like waiting in line, avoid mid-Sunday afternoon, as it can get very crowded after the church services finish.

Yorktown Deli & Coffee $6

2301 Yorktown (between San Felipe and Westheimer) 77056, (713) 552-0936

Cuisine - Sandwiches; Argentine
Hours - Mon-Fri 10AM to 4PM; Sat 10:30AM to 4PM
Credit Cards - Amex, MC, Visa
Service - Counter Service
Alcohol - NONE

Entrée Prices - $3 to $7 ($6 average)
Entrées $12 and less - 100%

Atmosphere & Décor - Spartan
Appeal - Friendly, tasty and cheap
Useful to Note - There's additional parking in back.
Menu Suggestions - Reuben Zinni Sandwich; empanadas

Though primarily serving the nearby office buildings, Yorktown Deli & Coffee is far more than a stop for busy workers to replenish calories. Due to the quality and value of the quick and casual fare, and the frendliness of the family that runs the place, it seems to have become part of the weekly routine for many people who work within walking distance. The offerings at Yorktown Deli are mostly familiar, but are interesting and possibly healthier takes on the soups, salads, and hot and cold sandwiches. Many have the readily likeable, straightforward Argentine-Italian flavors. There are also some tasty Argentine specialties like *empanadas* and *provelettas* (an Argentine-style grilled cheese sandwich). For a low price of a sandwich, usually around five dollars and less, you also receive a salad, and a choice among cole slaw, chips, pasta salad, and a fruit plate. There are over a dozen hot and cold sandwiches that are served daily, plus the occasional special. As with the other items, the sandwiches are slightly smaller than average, but are served with a choice of breads, white, wheat, French, rye or a croissant in customer-friendly fashion. One of the best is the Reuben Zinni with corned beef, sauerkraut and Swiss cheese. Other hot sandwiches include pastrami, a tuna melt, grilled cheese, chicken melt and roast beef. The cold sandwiches are the familiar chicken salad, tuna salad, ham and cheese, club, turkey, BLT, and a couple others featuring avocado. The sides are far more than the afterthought that they are at most humble sandwich shops. The side salads consist of a small collection of mixed greens, none of which are iceberg lettuce, tossed with a housemade light vinaigrette. The pasta salad of cold *fusilli* (corkscrew-shaped) pasta is loaded with plenty of spicy black pepper, and is the best choice among this, cole slaw and packaged chips, though the cole slaw is quite good and the fruit is fresh, too. For big appetites, an *empanada* might be worth an order in addition to the sandwich. For lighter appetites, there are several salads, each available with chicken breast for an additional dollar.

Befitting a place that has "Coffee" in the name, Yorktown Deli serves a very good daily drip coffee, and the many versions of the *espresso*-based drinks like *cappuccinos,* and *lattes.* Useful during the long summer months are iced and frozen *cappuccino* drinks. Unfortunately, like nearly every restaurant in this country, the *espresso* here is a far cry from what is served in Italy. But, you can get that gaucho favorite, *yerba maté* by the cup. Though nearly hidden behind a stairway in a small strip center on Yorktown, it is not too far south of San Felipe, in the midst of a neighborhood that somehow successfully incorporates tall office buildings. The amiability of the casual and quaint (it only seats about a dozen) Yorktown Deli makes this two-story retail complex a bit more inviting to newcomers. Even if not within strolling distance during the day, you should consider making a drive to Yorktown Deli for a good value and inexpensive lunch.

Zabak's $9

5901 Westheimer (at Fountain View) 77057, (713) 977-7676

Cuisine - Middle Eastern
Hours - Mon-Sat 11AM to 8PM
Credit Cards - Amex, Diners, Discover, MC, Visa
Alcohol - Beer & Wine
Service - Counter Service

Entrée Prices - $6 to $11 ($9 average)
Entrées $12 and less - 100%

Atmosphere & Décor - Functional, but pleasant and friendly
Appeal - Very good, casual Middle Eastern food in friendly small setting
Useful to Note - This is another one good for take-away.
Menu Suggestions - hummus; baba ganoush; Beef Shawarma Plate; Beef Shawarma Sandwich; namoura (flaky semolina pastry with syrup)

Cheerful and easy-to-like Zabak's is a great place in the Briagrove area for a well-made, quick and informal Middle Eastern food. The focused menu serves most of the casual eastern Mediterranean dishes that have become popular in Houston. There are succinct descriptions for each dish to help the uninitiated, who probably won't remain so for long. There is beer and wine, unlike restaurants of similar cuisine and caliber on nearby Hillcroft. *Hummus, tabouli,* spinach pies, Greek and Caesar salads are some of the starters and salads, beef and chicken *shawarmas,* gyros, kabobs and *falafel* (deep-fried patty of chickpeas and parsley) in plate and pita sandwich form make up most of the heartier fare. For every preparation, the ingredients are noticeably top quality and suitably fresh and ripe, and the resulting flavors are appropriately clean-tasting. The beef *shawarma,* one of the highlights is cooked in a unique fashion here, which works well. It begins with thinly sliced beef that is marinated and then cooked on a flat grill. The resulting beef is crisper than usual, and seems to mix even better with the onions and zesty *tahini* sauce. For beef-loving Houston, the *kafta* kabob here is made solely with ground beef rather than with lamb or a lamb and beef mixture, as at some other local places. The kabobs, served solely as plates, include versions with sirloin and chicken breast, and are skewered and grilled with tomatoes, onions and red and green bell peppers. These come with a choice of sides and pita bread. The *shawarmas, falafel* and *kafta* sandwiches are served with shredded lettuce, chopped tomatoes, *tahini* sauce and the mildly fruity and astringent spice sumac. There is also a gyro and Chicken Caesar Pita plus the heart-healthy *hummus* and *tabouli* combination. For the sweet tooth or as reward for eating healthier than usual, Zabak's not only has *baklava,* but also a good version of *namoura* and appealing White and Dark Chocolate Mousse Cake and Carrot Cake made with pineapple, walnuts and cream cheese icing.

Zydeco $8

1119 Pease (at San Jacinto) 77002, (713) 759-2001
910 Travis (Tunnel - at Walker) 77002, (713) 759-0404
1300 Broadway (east of Dixie Farm) Pearland, 77581, (281) 648-6500
www.zydecodiner.com

Cuisine - Cajun
Hours - Pease - Mon-Fri 11AM to 2PM (Tue-Fri 4:30 to 9PM from February to June); Travis - Mon-Fri 11AM to 2PM; Pearland - Mon-Wed 4 to 9:30PM; Thu-Fri 4 to 11PM; Sat 12 to 11PM; Sun 12 to 9PM
Credit Cards - Amex, Diners, Discover, MC, Visa
Service - Pease & Travis - Counter Service; Pearland - Table Service
Alcohol - Beer & Wine

Entrée Prices - $6 to $8 ($8 average)
Entrées $12 and less - 100%

Atmosphere & Décor - Spartan, but fitting
Appeal - Often delicious Cajun food downtown and Pearland
Useful to Note - At times, live music (zydeco, of course) at the Pease location.
Menu Suggestions - Chicken and Sausage Creole; Shrimp and Crab Étouffée; Chicken and Sausage Jambalaya; mashed potatoes; Chicken and Sausage Gumbo; fried shrimp; Maque Choux (creamed corn); bread pudding

Zydeco serves very tasty Cajun food in a couple of locations downtown and more recently, south in Pearland. The three restaurants support the sobriquets Louisiana Diner in a stand-alone structure on Pease, Louisiana

Joint in the tunnel and Louisiana Kitchen in Pearland; each seems appropriate for their address. The Pearland location has somewhat of a sports bar atmosphere, and is open just in the evening during the week. In an area of downtown that has still yet to be refurbished, the Pease location, opened since 1988, is somewhat dumpy, fitting for a Cajun food place. Though décor is not a high point at any of the locations, Zydeco is an informal and hospitable place to enjoy well-made, honest and zesty regional cooking on a nearby picnic bench with a cold beer or two and a group of friends. And, if that is not appealing, it is just as easy to get an order to go. The second location downtown is nicer, if more sterile, in the tunnels below the intersection of Travis and Walker, below the Bank One Building.

As the menu states Zydeco's food is southern Louisiana home cooking, served cafeteria-style. It is a steam table operation for most of the entrées. This is actually the best way to serve most of these dishes, as these are inherently stew-like in nature. The entrées change daily, and some, like the crawfish dishes, are just served seasonally. The featured steam table items are from a southern Louisiana culinary hit parade: Crawfish Étouffée, Shrimp and Crab Étouffée, Chicken and Sausage Creole, Chicken and Sausage Jambalaya, Snapper Creole, Fried Catfish Shrimp and Crab *Sauce Piquanté* (a spicy, stew-like dish), Stuffed Pork Chops with Jambalaya, Chicken Fricassee (a rich, buttery stew), Seafood *Courtbouillon* (seafood stew in a tomato sauce), and Baked Chicken. At least four of these are served each day, and cost between $6 and $8 and are served with two vegetables and cornbread. One of the best entrées is the Chicken and Sausage Creole. It is made with andouille sausage and steamed chicken in a spicy, somewhat heavy, tomato sauce. Most of the dishes with chicken and sausage are very good, and the seafood and crawfish dishes are no slouches either. The choices for the accompanying vegetable sides can be the creamed corn *maque choux*, garlic mashed potatoes, green beans, black-eyed peas, okra and tomatoes and broccoli. The mashed potatoes and corn are especially pleasing. One of the daily steam table items should be appealing, but if you crave another Cajun specialty or need a starter, Zydeco should be able to comply. Gumbos with shrimp or chicken and sausage, and red beans and rice are served in both cup and bowls. Served with cornbread or crackers, the decent-sized bowls can make for a meal. Other everyday items include fried seafood platters, po boys, a couple salads, and stuffed shrimp and crab. The fried platters are served with jambalaya and fries plus a choice among shrimp, oysters and catfish. Combinations of two or three are available if you have a tough time choosing just one. The classic New Orleans-style po boys are available also with fried shrimp, oysters or catfish. If you have room for dessert, their bread pudding is topped with a custard rum sauce and flecked with cinnamon for some more delicious calories.

Selected recommendations, selected eateries

Below is a selected list of recommended dishes from restaurants that are profiled in this guidebook plus ones listed in the aside, "25 a little too expensive for this guidebook". These more expensive restaurants are in italics. This list might not necessarily contain the best of each dish in the city, though it might be, and likely on the lower end of the price spectrum.

- ***baba ganoush*** - Café Pita+, Shawarma King, Zabak's
- **bagels** - New York Coffee Shop, Katz's, Kenny & Ziggy's
- ***barbacoa*** - Noemi's Tacos, Laredo Taqueria, El Hidalguense, Taqueria Del Sol, Taqueria Cancun
- **beef brisket** - see "Cuisine Guide" under "Barbecue" on page 457
- **beer selection** - Red Lion, Mucky Duck, *Café Montrose*
- **biscuits and gravy** - Lankford Grocery, Breakfast Klub, Frank's Grill
- **boiled crawfish** - *Mardi Gras Grill*, Ragin Cajun, *Floyd's Cajun Seafood*
- **boudin** - Maxey's Cajun Patio & Grill, Burt's Meat Market
- **breakfast tacos** - La Guadalupana, Porras, Villas Arcos, El Taquito Rico, Taqueria La Flor, Frank's Grill, Fiesta Tacos, Sunrise Taquitos, Porras
- **burritos** - Mission Burritos, Taqueria Arandas
- ***cabrito*** - Casa Grande, Cadillac Bar, El Hidalguense
- **calzones** - Ponzo's, Romano's
- ***carne guisada*** - Noemi's Tacos, Porras, Villa Arcos
- ***ceviche*** - Lemon Tree, Tampico, Ostioneria Puerto Vallarta, Mambo Seafood
- **cheesesteak** - Market Square Bar & Grill, Sandwich King, Texas Cheesesteaks
- **chicken fried steak** - Hickory Hollow, *Clementine's*, Armadillo Palace, Barbecue Inn, *Rudi Lechner's*
- **chicken *tikka masala*** - *Ashiana*, Himalaya, Mayuri, Gourmet India
- **Chinese dumplings** - San Dong Noodle House, Dumpling King, Doozo
- **desserts** - Ruggles Café Bakery, Empire Café, Paulie's
- **dim sum** - *Fung's Kitchen*, Kim Son (Stafford), Golden Palace, Ocean Palace
- **duck** - Goode Co. Barbecue, Sinh Sinh
- ***empanadas*** - Marini's, Marine's, Manena's, Yorktown Deli
- **fajitas** - Ninfa's (Original), Don Carlos, Lupe Tortilla, *El Tiempo, Santos*
- **fish tacos** - Berryhill Baja Grill, Cabo
- **fish and chips** - Red Lion, Mucky Duck
- **French fries** - *Café Montrose, Café Rabelais,* Goode Co. Taqueria, Niko Niko's
- **French toast** - Buffalo Grille, Breakfast Klub, Dot Coffee Shop
- **fried chicken** - Frenchy's, Henderson Chicken Shack, Spanish Village

- **fried shrimp** - Barbecue Inn, Kanomwan, Jasmine Asian Cuisine
- **frog legs** - Tampico, Cadillac Bar
- **goulash** - *Rudi Lechner's*, Polonia
- **green chicken curry** - Vieng Thai, Kanomwan, Thai Gourmet
- **gumbo** - *Mardi Gras Grill*, Ragin Cajun, *Floyd's Cajun Seafood*
- **gyros** - Niko Niko's, Andros Deli, Manny's Café
- **hamburgers** - see "Cuisine Guide" under "Hamburgers" on page 458
- **hot dogs** - Goode Co. Taqueria
- ***hummus*** - Jerusalem Halal Deli, Rita's Café, Fadi's Mediterranean Grill, Zabak's, Istanbul Grill, Phoenicia Deli, Café Pita+
- **Imperial rolls** - Saigon Pagaloc, Jasmine Asian Cuisine
- **lamb** - Niko Niko's, Bibas, Kasra, *Khyber, Rudi Lechner's*
- **lasagna** - Mandola's Deli, Giannotti's
- **linguini (or spaghetti) and clams** - *Perbacco*, Dolce Vita
- **margaritas** - *Pico's*, Spanish Village, Ninfa's (Original), *Santos*
- **Mexican breakfasts** - Goode Co. Taqueria, Gorditas Aguascalientes, Teotihuacan, La Mexicana, Jarro Café, Taqueria La Flor
- ***mole poblano*** - Otilias, La Mexicana, *Pico's*, Romero's Las Brazas, La Guadalupana
- **onion rings** - Maxey's Cajun Patio & Grill, Texas Cheesesteaks, Katz's, Pappas Burgers
- **pad Thai** - Vieng Thai, Thai Gourmet, Kanomwan
- **pancakes** - Buffalo Grille, New York Coffee Shop, Frank's Grill
- **pastries** - French Riviera Bakery & Café, Kraftsmen Baking, La Madeleine
- ***pho*** - Pho Danh, Pho Saigon, Tau Bay, Pho One, Jasmine Asian Cuisine
- ***pierogis*** - Polonia
- **pizza** - see "Cuisine Guide" under "Pizza" on page 460
- **pork chops** - Niko Niko's, Buffalo Grille
- **pork ribs** - Williams Smokehouse, Pizzitola, Pappas Barbecue
- **quail** - Teotihuacan, Cadillac Bar
- **red beans and rice** - Treebeards, Frenchy's, *Mardi Gras Grill*
- **reuben** - Kahn's, Katz's
- **rotisserie chicken** - Pollo Riko, El Rey, La Madeleine
- **sandwiches (cold)** - Antone's, Kojak's, Brown Bag Deli, Ponzo's
- **sandwiches (hot)** - Paulie's, Katz's, Kahn's, Giannotti's, Mexico's Deli, 100% Taquito, Panini
- ***shawarma*** - Jerusalem Halal Deli, Shawarma King, Phoenicia Deli, Zabak's
- **shrimp po boy** - Ragin Cajun
- **soup** - *Bayou City Seafood n' Pasta*, La Madeleine, *Mardi Gras Grill*, Jasmine Asian Cuisine, Kanomwan
- **spaghetti and meatballs** - *Perbacco*, Fratelli's, Giannotti's, Romano's, Pronto Cucinino

- **sushi** - see "Some reliable stops for sushi" aside on page 307
- **tamales** - Texas Tamale Co., Doña Tere, Villa Arcos
- ***thit nuong*** - Taydo, Thu Thu, Saigon Pagolac, Kim Son
- ***tres leches*** - Amazon Grill, 100% Taquito
- **Vietnamese sandwiches** - Hoang Son, Don Café, Thanh Noi, Givral, Les Givral, Lee's Sandwiches, Cali
- **wine selection** - *El Meson, Café Rabelais,* Dolce Vita, *divino*

Cuisine Guide

The restaurants are listed by main cuisine, but can be in more than one category.

There are listings for "Mexican" and "Tex-Mex". The differences in the food between the two can be slight, as these restaurants share many of the same dishes, and even every local taqueria serves at least a few Tex-Mex items. Though the classifications are less than perfect, I thought a distinction might be helpful for the purposes of this guide since these restaurants are generally different in feel and style. This is why "Mexican" is further divided between "restaurante" and "taqueria". Both "Italian" and "Italian-American" are also used, but this refers more to the level of authenticity of the cooking.

+ - More than one cuisine is served; these are listed under at least two headings.
★ - This restaurant is highly recommended.

American
Baba Yega
Barnaby's Café
Black Walnut Café
Brasil
Buffalo Grille
Café Artiste
Café Express
Café Mezza & Grille +
Daily Grind
Edloe Street Delicatessen
Empire Café
★ Goode Co. Taqueria +
Hobbit Café +
Java Java Café
Kojak's Timberbrook Café
McGonigel's Mucky Duck +
The Memorial Grill
Rudyard's
Ruggles Café Bakery
Rustika Café +
Sandy's Markets

Argentine / Uruguayan
Giannotti's +
Manena's Pastry Shop & Deli +
Marine's Empanadas +
Marini's Empanada House
Yorktown Deli & Coffee +

Barbecue
Baker's Ribs
Barbecue Inn +
Burns Bar BQ
★ Goode Co. Barbecue
Guy's Meat Market +
Hickory Hollow +
Houston Barbecue Company
Luling City Market Bar-B-Q
Lyndon's Pit Bar-B-Q
The Nickel Grill +
Nonmacher's Bar-B-Que
Pappas Bar-B-Q
Pizzitola Bar B Cue
Thelma's Bar-B-Que
★ Williams Smokehouse
Yo' Mama's Soul Food +

Bolivian
The Grill of the Andes

Bosnian
Café Pita+

Brazilian
Emporio

Café / Bakery
Chez Beignets
Dacapo's Café
French Riviera Bakery & Café +
Kraftsmen Baking
La Madeleine
Manena's Pastry Shop & Deli +
Rustika Café +

Cajun
Abe's Cajun Market

Burt's Meat Market +
Frenchy's +
Maxey's Cajun Patio & Grill +
Ragin Cajun
Treebeards +
Zydeco

Caribbean
Caribbean Cuisine
Reggae Hut

Chinese
Café Chino
Central China
China Garden
Chinese Café
Daniel Wong's Kitchen
Doozo Noodles & Dumplings
Dumpling King
Golden Palace
Hollywood +
Hunan Plus
Jade Village
Jasmine Asian Cuisine +
Kam's Fine Chinese Cuisine
Kim Son +
Lucky Pot
Mak Chin's +
Ocean Palace
Peking Cuisine
San Dong Noodle House
Shanghai
Sichuan Cuisine
Sinh Sinh +
Tan Tan +

Colombian
Colombian Cuisine
La Fogata
Marine's Empanadas +
Pollo Riko

Cuban
Café Piquet

Deli
Kahn's Deli
Katz's
Kenny & Ziggy's
New York Coffee Shop
Victor's Delicatessen

Diner
Avalon Diner
Bibas Greek Restaurant +
Dot Coffee Shop
Fountain View Café
Frank's Grill
Mama's Café

Ethiopian
Addisaba
Blue Nile

Fried Chicken
Frenchy's +
Henderson's Chicken Shack

Guatemalan
Guatemala
Lo Nuestro

Greek
Andros Deli +
Bibas Greek Pizza +
Bibas Greek Restaurant +
Manny's Café
Niko Niko's
Paw Paw's +
Yia Yia Mary's

Hamburgers
Adrian's Burger Bar +
Bellaire Broiler Burger
Cahill's on Durham
Champ Burger
Christian's Tailgate Bar & Grill
Guy's Meat Market +
Lankford Grocery
Kenneally's Irish Pub +
★ Market Square Bar & Grill
Maxey's Cajun Patio & Grill +
Pappas Burger
Southwell's Hamburger Grill
Tookie's

Indian
Bombay Sweets +
Gourmet India
Madras Pavilion +
Masala Wok
Mayuri
Pavani

Irish / British

McGonigel's Mucky Duck +
Red Lion

Italian

* Dolce Vita +
Fratelli's
Nundini Deli +

Italian-American

Antonio's Flying Pizza +
D'Amico's Italian Market Café
Giannotti's +
Mandola's Deli +
Palazzo's +
Paulie's +
Pronto Cucinino
Romano's +

Japanese

Nippon

Malaysian

Café Malay

Mexican (restaurante)

Berryhill Baja Grill
Casa Grande
El Hidalguense
El Paraiso
El Pueblito
Fiesta en Guadalajara
Fonda Doña Maria
Lila's
Maria Selma's
Mucho Mexico
Ostioneria Puerto Vallarta +
* Otilia's
Romero's Las Brazas
Taco Milagro
Tampico +
Teotihuacan

Mexican (taqueria)

Altamirano
Casa De Leon
Doña Tere Tamales
El Rey Taqueria
El Tapatio
El Taquito Rico
Gorditas Aguascalientes
Houston Tamale Company
Jarro Café
La Guadalupana Bakery & Café
La Tapatia Taqueria
Laredo Taqueria
Las Llardas
Los Dos Amigos
Mambo Parilla
Mambo Seafood +
Mexico's Deli
* Noemi's Tacos
* 100% Taquito
Ostioneria Arandas +
Porras
Sunrise Taquitos
Tacos del Julio
Taqueria Arandas
Taqueria Cancun
Taqueria Del Sol
Taqueria El Herradero
Taqueria La Flor
Taqueria Mexico
Sunrise Taquitos
Villa Arcos

Middle Eastern

Aladdin
Café Lili
Dimassi's Mediterranean Buffet
Droubi's
Fadi's Mediterranean Grill
Jerusalem Halal Deli
Mary'z
Mint Café
Phoenicia Deli
Rita's Café
Shawarma King
Zabak's

Pakistani

* Himalaya
La Sani
Royal
Savoy

Pan Asian

Bamboo House
Mak Chin's +

Pan Latin

Amazon Grill
* Café Red Onion

Persian
Bijan Persian Grill
Café Caspian
Darband Shishkabob
Kasra Persian Grill
Paw Paw's +

Peruvian
Lemon Tree

Pizza
Antonio's Flying Pizza +
Barry's Pizza & Italian Diner
Bibas Greek Pizza +
Candelari's Pizzeria
Collina's
* Dolce Vita +
* Kenneally's Irish Pub +
Palazzo's +
Panini +
Pizza Bella
Ponzo's +
Romano's +
Star Pizza

Polish
Polonia

Puerto Rican
Tex Chick

Salvadoran
El Pupusodromo
Los Ranchitos

Sandwiches
Andros Deli +
Antone's Import Co.
Brown Bag Deli
Busy Boy Sandwiches
Cali +
Carter & Cooley Co.
Don Café Sandwich +
French Riviera Bakery & Café +
Giannotti's +
Givral Hoang Sandwiches +
Hoang Son +
Lee's Sandwiches +
Leibman's Wine & Fine Foods
Les Givral's +
Mandola's Deli +
The Nickel Grill +
Nielsen's Delicatessen
Nundini Deli +
Panini +
Paulie's +
Ponzo's +
Sandwich King Deli & Grill
Texas Cheesesteaks
Thanh Noi Sandwich Shop +
Yorktown Deli & Coffee +

Seafood
Connie's Seafood House
Fountainview Fish Market
Mambo Seafood +
Ostioneria Arandas +
Ostioneria Puerto Vallarta +
Tampico +

Soul Food
Adrian's Burger Bar +
Burt's Meat Market +
This Is It
Yo' Mama's Soul Food +

Texan / Southern
Armadillo Palace
Barbecue Inn +
Breakfast Klub
Hickory Hollow +
Jax Grill
Treebeards +
Wunsche Bros. Café

Tex-Mex
Cabo
Cadillac Bar
Chacho's
Chuy's
Don Carlos
El Patio
Fiesta Tacos
* Goode Co. Taqueria +
La Escondida
La Hacienda
La Mexicana
Lopez
Los Gallitos
Lupe Tortilla's
Mission Burritos
* Ninfa's (Original location)
Poblanos
Rustika Café +
Santa Fe Flats (close enough)

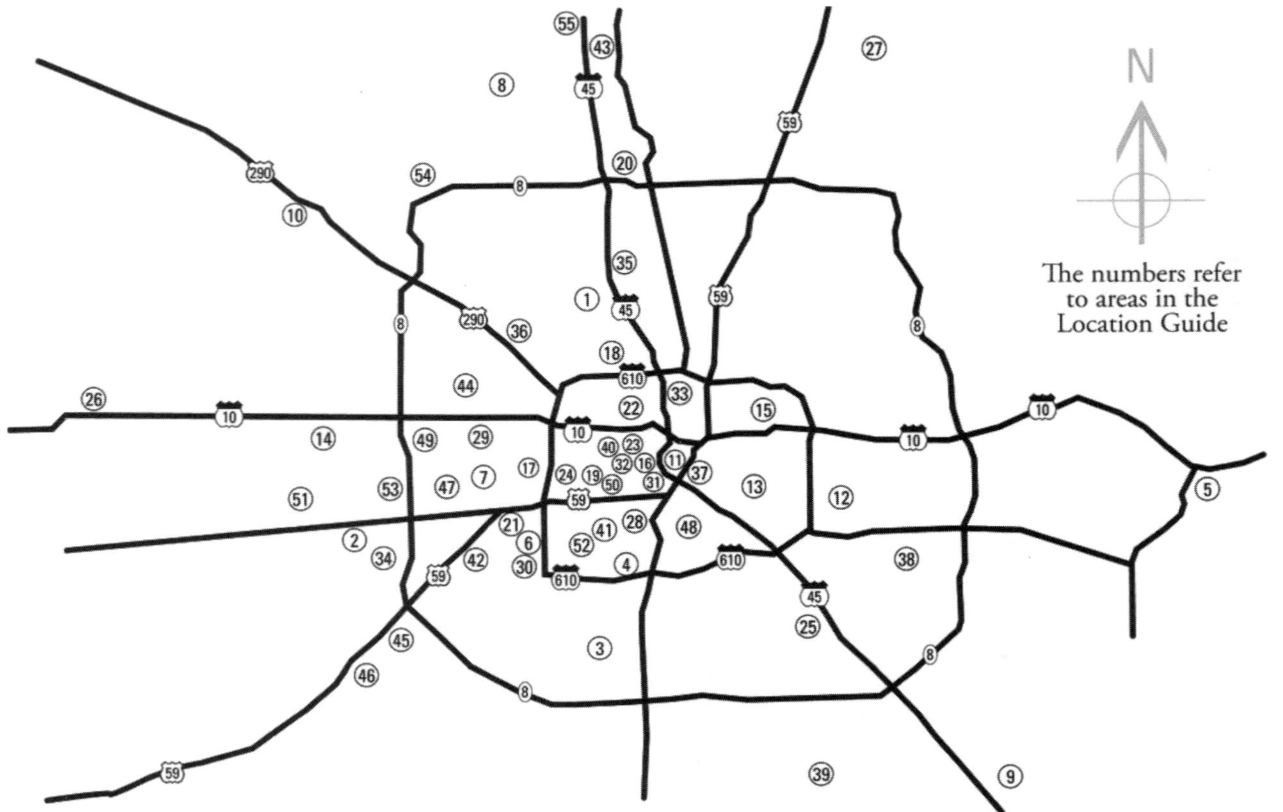
N
The numbers refer
to areas in the
Location Guide

Location Guide

The number after the name of the neighborhood refers to an area on the map on the preceding page.

+ - Indicates that this restaurant has more than one location.
★ - This restaurant is highly recommended.

Acres Homes - 1
Burns Bar BQ
Frenchy's +
★ Williams Smokehouse

Alief - 2
Doña Tere Tamales +
La Fogata
Lopez
Pollo Riko +
Royal
Savoy
Sunrise Taquitos +

Almeda - 3
Frenchy's +
Maxey's Cajun Patio & Grill

Astrodome / Reliant - 4
Antone's Import Co. +
Dimassi's Mediterranean Buffet +
Guy's Meat Market
Pappas Bar-B-Q +
Taqueria Arandas +

Baytown - 5
Taqueria Arandas +

Bellaire - 6
Bellaire Broiler Burger
Candelari's Pizzeria +
Daniel Wong's Kitchen
Jax Grill +
Thai Cottage +

Briargrove - 7
Antonio's Flying Pizza +
Baker's Ribs
Barry's Pizza +
Buffalo Grille +
Café Express +
Café Lili
Café Mezza & Grille
Chacho's
Droubi's +
Dumpling King
El Hidalguense +
El Patio +
Fountain View Café
Fountainview Fish Market
Guatemala
Jerusalem Halal Deli
La Madeleine +
Mama's Café
Marine's Empanadas & Bakery
Mary'z
Mayuri
Nit Noi +
Palazzo's +
Pappas Burger
Shawarma King
Southwell's Hamburger Grill +
Thai Restaurant
Vietnam Coast
Yorktown Deli & Coffee
Zabak's

Champions - 8
Berryhill Baja Grill +
Café Express +
El Pupusodromo +
La Madeleine +
La Tapatia Taqueria +
Nit Noi +
Pappas Bar-B-Q (2) +
Pho Danh +
Taqueria Arandas +
Tubtim Siam
Victor's Delicatessen

Clear Lake - 9
Abe's Cajun Market
Café Express +
La Madeleine +

Lupe Tortilla's +
Pappas Bar-B-Q +
Taco Milagro +
Taqueria Arandas +
Thai Cottage +
Tookie's

Copperfield - 10

La Hacienda +
La Madeleine +
Manny's Café
Pho Saigon +
Romero's Las Brazas
Taqueria Arandas +

Downtown - 11

Cabo
Café Express +
China Garden
Dimassi's Mediterranean Buffet +
Doozo Noodles & Dumplings
El Rey Taqueria +
Kim Son +
Les Givral's
★ Market Square Bar & Grill
Panini
Pappas Bar-B-Q (2) +
Ragin Cajun +
Treebeards (4) +
Zydeco (2) +

East / Galena Park - 12

Ostioneria Arandas +
Taqueria Arandas (2) +

East End - 13

Champ Burger
Connie's Seafood House +
Don Carlos +
Fiesta Loma Linda
Frank's Grill +
★ Kanomwan
Mambo Parilla
Mandola's Deli
Mucho Mexico
★ Ninfa's (Original location)
Ostioneria Puerto Vallarta
Taqueria Arandas +
Thelma's Bar-B-Que
Villa Arcos

Energy Corridor - 14

★ Café Red Onion +
Dimassi's Mediterranean Buffet +
Houston Barbecue Company
La Hacienda +
Leibman's Wine & Fine Foods
Lemon Tree
Lupe Tortilla's +
The Memorial Grill
Mexico's Deli
Rita's Café
Romano's +
Sandy's Markets
Taqueria Arandas +

Fifth Ward/Denver Harbor - 15

Adrian's Burger Bar
Burt's Meat Market
The Nickel Grill
Porras
Taqueria Arandas +

Fourth Ward - 16

This is It

Galleria / Uptown - 17

Berryhill Baja Grill +
Café Express +
Chinese Café +
Dimassi's Mediterranean Buffet +
Erawan
French Riviera Bakery & Café
Kenny & Ziggy's
La Madeleine +
La Tapatia Taqueria +
Miguelito's
Mint Café
Thai Gourmet
Yia Yia Mary's

Garden Oaks - 18

Barbecue Inn
El Rey Taqueria +
El Tapatio

Greenway Plaza - 19

Collina's +
Thai Cottage +

Greenspoint / IAH - 20

Lupe Tortilla's +
Pappas Bar-B-Q +

Taqueria Arandas +

Gulfton - 21

Café Piquet
Don Carlos +
Droubi's +
El Pupusodromo +
Gorditas Aguascalientes +
La Tapatia Taqueria +
Mambo Seafood +
Taqueria Mexico +

Heights (north of I-10) - 22

Berryhill Baja Grill +
Carter & Cooley Co.
Collina's +
Dacapo's Café
Houston Tamale Company
Java Java Café
Kojak's Timberbrook Café
Nundini Deli
Taqueria Arandas +
Thai Spice
Tony's Mexican

Heights (south of I-10) - 23

Cadillac Bar
Cahill's on Durham
Daily Grind
El Rey Taqueria +
Hickory Hollow +
Jax Grill +
Laredo Taqueria +
Mak Chin's
Mission Burritos +
Pizzitola Bar B Cue
Star Pizza +
Taqueria La Flor
Terlingua +

Highland Village - 24

Luling City Market Bar-B-Q
Nielsen's Delicatessen +
Ragin Cajun +

Hobby / Almeda Mall - 25

Connie's Seafood House +
Don Carlos +
Dot Coffee Shop
Frank's Grill
La Tapatia Taqueria +
* Noemi's Tacos
Pappas Bar-B-Q (2) +
Pho Saigon +
Taqueria Arandas +
Taqueria Del Sol
Taqueria El Herradero +
Taqueria Mexico +

Katy - 26

Candelari's Pizzeria +
Marini's Empanada House
Nonmacher's Bar-B-Que
Pho Saigon +
Pizza Bella
Taqueria Arandas +
Tony's Mexican +

Kingwood / Humble - 27

Berryhill Baja Grill +
La Madeleine +
Pappas Bar-B-Q +
Taqueria Arandas (2) +

Medical Center / Rice U - 28

Café Express +
Morningside Thai
Paulie's +
Pronto Cucinino +
Reggae Hut
Southwell's Hamburger Grill +
Spanish Village

Memorial - 29

Collina's +
* Goode Co. Barbecue +
Southwell's Hamburger Grill +

Meyerland - 30

Café Express +
Collina's +
Fadi's Mediterranean Grill +
La Madeleine +
New York Coffee Shop
Poblanos

Midtown - 31

Breakfast Klub
Cali
Christian's Tailgate Bar & Grill +
El Patio +
Les Givral's
Mai's
Pho Saigon +

Ponzo's
Van Loc

Montrose - 32

Aladdin
Baba Yega
Bamboo House
Barnaby's Café (2½) +
Berryhill Baja Grill +
Bibas Greek Restaurant
Brasil
Café Artiste
Café Express +
* Dolce Vita
El Paraiso
El Pueblito
Golden Room
Hollywood
Kam's Fine Chinese Cuisine
Katz's +
Kraftsmen Baking
La Guadalupana Bakery & Café
La Madeleine +
La Mexicana
La Tapatia Taqueria +
Lankford Grocery
Maria Selma's
Nidda
Niko Niko's
Nippon
Pronto Cucinino +
Romano's +
Rudyard's
Tex Chick

Near North - 33

Casa Grande
Connie's Seafood House +
El Taquito Rico
Fiesta en Guadalajara
Gorditas Aguascalientes (2) +
Laredo Taqueria +
Pappas Bar-B-Q +
Spanish Flowers
Tampico
Taqueria Arandas +
Teotihuacan (2) +

New Chinatown - 34

Central China
Chinese Café +
Don Café Sandwich
Givral Hoang Sandwiches
Golden Palace
Hunan Plus
Jade Village
Jasmine Asian Cuisine
Kim Son +
Lee's Sandwiches
Lucky Pot
Ocean Palace
Pho Danh +
Pho Saigon +
* Saigon Pagolac
San Dong Noodle House
Shanghai
Sichuan Cuisine
Sinh Sinh
Sunrise Taquitos +
Tan Tan
Taqueria El Herradero +
Taydo +
Thai Spice Express
Thanh Noi Sandwich Shop

North - 35

Fonda Doña Maria
Lupe Tortilla's +
Mambo Seafood (2) +
Ostioneria Arandas +
Pappas Bar-B-Q +
Pollo Riko +
Tacos del Julio +
Taqueria Arandas +

Northwest - 36

Brown Bag Deli +
* Café Red Onion +
Fiesta Tacos
Frank's Grill +
Fratelli's
Hickory Hollow +
Lyndon's Pit Bar-B-Q
Mambo Seafood +
Pappas Bar-B-Q +
Pho Saigon +
Sandwich King Deli & Grill +
Taqueria Arandas (2) +
Thu Thu
Yo' Mama's Soul Food

Old Chinatown - 37

Hoang Son
Jenni's Noodle House
Kim Son +

Pasadena - 38
Connie's Seafood House +
Tacos del Julio +
Taqueria Arandas +

Pearland - 39
Lila's
Taqueria Arandas +
Zydeco +

Rice Military - 40
Bibas Greek Pizza
Candelari's Pizzeria +
Christian's Tailgate Bar & Grill +
Los Dos Amigos

Rice Village - 41
Antone's Import Co. +
Black Walnut Café +
Brown Bag Deli +
Café Chino
Collina's +
D'Amico's Italian Market Café
Istanbul Grill
Kahn's Deli
La Madeleine +
Miss Saigon Cafe
Nit Noi +
Patu Thai Cuisine
Ruggles Café Bakery
Thai Spice

Sharpstown - 42
Addisaba
Altamirano
Bijan Persian Grill
Bombay Sweets
Busy Boy Sandwiches
Caribbean Cuisine
Darband Shishkabob
Doña Tere Tamales +
El Pupusodromo +
Giannotti's
★ Himalaya
La Sani
Lo Nuestro
Los Ranchitos
Pappas Bar-B-Q (3) +
Pavani
Peking Cuisine
Pollo Riko +
Taqueria Arandas +
Taqueria Cancun +
Tau Bay
Teotihuacan +

Spring - 43
Sunrise Taquitos +
Wunsche Bros. Café

Spring Branch - 44
Casa De Leon
Connie's Seafood House +
El Hidalguense +
Jarro Café
Las Llardas
Mambo Seafood +
★ Otilia's
Pho Saigon +
Polonia
Sandwich King Deli & Grill +
Tacos del Julio +
Taqueria Arandas (2) +
Taqueria Cancun (4) +
Thai Racha
★ Vieng Thai

Stafford - 45
Avalon Diner +
Barry's Pizza +
Frenchy's +
Kim Son +
Los Gallitos
Sandwich King Deli & Grill +

Sugar Land / First Colony - 46
Berryhill Baja Grill +
Café Express +
Chinese Café +
Dimassi's Mediterranean Buffet +
La Escondida
La Madeleine +
Lupe Tortilla's +
Madras Pavilion +
Pho Saigon +
Ragin Cajun +
Thai Cottage +

Tanglewilde - 47
Andros Deli
Blue Nile
Fadi's Mediterranean Grill +
La Tapatia Taqueria +
Nam

Miscellanea Guide

These are hopefully useful tidbits and such, objective and otherwise. The restaurants under each category include only the restaurants that are profiled and recommended in this guidebook.

* - Highly Recommended

All-You-Can-Eat

Bombay Sweets
Dimassi's Mediterranean Buffet
Gourmet India (lunch)
La Sani (lunch)
Mayuri (lunch)
Patu (lunch)
Pavani
Sandy's Markets
Thai Spice (lunch)

Breakfast - Nearly Daily

Andros Deli
Avalon Diner
Barnaby's (Fairview & Shepherd)
Bibas Greek Restaurant
Black Walnut Café
Brasil
Breakfast Klub
Buffalo Grille
Café Artiste
Casa de Leon
Casa Grande
Champ Burger
Chez Beignets
Daily Grind
Don Carlos
Dot Coffee Shop
El Paraiso
El Pupusodromo
El Rey Taqueria
El Tapatio
El Taquito Rico
Empire Café
Fonda Doña Maria
Fountain View Café
Frank's Grill
French Riviera Bakery & Café
Gorditas Aguascalientes
Guatemala
Java Java Café
Jarro Café
Katz's
Kenny & Ziggy's
Kojak's Timberbrook Café
Kraftsmen Baking
La Guadalupana Bakery & Café
La Madeleine
La Mexicana
Lankford Grocery
Lila's
Los Dos Amigos
Los Ranchitos
Mama's Café
Manena's Pastry Shop & Deli
Maria Selma's
Mexico's Deli
Mission Burritos
Mucho Mexico
* Noemi's Tacos
Porras
New York Coffee Shop
Sandwich King Deli & Grill
Sunrise Taquitos
Taqueria Arandas
Taqueria Cancun
Taqueria Del Sol
Taqueria El Herradero
Taqueria La Flor
Taqueria Mexico

Breakfast - Weekends Only

Baba Yega
Barnaby's Café (West Gray)
Berryhill Baja Grill
El Patio
El Pueblito
* Goode Co. Taqueria
Mission Burritos
* Otilia's
This is It

BYOB - might be an necessity

Aladdin
Café Malay
Café Mezza & Grille

Collina's (Richmond, Heights)
★ Himalaya
Java Java Café
★ Kanomwan
Lemon Tree
Mexico's Deli
Miguelito's
Rita's Café
Sichuan Cuisine
Thai Spice (Heights)
★ Vieng Thai

BYOB - an option

Café Lili
Collina's (all but Richmond)
Emporio
Erawan
Kojak's Timberbrook Café
Palazzo's
Ruggles Café Bakery

Delivery (limited, of course)

Bibas Greek Pizza
Café Chino
Café Malay
Candelari's Pizzeria
Empire Turkish Grill
Golden Room
Nit Noi
Miguelito's
Mint Café
Morningside Thai
Palazzo's
Ponzo's
Romero's Las Brazas (evening)
Teotihucan (Irvington)
Thai Spice (Heights)
This is It

Drive-Thrus

Antone's Import Co. (Kirby)
Chacho's
El Rey Taqueria (except downtown)
Frenchy's (except HEB location)
Lee's Sandwiches
Sunrise Taquitos (Spring)
Thai Racha

Highly Recommended - ★

★ Café Red Onion
★ Dolce Vita
★ Goode Co. Barbecue
★ Goode Co. Taqueria
★ Himalaya
★ Kanomwan
★ Kenneally's Irish Pub
★ Market Square Bar & Grill
★ Noemi's Tacos
★ Ninfa's (Original location)
★ 100% Taquito
★ Otilia's
★ Saigon Pagolac
★ Vieng Thai
★ Williams Smokehouse

Kids Menus

Abe's Cajun Market
Altamirano
Amazon Grill
Avalon Diner
Baker's Ribs
Barry's Pizza
Berryhill Baja Grill
Buffalo Grille
Cadillac Bar
Café Express
Café Mezza & Grille
Café Piquet
Candelari's Pizzeria
Chacho's
Colombian Cuisine
Connie's Seafood House
El Patio
Emporio
Fiesta Loma Linda
The Grill of the Andes
Guatemala
Hickory Hollow
Hollywood
Jarro Café
Jax Grill
Katz's (Woodlands)
Kojak's Timberbrook Café
Kraftsmen Baking
La Escondida
La Hacienda
La Mexicana
Leibman's
Lila's
Lopez
Mambo Parrilla
Manny's Café
Masala Wok
Mexico's Deli
Miguelito's
Mission Burritos

Mucho Mexico
New York Coffee Shop
Niko Niko's
Ostioneria Arandas
Pappas Burgers
Paulie's
Paw Paw's
Ragin Cajun
Romero's Las Brazas
Sandy's Market
Santa Fe Flats
Sylvia's Enchilada Kitchen
Tampico
Tony's Mexican

Open 24 Hours

Bibas Greek Restaurant
Chacho's
Dot Coffee Shop
Katz's
Las Llardas (weekends)
Spanish Flowers (nearly so)
Taqueria Arandas (Irvington)
Taqueria Cancun (weekends)

Patios

Aladdin
Amazon Grill
Baba Yega
Berryhill Baja Grill
Bibas Greek Pizza
Bibas Greek Restaurant
Brasil
Burns Bar BQ
Cabo
Candelari's Pizzeria (Washington)
Café Artiste
Chez Beignets
Café Express
Café Mezza & Grille
Christian's Tailgate (Bagby)
Collina's (Rice Village)
D'Amico's Italian Market Café
Daily Grind
★ Dolce Vita
El Patio (Brazos)
El Pueblito
Empire Café
French Rivieria Bakery & Café
★ Goode Co. Barbecue (Kirby)
★ Goode Co. Taqueria
Hobbit Café
Hollywood
Istanbul Grill
Jax Grill
Kahn's (a sidewalk, at least)
Kanomwan
Kraftsmen Baking
La Madeleine
La Mexicana
Mak Chin's
Marini's Empanada House
Mint Café
Mission Burritos
Niko Niko's
★ Otilia's
Palazzo (Westheimer)
Paulie's
Pronto Cucinino
Ragin Cajun (Sugar Land)
Red Lion
Romero's Las Brazas
Santa Fe Flats
Sylvia's Enchilada Kitchen
Taco Milagro
Tampico
Yia Yia Mary's

Pubs

Cahill's on Durham
Kenneally's
Market Square Bar & Grill
McGonigel's Mucky Duck
Red Lion
Rudyard's

Take-Away Only

Burt's Meat Market
Guy's Meat Market
Maxey's Cajun Patio & Grill (nearly)

Restaurant Review Form

Though we may disagree, feedback is encouraged. It is a big sprawling city, and can be difficult to cover adequately. Do you believe that some restaurant was missed, or that the book was too generous (or critical) in its inclusion and appraisal? If so, please send in your thoughts.

Based on my personal experience, I wish to recommend the following **restaurant** that is not on the list, or agree or disagree with a restaurant that is on the list. Please include the **address** and **telephone number**.

____

____

____

____

Please describe the restaurant and its merits and / or drawbacks:

____

____

____

____

____

____

Signing below affirms that I do **not work at the restaurant, nor am I connected with the ownership** or management of this restaurant.

Name: ______________________________

Address: ______________________________

____

Phone: ______________________________

E-Mail Address: ______________________________

Signed: ______________________________

Tempus Fugit Press
P.O. Box 540306
Houston, Texas 77254

Send a comment via e-mail at: Info@HoustonDiningontheCheap.com

Restaurant Review Form

Though we may disagree, feedback is encouraged. It is a big sprawling city, and can be difficult to cover adequately. Do you believe that some restaurant was missed, or that the book was too generous (or critical) in its inclusion and appraisal? If so, please send in your thoughts.

Based on my personal experience, I wish to recommend the following **restaurant** that is not on the list, or agree or disagree with a restaurant that is on the list. Please include the **address** and **telephone number**.

____

____

____

____

Please describe the restaurant and its merits and / or drawbacks:

____

____

____

____

____

____

Signing below affirms that I do **not work at the restaurant, nor am I connected with the ownership** or management of this restaurant.

Name: ______________________________________

Address: ____________________________________

____

Phone: ______________________________________

E-Mail Address: ______________________________

Signed: _____________________________________

Tempus Fugit Press
P.O. Box 540306
Houston, Texas 77254

Send a comment via e-mail at: Info@HoustonDiningontheCheap.com

Order Form

Houston Dining on the Cheap - 3rd Edition

To order a book, please fill out the following and include a check for the proper amount. Please copy this page as many times as needed.

Name: ______________________________

Address: ______________________________

____

Phone: ______________________________

E-Mail Address: ______________________________

Signed: ______________________________

Number of Books: ________

x $17.95 per book

Subtotal: $________

+ $3.50 shipping & handling **per book**

+ $1.48 sales tax **per book** - **Texas residents only**

Total: $ ________

Make checks payable to **Tempus Fugit Press.**

Tempus Fugit Press
P.O. Box 540306
Houston, Texas 77254